Commissioners for Administering Laws for

Commissioners for Administering Laws for Relief of Poor in Ireland : twenty-fifth annual report with appendix

Commissioners for Administering Laws for

Commissioners for Administering Laws for Relief of Poor in Ireland : twenty-fifth annual report with appendix

ISBN/EAN: 9783741104718

Manufactured in Europe, USA, Canada, Australia, Japa

Cover: Foto ©ninafisch / pixelio.de

Manufactured and distributed by brebook publishing software
(www.brebook.com)

Commissioners for Administering Laws for

Commissioners for Administering Laws for Relief of Poor in Ireland : twenty-fifth annual report with appendix

ANNUAL REPORT

OF

THE COMMISSIONERS

FOR

ADMINISTERING THE LAWS FOR RELIEF OF THE POOR IN IRELAND,

INCLUDING

THE TWENTY-FIFTH REPORT UNDER THE 10 & 11 VIC., c. 90,

AND

THE TWENTIETH REPORT UNDER THE 14 & 15 VIC., c. 68;

WITH

APPENDICES.

Presented to both Houses of Parliament by Command of Her Majesty.

DUBLIN:
PRINTED BY ALEXANDER THOM, 87 & 88, ABBEY-STREET,
FOR HER MAJESTY'S STATIONERY OFFICE.

1872.

[C.—577.] *Price 3s.*

TABLE OF CONTENTS.

APPENDIX.

APPENDIX A.—CIRCULARS OF INSTRUCTION, AND CORRESPONDENCE UNDER THE POOR LAW ACTS.

I.—CIRCULARS.

APPENDIX B.—TABLES CONNECTED WITH POOR RELIEF AND EXPENDITURE.

APPENDIX C.—Circulars of Instruction and Correspondence under the Medical Charities Act, the Vaccination Acts, and the Sanitary Acts.

I.—Circulars.

APPENDIX D.—Tabular Returns in connexion with Relief under the Medical Charities Act.

Index.

ANNUAL REPORT

OF THE

COMMISSIONERS

FOR

ADMINISTERING THE LAWS FOR RELIEF OF THE POOR IN IRELAND,

INCLUDING

THE TWENTY-FIFTH REPORT UNDER THE 10 & 11 VIC., c. 90,

AND

THE TWENTIETH REPORT UNDER THE 14 & 15 VIC., c. 68.

TO HIS EXCELLENCY JOHN POYNTZ EARL SPENCER, K.G.,
&c., &c., &c.,

Lord Lieutenant-General and General Governor of Ireland.

Poor Law Commission Office,
Dublin, 30th March, 1872.

MAY IT PLEASE YOUR EXCELLENCY,

WE, the Commissioners for administering the Laws for Relief of the Poor in Ireland, submit to your Excellency this the Twenty-fifth Annual Report of our proceedings under the Acts in force for the Relief of the Destitute Poor in Ireland.

1. We submit, in the first place, in continuation of similar returns in previous Annual Reports, a summary of weekly returns of persons relieved in the workhouse and out of the workhouse for fifty-two weeks, from the week ended 25th February, 1871, to the week ended 17th February, 1872, both inclusive; and we give, in illustration of these and previous returns, the two indoor and outdoor relief diagrams,* so as to afford a comparison of the fluctuations which have occurred in each year for the last seven years.

* See diagrams facing page 42.

SUMMARY of Weekly Returns of Persons relieved in Unions in Ireland, from the week

Week ended Saturday.	Relief in the Workhouse.														
	Able-bodied.			Healthy Children under 15 years of age.	Sick in Workhouse Hospitals.			All other Classes.			Total Number in Workhouses.	Average Weekly Cost per head for Maintenance (exclusive of clothing).		Deaths.	
	Males.	Females.	Total.		Fever Patients.	Other Cases.	Total.	Males aged 15 and upwards.	Females aged 15 and upwards.	Total.		s.	d.	No. in the Week.	Weekly rate of Mortality per 1,000.
1871.															
Feb. 25,	[illegible]	[illegible]	[illegible]	[illegible]	1,134	[illegible]	[illegible]	[illegible]	[illegible]	[illegible]	[illegible]	3	7	[illegible]	[illegible]
Mar. 4,	[illegible]	[illegible]	[illegible]	[illegible]	[illegible]	[illegible]	[illegible]	[illegible]	[illegible]	[illegible]	[illegible]	3	7	[illegible]	[illegible]
11,	[illegible]	[illegible]	[illegible]	[illegible]	[illegible]	[illegible]	[illegible]	[illegible]	[illegible]	[illegible]	[illegible]	[illegible]	[illegible]	[illegible]	[illegible]
18,	[illegible]	[illegible]	[illegible]	[illegible]	[illegible]	[illegible]	[illegible]	[illegible]	[illegible]	[illegible]	[illegible]	[illegible]	[illegible]	[illegible]	[illegible]
25,	[illegible]	[illegible]	[illegible]	[illegible]	[illegible]	[illegible]	[illegible]	[illegible]	[illegible]	[illegible]	[illegible]	[illegible]	[illegible]	[illegible]	[illegible]
April 1,	[illegible]	[illegible]	[illegible]	[illegible]	[illegible]	[illegible]	[illegible]	[illegible]	[illegible]	[illegible]	[illegible]	[illegible]	[illegible]	[illegible]	[illegible]
8,	[illegible]	[illegible]	[illegible]	[illegible]	[illegible]	[illegible]	[illegible]	[illegible]	[illegible]	[illegible]	[illegible]	[illegible]	[illegible]	[illegible]	[illegible]
15,	[illegible]	[illegible]	[illegible]	[illegible]	[illegible]	[illegible]	[illegible]	[illegible]	[illegible]	[illegible]	[illegible]	[illegible]	[illegible]	[illegible]	[illegible]
22,	[illegible]	[illegible]	[illegible]	[illegible]	[illegible]	[illegible]	[illegible]	[illegible]	[illegible]	[illegible]	[illegible]	[illegible]	[illegible]	[illegible]	[illegible]
29,	[illegible]	[illegible]	[illegible]	[illegible]	[illegible]	[illegible]	[illegible]	[illegible]	[illegible]	[illegible]	[illegible]	[illegible]	[illegible]	[illegible]	[illegible]
May 6,	[illegible]	[illegible]	[illegible]	[illegible]	[illegible]	[illegible]	[illegible]	[illegible]	[illegible]	[illegible]	[illegible]	[illegible]	[illegible]	[illegible]	[illegible]
13,	[illegible]	[illegible]	[illegible]	[illegible]	[illegible]	[illegible]	[illegible]	[illegible]	[illegible]	[illegible]	[illegible]	[illegible]	[illegible]	[illegible]	[illegible]
20,	[illegible]	[illegible]	[illegible]	[illegible]	[illegible]	[illegible]	[illegible]	[illegible]	[illegible]	[illegible]	[illegible]	[illegible]	[illegible]	[illegible]	[illegible]
27,	[illegible]	[illegible]	[illegible]	[illegible]	[illegible]	[illegible]	[illegible]	[illegible]	[illegible]	[illegible]	[illegible]	[illegible]	[illegible]	[illegible]	[illegible]
June 3,	[illegible]	[illegible]	[illegible]	[illegible]	[illegible]	[illegible]	[illegible]	[illegible]	[illegible]	[illegible]	[illegible]	[illegible]	[illegible]	[illegible]	[illegible]
10,	[illegible]	[illegible]	[illegible]	[illegible]	[illegible]	[illegible]	[illegible]	[illegible]	[illegible]	[illegible]	[illegible]	[illegible]	[illegible]	[illegible]	[illegible]
17,	[illegible]	[illegible]	[illegible]	[illegible]	[illegible]	[illegible]	[illegible]	[illegible]	[illegible]	[illegible]	[illegible]	[illegible]	[illegible]	[illegible]	[illegible]
24,	[illegible]	[illegible]	[illegible]	[illegible]	[illegible]	[illegible]	[illegible]	[illegible]	[illegible]	[illegible]	[illegible]	[illegible]	[illegible]	[illegible]	[illegible]
July 1,	[illegible]	[illegible]	[illegible]	[illegible]	[illegible]	[illegible]	[illegible]	[illegible]	[illegible]	[illegible]	[illegible]	[illegible]	[illegible]	[illegible]	[illegible]
8,	[illegible]	[illegible]	[illegible]	[illegible]	[illegible]	[illegible]	[illegible]	[illegible]	[illegible]	[illegible]	[illegible]	[illegible]	[illegible]	[illegible]	[illegible]
15,	[illegible]	[illegible]	[illegible]	[illegible]	[illegible]	[illegible]	[illegible]	[illegible]	[illegible]	[illegible]	[illegible]	[illegible]	[illegible]	[illegible]	[illegible]
22,	[illegible]	[illegible]	[illegible]	[illegible]	[illegible]	[illegible]	[illegible]	[illegible]	[illegible]	[illegible]	[illegible]	[illegible]	[illegible]	[illegible]	[illegible]
29,	[illegible]	[illegible]	[illegible]	[illegible]	[illegible]	[illegible]	[illegible]	[illegible]	[illegible]	[illegible]	[illegible]	[illegible]	[illegible]	[illegible]	[illegible]
Aug. 5,	[illegible]	[illegible]	[illegible]	[illegible]	[illegible]	[illegible]	[illegible]	[illegible]	[illegible]	[illegible]	[illegible]	[illegible]	[illegible]	[illegible]	[illegible]
12,	[illegible]	[illegible]	[illegible]	[illegible]	[illegible]	[illegible]	[illegible]	[illegible]	[illegible]	[illegible]	[illegible]	[illegible]	[illegible]	[illegible]	[illegible]
19,	[illegible]	[illegible]	[illegible]	[illegible]	[illegible]	[illegible]	[illegible]	[illegible]	[illegible]	[illegible]	[illegible]	[illegible]	[illegible]	[illegible]	[illegible]
26,	[illegible]	[illegible]	[illegible]	[illegible]	[illegible]	[illegible]	[illegible]	[illegible]	[illegible]	[illegible]	[illegible]	[illegible]	[illegible]	[illegible]	[illegible]
Sept. 2,	[illegible]	[illegible]	[illegible]	[illegible]	[illegible]	[illegible]	[illegible]	[illegible]	[illegible]	[illegible]	[illegible]	[illegible]	[illegible]	[illegible]	[illegible]
9,	[illegible]	[illegible]	[illegible]	[illegible]	[illegible]	[illegible]	[illegible]	[illegible]	[illegible]	[illegible]	[illegible]	[illegible]	[illegible]	[illegible]	[illegible]
16,	[illegible]	[illegible]	[illegible]	[illegible]	[illegible]	[illegible]	[illegible]	[illegible]	[illegible]	[illegible]	[illegible]	[illegible]	[illegible]	[illegible]	[illegible]
23,	[illegible]	[illegible]	[illegible]	[illegible]	[illegible]	[illegible]	[illegible]	[illegible]	[illegible]	[illegible]	[illegible]	[illegible]	[illegible]	[illegible]	[illegible]
30,	[illegible]	[illegible]	[illegible]	[illegible]	[illegible]	[illegible]	[illegible]	[illegible]	[illegible]	[illegible]	[illegible]	[illegible]	[illegible]	[illegible]	[illegible]
Oct. 7,	[illegible]	[illegible]	[illegible]	[illegible]	[illegible]	[illegible]	[illegible]	[illegible]	[illegible]	[illegible]	[illegible]	[illegible]	[illegible]	[illegible]	[illegible]
14,	[illegible]	[illegible]	[illegible]	[illegible]	[illegible]	[illegible]	[illegible]	[illegible]	[illegible]	[illegible]	[illegible]	[illegible]	[illegible]	[illegible]	[illegible]
21,	[illegible]	[illegible]	[illegible]	[illegible]	[illegible]	[illegible]	[illegible]	[illegible]	[illegible]	[illegible]	[illegible]	[illegible]	[illegible]	[illegible]	[illegible]
28,	[illegible]	[illegible]	[illegible]	[illegible]	[illegible]	[illegible]	[illegible]	[illegible]	[illegible]	[illegible]	[illegible]	[illegible]	[illegible]	[illegible]	[illegible]
Nov. 4,	[illegible]	[illegible]	[illegible]	[illegible]	[illegible]	[illegible]	[illegible]	[illegible]	[illegible]	[illegible]	[illegible]	[illegible]	[illegible]	[illegible]	[illegible]
11,	[illegible]	[illegible]	[illegible]	[illegible]	[illegible]	[illegible]	[illegible]	[illegible]	[illegible]	[illegible]	[illegible]	[illegible]	[illegible]	[illegible]	[illegible]
18,	[illegible]	[illegible]	[illegible]	[illegible]	[illegible]	[illegible]	[illegible]	[illegible]	[illegible]	[illegible]	[illegible]	[illegible]	[illegible]	[illegible]	[illegible]
25,	[illegible]	[illegible]	[illegible]	[illegible]	[illegible]	[illegible]	[illegible]	[illegible]	[illegible]	[illegible]	[illegible]	[illegible]	[illegible]	[illegible]	[illegible]
Dec. 2,	[illegible]	[illegible]	[illegible]	[illegible]	[illegible]	[illegible]	[illegible]	[illegible]	[illegible]	[illegible]	[illegible]	[illegible]	[illegible]	[illegible]	[illegible]
9,	[illegible]	[illegible]	[illegible]	[illegible]	[illegible]	[illegible]	[illegible]	[illegible]	[illegible]	[illegible]	[illegible]	[illegible]	[illegible]	[illegible]	[illegible]
16,	[illegible]	[illegible]	[illegible]	[illegible]	[illegible]	[illegible]	[illegible]	[illegible]	[illegible]	[illegible]	[illegible]	[illegible]	[illegible]	[illegible]	[illegible]
23,	[illegible]	[illegible]	[illegible]	[illegible]	[illegible]	[illegible]	[illegible]	[illegible]	[illegible]	[illegible]	[illegible]	[illegible]	[illegible]	[illegible]	[illegible]
30,	[illegible]	[illegible]	[illegible]	[illegible]	[illegible]	[illegible]	[illegible]	[illegible]	[illegible]	[illegible]	[illegible]	[illegible]	[illegible]	[illegible]	[illegible]
1872.															
Jan. 6,	[illegible]	[illegible]	[illegible]	[illegible]	[illegible]	[illegible]	[illegible]	[illegible]	[illegible]	[illegible]	[illegible]	[illegible]	[illegible]	[illegible]	[illegible]
13,	[illegible]	[illegible]	[illegible]	[illegible]	[illegible]	[illegible]	[illegible]	[illegible]	[illegible]	[illegible]	[illegible]	[illegible]	[illegible]	[illegible]	[illegible]
20,	[illegible]	[illegible]	[illegible]	[illegible]	[illegible]	[illegible]	[illegible]	[illegible]	[illegible]	[illegible]	[illegible]	[illegible]	[illegible]	[illegible]	[illegible]
27,	[illegible]	[illegible]	[illegible]	[illegible]	[illegible]	[illegible]	[illegible]	[illegible]	[illegible]	[illegible]	[illegible]	[illegible]	[illegible]	[illegible]	[illegible]
Feb. 3,	[illegible]	[illegible]	[illegible]	[illegible]	[illegible]	[illegible]	[illegible]	[illegible]	[illegible]	[illegible]	[illegible]	[illegible]	[illegible]	[illegible]	[illegible]
10,	[illegible]	[illegible]	[illegible]	[illegible]	[illegible]	[illegible]	[illegible]	[illegible]	[illegible]	[illegible]	[illegible]	[illegible]	[illegible]	[illegible]	[illegible]
17,	[illegible]	[illegible]	[illegible]	[illegible]	[illegible]	[illegible]	[illegible]	[illegible]	[illegible]	[illegible]	[illegible]	[illegible]	[illegible]	[illegible]	[illegible]

ended 25th February, 1871, to the week ended 17th February, 1872, both inclusive.

[illegible]	[illegible]	[illegible]	[illegible]	[illegible]	[illegible]	In Poor Law Hospitals	In other Hospitals	Blind	Deaf and Dumb	Relievable under section 1: No. of Cases	Relievable under section 1: No. of Persons	Not relievable under section 1: No. of Cases	Not relievable under section 1: No. of Persons	Under sec. 9: Males	Under sec. 9: Females	Under sec. 9: Total	Total Number of Persons in receipt of Out-door Relief	Total Number of Persons in receipt of Relief
[illegible]	[illegible]	[illegible]	[illegible]	[illegible]	[illegible]	[illegible]	[illegible]	[illegible]	[illegible]	[illegible]	[illegible]	[illegible]	[illegible]	[illegible]	[illegible]	[illegible]	[illegible]	[illegible]
[illegible]	[illegible]	[illegible]	[illegible]	[illegible]	[illegible]	[illegible]	[illegible]	[illegible]	[illegible]	[illegible]	[illegible]	[illegible]	[illegible]	[illegible]	[illegible]	[illegible]	[illegible]	[illegible]
[illegible]	[illegible]	[illegible]	[illegible]	[illegible]	[illegible]	[illegible]	[illegible]	[illegible]	[illegible]	[illegible]	[illegible]	[illegible]	[illegible]	[illegible]	[illegible]	[illegible]	[illegible]	[illegible]

2. The following tables represent in figures the maximum, minimum, and average daily numbers shown in each diagram for the whole series of seven years:—

RELIEF IN WORKHOUSE.

—		Maximum Numbers.	Date.	Minimum Numbers.	Date.	Average Daily Number.
1865-66,	.	63,009	25 February, 1865	41,698	2 September, 1865	52,191
1866-67,	.	60,255	9 February, 1867	47,785	1 September, 1866	50,741
1867-68,	.	62,170	8 February, 1868	51,869	7 September, 1867	53,017
1868-69,	.	61,941	11 March, 1869	46,835	29 August, 1868	53,757
1869-70,	.	60,024	6 March, 1869	43,637	4 September, 1869	50,964
1870-71,	.	55,462	26 February, 1870	41,701	20 August, 1870	47,910
1871-72,	.	51,927	25 February, 1871	39,606	26 August, 1871	45,383

OUT-DOOR RELIEF.

—		Maximum Numbers.	Date.	Minimum Numbers.	Date.	Average Daily Number.
1865-66,	.	12,895	11 March, 1865	8,803	7 October, 1865	10,049
1866-67,	.	18,816	9 February, 1867	9,949	13 October, 1866	12,953
1867-68,	.	18,666	15 February, 1868	11,975	28 September, 1867	14,940
1868-69,	.	18,674	20 February, 1869	14,217	3 October, 1868	16,863
1869-70,	.	21,320	19 February, 1870	15,859	2 October, 1869	18,296
1870-71,	.	25,363	18 February, 1871	18,967	1 October, 1870	21,476
1871-72,	.	28,490	17 February, 1872	22,655	7 October, 1871	23,859

3. These statistics, illustrated by the Indoor Relief Diagram, show a further decrease in the number of inmates of workhouses which on the 17th February, 1872, was less by 1,211 than the number at the corresponding date in the preceding year 1871, and less by 5,438 than the corresponding number in 1870. The difference between the present and preceding years has in the latter portion of the series of weeks been declining in consequence of the epidemic of small-pox; and at the latest date previous to the date of this Report the difference between 1871 and 1872 was only 931.

4. The number of persons receiving out-door relief has further increased from 25,363 to 28,490 in the course of the fifty-two weeks comprised in the table. In paragraphs 3 and 4 of our Report of 1869 we have entered fully into the considerations which oblige us to disregard any ordinary increase or decrease of out-door relief as indicative of the state of the population, and to look exclusively to the increase or decrease of the number of inmates of workhouses.

5. The number of children out at nurse has increased in the last twelve months from 1,428 to 1,540. On this subject we beg to refer to the views expressed in paragraphs 5, 6, 7, and 8 of our last Annual Report.

6. The following table exhibits the progress of the relief of "persons disabled from labour," &c., since 1857, in comparison with the other two classes for which out-relief is legalized by 1st section of 10 Vic. cap. 31.

RETURN showing the Number of Persons in receipt of Out-door Relief under the 1st Section of 10th Vic., cap. 31, on the last Saturday of February in each year from 1857 to 1872.

YEAR.	Persons permanently disabled from labour by reason of old age, infirmity, or bodily or mental defect.		Widows having two or more legitimate children dependent on them.		Persons being disabled from labour, by reason of severe sickness or serious accident.		Total.	
	Cases.	Persons.	Cases.	Persons.	Cases.	Persons.	Cases.	Persons.
1857,	296	541	34	120	181	435	511	1,096
1858,	424	466	79	253	320	878	823	1,642
1859,	413	559	83	167	281	692	777	1,418
1860,	609	728	87	361	434	1,004	1,130	2,093
1861,	1,197	1,317	375	848	961	2,548	2,533	4,713
1862,	1,591	2,180	783	1,035	1,260	3,287	3,634	6,502
1863,	2,050	3,541	614	1,584	1,359	3,924	4,023	9,049
1864,	2,990	3,695	486	1,939	1,808	4,682	5,284	10,316
1865,	3,357	4,336	606	2,353	2,045	5,324	6,008	12,013
1866,	3,515	4,369	696	2,771	1,915	4,670	6,126	11,810
1867,	4,648	6,021	920	3,684	2,781	6,758	8,349	16,463
1868,	5,171	7,026	1,075	4,398	3,072	6,900	9,318	18,324
1869,	5,816	7,472	1,137	4,878	2,652	6,503	9,605	18,853
1870,	6,992	8,912	1,183	5,045	3,545	7,368	11,720	21,325
1871,	7,069	9,746	1,260	5,829	3,359	7,969	12,688	23,544
1872,	9,229	11,231	1,463	6,347	3,911	9,432	14,603	27,010

The increase of out-door relief shown in this table, viz., from 23,544 last year to 27,010, amounting to 3,466 persons, is thus distributed—the permanently infirm class, 1,485; the widows 518; and the temporarily disabled by sickness or accident 1,463; the increase of the widow class being only one-third of the increase of each of the other two classes.

7. We here subjoin a tabular statement showing the number of "night-lodgers," a term corresponding to "casuals" in England for the past twelve months, in continuation of a similar table in last Report.

RETURN of NIGHT-LODGERS or CASUALS relieved.

Week ended	Number relieved during the week.				Number in Workhouse at close of week.			
	Males.	Females.	Children under 15.	Total.	Males.	Females.	Children under 15.	Total.
4th March, 1871, . .	992	293	253	1,538	122	49	55	270
1st April, 1871, . .	979	271	222	1,472	177	47	52	276
6th May, 1871, . .	975	247	254	1,476	93	44	31	168
3rd June, 1871, . .	863	288	216	1,367	111	34	34	179
1st July, 1871, . .	810	342	268	1,420	85	31	21	137
5th August, 1871, . .	836	333	272	1,441	100	29	37	166
2nd September, 1871, .	680	275	355	1,310	88	32	25	145
7th October, 1871, . .	819	264	198	1,281	97	33	49	179
4th November, 1871, .	891	251	247	1,389	113	31	41	185
2nd December, 1871, .	779	253	226	1,258	87	39	45	171
6th January, 1872, .	819	212	168	1,199	130	31	36	197
3rd February, 1872, .	894	231	234	1,359	161	42	42	245
2nd March, 1872, . .	1,145	295	243	1,683	193	44	57	294

Comparing this with the return for last year the numerical

force of this troublesome class of applicants appears to be now nearly stationary in Ireland.

8. As part of the statistics which are brought up very nearly to the date of this Report, the following table exhibits in the accustomed form:

CLASSIFICATION of Causes of Death in Workhouses, from 5th February, 1871, to 3rd February, 1872.

Causes of Death.	[illegible]														Previous Year.
	4th March.	1st April.	29th April.	27th May.	24th June.	22nd July.	19th Aug.	16th Sept.	14th Oct.	11th Nov.	9th Dec.	6th Jan.	3rd Feb.	Total.	
Age,	267	179	145	160	137	[illegible]	94	131	[illegible]	[illegible]	196	221	[illegible]	1,910	2,271
Apoplexy,	9	8	1	3	6	7	8	6	5	5	5	4	6	73	77
Asthma,	6	10	5	10	5	8	8	3	9	3	18	14	14	[illegible]	132
Atrophy,	71	68	[illegible]	63	64	60	48	71	40	45	44	[illegible]	111	[illegible]	[illegible]
Brain Disease,	40	39	[illegible]	23	34	73	18	34	18	[illegible]	31	37	49	379	377
Cancer,	13	13	[illegible]	14	15	10	27	11	19	14	17	[illegible]	18	[illegible]	[illegible]
Childbirth,	1	1	1	1	–	–	–	1	3	–	5	–	6	19	16
Cholera,	–	–	–	–	–	–	–	2	–	–	–	–	–	2	12
Consumption,	79	83	83	73	76	67	[illegible]	[illegible]	47	67	75	77	85	[illegible]	946
Convulsions,	14	16	17	18	16	6	13	13	8	9	10	10	15	151	218
Croup,	3	3	8	1	1	1	–	1	3	–	4	8	–	31	31
Diarrhoea,	43	40	53	23	[illegible]	23	[illegible]	31	35	[illegible]	30	43	41	414	471
Dropsy,	26	25	[illegible]	37	27	16	16	[illegible]	[illegible]	21	63	23	[illegible]	[illegible]	273
Dysentery,	6	11	11	4	10	6	6	6	8	6	9	8	6	[illegible]	109
Dyspepsia,	1	1	1	–	–	2	3	1	1	1	5	1	1	19	25
Epilepsy,	5	4	3	5	5	5	4	6	4	1	8	7	4	[illegible]	74
Fever,	57	56	73	[illegible]	49	67	54	[illegible]	49	[illegible]	45	67	47	[illegible]	[illegible]
Gangrene,	5	4	7	3	4	7	4	3	5	1	3	9	6	64	[illegible]
Heart Disease,	40	45	23	24	[illegible]	27	[illegible]	30	30	33	34	33	[illegible]	[illegible]	341
Hooping Cough,	4	6	10	3	6	1	3	1	8	5	6	1	17	[illegible]	75
Inflammation or other diseases of															
Bowels,	9	17	27	17	12	17	[illegible]	8	17	10	10	[illegible]	[illegible]	[illegible]	181
Kidneys,	15	17	11	13	7	10	8	11	9	11	11	13	10	149	[illegible]
Liver,	8	17	10	9	10	12	18	13	8	9	15	11	7	137	[illegible]
Lungs,	144	169	151	327	83	[illegible]	64	[illegible]	73	78	[illegible]	[illegible]	[illegible]	[illegible]	[illegible]
Measles,	7	15	10	3	1	–	–	–	–	7	5	5	1	67	[illegible]
Paralysis,	[illegible]	34	34	31	[illegible]	32	[illegible]	34	[illegible]	21	[illegible]	[illegible]	31	[illegible]	[illegible]
Pleurisy,	3	1	1	2	1	1	1	1	–	1	1	–	2	15	[illegible]
Rheumatism,	4	9	7	6	8	2	5	7	4	5	5	7	10	72	77
Scarlatina,	2	3	9	9	9	2	3	3	6	7	3	6	3	[illegible]	[illegible]
Scrofula,	13	15	18	9	11	13	[illegible]	11	9	10	15	5	17	[illegible]	[illegible]
Small-Pox,	2	3	4	6	6	6	5	11	13	[illegible]	[illegible]	[illegible]	[illegible]	[illegible]	[illegible]
Ulcer,	8	8	31	17	10	[illegible]	4	9	9	8	19	15	17	[illegible]	[illegible]
Other Diseases,	81	[illegible]	43	[illegible]	[illegible]	[illegible]	11	[illegible]	33	[illegible]	86	[illegible]	[illegible]	[illegible]	[illegible]
Total,	[illegible]	[illegible]	[illegible]	[illegible]	[illegible]	[illegible]	[illegible]	[illegible]	[illegible]	[illegible]	[illegible]	[illegible]	[illegible]	[illegible]	–
Previous year,	1,017	1,133	[illegible]	[illegible]	[illegible]	[illegible]	[illegible]	[illegible]	[illegible]	[illegible]	[illegible]	[illegible]	[illegible]	–	[illegible]

The total number of deaths in the workhouses in the fifty-two weeks comprised in the table has been 10,583. In the corresponding table in the last Annual Report the total number of deaths was 10,639, which, compared with the present numbers shows a decrease of 56 deaths and a decrease of 385, compared with the number in the preceding year.

The number of deaths by fever is 678 in comparison with 650 in the previous year, and with 774 in the year preceding.

It will be seen that no less than 462 deaths from small-pox have taken place in the workhouse hospitals of Ireland in the course of the year 1871–72 in comparison with only one single case recorded in our last Report for the year 1869–70, and with no more than 13 in the year 1870–71.

9. The whole number of deaths by small-pox registered in

Ireland in the year 1871 is now known to be 647, in comparison with 32 in 1870.

The present serious epidemic of small-pox will be dealt with in the Medical Branch of this Report; but in paragraph 13 of our last Report we alluded to the erroneous belief in the existence of a legal system of quarantine among the authorities at some points of the Irish and British coasts as interfering with the landing and proper treatment of small-pox patients in vessels coming into harbour. We give in the appendix some further correspondence bearing on this subject and illustrating the false impressions which still appear to prevail regarding it.*

In the same appendix will be found correspondence which took place regarding a proposal of the Mayor and Town Council of Cork to establish a small-pox quarantine as against vessels carrying coal from Newport in South Wales or elsewhere to the Cove of Cork.†

In this correspondence it was shown that the system of quarantine adopted in 1871 to prevent the importation of cholera from foreign infected ports was not applicable to an epidemic of small-pox existing in Great Britain for the purpose of preventing its extension to Ireland. We regret to have to observe that the erroneous impressions prevailing on this subject obtained publicity and professional sanction‡ in Dublin in the form of a complaint that no such measures were taken by the Government to prevent the introduction of small-pox as were taken in the year 1869 to prevent the introduction of the cattle plague.

It needs very little reflection to see that a disease which, like small-pox, lies dormant in the system from twelve to sixteen days after the contagion has been caught could not be prevented by any means whatever in the nature of quarantine from crossing the channel into Ireland, where a continuous stream of passenger traffic is going on daily and nightly at several points of the coast in a passage of only a few hours duration. With equal reason, and with equal chance of success, quarantine might be established between one town and another in the same Island.

It will be in your Excellency's recollection that one source of danger of the introduction of small-pox from Great Britain into Ireland in the beginning of the year 1871 was pointed out by us on the 3rd of March, and a suggestion made to the effect that removals under the removal laws should cease to take place from large towns, like London, Liverpool, and Glasgow to Ireland, which suggestion was communicated by your Excellency's command to the Secretary of State for the Home Department, and was sent forward to the Local Government Board in England, and to the Board of Supervision in Scotland.

The Local Government Board felt and admitted the reasonableness of this proposal, and it was, we presume, at its instance that the Select Vestry of Liverpool at once voluntarily suspended the removals to Ireland, as they had before done in 1866 during an invasion of cholera. This suspension took place on the 23rd

* Appendix A, II., page 44. † Appendix A, II., page 51.
‡ Dublin Journal of Medical Science, February, 1872.

March, 1871, and continued from that date until the 16th October following.

The Board of Supervision in Scotland observed in reply to the same proposal that no appreciable advantage could result from a suspension of Irish removals, so long as the ordinary passenger and commercial traffic between Scotland and Ireland remained uninterrupted. This remark is certainly borne out by the ascertained fact that in the year 1870 and the first half year of 1871 no less than 38 cases of small-pox are known to have been imported into Ireland from Liverpool, and 17 from Glasgow and Greenock. At the same time the Commissioners submit that there is a substantial difference between the voluntary transit of Her Majesty's subjects which cannot be prevented without an infringement of personal freedom, and the forcible deportation of paupers by a process of arrest and imprisonment which might easily be suspended with advantage and resumed at pleasure.

Moreover, there is a peculiar danger attending the class of persons who are the subjects of removal orders from large towns like Liverpool and Glasgow, and who before applying for relief, and perhaps subsequently to receiving it, may be presumed to have lived in the worst localities and were liable to contract there contagious disease, and to be sent over with the disease upon them undetected.

On this subject some correspondence, which will be found in the appendix, has taken place with the Liverpool Select Vestry regarding the removal to Ireland of tramps who come to that town from other parts of England with the purpose of obtaining conveyance to Ireland free of charge to themselves.*

10. The parochial authorities in Scotland continue to remove dangerous lunatics, hand-cuffed, from Scotch lunatic asylums to Irish workhouses. Recent instances of this practice are given in the appendix; and we may here observe that they are regarded in Ireland with feelings of great dissatisfaction.†

11. We conclude the series of recent statistics by repeating with one additional year the table showing the number of persons assisted by Boards of Guardians to emigrate, and the cost incurred for that purpose in each year, that is to say, for now twenty-two years past ended on the 25th of March.

* Appendix A, III., p. 53.
† Appendix A, V., p. 77.

[Table.

EMIGRATION under the Act 12 & 13 Vic. c. 104, sec. 26, dated 1 Aug. 1849.

Periods.		Amount authorized to be expended by Boards of Guardians.			Number of Persons assisted to Emigrate.			
					Men.	Women.	Children under 15 years of age.	Total.
		£	s.	d.				
Aug., 1849, to 25 Mar.,	1851,	11,131	14	11	561	1,244	787	2,592
Year ended 25 March,	1852,	21,010	5	4½	790	2,614	952	4,356
" "	1853,	14,517	0	11½	492	2,318	1,115	3,925
" "	1854,	12,416	17	6	163	1,320	918	2,401
" "	1855,	24,368	8	9½	189	2,847	768	3,794
" "	1856,	3,618	6	9	64	363	403	830
" "	1857,	2,719	15	1	76	363	363	802
" "	1858,	4,177	10	1½	58	469	302	829
" "	1859,	2,553	18	6	37	270	180	487
" "	1860,	1,729	19	2	45	178	141	364
" "	1861,	1,465	19	11	44	178	123	347
" "	1862,	628	17	4	19	73	38	132
" "	1863,	2,459	10	3	41	317	139	497
" "	1864,	4,770	4	5	123	501	345	969
" "	1865,	2,518	17	11	66	315	435	816
" "	1866,	3,425	9	11	109	364	660	1,133
" "	1867,	2,023	10	0	66	238	459	763
" "	1868,	1,983	9	6	71	253	485	810
" "	1869,	1,838	13	6	71	205	439	715
" "	1870,	1,830	13	3	48	219	449	717
" "	1871,	2,268	9	11	53	228	472	701
" "	1872,	2,094	3	10	34	223	339	596
Total,	£	123,610	10	9	3,447	14,915	10,365	28,727

12. We now proceed to the statistics arising out of the audited accounts of unions for the year ended 29th September, 1871.

We deal in the first place with that part of the union expenditure which relates exclusively to the relief of the poor, of which the following table affords an abstract for all Ireland for the year ended 29th September, 1871, in comparison with that for the year which ended on the same date in 1870:—

Year ended 29th September,	Net Annual Value.	Poor Rate Collected.	Poor Relief Expenditure during the Year.						Numbers relieved.			
			In-Maintenance and Clothing.	Out-Relief.	Cost of Relief in Blind and Deaf and Dumb Asylums and Extern Hospitals.	Salaries and Rations of Officers.	All other Expenses.	Total.	In Workhouse.	Out-door.	In Blind and Deaf and Dumb Asylums.	Total.
	£	£	£	£	£	£	£	£				
1871,	[illegible]	[illegible]	[illegible]	[illegible]	7,[illegible]	117,[illegible]	[illegible]	[illegible]	[illegible]	[illegible]	[illegible]	[illegible]
1870,	13,[illegible]	7[illegible]	[illegible]	[illegible]	7,[illegible]	1[illegible]	[illegible]	[illegible]	[illegible]	[illegible]	[illegible]	[illegible]
Increase,	[illegible]	–	682	[illegible]	[illegible]	4,[illegible]	1,[illegible]	17,[illegible]	–	[illegible]	[illegible]	–
Decrease,	–	14,[illegible]	–	–	–	–	–	–	4,919	–	–	[illegible]

An increase of expenditure has taken place under the head of In-maintenance, amounting to £682, notwithstanding that a considerable decrease, amounting to 4,919, has taken place in the total numbers receiving relief in the workhouse, and that the table on page 19 shows that the average daily number in the workhouse had decreased to the extent of 3,161. This increased expenditure arises from the considerable increase which has taken place in the cost of provisions, a comparison of several of the tables in the present with those of last year's Report showing such increase to be about 2*d*. per head per week for each person relieved. An increase of £4,357 has taken place under the head of Salaries and Rations of Officers, a portion of which increase is also accounted for by the increased price of provisions. But the most marked increase is that under the head of Out-door Relief, namely, £10,563, arising from the continuous increase in the numbers to whom such relief is extended, as previously referred to in par. 6.

13. The following is a tabulated account of admissions to the workhouse during the last year, in comparison with those of the thirteen preceding years:—

TABLE.

Year ended [illegible] September.	Number of Paupers in Workhouses at the commencement of the Year.	Number of Persons admitted during the Year. Number admitted in Sickness. Suffering from Fever or other contagious Disease.	Suffering under other Diseases.	Suffering from accidental Injury.	Total Number admitted in Sickness.	Number admitted [illegible]	Total Number admitted during the Year.	Number of Births in the Workhouses during the Year.	Total number of Persons relieved in the Workhouses during the Year.	Number of Deaths in the Workhouses during the Year.
1858,	79,[illegible]	11,101	[illegible]	2,231	67,519	47,[illegible]	166,218	2,454	177,[illegible]	9,[illegible]
1859,	54,[illegible]	9,335	52,[illegible]	2,107	64,[illegible]	79,[illegible]	111,[illegible]	2,770	153,[illegible]	6,[illegible]
1860,	53,[illegible]	7,107	35,[illegible]	2,[illegible]	47,[illegible]	46,[illegible]	[illegible]	2,140	170,[illegible]	9,677
1861,	36,[illegible]	9,765	69,378	2,[illegible]	[illegible]	111,[illegible]	161,[illegible]	2,135	[illegible]	10,[illegible]
1862,	43,[illegible]	13,110	41,[illegible]	2,[illegible]	56,[illegible]	145,[illegible]	[illegible]	2,615	[illegible]	15,750
1863,	45,101	14,[illegible]	46,347	2,431	61,[illegible]	279,370	340,[illegible]	3,077	[illegible]	13,[illegible]
1864,	69,477	15,781	53,[illegible]	2,[illegible]	82,[illegible]	151,[illegible]	217,771	2,[illegible]	[illegible]	12,768
1865,	45,[illegible]	15,410	61,[illegible]	2,[illegible]	67,[illegible]	[illegible]	[illegible]	2,741	[illegible]	10,[illegible]
1866,	41,[illegible]	13,[illegible]	[illegible]	2,[illegible]	64,117	[illegible],141	[illegible]	2,[illegible]	[illegible],104	11,341
1867,	46,575	11,742	44,175	2,431	57,[illegible]	154,[illegible]	211,[illegible]	2,[illegible]	[illegible]	15,[illegible]
1868,	44,819	11,[illegible]	41,[illegible]	2,[illegible]	65,[illegible]	164,[illegible]	240,[illegible]	2,[illegible]	[illegible]	11,679
1869,	47,776	9,878	41,[illegible]	2,441	54,[illegible]	161,[illegible]	155,[illegible]	2,410	[illegible]	12,[illegible]
1870,	46,012	8,153	59,[illegible]	2,510	69,760	153,[illegible]	183,135	2,[illegible]	[illegible]	10,697
1871,	49,373	8,718	59,717	2,610	69,310	161,[illegible]	191,[illegible]	2,[illegible]	[illegible],610	10,[illegible]

It will be observed from the above that a slight decrease has taken place in the total number admitted in sickness during the year. A considerable increase, however, has taken place under the head of Fever and other dangerous contagious diseases and cases of Accidental Injury, the number of cases under these heads having risen from 8,153 and 2,510 to 8,718 and 2,610 respectively.

14. The following is a statement of the result of the Weekly Summaries of Indoor Relief, showing the average daily number of recipients of relief for each of the twenty years ending 29th September, 1871:—

[TABLE.

Average Daily Number in receipt of Relief during the year, Average Number of Deaths per Week, and Rate of Mortality.

Year ended 29th Sept.	Estimated Population.	Able-bodied. Males.	Females.	Total.	[illegible] Children [illegible]	Sick in Workhouse Hospitals. Fever.	Other Cases.	Total.	All other Classes. Males.	Females.	Total.	Total [illegible] in Workhouses.	Deaths in Work-houses. [illegible]	[illegible]	[illegible]
1852.	6,[illegible]	14,918	37,332	52,251	73,961	3,518	[illegible]	[illegible]	4,428	7,618	12,143	166,821	601	2·7	[illegible]
1853.	[illegible]	10,[illegible]	[illegible]	37,[illegible]	37,164	[illegible]	20,410	[illegible]	[illegible]	[illegible]	10,791	[illegible]	[illegible]	3·0	[illegible]
1854.	6,1[illegible]	7,111	[illegible]	[illegible]	[illegible]	7,167	[illegible]	21,[illegible]	[illegible]	[illegible]	[illegible]	93,180	[illegible]	3·3	[illegible]
1855.	6,197,[illegible]	[illegible]	11,[illegible]	19,124	31,[illegible]	[illegible]	16,914	[illegible]	[illegible]	3,404	7,[illegible]	79,811	[illegible]	2·6	[illegible]
1856.	6,077,[illegible]	3,576	10,[illegible]	13,[illegible]	[illegible]	[illegible]	16,473	17,[illegible]	[illegible]	[illegible]	7,1[illegible]	63,[illegible]	[illegible]	[illegible]	[illegible]
1857.	6,041,[illegible]	[illegible]	7,[illegible]	10,[illegible]	17,[illegible]	[illegible]	14,376	16,[illegible]	[illegible]	4,137	6,[illegible]	50,[illegible]	175	3·5	[illegible]
1858.	6,012,[illegible]	[illegible]	7,111	[illegible]	[illegible]	[illegible]	14,[illegible]	14,[illegible]	[illegible]	4,013	6,14[illegible]	[illegible]	[illegible]	3·8	[illegible]
1859.	[illegible]	[illegible]	[illegible]	7,[illegible]	11,311	97[illegible]	13,[illegible]	1[illegible]	2,341	[illegible]	6,[illegible]	40,[illegible]	[illegible]	3·8	[illegible]
1860.	[illegible]	[illegible]	[illegible]	7,[illegible]	11,[illegible]	[illegible]	13,[illegible]	[illegible]	[illegible]	[illegible]	7,[illegible]	41,[illegible]	[illegible]	4·0	[illegible]
1861.	5,7[illegible]	[illegible]	[illegible]	[illegible]	12,[illegible]	1,[illegible]	14,[illegible]	15,[illegible]	[illegible]	[illegible]	[illegible]	46,[illegible]	[illegible]	4·0	[illegible]
1862.	5,7[illegible]	[illegible]	[illegible]	11,[illegible]	[illegible]	1,[illegible]	16,13[illegible]	17,[illegible]	[illegible]	6,031	10,[illegible]	[illegible]	[illegible]	4·3	[illegible]
1863.	5,[illegible]	[illegible]	[illegible]	11,[illegible]	14,[illegible]	1,[illegible]	[illegible]	18,[illegible]	[illegible]	[illegible]	11,[illegible]	57,310	[illegible]	4·4	[illegible]
1864.	5,[illegible]	[illegible]	7,[illegible]	10,[illegible]	14,11[illegible]	[illegible]	16,7[illegible]	18,[illegible]	[illegible]	[illegible]	11,[illegible]	[illegible]	[illegible]	4·3	[illegible]
1865.	5,673,[illegible]	[illegible]	[illegible]	8,1[illegible]	[illegible]	[illegible]	[illegible]	18,[illegible]	[illegible]	[illegible]	11,[illegible]	[illegible]	[illegible]	4·3	[illegible]
1866.	[illegible]	[illegible]	[illegible]	[illegible]	14,[illegible]	[illegible]	15,[illegible]	17,[illegible]	[illegible]	6,177	10,[illegible]	[illegible]	[illegible]	4·4	[illegible]
1867.	[illegible]	[illegible]	[illegible]	[illegible]	13,[illegible]	[illegible]	[illegible]	18,741	[illegible]	[illegible]	11,77[illegible]	[illegible]	[illegible]	4·6	[illegible]
1868.	5,[illegible]	[illegible]	[illegible]	[illegible]	16,[illegible]	1,1[illegible]	[illegible]	[illegible]	[illegible]	7,[illegible]	12,1[illegible]	[illegible]	731	4·1	[illegible]
1869.	5,[illegible]	[illegible]	[illegible]	[illegible]	16,[illegible]	[illegible]	[illegible]	[illegible]	[illegible]	[illegible]	12,[illegible]	[illegible]	[illegible]	4·1	[illegible]
1870.	5,[illegible]	[illegible]	[illegible]	7,[illegible]	12,[illegible]	946	15,[illegible]	16,[illegible]	[illegible]	[illegible]	11,[illegible]	[illegible]	[illegible]	4·1	[illegible]
1871.	5,[illegible]	[illegible]	[illegible]	[illegible]	12,[illegible]	[illegible]	14,[illegible]	15,[illegible]	[illegible]	[illegible]	11,[illegible]	[illegible]	[illegible]	4·3	[illegible]

15. The following is a statement of the Parliamentary Grant for Medical and Educational purposes, and of its distribution for the year ended 25th March, 1871:—

	Amount Claimed and Granted for the Year. £	s.	d.
Medical purposes, ...	64,280	17	0
Educational purposes, ...	7,563	15	7
Total, ...	71,844	12	7

The total amount claimed and allowed under the Parliamentary Grant for the year ended March, 1871, namely, £71,844 12s. 7d., is £1,835 1s. 4d. in excess of the claim for the previous year, and arises chiefly from increases of salary.

[STATEMENT.

16. STATEMENT of the Annual Collection and Expenditure of Poor Rates for twenty years, ended on the 29th September, 1871; showing the Net Annual Value of Property rated, the Amount of Poor Rate collected, and the Expenditure under the Poor Relief and Medical Charities Acts, &c., for each year ended 29th September, from 1852 to 1871, inclusive.

Year ended 29th September.	Net Annual Value of Property rated.	Amount of Poor Rate collected.	Expenditure for Relief of the Poor. In-Maintenance.	Out-door Relief.	Salaries and Rations of Officers.	Other Expenses.	Total Poor Relief Expenditure.	Expenditure under Medical Charities Acts.	Total of Poor Relief and Medical Charities.	Repayments under Annuities Acts.*	Expenses under Burial Grounds Acts, paid out of the Poor Rates.	Expenses under Registration Acts.	Expenses under the Sanitary Acts.	Expenses under Cattle Plague Act.	Total Expenditure.	Poundage of the Expenditure on Valuation. Poor Relief.	Total.
	£	£	£	£	£	£	£	£	£	£	£	£	£	£	£	s. d.	s. d.
1852. .	11,172,586	1,109,53	517,185	4,917	183,782	227,133	933,967	54,289	987,556	182,122	–	–		–	1,059,678	1 7	1 11½
1853. .	11,708,015	1,009,493	446,030	4,920	139,804	168,464	758,718	88,440	874,158	179,829	–	–	–	.	1,053,987	1 4½	1 10½
1854. .	11,463,595	923,154	453,858	3,715	127,417	165,192	750,182	89,707	842,889	71,925	–	–	–	–	921,594	1 4	1 7½
1855. .	11,563,466	835,594	432,842	4,702	119,853	127,882	685,249	89,898	774,647	14,228	–	–	–	–	788,878	1 2½	1 4½
1856. .	11,703,934	728,204	358,912	2,245	112,283	102,899	576,390	90,250	666,650	4,160	–	–	–	–	671,068	0 11½	1 1½
1857. .	11,877,038	585,583	292,685	2,612	103,743	101,047	499,889	90,160	589,849	1,416	–	–	–	–	590,765	0 10	1 0
1858. .	12,091,864	523,565	268,076	3,185	97,866	88,107	457,178	82,733	549,903	348	–	–	–	–	550,248	0 9	0 11
1859. .	12,213,650	525,063	234,202	3,229	93,903	82,866	413,712	69,336	513,048	568	–	–	–	–	513,616	0 8½	0 10
1860. .	12,280,029	525,880	372,682	4,514	97,841	82,491	454,531	104,217	558,778	57	–	–	–	–	558,835	0 9	0 11
1861. .	12,412,310	584,848	327,870	8,675	94,143	84,081	516,769	104,681	621,150	21	–	–	–	–	621,471	0 10	1 0
1862. .	12,567,498	686,716	379,316	14,750	98,809	85,825	578,709	106,858	685,467	12	117	–	–	–	685,770	0 11½	1 1
1863. .	12,623,539	729,843	370,737	18,372	96,223	110,650	663,981	109,206	715,187	25	1,011	–	–	–	718,525	0 11½	1 1½
1864. .	12,754,854	744,854	368,782	31,478	97,654	110,896	566,165	134,985	711,370	–	633	12,196	–	–	734,218	0 11½	1 1½
1865. .	12,935,165	749,429	385,189	28,333	89,467	110,837	600,849	117,859	717,889	–	714	13,850	–	–	731,843	0 11½	1 1½
1866. .	12,889,026	749,787	371,868	29,748	101,813	108,107	611,531	116,316	728,117	–	471	12,892	–	13,207	754,687	0 11½	1 2
1867. .	13,043,735	782,544	418,369	10,675	106,968	111,769	676,778	118,110	794,894	–	1,401	12,770	13,108	266	824,449	1 0½	1 3½
1868. .	13,117,769	860,070	438,832	14,785	108,758	117,171	707,330	121,963	829,891	–	2,060	12,452	8,067	–	847,888	1 1	1 3½
1869. .	13,153,485	818,450	408,255	18,184	111,061	113,884	674,884	123,716	798,607	–	2,459	12,425	8,286	–	817,772	1 0½	1 2½
1870. .	13,183,888*	733,845	381,884	49,181	113,467	118,870	668,207	129,838	798,189	–	1,488	12,903	8,898	–	816,973	1 0½	1 3½
1871. .	13,220,394	789,853	332,589	59,764	117,884	118,381	628,668	173,888	829,673	–	1,752	12,855	4,845	–	846,135	1 0½	1 3½

* All sums due from Unions in Ireland under the Consolidated Annuities Act had been levied and paid over before the close of the year 1863; there will be no further sums therefore to enter under this head in future years.

Hence it will be seen that the total disbursement of poor-rates for all purposes, viz., relief, medical relief, burial grounds, registration of births, deaths, and marriages, and sanitary measures was in 1870 £815,973, and the amount of poor-rate collected £753,345, the expenditure making a poundage of 1s. 2¾d. in the pound on the valuation. In 1871 the expenditure was £840,135, or 1s. 3¼d. in the pound, and the poor-rate collected only £739,053, the difference between the expenditure and collection being, to a great extent, covered by the Parliamentary Grant for Medical and Educational purposes.

17. The following four tables present some details for the eight years last past, which may be regarded with interest as showing the progressive operation of recent amendments of the law:—

Repayment of Relief.

Year ended 29th September.	From Paupers relieved by way of Loan.			From Poor Persons, under 6 & 7 Vic., c. 92, and 25 & 26 Vic., c. 83.			From Constabulary Patients.			Total.		
	£	s.	d.	£	s.	d.	£	s.	d.	£	s.	d.
1864, . .	843	8	2	189	2	1	155	17	1	1,188	7	4
1865, . .	804	8	9	292	5	5	131	19	4	1,228	8	6
1866, . .	817	9	4	324	9	10	180	19	7	1,322	11	9
1867, . .	986	18	10½	357	17	1	145	3	6	1,489	19	5½
1868, . .	805	5	4	487	12	0	167	16	7	1,464	11	11
1869, . .	1,048	4	9	411	13	3	157	7	4	1,617	5	8
1870, . .	1,216	4	6	392	11	1	196	14	10	1,804	10	7
1871, . .	1,346	1	3	500	13	1	225	11	3	1,[illegible]	5	7

Expenditure in Out-Door Relief.

Year ended 29th September.	In Money.			In Kind.			Cost of Orphans and Deserted Children, under [illegible] of 25 & 26 Vic., c. 83.			Total.		
	£	s.	d.	£	s.	d.	£	s.	d.	£	s.	d.
1864, . .	15,108	10	3	4,347	6	6	1,016	18	6	21,472	15	3
1865, . .	17,816	12	2	5,541	6	8½	1,377	5	9	23,[illegible]	19	7½
1866, . .	20,920	8	5	6,055	4	3¼	2,772	17	6¼	29,748	5	9
1867, . .	30,425	11	1½	6,294	11	6	3,357	1	7¼	40,075	3	9¼
1868, . .	33,868	2	2½	7,131	15	2	3,785	12	1	44,785	9	5½
1869, . .	39,014	12	4½	5,025	2	7½	4,143	12	9	48,181	7	3
1870, . .	45,431	8	2	6,445	9	6½	7,304	13	4½	59,181	8	1½
1871, . .	53,235	16	3	7,053	1	8½	8,885	4	8	69,744	2	7½

Maintenance in Asylums and Extern Hospitals.

Year ended 29th September.	In Blind Asylums.			In Deaf and Dumb Asylums.			Patients in Extern Hospitals.			Total.		
	£	s.	d.	£	s.	d.	£	s.	d.	£	s.	d.
1864, . .	2,444	0	0	1,551	14	10	1,698	14	5	5,694	9	3
1865, . .	2,817	8	9	1,783	17	3	2,018	2	3	6,618	8	3
1866, . .	2,435	8	9	1,560	2	9	3,779	13	2	6,176	4	8
1867, . .	2,588	13	11	2,319	5	5	1,098	13	8	6,148	11	0
1868, . .	2,458	13	1	3,065	10	5	755	10	1	6,280	0	7
1869, . .	2,427	1	7	3,548	5	5	720	1	2	6,693	8	2
1870, . .	2,549	6	10	3,720	6	9	736	10	7	7,006	4	2
1871, . .	2,503	8	8	4,059	18	2	664	11	4	7,227	18	2

*EXPENDITURE UNDER THE SANITARY ACTS.

Year ended 29th September.	Under Sewage Utilization Act.	Under Nuisances Removal Acts.	Under Diseases Prevention Acts.	Total.
	£ s. d.	£ s. d.	£ s. d.	£ s. d.
1867, . .	1,370 19 6	2,020 6 10	10,717 2 6½	14,108 5 10½
1868, . .	1,124 18 11	2,260 8 4	276 18 4	3,662 5 7
1869, . .	1,475 5 7	1,601 13 6	209 6 7	3,286 4 8
1870, . .	1,867 3 9	1,780 0 0	171 19 9	3,821 10 6
1871, . .	2,213 17 2	2,631 0 7	—	4,844 17 9

18. We here continue from last Report a form of table exhibiting for the last twenty-two years—the whole period, in fact, subsequent to the famine—the per-centage in each successive year of the several classes of workhouse inmates as compared with the whole number—

CLASSIFIED RETURN of the Number of Inmates of Workhouses in Ireland, on the first Saturday of January; and the per-centage of the several classes on the total Number of Inmates.

First Saturday of January.	Inmates not in Hospital: Able-bodied Males.	Able-bodied Females.	Children under 15 years of age.	Other classes.	Number in Hospital.	Total Number in Workhouses.	Per-centage on Total Number: Able-bodied Males.	Able-bodied Females.	Children under 15 years of age not in Hospital.	Other classes not in Hospital.	In Hospital.
4 Jan., 1851	23,179	49,758	91,569	14,083	38,923	[illegible]	10·7	21·1	41·1	6·5	[illegible]
3 ,, 1852	16,734	37,643	76,453	11,456	25,975	168,261	9·6	22·1	45·5	7·0	15·7
1 ,, 1853	12,291	[illegible]	61,844	10,825	31,826	130,764	9·6	23·0	41·7	7·8	15·5
7 ,, 1854	9,729	27,731	49,792	8,750	22,509	104,034	8·9	26·3	45·9	8·1	21·6
6 ,, 1855	8,157	16,167	34,794	2,827	17,106	[illegible]	7·3	19·1	[illegible]	8·3	[illegible]
5 ,, 1856	4,615	14,701	27,153	7,717	18,329	73,118	6·4	19·0	37·7	10·7	[illegible]
3 ,, 1857	3,512	9,740	19,187	6,011	16,771	56,123	6·4	16·8	34·9	11·9	30·0
2 ,, 1858	2,401	6,331	13,628	6,287	14,603	[illegible]	5·6	15·9	31·7	15·0	[illegible]
1 ,, 1859	2,317	[illegible]	12,531	6,147	13,833	41,509	5·1	15·6	[illegible]	14·8	[illegible]
7 ,, 1860	2,156	6,731	11,707	2,637	18,029	41,310	[illegible]	15·7	27·1	17·4	[illegible]
5 ,, 1861	[illegible]	7,199	[illegible]	6,616	14,766	42,372	5·5	16·5	[illegible]	17·9	[illegible]
4 ,, 1862	[illegible]	8,194	[illegible]	9,011	11,656	53,169	4·9	16·7	27·4	17·8	[illegible]
3 ,, 1863	[illegible]	9,644	16,750	11,192	18,481	[illegible]	5·7	16·1	27·8	19·4	[illegible]
2 ,, 1864	[illegible]	[illegible]	17,176	[illegible]	19,722	[illegible]	6·1	16·9	[illegible]	19·6	[illegible]
7 ,, 1865	[illegible]	[illegible]	[illegible]	12,101	19,345	60,178	5·7	[illegible]	[illegible]	[illegible]	[illegible]
6 ,, 1866	[illegible]	[illegible]	15,736	[illegible]	17,643	[illegible]	[illegible]	15·7	[illegible]	21·1	[illegible]
5 ,, 1867	3,013	[illegible]	14,731	[illegible]	[illegible]	[illegible]	[illegible]	17·2	[illegible]	[illegible]	[illegible]
4 ,, 1868	[illegible]	[illegible]	14,960	[illegible]	[illegible]	[illegible]	5·1	[illegible]	28·0	[illegible]	[illegible]
2 ,, 1869	[illegible]	7,062	14,344	13,176	15,815	[illegible]	5·1	17·4	29·0	[illegible]	[illegible]
1 ,, 1870	[illegible]	[illegible]	[illegible]	13,135	[illegible]	[illegible]	[illegible]	[illegible]	[illegible]	[illegible]	[illegible]
7 ,, 1871	[illegible]	6,070	[illegible]	[illegible]	[illegible]	[illegible]	4·8	[illegible]	[illegible]	[illegible]	[illegible]
6 ,, 1872	[illegible]	[illegible]	[illegible]	[illegible]	[illegible]	44,730	4·8	10·7	[illegible]	[illegible]	34·0

19. It has fallen to our lot in the course of the past year to be obliged to exercise once more the power of dissolving the Board of Guardians of a union, and of appointing instead paid officers to discharge the duties of the Board, and manage the business of the union. This power, which during the famine period was exercised in no less than forty-three cases, had not been used for more than twenty years, and the occasion for using it once more arose in the Millstreet Union, which is situate in the county of Cork. There were not, as in the cases of the famine period, any material difficulties to contend with in the management of the business of Millstreet Union. But the Board, consisting of fourteen ex-officio and the same number of elected Guardians, absolutely ceased to meet, the legal quorum of three having failed to be obtained no

* This table contains, for the year 1867, the extra expenditure during the last epidemic of cholera.

less than nine times in the course of twelve weeks, and after a long series of remonstrances addressed both to the Board collectively and to its members individually, it appeared with sufficient distinctness that, with one solitary exception, no member of the Board would willingly attend the weekly meetings. This person, an elected Guardian for one of the electoral divisions, had been from the time of his election a constant attendant at the weekly meetings, and so exercised his functions that after a certain lapse of time he and the Clerk of the Union had the board-room week after week entirely to themselves. We shall not enter into the particulars of that course of conduct of the elected Guardian which produced such a strange result, nor are we perhaps wholly acquainted with them, but we must say that the other members of the Board who abandoned the performance of their duty for a reason like this, did not act in a proper spirit, or acquit themselves creditably as guardians of the poor. At all events, we could not take upon ourselves the responsibility of permitting the interests of the ratepayers and the poor to remain without some form of legal management while the remedy was in our hands under provisions of the Legislature expressly enacted to meet such a contingency. The order of dissolution, and the correspondence which immediately preceded it will be found in the Appendix.* The order bears date 11th October, 1871, and still remains in force. The Vice-Guardians were warmly welcomed by the ratepayers, especially by those resident in Millstreet, at whose request they at once took in hand a project for providing both the workhouse and the town of Millstreet with a permanent supply of pure and wholesome water, that which hitherto it has been necessary to use being contaminated by sewage. This project had been for a long time under the consideration of the dissolved Board of Guardians, but they took no effectual steps in the matter. Two sources of supply having been pointed out, situate at about equal distances, little more than a mile from the town, the Vice-Guardians obtained from Dr. Cameron, public analyst in Dublin, a comparison of their respective qualities and acted upon his opinion, which was decisively in favour of one of the samples. Eight hundred pounds, the necessary cost of conveying this water by pipes to the workhouse, and to four fountains to be constructed equidistant from each other in the town, have been borrowed from the Public Works Loan Commissioners on the security of the rates, and the works are now in progress; and until this salutary business has been accomplished, we shall not entertain the question of recalling the Vice-Guardians from Millstreet and reconstituting the Board of Guardians for the purpose of again committing to its hands the management of the affairs of the union. We have entered into these particulars about the water supply, because they are suggestive of one of the modes of action by which the superintending authority in the administration of the Public Health Acts may be enabled to accomplish effectually the execution of necessary works; and at this time when the legislature has that subject under consideration, it seems not out of season to show an example of the successful working of the machinery referred to.

* Appendix A. VI., page 62.

PROCEEDINGS under the MEDICAL CHARITIES ACT, IRELAND (14th and 15th Vic., cap. 68); the Act of 1858, "To make further provision for the Practice of Vaccination in Ireland;" and the Act of 1863, "To further extend and make compulsory the Practice of Vaccination in Ireland."

20. We now proceed to submit to your Excellency the Report of our proceedings for the last year under the above-mentioned Acts of Parliament.

In the last line of the subjoined table is given a summary of the relief afforded under the Medical Charities Act for the year ended September 30th, 1871, in each Province and in all Ireland, distinguishing as usual the cases attended at the patients' homes from those attended at the Dispensaries; and also for the purpose of exhibiting the changes in the amount and description of relief afforded yearly, a similar summary for each of the nine previous years.

The comparison of the numbers for the two last years in this table shows, for the first time since the enactment of the Medical Charities Act in 1851, a diminution in the number of patients of both classes, both of those attended at their own homes and of those attended at the Dispensary stations, in all the provinces of Ireland. Of Dispensary cases, for the last compared with the previous year, there has been a decrease in Ulster of 8,192 cases, in Munster of 6,686, in Leinster of 12,451, and in Connaught of 6,404. Of domiciliary cases there has been a decrease for the latter year of 4,910 cases in Ulster, of 2,145 in Munster, of 762 in Leinster, and of 1,596 in Connaught;—giving for the whole of Ireland a decrease of 33,733 Dispensary cases and of 9,416 of those attended at the patients' homes.

The detailed statement of the expenses incurred in carrying the Medical Charities Act into execution in each Dispensary district, as required by the 20th section of the Act, and also the detail of the medical relief afforded in each district will be found in the Appendix.*

* Appendix D, No. 2, page [illegible].

SUMMARY of the NUMBER of CASES of MEDICAL RELIEF afforded under the Medical Charities Act.

Period.	Province of Ulster.			Province of Munster.			Province of Leinster.			Province of Connaught.			Total for Ireland.		
	Dispensary Tickets.	Visiting Tickets.	Total.	Dispensary Tickets.	Visiting Tickets.	Total.	Dispensary Tickets.	Visiting Tickets.	Total.	Dispensary Tickets.	Visiting Tickets.	Total.	Dispensary Tickets.	Visiting Tickets.	Total.
	(1.)	(2.)	(3.)	(4.)	(5.)	(6.)	(7.)	(8.)	(9.)	(10.)	(11.)	(12.)	(13.)	(14.)	(15.)
Year ended 30th Sept., 1862,	111,679	50,611	162,290	239,009	33,248	273,257	217,078	58,363	274,441	81,690	17,501	99,191	650,456	179,723	849,179
Year ended 30th Sept., 1863,	150,110	55,901	205,011	236,534	56,648	293,182	225,725	65,159	290,884	83,510	17,791	103,239	697,087	192,929	890,616
Year ended 30th Sept., 1864,	148,991	58,863	207,844	230,967	60,033	290,890	223,839	61,690	283,019	87,141	17,211	104,352	691,038	197,797	888,835
Year ended 30th Sept., 1865,	137,085	58,349	196,356	212,838	60,773	273,611	201,780	63,136	254,866	82,882	19,915	102,797	633,538	202,335	857,069
Year ended 30th Sept., 1866,	123,510	55,232	178,742	164,780	55,651	210,431	187,383	62,391	249,906	73,587	18,011	91,698	563,362	191,235	760,797
Year ended 30th Sept., 1867,	130,979	42,733	173,712	184,176	54,030	240,135	194,850	65,413	260,563	79,747	17,554	96,301	572,722	191,680	764,402
Year ended 30th Sept., 1868,	133,638	33,651	170,789	191,930	54,178	246,463	188,094	58,399	246,493	78,064	17,229	95,993	584,604	183,155	767,759
Year ended 30th Sept., 1869,	128,383	58,988	187,371	163,463	55,856	229,319	190,176	62,395	252,571	77,808	16,356	93,666	579,580	195,797	775,537
Year ended 30th Sept., 1870,	127,974	39,922	167,896	182,408	57,813	240,221	192,432	64,884	257,316	78,390	20,601	98,991	581,224	203,200	784,424
Year ended 30th Sept., 1871,	119,785	55,006	174,791	175,722	55,068	231,890	180,001	64,162	244,163	71,886	19,005	90,891	547,491	193,784	741,573

21. The next table gives the expenditure on medical relief under the Medical Charities Act in each province and for all Ireland in each of the last ten years ended September 29th, including, in addition to the original Medical Charities expenditure, the expense incurred in carrying out the Vaccination Acts, by which separate remuneration was awarded to the Dispensary Medical Officers for successful vaccinations, and a new expenditure rendered necessary for the provision of vaccinating stations, in addition to the Dispensary stations where vaccination is procurable continuously. At the vaccinating stations, of which two or more have been provided in each Dispensary district, in spring and autumn each year the Medical Officers attend to vaccinate all applicants.

Medical Charities Expenditure, Years ended 29th September.

Year.	Ulster.	Munster.	Leinster.	Connaught.	Total.
	£	£	£	£	£
1862,	28,979	31,991	31,748	14,190	106,858
1863,	29,676	32,263	32,646	14,598	109,208
1864,	31,264	34,367	34,136	15,118	114,905
1865,	31,493	34,983	34,762	15,841	117,058
1866,	31,749	34,464	34,439	16,243	116,915
1867,	32,020	35,341	34,683	16,072	118,118
1868,	34,017	35,431	36,401	16,136	121,985
1869,	34,623	35,644	36,634	16,835	123,716
1870,	34,464	37,686	38,130	17,676	129,936
1871,	34,881	38,862	41,151	18,111	135,005

The figures for the two last years in this table show an increased total expenditure for 1871 compared with 1870 of £5,069, nearly half of which, viz., £2,336, has been occasioned by the existing epidemic of small-pox, the panic caused by which has created an increase of applications for vaccination, and among the adult population a quite exceptional number of applications for re-vaccination, whereby the vaccination fees of the Dispensary Medical Officers have been increased from £6,384 for 1870 to £8,720 for 1871. A large proportion of the increased expenditure has fallen on Leinster, viz., £3,021. In Munster the increase has been £1,176, in Ulster, £417, and in Connaught £435. The disproportionate increase of expenditure in Leinster is also mainly attributable to the epidemic, which has hitherto more especially prevailed in this province.

22. The next table sets forth a comparative statement for the two years ended September 29th of the items of the general expenditure under the usual heads.

		1870.		1871.
1. Medicines and medical appliances,		£23,707		£23,489
2. Rent of Dispensary buildings,		7,353		7,563
3. Books, forms, stationery, printing, and advertising,		2,594		1,166
4. Salaries of { Medical Officers,		77,917		80,725
{ Apothecaries,		2,363		2,503
5. Fuel, porters, and incidental expenses,		8,763		10,001
Expenses under Vaccination Act:—				
6. Vaccination fees and other expenses:—				
Fees to Medical Officers,	6,384	7,140	8,720	9,627
Other expenses,	756		907	
		£129,936		£135,005

Under the first head in the above table there appears a decrease of expenditure for 1871 compared with 1870 on Medicines and Medical Appliances of £287. This decrease is in accordance with the above-mentioned diminution in the number of applicants for Dispensary relief in 1871. Under the head of Books, Stationery, Printing, and Advertising there has been a considerable decrease of expenditure, viz., £1,523. This item in 1870 was raised above the usual average by the expense incurred in that year in providing the new books and forms required by the Revised General Rules and Regulations for the Management of the Dispensaries of November 1869. The present expenditure under this head is rather under the average of late years. The item, Rent of Dispensary Buildings, shows the small increase of £210. The usual increase under Salaries of Medical Officers, which has occurred every year since the establishment of the present system of Dispensary relief, amounts for 1871 compared with 1870 to £2,949, and is rather greater than the corresponding increase for 1870, which was £2,558. Under the head of Fuel, Porters, and Incidental Expenses the expenditure for 1871 has been £1,238 above that of the previous year—an increase for which we are unable to assign any satisfactory explanation. The considerable increase of expense for 1871 in carrying out the Vaccination Acts, amounting to £2,467, results from the considerable increase during that year of vaccinations of children born since 1864, together with the large increase of applications for vaccination by persons born before that year, and the quite exceptional number of applicants for re-vaccination occasioned by the panic.

The average poundage on the Poor-Law Valuation of Ireland, now amounting to £13,239,394, to provide for the above-mentioned total expenditure, was 2·44*d*., which is slightly higher than that for the year before, viz., 2·36*d*.

23. The alterations which have been effected during the past year in the Dispensary arrangements have been very inconsiderable. In the Gort Union, the Ballinderoon Dispensary District, which was much above average both in area and population, was divided into the Kinvara and Ardrahan Districts, with a medical officer for each, the services of the apothecary of the former Ballinderoon Dispensary District being dispensed with.

24. In the course of the year, skilled midwives to attend on midwifery cases so long as the course of the labour is natural, were appointed in ten additional dispensary districts. Although these most useful appointments, of which there are now 178, increase from year to year, we think it is much to be regretted that they are not generally adopted by the dispensary committees.

25. The numbers of members of Committees of Management have been increased in 23 dispensary districts.

26. Since the date of the last Annual Report, fifteen Dispensary Medical Officers have been superannuated under the Poor Law Medical Officers Superannuation Act. With few exceptions, the

Guardians have awarded in all such cases two-thirds of the salaries as retiring allowance, the highest award permitted by the Act.

27. The next table sets forth the progress of the vaccination of the poor under the Medical Charities Act alone, from September 30th, 1853, to the same date 1858, and also the strikingly beneficial effects of the Acts for the promotion of vaccination in Ireland of the Acts of Lord Naas and Sir Robert Peel of 1858 and 1863; the former awarding payment in addition to their salaries to the Medical Officers for successful vaccinations, and the latter making compulsory the vaccination of children born in 1864 or subsequently. The large increase in the annual number of vaccinations recorded in this table—from 43,352 in the first year in the table to 140,220 for the last but one—may fairly be attributed to successful legislation, with the exception of 1856, in which year the numbers nearly doubled those of the year before, owing to panic caused by the epidemic of small-pox of 1855–56. The great increase in the numbers of vaccinations for the year ended September 30th, 1871, viz., 36,669, is also mainly owing to the panic occasioned by the far severer epidemic now prevailing.

TABLE.

			Number of Cases of Vaccination				Number of Cases of Vaccination
Year ended Sept. 30th,		1853, .	43,352	Year ended Sept. 30th,		1863, .	106,516
"	"	1854, .	52,644	"	"	1864, .	191,810
"	"	1855, .	46,711	"	"	1865, .	169,148
"	"	1856, .	84,131	"	"	1866, .	137,124
"	"	1857, .	47,855	"	"	1867, .	125,741
"	"	1858, .	54,954	"	"	1868, .	131,426
"	"	1859, .	140,411	"	"	1869, .	125,673
"	"	1860, .	107,305	"	"	1870, .	140,220
"	"	1861, .	90,254	"	"	1871, .	176,889
"	"	1862, .	59,[illegible]				

28. The next table exhibits the progress of vaccination by the Dispensary Medical Officers under the Compulsory Vaccination Act, for the last seven years; and shows the continuous decline yearly, except for the last year, in the number of persons vaccinated who were exempt from the operation of that Act. In the Annual Report for last year, we had occasion to express the satisfaction we experienced on account of the large increase of vaccination among children born since 1863. We said—"The comparison of the two last years affords very gratifying evidence of the progress of vaccination during the year ended September 30th, 1870. It shows indeed the usual decrease of vaccinations among the population born before January, 1864, amounting to 2,597 cases; but whereas in last year's Report we had to lament a decrease in Ulster of infant vaccinations amounting to 1,642, and but an inconsiderable increase in the other provinces, there has been, on the contrary, a considerable increase for the last year in all the provinces—viz., in Ulster an increase of 5,226 cases, in Munster of 3,575, in Leinster of 4,388, and in Connaught of 4,006; thus giving for all Ireland the highly gratifying result of an increase

of 17,145 cases of infant vaccinations." The table below shows for the last year not only a further increase of vaccinations of children subject to compulsory vaccination of 3,996, but, instead of the steady decrease year by year of the numbers vaccinated among those exempt from compulsory vaccination that has taken place since 1863, there has been the extraordinary increase for the year ended September 30th, 1871, of 35,673 cases. The explanation of this quite exceptional demand for the vaccination of children above seven years of age, and of adults, and for the re-vaccination of adults, which has contributed considerably to the increase in question, is to be found in the panic caused by the present small-pox epidemic. Accordingly it is remarkable that more than half of the increase,—viz., 18,741 cases—have occurred in Leinster, in which hitherto the disease has been more alarmingly prevalent than in the other provinces. There were in Leinster for the previous year only 895 vaccinations of persons born before 1864. In Ulster the vaccinations of the same class of cases have risen from 1,548 for 1870 to 8,953 for 1871; in Munster, from 1,491 for 1870 to 7,943 in 1871; and in Connaught, from 1,129 in 1870 to 4,204 in 1871. Thus the total number of vaccinations for the last year in the table, compared with the year before shows an increase of 39,000 vaccinations, 3,996 of which were those of children of seven years of age or under. The ascertained fact to which we have drawn attention formerly, that three-fourths of the entire mortality caused by small-pox falls upon children under five years old, makes manifest the great importance of early vaccination; and with the view to procure information on this important point, we requested the Dispensary Medical Officers, in making their vaccination returns for last year, to state the numbers of children vaccinated by them who were under one year old. We have accordingly learned that in 1871, of 44,897 children under eight years old vaccinated in Ulster, 37,003 were under one year old; in Munster, of 37,798 of the children under eight years, 30,018 were under one year old; in Leinster, of 31,943 of the former class, 24,486 were under one year; and in Connaught, of 24,415 children vaccinated under eight years, 17,240 were in their first year;—giving for all Ireland 109,413 infants vaccinated in their first year, out of the 139,053 vaccinated under eight years old. Notwithstanding this high proportion of early vaccination, so great is its importance, that we are earnestly desirous to urge the Guardians to use every effort to procure the vaccination of all children born within the year, in the first six months of their lives, by promptly enforcing against parents who neglect to have their children vaccinated within that time, the penalty imposed on defaulters by the Compulsory Vaccination Act.

The table gives a summary of the vaccinations performed by the Dispensary Medical Officers for seven years ending September 30th, 1871. The cases of persons born before 1864, and exempt from compulsory vaccination, and those of children born since January, 1864, and subject to compulsory vaccination, are registered separately in columns 1 and 2.

TABLE

Provinces.	No. of Cases of Vaccination performed during the year ended Sept. 30, 1865. Cases of Children born since 1st Jan., 1864. 1.	Other Cases. 2.	Total. 3.
Ulster, . . .	33,271	18,437	51,708
Munster, .	26,410	20,076	47,486
Leinster, .	24,011	17,686	41,697
Connaught, .	13,463	15,181	28,649
Total, Ireland, 1865, . .	97,160	71,989	169,149

Provinces.	No. of Cases of Vaccination performed during the year ended Sept. 30, 1866. Cases of Children born since 1st Jan., 1864. 1.	Other Cases. 2.	Total. 3.
Ulster, . .	36,008	8,704	44,712
Munster, .	28,363	8,894	37,457
Leinster, .	23,726	6,620	29,346
Connaught, .	16,933	8,176	25,109
Total, Ireland, 1866, . .	104,730	32,394	137,124

Provinces.	No. of Cases of Vaccination performed during the year ended Sept. 30, 1867. Cases of Children born since 1st Jan., 1864. 1.	Other Cases. 2.	Total. 3.
Ulster, . .	36,792	3,917	40,709
Munster, .	34,609	6,156	35,965
Leinster, .	22,600	2,732	25,332
Connaught, .	17,572	4,163	21,735
Total, Ireland, 1867, . .	107,473	18,268	125,741

Provinces.	No. of Cases of Vaccination performed during the year ended Sept. 30, 1868. Cases of Children born since 1st Jan., 1864. 1.	Other Cases. 2.	Total. 3.
Ulster, . .	41,093	3,429	44,522
Munster, .	32,008	4,211	36,224
Leinster, .	25,673	2,095	27,767
Connaught, .	19,845	2,048	21,893
Total, Ireland, 1868, . .	118,613	12,813	131,426

Provinces.	No. of Cases of Vaccination performed during the year ended Sept. 30, 1869. Cases of Children born since 1st Jan., 1864. 1.	Other Cases. 2.	Total. 3.
Ulster, . .	39,451	2,436	41,887
Munster, .	32,781	2,275	35,056
Leinster, .	25,781	1,183	26,969
Connaught, .	19,898	1,913	21,808
Total, Ireland, 1869, . .	117,912	7,768	125,677

Provinces.	No. of Cases of Vaccination performed during the year ended Sept. 30, 1870. Cases of Children born since 1st Jan., 1864. 1.	Other Cases. 2.	Total. 3.
Ulster, . .	44,577	1,348	45,925
Munster, .	36,357	1,491	37,848
Leinster, .	30,122	995	31,117
Connaught, .	23,901	1,129	25,030
Total, Ireland, 1870, . .	135,057	5,163	140,220

Provinces.	No. of Cases of Vaccination performed during the year ended Sept. 30, 1871. Cases of Children born since 1st Jan., 1864. 1.	Other Cases. 2.	Total. 3.
Ulster, . .	44,897	8,933	53,830
Munster, .	37,798	7,943	45,741
Leinster, .	31,943	19,736	51,679
Connaught, .	24,415	4,204	28,619
Total, Ireland, 1871, . .	139,053	40,826	179,889

Total, Ireland,	1.	2.	3.
1864,	25,354	166,456	191,810
" 1865,	97,160	71,989	169,149
" 1866,	104,730	32,394	137,124
" 1867,	107,473	18,268	125,741
" 1868,	118,613	12,813	131,426
" 1869,	117,919	7,760	125,679
" 1870,	135,057	5,163	140,220
" 1871,	139,053	40,826	179,889

We can draw no conclusion from the figures in the two tables for the two last years in regard to the ordinary operation of the Compulsory Vaccination Act, which hitherto, with the exception of 1869, has been so satisfactory, because the effect of the small-pox panic completely masks the operation of the Act; but it is at least gratifying to find that the numbers of children under eight years old vaccinated during the last exceed those for the year before in each province, giving a total increase for the whole country of 4,000 cases. There is good reason to believe that the small increase in cases of this class for the last year compared with the extraordinary increase of vaccinations among those exempt from the compulsory vaccination (viz. 35,673, the total number of persons of this class vaccinated the year before having been only 5,163) is to be explained by the fact that we are approaching a complete vaccination of the children born within the year. The number of children whose births were registered by the Registrar-General for the year ended September 30th, 1871, was 151,159, and the vaccinations under the Compulsory Vaccination Act for the same year were 139,053. It is true that of this number many must have been children between one and eight years of age whose parents had neglected to have them vaccinated in their first year; but it is also to be borne in mind that a large number of the 151,159 children would have died in their first year, or would have been vaccinated by private practitioners.

29. The two next tables exhibit the numbers of deaths occasioned by small-pox in the workhouse hospitals yearly from February, 1865 to February, 1872; the number of cases of small-pox treated by the Dispensary Medical Officers in each year of the eight, ending September 30th, 1871; and the numbers of deaths from small-pox registered by the Registrar-General in each quarter of the years 1864–71 inclusive. We have as usual to express our obligations to the Registrar-General for furnishing to us the return for the last quarter in anticipation of its publication.

DEATHS in WORKHOUSES from SMALL-POX and NUMBER of CASES of SMALL-POX treated by DISPENSARY MEDICAL OFFICERS.

Deaths in Workhouses from Small-pox.		Number of Cases of Small-pox treated by Medical Officers of Dispensary Districts.	
Period. 52 Weeks ended	Number of Deaths.	Period. 52 Weeks ended	Number of Cases.
11th February, 1865, . .	145	30th September, 1864, . .	1,965
10th February, 1866, . .	59	30th September, 1865, . .	2,000
9th February, 1867, . .	9	30th September, 1866, . .	470
8th February, 1868, . .	5	30th September, 1867, . .	105
6th February, 1869, . .	3	30th September, 1868, . .	135
5th February, 1870, . .	1	30th September, 1869, . .	37
4th February, 1871, . .	18	30th September, 1870, . .	61
3rd February, 1872, . .	452	30th September, 1871, . .	778

REGISTRAR-GENERAL'S RETURNS.

DEATHS from SMALL-POX registered in IRELAND, during dates undermentioned.

Year.	1st Quarter.	2nd Quarter.	3rd Quarter.	4th Quarter.	TOTAL.
1864	274	241	171	165	851
1865	123	110	53	63	317
1866	108	47	25	9	187
1867	7	5	4	4	20
1868	6	5	5	1	19
1869	8	9	2	1	20
1870	7	3	6	28	32
1871	38	67	101	441	647

30. In paragraph 42 of the Report for 1871, we stated that the marked increase of cases of small-pox, and of deaths caused by it, recorded in these tables for 1870 proved clearly that the epidemic which had previously prevailed severely in many places in Great Britain had reached this country by importation, especially from Liverpool, South Wales, and Glasgow. Many cases were specified in which such importation was clearly traced, and many more such cases have since been reported by the Dispensary Medical Officers. In the absence of any epidemic visitation of small-pox from 1863, when the Compulsory Vaccination Act was passed, to 1870; the deaths from small-pox in the workhouse hospitals were reduced from 145 in 1864 to 1 in 1869; and the numbers of cases treated by the Dispensary Medical Officers were reduced from 1,965 for 52 weeks ended September 30th, 1864 to 27 for 52 weeks ended September 30th, 1869. The second table affords the same evidence, recording the reduction of deaths registered from small-pox for all Ireland from 854 in 1864 to 20 in 1869. In last year's Report we had to announce that the existing epidemic had gained footing in Ireland, and it has now acquired, both in the number of cases and the virulence of the disease, a character of very unusual severity in late years. The contrast between the numbers of deaths and cases quoted above for 1869, and the corresponding numbers for the last year in these tables affords distressing evidence of the truth of this statement. The deaths from small-pox in the workhouse hospitals for that year having been 462, the cases treated by the Dispensary Medical Officers, 773, and the deaths recorded by the Registrar-General from the same disease, 647.

It is painful to contemplate the loss of life occasioned by any of the preventable diseases; but more especially is this true in regard to small-pox, against which we possess an antidote in successful infant vaccination and successful re-vaccination about puberty (to the importance, not to say the necessity of which, the experience of the present epidemic has borne strong evidence) which, with a near approach to certainty, either secures against the attack of the disease or deprives it of its fatal character; not to mention the partial or total loss of sight, the loss of hearing, the developement of scrofulous disease, and the ruin of the general health, which so often occur as the consequences of the disease when contracted by the unprotected.

31. In former Reports we have adverted to the motives which should induce all persons responsible for carrying out the Compulsory Vaccination Act to use every effort to secure the effective vaccination of the children born each year; but assuredly a motive more powerful than any of those formerly urged is to be found in the consideration of the deplorable loss of life and other evils which have already been caused by the present visitation of small-pox, and which will certainly be largely added to before the epidemic entirely subsides, together with the reflection that as regards the children under eight years of age, the calamity might have been nearly entirely prevented by the stringent enforcement of the excellent provisions of the Compulsory Vaccination Act. The well ascertained fact, moreover, should be borne in mind, that in those exceptional cases in which vaccination does not protect absolutely from the attack of small-pox, it seldom fails to mitigate the disease and prevent a fatal result. We are informed by one of our Medical Inspectors, Dr. King, that in the course of the present epidemic in the Cork Union, of 232 cases treated in the Union Hospital, the disease had been fatal in 32 of 100 unvaccinated patients, while only 3 deaths occurred among 132 who had been more or less perfectly vaccinated, a result in complete accordance with the uniform experience of the medical profession on this point. The outbreak and progress of the epidemic in Cork is described in Dr. King's Reports, which will be found in the Appendix.*

32. The returns of the numbers of cases of fever, scarlatina, and small-pox attended by the Dispensary Medical Officers for the year ended September 30th, 1871, show an inconsiderable decrease of cases of fever for this year compared with the year before from 13,744 to 15,574 cases. A considerable decrease in the number of cases of scarlatina has taken place during the same year from 7,424 for 1870 to 6,760 for 1871. The commencement of the small-pox epidemic in 1870 is declared by the increase in the number of cases for the year ended September 30th, 1870, to 51 from 27 for the year before, and its occurrence in various parts of the country is shown by the returns for the succeeding year, giving the serious increase to 773 cases. Of these cases 375 occurred in Leinster, 337 in Ulster, 30 in Munster, and 31 in Connaught;—proving that up to the end of last September the epidemic had hardly reached the two latter provinces.

33. Towards the middle of 1871, alarm having arisen from the fact that Asiatic cholera had appeared in several of the ports of the Baltic and Black Seas, between which and ports in Great Britain and Ireland considerable commercial intercourse exists, and from dread of consequent importation of the disease from some of the infected quarters, the Privy Council in England and your Excellency in Council in Ireland issued orders subjecting all ships arriving from any infected port to quarantine, and prescribing the duties of the masters of such ships, and of the nuisance authorities within whose jurisdiction such vessels might come, in regard to the treatment of persons on board labouring under cholera, and the

* Appendix C, II., p. 188.

disinfection of the vessels, and everything capable of communicating infection. On several occasions subsequently your Excellency directed that information received from the President of the Local Government Board in respect to the foreign ports in which cholera was prevalent should be communicated to us, and this information was at once transmitted to the Boards of Guardians affected by the Irish Order in Council. Soon after, however, the disease subsiding on the Continent, all apprehension of its invasion was at an end, and in no instance has it come to our knowledge that occasion has arisen to put the Order in Council in force.

34. On small-pox showing itself as an epidemic at Belfast, we lost no time in warning the Boards of Guardians of the adjacent populous unions of their danger, and in calling upon them to provide beforehand separate hospital accommodation for small-pox patients, so as to isolate any such cases as very probably might arise from intercourse with Belfast.—See Circular in Appendix.* We have systematically adopted a similar course in the cases of individual unions throughout Ireland in which small-pox made its appearance sporadically either by importation or otherwise.

The Boards of Guardians, almost without exception, attended promptly to these warnings, and with the aid and advice of their workhouse Medical Officers prepared themselves for the reception of small-pox patients, by making arrangements not likely to expose inmates of workhouses to any risk of contagion. The facility afforded by the ample margin of accommodation which generally exists in the unions in Ireland was necessarily of much value herein, especially in regard to the detention of convalescents until the danger of their spreading contagion had gone by.

In the dispensary practice cases would often occur in which the patients or their friends resisted all inducements to avail themselves of resort to the hospital, and on these occasions it fell to the duty of the Medical Officer to cause every precaution to be taken which could be taken against the spread of the disease, by isolating the case as far as practicable, by the free use of disinfecting processes, and, finally, by taking advantage of the popular alarm to vaccinate or revaccinate the residents.

These precautions have been attended by success in the greater part of Ireland, for there are very few unions in which the disease has become epidemic, although a considerable number have been visited by sporadic cases. Up to the date of 17th February last, the weekly returns of deaths in the union workhouses show 126 unions without any death by small-pox during the preceding fifty-two weeks; sixteen unions with only 1 death, and twelve in which the number of deaths has not exceeded 6. The remaining unions, being those in which the epidemic has been most severely felt, are the two Dublin Unions, Cork, Belfast, Antrim, Drogheda, Dundalk, Rathdown, and Wexford. Limerick has to this date escaped the epidemic.

35. In Dublin, as your Excellency is aware, the hospitals ordinarily open to the reception and treatment of dangerous contagious disease are not in connexion with the administration of the Poor

* Appendix A, I., No. 1, page 83.

Law, and the two Dublin Unions therefore form exceptions to the hospital system maintained elsewhere from the poor rate throughout Ireland. Some of the Dublin hospitals, as the Hardwicke, Cork-street, Meath, &c., are maintained wholly or in part by Parliamentary grant, while others, as Sir Patrick Dun's and the Mater Misericordiæ, are supported partly from endowment and partly from private subscriptions.

Under ordinary circumstances, therefore, the treatment of contagious disease in Dublin is not undertaken by the Poor Law authorities, but the latter are able to obtain admission to hospitals not under their own control for all contagious cases arising within the scope of their jurisdiction.

As soon, however, as the present epidemic began to show itself unmistakeably in Dublin, we instructed our Inspector, Mr. Robinson, to urge upon each of the Dublin Boards the necessity of immediately providing hospital accommodation for small-pox patients, which should be under their own control; and this was promptly effected in both Unions in the manner described in Mr. Robinson's Reports, which will be found in the Appendix.* In neither Union was that important adjunct to a contagious hospital, a convalescent department, unprovided for; so that from the commencement the patients have remained under medical authority until they could return to their homes without danger of giving contagion to their families or neighbours.

36. Correspondence, which is placed in the Appendix, shows beyond question the dangerous character of hospitals for contagious disease which are not provided with convalescent accommodation.† In epidemics, whether of small-pox, typhus, typhoid, or scarlatina, a pressure on the space for patients under treatment often causes the discharge of convalescents too soon after cure; and in small-pox, the most contagious of all diseases when not kept off by vaccination, this danger becomes greatly intensified as the epidemic advances towards its climax.

Regarded in its character as a protection from the spread of contagion, the convalescent ward should, for all practical purposes, be in connexion with the hospital itself; for thus only can the patients discharged from the wards for treatment be kept effectually under medical authority—detained, in fact, until pronounced safe.

In addition to the Hardwicke and Cork-street Fever Hospitals, Sir Patrick Dun's and the Mater Misericordiæ, as already mentioned, opened small-pox wards, as did also the City of Dublin Hospital, the Meath and Dr. Steevens' Hospitals; but none of these appear to have been provided with sufficient convalescent accommodation to meet their requirements. In the two Dublin Workhouse Small-pox Hospitals ample accommodation of this nature was provided from the commencement; and those two hospitals, therefore, have served the primary purpose of places of treatment, of isolation, and cure, without the danger of propagating the disease by discharging their convalescents too soon.

*Appendix C. III., page 195.
† Appendix C. IV., page 197.

37. The share of the burthen of the Dublin epidemic borne by the two Dublin Workhouse Hospitals will be seen from the following figures, abstracted from Mr. Robinson's weekly Reports of the progress of the epidemic. The total number treated in nine hospitals from 18th November up to the 23rd March, was 2,541; of which number, 1,152 were treated in the Workhouse Hospitals and 1,389 in the other seven hospitals. For such of the patients as are sent into the latter hospitals by poor law officers, the Guardians pay the cost of treatment and maintenance. The medical officers of the dispensary districts in Dublin and the suburbs were at the same time actively engaged in meeting the force of the epidemic, and most of the patients admitted into the various hospitals were sent there by them; but a large proportion were unwilling to go, and were therefore treated at their own homes.

The following two tables exhibit, the first of them the extent of the action of the Dispensaries, and the second that of the hospitals, in weekly summaries kept up from the 25th November, 1871, to the 23rd March, 1872; and it must be borne in mind that all those sent into hospital by the Dispensary Medical Officers are repeated in the Hospital Returns.

RETURN of the NUMBER of CASES of SMALL-POX treated in the CITY DISPENSARY DISTRICTS of NORTH and SOUTH DUBLIN UNIONS, from the Week ended Saturday, 25th November, 1871, to the Week ended Saturday, 23rd March, 1872.

Week Ended Saturday.	No. of Cases remaining under treatment at commencement of the Week.	No. of New Cases registered during the Week.	Total of two preceding Columns.	No. of Cases sent to Hospital during the Week.	No. of Cases discharged from treatment during the Week and included in Col. 4.	No. of Deaths during the Week while under charge of Dispensary Medical Officer.	Total of three preceding Columns.	No. of Cases remaining under treatment at close of the Week, being the difference between Cols. 3 & 7.
	1.	2.	3.	4.	5.	6.	7.	8.
1871.								
November 25, . .	16	63	79	10	17	4	31	48
December 2, . .	44	103	147	44	31	4	79	68
" 9, . .	68	75	143	38	45	5	88	55
" 16, . .	55	142	197	57	48	1	106	91
" 23, . .	91	124	215	65	48	5	118	97
" 30, . .	97	143	240	44	93	6	144	96
1872.								
January 6, . .	96	118	214	41	48	5	94	116
" 13, . .	116	104	220	60	47	6	113	107
" 20, . .	107	142	249	50	60	3	113	136
" 27, . .	136	104	240	63	60	7	130	110
February 3, . .	110	142	252	59	59	7	125	127
" 10, . .	127	137	264	65	60	15	140	124
" 17, . .	124	151	275	50	78	7	135	140
" 24, . .	140	162	302	76	80	6	162	138
March 2, . .	138	110	248	49	60	11	120	128
" 9, . .	128	142	270	66	63	10	139	131
" 16, . .	131	178	309	80	77	7	149	160
" 23, . .	160	118	278	64	83	9	156	122

RETURN of the NUMBER of CASES of SMALL-POX treated in HOSPITALS in DUBLIN from the Week ended Saturday, 25th November, 1871, to the Week ended Saturday, 23rd March, 1872.

Week Ended Saturday.	No. of Cases under treatment at the end of previous Week.	Admitted into Hospital during the Week.			Total of Columns 1 and 4.	Discharged during the Week.	Died during the Week.	Remaining under treatment on Saturday Night.
		Sent in by Medical Officers of Dispensary Districts.	Sent in by other Persons.	Total Admitted during the Week.				
	1.	2.	3.	4.	5.	6.	7.	8.
1871.								
November 25,	108	24	37	61	169	59	10	100
December 2,	100	30	87	117	217	49	18	150
" 9,	150	39	61	100	250	15	27	208
" 16,	208	56	84	140	348	40	19	289
" 23,	269	64	87	151	420	43	73	304
" 30,	304	65	77	142	446	63	48	335
1872.								
January 6,	335	73	73	146	481	104	34	343
" 13,	343	84	83	167	510	131	30	349
" 20,	349	48	73	157	501	107	40	350
" 27,	350	66	78	144	494	141	77	276
February 3,	331	44	86	142	477	118	31	431
" 10,	324	46	66	111	435	100	75	260
" 17,	340	53	67	170	430	104	77	249
" 24,	331	57	87	140	465	109	77	277
March 2,	377	44	83	127	459	111	77	271
" 9,	391	72	66	138	459	127	70	317
" 16,	317	105	70	175	492	127	39	318
" 23,	316	80	57	137	453	90	31	330

38. The following tables show in a similar form the progress of the epidemic in Belfast from 2nd December, 1871, as recorded in the Weekly Returns of the Dispensary Districts in Belfast Union, and also as recorded in the returns from Belfast Union Fever Hospital from 25th November, 1871 to the 23rd March, 1872.

RETURN of the NUMBER of CASES of SMALL-POX treated in BELFAST UNION FEVER HOSPITAL from the Week ended Saturday the 2nd December, 1871, to the Week ended Saturday, 23rd March, 1872.

Week Ended Saturday.	No. of Cases under treatment at the end of previous Week.	Admitted into Hospital during the Week.			Total of Columns 1 and 4.	Discharged during the Week.	Died during the Week.	Remaining under treatment on Saturday Night.
		Sent in by Medical Officers of Dispensary Districts.	Sent in by other Persons.	Total Admitted during the Week.				
	1.	2.	3.	4.	5.	6.	7.	8.
1871.								
December 2,	121	—	–	35	156	34	6	116
" 9,	116	21	–	21	137	14	7	117
" 16,	117	71	–	71	188	26	4	158
" 23,	158	41	–	41	199	78	9	112
" 30,	112	44	–	44	156	16	9	131
1872.								
January 6,	142	31	–	31	173	21	15	137
" 13,	134	48	–	43	177	27	10	140
" 20,	140	29	–	29	169	24	10	134
" 27,	134	26	–	26	160	30	7	123
February 3,	127	19	–	19	146	36	3	106
" 10,	106	22	–	22	179	24	5	107
" 17,	107	17	–	12	114	18	5	86
" 24,	86	10	–	10	96	20	5	71
March 2,	71	8	–	8	79	10	5	67
" 9,	67	11	–	11	78	23	2	53
" 16,	53	10	–	10	63	6	7	43
" 23,	43	4	–	4	47	11	3	13

RETURN of the NUMBER of CASES of SMALL-POX treated in the DISPENSARY DISTRICTS of BELFAST UNION, from the Week ended Saturday, 25th November, 1871, to the Week ended Saturday, 23rd March, 1872.

Week Ended Saturday.	No. of Cases remaining under treatment at commencement of the Week.	No. of New Cases registered during the Week.	Total of two preceding Columns.	No. of Cases sent to Hospital during the Week.	No. of Cases discharged from treatment during the Week not included in Col. 4.	No. of Deaths during the Week while under charge of Dispensary Medical Officers.	Total of three preceding Columns.	No. of Cases remaining under treatment at close of the Week, being the difference between Cols. 3 & 7.
	1.	2.	3.	4.	5.	6.	7.	8.
1871.								
November 25.	40	25	65	16	11	1	31	34
December 2.	34	24	58	18	11	8	37	21
" 9.	21	19	40	7	11	1	19	21
" 16.	21	25	46	11	14	1	26	20
" 23.	20	37	57	14	12	—	26	31
" 30.	30	11	41	18	11	1	31	16
1872.								
January 6.	16	30	46	16	9	—	26	20
" 13.	20	29	49	15	17	7	37	12
" 20.	22	15	37	11	17	1	29	8
" 27.	8	14	22	1	7	6	14	10
February 3.	10	18	28	3	8	1	12	20
" 10.	20	21	41	4	11	6	21	20
" 17.	20	11	31	8	10	—	18	13
" 24.	13	12	25	6	11	3	21	9
March 2.	9	3	12	4	9	—	13	5
" 9.	5	5	10	2	3	—	5	5
" 16.	5	5	10	2	3	1	7	3
" 23.	3	2	5	2	—	—	2	5

The cases sent to hospital by the Dispensary Medical Officers were all sent to the Belfast Workhouse Fever Hospital.

It will be seen with satisfaction that the epidemic has been gradually declining for the last twelve weeks in Belfast; and that on the 23rd March the number remaining under treatment in the Hospital was only 42 in comparison with 142 on the 30th December; also that the deaths for several weeks past have not exceeded an average of 2. We may derive from the precedent of Belfast some hope that the Dublin epidemic will shortly decline in a similar manner, though we cannot unfortunately affirm at the present date that the decrease in the number of cases or deaths has actually yet begun.

DEPARTMENTAL ARRANGEMENTS.

39. In the 39th paragraph of our Annual Report for 1869, we mentioned that the duty of auditing the accounts of lunatic asylums in Ireland had been transferred to the Auditors of Poor Law Unions, the number of Auditors having at the same time been increased from four to five. By an Act of the last session of Parliament the auditing of the accounts of the municipal authorities of most of the towns in Ireland has been now added to the duties of the Poor Law Auditors. We have not as yet asked for any increase of the number of these officers on account of this accession of duty, but we apprehend that before long we shall find it necessary to do so.

40. It may not be out of season if we conclude the present Report to Your Excellency with a short *resumé* of the history of the administration of the Poor Law since its introduction in 1838. From 1838 until 1847 the administration was carried on under the English Poor Law Commission, and one of those Commissioners resided permanently in Ireland until 1843, when two assistant Commissioners were substituted under a delegation of authority to conduct the business of the department in Dublin. In 1845 this arrangement was superseded, and a fourth member was added to the English Commission, who took charge of the Poor Law administration in Ireland.

During the whole of this time relief in the workhouse was the only form of relief permitted by the law; but in 1847, two years after the commencement of the Irish famine, out-door relief was made legal under certain restrictions, and the connexion with the English Commission at the same time ceased; a separate Irish Commission being established, consisting of a Chief Commissioner, the Chief Secretary and Under Secretary of the Lord Lieutenant, aided by the services of an Assistant Commissioner, who, in the absence of the Chief Commissioner, was invested with his powers and duties.

This continued until 1851, when the Medical Charities Act was passed. The Commission was then increased from one to three paid members in addition to the two ex-officio members, the office of Assistant Commissioner being abolished, and in this form it exists to the present day.

The changes made in the law from time to time, as well as the course pursued in the administration of relief to the poor, are to be found recorded in detail in thirty-three Annual Reports submitted to Parliament, from 1839 to the present year inclusive. The salient points are the building of 131 workhouses, which were completed in 1844, the year before the first potato blight; the Relief Extension Act of 1847; the additional workhouses built for the thirty-two new unions established in 1850–51; the passing of the Medical Charities Act in that year; and, finally, the fluctuations in the number of paupers, and the amount of expenditure from 1850–51 to 1871–72, a period commencing when the abnormal state of things which existed during the famine period had passed away.

The periodical fluctuations will be found exhibited with sufficient distinctness in the tables given in this Report at pages 19, 20, and 22 respectively. For the year ended 29th September, 1852, the relief expenditure, excluding the medical charities, was £883,267, the average daily number of in-door poor being 166,821. In 1859 these figures had decreased to £413,712 as the relief expenditure, and to 40,380 as the average daily number of in-door poor; that is to say, the expenditure was reduced little more than 50 per cent., while the pauperism had decreased 75 per cent. The explanation is, that in the first place the cost of in-maintenance was greater in 1859 than in 1852, the proportion of inmates relieved through sickness had increased, the dietaries for both sick and healthy were more liberal, and the establishment charges could not be diminished in direct proportion to the number relieved. Comparing 1859 with 1871, the average daily number of inmates has increased by 3,625, or nearly 14 per cent.; but the expenditure in relief has increased by £271,956, or nearly 66 per cent. This disproportion arises in much the same way as that above described, that is to say, from the further increased cost of in-maintenance, which in 1859 was £234,202, and in 1871 382,366—amount of increase £148,364; from increase in salaries of officers, £23,919; from increase in other expenses, £33,168; and finally, from an increase of out-door relief of £66,505. The out-door relief, which in the year 1850 was £120,773, dispensed to an average daily number of more than 100,000 persons, had in 1856 diminished to £2,245, dispensed to an average daily number of 886 persons. Since 1856 the out-door relief has continuously increased and is now £69,744 per annum, dispensed to an average daily number of 23,400 persons.

This rapid increase of expenditure on relief purposes it is fair to observe has taken place concurrently with the maintenance of the Electoral Division system of rating; and it is our conviction that the proposed change to Union rating would have a salutary effect in checking the progress of any expenditure which may, perhaps, be unnecessary.

41. The total accommodation in the 163 workhouses in Ireland is reckoned at 150,000, or about three times the amount of the average daily number relieved; but this number is much greater at one season of the year than another; it is liable also to sudden increase by failure of crops or outbreak of epidemic disease, either local or general. Considering how much the secure and successful working of the system of relief in Ireland depends upon the sufficiency of workhouse accommodation; considering also how important it is to health and comfort that each of these establishments should at all times possess an unoccupied margin of space not only as a whole, but in each of its classified departments, the present margin of two-thirds, which may in a single calamitous season be seriously reduced or even wholly annihilated, ought not, in our opinion, to be regarded in any other light than as a most favourable and fortunate circumstance, so long as it lasts, in the administration of the Irish Poor Law.

The ownership of the workhouses is vested in the Poor Law Commission, and the Board of Guardians in each case possess a right of occupancy only under the Commissioners as proprietors of the legal estate. The cost of purchasing the land and of erecting the buildings was defrayed in the first instance from the Imperial Exchequer, and made repayable from the poor-rates of the union by equal instalments spread over twenty years, without interest for the first ten years. Repayment of these instalments was actually made in very few cases; and towards the close of the famine period £1,321,360 was due from Irish Unions to the Exchequer under the head of Workhouse Loans. There were at this time other debts, chiefly famine debts, due to the Exchequer from Irish counties, baronies, half-baronies, and townlands, which amounted to a total of £3,722,353. It was determined to consolidate these debts and to charge each of the 60,760 townlands in Ireland with its own proper share, payable by instalments spread over different periods according to the exigencies of the case. This work was accomplished with great labour, and the poor-rate became the medium for payment of the annual instalments, a special poundage in respect thereof being included in every rate on the townland, which when collected became the property of the Electoral Division comprising it, and the Electoral Division thereafter lay under the obligation to pay the collective debt of all its townlands to the Imperial Treasury.

For about two years these instalments were duly paid, and would have continued to be so, but in the year 1853 the Government remitted the remainder of the debt; and from that date it will be found to disappear from the accounts of the Union expenditure as detailed in the Annual Reports. The result of these operations has been to leave the proprietorship of the workhouses as it was before; that is to say, vested in the Commissioners; subject to a constructive right of occupancy by the Board of Guardians in each case, and free from all debt and incumbrance.

There is only one exception to this state of affairs, and that is the case of the Clonmel Union, in the county of Tipperary, which possesses one of the finest workhouses in Ireland, but which, unfortunately, was obliged to borrow the cost of erecting it from private sources, the fund at the command of the Exchequer Loan Commissioners being at that time (1851) exhausted.

Memorials from Clonmel Union praying to be placed on the same footing as the other Unions in Ireland, have been addressed to the Lords Commissioners of Her Majesty's Treasury, but without effect hitherto.

We have the honour to be,

Your Excellency's very obedient, faithful servants,

A. Power.
Hartington.
T. H. Burke.
J. M'Donnell, M.D.
R. M. Bellew.

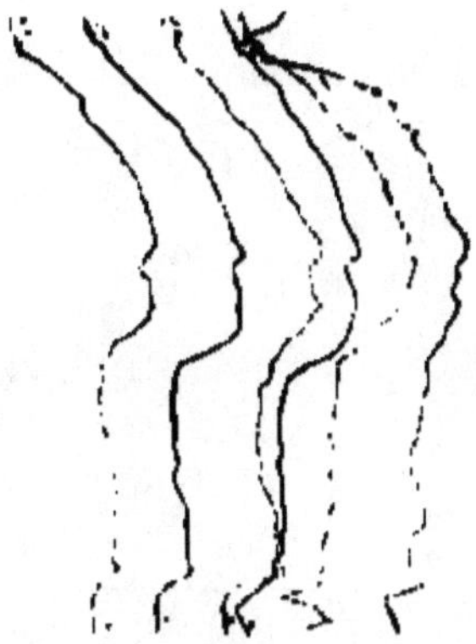

APPENDIX.

APPENDIX A.

CIRCULARS OF INSTRUCTION AND CORRESPONDENCE UNDER THE POOR LAW ACTS.

I.—CIRCULARS.

No. 1.—Provision of Small-Pox Wards.

Poor Law Commission Office, Dublin,
9th December, 1870.

Sir,

The Commissioners for administering the Laws for Relief of the Poor in Ireland desire to inform the Board of Guardians of Union that small-pox exists now at Belfast, and that cases have occurred in which it appears to have been communicated from Belfast to towns in the neighbourhood.

It has been found that when small-pox is treated in the general wards of a workhouse fever hospital, great danger is incurred of its spreading; and the Commissioners are anxious that special wards for the treatment of small-pox should be found ready for the protection of every Workhouse in which it may possibly hereafter make its appearance.

The Guardians will therefore have the goodness to take into immediate consideration the propriety of providing two separate wards for male and female patients. Much mischief is known to have arisen from the absence of such preparation when the disease has suddenly been admitted, or made its appearance in a Workhouse.

By order of the Commissioners,

D. Dakes, Chief Clerk.

To the Clerk, Union.

No. 2.—Duties of Clerks of Unions under "The Juries (Ireland) Act, 1871."

"Juries (Ireland) Act."

Poor Law Commission Office, Dublin,
12th October, 1871.

Sir,

The Commissioners for administering the Laws for Relief of the Poor in Ireland desire to state that as some additional duties devolve upon Clerks of Unions and Poor Rate Collectors under the provisions of "The Juries (Ireland) Act, 1871," (34 & 35 Vic., c. 71), they have thought it advisable to furnish to you, for your information and that of the Board of Guardians, extracts from the Act in question, comprising

D 2

those sections which relate to the duty of Clerks of Unions and Poor Rate Collectors, and the remuneration to be allowed for those duties.

Extracts from the Act are accordingly forwarded to you herewith.

By order of the Commissioners,

B. Banks, Chief Clerk.

To the Clerk of each Union.

No. 3.—Grant for Medical and Educational Purposes.

Poor Law Commission Office, Dublin,

Sir, 23rd October, 1871.

The Commissioners for administering the Laws for Relief of the Poor in Ireland transmit to you herewith a form to be filled up and returned to this office, duly certified, as soon as the expenses chargeable on the parliamentary grant for medical and educational purposes in Unions in Ireland for the half-year ended the 29th September last, shall have been accurately ascertained.

The statement, as already pointed out, should comprise only those items which correspond to those included in the estimate on which the grant was made, viz.:—

1. The actual salary which became due to each Medical Officer and Apothecary (if any) for the half-year.
2. The actual cost during the half-year of medicine and medical and surgical appliances, not, however, including therein the cost of stimulants, such as wines and spirits.
3. The actual salary which became due to each schoolmaster and schoolmistress for the half-year, but not including under this head the cost of rations.

These particulars to be given separately for each dispensary district and for the Workhouse, and care must be taken that no other expenses than those above mentioned are included.

By order of the Commissioners,

B. Banks, Chief Clerk.

To the Clerk of each Union.

II.—Correspondence on the Subject of a Supposed Legal System of Quarantine as Affecting Intercourse Between Ports in Great Britain and Ports in Ireland.

Inishowen Union.

No. 1.—Letter from Dr. Sproulle, Medical Officer of Moville Dispensary District, to Mr. R. Hamilton, Poor Law Inspector.

Sir, Moville, 8th May, 1871.

I beg to report that I visited the ship *Unanimo* now in quarantine in Lough Foyle, off Moville, on Saturday the 6th May inst., and also to-day. There are as you are already aware two cases of small-pox on board. In so far the disease does not appear to extend itself to the other members of the crew, which, as a preventive, have all been carefully re-vaccinated with good fresh lymph. On making inquiry as to the origin of the disease, I find that in the house in which the man first attacked lodged before joining the ship there was a person ill of small-pox, and that the second man labouring under the disease was in the habit of occasionally lying in the other man's "bunk," from the time he joined the ship up to the time when the disease presented itself. The ship was seven days at sea, when the person first attacked complained of being ill, and the captain put about for this port the moment he saw by the rash what the illness had resulted in. The second man sickened four days after the symptoms of illness first presented themselves in the other case. The man first attacked is now quite convalescent; the disease is of a very mild and mitigated character in his case, and he mentions the extraordinary fact that this is his *third* attack of small-pox. In the other case the disease is of a very severe confluent character; the disease has now arrived at its most dangerous period, and for the next three days it will be impossible to say how it may terminate.

As I informed you in my last communication, the captain quite refused the offered services of the relieving officer when he visited the ship for the purpose of offering to have the men removed to the workhouse hospital, but you will see by the enclosed letters that he changed his mind. I showed the letter to Captain Salwey, District Commander of Coast-guards, who wrote to the captain saying that it would be impossible for him to permit the landing of *any* person from his ship, much less those labouring under disease. The captain requested me to continue in attendance on the men, not as dispensary but private patients. Should any other case occur on board, I shall immediately report the circumstance.

I am, sir, your obedient servant,

Thomas W. Sproulle.

R. Hamilton, esq., Poor Law Inspector.

Enclosure in No. 1.

Dr. Sproulle.

Moville Roads,
May 5th, 1871.

Dear Sir,

I am desirous to land the two men who are now suffering from small-pox on board of the *Umaina* and placing them in some hospital, thereby preventing any unnecessary delay to the ship and expense to my owners. If you will kindly inform me if this can be accomplished, you will greatly oblige your obedient servant,

Benj. Mesta, Master, Barque *Umaina*.

Doctor Sproulle has shown me your letter, hoping that probably it could be complied with, but I assure you it is quite impossible, the quarantine laws are so stringent and imperative that they must be complied with. It cannot be granted according as you wish.

J. Fitzpatrick, Station Officer.

No. 2.—Report from Mr. R. Hamilton to the Commissioners.

Gentlemen,

Strabane, May 20, 1871.

In reference to previous correspondence respecting an outbreak of small-pox on board a vessel lying off Moville, in Lough Foyle, I have the honour to forward a report from the medical officer of the district, from which you will observe one of the sailors first attacked has died, and that a third case has occurred, but Dr. Sproulle does not apprehend further spread of the disease.

I have the honour to be, gentlemen,

Your obedient servant,

R. Hamilton.

The Poor Law Commissioners, Dublin.

Enclosure in No. 2.—Letter from Dr. Sproulle.

Sir, Moville, 18th May, 1871.

I have to report the occurrence of a third case of small-pox on board the barque *Unanima* still lying off Moville, and would have reported the case sooner but that I have been watching it with great interest, inasmuch as it has occurred in one of the crew (the cook) whom I had carefully re-vaccinated, and who had on his arm at the time the disease manifested itself (the eighth day of the re-vaccination) two most perfect vaccine vesicles in every way as perfect as those usually seen on the arms of infants. The premonitory fever was rather smart, and the eruption began to appear at the end of the second day on the face and neck. On the third day there was an increase in the number of papules on the face, neck, and arms, to which the eruption has limited itself. On to-day (the fifth day of the rash) the pustules are still fewer in number, quite distinct, and very few of them presenting the well-marked characteristics of the small-pox pustule; and those first appearing are now beginning to form black crusts in the centre and die away, and the man is so well that he could resume his work, if allowed. This favourable state of the case may, I think, be most fairly attributed to the prophylactic effects of the re-vaccination, which not only thus mitigated the disease, but very nearly put out the variolous poison evidently existing in the man's constitution at the time of his re-vaccination, and had the latter been earlier performed it would, I have no doubt, have altogether prevented the appearance of the disease.

The poor man who had the disease in the confluent form died on the sixteenth day of his illness, and was, at the instance of the coast-guard authorities, buried out at sea. The rest of the crew still healthy, and all means have been adopted for the cleaning and disinfecting of the vessel. I do not apprehend any further spread of the disease.

I am, sir, yours faithfully,

Thos. W. Sproulle.

R. Hamilton, esq., Poor Law Inspector.

No. 3.—Letter from Dr. Browne, Officer of Health for the City of Derry.

Gentlemen, Londonderry, May 2, 1871.

I have the honour to inform you that I was called on this morning by Mr. Benjamin Minta, master of the barque *Unanima*, who, when on his voyage from North Shields to New York with a cargo of iron, put back to this port, in consequence of supposed small-pox having made its appearance among his crew. With him I at once proceeded to Moville,—sixteen miles distant, where the barque lies, and found two of the sailors suffering from variola, viz., V. Ludovic Bernard, aged twenty-one, a Norwegian, who was attacked on the 26th April, and John M'Donald, aged twenty-five, a native of Prince Edward's Island, who sickened on the 27th April.

Bernard has the eruption all over him, but in a distinct form. M'Donald is not so generally covered, but the pustules, especially on the face, are so close as to be nearly confluent. His throat is somewhat but not severely affected.

In neither of the patients is there much fever, and neither of them has a detectable cicatrix from vaccination.

I examined every person on board the barque, who, exclusive of the two sick men, but, including the master, his wife and child, are fifteen in number; and finding three of the crew without satisfactory marks of vaccination, I at once vaccinated them.

I then gave minute directions about having the barque, as well as the patients' clothes, bedding, &c., thoroughly disinfected by means of carbolic acid, sulphurous acid vapour, and lime-washing, and undertook to retain medical charge of the vessel and crew.

The barque is in strict quarantine, and is not to hold communication with any other ship or the shore, except through myself or the Coast-guard station, with which I have arranged a system of signals to be used in case of emergency.

I have the honour to be, gentlemen,

Your obedient servant,

William Browne, M.D.,
Officer of Health for City of Derry.

The Poor Law Commissioners, Dublin.

P.S.—I have neglected to mention that the barque arrived at Moville yesterday.

No. 4.—Letter from the Commissioners to Dr. Browne.

Poor Law Commission Office, Dublin,
22nd May, 1871.

Sir,

Adverting to your letter of the 2nd inst., relating to the cases of small-pox on board the barque *Unanima*, lying off Moville, the Commissioners for administering the Laws for Relief of the Poor in Ireland request that you will be good enough to state by what authority quarantine has been established in Lough Foyle, so as to prevent communication between a ship containing cases of small-pox and the shore.

One of the patients on board the *Unanima* having died after landing had been refused by the commanding officer of coast-guards, it is important to the Commissioners to understand by what authority quarantine is supposed to exist in Lough Foyle, and they will feel obliged by your informing them of any ground for that supposition which may be known to you.

By order of the Commissioners,

D. Banks, Chief Clerk.

To W. Browne, esq., M.D., Officer of Health,
Londonderry.

No. 5.—Letter from the Commissioners to Mr. Hamilton.

Poor Law Commission Office, Dublin,
23rd May, 1871.

Sir,

The Commissioners for administering the Laws for Relief of the Poor in Ireland acknowledge the receipt of your report of the 20th inst., forwarding a communication from Dr. Sproulle, the medical officer of the Moville Dispensary District, relating to the cases of small-pox which have occurred on board the barque *Unanima* at present lying off Moville. The Commissioners at the same time forward for your information a copy of a letter which they have addressed to Dr. Browne, the officer of health for the city of Derry, relating to the course adopted in this case of regarding the vessel as in quarantine, and the Commissioners have to state that they do not believe that any such thing as quarantine exists on any part of the coast of Ireland, nor could exist, except by an order of the Lord Lieutenant in Council.

The coast-guard officer who prevented the landing of the small-pox patients from the *Unanima*, when the captain was desirous to land them, has therefore incurred a most serious responsibility, as one of the men subsequently died on board ship, and it is doubtful to the Commissioners whether an inquest ought not to have been held.

The Commissioners request that you will be so good as to report to them the name and address of the officer in question.

By order of the Commissioners,

B. Banks, Chief Clerk.

To R. Hamilton, esq.,
Poor Law Inspector, Dungannon.

No. 6.—Letter from Dr. Browne to the Commissioners.

Londonderry, 25th May, 1871.

Gentlemen,

Absence from home has been the cause of my not sooner replying to your letter of the 22nd inst.

I now beg to inform you that on her first arrival the barque *Unanima* was ordered into quarantine by the chief officer of the coast-guard station at Moville, and that I did not in any way interfere in this matter further than to suggest arrangements for facilitating communication with the shore.

I am, gentlemen, your obedient servant,

William Browne,
Officer of Health for City of Derry.

The Poor Law Commissioners, Dublin.

No. 7.—Report from Mr. R. Hamilton, Poor Law Inspector.

Strabane, July 1, 1871.

Gentlemen,

In returning the accompanying correspondence on the subject of the quarantine placed on the barque *Unanima* while lying off Moville, in Lough Foyle, I have the honour to inform you that on the 20th ult. I heard Captain Salwey had returned to his district.

On the 21st I wrote asking him to fix a day for a personal interview, and he replied he could not meet me before the 1st of July. I accordingly met him this day.

He was courteous in his manner, and appeared to be anxious to afford every information as to the authorities under which he acted.

The title of the instructions referred to is "Special Instructions for the Coast-guard of the United Kingdom," dated 1866, signed by the then Lords of the Admiralty, and addressed to the respective captains, commanders, and officers of the coast-guard.

Captain Salwey stated that in placing the *Unanima* under quarantine he acted under chapter 23, page 86, of these instructions, and in carrying out the quarantine he acted under the "Queen's Regulations" and "Admiralty Instructions for the Government of the Naval Service."

Evidently the attention of the coast-guard has never been drawn to the Sanitary Act of 1866.

I have the honour to be, gentlemen,

Your obedient servant,

R. Hamilton.

The Poor Law Commissioners, Dublin.

No. 8.—LETTER from the COMMISSIONERS to the UNDER SECRETARY of the LORD LIEUTENANT.

Poor Law Commission Office, Dublin,
10th July, 1871.

SIR,

The Commissioners for administering the Laws for Relief of the Poor in Ireland deem it their duty to bring under the consideration of his Excellency the Lord Justice the following statement relating to the barque *Unanimo*, from North Shields to New York, which put back with small-pox on board, and arrived in Lough Foyle on the 1st May last.

Mr. Hamilton, the Inspector in charge of the district, having learnt that on the arrival of the ship application had been made for medical assistance, and having reason to believe that there was small-pox on board, directed the Relieving Officer to proceed to the ship, taking with him the Medical Officer, and to explain to the captain the particulars of the existing arrangements for affording medical relief in the district; and, in the event of its being considered necessary to remove any of the patients to the Union Fever Hospital, to make the necessary arrangements for that purpose. The Relieving Officer accordingly visited the ship, in company with the Medical Officer, on the 2nd May, and found that there were two cases of small-pox on board; but the captain declined any assistance from him, stating that he had obtained the services of Dr. Browne from Derry.

Dr. Browne, who is Officer of Health for the city of Derry, also reported the case to the Commissioners, stating that the barque was in strict quarantine, and was not to hold communication with any other ship or the shore, except through himself or the coast guard station.

On the 5th May the captain applied to the coast guard officer for permission to land the two men who were suffering from small-pox; and this application appears to have been supported by Dr. Sproule, the Dispensary Medical Officer, who was then at the request of the captain, in attendance on the cases; but the request was peremptorily refused in the following terms:—

"Dr. Sproulle has shown me your letter, hoping that possibly it could be complied with, but I assure you it is quite impossible. The quarantine laws are so stringent and imperative that they must be complied with. It cannot be granted according to your wish."

On the 18th May Dr. Sproulle reported that a third case had occurred on board, and that one of the two men first attacked had died, and at the instance of the coast guard had been buried out at sea.

The Commissioners have, in vain, endeavoured to ascertain by what authority quarantine was established, as above described, in Lough Foyle. They wrote to Dr. Browne, who was first in charge of the cases, and he informed them in reply that on her first arrival, the barque *Unanima* was ordered into quarantine by the chief officer of the coast guard station at Moville, and that he (Dr. Browne) did not in any way interfere in the matter, further than to suggest arrangements for facilitating communication with the shore. Mr. Hamilton, Poor Law Inspector, has since had an interview with Captain Salwey, Inspecting Commander of coast guards at Moville, who referred to instructions entitled "Special Instructions for the Coast Guards of the United Kingdom," dated 1866, signed by the then Lords of the Admiralty, and addressed to the respective captains, commanders, and officers of the coast guard. Captain Salwey stated that in placing the *Unanima* under quarantine, he acted under chapter 23, page 86, of these instructions; and that in carrying out the quarantine, he acted under the "Queen's Regulations" and "Admiralty Instructions for the government of the Naval Service."

The Commissioners, after inquiry, cannot discover that in the last of the documents referred to by Captain Salwey, there was any instruction which gave him to understand that he had any authority to prevent a person in small-pox on board ship in the Foyle from being landed; but they have not the means of reference to the instructions issued to coast guard officers in 1866. As one of the cases on board the *Unanima* terminated fatally, the question of the conduct of the coast guard appears to the Commissioners to assume a very serious complexion, and they have therefore laid the particulars before the Government for such further action as may be thought necessary. The Commissioners at the same time desire to refer to paragraph 13 in their last Annual Report, in which reference is made to the subject of quarantine and the misunderstanding which appears to prevail in regard to it.

By order of the Commissioners,

B. Banks, Chief Clerk.

To T. H. Burke, esq., &c.,
Dublin Castle.

No. 9.—Letter from the Under Secretary of the Lord Lieutenant to the Commissioners.

Dublin Castle,
29th September, 1871.

Gentlemen,

Referring to your letter of the 10th July last relative to the coast guard at Lough Foyle having prevented the landing from the barque *Unanima* of certain men who were suffering from small-pox, I am directed by the Lords Justices to acquaint you that their Excellencies having caused inquiry to be made in the matter, find that the barque in question was placed in quarantine by the inspecting commander of coast guard (it is believed after consultation with the collector of customs at Londonderry) under a misapprehension of his duty, he not being aware that small-pox is not one of the diseases the presence of which on board a ship renders her liable to quarantine.

I am to add that in order to guard against the recurrence of such misunderstanding, instructions have been issued by the Admiralty to the coast guard with regard to vessels liable to quarantine.

I am, gentlemen, your obedient servant,

T. H. Burke.

The Poor Law Commissioners, Custom House.

Londonderry Union.

No. 10.—Letter from the Mayor of Derry to the Under Secretary of the Lord Lieutenant, referred to the Commissioners for Report.

Londonderry,
3rd October, 1871.

Sir,

With reference to the Order in Council, dated 9th August, 1871, regarding infectious diseases on board ship, the introductory portion of that proclamation appears to be very full, but his Excellency's order seemed to be entirely confined to cholera.

Yesterday it was discovered by the Officer of Health that there was a case of small-pox on board; the man was immediately removed to the hospital at the Union Workhouse, after which the Medical Officer sent some of his assistants to purify the ship, who were met by the master thereof, who declined to permit them to enter his vessel for such a purpose.

The matter was brought before the magistrates and also a large committee of the Corporation, and neither of these bodies could see what authority they had to punish the master.

I have therefore to request the advice of the Law Officers of the Crown how to proceed in such a case. Can we, under the provisions of the 6th of George 4th, c. 78? or must we await the extension of his Excellency's order to small-pox and other infectious diseases?

Waiting your instructions,

I have, &c.,

PITT SKIPTON, Mayor of Derry.

To T. H. Burke, esq.

No. 11.—LETTER from the COMMISSIONERS to the UNDER SECRETARY of the LORD LIEUTENANT.

Poor Law Commission Office, Dublin,
9th October, 1871.

SIR,

The Commissioners for administering the Laws for Relief of the Poor in Ireland return herewith the file of papers referred to them on the 6th instant with a request for their opinion and report in regard to a letter from the Mayor of Derry, from which it appears that a question has arisen as to whether the Order in Council of the 9th August last applies to the case of a vessel arriving with small-pox on board; and in reference thereto the Commissioners have the honour to state for the information of their Excellencies the Lords Justices, that the authorities at Londonderry appear to have been mistaken in attempting to deal with a case of small-pox under the Privy Council Order, which refers to cholera only.

It would be quite in vain, at this time, to attempt to keep small-pox out of the country by any measure of quarantine, and, probably, any attempt to do so at an earlier period would not have been attended with success when the disease was prevalent at Glasgow and Liverpool, and at other places on the western coast of Great Britain, inasmuch as the passage by steamer is only of a few hours duration, while the usual time of incubation of small-pox is about fourteen days.

By order of the Commissioners,

B. BANKS, Chief Clerk.

To Thomas H. Burke, esq., &c.,
Dublin Castle.

CORK UNION.

No. 12.—LETTER from the TOWN CLERK of CORK to the UNDER SECRETARY of the LORD LIEUTENANT—referred to the COMMISSIONERS for their OPINION.

Town Clerk's Office, 7, South Mall, Cork,
5 January, 1872.

SIR,

The attention of the Mayor has been called to the fact that Newport is very much affected with small-pox. Two colliers belonging to Messrs. Sutton of this city, coal merchants, left Newport some time since, and are now weather-bound at New Milford. The captain of one of them (the *Ocean*) is now laid up with that disease. The captain of the other (the *Perilla*) died of the disease. A vessel recently arrived from Newport, in Cork Harbour and the captain was removed to Hospital in Queenstown suffering from small-pox. Under these circumstances the Mayor begs to suggest that the quarantine laws be enforced and made applicable to all vessels from Newport, otherwise there is much danger of the disease spreading in this city where several cases are now under treatment.

I am, sir, your obedient servant,

Alex. MacCarthy, jun., Town Clerk.

The Under Secretary, Dublin Castle.

No. 13.—Letter from the Commissioners to the Under Secretary of the Lord Lieutenant.

Poor Law Commission Office, Dublin,
9th January, 1872.

Sir,

The Commissioners for administering the Laws for Relief of the Poor in Ireland acknowledge the receipt of a file of papers referred to them on the 8th instant containing a letter from the Town Clerk of Cork, in which he refers to the prevalence of small-pox at Newport, South Wales, and suggests that the quarantine laws be enforced in regard to vessels arriving at Cork Harbour from Newport, in order to meet the danger of a probable spread of the disease in the city, and in reference thereto the Commissioners have the honour to state for the information of His Excellency the Lord Lieutenant, that they doubt the applicability of any system of quarantine to the disease of small-pox, which usually undergoes a period of incubation of about fourteen days before it makes its appearance.

With regard to the particular case in question, that of the city of Cork, the provision made for treatment in a hospital at Queenstown of cases on board ship in which the disease was developed, preserved the city from an outbreak of small-pox during nearly the whole of the year, 1871, but it was at length introduced there by a sailor who took it at Newport, and on whom it broke out after his return to Cork, when he refused to be taken into hospital.

Quarantine provisions like those provided against cholera could not prevent persons having the disease latent in them in this way, landing and spreading it.

As regards the city of Dublin, to which reference is made in the papers, there is this additional reason for doubting the value of quarantine at present, that the disease which, it is believed, travelled by land down the eastern coast from Belfast, is now present in every quarter of the city, and in most of the suburbs.

It appears to the Commissioners that what is most wanted in regard to small-pox is an effectual power of compelling the individual patient to go to hospital, and a power of detention until the danger of spreading the contagion has ceased.

The file of papers is returned herewith.

By order of the Commissioners,

B. Banks, Chief Clerk.

To Thomas H. Burke, esq., &c.,
Dublin Castle.

No. 14.—LETTER from the LOCAL GOVERNMENT BOARD to the UNDER SECRETARY of the LORD LIEUTENANT—referred to the COMMISSIONERS for their OBSERVATIONS.

Local Government Board, Whitehall, S.W.
SIR, 10th January, 1872.

I am directed by the Local Government Board to acknowledge the receipt of your letter of the 6th instant, in which, by direction of the Lord Lieutenant of Ireland, you transmit to the Board a copy of a letter from the Town Clerk of Cork, reporting the existence of small-pox at Newport (South Wales) and the danger of its propagation by colliers arriving thence in Cork Harbour, and suggesting also that the quarantine laws be enforced and applicable to all vessels from Newport. The attention of the Board is further drawn to the fact that small-pox prevails to an alarming extent in Dublin, and that grave apprehensions are entertained as to the aggravation of the disease by the expected arrival of a fleet of colliers now weather-bound in England.

I am directed to state that the Board have considered the suggestions in your letter, but they desire to point out that neither the Quarantine Act nor the 52nd section of the 29 and 30 Vic., cap. 90, referred to by you, has ever been applied to small-pox or any other current contagious disease in the United Kingdom, neither would it be practicable, as the Board are advised, to issue under the above quoted section of the Act any general regulations applying to coasting vessels, which should be capable of satisfactorily meeting the danger to which your letter refers.

It appears to the Board that the only practicable method of dealing with the evil to which attention has been directed is the plan of local action, under section 29 of the Sanitary Act, 1866, and they would, therefore, desire that the attention of the Lord Lieutenant should be directed to the provisions of this section. The Act is the same as that referred to in your letter.

The Board consider that the prompt provision of ample hospital accommodation for small-pox cases at each threatened port is the first thing to be attended to, as no regulation can be conceived to be operative at any port which does not presuppose the existence of such accommodation.

The Board think it right to direct the attention of His Excellency to section 68 of the 29 and 30 Vic., cap. 90, which provides that all powers relating to the execution of the Act, and by the Act vested in the Privy Council in England shall, with regard to the execution of the Act in Ireland in all cases not therein expressly provided for, be vested in the Lord Lieutenant in Council in Ireland.

I am, &c.,

JOHN LAMBERT, Secretary.

To T. H. Burke, esq., &c.,
Dublin Castle, Dublin.

No. 15.—LETTER from the COMMISSIONERS to the UNDER SECRETARY of the LORD LIEUTENANT.

Poor Law Commission Office, Dublin,
13th January, 1872.

SIR,

The Commissioners for administering the Laws for Relief of the Poor in Ireland return to you herewith the letter from the Local Government Board, referred to them for any observations they might wish to make thereon on the subject of a suggestion made by the Mayor of Cork that the quarantine laws be enforced and made applicable to all vessels from Newport (South Wales), which is stated to be very much affected with small-pox.

The only observation which the Commissioners wish to make upon the letter relates to the paragraph in which the attention of His Excellency the Lord Lieutenant is directed to the 29th section of the Sanitary Act, 1866.

That section empowers a nuisance authority, with the sanction of the Lord Lieutenant in Council, "to lay down rules for the removal to any hospital, to which such authority is entitled to remove patients, and for keeping in hospital so long as may be necessary persons brought within their district by any ship or boat who are infected with any dangerous and infectious disorder."

The Commissioners are not aware whether this section has any practical operation in England, but in Ireland generally the treatment of infectious diseases in hospital is conducted by the Poor Law Boards, who are not usually the nuisance authority in seaport towns, and it would not be expedient that this function should be assumed by the nuisance authority in such places.

The city of Dublin is exceptional in this respect; there are in addition to Poor Law Hospitals, many hospitals supported by parliamentary grant, by private subscriptions, or otherwise, which are not under the control of any Poor Law authority; but even in regard to these the Corporation, which is the nuisance authority in Dublin, is not entitled, so far as the Commissioners are aware, to remove patients to hospital, and probably is not exercising any such authority at present.

If, however, the Corporation should by arrangement with any of the Dublin hospitals, not being Poor Law hospitals, entitle themselves to remove patients to such hospitals, it would then be in a situation to "lay down rules" under section 29 of the Sanitary Act.

With regard to the paragraph of the letter of the Local Government Board, in which the prompt provision of ample hospital accommodation is recommended, the Commissioners desire to assure his Excellency that the necessary steps to provide sufficient accommodation for small-pox patients on the outbreak of that disease in any Union are taken by them from time to time as occasion demands. The Guardians of Unions in Ireland are well acquainted with their duties in this respect, and have generally evinced great readiness in promptly meeting every emergency of the kind referred to.

By order of the Commissioners,

B. BANKS, Chief Clerk.

To T. H. Burke, esq., &c.,
Dublin Castle.

III.—CORRESPONDENCE ON THE SUBJECT OF REMOVALS FROM PLACES IN ENGLAND AND SCOTLAND WHERE SMALL-POX PREVAILS TO IRELAND, AND AS TO THE REMOVAL OF TRAMPS FROM LIVERPOOL.

No. 1.—LETTER from the HOME OFFICE to the UNDER SECRETARY of the LORD LIEUTENANT—referred to the COMMISSIONERS for their information.

SIR,

Whitehall, 21st March, 1871.

I am directed by Mr. Secretary Bruce to acknowledge the receipt of your letter of the 8th instant, transmitting a copy of a letter from the Irish Poor Law Commissioners as to the suspension of the removal of Irish paupers from Great Britain to Ireland during the prevalence of small-pox in those places from which such removals most frequently take place;* and I am to inform you that Mr. Bruce has communicated with the Poor Law Board upon the subject, and to transmit to you, herewith, to be laid before the Lord Lieutenant, a copy of their reply to his communication.

I am, &c., &c.,

HENRY WINTERBOTHAM.

T. H. Burke, esq., &c., &c.

ENCLOSURE in foregoing LETTER.

LETTER from the POOR LAW BOARD in ENGLAND to the SECRETARY of STATE for the HOME DEPARTMENT.

Poor Law Board, Whitehall, S.W.,
17th March, 1871.

SIR,

I am directed by the Poor Law Board to acknowledge the receipt of your letter of the 10th instant, in which, by direction of Mr. Secretary Bruce, you transmit a communication from the Irish Poor Law Commissioners suggesting the suspension of the removal of poor persons to Ireland during the present prevalence of small-pox in those places from which such removals frequently take place, and you request the opinion of the Board upon the proposal.

In reply the Board direct me to explain that they do not possess any power which enables them to suspend the removal of poor persons from England to Ireland. They are, however disposed to consider that, having regard to the prevalence at the present time of small-pox in some of the principal unions and towns from which such removals most frequently take place, it might be prudent if the authorities were to abstain at present from effecting such removals.

The Board will accordingly bring the subject under the notice of the several Boards of Guardians of such places.

As regards removals from Glasgow Mr. Secretary Bruce is, no doubt, aware that any communication upon the subject to the authorities of that place should be made by the Board of Supervision in Scotland.

The enclosures which accompanied your letter are returned herewith.

I am, sir, your obedient servant,

(Signed), JOHN HIBBERT, Secretary.

The Hon. A. F. O. Liddell, &c., &c.,
Home Office, Whitehall.

* See Annual Report for 1871, page 185.

No. 2.—Letter from the Home Office to the Under Secretary of the Lord Lieutenant—referred to the Commissioners for their information.

Sir, Whitehall, 29th March, 1871.

In acknowledging the receipt of your letter of the 25th instant, and with reference to the communication from this department of the 21st instant, I am directed by Mr. Secretary Bruce to transmit to you, to be laid before his Excellency the Lord Lieutenant, the accompanying copy of the reply which has been received from the Board of Supervision, together with the enclosure contained therein, relative to the proposal of the Irish Poor Law Commissioners to suspend the removal of poor persons to Ireland from Great Britain during the prevalence of small-pox.

I am, &c.,

A. F. O. Liddell.

T. H. Burke, esq., Irish Office.

Enclosures in foregoing Letter.

(a.)—Letter from the Board of Supervision to the Home Office.

Board of Supervision, Edinburgh.
Sir, 27th March, 1871.

I have the honour to acknowledge the receipt of your letter of the 21st instant transmitting a copy of a letter from the Irish Poor Law Commissioners, which suggests the suspension of the removal of poor persons to Ireland from Great Britain during the prevalence of small-pox in those places from which such removals most frequently take place, and requesting the opinion of the Board of Supervision thereon, with special reference to the Port of Glasgow.

I am directed by the Board of Supervision to state, for the information of Mr. Secretary Bruce, that they are of opinion that they have no power to suspend the removal of poor persons from Scotland to Ireland, the power of removal being vested by statute in the Parochial Boards exclusively. But as the exercise of that power is left to the discretion of the Parochial Boards, the Board have no doubt that any recommendation which might be made upon the subject by the Home Secretary or the Board of Supervision would receive their attentive consideration. If such a recommendation should be made, it would probably be equitable and advisable to intimate that the cost of maintaining in Scotland those paupers against whom warrants of removal are obtained, and who are not removed, will be defrayed by the Irish Government during the period of suspension.

I am, however, directed to state further that it does not appear to the Board that the suspension suggested by the Irish Poor Law Commissioners would be of any appreciable value unless it were accompanied by a total cessation of intercourse between Great Britain and Ireland, the liability of paupers to contract and convey the disease of small-pox not being greater than that of the ordinary population of the country.

With reference to the port of Glasgow in particular, the Board have to state that small-pox has not yet prevailed in the city of Glasgow to any alarming or serious extent, and the local authority there has all along taken active measures of a precautionary and preventive nature regarding it. In order to furnish Mr. Secretary Bruce with the most recent information upon this subject, the Board communicated on the 23rd instant with Dr. Gairdner, the Medical Officer in Glasgow under the Public Health (Scotland) Act, 1867; and I am directed to transmit herewith a copy of the reply, dated the 24th instant, from Dr. Dunlop, the Assistant Medical Officer. It will be observed from Dr. Dunlop's letter that the total number of deaths from small-pox in Glasgow from November last to the 24th instant, has been only 77, or about one in every 6,128 of the population according to the census of 1861; whereas the returns of the Registrar-General of England show a total of 2,003 deaths from small-pox in London from the week ending 17th January to the week ending 18th March (both inclusive), or about one in every 1,400 of the population according to the census of 1861

I am, sir, your obedient servant,

(Signed) JOHN SKELTON, Secretary.

Henry Winterbotham, esq.,
Home Office, Whitehall, London.

(*b*).—LETTER from the MEDICAL OFFICER in GLASGOW under the Public Health Act to the BOARD of SUPERVISION.

Sanitary Department Chambers,
1, Montrose-street, Glasgow,
24th March, 1871.

SIR,

I am directed by Dr. Gairdner to acknowledge receipt of your note of 23rd instant, requesting information in regard to the epidemic of small-pox; and in reply, I take the liberty of enclosing the following extract from the Medical Report of the Officer of Health, submitted to the Health Committee of the Police Board at its meeting on Monday last.

"During the fortnight ending Saturday, the 18th current, there were reported 74 cases of small-pox, as against 120 in the previous two weeks; and to-day there are 124 cases of small-pox under hospital treatment, and 22 treated at home—in all, 146. Of the 124 cases of small-pox in hospital, 82 were vaccinated and 42 unvaccinated.

"Since the month of November last, when the epidemic may be said to have commenced, till the end of February, 328 cases of small-pox and 77 deaths were known to this department; but, as every death from small-pox is known to us, and every recovery from the same disease is not known, it would follow that a calculation of the mortality from small-pox in the city based upon these figures would be fallacious. Taking, however, the rate of the mortality in the small-pox wards of the Fever Hospital, Parliamentary Road, which is between 12 and 13 per cent., or 1 in 8 or 1 in 7, as the general rate over the city, then these 77 deaths represent at least 600 cases of small-pox.

"From information derived from Dr. Russell, it is observed that during January and February there were 157 cases of small-pox admitted into the Parliamentary Road Hospital, and of these, sixty-nine were unvaccinated and nineteen died (27·5 per cent.), and eighty-eight were vaccinated and three died (3·4 per cent). Of these vaccinated persons who died, all were adult males—one aged 24, with two very imperfect vaccine marks; one aged 27, with one good vaccine mark: and one aged 32, with a distinct but indifferent mark.

"The vaccination stations of the Board have now been in operation for two weeks, and during that time 2,115 persons have had their arms, &c., carefully examined; and of these, 310 have been vaccinated, 160 being children, 150 being adults, young men and women. The house to house visitation in infected localities, and in tenements where an unvaccinated population may be expected to be found, is being attended with considerable success, many having no objections to submit to the operation when it is brought without any trouble and expense to them—to their very homes."

It may be mentioned in conclusion that to prevent the spread of small-pox among seamen at the harbour, arrangements are being made, with consent of the local marine board, for the re-vaccination of all applicants at the port of Glasgow.

I am, &c.,

(Signed) JAMES DUNLOP, M.D.,
Assistant Medical Officer.

To John Skelton, esq., Secretary,
Board of Supervision.

No. 3.—LETTER from the COMMISSIONERS to the CHIEF SECRETARY of the LORD LIEUTENANT.

Poor Law Commission Office, Dublin,
MY LORD, 28th November, 1871.

The Commissioners for administering the Laws for Relief of the Poor in Ireland desire to state, for the information of his Excellency the Lord Lieutenant, that they have received a copy of a warrant for the removal of a man named Matthew M'Guire from the parish of Liverpool to the Cavan Union, together with replies to queries respecting the circumstances under which the pauper was removed; and from which it appears that the pauper had resided for five or six years in London, and had come as a tramp to Liverpool; that he was relieved for two days in Liverpool Workhouse previously to being sent to Ireland; and he states that he designedly sought relief in Liverpool in order to get sent to Ireland.

The Commissioners, in the Appendix to their last Annual Report, adverted to the practice which existed in Liverpool of persons applying for relief to the authorities there for the purpose of getting sent to Ireland, and being detained in the Workhouse until there is a batch of them to be sent over to any particular place, and probably this is one of such cases.*

The Commissioners at the same time wish to state that they entertain no doubt that this practice of the Liverpool authorities has been one of the many sources from which the small-pox contagion in Ireland proceeded, two instances at least having come to their knowledge of the disease having been imported in this way, and both at a time when Ireland was comparatively free from it.

By order,

D. BANKS, Chief Clerk.

The Marquis of Hartington, M.P., &c.,
Dublin Castle.

No. 4.—LETTER from the HOME OFFICE to the UNDER SECRETARY of the LORD LIEUTENANT, referred to the COMMISSIONERS for their information.

SIR, Whitehall, 12th January, 1872.

With reference to your letter of the 2nd ultimo, I am directed by Mr. Secretary Bruce to transmit to you herewith, to be laid before the Lord Lieutenant, the enclosed copy of a letter which has been addressed to the Local Government Board by the Clerk to the Select Vestry of the Parish of Liverpool, with reference to the possible danger of spreading the contagion of small-pox alleged to exist by the Irish Poor Law Board, owing to the removal from that parish of Irish paupers back to Ireland.

I am, &c.,

A. F. O. LIDDELL.

To the Under Secretary, Dublin Castle.

*See Annual Report for 1871, page 23.

ENCLOSURE in No. 4.—LETTER from the SELECT VESTRY of the PARISH of LIVERPOOL to the LOCAL GOVERNMENT BOARD.

MY LORDS AND GENTLEMEN, Liverpool, 22nd December, 1871.

I am instructed by the Select Vestry of this parish to acknowledge the receipt of your letter of the 12th instant, relative to the removal from this parish to the Cavan Union of a pauper named Matthew M'Guire.

This man was admitted to the vagrant department of the Workhouse upon the 10th October last, his statement then being that he had been in Liverpool but one day. He was, in consequence of his age (he being entered as 65 years old), relieved from the labour task ordinarily required from vagrants, and was discharged from the department in the usual way. He applied for re-admission, and was admitted upon the 20th October, and again upon the 22nd, the 23rd, and the 24th days of the same month. Upon his discharge from the vagrant wards upon the morning of the 25th October, he applied for relief to the Relieving Officer; and as it was clear that the man was destitute and not able-bodied, he was offered an order for the Workhouse. This he accepted, and entered the house on the same day. He was located in the aged men's division of the Workhouse, where he remained until the 13th November, the day upon which he was removed to Ireland. It will thus be seen that his chargeability extended over a period of *twenty-six days* instead of *two days*, as alleged. The Select Vestry are quite at a loss to know the grounds upon which this man's removal can be complained of. At first sight it seems that the complaint is founded upon the statement that the removal was effected only two days after he first became chargeable, but from a subsequent passage in the Commissioners' letter the practice of "detaining paupers in the Workhouse until there is a batch of them to be sent over to any particular place" appears to be the subject of complaint.

That Irish paupers very frequently come to Liverpool for the express purpose of being removed to Ireland, the Select Vestry know only too well; and if the Poor Law Commissioners of Ireland will state how this is to be prevented, or how, when they have come, such paupers are to be dealt with other than by sending them home or keeping them altogether, the Select Vestry will gratefully accept the information.

As regards the alleged detention of paupers, it is only necessary to state that the Select Vestry have no power to detain any pauper for the purpose stated.

It is true that the removal of a pauper is sometimes delayed in order that it may be seen if other cases arise requiring removal to the same place; but this, the Select Vestry submit, is perfectly justifiable.

Through the reiterated complaints of the Irish authorities, the law was so altered as to require that in all cases paupers removed should be accompanied to their place of destination by an officer; and it has consequently become necessary, either that the number of removing officers should be largely increased, or that the work should be so regulated as that the one journey of the officer should be utilized to the fullest extent. The Select Vestry have chosen to adopt the latter alternative, and they fail to see that the course they have taken affords any reasonable ground of complaint to the Irish authorities.

The statement that the action of the Liverpool authorities has conduced to the spread of small-pox in Ireland, the Select Vestry feel to be particularly ungracious, and they will be glad to be furnished with the particulars of the "two instances" referred to by the Commissioners. The fact is that during the prevalence of the small-pox epidemic in Liverpool, the Select Vestry voluntarily suspended removals to Ireland upon this very account. From the 23rd March last (the date of the resolution of suspension) to the 20th October (when the suspension was removed) no Irish removals were made from this parish; and during the period named no fewer than 440 cases (i.e., families) were admitted to the Workhouse as Irish removable poor, many of which are still chargeable. Since the resumption of the removals thirty-three cases have been removed, and the average period of chargeability previous to removal has, on these cases, been fifty-seven days.

The Select Vestry cannot but consider that the complaint in this case, as well as other complaints equally unreasonable, forms part of a systematized plan for arousing a feeling against these removals with the evident object of inducing Parliament to withdraw the powers now possessed by English and Scotch Boards of Guardians—powers which it is believed it is, for the protection of English ratepayers, absolutely necessary to retain.

Two accidental facts may be stated in connexion with this particular case. One is that Maguire expressed no wish here to be removed to Cavan—in fact, he objected to go there, as he wanted to go to Dublin; the other is that during the small-pox epidemic, no case of small-pox occurred in the Workhouse itself, nor was a single case treated in the Workhouse, the Small-pox Hospitals being, as the Board are aware, some miles distant from the Workhouse.

I have, &c.,

(Signed), H. J. Hagger.

The Local Government Board,
Whitehall, London.

For the purposes of future reference, it is thought to be desirable to direct attention here to a letter of even date herewith, respecting the case of Mary Keating.*

No. 5.—Letter from the Commissioners to the Under Secretary of the Lord Lieutenant.

Poor Law Commission Office, Dublin,
20th March, 1872.

Sir,

The Commissioners for administering the Laws for Relief of the Poor in Ireland return to you herewith the file of papers referred to them, relating to the case of Matthew M'Guire, a person 65 years of age, who after five or six years residence in London, made his way as a tramp to Liverpool and applied there for relief, as he states, for the purpose of being removed to Ireland.

This case was brought under the notice of His Excellency by the Commissioners in their letter of the 28th November, 1871, and there appears to have been some misapprehension in dealing with it as a complaint against the Select Vestry of Liverpool, and especially on the part of the Select Vestry in replying to it as a complaint preferred against them in regard to their administration of the English law of removal to Ireland.

It is necessary, in order to make the matter clear, to refer to events which occurred some time since. On the 3rd December, 1869, a person named Joseph Wilson, was received into the Fever Hospital of Belfast Workhouse. The account which he gave of himself was, that he had tramped from Dublin to Belfast, having slept night after night at four Workhouses in succession of the following unions, Balrothery, Drogheda, Dundalk, and Newry; arriving at Belfast on the 25th November. Falling ill, he applied to the Relieving Officer on the 1st December following, for admission to the Workhouse Hospital, and was admitted on the 3rd December with an eruption on him, pronounced at once to be small-pox. This was precisely 15 days after he had left Liverpool for Dublin. When questioned as to where and how he took the contagion of small-pox, he could not assign any probable way of having caught it, except that he had slept in Liverpool Workhouse the night before he came over to Dublin, where he arrived on the 18th November, and after sleeping a night there in a lodging-house, resumed his journey on tramp to Belfast. There was no small-pox in Dublin at this time.

This was the first case of small-pox which had occurred at Belfast for many months, that town as well as the rest of Ireland possessing at that time almost total immunity from the disease.

Shortly after Wilson's case, two other cases broke out in the Belfast

* See No. 11, page 65.

Workhouse, and were treated in the Fever Hospital, and the first spread of small-pox, as an epidemic in Belfast, from which town it has never since been absent, was occasioned at this time by convalescent patients from the Workhouse Fever Hospital, carrying the disease with them into the town.

Notwithstanding the out-break at Belfast, and its subsequent spread to Dundalk and Drogheda, the rest of Ireland, including Dublin, continued free from small-pox during the year 1870, with the exception of certain cases directly traceable to importation, the number of deaths in that year not having exceeded in the whole 32. But early in 1871 there was reason to apprehend, from the increasing number of cases imported, the approach of that epidemic which caused no less than 647 deaths in that year, and is at this time causing a very much greater annual rate of mortality. The known cases of imported small-pox from Liverpool in the year 1870, and the first half of 1871, were 38, and from Glasgow in the same period, 17.

On the 9th February, 1871, the Select Vestry of Liverpool applied for, and obtained an order, removing John Green, a youth of 18, then an inmate for seven days of the Brownlow Hill Workhouse, to Dublin. He arrived in charge of an officer on the 10th February, and slept that night in North Dublin Workhouse, and the next three successive nights he slept in the Workhouses of Balrothery, Drogheda, and Ardee Unions. In the last he became ill, and broke out in small-pox on the 17th February, just 14 days after the time when he became an inmate of Liverpool Workhouse.

Upon this case the Commissioners founded their representation to His Excellency of the 4th March, 1871, recommending that if practicable, a suspension of removal orders from Great Britain to Ireland should be effected in towns such as London, Liverpool, and Glasgow, in which small-pox was then epidemic, and from which removals to Ireland were very frequently taking place. By His Excellency's command this proposal was communicated, through the Home Department, to the Local Government Board in England, and to the Board of Supervision in Scotland. By a letter of the Local Government Board, dated 17th March, the Commissioners were apprized that the Local Government Board considered that it had no authority to effect the arrangement in question, but they would suggest the expediency of suspending the removals to the Boards of Guardians of the places referred to.

No further communication was made to the Commissioners on this subject, nor were they made aware in any way that the Select Vestry of Liverpool had adopted, on the 23rd March following, the suggestion, and had suspended the removal of paupers to Ireland from that date to the 20th October, when the suspension was removed.

On the 15th November following, Matthew Maguire was removed under warrant from Liverpool to Cavan, to which place, having been born there, he was properly removable; and the representation of this case to the notice of His Excellency had no reference to the propriety of his removal, or the manner in which he was removed, but was sent as an additional example and proof of what was then only imperfectly known in this country, namely, that an extensive practice prevailed, of Irish persons in a low rank of life in England, coming to Liverpool, and applying for relief there in order to obtain by legal process of removal conveyance to Ireland without cost to themselves.

In the letter of the Select Vestry, the great frequency of these cases is admitted, and the question is asked, how they can be prevented, and how, when they have come to Liverpool, such persons are to be dealt with otherwise than by sending them home or keeping them altogether. The answer to this question appears to be, that if the system of removal did not exist no persons would come to Liverpool and seek relief there in order to be conveyed free of expense to Ireland; so clear it is that the existence of the law of the removal itself is the cause of this great inconvenience to the Poor Law Authorities at Liverpool, and of this part of the danger of contagious diseases, such as cholera and small-pox, and probably also typhus-fever, being conveyed from Liverpool to Ireland. The Commissioners have now to repeat, that there was nothing to complain of in this particular case of removal from Liverpool, and that the attention of His Excellency was called to it merely as an additional instance of a system of practice, dangerous to this country, arising out of the Removal Law.

It does not appear desirable that any further correspondence should take place with the Liverpool Vestry on this matter. Whatever may be necessary for their vindication in the case, will be effected by the publication of their letter, and of this reply to it, in the appendix to the Annual Report of the Commissioners to His Excellency, which is now in course of preparation.

By Order of the Commissioners,

B. BANKS, Chief Clerk.

To T. H. Burke, esq.,
Dublin Castle.

No. 6.—EXTRACT from MINUTES of PROCEEDINGS of the BOARD of GUARDIANS of SOUTH DUBLIN UNION, on Thursday 9th NOVEMBER, 1871.

MASTER'S REPORT.

That on yesterday morning, at 9 a.m., he admitted on Removal Warrant from Brownlow Hill Workhouse, a woman named Mary Keating, who was near her confinement, and who stated to the Doctor at Brownlow Hill Workhouse, "she did not know the moment she would be confined." She appeared to be in labour when presented at the gate, and was confined in six hours after her admission.

Referred to Poor Law Commissioners.

No. 7.—WARRANT of REMOVAL.

To the Select Vestry of the Parish of Liverpool, in the Borough of Liverpool, in the County of Lancaster, being the Guardians of the Poor of the said Parish, and to the Guardians of the Poor of the South Dublin Union, in the County of Dublin in Ireland.

Borough of Liverpool, to wit.

At a petty sessions of Her Majesty's justices of the peace for the borough of Liverpool, holden in and for the said borough, at the police court, in the said borough, on the 7th day of November, 1871, before us, the undersigned, Her Majesty's justices of the peace for the said borough.

Whereas complaint is now made by the Select Vestry of the parish of Liverpool, in the borough of Liverpool, in the county of Lancaster, as Guardians of the Poor of the said parish, that Mary Keating hath become and is now chargeable to the said parish of Liverpool. And whereas the said Mary Keating having been brought before us, and application having been made to us in petty sessions assembled, by Edward Ams, as officer of the said Select Vestry on their behalf, we have made due examination on oath, and find that the said Mary Keating is of the reputed age of twenty-nine years, and was born in Ireland, in the parish or townland of Rathfarnham, in the county of Dublin, now contained in the said union of South Dublin, and she hath not a settlement in England, and is not otherwise exempt from removal from the said parish of Liverpool; and we have seen the said Mary Keating, and are satisfied that she is in such a state of health as not to be liable to suffer bodily or mental injury by the removal to Ireland.

These are therefore to require you, the said Select Vestry of the said parish of Liverpool, as such Guardians as aforesaid, to cause the said Mary Keating to be safely conveyed to the said union of South Dublin, and to be delivered at the workhouse of such union.

Given under our hands and seals at the sessions aforesaid.

(Signed), HENRY DUCKWORTH.
HENRY C. BELOE.

No. 8.—STATEMENT made by MARY KEATING in reply to inquiries on admission at the SOUTH DUBLIN WORKHOUSE.

Name of pauper removed—Mary Keating; aged twenty-nine.

1. Date of warrant or copy? (Send copy if received).[1]—7th November, 1871.
2. Date of embarkation?—7th November, 1871.
3. Name of the port at which the embarkation took place?—Liverpool.
4. How sent, as a deck passenger or otherwise?—Second cabin.
5. When and by whom delivered at the workhouse?—8th November, 1871; Edward Aris, Assistant Removing Officer.
6. How long is it since the pauper left Ireland?—Ten weeks.
7. Where was the pauper born in Ireland? (Giving, if possible, the name of the parish, and the name of the townland.)—Rathfarnham, county Dublin, South Dublin Union.
8. What was the pauper's last place of residence in Ireland? (Giving, if possible, the name of the parish, and the name of the townland.)—Sandymount-strand, Dublin, South Dublin Union.
9. How long had the pauper resided in such place before leaving Ireland?—Five years.
10. Where was the pauper residing in England or Scotland when she became chargeable? (Give the name of the union, and also of the parish or township, if possible.)—5, Halbert-street, Park-road, Brownlow-hill Workhouse.
11. How long had she resided there?—Four weeks.
12. If less than three years, give as accurately as possible the particulars of previous residence for at least three years, stating in all cases, if possible, the name of the union, and of the parish or township.—Six weeks in workhouse.

Mary Keating states she went to the Brownlow Hill Workhouse about six weeks ago, as she believed she was near her confinement. On the morning of the 7th inst. she told the doctor that she was then ill, and asked that she would not be removed, as she could not tell the moment she would be confined. She was in labour when she arrived, and was confined in six hours after her admission.

No. 9.—LETTER from the COMMISSIONERS to the BOARD of GUARDIANS.

Poor Law Commission Office, Dublin,
SIR, 16th November, 1871.

The Commissioners for administering the Laws for Relief of the Poor in Ireland have had before them the minute of the Board of Guardians of South Dublin Union of the 9th inst., referring to them the report of the master of the workhouse, relating to the admission on the 8th inst. of a woman named Mary Keating on her removal from Liverpool Workhouse, the woman appearing to be in labour when presented at the gate, and having been confined in six hours after her admission.

The Commissioners have also had before them a copy of the Warrant of Removal, dated the 7th inst., and of the statement made by Mary Keating on her admission to the South Dublin Workhouse, in which she states that on the morning of the 7th instant (the day on which the Removal Warrant was obtained, and the removal effected), she told the doctor that she was then ill, and asked that she might not be removed, as she could not tell the moment she would be confined.

In reference to this case, the Commissioners have to observe that the woman's statement that she believed herself to be on the eve of her confinement at the time of removal, and that she stated herself to be so to the Medical Officer of Liverpool, is corroborated by the subsequent fact that she was actually in labour when presented at the gate of the workhouse, and assuming her statement to be correct, she ought not to have been removed by the authorities at Liverpool until after her confinement.

The Commissioners will bring the case, like other previous cases, under the notice of His Excellency the Lord Lieutenant.

By order of the Commissioners,

B. BANKS, Chief Clerk.

To the Clerk of South Dublin Union.

No. 10.—LETTER from the COMMISSIONERS to the UNDER SECRETARY of the LORD LIEUTENANT.

Poor Law Commission Office, Dublin,
SIR, 16th November, 1871.

The Commissioners for administering the Laws for Relief of the Poor in Ireland have the honour to forward, for the information of His Excellency the Lord Lieutenant, the accompanying copy of papers relating to the case of a poor woman named Mary Keating, aged 29 years, who was removed under warrant, dated the 7th inst., from the parish of Liverpool to the workhouse of South Dublin Union, where she arrived on the 8th inst., being then in labour, and where she gave birth to a child in six hours after her admission.

The object of the Commissioners in submitting this case to His Excellency is that the Liverpool authorities may be afforded an opportunity of explanation.

By order of the Commissioners,

B. BANKS, Chief Clerk.

To the Under Secretary of His Excellency the
Lord Lieutenant, Dublin Castle.

No. 11.—LETTER from the HOME OFFICE to the UNDER SECRETARY of the LORD LIEUTENANT, referred to the COMMISSIONERS for their information.

SIR, Whitehall, 13th January, 1872.

With reference to your letter of the 21st November last, I am directed by Mr. Secretary Bruce to transmit to you herewith, as received from the Local Government Board, the accompanying copy of a letter, together with enclosures, from the Select Vestry of the parish of Liverpool, on the subject of the removal of Mary Keatinge from that parish to the South Dublin Union. And I am to request that you will lay the same before the Lord Lieutenant for His Excellency's directions thereon.

I am, &c.,

A. F. O. LIDDELL.

The Under Secretary, Dublin Castle.

ENCLOSURE in No. 11.—LETTER from the SELECT VESTRY of LIVERPOOL to the LOCAL GOVERNMENT BOARD.

Liverpool, 22nd December, 1871.

MY LORDS AND GENTLEMEN,

I am directed by the Select Vestry of this parish to acknowledge the receipt of your letter of the 4th instant relative to the removal, upon the 7th ultimo, from this parish to the South Dublin Union, of a pauper named Mary Keating.

I now beg to forward to you herewith the following documents, namely :—

1. Copy statement of pauper at her preliminary examination.
2. Copy of pauper's examination before the magistrates.
3. Copy statement made by Mary E. Platt, a pauper inmate of the Brownlow Hill Workhouse.
4. Statement of two officers present in court during pauper's examination.
5. Copy statement of the officer who effected the removal.
6. Copy statement of Medical Officer.

From these statements it appears clear that whatever Keating may now say to the contrary, she, whilst in Liverpool, did not believe her delivery to be so imminent as it afterwards proved to be, and the Select Vestry in corroboration of this view would simply direct attention to the statement made to two persons by the pauper, that if removed she would return to this neighbourhood, in order that her confinement might not take place in Dublin. The Select Vestry consider that this view quite agrees with the probabilities of the case, as they consider it in the highest degree improbable that their officers would remove a woman whose delivery was expected to take place in the course of a few hours, or even in the course of a day or two. To take no higher ground, they are confident that the trouble and annoyance that such an event as the delivery of a woman after a passage would cause to the officer making the removal, and the outcry against English "barbarity" which would in that case inevitably follow, would be sufficient to prevent a removal being made under such circumstances.

Referring to the final paragraph of the Commissioners' letter, the Select Vestry have only to observe that the fact is that Irish Boards of Guardians are determined, so long as any removals of Irish poor are made, to represent themselves as injured parties in the matter, with the evident object by their pertinacious complaints of inducing Parliament to repeal the existing law. Under these circumstances the Select Vestry think it only right to take this opportunity of pointing out to you that Liverpool has grievances in connexion with the chargeability of Irish poor far greater in extent than anything they have heard of as existing elsewhere. They content themselves upon the present occasion by naming two—first, there is the practice, of which the case of Mary Keating is an instance of pregnant women coming over here from Ireland for the express purpose of being confined here. During the present year thirty-three women (twenty-one of them admitting themselves to be single) have been received into the workhouse as Irish removable cases, and have been confined within a short period of their admission—twenty-two of them within twenty-four hours. Many of these women avowed their object in coming to Liverpool to be as here stated.

Another instance may be cited in the action of certain charitable organizations, notably, that of the Mendicity Societies of Dublin and other large towns. These frequently pay for the passage to Liverpool of persons in pauper circumstances, who become chargeable within a very short time of their arrival. It is often alleged, and the Select Vestry believe it to be true, though it is necessarily very difficult of proof that guardians and their officers do not scruple to avail themselves occasionally of these agencies to send upon one pretext or another Irish paupers to this country.

One such instance occurred during the present year in the case of this very South Dublin Union, and I am instructed to send to you herewith copy letter addressed to the Clerk to the Guardians upon that occasion. To that letter no reply has been received. The woman, in that case as a deserted woman, was irremovable, and she remained for nearly five months chargeable to the parish.

As regards the general question the Select Vestry wish to add that it is their desire that their officers should upon all occasions act strictly within the law bearing upon this matter, and should carry out its provisions with all reasonable regard for the feelings of the paupers. In proof of this they may state that there are constantly upon the Relief lists, both indoor and outdoor, of the parish families of removable Irish poor, whom there is no attempt made to remove because from special circumstances it is thought that the removal would press with great and peculiar hardship upon the families concerned.

I have the honour to be, my lords and gentlemen,

Your obedient servant,

(Signed) H. J. Hagger.

For the purposes of future reference it is thought desirable to direct attention to another letter of even date herewith respecting the case of Matthew Maguire.*

The Local Government Board, Whitehall, London.

Statements referred to in foregoing Letter.

1.—Examination of the undernamed Pauper, taken the 19th day of October, 1871.

Mary Keating, a servant, aged twenty-nine, single, pregnant, says—I was born at Rathfarnham; I believe that I was christened at the Roman Catholic Chapel; I went to live in Dublin with my parents when I was very young, and when about fifteen I went to service and continued earning my living in various situations in various families in Dublin until I left it, and came to Liverpool about five weeks ago, and came to the sheds and then into the Workhouse. I should think my parents were born in Dublin; they were both Irish.

I came over here to be confined, because I did not want my people to know the state I was in.

I do not want to be sent back to Dublin. If I am sent I will come back again.

2.—Borough of Liverpool, to wit.

The examination of Mary Keating, taken on oath before us, the undersigned, two of Her Majesty's Justices of the Peace, in and for the said borough of Liverpool in Petty Sessions assembled this 7th day of November in the year of

* See No. 4, page 53.

our Lord one thousand eight hundred and seventy-one, who on her oath saith that she hath become and is now chargeable to the parish of Liverpool in the said borough; that according to the best of her knowledge and belief she is about twenty-nine years of age, and was born in Ireland, in the parish or townland of Rathfarnham, in the county of Dublin, now contained in the South Dublin Union, in the county of Dublin, in Ireland aforesaid; that she hath not a settlement in England, and is not otherwise exempt from removal from the said parish of Liverpool, and that the said Mary Keating is in such a state of health as not to be liable to suffer any bodily or mental injury by removal to Ireland.

her
MARY + KEATING
mark.

Sworn the day and year first above written before us at Liverpool in the said borough.

(Signed), HENRY DUCKWORTH.
HENRY C. BELOE.

3.—STATEMENT of MARY ELLEN PLATT

Says—I remember Mary Keating; she was in the class division; it is about ten weeks since she first came in; she was in about two weeks before I took much notice of her; she sat alongside of me; she told me she left her situation in Dublin to come to Liverpool, because she was pregnant, and she did not want to be confined in Dublin for fear of her parents getting to know the state she was in; she said her father and mother were living in Dublin, and that she had lived all her life in Dublin, and that was her native place; she also told me that she was about two months off her time; when she went out the first time, she was only out two days; a few days after she came in the second time she told me she was going to be passed home to Ireland, and that the pass-master asked her how far she was off her time, and that she told him about five weeks; the day she went to the Court she said, if she had known she would have gone out to prevent them sending her home; she said she would go to Ireland, and come back again and go to Toxteth Park Workhouse to be confined; she said when she got to Dublin she would try and find the father of her child, and get money from him to bring her back.

(Signed), MARY ELLEN PLATT.

18th December, 1871.

4.—STATEMENT of TWO OFFICERS.

We, the undersigned, James Alexander M'Innes and Edward Aris, officers in the employ of the select vestry of the parish of Liverpool, in the county of Lancaster, hereby severally and respectively declare that on the 7th day of November last, complaint was made to Henry Duckworth and Henry Christie Beloe, esquires, two of Her Majesty's justices of the peace in and for the borough of Liverpool, by the said select vestry of the chargeability to the said parish of one Mary Keating, and application was made to the said justices for an order for her removal to Ireland. That we, the said James Alexander M'Innes and Edward Aris were present when the said Mary Keating was examined by the said justices touching such removal. That the whole of her examination (copy of which is hereto annexed) was carefully and distinctly read over to her by Peter Lucas Stubbs, one of the clerks to the said justices, and that she appeared perfectly to understand the same. After the same had been read over to her she was asked by Mr. Stubbs, "Is it true?" she answered "Yes," and was thereupon sworn thereto.

Dated this 18th day of November, 1871.

(Signed), JAMES ALEXANDER M'INNES,
EDWARD ARIS.

5.—STATEMENT of the OFFICER who effected the REMOVAL.

I, the undersigned, Edward Aris, an officer in the employ of the select vestry of the parish of Liverpool, in the county of Lancaster, hereby declare that on the 7th day of November last I removed Mary Keating, the person referred to in the order made by Henry Duckworth and Henry Christie Beloe, esquires, two of Her Majesty's justices of the peace for the borough of Liverpool, in the county of Lancaster, bearing date the 7th day of November last, from the Liverpool Workhouse to the South Dublin Union Workhouse, in Ireland. That I took her in a car from the Liverpool Workhouse to the City of Dublin Steam Packet Company's steamer, then lying in the Clarence Dock, on board of which she was provided with a cabin passage; that I saw her several times during the passage to Ireland, and that although she complained of sea sickness, she made no other complaint. That immediately on landing at Dublin, I took her to the workhouse of the South Dublin Union in a covered car. That at the time I removed her from the Liverpool Workhouse, I had no idea that she was near her confinement. That neither prior to her removal nor during the passage did the said Mary Keating state to me or in my hearing that she could not tell the moment she would be confined, or anything to that effect.

(Signed), EDWARD ARIS.

18th December, 1871.

6.—STATEMENT OF MEDICAL OFFICER.

I, the undersigned, John Wilson Steele, doctor of medicine and Assistant Medical Officer of the Workhouse, Brownlow Hill, hereby declare that upon the 7th day of October last I examined Mary Keating, and considered her to be in a fit state of bodily health to undergo removal to Ireland; and I further declare that upon the occasion of my said examination, she, in reply to my question as to when she expected her delivery to take place, stated that she expected to be delivered in about a month from that time, but said she did not wish to go to Ireland, her reason being that she came over here to be confined in order to forego the shame of remaining at home in Ireland.

(Signed), JOHN WILSON STEELE, M.D.

21st December, 1871.

COPY LETTER to the GUARDIANS of the SOUTH DUBLIN UNION as to the case of MARGARET M'KENNA.

Liverpool, 15th February, 1871.

SIR, Margaret M'Kenna.

I am instructed by the select vestry of this parish to inform you that this woman has become chargeable to the parish, and has made a statement which it is thought should, as a matter of courtesy, be communicated to your Board before other action (should it be thought desirable to proceed further) is taken in the matter.

Her statement in substance is that she was an inmate of the South Dublin Workhouse until the 6th instant; that upon that day, in pursuance of a former conversation she had had with the master of the Workhouse, Mr. John Hornett, she told him that she was ready to leave, he having previously promised to get her a pass to Liverpool from the Mendicity Society; that upon the evening of the 6th Mr. Cavan, Relieving Officer, took her from the Workhouse to the society's office, and after she had waited for some time, Mr. Cavan gave her a note which served as a passage ticket, and also gave her 2s. and a loaf. She arrived in Liverpool on Tuesday morning and became chargeable on Thursday.

The woman herself belongs to Ireland, and her husband, for whom, according to her statement, she came to look, also belongs to Ireland.

If this statement be correct, there can be no doubt that the woman has been irregularly removed to Liverpool, and that two of your officers have been cognizant of and have participated in the irregularity.

I am, &c.,
(Signed), H. J. HAGGER.

No. 12.—LETTER from the COMMISSIONERS to Mr. ROBINSON, Poor Law Inspector.

Poor Law Commission Office, Dublin,
SIR, 13th March, 1872.

Referring to the case of Mary Keating, who was removed under warrant, dated 7th November last, from the parish of Liverpool to the Workhouse of South Dublin Union, the Commissioners for administering the Laws for Relief of the Poor in Ireland desire to state that they wish to return the papers containing the explanation given by the select vestry of Liverpool regarding the case to the Chief Secretary's office, but before doing so they will be glad to receive the clerk's explanation as to the case of Margaret M'Kenna (which is referred to in the latter part of the letter from Mr. H. J. Hagger to the Local Government Board, dated the 22nd December last), both as to what is known by him regarding the particulars of that case, and whether the letter of the 15th February, 1871, was laid before the Board of Guardians, and if so, what was their action upon it.

The file of papers is forwarded to you herewith, and you will be good enough to return it with your report.

By order of the Commissioners,

B. BANKS, Chief Clerk.

To Henry Robinson, esq.,
Poor Law Inspector,
31, Cambridge-terrace, Kingstown.

No. 13.—REPORT from Mr. ROBINSON to the COMMISSIONERS.

GENTLEMEN, Kingstown, March 19, 1872.

I have the honour to acknowledge the receipt of your letter of the 13th inst., in which you express a wish to receive an explanation from the Clerk of the South Dublin Union as to the case of a woman named Margaret M'Kenna (which is referred to in the latter part of the letter from Mr. H. T. Hagger to the Local Government Board, dated the 22nd of December last), both as to what is known by him regarding the particulars of that case, and whether the letter of the 15th February, 1871, was laid before the Board of Guardians, and if so, what was their action upon it.

I have had an interview with the Clerk of the Union and obtained an explanation in writing from him on the subject, together with reports from the assistant master of the Workhouse, and from Mr. Campbell, Relieving Officer, who probably is the person referred to in Mr. Hagger's letter as Mr. Cavan. Mr. Hornidge, who was Workhouse Master in February, 1871, and who is alluded to by Mr. Hagger as Mr. John Hornets, is not now alive.

From the documents forwarded to me by the clerk, which I enclose for your information, it appears that Margaret M'Kenna left the South Dublin Workhouse on the 14th of January, 1871, and not on the 6th of February, as stated by her in Liverpool, and consequently that more than three weeks elapsed between the time of her discharge from the South Dublin Workhouse and her application for relief in Liverpool.

Mr. Campbell denies having in any way assisted her to proceed to Liverpool.

The only excuse the Clerk of the Union can offer for omitting to lay Mr. Hagger's letter before the Board of Guardians, and to acknowledge its receipt is, that he gave the letter to the late Master of the Workhouse who did not return it, and that consequently the matter escaped his memory.

The papers forwarded to me with your communication of the 13th inst. are herewith returned.

I have the honour to be, gentlemen,
Your obedient servant,
Henry Robinson.

The Poor Law Commissioners.

Enclosures in No. 13.

(*a.*)—Letter from Clerk of South Dublin Union to Mr. Robinson.

South Dublin Union,
Clerk's Office, Board Room, James's-street,
16th day of March, 1872.

Sir,

With reference to the case of Margaret M'Kenna, on which you requested me to report, I beg leave to inform you that I have caused every inquiry in my power to be made, and now send you the annexed statements of the assistant master and relieving officer Campbell.

I have a distinct recollection of receiving Mr. Hagger's letter and handing it to Mr. Hornidge for explanation of the charges contained in it. I have made diligent and careful search for but cannot find the letter, nor do I find any entry of it on the minutes, and I can only account for this by the fact that the letter was never returned to me by Mr. Hornidge, and that, in consequence, the matter unfortunately escaped my memory.

I have the honour to be, sir,
Your obedient servant,
George Hepburn, Clerk of the Union.

Henry Robinson, esq.,
Poor Law Inspector.

(*b.*)—Letter from Mr. Sullivan, Assistant Master of the Workhouse.

South Dublin Union,
16th March, 1872.

Sir,

In reply to the annexed letter I have to state that there was no inmate of the name of Margaret M'Kenna discharged from the Workhouse on the 6th February, 1871, but a woman of that name, aged forty-five years, and who is described on the workhouse books as a *widow*, was discharged on the 14th January, 1871, having been an inmate from the 16th December, 1869; this is the only person of that name discharged during the months of January or February of that year. When leaving the Workhouse she gave as the address, she was going to 16, Liverpool-road. This would appear to contradict her statement that she went to the mendicity, accompanied by one of our relieving officers. I may mention that the committee of the Mendicity Institution entertain applications for the sending of poor people to their homes only on Tuesdays, and the 14th January, the day of her discharge from here, was on Saturday, so that if this be the same person, her application would not have been entertained till the 18th, that is four days after her discharge from the Workhouse.

The late master Mr. Hornidge never in any way to my knowledge assisted in the removal of inmates or persons who had been inmates to England or Scotland, nor was there any funds at his disposal for that purpose.

On the occasion when the correspondence took place on the subject, I distinctly recollect Mr. Hornidge and Mr. Campbell denying that they in any way assisted this woman in obtaining her passage to Liverpool.

I am, sir, your obedient servant,

J. Sullivan, Assistant Master.

G. Hepburn, esq., Clerk of the Union.

(c.)—Letter from Mr. Samuel Campbell, Relieving Officer.

Sir, 16th March 1872.

The only recollection I have of this woman Margaret M'Kenna is that about a year ago the late master, Mr. Hornidge, showed me a letter respecting her; the letter stated that he the late master sent her to Liverpool, and that I gave her a loaf of bread and 2s. in money, which both of us at the time denied, as I do now distinctly.

I never by any chance gave an inmate money on leaving this house, neither did I ever accompany any inmate from this house to procure a passage to Liverpool.

The following entry appears in my application and report-book under date 10th December, 1869:—Margaret M'Kenna, aged forty-five years, a widow, a charwoman, living at 45, James's-street, having a sore hand, was admitted provisionally on the above date by me.

Samuel J. Campbell.

No. 14.—Letter from the Commissioners to the Under Secretary of the Lord Lieutenant.

Poor Law Commission Office, Dublin,
Sir, 21st March, 1872.

The Commissioners for administering the Laws for Relief of the Poor in Ireland return herewith the file of papers relating to the case of Mary Keating, a young single woman, nineteen years of age, who was brought from Liverpool, under warrant of removal, to the South Dublin Workhouse, and was delivered of a full-grown child in six hours after her arrival.

She stated that she had been in service in Dublin, and, becoming pregnant, had gone to Liverpool to be confined, so as to keep her disgrace from the knowledge of her friends; and that when it was proposed to remove her back to Dublin, she had told the authorities at Liverpool that she was expecting to be confined immediately.

The case was represented by the Commissioners to his Excellency the Lord Lieutenant, expressly in order that the removing authorities at Liverpool might have the opportunity of giving an answer to these statements.

The select vestry of the parish of Liverpool, at whose instance the removal was ordered, and whose officers carried out the order, replied to the statements of Mary Keating by several depositions, which went to show that so far from stating at Liverpool that she was in expectation of immediate confinement, she told the officers and others that she was expecting that event in a month or five weeks; and that relying on this, they had taken steps for her removal without delay.

One of these depositions, made by Dr. Steele, the Medical Officer at Liverpool, states that Mary Keating made such a declaration to him on the 7th October; and, as she was removed on the 7th November, this would so far support her story. But there is reason to suppose that the word "October" has been used in error for November, and that the young woman, whose object it was to be confined at Liverpool, deceived the officers as to the time when she was expecting it to take place.

The Commissioners would have willingly given publicity to this explanation at the time, but unfortunately it was conveyed in such a tone, accompanied by recrimination upon subjects having little or no connexion with the case of Mary Keating, that if it had been communicated at that time to the South Dublin Board, it would have probably resulted in a controversy neither relevant nor useful in any point of view.

The Select Vestry say that Liverpool has grievances in connexion with the chargeability of Irish poor, far greater in extent than anything they have heard of as existing elsewhere; and they complain, in the first place, that pregnant women come over from Ireland to be confined there, as exemplified in the case of Mary Keating. In the next place, they complain of the action of certain charitable organizations, and notably of the mendicity societies in Dublin and other large towns—paying the passage to Liverpool of persons in pauper circumstances, who become chargeable there in a short time after their arrival; and that Guardians and their officers do not scruple to avail themselves of these agencies to send upon one pretext or another paupers into England.

The example given in regard to this alleged practice is the case of Margaret M'Kenna, who appears to have stated to the authorities of Liverpool parish that she was an inmate of South Dublin Workhouse on the 6th February, 1871, the master of which, Mr. John Hornett, promised to get her a pass to Liverpool from the Mendicity Society, and that on the evening of the 6th February Mr. Cavan, Relieving Officer, took her from the Workhouse to the society's office, and gave her there a passage ticket, with 2s. and a loaf. She was admitted to the Liverpool Workhouse on the 9th February, and she stated that both herself and her husband, whom she went to England to look for, belonged to Ireland.

It appears upon inquiry from the Workhouse officers of South Dublin Union, that Margaret M'Kenna left the Workhouse on the 14th January, 1871, and not on the 6th February, and that more than three weeks therefore elapsed between the time of her discharge and the time of her application for relief at Liverpool.

Both Mr. Hornidge (not Hornett) the Master, and Mr. Campbell (not Cavan) the Relieving Officer, absolutely denied that they in any way assisted this woman in obtaining her passage to Liverpool; and from the character of those officers (the former of whom is now dead), the Commissioners place implicit reliance on their statements.

It is very likely that Margaret M'Kenna, presenting herself to the Dublin Mendicity Society as a woman whose husband was in England, and as being anxious to go there and join him, would obtain assistance for the purpose from that society; and there may be other charitable institutions and many charitable individuals in Dublin willing to expend the money at their command in the same manner. At the same time the Commissioners are able to affirm most confidently that no such expenditure from the poor-rate has ever taken place in Ireland without being disallowed by the auditor, and repayment of the amount rigidly enforced from those who expended it. It does not, however, seem reasonable to expect that either Liverpool or any other large town in the United Kingdom, could take effective measures in any way to protect itself against the occurrence of such cases as that of Mary Keating, or such cases as that of Margaret M'Kenna, so long as persons are permitted to go of their own free will from one place to another for any lawful purpose; or, secondly, so long as benevolent individuals are not prevented by law from assisting persons desiring so to do, but unable to do so from want of funds. That Liverpool should, from her geographical position in relation to Ireland, be peculiarly exposed to such inconveniences, may, from one point of view, be a subject of regret; but, on the other hand, it must be allowed that she has enjoyed, and still enjoys, incalculable material advantages from her proximity to and connexion with the coasts of Ireland.

(By order.) B. Banks, Chief Clerk.

To T. H. Burke, esq., &c., &c.,
Dublin Castle.

IV.—CORRESPONDENCE ON THE SUBJECT OF THE REFUSAL OF THE AUTHORITIES AT MARYPORT TO ALLOW AN IRISH SEAMAN, SUFFERING FROM SMALL-POX, TO LAND AT THAT PLACE (IN CONTINUATION OF CORRESPONDENCE IN REPORT FOR 1871, APPENDIX A. III., P. 51.)

LETTER from the HOME OFFICE to the UNDER SECRETARY of the LORD LIEUTENANT.

Sir, Whitehall, 20th May, 1871.

Referring to your letter of the 17th February last, stating that in the opinion of the Irish Government the explanation given with respect to the refusal of the authorities at Maryport to render assistance to a seaman named George Ritchie, who was taken ill with small-pox on board the ship *Slaney* in that port, is unsatisfactory, I am directed by Mr. Secretary Bruce to transmit to you herewith a report by Dr. Buchanan, of the Medical Department of the Privy Council, upon this case, and to state, for the information of the Irish Government, that the amendments of the law necessary to prevent the recurrence of similar scandals is under consideration.

I am, &c.,
A. F. O. Liddell.

ENCLOSURE in foregoing LETTER.

REPORT by Dr. BUCHANAN on the alleged misconduct or neglect of the Sanitary Authority at Maryport and its Officer, in the case of George Ritchie, a sailor, taken into that port suffering from small-pox.

In accordance with my instructions, I have visited Maryport, in Cumberland, and have inquired into the circumstances under which, as alleged, a seaman named Ritchie, who was suffering from small-pox on board the ship *Slaney*, was not allowed to be landed at that port in December last.

I conducted my inquiry on April 18th, 1871, at the office of the harbour trustees; and there were present—J. P. Lenhoum, esq., chairman of the Board of Trustees; Mr. Harwise, clerk of the Board; Dr. Pearson and Mr. Johnstone,—the last two being the gentlemen concerning whose course of action question has arisen.

The *Slaney* was in harbour on my arrival at Newport on the evening of the

17th, and the purpose of my inquiry was notified to the master, who, however, found himself obliged to leave Maryport early on the morning of the 28th, before the inquiry began.

I read to the gentlemen present the papers relating to the case, and invited their comments upon the allegations therein made. Mr. Johnstone, the collector of customs, stated that he was satisfied that he had not, in the absence of an Order in Council, any duty of providing for a seaman sick of small-pox; but he believed that the local health authority had some duty of the kind. He had heard in general terms of Dr. Pearson's appointment as Medical Consultee of the trustees, and understanding the question to be of a medical nature, he sent the master of the *Slaney* to Dr. Pearson, and considered that his functions were at an end. In this view of his duties I believe that Mr. Johnstone was essentially right, and that if he committed any error it was in referring the master to Dr. Pearson instead of to the clerk of the trustees, who legally is their proper representative.

Dr. Pearson, upon hearing the statements of the papers, positively denied that he had in any sense ordered the removal of the *Slaney*, but says that he did point out to the master that, medically speaking, there was need for the vessel being placed in quarantine, and that there was no provision for quarantine in Maryport. He made this statement, he alleges, as a medical practitioner knowing the town, and not as a public officer. He understands by quarantine the isolation of a ship having infectious disease on board. He states that he did not indicate Liverpool as the place to which the ship ought to have been taken, and he denies, and holds to be ridiculous as well as false, the allegation that he threatened the captain with any consequences if the sick sailor were landed. He did not visit the sick seaman, and was not, he says, requested to do so.

In view of this statement, a part of which had been anticipated in the inquiry before the Maryport magistrates, I pointed out that a public officer could not, unless he specially guarded himself, dissociate his private action from his action in his public capacity, and I then learnt that Dr. Pearson had not, and acted in the knowledge that he had not, in the sense which the papers in the case suggested, the functions of "Officer of Health" in Maryport.

The sanitary authority, both sewer and nuisance authority for the town is under a local Act, the board of trustees for the district and harbour of Maryport, and this Board, having at various times had occasion for the services of a medical practitioner to inspect nuisances, had retained Dr. Pearson to act as their officer as occasion arose, reserving to themselves and their other officers the initiation and conduct of all sanitary action, but calling in Dr. Pearson's services as they thought fit, and remunerating those services by a fee paid in the particular case.

The Chairman and Clerk of the Board assured me that it was no part of Dr. Pearson's duty as an officer of the Board to take cognizance of the health of the town, nor, unless specially summoned in writing, to be a party to any sanitary action which the Board might see fit to take.

The following are the proceedings relating to Dr. Pearson's appointment:—

1. At a committee meeting, November 15, 1869—

"Read letter from Dr. Pearson, dated November 15, 1869, being reply to a letter from the clerk, dated November 13, 1869, on the subject of the nuisance in Smith's yard in Fleming-square, stating that if the trustees will give him written authority to act as their Medical Officer in all cases in which the Inspector may require it, he will do so."

"Resolved—That Dr. Pearson's letter be referred to the Board."

2. At a meeting of the trustees, December 15, 1869—

Dr. Pearson, at the request of the Board, attended the meeting, and explained that he wished to be appointed Medical Officer under the common seal of the trustees before he made any inspection of nuisances, and that his remuneration would be by fees, according to services rendered.

"Resolved—That Dr. Pearson be appointed Medical Officer, and that his appointment be sealed at the next Board meeting."

3. At a meeting of the trustees, January 11, 1870—

The clerk having prepared a document appointing Dr. Pearson the Medical Officer of the trustees, it was

"Resolved—That the common seal be affixed to the same, which was accordingly done in the presence of the meeting."

District of Maryport.

The trustees for the district and harbour of Maryport, in pursuance of the "Maryport Improvement and Harbour Act 1866," and the "Maryport District and Harbour Act, 1868," being the local authority charged with the jurisdiction over matters of common nuisance, do hereby appoint Joseph Pearson, of Maryport, M.D., their Medical Officer for the said district.

Given under the common seal of the said trustees the 11th day of January, 1870.

JOHN BARWISE, Clerk to the Trustees.

[*Common Seal.*]

It will be observed that this appointment of Dr. Pearson to be Medical Officer is not made in accordance with the 10th and 11th Vic., cap. 34, (incorporated with the "Maryport Local Act,") sec. 14 of which empowers the trustees to appoint, "subject to the approval of one of Her Majesty's Principal Secretaries of State," a person of competent skill and experience, who shall be styled the "Officer of Health;" the duties of such officer being defined to be *inter alia* to ascertain the existence of disease, especially epidemics, and to point out the best means of checking the spread of such diseases; and such officer to be paid by "salary out of the rates."

Now, Dr. Pearson was not appointed an "officer of health" with these functions, but as the chairman and clerk of the trustees both testify, his duties were not to arise until he was specially called on in writing to advise in each particular case. His appointment was never submitted to the Secretary of State for approval, and it was arranged that payment was to be made to him, not by salary, as in the case of an officer of health, but only according as the Board saw fit to put his services into requisition.

I am therefore of opinion that thus far, for the purpose of dealing with such a case as that now under investigation, Dr. Pearson was in the position of any other medical practitioner in the town.

It is a matter for consideration however, in the next place, whether Dr. Pearson's connexion with the Board was not such as to require of him a general knowledge of the sanitary laws. If he had had such knowledge, it would be expected that upon application being made to him he would have referred the master of the *Skerry* to the chairman or clerk of the harbour trustees. Dr. Pearson appears, however, to know hardly anything of sanitary law, and certainly not to have been aware that the trustees, as sanitary authority, had any functions in respect of vessels in the harbour. The only action which he has taken since his appointment in January, 1870, has been on one occasion to examine and report in pursuance of a special minute of the trustees about the injury to health that might be produced by a particular nuisance. In the discharge of this duty no knowledge of the law was required, and Dr. Pearson has never on that or any other occasion, had to refer to the "Sanitary Act, 1866," under certain sections of which the powers of the sanitary authority in dealing with ships arise.

Meanwhile Dr. Pearson's appointment as Medical Officer to the trustees has doubtless led to a belief in the town that he had some general duties and powers, and public expectation has probably invested him with still more of such. In truth he appears to have had no powers, no duties but such as from time to time were given him in relation to particular cases, and neither to have had, nor to have supposed himself to have had, any general functions whatever.

It may be questioned whether Dr. Pearson should have allowed himself to be placed in the false position of having the title of Medical Officer while his duties were but those of occasional referee.

A part of the reference made to my Lords of the Council by the Home Secretary, is to advise whether in the case of the *Sisney* Dr. Pearson neglected his duty, and if so, whether any steps should be taken to mark the disapproval of the Secretary of State as to his conduct.

The foregoing part of the report will probably enable my Lords to decide on the answer to be given to the question.

The other reference made by the Home Secretary to my Lords is the more important one of advising what steps should be taken to prevent the recurrence of such a case as that under investigation, where the master of a vessel, having on board a person suffering from a dangerous infectious disease, can find on shore no place for the reception of such a case. This is a matter which concerns the whole kingdom. The difficulty that has arisen at Maryport has occurred elsewhere; and generally there are not at English ports any places, such as appear by the letter of January 31st of the Irish Poor Law Commissioners, to be universally available in Ireland, into which sick seamen can be taken for treatment.

Section 37 of the "Sanitary Act, 1866," gives to every sewer authority power "to provide for the use of the inhabitants within its district hospitals or temporary places for the reception of the sick;" and section 26 of the same Act enacts that, where such an hospital is provided, a justice may direct the removal to it "of any person suffering from any dangerous contagious or infectious disorder, being without proper lodging or accommodation, or lodged in a room occupied by more than one family, or being on board any ship or vessel."

It will be seen that the provision of such an hospital, important as for sanitary reasons it is in every health district, is of double importance in the case of seaport districts.

Unhappily, hardly any sewer authority has availed itself of the powers thus conferred on it; and Maryport, like other districts, has no such place for the reception of the sick. It is stated by the chairman and the clerk of the Board of Trustees, that since that body has had authority to provide such a place, no occasion for the exercise of its powers, in regard of persons brought by vessels, had arisen before that which is the subject of the present inquiry. If the case of Ritchie on board the *Sisney* had been represented to the clerk of the trustees, that gentleman would, he says, although he has no instructions to meet such a case, have summoned Dr. Pearson to consider with him the steps necessary to be taken, and would have prepared himself to advise the trustees as to their course of action.

It is evident, however, that the intention of the Legislature has been to confer on every sewer authority power to be prepared beforehand to meet the contingency of a case of dangerous infectious disease imported into its district, and not that it should think for the first time, when the contingency has actually occurred, of what ought to be done.

The steps to be taken to prevent the recurrence at Maryport and elsewhere of such a case as the present, and for insuring generally that there shall be provision for the due treatment in isolation of any person importing dangerous infectious disease, appear, therefore, to be, first, that the health authority should, in all such cases have some place for the reception and treatment of such disease; second, that the health authority should in all cases have a medical practitioner, with the full functions of an "officer of health," to take cognizance of occurrences affecting the health of the district, and to originate advice as to the proper way of meeting such occurrences. If these two wants had been supplied at Maryport, the events under investigation could not have occurred. But it is hardly to be hoped that action of the sort here indicated will be taken by local authorities, so long as the Legislature leaves it optional with them whether or not they shall incur the expense therein involved.

(Signed) George Buchanan.

Medical Department of the Privy Council
Office, May 3rd, 1871.

V.—CORRESPONDENCE ON THE SUBJECT OF THE REMOVAL OF DANGEROUS LUNATICS FROM SCOTCH LUNATIC ASYLUMS TO IRISH WORKHOUSES.

No. 1.—REPORT from Mr. ROBINSON, Poor Law Inspector, to the COMMISSIONERS.

GENTLEMEN, Dublin, February 22nd, 1872.

I would beg to bring under your notice two cases of removal from the parish of Glasgow to this country; one case is that of a man named John Flinn, who has been removed to the South Dublin Union, and the other of a man named William Smith, who, with his three children, is now on his way to Castleblayney in charge of a removing officer.

On going into the South Dublin Workhouse this day, I observed these two men handcuffed together, and on making inquiry from the removing officer, who was there at the time, he informed me that they were both dangerous lunatics, and had been taken out of the lunatic asylum in Glasgow, and sent direct from that institution to Ireland. I also learned from him that he considered it necessary to restrain them with handcuffs in consequence of the information he obtained from the officers of the lunatic asylum regarding their dispositions, as they were described to him as dangerous and violent.

He also told me that the father of John Flinn and two brothers of William Smith reside in Scotland, and that the removal orders were obtained on the depositions of these persons.

The admission of John Flinn having been reported by the master of the South Dublin Workhouse to the Board of Guardians at their meeting held this day, I advised them to apply for the depositions taken in the case, and to forward them, with the removal warrant, to you; if the Castleblayney Board of Guardians will adopt the same course in regard to William Smith, you will have all the particulars of both removals before you.

I have the honour to be, gentlemen,

Your obedient servant,

HENRY ROBINSON.

The Poor Law Commissioners.

No. 2.—EXTRACT from MINUTES of PROCEEDINGS of the BOARD of GUARDIANS of SOUTH DUBLIN UNION, on the 22nd February, 1872.

The master reported that a man named James Flinn certified as a dangerous lunatic was removed under warrant from the Glasgow Union to this Workhouse this morning, and that he has been placed in the lunatic department, and has asked his discharge, and that he requested the instructions of the Board.

Ordered—That he be not discharged, but that steps be taken to have him committed as a dangerous lunatic, and that application be made to the Guardians of Glasgow Union for copies of the depositions and documents on which the removal order was obtained, pursuant to the 25th and 26th Vic., cap. 113, section 3, which the clerk is to send at once to the Poor Law Commissioners along with the removal warrant.

No. 3.—LETTER from the CLERK of the UNION to the COMMISSIONERS.

South Dublin Union,
Clerk's Office, Board Room, James's-street,
27th February, 1872.

GENTLEMEN,

I have just received and now beg to forward herewith copy petition, medical certificate and deposition on which the removal order in the case of John Flinn was granted by the sheriff of Lanarkshire, referred to in the minutes of proceedings of 22nd, as also a copy of the removal order.*

I have the honour to be, gentlemen,
Your obedient servant,
GEORGE HEPBURN, Clerk of the Union.

The Poor Law Commissioners,
Poor Law Office, Custom House.

No. 4.—LETTER from the COMMISSIONERS to the BOARD of GUARDIANS.

Poor Law Commission Office, Dublin,
5th March, 1872.

SIR,

The Commissioners for administering the Laws for Relief of the Poor in Ireland acknowledge the receipt of your letter of the 27th ult., forwarding copy of the depositions and other documents in the case of John Flinn, a lunatic pauper, who was removed under warrant, dated 20th ult., from the Gartnavel Lunatic Asylum, Glasgow, to the Workhouse of South Dublin Union; and in reference thereto the Commissioners desire to state that according to the view taken by the legal authorities in Scotland, removals of lunatics from Scotch Asylums to Irish Union Workhouses, are in accordance with the law authorizing removals from Scotland to Ireland; nor is there any appeal against such warrants of removal.

By order of the Commissioners,
B. BANKS, Chief Clerk.

To the Clerk of South Dublin Union,
James's-street.

No. 5.—LETTER from the CLERK of the UNION to the COMMISSIONERS.

South Dublin Union,
Clerk's Office, Board Room, James's-street,
8th day of March, 1872.

GENTLEMEN,

The Guardians have (in reference to your letter 5,746 of 5th inst.), respecting the case of John Flinn, directed that the documents and correspondence be laid before his Excellency the Lord Lieutenant and the Chief Secretary for Ireland, with request to induce Her Majesty's Government to alter the existing unjust law, and make such amendments therein as will operate justly towards the ratepayers of this country.

* The documents which accompanied this letter were returned to the Board of Guardians, who applied for them after the receipt of the Commissioners' letter of the 5th March with a view to laying correspondence before the Lord Lieutenant (see No. 5).

I have therefore to request that you will have the goodness to direct that the documents I forwarded to you in this matter be sent to me to enable me to carry out the order of the Board.

I have the honour to be, gentlemen,

Your obedient servant,

Geo. Hepburn, Clerk of the Union.

The Poor Law Commissioners, Custom House.

Note.—The documents were returned as requested.

No. 6.—Letter from the Commissioners to the Board of Guardians of Castleblayney Union.

Poor Law Commission Office, Dublin,
24th February, 1872.

Sir,

The Commissioners for administering the Laws for Relief of the Poor in Ireland have received a report from their Inspector, Mr. Robinson, in which he states that on going into the Workhouse of South Dublin Union on the 22nd inst., he observed two men handcuffed together, and that on making inquiry concerning them, he found that they had been removed from Glasgow; and the removing officer informed him that they were both dangerous lunatics, and had been taken out of the lunatic asylum in Glasgow and sent direct from that institution to Ireland. The removing officer also stated that he considered it necessary to restrain them with handcuffs in consequence of the information he obtained from the officers of the lunatic asylum regarding their dispositions, as they were described to him as dangerous and violent.

One of these men, Wm. Smith, with his three children, was about to be taken on by the removing officer to Castleblayney. His brother resides in Scotland, and it was stated that the removal order was obtained on the deposition of the brother.

If the family have arrived at the Workhouse, the Commissioners presume that a copy of the removal order has been forwarded to the Board of Guardians; and the Commissioners recommend the Guardians to apply at once to the parochial authorities in Glasgow, on whose behalf the warrant was obtained, for a copy of the depositions on which it was granted, which they are bound by the 3rd sec. of the 25th & 26th Vic., c. 83, to furnish if applied for within three months from the date of the warrant.

The copy of the depositions and warrant should then be forwarded to the Commissioners, with any information that may be obtained regarding the facts of the case.

By order, &c.,

B. Banks, Chief Clerk.

To the Clerk, Castleblayney Union.

No. 7.—Warrant for the Removal of Wm. Smith and Family from Glasgow to Castleblayney.

To Ebenezer Adamson, Inspector of the Poor for the Parish of City Parish, Glasgow, and to the Guardians of the (Union or Parish) of Castleblayney.

Order for Removal to Castleblayney Union, Ireland.

Glasgow, 20th February, 1872.

I, Alexander Erskine Murray, Sheriff-Substitute of the county of Lanark, having considered the foregoing petition and certificate, and the depositions of the said James Smith, Hercules Smith, and Archibald Dempster; and having examined into the state of the health of the said William Smith, senior, find that the said William Smith, senior, is of the reputed age of 34 or 35 years; that the said William Smith, junior, Hannah Smith, and Christina Smith are of the reputed ages of 9 or 10, 7 or 8, and 5 or 6, respectively; find that the said William Smith, senior, was born in the parish of Ballybay, within the Union of Castleblayney, in Ireland; find that the said William Smith, senior, has become, and is now actually chargeable to the parochial board of the parish of Glasgow; and that the said William Smith, senior, has not acquired and retained a settlement in Scotland: find that none of the said persons would suffer bodily or mental injury by being removed as herein ordered: Therefore, I do hereby order that William Smith, senior, be removed with William Smith, junior, Hannah Smith, and Christina, his said children, and conveyed to, and delivered safely at, the Workhouse of the Union of Castleblayney, Ireland; and I do order you, the said Ebenezer Adamson, Inspector of Poor, to cause the said persons to be so safely conveyed and delivered.

(Signed), A. Erskine Murray.

No. 8.—Depositions referred to in the Warrant of Removal.

Glasgow, 19th February, 1872.

Deposition of James Smith, 32 King-street, Calton, who being solemnly sworn, depones that, I am an older brother of William Smith. He is about thirty-four years old, and was born in the parish of Ballybay, townland of Carnaboe, county Monaghan, Ireland. He first came over to Scotland when about three years old with his parents, but in two years they returned to Ireland and he came back about 1853. He first lived with me in Muslin-street, Bridgeton Barony Parish, one year, then in New-street, Calton, about a year or two, where he was learning his trade, then he was in lodgings in different places some time, till he got married to Mary Anne Gillard, and stopped in different places. The first place I remember of would be in Great Hamilton-street, (Barony Parish). The next place I remember was in Gallowgate City Parish, this was about two or three years after his marriage. He was only there some months. Then he went to Partick, and remained more than five years in it, Govan Parish. When he left Partick he came to West Campbell-street Barony Parish, and was there some months. Then he went to America for about a year, then he came back and stayed in Whitevale-street Barony Parish some months, then in Marlborough-street City Parish a few months. Then he went to Govan for a few months. Then he went to England for more than a year. Then he and his wife were in lodgings for a few weeks till his wife got ill, and they being in King-street, Calton (south side of street), she was sent to Barnhill Poorhouse at the expense of Barony Parish, and died there. Then he lodged in different places a year, but not in Govan Parish, then married again a Mrs. M'Mahon, a widow. Then they lived in Hill-street City Parish scarcely a year, but for the last year and a half I don't know where he has been. He has four children by the first wife: Elizabeth, about twelve, William, about nine or ten, Hannah, about seven or eight, and Christina, about five or six, all born in Scotland. I don't know where the second wife is. He and she have been separated for more than a year. The children remained with him. All which is truth, as I shall answer to God. I know that he at present is living in Gartnavel at the expense of the City Parish. His eldest child is in service, and the other three are in the City Poorhouse, Truth.

(Signed), JAMES SMITH.
A. ERSKINE MURRAY.

Hercules Smith, brother of William Smith, residing at 58 King-street, Calton, sworn, depones, William was born in Ballybay parish, county Monaghan, Ireland. I think the union is Castleblaney. I think his age is about thirty-five years, but I am not sure. He came to Scotland in 1853, after being away some years, after living in different places, he and his wife Mary Anne Gillard went to live in Partick, parish of Govan. They were fully five years there. When they left they came to West Campbell-street Barony Parish, and was there a few months; then he went to America for eighteen months, then he came and lived in E. John-street City Parish for a few months, then in Marlborough-street City Parish, a few months, then in Govan three or four months, then in England about one year, then in different places (but not in Govan parish) for a fortnight or so, when his wife died. He tossed about in different places for about a year, but not in Govan parish, and then married again and lived in Hill-street City Parish for less than a year, then getting ill he was sent to Gartnavel at the expense of the City Parish, who have also charge of his three younger children. The wife left him when he was ill, all which is truth.

(Signed), HERCULES SMITH.
A. ERSKINE MURRAY.

Archibald Dempster, inspector's clerk, City Parish, sworn, depones, notice was given to the City Parish on 14th April, 1871, to remove William Smith from the central police office, he being supposed to be insane; he was removed to the poorhouse the same day, and on 24th April, 1871, sent to Gartnavel at the expense of the parish, under warrant, where he remains. His three younger children, Hannah, aged twelve, William, ten, and Christina, aged eight, are in the City Poorhouse, all which is truth, as I shall answer to God. We do not know anything about his second wife, or where she is.

(Signed), ARCHIBALD DEMPSTER.
A. ERSKINE MURRAY.

No. 9.—EXTRACT from MINUTES of PROCEEDINGS of the BOARD of GUARDIANS of CASTLEBLAYNEY UNION on the 6th March, 1872.

Read letter from the secretary of the Poor Law Board, Glasgow, enclosing a copy of the depositions in the case of the removal of William Smith from Glasgow to the Workhouse here.

Ordered that these depositions and the removal order be enclosed to the Commissioners in accordance with their request.

With regard to the removal of William Smith already referred to, it was resolved that, in the opinion of this Board, the course adopted was both harsh and illegal, and the Guardians hope the Commissioners will take such steps as will be most likely to prevent a recurrence of such a case. The Guardians feel that Captain Robinson is entitled to their thanks for promptly calling attention to the matter.

No. 10.—Letter from the Commissioners to the Board of Guardians.

Poor Law Commission Office, Dublin,
19th March, 1872.

Sir,

The Commissioners for administering the Laws for Relief of the Poor in Ireland have had before them the copy of the warrant of removal and of the depositions taken in the case of William Smith, a pauper lunatic, who, with his three children, was recently removed from Glasgow to the Workhouse of the Castleblayney Union, and with reference to the Guardians' resolution on the subject (a copy of which was entered on the minutes of their proceedings on the 6th inst.), the Commissioners have to state that according to the view taken by the legal authorities in Scotland, removals of lunatics from Scotch asylums to Irish workhouses are in accordance with the law authorising removals from Scotland to Ireland, nor is there any appeal against such warrants of removal.

By order,

B. Banks, Chief Clerk.

To the Clerk, Castleblayney Union.

VI.—CORRESPONDENCE WITH THE GUARDIANS OF MILLSTREET UNION, PREVIOUSLY TO THE DISSOLUTION OF THE BOARD AND COPY ORDER OF DISSOLUTION.

No. 1.—Letter addressed to each Member of the Board of Guardians individually.

Poor Law Commission Office, Dublin,
28th August, 1871.

Sir,

The Commissioners for administering the Laws for Relief of the Poor in Ireland have to inform you that their attention has been drawn to the fact that there was not a sufficient number of Guardians present on the 17th inst. to form a board, and that they find on reference to the records of this department that, owing to the failure of Guardians to attend in a sufficient number to constitute a board, there was no meeting held on sixteen occasions during the present year, and that several of the Guardians, although resident in the Union, fail to attend.

The Commissioners wish to point out the importance of holding regular meetings each week for the discharge of the usual business of the Union, the proper and efficient management of the Workhouse, the necessary control of the paid officers of the Union, and the receipt and consideration of applications for relief from the sick and destitute poor. Punctual and constant attention to these objects will tend not only to the due and effectual relief of the destitute poor in the Union who should be assured that they can, at least weekly, make known their wants to the Guardians, but to the interest of the ratepayers in an economical point of view.

By order, &c.,

D. Banks, Chief Clerk.

No. 2.—Extract from Guardians' Minutes of 24th August, 1871.

Read letter from Poor Law Commissioners enclosing a communication from Mr. Cooper, wherein he complained of the water supply for the town of Millstreet, and drawing the attention of the Guardians to the immediate necessity of adopting either of the two plans mentioned by the County Surveyor for procuring the necessary supply.

A deputation of the inhabitants of the town of Millstreet waited on the Board for the purpose of urging them to adopt some means of supplying the inhabitants of the town with pure water. After some discussion, a report from the Medical Officer on the same subject was handed in. It was then resolved to direct the clerk to call on two persons named Daniel Murphy and Denis Horgan, who had claims on the stream of water running from Mount Leader to the Workhouse, with a view of getting them to surrender their right to the stream into the hands of the Guardians. He was also directed in case he succeeded to write to the County Surveyor for plans and estimates of the necessary works.

The Medical Officer's report was as follows:—

Gentlemen,

It may not be inconsistent with my duty as Medical Officer (with reference to the supplying of the town of Millstreet with pure water) to remind you that we are threatened by the danger of an outbreak of cholera. This scourge has made its appearance in some of the coasts of the Baltic, and it is now within a few days' easy sail of these shores. It would be wise to prepare in time against its arrival, and fortunately the means of protection from its ravages are available and efficacious if adopted; consisting especially and above all things in the supply for drinking and for culinary purposes of pure water, untainted with the leakage from privies or cesspools, house refuse, or any sort of filth. Cholera is not contagious in the same way that other zymotic diseases are, contact with persons suffering from typhus, small-pox, &c., is sufficient to communicate the disease, and the atmosphere surrounding the patients is rendered dangerous by the infections emanating from their persons; not so with cholera, the peculiarity of which is that the infecting matter exists only in the discharges from the bowels and stomachs of those attacked, and in such discharges alone the germ of cholera disease resides, which germ is disseminated by means of water. These are well ascertained facts, from which it follows that the perfect exclusion of all filth, excremental matter, and discharges from the sewers, of water supplies is indispensable as a precaution against and a certain means of checking the spread of this fatal disease; and it follows that it is incumbent on all local authorities during the prevalence of epidemic cholera to take care that "Ro allis" supply of drinking water be pure and protected from all contamination; and happily you have it in your power in your locality to take the necessary precautions and effect a most desirable object by having conveyed in pipes from its mountain source pure unpolluted water to supply the town and workhouse.

I remain, gentlemen, your obedient servant,

John Leader, M.D.

No. 3.—Letter from the Commissioners to the Board of Guardians.

Poor Law Commission Office, Dublin,
30th August, 1871.

Sir,

The Commissioners for administering the Laws for Relief of the Poor in Ireland acknowledge the receipt of the minutes of proceedings of the Board of Guardians of the Millstreet Union on the 24th instant, containing an entry of their letter of the 3rd instant, drawing the attention of the Guardians to the necessity which exists for adopting measures to obtain a supply of water for the town of Millstreet and the Workhouse.

It appears from the minutes that a deputation of the inhabitants of the town waited on the Board for the purpose of urging them to adopt some steps for supplying the town with pure water; and that a report from Dr. Leader, Medical Officer, on the same subject was handed in, which was as follows—"It may not be inconsistent with my duty as Medical Officer to remind you that we are threatened by the danger of an outbreak of cholera. This scourge has made its appearance in some of the coasts of the Baltic, and it is now within a few days' easy sail of these shores. It would be wise to prepare in time against its arrival, and fortunately the means of protection from its ravages are available and efficacious, if adopted; consisting especially and above all things in the supply of pure water for drinking and for culinary purposes; and happily you have it in your power in your locality to take the necessary precautions and effect a most desirable object, by having conveyed in pipes from its mountain source pure unpolluted water to supply the town and Workhouse."

It seems that having read the Medical Officer's report, the Guardians passed a resolution directing the clerk to call on two persons who had claims on the stream of water running from Mount Leader to the Workhouse, with a view to getting them to surrender their right to the stream into the hands of the Guardians. He was also directed, in case he succeeded, to write to the county surveyor for plans and estimates of the necessary works.

The Commissioners fear that the steps adopted at the last meeting of the Guardians will not be effectual in procuring a supply of pure water for the Millstreet Workhouse and the town of Millstreet, so long needed and so long postponed; but they await the result of the instructions which have been given to the clerk.

In the meantime the Commissioners have under their serious consideration the constantly recurring default of the Guardians to meet as a Board for the execution of their duties; a failure to do so having occurred no less than sixteen times in the course of the present year.

At the present critical period the Commissioners feel that by the appointment of paid officers to perform the duties of the Guardians, they might possibly save the lives of many of the poor inhabitants destined to become the victims of cholera or other epidemic disease, if matters are allowed to proceed longer in the same course.

On the receipt of the minutes of the meeting of the Guardians which should take place to-morrow, the Commissioners will take this subject into further consideration.

By order, &c.,

B. Banks, Chief Clerk.

To the Presiding Chairman, Board of
Guardians, Millstreet Union.

No. 4.—LETTER from W. H. MASSY, esq., J.P., to the COMMISSIONERS.

Mount Massy, Macroom,
SIR, 31st August, 1871.

In answer to letter of above No., I beg to say I reside about sixteen miles from Millstreet Workhouse, and consider it is more the duty of those who are close to it or are elected Guardians to attend than it is mine.

I am not aware that I am in any way called on to attend either; and must remark that the cause of the bad attendance of Guardians is simply that subjects day after day are brought forward there which to many of the *Guardians are offensive and insulting*, and are totally irrelevant to the Workhouse business or the administering of the Poor Laws; and I cannot but add that if the Poor Law Commissioners sanction, as they have to a certain extent, such irrelevant matter being entertained at Poor Law Boards, they should not be so ready to address such a letter to any individual such as the one I have received, as I do not conceive I am called on to attend if I do not choose so to do, as most assuredly I don't mean to as long as I see no way of preventing subjects being brought forward which should not.

I will say I do believe if a paid Guardian was appointed to the Millstreet Union, it would be a step in the right direction.

I have the honour to be, sir,
Your very obedient servant,
W. HUTCHINSON MASSY.

B. Banks, esq., Chief Clerk,
Poor Law Commission Office, Dublin.

No. 5.—LETTER from the COMMISSIONERS to Mr. HORSLEY, Poor Law Inspector.

Poor Law Commission Office, Dublin,
SIR, 8th September, 1871.

The Commissioners for administering the Laws for Relief of the Poor in Ireland transmit to you the accompanying papers relating to the frequent failures of the Guardians of the Millstreet Union to attend in a sufficient number to form a Board; and the Commissioners request that you will be good enough to report to them whether you see any other course for the Commissioners to adopt under the circumstances presented by this Union, than the dissolution of the Board of Guardians and the appointment of paid officers.

By order, &c.,
B. BANKS, Chief Clerk.

To H. Horsley, esq.,
Poor Law Inspector, Killarney.

No. 6.—REPORT from Mr. HORSLEY to the COMMISSIONERS.

GENTLEMEN, September 9th, 1871.

In reply to your communication of the 8th instant, with enclosures, I beg to report that I think it may be desirable before taking the extreme step of dissolving the Board of Guardians of the already very heavily taxed Union of Millstreet, to make a last effort to bring the individual members of it to a sense of the heavy responsibility which they will incur towards their constituents, the ratepayers, if by wilfully and persistently absenting themselves from the weekly meetings of the Board, they compel the Poor Law Commissioners, in the interests of the poor and the general ratepayers alike, to provide for the administration of the affairs of the Union by the appointment of paid officers, under sec. 26 of the Irish Poor Relief Act.

And I would therefore respectfully suggest that the three Chairmen of the Board should be written to, and recommended to meet together without delay for the purpose of calling an extraordinary meeting of all the Guardians, to consider the present unbecoming position of the body, before their constituents and the public, and to determine whether they will, by more frequent and regular attention to the discharge of their official duties and of the trust reposed in them, render it unnecessary for the Poor Law Commissioners to adopt the otherwise unavoidable course indicated in their letter of the 28th ultimo.

I return herewith the file of papers sent to me with the Commissioners' letter.

I have the honour to be, gentlemen,

Your very obedient servant,

S. HORSLEY.

To the Poor Law Commissioners,
Poor Law Office, Dublin.

No. 7.—LETTER from the COMMISSIONERS to each of the three CHAIRMEN of the UNION.

Poor Law Commission Office, Dublin,
11th September, 1871.

SIR,

Adverting to their letter of the 28th ultimo, the Commissioners for administering the Laws for Relief of the Poor in Ireland forward for your information the accompanying copy of a letter, which they addressed to the presiding Chairman of the Board of Guardians of the Millstreet Union on the 30th ultimo, on the subject of the frequent failures of the Guardians to meet in a sufficient number to form a board, and the necessity which exists for adopting measures to obtain a supply of water for the town of Millstreet and the Workhouse.

It appears that this letter has remained unopened, in consequence of no meeting of the Board having been held on either of the two days of meeting which have since arrived.

The Commissioners request that you will have the goodness to meet, with the Vice-Chairman and Deputy Vice-Chairman,* without delay, for the purpose of calling an extraordinary meeting of all the Guardians to consider the present unbecoming position of the body before their constituents and the public, and to determine whether Guardians will, by more frequent and regular attention to the discharge of their official duties and of the trust reposed in them, render it unnecessary for the Commissioners to adopt the otherwise unavoidable course indicated in their letter of the 30th ultimo.

By order, &c.,

B. BANKS, Chief Clerk.

To M'Carthy O'Leary, esq., D.L., Coomleague, Millstreet, Chairman of the Board of Guardians.

* Similar letters were addressed to Captain Leader, the Vice-Chairman, and to J. D. Cronin, esq., Deputy Vice-Chairman.

No. 8.—LETTER from the COMMISSIONERS to Mr. HORSLEY.

Poor Law Commission Office, Dublin,
SIR, 6th October, 1871.

The Commissioners for administering the Laws for Relief of the Poor in Ireland forward to you the accompanying paper, which they have received from the Clerk of the Millstreet Union, notifying that there was no meeting of the Board of Guardians on the 5th instant; and the Commissioners request that you will again be good enough to report on the question of the propriety of dissolving this Board and appointing two paid officers.

The former papers on the subject are also enclosed herewith.

By order, &c.,
B. BANKS, Chief Clerk.

S. Horsley, esq.,
Poor Law Inspector, Killarney.

No. 9.—REPORT from Mr. HORSLEY to the COMMISSIONERS.

GENTLEMEN, October 9th, 1871.

I beg to acknowledge the receipt of your communication of the 6th instant together with a file of papers relating to the persistent failure of the Millstreet Board of Guardians to attend with sufficient frequency or in sufficient numbers for the transaction of the affairs of the Union on the appointed days of meeting; and I have now the honour to report that as all remonstrances on this subject with the Guardians individually and collectively appear to have been disregarded, inasmuch as there has been no meeting of the Board since the 21st ultimo, although in addition to the ordinary routine business of the Union, there are many special matters, such as the introduction of a supply of pure water for the town of Millstreet, the abatement of nuisances in the town and other localities, requiring immediate and assiduous attention, I see no course left open to the Commissioners except to exercise the powers given them under the 26th section of the Irish Poor Relief Act, in order that due attention may be given to the interests of the poor and of the ratepayers of this Union, and that due provision may be made for the regular and punctual despatch of all business relating to the internal economy of the Workhouse, and to the observance of the Commissioners' regulations with reference to the Workhouse and Union officials.

I have the honour to be, gentlemen,
Your very obedient servant,
S. HORSLEY.

To the Poor Law Commissioners,
Poor Law Office, Dublin.

No. 10.—LETTER from the COMMISSIONERS to the BOARD of GUARDIANS.

Poor Law Commission Office, Dublin,
SIR, 11th October, 1871.

Adverting to previous correspondence the Commissioners for administering the Laws for Relief of the Poor in Ireland have to inform the Board of Guardians that they have again received the usual form of minutes without any proceedings being entered upon it, a quorum of three Guardians not having attended for the transaction of business.

The Commissioners have also before them a report from their inspector Mr. Horsley, in which he states "that as all remonstrances on this subject with the Guardians individually and collectively appear to have been disregarded, inasmuch as there has been no meeting of the Board since the 21st ultimo, although in addition to the ordinary routine business of the Union, there are many special matters, such as the introduction of a supply of pure water for the town of Millstreet, the abatement of nuisances in the town and other localities requiring immediate and assiduous attention, I see no course left open to the Commissioners except to exercise the powers given them under the 26th section of the Irish Poor Relief Act, in order that due attention may be given to the interests of the poor and of the ratepayers of this Union, and that due provision may be made for the regular and punctual despatch of all business relating to the internal economy of the Workhouse, and to the observance of the Commissioners' regulations with reference to the Workhouse and Union officials."

The Commissioners under these circumstances feel that they had no alternative but to exercise the power in question, and they have signed and forward herewith an order dissolving the Board of Guardians of Millstreet Union, and will proceed at once to appoint paid officers to carry into execution the provisions of the Acts in force for the relief of the poor therein.

By order, &c.,

B. Banks, Chief Clerk.

To the Clerk, Millstreet Union.

No. 11.—Order dissolving the Board of Guardians of Millstreet Union.

To the Guardians of the Poor of the Millstreet Union; to the Clerk of the said Union, and to all other persons whom it may concern:

Whereas regular meetings of the Board of Guardians of the Millstreet Union have not been holden at the times enjoined by our general order for regulating the meetings and proceedings of Boards of Guardians in Ireland, bearing date the 10th day of January, 1852; and whereas through the default of the said Guardians the duties of the Board of Guardians of the said Union have not been duly and effectually discharged according to the intention of the Acts in force for the Relief of the Destitute Poor in Ireland:

Now, therefore, we, the Commissioners for administering the Laws for Relief of the Poor in Ireland, do hereby, in exercise of the powers by the said Acts vested in us in this behalf, declare the said Board of Guardians to be dissolved, and the said Board is hereby dissolved accordingly.

Sealed with our Seal this Eleventh day of October, in the year of Our Lord One Thousand Eight Hundred and Seventy-one.

(Signed), A. Power.
J. M'Donnell.

APPENDIX B.

TABLES CONNECTED WITH POOR RELIEF AND EXPENDITURE.

No. 1.—A Return (in pursuance of the 29th Section of the Act 10 Vic., c. 31) of the ... and Out of the Workhouse in each Union in Ireland, for the Year ended ... Registration, Sanitary, and Burial Grounds Acts, and Total Expenditure out of ...

Part I.—Return showing the Expenditure of Unions ...

Expenditure during the Year ended 29th September, 1871.

Names of Counties and Unions.	In-Maintenance.	Out-Relief.	Maintenance of Blind and Deaf and Dumb ... in Asylums ... in Lunatic Hospitals.	Salaries and Rations of Officers.	All other Poor Relief Expenses.	Total Poor Relief Expenditure.	Expenses under Medical Charities Acts.
PROVINCE OF ULSTER.	£ s. d.	£ s. d.	£ s. d.	£ s. d.	£ s. d.	£ s. d.	£ s. d.
ANTRIM.							
Antrim,	2,628 19 10	175 3 8	30 18 0	733 1 1	1,[illegible] 2 8	4,[illegible] 17 6	[illegible] 4 3
Ballycastle,	912 14 10	—	—	339 5 10	330 5 5	1,579 8 2	539 7 7
Ballymena,	3,[illegible] 2 7	1,191 7 8	69 18 8	900 6 4	[illegible] 0 11	[illegible] 16 2	1,[illegible] 18 9
Ballymoney,	970 11 2	159 3 0	37 3 11	541 18 7	504 19 4	2,164 17 6	783 8 0
Belfast,	16,513 16 7	886 11 7	107 15 3	2,107 2 6	[illegible] 0 7	25,576 11 6	3,[illegible] 0 6
Larne,	1,379 15 10	158 [illegible] 5	—	738 1 0	301 1 4	2,577 10 7	955 10 6
Lisburn,	1,782 6 6	85 17 0	17 0 0	612 15 9	577 11 2	3,168 6 11	1,004 15 10
ARMAGH.							
Armagh,	2,[illegible] 2 8	5 14 0	—	856 18 10	836 7 11	4,0[illegible] 1 6	1,387 8 6
Lurgan,	2,450 0 0	160 18 7	14 6 8	730 6 9	726 18 0	4,129 2 3	1,[illegible] 0 7
CAVAN.							
Bailieborough,	626 4 0	166 7 2	—	632 1 1	311 14 2	1,900 2 2	842 0 6
Bawnboy,	808 11 11	375 16 8	90 4 8	750 0 0	410 9 6	2,101 16 11	488 10 1
Cavan,	2,011 0 5	63 3 11	96 12 9	724 9 7	866 2 5	3,[illegible] 4 4	1,[illegible] 14 11
Cootehill,	810 1 11	30 0 0	30 0 0	154 1 6	576 12 6	1,601 4 6	[illegible] 0 9
DONEGAL.							
Ballyshannon,	1,037 1 7	—	—	374 15 0	343 8 9	1,756 0 4	617 7 6
Donegal,	613 10 2	116 13 6	15 0 0	433 13 0	349 10 4	1,[illegible] 16 6	585 5 9
Dunfanaghy,	815 16 9	—	—	280 3 8	136 3 8	[illegible] 3 3	389 3 5
Glenties,	610 13 4	48 10 3	15 0 0	380 18 1	814 0 4	1,867 18 4	772 16 11
Inishowen,	822 4 9	276 7 5	37 10 0	111 16 6	311 4 1	1,[illegible] 4 11	738 5 6
Letterkenny,	930 1 10	6 8 0	—	280 0 1	398 13 0	1,[illegible] 11 11	440 19 9
Milford,	380 6 5	135 17 2	—	110 10 7	670 1 3	1,[illegible] 9 5	722 8 1
Stranorlar,	356 13 1	10 5 0	—	173 8 11	[illegible] 10 0	1,[illegible] 13 0	487 11 9
DOWN.							
Banbridge,	1,490 4 8	485 8 8	36 0 0	790 11 6	670 17 2	3,449 1 9	[illegible] 16 10
Downpatrick,	2,307 13 6	65 7 0	—	855 9 2	707 10 1	3,712 19 9	1,0[illegible] 17 0
Kilkeel,	[illegible] 0 6	13 6 6	7 10 0	602 3 5	176 1 1	1,[illegible] 0 9	354 17 0
Newry,	2,117 15 3	617 9 4	130 17 1	930 17 7	1,[illegible] 3 9	4,[illegible] 1 7	1,[illegible] 11 9
Newtownards,	2,[illegible] 9 10	[illegible] 15 6	30 0 0	847 6 11	616 7 4	3,[illegible] 19 7	1,0[illegible] 16 3
FERMANAGH.							
Enniskillen,	1,697 12 8	4 11 7	—	[illegible] 8 2	420 18 6	2,787 15 5	579 12 8
Irvinestown,	601 19 9	30 2 6	—	356 2 2	861 19 0	1,849 15 6	534 1 8
Lisnaskea,	735 5 9	158 18 0	—	476 18 2	276 4 4	1,[illegible] 6 3	[illegible] 11 9
LONDONDERRY.							
Coleraine,	1,[illegible] 0 8	[illegible] 3 4	—	815 19 10	1,139 17 8	3,[illegible] 0 4	[illegible] 0 11
Londonderry,	2,[illegible] 3 1	69 8 9	104 5 7	816 11 4	705 16 11	4,351 8 8	1,331 18 8
Magherafelt,	1,[illegible] 3 5	17 14 6	11 0 0	854 16 4	630 5 0	2,109 7 3	842 19 8
N.-T.-Limavady,	657 19 3	14 14 0	15 0 0	587 19 8	437 16 11	1,643 0 4	790 3 3
MONAGHAN.							
Carrickmacross,	781 3 6	11 13 9	41 8 10	420 10 6	801 17 11	1,448 11 0	416 0 10
Castleblayney,	1,175 11 0	134 10 0	17 7 9	875 18 10	[illegible] 8 7	2,770 16 2	760 4 0
Clones,	735 11 3	6 13 11	6 13 2	381 15 6	423 17 8	1,548 [illegible] 8	788 19 7
Monaghan,	283 6 6	—	—	897 5 1	311 0 9	1,500 1 10	619 10 4
TYRONE.							
Castlederg,	318 11 7	8 8 8	—	244 4 1	173 18 10	[illegible] 8	887 2 1
Clogher,	840 3 9	22 15 10	—	437 11 6	337 5 11	1,703 0 0	624 3 7
Cookstown,	468 10 5	8 13 10	—	430 4 7	190 17 8	1,[illegible] 16 11	670 3 1
Dungannon,	1,295 6 11	381 5 2	30 18 8	881 3 7	320 19 4	2,[illegible] 6 0	823 9 5
Gortin,	340 9 7	3 0 0	6 10 8	311 16 6	141 6 9	[illegible] 3 1	580 19 2
Omagh,	1,1[illegible] 0 4	77 4 0	—	713 4 8	348 16 0	2,[illegible] 3 6	840 7 3
Strabane,	1,[illegible] 1 6	498 5 10	8 14 0	879 0 0	636 7 1	3,[illegible] 13 9	[illegible] 3 3
Total, Ulster, 1871,	68,645 17 7	6,743 19 11	1,077 1 1	27,[illegible] 6 9	24,781 9 3	[illegible] 9 7	38,[illegible] 10 9
Total, Ulster, 1870,	72,087 11 7	7,177 8 0	930 0 9	26,[illegible] 9 6	24,356 10 4	131,[illegible] 0 8	38,[illegible] 13 9
Increase,	—	1,616 1 11	179 0 4	884 10 3	424 18 11	—	416 17 0
Decrease,	3,441 14 0	—	—	—	—	578 10 7	—

EXPENDITURE on the RELIEF of the POOR, and of the TOTAL NUMBERS RELIEVED in 29th September, 1871; also showing the EXPENSES under the Medical Charities, the POOR RATE during the Year.

during the Year ended 29th September, 1871.

Payments under the Acts for Prevention of Births, Deaths, and Marriages.	Payments under the Sanitary Acts.	Expenses under Burial Grounds Act, paid out of the Poor Rate.	Total Expenditure out of the Poor Rate.	Valuation on 29th Sept., 1871.	Poundage on the Valuation: Of the Expenditure on Relief of the Poor.	Poundage on the Valuation: Of Total Expenditure.	Names of Counties and Unions.
£ s. d.	£ s. d.	£ s. d.	£ s. d.	£ s. d.	s. d.	s. d.	PROVINCE OF ULSTER.
							ANTRIM.
94 15 9	0 6 0	—	4,052 7 6	122,186 5 0	0 7½	0 8	Antrim.
37 11 8	—	—	2,153 5 8	63,028 15 0	0 7¾	0 11	Ballycastle.
193 9 0	4 [illegible] 6	65 5 5	6,303 7 8	122,697 15 0	0 9½	1 0½	Ballymena.
73 12 4	10 0 0	—	2,801 18 7	81,017 18 0	0 6½	0 9	Ballymoney.
403 7 0	5 11 8	—	20,815 14 6	651,[illegible] 16 0	0 11½	1 3½	Belfast.
83 8 9	70 4 4	—	4,265 17 8	98,886 11 0	0 8½	0 11	Larne.
163 10 9	8 7 0	—	6,227 5 5	167,767 0 0	0 6½	0 8½	Lisburn.
							ARMAGH.
159 3 3	91 13 8	—	6,028 0 10	203,657 1 0	0 4½	0 6½	Armagh.
186 3 0	5 7 8	—	5,626 16 6	136,597 0 0	0 7½	0 9½	Lurgan.
							CAVAN.
19 9 4	20 15 0	—	2,510 6 9	39,888 17 0	0 11½	1 3½	Bailieborough.
40 15 3	—	—	2,097 1 3	39,499 19 0	1 0½	1 4½	Bawnboy.
113 0 8	20 0 0	—	6,360 0 3	111,786 5 0	0 7½	0 11½	Cavan.
76 19 3	7 10 0	—	2,326 8 8	72,159 19 0	0 5½	0 7½	Cootehill.
							DONEGAL.
54 4 9	—	—	2,720 11 7	60,356 10 0	0 8½	0 11	Ballyshannon.
51 12 3	—	—	2,103 16 5	34,130 0 0	0 10½	1 5	Donegal.
42 6 3	—	—	1,037 9 11	11,427 15 0	1 1½	1 9	Dunfanaghy.
64 15 0	—	—	2,025 4 3	19,[illegible] 10 0	1 3½	[illegible]	Glenties.
77 11 6	17 0 0	—	2,708 13 11	39,675 1 0	0 11½	1 4½	Inishowen.
83 9 3	—	—	2,147 3 10	32,046 0 0	1 1	1 4½	Letterkenny.
53 18 8	4 11 8	85 7 6	2,349 14 5	29,618 5 0	1 0½	1 7	Milford.
37 15 8	—	—	1,579 4 6	29,960 15 0	0 9½	1 0½	Stranorlar.
							DOWN.
165 5 9	—	—	5,619 4 4	150,[illegible] 3 0	0 5½	0 7	Banbridge.
117 5 6	87 0 8	—	4,910 2 3	171,107 10 0	0 5	0 6½	Downpatrick.
63 7 8	1 0 0	—	1,780 5 2	41,043 5 0	0 8½	0 10	Kilkeel.
158 12 8	15 0 0	—	7,821 7 11	163,507 11 0	0 9½	0 11½	Newry.
116 12 6	—	—	6,171 10 4	133,[illegible] 11 0	0 9	0 11	Newtownards.
							FERMANAGH.
98 6 8	20 0 8	—	3,776 13 7	109,136 15 0	0 6½	0 8½	Enniskillen.
38 7 9	11 6 3	—	1,630 18 4	39,380 15 0	0 8½	0 9	Irvinestown.
35 9 8	—	28 6 8	2,[illegible] 7 9	67,795 14 0	0 6½	0 9½	Lisnaskea.
							LONDONDERRY.
91 17 3	—	—	1,833 7 6	37,[illegible] 3 0	0 9½	1 0	Coleraine.
127 1 0	—	—	4,980 1 10	149,716 0 0	0 7	0 9½	Londonderry.
125 11 9	19 10 9	—	3,098 8 1	91,[illegible] 16 0	0 5½	0 8½	Magherafelt.
55 11 0	8 15 0	—	2,409 18 7	66,287 10 0	0 5½	0 8½	N.-T.-Limavady.
							MONAGHAN.
62 8 0	—	—	2,[illegible] 3 7	49,071 5 0	0 7½	0 10	Carrickmacross.
92 14 3	97 4 0	—	3,728 10 7	71,[illegible] 0 0	0 7½	0 10½	Castleblayney.
45 6 0	—	—	1,[illegible] 10 0	56,[illegible] 1 0	0 5½	0 8	Clones.
79 9 8	—	—	2,707 10 7	93,[illegible] 3 0	0 4½	0 7½	Monaghan.
							TYRONE.
32 11 3	20 11 6	—	1,171 9 0	25,801 8 0	0 7½	0 10½	Castlederg.
84 7 0	6 13 0	—	2,[illegible] 19 1	56,117 10 0	0 7½	0 10½	Clogher.
69 [illegible] 0	—	—	2,073 10 0	63,[illegible] 11 0	0 5½	0 8	Cookstown.
65 11 0	10 0 0	—	3,[illegible] 6 5	92,[illegible] 4 0	0 6	0 9½	Dungannon.
29 2 9	—	—	1,136 2 5	14,477 7 0	0 10½	1 2½	Gortin.
95 15 7	10 14 10	—	2,[illegible] 0 0	68,[illegible] 11 0	0 [illegible]	0 9½	Omagh.
63 16 6	20 0 0	—	4,331 11 1	96,[illegible] 0 0	0 8½	0 10½	Strabane.

7	88	19	0	623	3	9	384	5	8	3,177	18
0	—			202	19	9	158	19	1	1,099	0
8	6	13	8	197	15	11	138	14	8	1,083	13
8	32	8	0	687	6	8	483	19	11	3,413	6
6	388	18	0	3,729	6	11	6,379	7	7	31,358	19
9	9	13	0	319	15	0	236	19	7	1,859	15
11	34	0	9	412	18	5	326	19	1	2,560	15
8	117	0	0	920	10	4	765	13	6	5,035	6
	—			470	3	4	388	8	10	1,213	6
6	50	19	0	997	7	10	663	4	0	5,333	14
11	163	17	11	711	2	9	264	11	7	3,380	0
0	61	17	6	693	7	9	533	17	4	4,037	4
2	19	6	6	530	3	8	323	19	11	2,560	9
4	16	7	7	560	14	0	151	3	11	2,129	14
6	59	10	0	263	7	1	782	11	7	3,053	16
8	—			255	11	2	163	3	10	1,226	13
6	87	9	9	785	10	6	824	6	7	6,440	0
4	—			365	6	7	248	0	6	1,801	16
0	13	0	0	604	13	10	362	1	1	3,016	1
8	—			301	13	11	337	17	6	1,448	7
0	70	16	0	1,083	7	3	1,758	9	0	8,173	17
	31	10	0	479	17	1	273	5	7	2,605	19
0	169	5	4	1,046	16	8	787	16	6	5,613	17
7	3	18	8	585	7	8	468	0	5	3,528	0
0	56	18	11	568	12	11	815	17	10	1,889	4
11	162	9	3	1,016	13	9	938	3	6	8,083	3
6	725	7	3	2,109	15	10	2,309	1	11	17,732	9
8	73	10	9	911	15	4	795	6	5	6,848	6
0	83	0	0	739	18	9	770	17	1	6,221	10
8	—			291	4	8	221	9	5	1,811	19
0	35	15	7	595	16	8	765	17	10	5,166	3
8	60	19	6	916	11	8	863	13	3	7,227	14
	88	0	8	641	0	6	369	16	6	3,315	0
6	77	16	0	1,130	0	4	1,795	18	1	6,639	0
7	3	10	0	795	5	6	349	18	5	5,161	0
0	1	13	0	657	4	4	448	11	0	3,260	19
0	79	1	0	731	10	0	414	17	5	3,263	17
0	75	18	0	677	19	3	728	11	4	5,775	18
5	99	18	0	983	16	10	658	14	8	4,624	10
8	93	3	9	320	14	6	469	3	10	2,229	14
11	55	2	0	614	11	9	570	16	6	3,104	8
0	437	19	0	3,280	15	11	1,215	9	7	11,607	3
9	3,985	0	6	37,690	4	0	32,086	4	8	258,024	5

8	72,388	6
8	21,273	12
8	15,899	8
5	65,891	8
7	227,916	7
4	32,085	10
8	188,289	10
7	72,281	6
5	60,151	10
1	62,077	10
1	169,465	[illegible]
8	125,893	15
8	87,139	6
8	60,365	12
5	280,839	8
3	14,778	6
4	52,611	6
6	23,987	6
3	192,183	6
10	19,787	6
8	73,136	10
1	15,046	10
5	84,377	10

No. I. Part 1.—Return showing the Expenditure of Unions

Expenditure during One Year ended 29th September, 18..

d.	Out-Relief. £ s. d.	Maintenance of Blind and Deaf and Dumb, in Asylums, and cost of Relief in Fever Hospitals. £ s. d.	Salaries and Rations of Officers. £ s. d.	All other Poor Relief Expenses. £ s. d.	Total Poor Relief Expenditure. £ s. d.	Expenses under Medical Charities Act. £ s. d.
8	1,773 8 6	[illegible] 3 7	1,164 11 8	[illegible] 16 4	7,[illegible] 13 5	1,[illegible] 3 11
6	391 16 5	—	307 13 0	612 2 10	3,176 1 8	1,017 15 0
4	7,304 4 6	441 5 5	3,[illegible] 4 8	3,117 1 5	15,773 8 9	3,353 1 6
8	4,620 9 10	[illegible] 8 7	3,913 19 8	6,760 10 6	60,216 12 5	3,976 16 1
9	122 8 6	129 8 8	1,116 13 8	8,[illegible] 12 9	9,313 17 5	8,217 10 11
9	1,173 8 8	46 16 10	738 8 1	833 17 5	5,171 8 1	1,[illegible] 10 3
5	930 19 6	33 10 0	713 10 9	555 10 0	4,150 18 9	916 0 6
1	1,511 1 7	83 1 6	805 11 1½	979 18 0	5,873 4 9½	1,[illegible] 17 7
7	890 16 9	88 18 6	795 5 6	880 8 1	4,625 3 7	819 11 8
9	553 17 8	93 10 8	828 17 4	411 3 7	3,[illegible] 8 6	175 6 6
0	3,350 1 7	[illegible] 10 8	3,[illegible] 3 10	1,207 11 10	9,049 11 3	1,011 5 6
6	971 17 6	16 9 6	635 1 6	505 17 1	3,177 17 3	496 19 6
1	329 3 10	30 6 6	468 8 1	856 6 7	8,[illegible] 5 8	637 15 0
9	995 7 9	27 8 6	880 16 7	461 9 6	2,485 14 6	863 14 6
0	4 8 10	101 1 8	674 14 6	480 19 11	3,418 19 11	924 13 6
6	1,600 13 9	40 6 8	749 2 7	653 11 5	4,[illegible] 6 6	937 18 10
7	185 16 6	30 1 8	612 19 4	660 11 7	8,983 7 6	479 1 9
9	1,172 10 10	1 17 9	846 13 6	891 6 10	4,980 8 4	931 6 6
4	973 17 5	19 7 6	890 18 4	489 17 3	4,131 8 8	473 15 6
8	1,649 10 4	30 9 6	717 16 5	880 6 10	6,354 10 3	917 17 6
8	2,479 4 6	75 2 5	830 12 7	366 14 1	7,819 6 11	1,340 19 6
3	1,170 19 0	8 8 9	771 15 11	580 4 9	4,243 11 1	1,140 14 1
6	479 16 8	6 11 6	442 8 10	428 1 10	3,[illegible] 8 8	676 9 6
7	420 13 6	60 8 8	735 16 6	303 16 9	3,954 5 8	981 1 5
1	1,775 8 8	80 6 3	791 1 4	621 9 10	6,139 3 3	655 9 5
6	17 3 0	15 6 6	940 13 5	374 15 1	5,440 0 8	577 16 1
0½	910 17 0	7 16 9	787 8 8	327 14 10½	4,845 12 7½	643 6 8
7	558 13 9	30 16 6	893 13 11	901 3 1	3,976 15 6	665 1 10
4	987 4 9	11 15 6	474 3 8	320 11 8	8,673 7 6	318 4 11
9	1,390 1 11	75 6 6	1,044 11 7	949 9 6	6,[illegible] 9 9	940 15 0
9	135 16 1	15 6 6	786 17 5	648 16 4	2,401 9 7	1,096 10 2
1	80 13 6	16 5 8	674 1 3	481 6 6	2,080 15 6	374 6 8
1	879 16 3	91 12 6	1,812 6 3	1,130 5 3	6,004 7 6	1,185 14 11
3	1,338 5 3	60 16 8	778 13 6	689 7 1	3,640 2 1	1,075 5 7
9	182 13 7	4 15 0	835 3 6	356 8 6	2,403 15 4	749 5 6
9	1,601 8 9	47 10 6	787 15 6	753 14 8	8,791 6 9	1,157 19 1
1	1,314 8 6	107 16 8	830 8 3	636 6 1	7,351 16 4	1,117 1 10
1	831 17 7	96 11 6	730 14 1	782 6 7	4,010 17 6	611 4 6
3	1,463 3 11	103 4 6	641 11 11	918 14 3	6,180 16 11	1,360 0 5
7	93 15 7	—	558 15 1	397 5 4	2,617 19 7	471 14 10
1½	35,[illegible] 19 10	2,[illegible] 11 11	37,[illegible] 9 11½	35,477 10 6½	[illegible],734 6 1½	41,351 7 7

during the Year ended 29th September, 1871—*continued.*

Expenses under the Acts for Registration of Births, Deaths, and Marriages.	Expenses under the Sanitary Acts.	Expenses under Burial Grounds Acts, paid out of the Poor Rate.	Total Expenditure out of the Poor Rate.	Valuation on 29th Sept., 1871.	Poundage on the Valuation: Of the Expenditure on Relief of the Poor.	Of Total Expenditure.	Names of Counties and Unions.
£ s. d.	£ s. d.	£ s. d.	£ s. d.	£ s. d.	s. d.	s. d.	PROVINCE OF LEINSTER.
							CARLOW.
110 6 3	34 6 11	85 17 3	6,282 7 9	150,035 10 0	1 0½	1 2½	Carlow.
							DUBLIN.
85 14 6	685 16 7	—	6,788 7 9	94,818 5 0	0 8	1 0½	Balrothery.
182 7 9	62 9 10	—	30,611 1 9	332,255 5 0	1 7½	1 10½	Dublin, North.
455 15 0	382 11 9	—	31,556 0 1	367,295 0 0	1 7½	1 8½	Dublin, South.
168 5 8	80 5 2	—	13,632 17 3	325,670 5 0	0 10	1 0½	Rathdown.
							KILDARE.
70 19 6	250 7 8	119 19 6	7,888 8 11	108,165 7 0	1 0	1 3½	Athy.
38 4 0	88 13 8	—	5,177 1 2	114,880 10 0	0 9½	0 10½	Celbridge.
94 10 9	170 9 8	—	7,643 0 9½	151,801 0 0	0 8½	0 11½	Naas.
							KILKENNY.
51 12 0	27 10 3	50 0 0	5,437 17 1	75,161 5 0	1 3½	1 4½	Callan.
34 0 0	12 15 1	15 0 0	3,480 9 0	62,228 15 0	1 1	1 5	Castlecomer.
87 9 9	27 0 8	—	10,164 4 0	108,945 0 0	1 9½	[illegible] 9½	Kilkenny.
43 10 0	15 0 0	114 0 1	5,480 5 0	83,942 0 0	0 11½	1 3	Thomastown.
22 0 3	5 7 6	85 16 7	3,235 10 6	55,460 0 0	1 1½	1 2½	Urlingford.
							KING'S CO.
83 3 0	80 7 6	—	3,702 1 7	85,170 4 0	0 7½	0 9½	Edenderry.
88 10 0	1 8 4	—	4,535 15 11	102,313 3 0	0 7½	0 10½	Parsonstown.
38 9 3	—	—	5,169 7 7	82,083 4 0	1 2½	1 3½	Tullamore.
							LONGFORD.
26 3 0	84 1 6	—	2,328 0 2	63,677 12 0	0 8½	0 11½	Ballymahon.
71 14 0	33 10 0	—	5,005 17 6	84,804 18 0	1 1½	1 2½	Granard.
63 2 0	4 10 0	—	4,421 17 0	60,777 10 0	1 4½	1 4½	Longford.
							LOUTH.
79 15 2	107 10 3	2 0 0	6,931 13 6	84,586 10 0	1 7½	1 8	Ardee.
74 4 0	178 1 4	34 19 6	7,723 1 4	121,704 7 0	1 2	1 3	Drogheda.
165 3 6	47 4 6	—	6,280 17 4	100,080 0 0	0 11	1 1½	Dundalk.
							MEATH.
76 2 6	87 10 6	—	3,730 19 7	105,620 10 0	0 7	0 8½	Dunshaughlin.
63 16 4	6 0 0	134 10 4	5,070 1 0	85,454 17 0	0 10	1 0½	Kells.
72 3 10	—	55 17 6	5,796 18 3	97,872 6 0	1 0½	1 2½	Navan.
65 10 8	—	—	3,062 0 9	62,391 1 0	0 9½	1 0	Oldcastle.
43 0 0	3 1 0	—	5,311 10 1½	104,943 0 0	0 10½	0 11½	Trim.
							QUEEN'S CO.
19 0 0	—	—	4,140 7 6	68,017 3 0	0 11½	1 2½	Abbeyleix.
213 11 0	30 0 0	—	8,641 17 11	80,200 0 0	1 0½	1 7½	Donaghmore.
21 1 0	—	—	7,804 16 0	101,941 7 0	1 4½	1 7½	Mountmellick.
							WESTMEATH.
75 0 0	10 0 0	—	5,420 1 0	88,562 1 0	0 10½	1 1½	Athlone.
49 5 6	30 7 0	—	2,403 17 8	43,811 3 0	0 8	0 11½	Delvin.
47 17 0	60 10 6	—	7,250 10 1	157,997 10 0	0 9½	0 11½	Mullingar.
							WEXFORD.
66 10 6	41 1 1	—	6,707 16 3	109,786 0 0	0 11½	1 0	Enniscorthy.
52 10 6	0 16 0	—	4,349 10 8	79,216 10 0	0 11½	1 1	Gorey.
80 7 6	8 0 0	—	6,044 12 4	101,783 6 0	1 2½	1 2½	New Ross.
102 17 3	12 0 5	—	8,614 3 10	107,164 15 0	1 4½	1 7½	Wexford.
							WICKLOW.
46 1 6	—	—	5,281 4 0	78,772 16 0	1 3	1 4½	Baltinglass.
63 13 6	41 1 4	—	7,780 14 1	127,834 1 0	0 11½	1 2½	Rathdrum.
35 10 0	0 0 8	—	3,180 6 4	58,541 15 0	1 0½	1 3	Shillelagh.
3,361 0 11	2,160 10 11	677 7 8	280,623 3 0½	4,443,527 17 0	1 1½	1 4	1871, Total, Leinster.
3,278 1 1	1,028 [illegible] 5	321 16 10	261,626 17 5½	4,427,100 5 0	1 0½	1 3	1870, Total, Leinster.
82 19 10	1,132 11 6	355 11 10	18,334 5 0	15,684 10 0	0 0½	0 1	Increase.
—	—	—	—	—	—	—	Decrease.

[*continued.*

No. 1. Part 1.—Return showing the Expenditure of Unions

Expenditure during the Year ended [illegible] September, [illegible].

[illegible]	Out-Relief.			[illegible]			Salaries and Rations of Officers.			All other Poor Relief Expenses.			Total Poor Relief Expenditure.			[illegible]		
d.	£	s.	d.	£	s.	d.	£	s.	d.	£	s.	d.	£	s.	d.	£	s.	d.
4	9	10	1	—			771	7	10	481	4	4	8,878	12	9	[illegible]	1	4
3	89	19	5	22	10	0	968	1	9	280	11	4	1,[illegible]	0	1	716	16	6
9	362	10	9	[illegible]	15	3	1,[illegible]	19	0	497	0	9	4,978	15	7	1,012	7	3
6	133	1	8	—			451	0	11	316	18	9	[illegible]	15	11	177	16	11
9	17	4	4	17	7	0	415	[illegible]	1	324	11	9	8,014	[illegible]	5	394	[illegible]	11
2	84	3	2	18	0	0	179	12	0	871	16	10	1,[illegible]	16	11	505	11	11
5	30	16	9	—			499	7	0	220	1	2	1,774	11	1	673	[illegible]	6
8	150	9	7	—			300	9	4	187	19	3	1,[illegible]	19	8	917	10	11
5	43	0	0	—			420	0	0	[illegible]	19	10½	1,150	5	5½	273	0	9
1	457	13	0	36	0	0	700	16	11	548	14	3	1,163	19	1	320	10	2

				GALWAY.
0	[illegible]	1	0[illegible]	Ballinasloe.
[illegible]	1	0	11[illegible]	Clifden.
1	4[illegible]	1	4[illegible]	Galway.
1	3[illegible]	1	7	Glennamaddy.
0	11[illegible]	1	1[illegible]	Gort.
0	9	0	8	Loughrea.
0	10[illegible]	1	[illegible]	Mountbellew.
1	7[illegible]	2	2	Oughterard.
0	11[illegible]	1	[illegible]	Portumna.
1	[illegible]	1	[illegible]	Tuam.
				LEITRIM.
1	0[illegible]	1	[illegible]	Car-on-Shan.
0	[illegible]	1	[illegible]	Manorhamilton.
1	[illegible]	1	[illegible]	Mohill.
				MAYO.
0	10[illegible]	1	1	Ballina.
1	[illegible]	1	[illegible]	Ballinrobe.
[illegible]	[illegible]	0	[illegible]	Belmullet.
0	11	1	[illegible]	Castlebar.
0	[illegible]	1	[illegible]	Claremorris.
1	[illegible]	1	[illegible]	Killala.
1	[illegible]	1	[illegible]	Newport.
1	[illegible]	1	[illegible]	Swineford.
1	[illegible]	1	[illegible]	Westport.
				ROSCOMMON.
1	[illegible]	1	[illegible]	Boyle.
0	[illegible]	1	[illegible]	Castlerea.
1	[illegible]	1	[illegible]	Roscommon.
1	[illegible]	1	[illegible]	Strokestown.
				SLIGO.
0	7[illegible]	0	[illegible]	Dromore, West.
1	[illegible]	1	6	Sligo.
0	[illegible]	0	11[illegible]	Tobercurry.
1	0[illegible]	1	4[illegible]	1851, } Total, Connaught.
1	0[illegible]	1	4[illegible]	1850, }

SUMMARY OF FOREGOING TABLE, No. I.—Part I.

	Ulster.	Munster.	Leinster.	Connaught.	Total Ireland. 1871.	Total Ireland. 1870.	Increase.	Decrease.
	£ s. d.	£ s. d.	£ s. d.	£ s. d.	£ s. d.	£ s. d.	£ s. d.	£ s. d.
Expenditure during the year ended 29th September, 1871:								
In-Maintenance,	68,445 17 7	152,994 6 1	141,122 19 1½	30,702 0 8	[illegible]	[illegible]	[illegible] 1 0½	—
Out-Relief,	8,713 18 11	18,116 5 4½	[illegible] 19 10	[illegible] 4 1	69,744 6 7½	[illegible] 6 1	[illegible] 16 6	—
Maintenance of Blind and Deaf and Dumb, in Asylums, and cost of Relief in Extern Hospitals,	1,020 1 1	[illegible] 0 5	[illegible] 16 11	495 1 8	7,223 18 2	[illegible] 4 9	211 15 6	—
Salaries and Rations of Officers,	27,407 8 9	27,483 1 9	[illegible] 9 11½	15,618 11 1½	117,834 8 4½	113,487 7 1½	4,347 1 3½	—
All other Poor Relief Expenses,	31,763 9 8	37,026 1 9½	35,177 18 6½	11,041 10 3½	[illegible] 2 4½	[illegible]	1,643 1 3	—
Total Poor Relief Expenditure,	[illegible] 9 7	190,914 1 10	[illegible] 8 1½	[illegible] 6 9½	[illegible] 6 8	[illegible] 14 9	[illegible] 14 1	—
Expenses under Medical Charities Acts,	[illegible] 10 9	[illegible] 3 8	41,151 7 7	10,110 16 0	[illegible] 17 2	[illegible] 6 8	[illegible] 10 11	—
Expenses under the Acts for Registration of Births, Deaths, and Marriages,	4,310 6 4	3,679 7 7	[illegible] 6 11	1,853 1 7	[illegible] 16 7	[illegible] 11 1	—	67 14 7
Expenses under the Sanitary Acts,	410 6 9	1,780 13 10	1,360 10 11	[illegible] 18 3	4,514 17 9	[illegible] 16 6	[illegible] 19 8	—
Expenses under Burial Grounds Acts, paid out of the Poor Rate,	[illegible] 13 11	922 11 9	677 7 8	46 10 6	1,762 11 10	[illegible] 5 9	170 7 1	—
Total Expenditure out of the Poor Rates,	172,313 9 6	[illegible] 12 3	[illegible] 3 2½	[illegible] 2 0½	[illegible] 13 0	[illegible] 8	[illegible] 8 9	—
Valuation at 29th September, 1871,	[illegible] 5 0	[illegible] 15 3	[illegible] 17 0	[illegible] 19 8	[illegible] 16 3	[illegible] 11 0	[illegible] 6 8	—
Poundage on the Valuation:								
Of the Expenditure on Relief of the Poor,	0 0 7½	0 1 4½	0 1 1½	0 1 0½	0 1 0½	0 1 0½	0 0 0½	—
Of Total Expenditure,	0 0 10½	0 1 7½	0 1 4	0 1 1½	0 1 3½	0 1 0½	0 0 0½	—

PART 2.—RETURN of the Number of Persons who received Poor Relief during the Year ended 20th September, 1871.

Names of Counties and Unions.		Number of Persons who received Relief under the Poor Relief Acts during the Year. In Workhouse.	Out-door.	In Blind and Deaf and Dumb Asylums.	Total.	Average Daily Number of Paupers in the Workhouse.
PROVINCE OF ULSTER.						
ANTRIM,	Antrim,	1,568	86	2	1,656	287
	Ballycastle,	491	–	–	491	114
	Ballymena,	1,091	1,082	6	2,179	277
	Ballymoney,	909	397	5	1,311	147
	Belfast,	13,211	461	17	13,689	2,286
	Larne,	779	125	–	901	211
	Lisburn,	1,916	138	3	2,057	272
ARMAGH,	Armagh,	1,318	42	–	1,360	361
	Lurgan,	2,893	42	1	2,936	302
CAVAN,	Bailieborough,	638	165	–	803	132
	Bawnboy,	517	301	3	821	98
	Cavan,	1,379	146	3	1,528	268
	Cootehill,	601	49	2	652	130
DONEGAL,	Ballyshannon,	534	–	–	534	179
	Donegal,	289	110	1	400	76
	Dunfanaghy,	73	–	–	73	33
	Glenties,	283	40	1	324	108
	Inishowen,	378	122	3	503	130
	Letterkenny,	405	1	–	406	100
	Milford,	233	107	–	340	87
	Stranorlar,	349	3	–	352	72
DOWN,	Banbridge,	1,938	217	3	2,158	201
	Downpatrick,	1,318	142	–	1,460	240
	Kilkeel,	504	10	1	515	88
	Newry,	3,303	600	6	3,909	415
	Newtownards,	1,721	475	3	2,199	364
FERMANAGH,	Enniskillen,	600	14	–	614	210
	Irvinestown,	454	9	–	463	91
	Lisnaskea,	617	189	–	806	80
LONDONDERRY,	Coleraine,	1,341	207	–	1,548	278
	Londonderry,	2,054	15	–	2,069	578
	Magherafelt,	980	16	1	990	178
	Newtownlimavady,	902	6	1	909	150
MONAGHAN,	Carrickmacross,	690	4	–	694	99
	Castleblayney,	1,294	154	1	1,449	170
	Clones,	820	3	–	823	112
	Monaghan,	405	–	–	405	154
TYRONE,	Castlederg,	217	2	–	219	71
	Clogher,	657	50	–	707	108
	Cookstown,	501	6	–	507	149
	Dungannon,	1,248	299	3	1,550	202
	Gortin,	379	2	1	382	58
	Omagh,	924	29	–	953	109
	Strabane,	1,762	419	1	2,182	235
Total Ulster, Year 1871,		54,344	6,581	68	60,993	10,116
Do. do. 1870,		59,230	6,172	60	65,462	11,065
Increase,		–	409	8	–	–
Decrease,		4,886	–	–	4,499	949

No. 1. PART 2.—RETURN of the Number of Persons who received Poor Relief—*con.*

NAMES OF COUNTIES AND UNIONS.		Number of Persons who received Relief under the Poor Relief Acts during the Year.				Average Daily Number of Paupers in the Workhouse.
		In Workhouse.	Out-door.	In Blind and Deaf and Dumb Asylums.	TOTAL.	
PROVINCE OF MUNSTER.						
CLARE, . . .	Ballyvaghan, .	274	–	–	274	160
	Corrofin, . .	432	20	–	452	111
	Ennis, . . .	1,490	349	–	1,848	404
	Ennistymon, .	718	232	3	953	257
	Killadysert, . .	371	260	1	538	180
	Kilrush, . .	883	440	1	1,339	295
	Scariff, . .	480	–	5	494	167
	Tulla, . . .	879	155	2	1,036	243
CORK, . . .	Bandon, . .	748	2	6	756	162
	Bantry, . .	351	50	–	401	91
	Castletown, . .	536	4	–	540	147
	Clonakilty, . .	674	1	2	677	211
	Cork, . . .	9,630	2,558	77	12,201	2,100
	Dunmanway, .	447	68	–	515	125
	Fermoy, . .	1,338	14	2	1,354	238
	Kanturk, . .	1,571	701	8	2,280	393
	Kinsale, . .	715	–	–	715	136
	Macroom, . .	814	18	2	834	223
	Mallow, . .	1,920	767	11	2,698	370
	Midleton, . .	1,838	568	6	2,412	298
	Millstreet, . .	1,086	334	1	1,421	245
	Mitchelstown, .	1,833	89	3	1,925	280
	Skibbereen, . .	864	40	6	910	250
	Skull, . . .	238	31	1	270	98
	Youghal, . .	1,493	535	6	2,034	209
KERRY, . . .	Cahersiveen, .	604	128	–	732	120
	Dingle, . . .	642	4	1	647	150
	Kenmare, . .	671	51	–	722	131
	Killarney, . .	999	431	5	1,435	317
	Listowel, . .	981	–	5	986	148
	Tralee, . . .	1,691	1	14	1,706	490
LIMERICK, . .	Croom, . . .	790	250	–	1,039	219
	Glin, . . .	480	89	6	575	110
	Kilmallock, . .	2,391	1,183	17	3,591	552
	Limerick, . .	7,840	675	17	8,532	1,464
	Newcastle, . .	1,055	416	3	1,481	232
	Rathkeale, . .	1,217	684	6	1,907	319
TIPPERARY, .	Borrisokane, .	459	1	–	460	129
	Carrick-on-Suir, .	1,762	439	3	2,204	358
	Cashel, . . .	1,849	865	7	2,721	609
	Clogheen, . .	966	–	2	968	250
	Clonmel, . .	2,202	424	7	2,633	471
	Nenagh, . .	1,944	361	–	2,305	387
	Roscrea, . .	647	193	–	840	167
	Thurles, . .	908	45	7	960	637
	Tipperary, . .	2,061	1,231	8	3,300	421
WATERFORD, .	Dungarvan, . .	1,755	564	6	2,325	377
	Kilmacthomas, .	876	436	4	1,316	102
	Lismore, . .	940	342	3	1,285	170
	Waterford, . .	3,400	1,963	5	5,368	840
Total Munster, Year 1871, .		69,368	18,476	272	88,116	15,969
Do. do. 1870, .		70,002	16,811	276	87,089	17,134
Increase, ...		–	1,665	–	127	–
Decrease, ...		1,634	–	4	–	1,165

No. 1. Part 2.—Return of the number of Persons who received Poor Relief—*con.*

Names of Counties and Unions.		Number of Persons who received Relief under the Poor Relief Acts during the year.				Average Daily Number of Paupers in the Workhouse.
		In Workhouse.	Out-door.	In Blind and Deaf and Dumb Asylums.	Total.	
PROVINCE OF LEINSTER.						
Carlow,	Carlow,	2,271	1,039	5	3,315	319
Dublin,	Balrothery,	4,098	500	—	4,598	214
	Dublin, North,	6,402	231	33	6,666	1,033
	Dublin, South,	8,899	1,287	38	10,224	2,093
	Rathdown,	2,846	40	12	2,898	502
Kildare,	Athy,	1,514	586	3	2,103	200
	Celbridge,	966	515	3	1,484	105
	Naas,	2,504	1,066	6	3,576	277
Kilkenny,	Callan,	1,426	738	3	2,167	256
	Castlecomer,	773	509	2	1,284	146
	Kilkenny,	2,837	1,335	3	4,175	463
	Thomastown,	1,203	292	1	1,496	227
	Urlingford,	666	238	1	905	169
King's Co.	Edenderry,	1,328	271	2	1,601	180
	Parsonstown,	842	33	5	880	274
	Tullamore,	2,250	519	8	2,777	353
Longford,	Ballymahon,	805	205	4	1,014	122
	Granard,	778	1,071	—	1,849	217
	Longford,	1,560	539	2	2,101	278
Louth,	Ardee,	3,252	1,118	2	4,372	265
	Drogheda,	5,247	2,883	5	8,135	290
	Dundalk,	2,647	1,089	—	3,736	280
Meath,	Dunshaughlin,	2,389	356	—	2,745	151
	Kells,	888	237	4	1,129	207
	Navan,	3,335	689	1	4,025	216
	Oldcastle,	661	61	1	723	181
	Trim,	1,974	583	1	2,558	220
Queen's Co.	Abbeyleix,	845	310	4	1,159	136
	Donaghmore,	415	103	1	519	88
	Mountmellick,	1,919	812	6	2,737	378
Westmeath,	Athlone,	1,510	259	1	1,770	305
	Delvin,	1,007	111	1	1,119	116
	Mullingar,	1,417	579	7	2,003	327
Wexford,	Enniscorthy,	1,658	1,381	5	3,044	266
	Gorey,	1,151	213	—	1,364	251
	New Ross,	1,629	1,015	3	2,647	431
	Wexford,	1,858	1,051	10	2,919	420
Wicklow,	Baltinglass,	1,620	610	8	2,238	213
	Rathdrum,	2,110	1,280	1	3,391	306
	Shillelagh,	792	23	—	815	169
Total Leinster, Year 1871,		83,281	26,361	181	109,823	14,831
Do. do. 1870,		80,975	26,239	163	107,377	15,431
Increase,		2,306	122	18	2,446	—
Decrease,		—	—	—	—	600

No. 1. Part 2.—Return of the number of Persons who received Poor Relief—*con.*

Names of Counties and Unions.		Number of Persons who received Relief under the Poor Relief Acts during the year.				Average Daily Number of Paupers in the Workhouse.
		In Workhouse.	Out-door.	In Blind and Deaf and Dumb Asylums.	Total.	
PROVINCE OF CONNAUGHT.						
Galway,	Ballinasloe,	901	25	–	1,010	260
	Clifden,	419	286	2	702	185
	Galway,	1,077	230	2	1,309	383
	Glennamaddy,	642	144	–	786	171
	Gort,	566	10	5	581	108
	Loughrea,	674	36	1	711	188
	Mount Bellew,	640	20	–	660	147
	Oughterard,	256	300	–	556	137
	Portumna,	387	75	–	462	137
	Tuam,	1,129	503	4	1,636	279
Leitrim,	Carrick-on-Shannon	700	89	1	790	188
	Manorhamilton,	513	–	3	516	120
	Mohill,	765	454	–	1,219	176
Mayo,	Ballina,	713	188	–	901	164
	Ballinrobe,	888	63	2	953	247
	Belmullet,	333	58	–	391	98
	Castlebar,	472	337	1	810	133
	Claremorris,	435	78	6	519	128
	Killala,	190	107	–	297	63
	Newport,	247	49	–	296	74
	Swineford,	689	94	1	784	134
	Westport,	622	10	–	632	172
Roscommon,	Boyle,	790	459	4	1,253	206
	Castlerea,	838	48	1	887	213
	Roscommon,	1,019	354	2	1,375	330
	Strokestown,	745	315	2	1,062	200
Sligo,	Dromore, West,	190	48	2	240	67
	Sligo,	1,042	511	4	1,557	330
	Tobercurry,	359	147	3	509	90
	Total Connaught, Year 1871,	18,517	4,998	45	23,560	5,130
	Do. do. 1870,	19,322	4,663	43	24,028	5,570
	Increase,	–	335	2	–	–
	Decrease,	805	–	–	468	440
SUMMARY OF PROVINCES.						
Ulster,		64,344	6,381	69	60,893	10,115
Munster,		69,368	19,476	272	89,116	15,260
Leinster,		83,281	26,301	161	109,823	14,531
Connaught,		18,517	4,998	45	23,560	5,130
	Total Ireland, Year 1871,	225,510	56,416	566	282,492	40,045
	Do. do. 1870,	230,429	53,885	542	284,856	49,195
	Increase,	–	2,531	24	–	–
	Decrease,	4,919	–	–	[illegible]	3,150

[illegible]

[illegible]

No. 4.—SUMMARIES of Tables Nos. 2 and 3, showing the TOTAL RECEIPTS, EXPENDITURE, and BALANCES, for the HALF-YEARS ended 25th MARCH and 29th SEPTEMBER, 1871, respectively.

I.—SUMMARY of Table No. 2:—HALF-YEAR ended 25th March, 1871:—163 Unions.

Dr.	£ s. d.	£ s. d.	Cr.	£ s. d.	£ s. d.
To balances in favour of Electoral Divisions at the close of previous half-year,	—	[illegible]	By balances against Electoral Divisions at the close of previous half-year,	—	[illegible]
„ Amount of poor-rate collected and lodged during the half-year ended 25th March, 1871,	[illegible]		„ In-maintenance and Clothing of Electoral Division Paupers during the half-year ended 25th March, 1871,	[illegible]	
„ Amount of repayment of relief,	[illegible]		„ Ditto, for Union Paupers,	[illegible]	
„ Amount of other receipts,	[illegible]	[illegible]	„ Out-door relief for Electoral Division Paupers during the above half-year,	[illegible]	
			„ Ditto, for Union Paupers,	[illegible]	
			„ Maintenance of Idiots, Deaf, Dumb, and Blind in Asylums during the above half-year,	[illegible]	[illegible]
			„ Establishment charges,	[illegible]	
			„ Repayment of loans under Act [illegible],	[illegible]	
			„ Amount of Collectors' poundage or salary as remuneration,	[illegible]	
			„ Registration expenses,	[illegible]	
			„ Workhouse Burial expenses,	[illegible]	
			„ Election, law, and other expenses,	[illegible]	[illegible]
			Total Poor Relief Expenditure,	—	[illegible]
			„ Expenses under Medical Charities and Vaccination Acts,	[illegible]	
			„ Expenses under the Acts for Registration of Births, Deaths, and Marriages,	[illegible]	
			„ Expenses under Sanitary Acts,	[illegible]	
			„ Expenses under Miscellaneous Acts, paid out of the Poor Rates,	[illegible]	[illegible]
			Total Expenditure out of the Poor Rates,	—	[illegible]
„ Balances against Electoral Divisions at the close of this half-year,	—	[illegible]	„ Balances in favour of Electoral Divisions at the close of this half-year,	—	[illegible]
Total,	—	[illegible]	Total,	—	[illegible]

II.—SUMMARY of Table No. 3:—HALF-YEAR ended 29th Sept., 1871:—163 Unions.

Dr.	£ s. d.	£ s. d.	Cr.	£ s. d.	£ s. d.
To balances in favour of Electoral Divisions at the close of previous half-year,	—	[illegible]	By balances against Electoral Divisions at the close of previous half-year,	—	[illegible]
„ Amount of poor-rate collected and lodged during the half-year ended 29th September, 1871,	[illegible]		„ In-maintenance and Clothing of Electoral Division Paupers during the half-year ended 29th September, 1871,	[illegible]	
„ Amount of repayment of relief,	[illegible]		„ Ditto for Union Paupers,	[illegible]	
„ Parliamentary Grant,	[illegible]		„ Out-door relief for Electoral Division Paupers during the above half-year,	[illegible]	
„ Amount of other receipts,	[illegible]	[illegible]	„ Ditto for Union Paupers,	[illegible]	
			„ Maintenance of Idiots, Deaf, Dumb, and Blind in Asylums during the above half-year,	[illegible]	[illegible]
			„ Establishment charges,	[illegible]	
			„ Repayment of loans under Act [illegible],	[illegible]	
			„ Amount of Collectors' poundage or salary as remuneration,	[illegible]	
			„ Registration expenses,	[illegible]	
			„ Workhouse Burial expenses,	[illegible]	
			„ Election, law, and other expenses,	[illegible]	[illegible]
			Total Poor Relief Expenditure,	—	[illegible]
			„ Expenses under Medical Charities and Vaccination Acts,	[illegible]	
			„ Expenses under the Acts for Registration of Births, Deaths, and Marriages,	[illegible]	
			„ Expenses under Sanitary Acts,	[illegible]	
			„ Expenses under Miscellaneous Acts, paid out of the Poor Rates,	[illegible]	[illegible]
			Total Expenditure out of the Poor Rates,	—	[illegible]
„ Balances against Electoral Divisions at the close of this half-year,	—	[illegible]	„ Balances in favour of Electoral Divisions at the close of this half-year,	—	[illegible]
Total,	—	[illegible]	Total,	—	[illegible]

No. 5.—TABLE showing the PARTICULARS included under the head of Audited Accounts of Unions, for the HALF-YEAR

NAMES OF UNIONS.	Salaries and Rations of Officers.			Repairs, Improvements, and additional Buildings.			Furniture, Utensils, and Implements of Work.			Proportion of Fuel, &c., debited to Establishment.			Printing, Stationery, Advertising, and Postage.		
PROVINCE OF ULSTER:	£	s.	d.	£	s.	d.	£	s.	d.	£	s.	d.	£	s.	d.
Co. of Antrim.															
Antrim,	361	9	9	96	0	5	48	2	3	12	14	11	78	11	5
Ballycastle,	191	7	6	53	15	9	30	16	10	10	1	3	12	8	7
Ballymena,	495	15	0	146	18	11	25	2	6	31	5	0	82	14	8
Ballymoney,	294	2	4	10	14	11	9	2	3	0	18	11	10	17	10
Belfast,	1,704	7	11	658	12	4	349	2	0	60	5	7	165	5	2
Larne,	383	0	9	81	9	0	30	5	0	27	1	6	33	16	3
Lisburn,	294	13	7	118	6	9	53	12	4	12	4	4	21	16	8
Co. of Armagh.															
Armagh,	450	2	5	260	14	4	16	7	2	10	12	6	19	10	5
Lurgan,	357	19	2	140	16	2	11	16	4	16	10	1	62	1	10
Co. of Cavan.															
Bailieborough,	212	3	2	29	1	2	5	19	9	29	10	1	12	6	10
Bawnboy,	208	6	8	44	16	10	28	9	6	17	19	1	33	8	5
Cavan,	353	1	9	41	9	9	41	0	4	24	5	6	42	4	1
Cootehill,	227	19	1	23	4	1	5	1	6	9	7	8	16	14	4
Co. of Donegal.															
Ballyshannon,	190	16	0	28	10	11	21	2	0	16	0	0	37	4	0
Donegal,	212	14	1	97	0	3	20	18	5	1	18	1	58	7	6
Dunfanaghy,	183	1	8	5	19	4	9	16	8	10	17	3	12	8	4
Glenties,	179	17	9	24	10	7	5	9	10	10	6	1	14	4	7
Inishowen,	217	9	11	42	10	4	20	10	4	12	7	0	97	11	6
Letterkenny,	171	0	7	34	11	2	19	5	8	10	4	5	20	11	10
Milford,	198	13	1	66	1	4	17	12	4	12	4	2	27	5	6
Stranorlar,	241	14	6	23	1	10	9	9	9	11	0	0	16	17	1
Co. of Down.															
Banbridge,	369	10	7	70	18	5	29	11	7	20	16	0	47	10	9
Downpatrick,	395	5	3	25	14	3	20	16	7	17	11	9	37	10	0
Kilkeel,	200	12	0	9	2	0	6	1	3	8	11	6	14	14	2
Newry,	448	5	6	90	0	7	25	0	7	35	16	7	51	9	9
Newtownards,	434	14	9	72	0	8	15	4	2	21	9	5	39	17	8
Co. of Fermanagh.															
Enniskillen,	324	15	5	47	19	1	10	2	2	9	10	3	21	16	10
Irvinestown,	173	4	5	21	0	11	—			17	7	8	10	12	5
Lisnaskea,	210	10	3	18	1	10	15	14	9	10	5	8	18	19	5
Co. of Londonderry.															
Coleraine,	306	8	1	232	1	10	28	11	0	16	14	8	64	17	4
Londonderry,	399	16	1	46	1	7	56	7	4	31	12	6	54	10	2
Magherafelt,	279	11	3	78	5	0	4	13	7	12	14	3	24	1	3
Newtownlimavady,	263	6	11	87	18	0	7	16	8	21	6	5	25	2	9
Co. of Monaghan.															
Carrickmacross,	216	4	8	105	19	3	20	12	2	12	10	9	18	0	4
Castleblayney,	264	1	10	25	18	9	15	11	9	11	16	7	24	9	1
Clones,	185	8	5	17	9	4	11	12	0	15	1	0	18	0	10
Monaghan,	303	16	8	18	7	11	8	3	10	17	13	10	29	17	8
Co. of Tyrone.															
Castlederg,	161	7	1	5	13	4	6	18	7	6	14	5	10	12	7
Clogher,	222	8	1	82	13	1	11	18	6	20	11	0	24	0	9
Cookstown,	216	15	5	5	18	0	7	7	9	2	17	0	14	17	0
Dungannon,	300	11	10	67	0	8	23	14	4	6	0	0	20	10	4
Gortin,	149	11	6	16	1	10	4	10	6	8	7	10	10	13	8
Omagh,	355	17	11	37	14	6	15	2	4	37	18	4	27	2	0
Strabane,	340	8	10	53	6	7	44	4	1	18	16	10	26	11	4
Total Ulster (44 Unions),	12,841	18	1	3,115	4	8	1,127	7	0	798	18	4	1,467	6	9

ESTABLISHMENT CHARGES in the Summary (Table No. 2) of the ended 25th MARCH, 1871:—163 Unions.

Drugs and Medical or Surgical Appliances.	Rent and Taxes.	Insurance.	Other Charges.	Amount debited to Establishment.	Credits Deducted.	Amount of Establishment Charges apportioned.
£ s. d.	£ s. d.	£ s. d.	£ s. d.	£ s. d.	£ s. d.	£ s. d.
60 19 9	–	–	9 17 1	650 15 0	8 0 0	642 15 0
29 1 8	1 10 0	–	11 14 11	310 16 0	–	310 16 0
33 11 6	–	8 16 9	3 13 6	700 17 0	–	700 17 0
1 14 11	9 0 0	6 0 0	0 3 0	325 14 2	5 0 0	320 14 2
331 13 10	29 17 8	3 0 0	10 12 6	3,309 17 2	102 12 3	3,207 4 11
18 0 9	8 15 1	7 8 0	13 11 9	562 16 10	21 11 5	541 5 5
27 7 1	17 10 0	9 0 0	22 0 6	508 10 4	49 8 4	459 2 0
30 14 9	0 14 0	–	3 8 10	777 9 3	29 3 11	748 5 4
44 18 1	23 18 1	–	7 17 6	655 1 3	25 1 0	630 0 3
14 7 8	12 0 0	0 6 9	1 4 10	313 18 10	3 13 0	310 5 10
–	–	4 8 8	0 15 8	337 8 6	–	337 8 6
49 10 11	–	1 11 6	5 14 10	661 18 5	19 1 8	642 16 9
17 0 5	–	–	0 18 8	290 5 10	–	290 5 10
2 9 9	10 7 6	1 0 0	7 6 7	304 5 9	–	304 5 9
9 0 8	–	3 10 0	2 10 0	330 12 6	5 0 0	325 12 6
1 5 3	–	–	1 0 0	174 10 6	–	174 10 6
16 18 6	–	3 4 11	–	259 4 3	–	259 4 3
0 3 3	–	–	15 11 7	330 12 11	–	330 12 11
16 17 4	–	–	11 11 11	278 3 11	–	278 3 11
–	–	0 16 0	–	321 12 7	–	321 12 7
12 10 11	–	–	0 19 3	316 2 4	1 1 10	315 0 6
0 1 0	17 5 0	–	23 0 7	675 13 8	69 4 6	606 9 2
69 3 0	–	11 11 0	5 12 8	602 2 9	19 2 9	583 0 0
0 2 3	2 11 11	–	8 5 4	249 0 7	31 15 6	217 5 1
3 16 8	2 0 0	–	–	666 17 8	18 16 0	647 1 8
40 0 8	12 16 3	–	5 5 9	634 18 2	2 11 0	632 7 2
23 5 9	–	8 0 0	6 1 0	425 1 4	11 7 4	413 14 0
42 2 1	–	4 8 6	10 19 9	280 4 0	–	280 4 0
6 16 5	–	6 3 0	0 4 5	272 0 0	–	272 0 0
7 7 10	5 19 11	–	15 0 0	625 8 8	–	625 8 8
4 1 10	–	–	15 10 0	580 15 3	43 4 10	537 10 5
21 7 6	–	2 11 0	8 8 10	431 13 5	–	431 13 5
–	–	1 6 3	19 0 0	373 15 7	7 10 0	366 5 7
1 1 0	1 19 4	8 10 9	2 13 8	387 10 4	–	387 10 4
20 5 4	11 15 8	0 19 6	6 18 3	414 0 8	14 10 6	399 10 2
11 18 11	–	3 0 0	1 12 6	259 3 0	8 1 2	251 1 10
23 13 3	9 5 0	6 19 0	1 13 5	415 9 7	–	415 9 7
18 1 2	–	3 8 3	1 13 10	234 8 3	–	234 8 3
26 9 11	–	5 9 3	–	343 0 7	–	343 0 7
–	11 19 0	1 1 0	1 12 8	202 9 7	–	202 9 7
–	25 0 0	0 7 6	0 12 6	478 17 2	47 17 8	430 19 6
4 13 4	–	3 16 0	1 14 0	194 8 9	–	194 8 9
14 19 4	13 0 10	5 7 4	0 17 7	508 6 2	–	508 6 2
30 3 9	–	9 10 0	–	526 17 2	15 0 0	511 17 2
1,118 7 10	218 6 3	137 15 9	385 11 5	31,445 10 6	560 [illegible]	31,055 [illegible]

[continued.

No. 5.—Table showing the Particulars included under the head of

Audited Accounts of Unions, for the

Names of Unions.	Salaries and Rations of Officers.			Repairs, Improvements, and additional Buildings.			Furniture, Utensils, and Implements of Work.			Proportion of Fuel, &c., debited to Establishment.			Printing, Stationery, Advertising, and Postage.		
Province of Munster.	£	s.	d.	£	s.	d.	£	s.	d.	£	s.	d.	£	s.	d.
Co. of Clare.															
Ballyvaghan,	171	16	3	32	17	1	56	18	9	9	6	6	26	17	2
Corrofin,	183	19	6	26	16	7	4	2	1	7	13	6	16	6	3
Ennis,	456	18	6	177	9	6	55	8	7	31	4	3	45	14	2
Ennistymon,	215	5	9	123	2	3	17	19	2	17	14	6	50	0	2
Killadysart,	205	14	0	70	1	9	9	14	5	19	4	7	21	3	6
Kilrush,	395	3	6	35	9	9	7	1	1	22	0	2	32	0	9
Scariff,	253	4	9	40	0	3	9	6	9	22	8	4	15	13	10
Tulla,	259	13	9	47	1	11	15	0	6	12	18	1	24	7	0
Co. of Cork.															
Bandon,	309	16	8	44	12	11	32	13	2	14	14	8	69	13	6
Bantry,	171	5	6	12	15	4	11	16	6	11	10	9	13	11	1
Castletown,	166	3	9	8	10	9	6	6	5	8	9	6	5	9	6
Clonakilty,	309	1	0	105	6	5	19	0	7	5	2	0	15	18	10
Cork,	1,769	19	7	2,087	11	0	440	10	10	68	5	8	155	4	6
Dunmanway,	177	2	5	30	17	1	17	10	3	17	4	9	26	4	6
Fermoy,	400	5	7	177	1	4	39	8	5	21	18	2	13	16	3
Kanturk,	451	18	4	170	15	8	27	12	5	39	16	10	63	8	5
Kinsale,	231	1	4	74	6	9	12	6	9	12	4	0	11	5	0
Macroom,	242	2	0	100	4	6	23	0	9	13	18	0	19	0	3
Mallow,	343	5	6	63	4	9	30	14	7	29	0	6	54	9	11
Midleton,	330	14	9	15	5	6	17	6	11	60	8	6	32	2	11
Millstreet,	261	0	7	20	4	9	19	15	8	16	16	10	28	4	9
Mitchelstown,	310	11	7	37	15	4	23	14	4	23	10	6	17	16	5
Skibbereen,	291	8	7	94	11	2	20	16	1	13	9	3	31	14	6
Skull,	177	4	10	16	16	0	2	1	9	6	10	0	8	9	3
Youghal,	393	10	1	113	16	9	57	19	4	11	14	0	91	7	10
Co. of Kerry.															
Cahersiveen,	256	15	8	31	18	11	6	11	5	8	0	0	24	10	8
Dingle,	298	2	2	16	4	7	19	10	10	9	14	1	2	17	5
Kenmare,	216	0	5	56	14	4	9	14	1	19	7	0	15	5	9
Killarney,	547	10	3	107	16	9	61	4	11	78	15	10	36	11	9
Listowel,	286	0	9	37	5	10	7	16	2	14	2	7	20	15	4
Tralee,	510	10	10	22	2	10	67	0	6	63	15	1	42	6	4
Co. of Limerick.															
Croom,	291	13	0	36	17	8	32	6	11	15	16	3	39	4	1
Glin,	256	16	9	16	7	7	3	2	1	19	16	10	16	0	2
Kilmallock,	493	8	4	64	12	5	57	4	8	37	10	4	53	5	10
Limerick,	909	6	11	166	15	6	49	2	3	61	0	6	123	7	10
Newcastle,	752	16	9	165	3	10	69	9	9	31	4	0	25	10	2
Rathkeale,	387	4	3	120	19	5	16	10	11	25	3	9	52	8	5
Co. of Tipperary.															
Borrisokane,	192	14	2	15	19	5	13	10	3	29	6	6	19	4	5
Carrick-on-Suir,	464	11	1	133	6	6	20	1	0	24	8	0	53	9	6
Cashel,	465	15	11	80	5	8	22	6	2	55	3	4	36	9	1
Clogheen,	397	16	4	40	0	10	40	8	11	16	16	10	20	7	8
Clonmel,	545	0	6	140	4	0	67	16	0	37	13	9	42	0	11
Nenagh,	352	15	11	60	0	7	17	6	11	27	10	0	28	13	5
Roscrea,	331	0	3	85	12	6	38	17	11	9	0	0	25	3	7
Thurles,	356	6	3	40	19	7	4	15	7	31	16	5	17	17	2
Tipperary,	401	12	7	70	0	0	16	10	4	13	13	0	45	15	6
Co. of Waterford.															
Dungarvan,	369	3	5	78	0	11	5	1	11	2	16	0	29	6	2
Kilmacthomas,	254	7	3	8	4	6	28	6	11	12	6	3	72	14	0
Lismore,	363	15	11	60	4	7	15	15	3	16	10	10	6	4	7
Waterford,	560	5	0	147	6	6	50	12	2	26	16	3	86	15	6
Total Munster (53 Unions),	16,906	16	4	4,847	18	1	1,770	19	1	1,180	8	5	1,531	19	7

Establishment Charges in the Summary (Table No. 2) of the Half-year ended 25th March, 1871—*continued.*

Drugs and Medical or Surgical Appliances.	Rent and Taxes.	Insurance.	Other Charges.	Amount debited to Establishment.	Credits Deducted.	Amount of Establishment Charges apportioned.
£ s. d.	£ s. d.	£ s. d.	£ s. d.	£ s. d.	£ s. d.	£ s. d.
90 11 6	–	9 10 0	6 18 9	331 10 9	21 7 1	310 12 1
5 5 8	18 0 0	–	2 6 11	206 4 5	1 15 0	204 9 5
40 13 8	25 19 5	8 0 0	20 5 11	788 10 5	20 5 10	768 4 7
14 19 1	11 10 9	0 5 0	22 14 0	488 5 5	–	488 5 5
0 14 0	–	7 15 4	9 10 3	343 18 0	26 8 6	317 9 9
88 11 11	2 12 6	0 16 0	3 9 0	583 8 7	19 19 0	560 4 7
5 2 1	–	–	19 10 1	305 12 0	–	305 12 0
28 10 6	–	0 5 0	20 2 8	398 6 3	23 4 11	393 1 4
20 9 1	10 13 4	4 13 9	8 2 4	513 8 1	42 10 0	499 18 1
11 16 8	6 0 0	–	0 6 9	239 2 7	11 16 9	291 5 10
23 0 11	–	9 2 6	0 9 5	244 19 0	–	244 19 0
27 10 1	–	4 19 6	2 13 0	369 11 5	0 19 6	368 11 11
300 0 8	86 5 5	88 18 3	95 4 3	5,130 4 2	100 15 0	5,010 9 2
–	–	7 15 0	0 15 10	277 9 10	18 9 0	259 0 10
22 8 1	33 8 1	4 8 3	6 1 8	712 9 10	44 6 9	668 3 1
23 0 10	5 0 0	13 3 6	6 0 8	600 14 0	–	600 11 0
5 9 6	8 13 7	–	7 17 6	397 4 0	18 8 10	349 1 7
15 19 9	15 0 0	4 2 0	–	432 7 2	2 14 0	429 13 2
29 1 9	16 10 6	11 7 3	27 10 6	571 5 9	3 16 7	567 9 2
1 6 3	11 16 3	0 9 5	15 11 2	505 1 9	25 12 1	479 9 8
28 16 7	–	5 17 0	6 13 0	407 14 2	3 2 10	404 11 4
10 3 6	1 17 6	9 13 0	16 8 5	461 10 8	13 2 1	448 8 7
21 17 5	10 0 0	11 6 0	20 5 3	518 9 2	–	518 9 2
16 10 7	6 10 0	5 2 0	5 17 6	246 1 11	–	246 1 11
46 4 4	43 13 9	11 2 6	11 16 10	720 4 5	66 3 1	654 1 4
1 1 0	–	–	6 9 6	339 12 9	3 15 7	335 17 2
9 7 4	–	–	7 8 9	335 5 0	–	335 5 0
10 4 11	1 5 0	0 12 0	6 8 2	367 12 8	0 0 5	367 12 3
3 15 1	10 0 0	15 10 0	19 4 2	907 17 2	2 12 8	905 4 6
30 8 8	–	13 4 6	3 10 0	413 14 5	3 19 10	409 14 7
22 0 10	40 19 5	15 10 0	8 14 6	788 18 4	94 11 10	694 6 6
13 11 7	–	–	14 13 6	437 4 6	6 10 4	430 14 2
6 7 5	–	4 14 0	9 0 6	324 0 6	–	324 0 6
10 2 6	85 1 9	–	76 15 7	828 5 2	397 14 11	430 10 3
138 3 11	87 10 0	21 1 0	105 15 5	1,763 6 5	131 11 6	1,631 14 11
23 10 9	–	–	39 7 10	743 4 6	14 3 1	729 1 5
34 14 4	–	8 18 0	0 8 4	605 12 6	–	605 12 6
–	8 0 0	4 1 9	9 2 8	284 19 3	40 3 1	235 16 2
49 13 8	73 1 6	7 14 0	11 4 4	826 11 0	84 12 1	745 18 11
5 11 4	116 10 0	–	10 0 10	781 1 11	70 3 0	710 18 11
7 9 4	10 19 6	–	56 0 4	630 0 4	7 7 4	622 13 0
21 6 2	25 19 7	19 6 2	92 0 11	1,005 9 0	0 16 6	1,004 12 6
9 3 4	42 14 10	9 6 0	11 16 9	557 0 7	19 6 3	538 4 4
33 10 10	–	–	6 6 2	529 8 3	45 7 1	484 1 2
–	4 3 6	7 10 8	24 10 5	477 19 5	45 2 2	432 17 3
21 8 2	20 11 1	0 15 0	22 12 3	618 12 1	10 9 3	607 6 10
17 4 7	13 3 6	1 9 0	11 18 8	548 6 5	6 4 2	542 2 3
13 0 9	–	7 15 4	14 0 11	307 17 11	1 1 2	306 16 9
6 15 0	12 12 6	–	29 2 0	465 0 8	6 13 3	458 7 5
46 19 2	73 0 0	2 5 6	26 6 5	1,071 9 8	38 6 1	1,033 3 7
1,412 13 7	850 5 9	[illegible] 10 0	1,091 1 8	33,894 4 10	1,675 13 5	30,601 11 6

[*continued.*

H 2

No. 5.—Table showing the Particulars included under the head of
Audited Accounts of Unions, for the

Names of Unions.	Salaries and Rations of Officers.			Repairs, Improvements, and additional Buildings.			Furniture, Utensils, and Implements of Work.			Proportion of Fuel, &c., debited to Establishment.			Printing, Stationery, Advertising, and Postage.		
Province of Leinster:	£	s.	d.	£	s.	d.	£	s.	d.	£	s.	d.	£	s.	d.
Co. of Carlow.															
Carlow,	520	14	0	78	18	10	41	15	0	51	11	6	31	16	0
Co. of Dublin.															
Balrothery,	319	0	6	23	6	8	20	9	9	19	1	3	22	9	1
Dublin, North,	1,938	3	4	493	16	2	261	17	9	152	2	2	120	17	6
Dublin, South,	2,491	16	1	1,255	16	6	710	6	7	79	6	11	322	8	3
Rathdown,	563	4	9	1,020	17	4	57	19	5	22	12	11	97	16	4
Co. of Kildare.															
Athy,	377	4	6	114	10	1	30	7	5	20	10	0	38	12	11
Celbridge,	376	12	9	58	14	11	87	17	5	30	2	1	23	12	6
Naas,	458	12	6¼	43	1	6	25	16	1	22	6	11	41	1	7
Co. of Kilkenny.															
Callan,	302	16	3	58	11	8	11	17	0	22	3	9	37	6	4
Castlecomer,	300	4	8	42	6	1	35	16	2	12	6	5	21	7	5
Kilkenny,	657	6	1	155	0	0	58	13	9	39	1	11	38	3	0
Thomastown,	209	16	5	24	15	6	19	6	6	27	17	6	17	19	3
Urlingford,	284	17	0	12	14	2	21	6	6	11	9	10¼	25	11	0
King's County.															
Edenderry,	276	19	9	40	16	3	20	19	10	16	7	10	25	7	4
Parsonstown,	325	19	4	37	1	10	47	0	8	17	17	11	62	8	0
Tullamore,	420	9	1	60	16	1	15	10	7	34	6	11	21	17	4
Co. of Longford.															
Ballymahon,	255	16	0	58	10	10	24	7	1	21	2	0	21	11	0
Granard,	303	14	6	133	9	1	57	11	0	13	6	7	26	0	8
Longford,	337	11	7	41	1	6	32	3	1	20	0	6	32	14	3
Co. of Louth.															
Ardee,	353	1	11	52	7	6	16	16	9	18	14	5	27	4	9
Drogheda,	402	1	6	70	9	3	22	11	8	17	3	6	28	6	8
Dundalk,	357	8	6	33	8	9	48	4	6	16	5	2	46	4	8
Co. of Meath.															
Dunshaughlin,	330	6	6	32	15	4	6	16	11	26	4	8	19	10	5
Kells,	367	15	3	49	12	6	40	4	5	10	5	6	21	10	7
Navan,	576	12	5	77	11	8	22	11	9	27	16	0	20	1	6
Oldcastle,	246	19	7	42	1	8	14	9	5	11	17	9	20	10	9
Trim,	355	9	3	41	11	6	56	12	9	22	10	8¼	37	14	1
Queen's County.															
Abbeyleix,	266	10	11	69	12	9	58	9	9	20	1	4	21	17	6
Donaghmore,	291	0	9	19	1	6	28	15	2	22	10	1	17	14	9
Mountmellick,	496	14	7	56	16	4	30	17	11	34	10	10	12	7	5
Co. of Westmeath.															
Athlone,	860	16	2	87	11	8	37	17	4	44	19	11	46	13	7
Delvin,	217	14	11	88	14	6	4	0	6	97	13	9	84	1	8
Mullingar,	468	9	0	141	19	1	41	10	6	31	5	11	60	19	3
Co. of Wexford.															
Enniscorthy,	386	6	6	131	9	6	75	2	7	25	6	1	41	5	9
Gorey,	512	4	9	40	6	7	14	10	6	16	15	6	34	6	8
New Ross,	392	10	2	56	2	3	59	5	11	14	12	6	30	14	6
Wexford,	415	14	1	198	15	3	45	10	6	9	16	8	40	11	7
Co. of Wicklow.															
Baltinglass,	353	13	0	116	12	1	32	15	2	24	4	11	17	19	8
Rathdrum,	330	11	11	158	2	4	15	17	2	93	9	7	42	12	5
Shillelagh,	266	6	1	52	18	2	37	2	3	22	8	3	13	7	1
Total Leinster (40 Unions).	[illegible]	13	[illegible]	5,111	11	1	[illegible]	0	4	1,1[illegible]	7	[illegible]	1,726	17	5

ESTABLISHMENT CHARGES in the Summary (Table No. 2) of the HALF-YEAR ended 25th MARCH, 1871—*continued.*

Drugs and Medical or Surgical Appliances.	Rent and Taxes.	Insurance.	Other Charges.	Amount debited to Establishments.	Credits Deducted.	Amount of Establishment Charges apportioned.
£ s. d.	£ s. d.	£ s. d.	£ s. d.	£ s. d.	£ s. d.	£ s. d.
20 13 5	40 7 10	11 18 0	39 4 0	817 0 9	7 0 1	810 0 8
45 11 8	23 3 5	–	57 1 0	510 5 2	51 18 6	458 17 8
168 9 1	114 13 6	37 1 9	124 6 11	3,430 0 10	108 18 9	3,321 2 1
250 16 7	108 16 11	–	194 18 2	5,304 6 2	210 6 5	5,093 19 9
50 19 10	43 10 7	10 8 0	58 4 5	1,983 19 7	13 9 3	1,960 10 4
28 11 4	83 8 11	7 10 0	36 13 9	680 17 11	39 7 5	641 10 6
74 1 5	–	5 15 0	7 8 1	573 7 9	–	573 7 9
34 17 9	28 3 0	–	18 19 5	669 18 11½	131 14 1	538 4 10½
23 19 2	–	–	59 9 1	595 2 8	2 1 6	593 1 2
15 8 7	2 0 0	8 16 3	9 13 9	417 13 4	17 18 8	399 14 8
70 8 8	10 13 8	12 11 8	10 16 0	1,052 14 1	0 12 0	1,052 2 1
11 14 7	6 13 11	1 3 9	3 2 10	415 12 8	20 2 0	395 10 8
9 6 2	–	8 0 0	7 7 4	328 18 0½	9 16 4½	319 15 8
10 10 10	3 7 9	8 5 9	5 8 8	407 17 0	6 14 5	401 2 7
15 10 2	7 1 8	–	6 3 7	510 4 8	2 3 10	508 0 5
23 4 11	10 7 6	0 10 6	11 11 8	614 4 1	22 9 6	591 14 7
0 18 4	5 11 0	0 0 4	43 4 9	447 3 10	9 0 0	438 3 10
6 7 0	–	8 19 6	18 17 1	573 17 7	–	573 17 7
10 10 8	29 10 7	6 13 6	5 15 11	525 7 7	40 9 7	484 18 0
27 10 0	10 10 8	0 4 6	1 4 1	508 0 7	4 4 10	504 1 9
23 10 8	18 7 3	–	16 1 2	598 14 8	9 4 1	589 10 1
4 4 4	–	7 1 0	19 9 9	540 6 7	15 17 0	524 9 7
18 13 4	–	1 17 0	6 12 3	437 19 8	19 6 8	418 13 0
1 1 6	10 0 0	–	13 15 6	522 11 2	4 17 7	517 13 7
38 1 5	10 0 0	17 7 6	87 11 5	624 13 3	4 12 8	620 0 7
17 5 1	–	–	4 14 1	358 3 9	16 2 9	342 11 0
30 2 7	–	9 15 6	22 19 10	576 8 0½	8 9 8	567 19 11
10 1 5	4 1 10	7 19 3	12 7 0	480 16 6	0 10 7	480 5 7
0 4 9	–	3 3 0	6 3 8	396 19 7	2 1 11	394 17 8
24 9 4	19 15 6	7 16 3	13 9 4	764 17 4	9 3 0	755 14 4
20 14 6	0 6 8	8 0 0	8 0 0	617 1 10	24 15 7	592 6 3
23 0 4	–	3 11 6	11 6 11	410 8 9	5 17 4	404 6 1
19 1 11	–	9 6 0	70 16 3	863 9 1	20 13 1	842 0 0
3 13 4	40 6 6	8 0 0	45 9 1	776 17 4	125 0 7	651 16 9
29 6 0	24 10 10	–	23 15 5	601 5 9	17 4 3	584 1 6
37 4 4	29 5 1	6 14 0	13 16 9	630 7 8	18 4 10	612 2 5
23 16 4	51 6 0	–	9 16 8	838 7 1	40 6 1	798 1 0
23 10 5	14 17 8	–	9 6 3	390 19 6	15 8 2	375 11 4
22 19 0	18 8 5	–	20 4 0	651 17 11	–	651 17 11
12 7 11	10 5 0	–	26 4 8	440 19 4	35 0 8	405 18 8
[illegible] 11 9	[illegible] 17 8	224 15 10	[illegible] 6 5	[illegible] 4 0½	1,0[illegible]4 5 6½	[illegible] 19 6

[*continued.*

No. 5.—Table showing the Particulars included under the head of Audited Accounts of Unions, for the

Names of Unions.	Salaries and Rations of Officers. £	s.	d.	Repairs, Improvements, and additional Buildings. £	s.	d.	Furniture, Utensils, and Implements of Work. £	s.	d.	Proportion of Food, &c., debited to Establishment. £	s.	d.	Printing, Stationery, Advertising, and Postage. £	s.	d.
Province of Connaught:															
Co. of Galway.															
Ballinasloe,	348	11	2	63	15	8	26	2	6	46	15	11	41	3	2
Clifden,	247	0	2	16	9	1	12	7	1	7	0	0	18	5	3
Galway,	502	16	0	27	11	4	12	14	3	12	10	0	43	1	11
Glennamaddy,	228	10	0	24	5	8	6	7	8	16	16	0	31	14	9
Gort,	255	7	4	42	6	10	42	1	6	18	15	2	22	12	4
Loughrea,	249	12	8	61	12	8	42	10	3	18	1	11	16	5	0
Mount Bellew,	216	15	8	14	2	1	10	13	1	10	9	1	13	4	2
Oughterard,	176	13	4	20	4	1	5	7	9	7	10	5	12	4	6
Portumna,	189	10	4	6	0	5	11	13	0	10	8	8	14	7	3
Tuam,	320	18	6	53	1	11	18	12	2	11	3	0	29	7	9
Co. of Leitrim.															
Carrick-on-Shannon,	235	2	3	44	16	7	25	7	8	17	7	11	22	10	1
Manorhamilton,	221	2	8	41	5	7	10	1	1	6	17	6	25	10	3
Mohill,	305	18	6	43	12	11	39	10	7	19	7	2	27	18	8
Co. of Mayo.															
Ballina,	298	0	10	18	14	3	9	6	0	10	6	9	17	10	10
Ballinrobe,	329	6	8	38	14	2	28	12	0	11	8	1	62	3	5
Belmullet,	178	17	9	19	12	4	6	7	3	9	15	1	13	11	7
Castlebar,	237	8	11	67	6	7	16	3	11	12	5	0	15	11	2
Claremorris,	220	16	4	22	7	3	18	8	2	10	5	1	29	18	4
Killala,	149	5	6	7	16	11	7	19	0	10	9	10	11	2	10
Newport,	187	10	3	9	5	8	5	11	4	8	8	8	10	18	1
Swineford,	229	16	6	5	1	8	64	18	9	10	6	0	23	16	7
Westport,	279	17	11	40	11	9	20	17	6	9	12	10	36	3	1
Co. of Roscommon.															
Boyle,	377	8	2	45	19	11	85	10	6	16	19	5	82	15	7
Castlerea,	238	12	2	24	5	0	51	17	8	21	12	5	38	7	0
Roscommon,	313	11	1	120	6	2	37	9	11	6	0	0	39	16	4
Strokestown,	236	5	0	43	2	8	26	4	6	8	0	0	27	10	4
Co. of Sligo.															
Dromore, West,	167	13	9	15	15	0	–			8	5	11	17	17	10
Sligo,	436	11	11	26	12	2	41	5	3	55	8	7	79	5	8
Tobercurry,	163	13	10	7	5	6	–			11	5	2	16	8	11
Total Connaught (29 Unions),	7,783	9	7	1,040	5	5	583	15	7	441	8	1	769	7	8

SUMMARY

	£	s.	d.	£	s.	d.	£	s.	d.	£	s.	d.	£	s.	d.
Ulster,	13,341	16	1	3,113	4	0	1,137	7	0	708	18	4	1,402	9	9
Munster,	15,408	18	5	5,537	13	1	1,770	15	1	1,180	8	5	1,584	19	7
Leinster,	19,891	13	9½	4,411	14	1	2,208	0	4	1,186	7	9½	1,734	17	5
Connaught,	7,783	9	7	1,040	5	5	583	15	7	441	8	1	769	7	8
Total Ireland (163 Unions),	[illegible]	19	9½	14,183	16	7	[illegible]	16	0	3,516	17	6½	5,491	14	3

ESTABLISHMENT CHARGES in the Summary (Table No. 2) of the HALF-YEAR ended 25th MARCH, 1871—*continued*.

Drugs and Medical or Surgical Appliances	Rent and Taxes	Insurance.	Other Charges.	Amount debited to Establishment.	Credits Deducted.	Amount of Establishment Charges apportioned.
£ s. d.	£ s. d.	£ s. d.	£ s. d.	£ s. d.	£ s. d.	£ s. d.
28 3 0	15 3 0	13 0 6	3 4 7	586 18 8	24 11 6	562 7 0
1 4 6	7 0 0	–	2 18 10	306 5 1	–	306 5 1
17 0 6	0 5 5	8 10 0	4 4 8	627 3 7	–	627 3 7
14 0 1	–	0 3 0	13 14 11	336 16 0	6 11 0	329 5 0
22 7 3	30 8 8	5 2 5	0 9 3	439 5 3	31 19 3	407 6 0
1 16 8	15 10 1	–	2 19 3	404 7 6	10 10 0	393 17 0
9 12 3	–	6 7 6	22 3 4	309 7 2	33 0 8	271 6 6
17 9 10	–	4 19 0	13 1 10	257 10 0	–	257 10 0
15 5 6	–	2 16 6	23 0 4½	283 11 6½	23 15 9	259 15 9½
20 1 8	9 0 9	7 2 0	10 1 0	505 9 3	–	505 9 3
14 3 3	41 6 2	–	–	600 13 11	–	600 13 11
4 0 5	11 10 11	8 16 0	–	388 9 6	–	388 9 6
1 1 0	7 16 0	–	0 0 4	444 0 2	–	444 0 2
17 17 6	21 18 10	–	6 19 6	358 14 6	32 6 4	326 8 2
20 16 3	6 15 8	–	17 15 6	492 9 8	16 1 11	476 7 9
1 7 4	–	–	11 0 4	243 11 8	13 8 0	230 3 8
0 18 8	12 8 6	0 7 9	5 18 9	379 8 5	–	379 8 5
5 6 2	1 0 0	–	15 17 6	331 16 10	32 6 0	299 9 10
0 2 9	–	–	1 8 3	188 6 3	21 0 0	167 6 3
9 16 2	–	–	2 11 1	253 17 10	–	253 17 10
11 0 0	2 10 9	0 11 6	4 0 2	340 8 1	23 14 6	316 13 7
3 9 8	0 10 5	–	8 17 11	400 1 1	20 17 10	379 3 3
33 14 0	–	9 18 9	–	550 4 4	–	550 4 4
16 10 0	2 3 9	7 13 6	10 1 4	433 8 10	29 18 6	403 10 4
–	28 6 4	10 16 0	11 15 0	568 1 5	–	568 1 5
20 4 7	6 6 0	2 0 2	17 9 11	413 7 9	18 16 1	394 11 8
2 10 10	–	0 7 6	0 0 0	274 2 7	–	274 2 7
10 16 10	21 1 3	16 7 6	1 0 0	767 10 2	1 1 0	766 9 2
0 15 7	–	–	4 19 8	228 8 8	–	228 8 8
[illegible]	[illegible]	112 10 10	[illegible]	11,530 1 9¼	357 19 0	11,172 2 9¼

OF PROVINCES.

1,119 8 10	216 4 8	137 15 0	286 11 5	21,655 10 8	600 9 8	21,055 8 0
1,412 13 7	650 3 9	295 16 6	1,031 1 3	32,082 4 10	1,478 13 5	30,603 11 5
1,250 11 9	645 17 8	224 15 10	1,065 6 8	32,265 4 0¼	1,084 5 0¼	31,200 19 0
237 6 5	241 4 5	112 10 10	220 4 9¼	11,530 1 9¼	357 19 0	11,172 2 9¼
[illegible]	[illegible]	771 [illegible]	[illegible]	[illegible]	[illegible]	[illegible]

No. 6.—Table showing the Particulars included under the head of

Audited Accounts of Unions, for the Half-year

Names of Unions.	Salaries and Rations of Officers.	Repairs, Improvements, and additional Buildings.	Furniture, Utensils, and Implements of Work.	Proportion of Fuel, &c., debited to Establishment.	Printing, Stationery, Advertising, and Postage.
Province of Ulster:	£ s. d.	£ s. d.	£ s. d.	£ s. d.	£ s. d.
Co. of Antrim.					
Antrim, . . .	371 11 4	368 2 2	91 0 1	11 19 1	87 15 11
Ballycastle, . .	198 15 4	79 8 2	11 9 1	6 19 9	21 5 10
Ballymena, . .	471 11 4	154 11 3	32 8 10	37 11 8	87 10 6
Ballymoney, . .	277 14 3	44 12 2	2 9 6	6 3 4	27 4 1
Belfast, . .	1,804 15 7	538 16 11	148 10 0	60 9 4	170 10 8
Larne, . . .	318 0 3	78 19 1	31 5 0	23 1 8	46 12 0
Lisburn, . .	348 8 8	65 2 8	11 15 6	11 11 6	33 18 10
Co. of Armagh.					
Armagh, . . .	428 14 7	190 2 4	17 6 1	19 14 10	60 13 2
Lurgan, . . .	341 10 7	138 1 4	5 6 6	17 6 9	79 18 1
Co. of Cavan.					
Bailieborough, . .	220 18 2	46 10 8	7 2 4	27 2 0	21 15 4
Bawnboy, . .	221 3 6	136 19 5	7 0 7	11 10 0	21 17 0
Cavan, . . .	391 7 10	122 12 9	24 0 8	23 13 6	28 3 9
Cootehill, . . .	326 2 4	46 7 2	5 12 7	6 18 0	10 10 0
Co. of Donegal.					
Ballyshannon, . .	181 0 0	68 7 7	13 17 10	10 0 0	11 9 8
Donegal, . .	240 16 11	50 10 0	15 17 1	—	19 17 0
Dunfanaghy, . .	130 1 10	3 9 9	9 7 11	10 4 0	8 10 0
Glenties, . .	181 0 1	8 7 0	2 3 11	8 15 6	20 5 0
Inishowen, . .	224 6 9	8 11 3	3 4 8	7 16 11	10 1 0
Letterkenny, . .	177 10 0	68 2 2	46 19 2	9 8 0	10 18 11
Milford, . .	211 17 6	117 5 2	11 6 9	12 2 0	8 4 1
Stranorlar, . .	231 6 5	40 17 10	7 5 0	9 11 0	15 13 9
Co. of Down.					
Banbridge, . .	394 0 11	118 13 3	43 2 9	16 12 2	37 16 8
Downpatrick, . .	410 3 11	168 1 7	16 4 10	16 4 5	34 2 8
Kilkeel, . . .	209 10 5	39 0 5	2 11 8	6 12 10	15 17 6
Newry, . . .	467 12 1	613 15 2	19 1 5	27 16 9	51 2 5
Newtownards, . .	419 12 8	168 14 11	26 0 11	31 9 3	41 6 10
Co. of Fermanagh.					
Enniskillen, . .	337 13 6	61 0 8	5 1 1	6 16 9	40 16 2
Irvinestown, . .	189 17 0	84 10 8	–	16 1 8	26 10 11
Lisnaskea, . .	219 2 11	47 16 9	13 12 10	12 5 9	10 11 8
Co. of Londonderry.					
Coleraine, . .	309 16 9	367 11 7	41 3 11	16 8 9	64 3 4
Londonderry, . .	423 16 2	118 9 11	110 4 1	14 10 4	49 4 11
Magherafelt, . .	279 5 1	28 7 7	15 19 2	18 14 8	36 9 9
Newtownlimavady, .	264 5 3	88 8 2	14 19 10	19 7 0	29 11 7
Co. of Monaghan.					
Carrickmacross, .	217 6 7	11 4 5	19 15 9	12 3 8	11 19 6
Castleblayney, .	201 11 0	59 4 6	10 14 8	12 4 9	34 0 5
Clones, . . .	170 7 5	9 7 4	24 9 9	18 2 9	19 10 7
Monaghan, . .	303 10 5	69 6 8	10 12 11	11 10 1	5 17 9
Co. of Tyrone.					
Castlederg, . .	179 17 0	81 16 6	3 0 7	4 6 4	7 9 5
Clogher, . .	215 8 5	48 10 3	16 1 11	14 10 1	91 6 10
Cookstown, . .	212 9 9	6 11 2	4 19 4	1 5 6	8 14 5
Dungannon, . .	314 11 9	100 15 7	20 7 11	7 19 0	49 12 10
Gortin, . . .	169 4 11	7 11 10	9 8 8	9 13 5	13 4 7
Omagh, . . .	357 6 9	97 6 1	7 6 7	40 19 0	45 5 9
Strabane, . .	379 2 11	77 8 5	48 9 11	10 19 0	49 10 4
Total Ulster (44 Unions),	12,384 10 8	4,670 17 4	991 7 6	687 12 5	1,865 7 8

Establishment Charges in the Summary (Table No. 3) of the ended 29th September, 1871:—163 Unions.

Drugs and Medical or Surgical Appliances.	Rent and Taxes.	Insurance.	Other Charges.	Amount debited to Establishment.	Credits Deducted.	Amount of Establishment Charges apportioned.
£ s. d.	£ s. d.	£ s. d.	£ s. d.	£ s. d.	£ s. d.	£ s. d.
34 10 9	–	8 10 0	12 14 1	937 1 5	8 0 0	929 1 5
5 3 9	1 10 0	4 3 6	7 5 10	335 15 3	–	335 15 3
22 6 4	–	2 0 0	9 3 11	756 18 0	–	756 18 0
18 13 11	6 0 0	0 12 6	–	377 6 9	5 0 0	372 6 9
316 18 1	93 0 5	20 0 0	56 15 10	3,180 10 4	102 19 11	3,077 10 5
13 11 7	8 15 1	–	32 0 1	607 10 10	47 18 5	559 12 7
19 1 6	–	–	12 14 0	522 6 6	10 4 8	508 3 10
16 16 0	2 0 7	17 14 6	29 16 6	765 0 4	60 9 4	704 10 11
33 2 0	–	10 6 5	19 19 5	683 15 4	13 11 5	670 3 11
3 18 6	–	9 5 0	6 15 11	343 17 3	7 1 10	336 15 5
–	–	–	4 1 3	402 17 9	1 2 6	401 15 3
32 9 6	–	8 3 6	5 0 10	633 11 11	12 5 0	621 6 11
13 16 1	–	5 5 3	9 0 6	316 13 5	1 7 1	315 6 4
1 2 8	10 7 6	2 5 0	26 10 0	307 19 10	–	307 19 10
35 0 4	–	–	4 2 4	546 14 6	5 0 0	541 14 6
11 5 4	–	3 15 0	2 5 5	179 18 3	–	179 18 3
–	–	–	2 0 0	222 11 9	–	222 11 9
22 17 1	1 9 0	4 5 0	16 10 11	299 3 2	5 1 5	294 1 9
12 9 8	–	4 15 0	9 15 7	360 3 0	–	360 3 0
20 10 6	–	4 5 3	16 3 8	404 13 11	4 10 8	400 3 3
–	–	3 16 0	1 18 0	310 9 0	–	310 9 0
10 6 9	5 18 0	8 16 6	38 7 5	653 10 5	25 8 6	628 1 11
64 19 11	–	–	16 10 0	728 7 9	10 2 0	718 5 9
13 1 10	2 12 7	4 0 0	16 14 9	309 8 0	9 5 7	300 2 5
7 17 3	3 0 0	6 9 0	3 0 0	1,163 16 1	8 14 0	1,155 2 1
115 6 9	12 3 0	10 17 0	37 6 9	820 2 1	50 12 7	770 0 6
27 11 6	–	–	6 6 0	491 7 6	25 10 3	465 17 3
–	–	–	5 6 2	275 18 3	4 9 0	271 9 3
16 18 6	–	–	4 11 1	231 19 2	–	231 19 2
14 9 6	4 15 0	5 9 3	19 17 6	842 15 7	–	842 15 7
22 19 7	–	6 6 2	128 3 10	734 2 3	126 5 10	607 16 5
10 19 0	–	3 6 9	5 17 0	391 7 0	1 15 4	389 11 8
–	–	3 17 6	24 6 9	434 15 6	6 12 6	428 3 0
13 16 4	–	–	6 0 4	258 5 0	3 5 2	254 19 10
20 10 5	–	–	5 6 6	430 19 8	7 9 7	423 10 1
0 6 7	–	–	0 16 11	244 1 1	2 13 2	241 7 11
6 12 10	1 17 5	–	11 15 7	414 8 9	32 18 2	351 5 7
6 10 7	–	–	1 14 0	217 12 5	–	217 12 5
12 14 7	–	0 10 0	1 10 0	330 7 10	2 10 0	327 17 10
23 2 4	6 15 10	3 15 0	1 10 7	272 9 4	–	272 9 4
12 9 0	–	3 2 6	–	501 18 7	68 14 0	433 4 7
6 7 9	–	–	0 19 0	197 9 7	0 8 11	197 0 8
19 10 1	13 6 10	–	1 2 0	643 13 1	–	643 13 1
66 11 1	1 6 9	–	37 15 9	863 11 7	19 10 7	843 1 0

No. 6.—Table showing the Particulars included under the head of Audited Accounts of Unions, for the

Names of Unions.	Salaries and Rations of Officers.			Repairs, Improvements, and additional Buildings.			Furniture, Utensils, and Implements of Work.			Proportion of Fuel, &c., debited to Establishment.			Printing, Stationery, Advertising, and Postage.		
ovince of Munster:	£	s.	d.	£	s.	d.	£	s.	d.	£	s.	d.	£	s.	d.
Co. of Clare.															
llyvaghan,	163	6	2	39	1	8	11	1	0	7	11	0	20	12	0
rrofin,	164	4	0	26	8	2	4	7	6	6	17	2	12	5	10
nnis,	457	12	8	46	10	10	29	15	2	16	17	3	38	19	8
nnistymon,	254	17	7	131	1	7	9	14	0	6	2	9	30	11	9
Kildysart,	207	11	5	6	18	2	3	0	2	10	8	9	16	11	7
lrush,	404	7	1	22	1	11	1	0	10	16	8	0	27	15	11
ariff,	263	11	10	60	12	9	4	16	6	14	11	0	11	8	6
lla,	260	1	0	63	10	9	16	6	4	12	3	6	24	19	10
Co. of Cork.															
ndon,	309	4	3	122	15	10	38	9	11	13	3	6	51	4	0
ntry,	161	16	6	6	8	11	4	0	4	11	6	4	10	6	3
stletown,	165	12	2	6	14	1	2	6	0	6	0	0	9	1	1
nakilty,	216	4	0	24	11	6	11	11	6	5	10	0	19	16	2
rk,	1,932	7	4	2,361	7	3	379	19	7	53	17	0	203	19	9
nmanway,	162	15	9	33	12	10	10	1	8	11	10	3	31	5	6
rmoy,	413	5	10	42	12	0	25	15	7	16	13	4	107	7	6
nturk,	460	5	0	100	3	3	22	6	2	33	19	6	68	6	0
nsale,	248	2	0	60	1	3	5	5	10	9	6	5	44	13	4
acroom,	240	5	10	15	12	10	9	10	0	12	12	11	24	16	8
llow,	371	2	1	43	1	6	22	16	3	23	10	0	67	4	7
dleton,	306	15	0	52	13	8	15	11	4	13	13	2	59	3	3
llstreet,	240	0	7	24	9	0	16	1	9	18	18	10	38	12	7
tchelstown,	216	7	1	39	6	10	24	10	0	57	12	11	21	15	10
ibbereen,	293	18	6	123	3	2	14	11	10	15	10	6	41	19	0
ull,	178	6	5	5	3	9	6	15	0	4	10	0	15	16	11
ughal,	412	9	7	25	13	8	17	5	9	12	9	0	36	12	9
Co. of Kerry.															
hercivcen,	256	12	11	6	8	6	–			5	0	0	28	3	9
ngle,	300	10	8	16	8	3	16	0	5	9	16	9	18	15	4
nmare,	453	15	0	29	18	7	12	15	10	21	15	1	39	2	3
llarney,	497	8	0	620	10	8	25	14	11	52	14	7	66	16	10
stowel,	202	15	4	6	10	9	0	13	5	12	17	11	26	4	11
alee,	538	3	4	34	14	8	22	3	5	51	6	7	47	11	1
Co. of Limerick.															
oom,	301	14	9	28	8	10	23	17	11	18	16	9	30	15	0
n,	271	17	2	21	6	11	1	6	0	11	1	6	8	5	0
mallock,	523	9	10	71	4	7½	101	17	6	26	17	0	64	6	3½
merick,	1,159	6	11	239	2	4	64	19	6	66	16	5	112	9	3
wcastle,	429	14	7	80	8	6	50	5	7	54	15	5	54	0	1
thkeale,	365	13	11	104	1	5	47	4	0	40	4	1	25	1	1
Co. of Tipperary.															
rrisokane,	108	13	10	8	5	9	11	18	0	16	19	3	20	8	5
rrick-on-Suir,	602	5	5	66	16	4	16	10	5	16	15	3	29	16	1
shel,	450	15	9	75	9	8	[illegible]	6	7	30	7	10	54	11	9
gheen,	318	13	1	28	1	9	13	8	9	18	1	6	21	12	5
nmel,	505	5	8	104	19	7	31	3	2	35	18	2	55	17	0
nagh,	371	19	7	28	13	11	7	16	8	22	10	7	24	14	6
screa,	341	4	1	54	11	9	24	11	8	0	0	0	27	15	4
urles,	575	13	0	33	18	7	4	0	6	21	16	4	45	19	1
pperary,	416	4	8	147	11	6	13	0	8	15	12	6	47	9	9
Co. of Waterford.															
ngarvan,	394	10	4	48	13	11	14	4	2	9	4	6	41	14	8
lmacthomas,	266	9	3	19	12	1	15	1	2	13	13	6	15	7	9
smore,	311	16	7	206	14	6	116	0	6	11	2	9	22	5	8
aterford,	624	11	11	131	13	3	92	0	6	16	5	2	63	4	8

ESTABLISHMENT CHARGES in the Summary (Table No. 3) of the HALF-YEAR ended 29th SEPTEMBER, 1871—*continued.*

Drugs and Medical or Surgical Appliances.			Rent and Taxes.			Insurance.			Other Charges.			Amount debited to Establishment.			Credits Deducted.			Amount of Establishment Charges apportioned.		
£	s.	d.	£	s.	d.	£	s.	d.	£	s.	d.	£	s.	d.	£	s.	d.	£	s.	d.
11	16	6	10	19	0		–		3	4	0	290	14	0	11	19	7	274	14	6
5	6	5	16	0	0	7	6	6	0	10	0	267	18	9	14	6	7	256	18	2
63	2	4	20	19	3	1	10	5	7	1	2	687	8	0	16	5	9	671	2	3
40	3	7	11	10	5	6	1	1	62	4	7	570	6	10	13	17	0	556	9	10
0	16	2		–			–		2	6	2	253	7	10		–		253	7	10
84	8	0	2	12	6	8	5	6	5	6	3	565	18	0	3	7	0	562	11	0
11	18	8		–		4	16	9	35	5	5	397	3	2	49	1	3	348	1	11
22	3	7		–		7	2	5	20	1	2	402	8	8	2	19	2	399	9	6
17	12	1	10	15	4		–		1	18	10	601	1	11	15	0	0	586	1	11
11	1	6	6	0	0	0	8	9	0	4	0	245	8	7	14	11	0	230	17	7
	–			–			–		0	10	6	212	8	10	23	18	6	188	10	4
0	2	9		–			–		4	8	4	303	3	4		–		303	3	4
397	0	1	100	2	1	10	0	0	256	10	2	6,677	18	3	136	9	6	6,541	8	9
	–			–			–			–		209	5	9		–		209	5	9
19	3	1	32	8	1	7	0	0	21	10	1	689	9	6	73	13	0	616	9	6
56	9	1	5	2	0		–		6	19	5	730	10	11		–		730	10	11
	–		1	15	0	6	9	0	6	17	0	404	9	10	26	5	4	378	4	6
30	19	0	3	0	0		–		7	10	6	337	16	9	5	10	6	332	6	3
29	15	10	15	10	6		–		46	18	0	620	0	9	6	5	10	613	14	11
40	11	8	11	0	2	6	11	5	29	13	7	594	0	4	16	5	0	577	15	4
31	7	6		–			–		26	16	2	398	6	11	39	12	9	358	14	2
16	0	4	1	17	6		–		20	3	10	417	19	4	7	14	1	410	5	3
91	18	7		–			–		7	14	4	518	16	7	4	0	0	514	16	7
0	1	6	7	11	0		–		6	13	1	223	16	1	0	17	6	222	18	7
27	1	8	59	4	0	3	0	0	46	12	5	641	12	7	42	17	9	598	14	10
1	1	0	0	5	0	10	10	6	6	5	7	326	8	3	17	19	4	308	8	11
36	1	8		–		6	5	0	9	2	1	421	0	9		–		421	0	9
16	1	8	1	6	0	8	1	0	6	5	1	571	10	0	3	10	3	568	3	9
1	2	5		–		1	10	0	13	15	6	1,259	4	0	1	1	1	1,258	2	11
1	16	8		–			–		4	18	6	346	1	4	15	16	0	330	5	4
20	2	3	47	19	5		–		20	14	0	782	18	9	26	14	4	756	19	5
65	2	10		–		10	2	8	91	17	7	485	11	4	9	14	3	475	17	1
1	16	4		–			–		8	10	4	328	2	9	25	13	7	302	9	6
45	16	1	86	2	10	10	16	10	154	1	2	1,018	16	2	19	14	5	999	1	9
183	5	0	87	10	0	1	0	0	146	4	7	1,934	13	11	64	5	0	1,870	8	11
22	7	4		–		12	10	7	6	6	0	651	3	4	33	0	0	618	3	4
40	14	7		–			–		3	6	4	633	5	5	0	10	0	632	15	5
25	19	4	1	4	8		–		20	19	5	303	3	8	6	7	8	296	16	0
20	16	1	73	1	6	6	0	0	0	7	4	753	4	5	2	5	0	750	19	5
69	5	7	114	15	0	19	14	4	11	6	1	817	13	0	42	11	1	804	1	11
12	18	11	10	9	3	7	10	0	9	12	9	440	10	10	3	9	8	437	1	2
16	11	6	25	10	8	7	10	0	130	17	9	996	2	11	157	9	11	838	13	0
10	17	6	38	16	9	1	7	0	40	13	4	652	8	10	39	6	8	612	17	9
10	8	10		–		6	6	0	1	0	0	481	17	9	27	13	3	454	4	6
18	10	11	0	1	0	2	6	0	23	0	6	626	6	11	7	7	11	618	19	0
30	19	11	20	11	1	12	5	0	11	15	6	714	0	2	32	13	2	681	7	0
21	9	7	13	16	7	6	2	6	21	7	11	564	0	4	6	4	4	557	16	0
69	18	1		–			–		21	1	4	379	17	1	23	2	6	356	14	7
10	13	1	15	18	6	5	10	1	20	11	2	715	6	10	27	0	0	688	6	10
53	2	6	77	18	0	9	17	9	83	16	2	1,078	14	11	41	4	5	1,037	10	6

No. 6.—Table showing the Particulars included under the head of

Audited Accounts of Unions, for the

Names of Unions.	Salaries and Rations of Officers.			Repairs, Improvements, and additional Buildings.			Furniture, Utensils, and Implements of Work.			Proportion of Fuel, &c., debited to Establishment.			Printing, Stationery, Advertising, and Postage.		
Province of Leinster:	£	s.	d.	£	s.	d.	£	s.	d.	£	s.	d.	£	s.	d.
Co. of Carlow.															
rlow,	625	17	0	151	2	6	64	9	10	38	18	11	78	14	10
Co. of Dublin.															
lbrothery,	279	18	8	36	16	11	14	12	6	16	8	6	63	11	8
ublin, North,	1,922	1	11	330	15	0	180	17	5	105	2	4	[illegible]	7	6
ublin, South,	2,551	3	7	1,166	14	6	485	6	8	63	9	0	209	18	7
thdown,	577	8	8	250	0	0	79	6	5	21	16	5	125	14	9
Co. of Kildare.															
hy,	390	15	7	131	4	0	35	0	0	25	0	0	38	0	0
lbridge,	307	5	0	24	12	1	49	17	5	21	5	4	44	12	0
as,	451	18	7	51	9	2	11	17	7	23	16	10	49	19	11
Co. of Kilkenny.															
llan,	405	9	5	46	7	10	17	16	2	20	1	8	28	16	9
stlecomer,	508	19	8	60	18	1	16	10	10	14	2	4	40	3	0
lkenny,	704	17	9	62	16	6	44	3	9	23	13	5	64	19	11
omastown,	325	7	7	18	17	0	11	17	11	17	10	3	19	14	3
lingford,	245	11	1	30	18	9	18	5	11	10	9	9	32	12	2
King's County.															
lenderry,	305	10	10	116	1	3	—			15	3	2	40	11	6
rsonstown,	347	14	4	46	17	11	35	7	0	18	2	2	66	1	0
llamore,	439	13	6	55	3	3	20	15	1	25	5	10	46	3	9
Co. of Longford.															
llymahon,	202	1	4	118	16	3	34	8	11	11	14	3	28	10	2
anard,	328	18	10	93	5	6	11	13	1	14	4	10	41	9	0
ngford,	943	8	9	86	19	5	33	1	5	30	19	6	35	6	10
Co. of Louth.															
dee,	354	11	8	20	8	3	14	3	3	17	4	11	28	0	0
ogheda,	419	11	2	33	0	0	11	0	8	15	9	4	50	10	0
ndalk,	385	7	6	41	8	2	22	11	10	19	18	1	37	0	1
Co. of Meath.															
nshaughlin,	330	16	9	62	19	0	26	13	0	18	0	3	20	18	6
lls,	358	0	9	47	4	6	103	19	4	15	13	8	26	17	11
van,	414	8	11	54	5	5	39	0	2	10	14	5	25	17	10
dcastle,	242	18	10	20	0	0	12	9	2	10	7	9	21	19	5
im,	372	0	5	60	2	6	30	10	8	20	9	2	56	13	10
Queen's County.															
beyleix,	228	3	0	230	8	1	44	10	5	60	0	0	31	11	4
naghmore,	265	16	7	84	11	11	22	14	8	19	14	0	20	1	6
untmellick,	515	17	0	200	10	7	19	0	5	10	0	0	69	4	0
Co. of Westmeath.															
hlone,	405	1	3	17	14	5	59	18	5	6	3	7	34	14	1
lvin,	210	8	4	41	15	1	9	1	0	28	18	11	97	15	1
llingar,	524	0	3	151	5	5	40	15	1	65	10	7	43	17	4
Co. of Wexford.															
niscorthy,	369	6	8	115	3	10	71	11	4	10	5	8	45	9	8
rey,	391	10	0	45	2	9	9	14	10	17	15	5	63	7	2
w Ross,	395	5	4	73	14	4	35	12	6	13	10	10	57	2	2
xford,	490	14	3	95	5	1	55	4	10	16	2	6	51	5	0

£	s.	d.	£	s.	d.	£	s.	d.	£	s.	d.	£	s.	d.	£	s.	d.
12	0	9	12	0	6		–		31	4	11	1,014	15	8	41	3	11
40	5	5	33	3	5	5	5	0	116	9	2	607	11	10	68	1	6
167	13	10	104	1	3	0	15	0	61	10	11	3,260	5	1	30	7	5
223	7	4	276	6	11	35	16	10	166	15	0	5,227	6	7	227	6	0
56	1	8	42	10	7		–		84	13	6	1,289	11	9	6	11	0
43	3	7	20	0	0		–		47	14	6	723	17	8	60	14	1
30	6	2		–			–		4	10	3	672	11	5		–	
36	0	5	26	3	1	6	9	6	12	14	6	672	15	6	41	9	3
	–			–			–		75	16	11	604	12	9	2	1	6
23	17	6		–			–		11	4	5	475	5	10	25	17	6
50	0	4	11	0	4		–		13	17	6	975	14	5	41	0	1
12	10	5	4	8	10	0	0	0	1	17	5	421	3	8	45	14	10
11	12	0		–		0	5	0	1	1	7	354	17	3	16	6	3
14	16	7		–		3	7	8	16	6	11	512	18	0	2	10	7
18	5	8	6	15	2	6	6	10	12	16	11	559	8	0	1	5	4
30	5	2	10	17	4	10	14	6	13	1	5	851	16	10	101	0	5
14	2	1	5	11	6		–		20	6	10	490	10	4		–	
14	16	1		–			–		14	19	4	527	6	6		–	
0	6	6	20	10	7		–		0	12	11	546	9	1	28	10	5
20	7	6	12	12	8	12	13	6	4	15	1	503	12	5	6	12	6
42	1	7	16	7	3	7	13	0	7	6	11	609	11	9	5	17	4
1	4	5		–		0	4	6	30	14	3	530	6	10	15	16	6
20	12	1		–		6	10	6	12	0	9	616	11	2	11	9	0
25	16	4		–		6	17	0	16	5	3	614	6	9	3	15	0
68	5	10	9	4	2		–		20	9	0	627	6	11	20	10	9
35	3	10		–		10	7	0	3	17	1	306	6	7	0	10	0
17	17	4		–			–		25	5	7	503	6	2	40	10	0
0	13	2		–		0	0	8	20	12	11	604	15	11		–	
16	15	8		–			–		0	17	7	429	11	5	17	19	10
20	15	9	22	7	1		–		34	4	6	591	6	0	62	5	9
27	3	11		–		1	0	0	24	18	0	576	13	6	11	4	6
0	10	6		–			–		27	6	0	351	12	11	3	8	3
12	12	0		–			–		77	6	11	545	5	7	6	12	0
6	8	0	60	8	1		–		36	7	2	734	1	1	141	14	2
24	3	5	49	16	8	6	17	6	53	3	3	544	8	3	48	13	0
7	0	2	27	10	1	0	4	6	4	0	2	654	0	1	9	17	2
60	0	11	51	6	0	6	0	0	25	9	5	643	8	11	6	6	0
27	0	11	14	17	8	7	17	5	4	14	7	615	0	10		–	
38	15	4		–		10	16	6	10	16	3	635	18	11		–	
30	17	6		–		7	0	0	24	1	5	416	11	7	10	1	0

No. 6.—Table showing the Particulars included under the head of

Audited Accounts of Unions, for the

Names of Unions.	Salaries and Rations of Officers. £	s.	d.	Repairs, Improvements, and additional Buildings. £	s.	d.	Furniture, Utensils, and Implements of Work. £	s.	d.	Proportion of Fuel, &c., debited to Establishment. £	s.	d.	Printing, Stationery, Advertising, and Postage. £	s.	d.
Province of Connaught:															
Co. of Galway.															
Ballinasloe,	372	16	8	24	4	10	22	16	6	14	18	3	30	18	7
Clifden,*	245	1	0	16	8	6	14	8	3	7	10	0	14	8	6
Galway,*	507	9	6	25	16	4	19	4	0	12	7	0	49	8	1
Glennamaddy,	222	18	11	41	1	0	10	14	6	16	10	11	31	10	6
Gort,	253	19	9	21	8	6	14	5	4	15	1	6	17	1	10
Loughrea,	237	0	0	16	12	6	9	15	10	11	5	9	19	1	2
Mount Bellew,	232	12	1	20	7	5	25	16	1	9	10	9	18	15	7
Oughterard,*	179	16	4	5	16	6	2	7	7	8	8	1	12	9	7
Portumna,	206	10	4	3	6	8	4	19	10	10	3	2	10	3	10
Tuam,	340	18	5	81	12	6	13	0	5	10	1	1	61	6	3
Co. of Leitrim.															
Carrick-on-Shannon,	313	8	5	59	1	8	16	10	2	10	11	6	37	1	5
Manorhamilton,	225	17	4	19	6	0	6	19	9	8	0	0	20	10	11
Mohill,	307	13	6	48	1	10	20	18	9	13	12	9	67	10	11
Co. of Mayo.															
Ballina,	288	0	1	26	17	11	20	7	0	10	19	6	18	18	2
Ballinrobe,	316	15	2	53	12	2	6	8	11	8	14	1	57	6	0
Belmullet,	178	4	7	51	17	6	6	5	10	8	5	10	16	12	8
Castlebar,	247	19	1	29	17	0	22	0	7	16	12	0	27	11	0
Claremorris,	224	17	2	78	17	1	20	7	5	9	19	4	22	6	1
Killala,	154	11	2	1	10	0	0	19	0	8	3	7	14	8	3
Newport,	166	7	1	16	8	10	6	13	0	7	15	6	20	7	7
Swineford,	260	8	7	11	0	7	28	8	4	9	11	3	28	16	7
Westport,	251	1	1	39	5	9	15	5	0	6	17	5	25	6	6
Co. of Roscommon.															
Boyle,	308	8	0	19	8	7	24	12	6	14	8	2	54	3	7
Castlerea,	279	7	10	35	6	0	29	8	4	21	10	6	30	5	8
Roscommon,	308	0	0	173	3	8	86	16	7	6	9	10	61	1	6
Strokestown,	372	4	8	84	11	11	16	1	7	5	0	0	21	17	5
Co. of Sligo.															
Dromore, West,	190	17	6	91	16	11	–			9	14	5	24	16	7
Sligo,	380	5	3	83	11	5	40	14	11	60	4	11	46	10	9
Tobercurry,	190	19	2	97	8	0	2	19	9	7	6	1	16	14	11
Total Connaught (26 Unions),	7,920	8	4	1,005	16	6	456	19	7	371	10	4	777	0	10

SUMMARY

	£	s.	d.	£	s.	d.	£	s.	d.	£	s.	d.	£	s.	d.
Ulster,	13,955	10	6	4,670	17	4	801	7	6	687	12	9	1,396	7	8
Munster,	10,074	6	4	5,718	4	9½	1,455	4	0	982	9	3	1,997	9	9½
Leinster,	16,808	9	9	4,615	16	11	1,805	0	8	1,045	16	11	2,020	0	1
Connaught,	7,920	8	4	1,005	10	0	456	19	7	371	10	4	777	0	10
Total Ireland (163 Unions),	[illegible]	5	1	[illegible]	11	6½	[illegible]	17	9	[illegible]	1	6	[illegible]	7	4½

* The accounts of the Clifden, Galway, and Oughterard Unions have not yet been

Establishment Charges in the Summary (Table No. 3) of the Half-year ended 29th September, 1871—*continued*.

Drugs and Medical or Surgical Appliances.			Rent and Taxes.			Insurance.			Other Charges.			Amount debited to Establishment.			Credits Deducted.			Amount of Establishment Charges apportioned.		
£	s.	d.	£	s.	d.	£	s.	d.	£	s.	d.	£	s.	d.	£	s.	d.	£	s.	d.
6	7	9	6	14	0	1	2	6	6	14	10	487	7	10	9	15	6	477	12	4
31	3	6	–			6	10	0	2	6	7	337	16	3	–			337	16	3
41	8	11	–			–			8	3	3	657	9	10	17	3	0	640	6	10
12	10	7	–			2	0	0	14	10	11	354	12	4	21	18	4	332	14	0
3	11	0	30	2	2	–			–			361	14	2	33	8	8	320	5	6
40	10	5	15	4	0	4	14	6	1	8	4	318	7	7	–			318	7	7
31	5	2	–			–			16	13	9	343	6	10	19	9	9	323	17	1
5	14	5	–			–			12	19	6	226	19	11	24	2	3	202	17	8
12	9	10	–			–			8	11	8	250	5	4	7	3	6	243	1	10
36	13	6	6	16	7	1	1	0	7	2	8	548	11	5	–			548	11	5
1	10	0	–			6	16	0	–			455	19	2	15	2	6	440	16	8
46	16	11	–			0	12	0	0	17	2	338	16	6	–			338	16	6
8	10	5	7	16	0	8	19	6	3	7	6	455	10	3	0	12	6	454	17	9
20	17	9	22	10	6	17	5	0	0	14	1	446	4	9	34	12	10	411	11	11
25	6	6	6	15	8	9	9	0	25	9	7	502	17	10	25	0	0	477	17	10
–			–			3	0	0	36	16	5	309	1	10	–			309	1	10
16	6	10	12	8	6	–			27	0	4	396	16	1	33	19	0	362	17	1
17	16	5	1	0	0	3	16	6	18	12	4	370	11	4	11	16	6	358	14	10
19	15	0	–			5	0	0	1	5	0	205	7	0	6	0	0	199	7	0
6	6	9	–			3	15	0	3	18	9	263	6	6	–			263	6	6
14	1	6	–			0	15	0	11	18	4	363	15	2	13	14	7	350	0	7
7	9	5	14	10	10	7	10	0	6	3	4	407	18	1	26	16	9	381	1	4
43	0	6	–			–			25	10	11	549	16	3	6	8	10	543	7	5
30	3	5	2	3	9	–			9	8	5	456	7	9	5	8	2	450	19	7
71	12	9	26	6	5	0	10	10	22	16	6	700	0	0	–			700	0	0
54	9	1	–			–			33	7	1	439	11	3	78	5	4	361	5	11
7	11	11	–			1	16	8	11	2	8	288	0	6	–			288	0	6
20	8	10	18	19	3	–			10	0	0	678	11	4	0	12	11	677	18	5
–			–			3	3	5	6	6	0	253	15	4	–			253	15	4
681	5	8	174	6	8	87	10	0	859	17	6	11,706	18	5	403	10	9	11,303	7	8

OF PROVINCES.

1,156	19	11	175	11	6	170	3	2	638	12	6	23,676	2	6	708	15	3	22,967	7	3
1,626	5	3	635	16	11	212	3	6	1,390	4	4½	33,286	19	1½	1,148	8	0½	32,138	10	4
1,343	16	7	647	10	2	174	14	5	1,209	2	2	32,010	16	6	1,272	4	0	30,738	14	6
681	5	8	174	6	8	87	10	0	859	17	6	11,706	18	5	403	10	9	11,303	7	8
4,769	4	5	2,633	[illegible]	3	645	0	1	6,291	16	6½	100,770	10	8½	3,533	18	9½	97,237	19	11

omitted, but the above particulars have been obtained from the Clerks of the Unions.

No. 7.—Table showing the Expenditure for Provisions, Necessaries, and Clothing of Workhouse Inmates, during the Half-year ended 25th March, 1871 (included in Table No. 2); also, the Number relieved in the Half-year, and the Average Weekly Cost per Head:—163 Unions.

Name of Union.	Cost of Provisions consumed.	Cost of Necessaries consumed.	Cost of Clothing.	Total Cost of Provisions, Necessaries, and Clothing.	Total Number of Paupers relieved.	Collective No. of Days for all Paupers relieved in the Half-year.	Average No. of Days of Relief to each Pauper.	Average Daily No. of Paupers in Workhouse.	Average Weekly Cost per head: Provisions and Necessaries.	Average Weekly Cost per head: Clothing.	Average Weekly Cost per head: Total.
Province of Ulster:	£ s. d.	£ s. d.	£ s. d.	£ s. d.					s. d.	s. d.	s. d.
Co. of Antrim.											
Antrim, . . .	606 0 7	134 3 11	187 3 6	928 17 0	601	59,109	58	279	1 11¼	0 6	2 6¼
Ballycastle, . .	267 16 5	60 13 6	73 2 10	891 10 6	271	20,511	76	109	2 2	0 6	2 8
Ballymena, . .	711 0 4	114 13 10	178 16 0	1,004 12 2	669	50,094	76	266	2 3¼	0 6	2 9¼
Ballymoney, . .	216 10 4	96 10 10	96 13 0	410 0 2	329	27,043	62	147	1 7¼	0 6	2 1¼
Belfast, . . .	6,234 9 8	812 9 1	1,406 8 7	8,453 7 4	7,909	450,058	57	2,504	2 2	0 5½	2 7½
Larne, . . .	596 7 8	116 11 6	194 18 11	912 12 7	620	46,727	60	248	2 1	0 7	2 8
Lisburn, . . .	573 15 2	117 6 8	215 2 11	906 4 9	1,069	51,635	47	275	1 10	0 7	2 5
Co. of Armagh.											
Armagh, . . .	813 12 1	123 17 6	276 11 3	1,214 0 10	830	69,177	83	369	1 10¼	0 6½	2 5¼
Lurgan, . . .	956 16 8	249 7 5	104 15 6	1,307 2 7	1,719	72,130	42	387	2 3¼	0 4½	2 8
Co. of Cavan.											
Bailieborough, . .	364 0 1	44 12 8	81 6 3	516 10 0	343	24,811	69	132	2 5½	0 5½	2 11
Bawnboy, . . .	242 6 2	45 16 8	73 11 5	386 16 3	273	18,140	66	96	2 4	0 7	2 11
Cavan, . . .	702 12 8	123 16 5	211 3 0	1,037 10 8	606	60,676	68	270	2 3	0 7	2 10
Cootehill, . . .	202 18 8	67 5 8	81 19 9	411 18 1	361	22,968	64	122	2 0	0 6	2 6
Co. of Donegal.											
Ballyshannon, . .	354 4 11	120 9 0	74 7 1	548 1 0	324	33,813	100	177	1 11	0 3½	2 3½
Donegal, . . .	207 1 10	89 3 10	61 19 8	348 4 11	180	14,371	63	79	2 6	0 7	3 1
Dunfanaghy, . .	78 10 10	30 16 6	29 10 0	128 10 4	58	6,057	115	33	2 3	0 8	2 11
Glenties, . . .	207 16 6	47 4 0	47 13 0	301 13 0	124	14,991	104	108	1 9	0 4	2 1
Inishowen, . . .	272 16 10	47 12 7	60 10 0	380 0 11	221	23,937	108	137	1 10	0 4	2 2
Letterkenny, . .	307 12 7	90 1 8	75 9 0	471 2 3	250	20,377	81	109	2 9	0 6½	3 3

191	19	1	44	10	9	67	11	10	304	3	8	166	14,278	103	86
110	4	6	40	7	6	28	10	0	179	11	2	210	10,606	68	74
409	12	9	189	18	9	77	18	5	700	7	11	930	37,402	40	189
601	18	4	104	9	3	105	1	3	1,101	2	10	670	54,616	63	221
176	16	9	85	7	9	40	5	6	252	9	0	260	10,035	66	80
999	8	11	166	6	5	408	6	9	1,569	2	1	1,767	64,223	48	448
886	9	6	141	18	9	178	19	1	1,187	8	4	1,074	74,829	69	386
686	7	8	160	6	9	149	7	7	626	0	7	581	46,080	66	243
528	6	7	40	13	3	64	19	2	322	1	0	794	18,751	64	100
217	14	9	73	0	9	103	15	1	394	10	0	347	17,008	48	80
353	2	1	180	19	4	278	9	4	726	11	9	654	38,892	68	284
761	19	4	148	8	8	316	19	1	1,241	7	1	1,243	72,364	60	666
306	9	8	94	0	1	139	13	7	533	8	4	532	31,843	54	189
139	9	10	68	1	9	75	4	10	275	9	5	522	29,063	65	162
654	18	1	65	16	7	84	1	8	896	19	10	859	17,937	60	95
356	7	9	85	1	8	96	12	0	551	1	11	671	60,920	46	164
292	2	5	57	6	5	67	6	5	417	10	3	489	21,639	47	115
856	16	4	79	12	11	88	7	4	494	16	7	859	26,065	104	144
104	4	9	69	12	8	25	9	1	185	6	6	185	16,069	97	70
294	8	8	74	9	0	107	16	1	476	11	3	409	91,150	52	113
251	10	7	80	2	7	54	7	6	386	0	10	311	28,109	64	139
432	16	1	97	8	2	78	16	10	607	16	1	644	38,847	53	173
134	11	4	89	9	8	31	0	9	179	1	4	818	11,234	51	60
375	7	4	92	16	8	97	0	5	565	8	0	529	38,597	69	194
520	16	0	118	8	11	160	3	2	793	7	1	939	44,814	47	259
23,594	17	5	4,738	0	4	6,349	9	8	34,900	7	5	22,097	1,026,201	60	10,245

No. 7.—Table showing the Expenditure for Provisions, Necessaries, and Clothing of Workhouse Inmates, during the Half-year ended 25th March, 1871 (included in Table No. 2); also, the Number relieved in the Half-year, and the Average Weekly Cost per Head:—163 Unions—*continued.*

Names of Unions.	Cost of Provisions consumed.	Cost of Necessaries expended.	Cost of Clothing.	Total Cost of Provisions, Necessaries, and Clothing.	Total Number of Paupers relieved.	Collective No. of Days for all Paupers relieved in the Half-year.	Average No. of Days of Relief to each Pauper.	Average Daily No. of Paupers in Workhouse.	Average Weekly Cost per head: Provisions and Necessaries.	Average Weekly Cost per head: Clothing.	Average Weekly Cost per head: Total.
Province of Munster:	£ s. d.	£ s. d.	£ s. d.	£ s. d.					s. d.	s. d.	s. d.
Co. of Clare.											
Ballyvaghan,	403 16 0	57 14 2	115 15 4	612 5 6	209	26,794	128	149	2 6½	0 8	3 2½
Corrofin,	291 14 1	50 3 6	86 0 0	428 17 7	278	20,089	74	107	2 4	0 7	2 11½
Ennis,	1,250 11 0	185 13 11	215 0 0	1,655 4 11	908	78,108	81	399	2 9	0 5	3 2
Ennistymon,	745 16 9	131 9 9	201 9 10	1,081 16 6	493	48,856	98	257	2 6½	0 7	3 1
Killadysert,	430 10 8	66 10 9	104 9 8	577 11 1	247	21,911	89	117	3 1	0 8	3 9
Kilrush,	1,028 16 11	108 6 7	115 11 6	1,258 17 0	610	54,596	90	290	2 11	0 3½	3 2½
Scariff,	489 11 4	84 5 4	94 14 6	667 11 1	337	28,975	86	154	2 9	0 5½	3 2½
Tulla,	709 0 6	68 9 0	149 15 7	1,027 6 5	657	44,634	80	239	2 8½	0 5½	3 2
Co. of Cork.											
Bandon,	590 9 10	81 2 6	71 0 7	751 5 11	408	34,094	84	161	2 9½	0 3½	3 1
Bantry,	620 0 11	24 0 6	29 16 8	673 16 1	209	16,707	80	80	5 4	0 3	5 8
Castletown,	384 16 0	34 18 0	64 3 0	484 10 0	859	28,710	34	156	1 11	0 3½	2 3
Clonakilty,	645 19 4	64 16 1	78 15 9	789 9 7	480	37,803	90	201	2 7	0 3½	2 11
Cork,	7,478 1 4	711 19 2	1,414 5 8	9,604 6 2	5,574	396,100	71	2,107	2 10½	0 6	3 4½
Dunmanway,	334 9 5	45 1 6	145 2 9	524 13 11	373	23,917	63	128	2 8	0 10½	3 6
Fermoy,	685 10 5	132 16 2	159 11 9	977 17 0	745	44,678	60	238	2 5	0 6	2 11
Kanturk,	1,286 11 6	259 9 10	235 8 0	1,774 9 4	1,015	75,387	74	401	2 10½	0 5½	3 3½
Kinsale,	451 12 11	72 9 5	89 8 7	614 9 11	481	26,345	55	140	2 10	0 5½	3 3½
Macroom,	475 8 6	73 8 6	109 1 0	652 18 9	498	42,879	86	223	2 5½	0 4	2 9½
Mallow,	1,317 15 6	155 11 3	118 3 4	1,615 19 0	1,116	71,075	61	379	2 10	0 3½	3 2
Midleton,	778 8 0	143 13 6	161 1 3	1,083 9 9	1,001	64,110	64	288	2 4	0 5	2 9
Millstreet,	858 19 8	114 17 11	200 4 3	1,166 1 5	630	49,061	74	250	2 9	0 7	3 4
Mitchelstown,	500 11 1	104 16 5	136 5 9	741 13 3	746	43,618	58	232	1 11	0 5½	2 4½

790	1	2	148	19	7	192	17	7	1,119	16	4	360	46,395	83	948	2	8¾	0	7	3	4¾
985	5	0	36	1	11	56	6	11	379	13	10	177	16,708	106	99	2	4½	0	3½	2	10
668	10	4	142	2	7	257	12	4	1,842	6	8	816	56,031	69	305	2	3¾	0	7	3	0½
884	5	5	51	10	2	50	10	4	486	6	11	372	24,240	65	192	2	6½	0	3½	2	9½
431	10	10	78	11	6	56	13	4	564	15	5	354	27,800	77	145	2	7½	0	3½	2	11
378	1	11	97	17	7	110	0	7	616	0	1	857	36,407	79	140	2	1¾	0	7	2	8¾
1,081	7	8	147	1	8	603	17	8	1,448	6	10	800	57,087	93	304	5	0¼	0	6	3	6½
471	6	0	35	15	6	99	6	0	569	9	6	407	26,984	66	143	2	7½	0	5½	3	1¼
1,126	9	5	274	15	2	310	0	9	1,748	18	4	1,098	81,609	74	434	2	5	0	7	3	0
741	0	11	76	18	6	117	5	2	936	5	7	437	37,082	86	200	3	0½	0	5½	3	5½
879	17	1	74	14	1	107	6	10	501	18	0	310	21,828	70	116	2	11	0	8½	3	7¼
1,789	16	6	171	14	3	430	1	10	2,394	12	9	1,337	100,252	67	549	2	6¾	0	7	3	1¾
4,757	4	7	419	11	0	881	11	6	6,058	7	1	4,831	288,104	59	1,601	2	6½	0	5½	3	0
828	10	10	134	9	10	616	10	7	1,577	11	3	639	43,450	69	231	2	1¼	*1	11½	5	1
683	15	6	128	8	0	131	16	9	1,148	14	8	729	44,176	56	284	3	4½	0	5½	3	9½
289	13	11	84	0	10	42	0	0	495	18	9	250	23,429	91	125	2	6½	0	5	2	11½
1,073	19	11	307	19	11	249	9	3	1,631	9	3	1,081	68,745	64	366	2	7½	0	6	3	1½
1,817	18	9	310	1	5	347	2	0	2,375	2	2	1,142	97,193	85	517	2	9¼	0	6	3	3½
771	1	4	131	16	9	162	15	6	1,065	13	7	839	45,676	82	242	2	9½	0	6	3	3½
1,301	14	6	265	17	6	261	6	2	2,128	16	3	1,385	90,991	66	461	2	8½	0	6½	3	3½
1,139	15	6	201	18	2	149	14	10	1,344	8	5	864	72,033	83	383	2	8½	0	3½	3	0
328	5	11	130	17	8	180	15	0	639	16	7	433	31,147	73	167	2	11½	0	9½	3	9
722	0	5	129	0	5	138	5	9	1,001	6	7	589	43,267	73	233	2	8½	0	6	3	2½
1,330	2	3	134	16	0	631	8	6	1,890	6	9	1,253	79,316	63	423	2	8½	0	7	3	3½
1,191	14	6	134	15	8	247	0	0	1,565	9	8	1,133	67,280	60	336	2	9	0	6	3	3
349	7	5	68	11	8	116	8	4	734	7	5	498	26,840	54	143	3	2½	0	7½	3	10
351	6	11	65	6	11	143	11	2	760	7	0	359	34,154	65	183	2	6	0	7	3	1
2,836	16	3	209	11	6	471	19	6	8,317	10	5	2,107	137,864	73	617	2	6½	0	5½	3	2½
51,019	7	0	6,780	1	9	10,743	14	10	68,384	3	7	42,304	2,972,930	71	15,720	2	8½	0	6	3	2½

No. 7.—Table showing the Expenditure for Provisions, Necessaries, and Clothing of Workhouse Inmates, during the Half-year ended 25th March, 1871 (included in Table No. 2); also, the Number relieved in the Half-year, and the Average Weekly Cost per Head:—163 Unions—*continued.*

Names of Unions.	Cost of Provisions consumed.	Cost of Necessaries consumed.	Cost of Clothing.	Total Cost of Provisions, Necessaries, and Clothing.	Total Number of Paupers relieved.	Collective No. of Days for all Paupers relieved in the Half-year.	Average No. of Days of Relief to each Pauper.	Average Daily No. of Paupers in Workhouse.	Average Weekly Cost per head: Provisions and Necessaries.	Average Weekly Cost per head: Clothing.	Average Weekly Cost per head: Total.
Province of Leinster.	£ s. d.	£ s. d.	£ s. d.	£ s. d.					s. d.	s. d.	s. d.
Co. of Carlow.											
Carlow,	1,839 17 2	244 14 9	342 18 4	1,887 10 6	1,462	65,840	45	360	3 1½	0 6½	3 10½
Co. of Dublin.											
Balrothery,	636 6 5	92 0 9	160 14 5	888 10 7	1,045	38,673	90	205	2 7½	0 7	3 2½
Dublin, North,	6,892 11 7	683 16 11	940 5 0	8,461 18 6	4,058	350,809	68	1,885	3 0	0 4½	3 4½
Dublin, South,	11,934 2 10	1,394 0 7	2,210 6 9	15,534 10 2	5,791	533,773	93	2,946	3 4½	0 6	3 11½
Rathdown,	2,005 5 1	204 17 3	489 10 0	2,163 17 4	1,809	94,032	68	500	3 4½	0 6½	4 1½
Co. of Kildare.											
Athy,	971 16 1	140 19 5	239 10 1	1,348 9 7	798	55,189	69	294	2 9½	0 7	3 4½
Celbridge,	624 9 6	30 2 1	132 9 2	1,007 0 9	853	51,697	57	169	3 9½	0 6	4 0½
Naas,	829 16 1	178 0 10	163 7 5	1,671 4 4	1,308	80,589	43	271	3 0½	0 5½	3 6
Co. of Kilkenny.											
Callan,	926 9 9	169 12 7	202 7 8	1,311 10 0	794	48,579	62	256	2 11	0 7	3 6
Castlecomer,	496 6 10	140 11 9	164 13 0	808 10 7	393	25,844	61	187	3 4½	1 0	4 4½
Kilkenny,	1,798 6 4	276 6 8	578 17 1	2,869 9 7	1,541	88,614	60	488	3 1½	0 10½	4 0
Thomastown,	686 14 9	97 19 5	157 1 11	941 16 1	662	41,607	63	232	2 7½	0 6½	3 1½
Urlingford,	631 3 2	69 7 7	184 0 11	884 11 8	429	84,030	76	170	3 0½	0 6½	3 7½
King's County.											
Edenderry,	619 3 1	54 14 3	102 2 7	775 19 11	716	35,034	49	190	2 8½	0 5	3 1½
Parsonstown,	819 12 7	164 9 3	105 9 10	1,089 11 8	531	50,536	92	209	2 6½	0 6½	3 0
Tullamore,	1,131 17 5	151 9 3	200 17 5	1,484 4 1	1,365	67,657	49	369	2 8	0 5	3 1

Co. of Longford.											
Ballymahon, . .	335 14 2	91 16 11	89 11 9	517 8 3	408	91,501	53	114	9 0½	0 7	3 4½
Granard, . .	735 3 11	188 9 5	132 5 0	983 18 4	608	41,844	51	219	2 11	0 5½	3 1½
Longford, . .	771 11 1	160 5 7	249 0 0	1,180 17 6	946	53,192	58	263	2 0½	0 7½	3 1½
Co. of Louth.											
Ardee, . .	1,110 16 6	130 16 10	217 18 5	1,458 18 8	1,745	56,277	80	278	3 4½	0 7	3 11½
Drogheda, . .	1,308 14 7	110 10 4	239 18 8	1,646 3 7	2,089	72,619	68	388	2 8	0 6	3 2
Dundalk, . .	904 15 6	187 14 8	170 16 11	1,199 6 1	1,468	64,619	86	281	3 0½	0 5½	3 2
Co. of Meath.											
Dunshaughlin, . .	399 5 6	102 4 7	129 10 0	747 0 0	1,169	99,216	24	161	3 1	0 7½	3 6½
Kells, . .	639 9 11	176 4 11	246 1 0	1,104 15 10	638	39,083	70	208	3 1	0 10½	3 11½
Navan, . .	648 7 6	114 1 1	150 5 9	1,101 14 4	1,049	40,370	91	216	3 6½	0 6½	3 10
Oldcastle, . .	516 8 6	149 11 3	116 0 6	773 15 8	409	38,047	81	176	2 9½	0 8	3 3½
Trim, . .	880 15 9½	154 16 9	184 16 1	1,280 8 0½	1,006	41,180	69	210	3 6½	0 7½	4 1½
Queen's County.											
Abbeyleix, . .	492 17 1	196 5 8	98 15 9	648 15 11	495	23,918	56	187	5 2½	0 7	3 9½
Donaghmore, . .	397 13 10	63 19 1	48 10 8	510 3 7	419	14,605	62	77	4 8½	0 8½	4 11½
Mountmellick, . .	1,396 18 2	258 9 7	330 19 9	1,918 13 0	1,141	71,919	63	379	3 1	0 8	3 9
Co. of Westmeath.											
Athlone, . .	696 10 7	160 16 11	283 6 5	1,311 3 11	808	58,764	65	310	2 8	0 7	3 1
Delvin, . .	401 15 11	74 1 8	100 0 0	575 17 7	680	29,319	88	110	2 11½	0 7½	3 7½
Mullingar, . .	949 1 2	220 4 9	297 10 11	1,459 16 10	958	68,309	68	335	3 7½	0 8	3 3½
Co. of Wexford.											
Enniscorthy, . .	730 6 11	148 15 8	257 10 10	1,137 3 5	985	57,118	58	304	2 3	0 7	2 10
Gorey, . .	900 18 5	111 0 9	198 11 3	1,210 17 5	710	47,665	67	253	2 11½	0 7	3 6½
New Ross, . .	1,479 17 6	181 16 6	337 0 0	1,998 16 0	1,012	60,580	80	489	2 10½	0 7	3 5½
Wexford, . .	1,223 10 0	136 14 0	400 0 0	1,820 4 0	1,041	74,567	71	397	3 6½	0 9	3 5½
Co. of Wicklow.											
Baltinglass, . .	793 6 11	103 10 1	235 1 9	1,131 18 9	839	30,895	47	310	3 3	0 10	4 1
Rathdrum, . .	1,207 4 5	114 0 0	377 9 7	1,798 14 0	1,282	60,397	49	891	3 1½	0 10½	4 0
Shillelagh, . .	553 6 5	110 8 3	120 0 0	788 8 8	619	34,385	57	184	3 8½	0 6½	3 2½
Total Leinster (40 Unions),	52,752 13 7½	7,505 7 1	11,330 3 6	71,147 4 9½	17,238	2,757,010	58	14,010	3 0½	0 7	3 7½

[continued.

No. 7.—Table showing the Expenditure for Provisions, Necessaries, and Clothing of Workhouse Inmates, during the Half-year ended 25th March, 1871 (included in Table No. 2); also, the Number relieved in the Half-year, and the Average Weekly Cost per Head;—163 Unions—*continued*.

Names of Unions.	Cost of Provisions consumed.	Cost of Necessaries consumed.	Cost of Clothing.	Total Cost of Provisions, Necessaries, and Clothing.	Total Number of Paupers relieved.	Collective No. of Days for all Paupers relieved in the Half-year.	Average No. of Days of Relief to each Pauper.	Average Daily No. of Paupers in Workhouse.	Average Weekly Cost per head: Provisions and Necessaries.	Average Weekly Cost per head: Clothing.	Average Weekly Cost per head: Total.
PROVINCE OF CONNAUGHT:	£ s. d.	£ s. d.	£ s. d.	£ s. d.					s. d.	s. d.	s. d.
Co. of Galway.											
Ballinasloe, . .	798 8 1	104 9 9	139 10 5	1,018 7 3	606	48,578	80	267	2 6½	0 5	2 11½
Clifden, . . .	394 2 9	48 13 3	51 0 2	496 10 9	289	23,928	80	188	2 4	0 3½	2 7½
Galway, . . .	1,155 15 1	132 18 9	128 2 0	1,416 15 10	625	71,734	67	391	2 6	0 3	2 9
Glennamaddy, . .	463 10 0	43 5 0	93 15 8	600 14 9	387	31,504	81	168	2 2½	0 5	2 7½
Gort, . . .	446 9 6	75 9 3	58 6 5	580 5 5	339	27,996	83	149	2 7½	0 3½	2 10½
Loughrea, . .	379 8 3	63 17 11	71 7 8	525 18 10	440	25,424	58	136	2 6	0 4½	2 10½
Mount Bellew, . .	353 9 11	59 5 5	93 3 9	505 18 1	390	26,670	68	142	2 9½	0 5½	2 8
Oughterard, . .	370 0 0	40 12 5	43 0 11	474 13 4	183	24,990	129	133	2 5½	0 2½	2 8
Portumna, . .	397 12 6	60 5 8	76 19 2	534 10 7	258	21,316	85	180	2 7½	0 5½	3 0½
Tuam, . . .	841 4 10	139 10 0	168 14 6	1,159 9 8	080	61,765	75	078	2 7½	0 0	2 1½
Co. of Leitrim.											
Carrick-on-Shannon, .	488 5 5	60 0 1	102 10 1	650 19 5	441	32,698	75	178	2 3½	0 5½	2 8
Manorhamilton, .	297 5 3	73 3 0	92 11 9	463 0 0	280	22,132	77	118	2 4	0 7	2 11
Mohill, . . .	440 8 0	88 0 0	169 11 0	668 5 0	405	31,092	67	165	2 4½	0 7	2 11½
Co. of Mayo.											
Ballina, . . .	371 12 9	60 16 0	67 18 6	500 7 3	411	28,522	69	157	2 1½	0 4	2 6½
Ballinrobe, . .	693 1 1	128 8 8	119 8 7	941 18 4	503	41,509	79	227	2 7	0 4½	2 11½
Belmullet, . .	231 16 7	53 8 9	45 5 4	335 10 8	217	19,480	90	103	2 1	0 4	2 5
Castlebar, . .	530 7 6	53 4 0	70 8 9	653 0 9	281	23,007	84	126	2 4	0 5	2 9
Claremorris, . .	370 14 5	55 5 11	54 5 5	480 6 9	283	23,816	81	131	2 7½	0 4	2 11½
Killala, . . .	246 5 11	30 1 8	30 14 5	306 0 0	145	14,740	102	76	2 7½	0 3½	2 10½
Newport, . . .	198 8 3	63 15 6	57 8 11	329 12 10	149	12,580	84	67	2 3	0 5	2 8
Swinford, . .	345 16 0	61 19 9	136 7 4	574 3 1	394	34,696	63	181	2 6½	0 8½	3 3
Westport, . .	425 8 8	51 13 0	136 0 2	613 10 10	370	32,750	89	174	2 0½	0 7	2 7½

	£	s.	d.	£	s.	d.	£	s.	d.	£	s.	d.					s.	d.	s.	d.	s.	d.
Co. of Roscommon.																						
Boyle, . . .	687	0	5	188	17	5	223	14	5	1,049	18	4	514	47,728	63	234	2	5	0	8	3	1
Castlerea, . . .	643	10	1	180	10	10	125	5	7	889	12	6	647	39,582	73	210	2	6½	0	5½	3	1½
Roscommon, . .	1,022	19	0	196	0	0	216	6	8	1,486	6	8	708	60,758	86	323	2	5½	0	6	3	3¼
Strokestown, . .	621	17	9	122	1	8	112	4	11	856	4	4	615	37,490	78	200	2	9¾	0	5	3	2¾
Co. of Sligo.																						
Dromore, West, .	185	1	1	23	9	2	28	15	3	811	5	0	113	10,686	97	68	2	6	0	3½	3	0½
Sligo, . . .	728	10	3	161	1	4	400	7	8	1,209	19	3	889	68,085	94	314	2	1½	0	11¼	3	1
Tobercurry, . .	225	7	0	21	9	8	29	4	8	278	1	4	221	16,370	72	87	2	1½	0	3	2	4½
Total Connaught (39 Unions).	14,163	17	0	2,285	19	0	3,079	10	9	19,529	18	9	11,863	940,460	81	5,008	2	5¼	0	5½	2	11

SUMMARY OF PROVINCES.

	£	s.	d.	£	s.	d.	£	s.	d.	£	s.	d.					s.	d.	s.	d.	s.	d.
Ulster, . .	23,504	17	5	4,755	0	4	6,549	9	8	34,900	7	5	32,697	1,926,201	60	10,246	2	0½	0	5¼	2	0½
Munster, . .	51,019	7	0	6,790	1	0	10,785	14	10	68,683	8	7	42,364	2,092,030	71	15,920	2	8¼	0	6	3	2¼
Leinster, . .	52,288	13	7½	7,505	7	1	11,859	3	6	71,147	4	2½	47,289	2,757,970	56	14,670	3	0½	0	7	3	7½
Connaught, . .	14,163	17	6	2,285	10	0	3,079	10	6	19,529	12	8	11,863	940,466	81	6,004	2	5¼	0	5½	2	11
Total Ireland (163 Unions),	111,600	13	6½	21,317	6	2	31,712	4	9	194,110	6	5½	133,362	6,817,370	65	45,638	2	7¼	6	6¼	3	1¾

No. 8.—Table showing the Expenditure for Provisions, Necessaries, and Clothing of Workhouse Inmates, during the Half-year ended 29th September, 1871 (included in Table No. 3); also, the Number relieved in the Half-year, and the Average Weekly Cost per Head:—163 Unions.

Name of Union.	Cost of Provisions consumed.	Cost of Necessaries consumed.	Cost of Clothing.	Total Cost of Provisions, Necessaries, and Clothing.	Total Number of Paupers relieved.	Collective No. of Days for all Paupers relieved in the Half-year.	Average No. of Days of Relief to each Pauper.	Average Daily No. of Paupers in Workhouse.	Average Weekly Cost per head. Provisions and Necessaries.	Average Weekly Cost per head. Clothing.	Average Weekly Cost per head. Total.
Province of Ulster:	£ s. d.	£ s. d.	£ s. d.	£ s. d.					s. d.	s. d.	s. d.
Co. of Antrim.											
Antrim, . . .	770 9 9	153 3 7	187 10 6	1,110 2 10	963	53,007	55	279	2 5½	0 6	2 11½
Ballycastle, . .	286 2 11	60 9 5	84 6 9	430 18 1	231	20,917	68	111	2 3½	0 6½	2 10½
Ballymena, . .	555 14 7	120 0 4	185 15 6	861 10 5	681	51,018	76	271	1 10½	0 6	2 4½
Ballymoney, . .	207 6 8	67 10 7	129 16 9	404 14 0	537	26,105	49	139	1 5	0 9	2 2
Belfast, . . .	5,968 7 10	890 18 3	1,201 5 2	8,060 11 3	7,804	384,403	49	2,045	2 6	0 5½	2 11½
Larne, . . .	600 4 8	98 8 4	169 15 3	867 3 3	514	41,360	80	220	2 4½	0 7	2 11½
Lisburn, . . .	663 8 9	114 19 7	197 18 3	975 10 7	1,113	47,499	43	253	2 0	0 7	2 7
Co. of Armagh.											
Armagh, . . .	806 10 0	153 13 0	145 18 10	1,106 1 10	876	62,709	72	334	2 1½	0 4	2 5½
Lurgan, . . .	786 9 1	169 5 6	102 0 8	1,060 16 7	1,541	59,608	39	317	2 3	0 3	2 6
Co. of Cavan.											
Bailieborough, . .	341 15 6	56 12 8	67 18 1	419 3 0	407	48,177	57	125	2 5½	0 5	2 10½
Bawnboy, . . .	236 14 11	50 8 8	184 18 7	472 1 6	347	17,485	50	93	2 8½	1 1	3 9½
Cavan, . . .	706 18 4	99 8 5	196 18 2	1,002 19 0	867	47,256	55	261	2 4½	0 7	2 11½
Cootehill, . .	478 2 10	48 9 7	78 11 5	605 3 10	804	20,831	58	111	2 6	0 5½	2 7½
Co. of Donegal.											
Ballyshannon, . .	334 6 4	90 14 4	66 19 11	491 0 7	336	32,156	61	171	1 10½	0 3½	2 1½
Donegal, . . .	187 3 1	44 17 3	53 14 6	285 14 10	191	18,024	68	89	2 5½	0 7	3 0½
Dunfanaghy, . .	78 12 3	19 5 2	18 0 0	116 17 5	65	5,047	108	34	2 4	0 5	2 9
Glenties, . . .	226 0 1	36 8 3	46 12 4	309 0 8	204	18,680	90	106	1 10½	0 4	2 2½
Inishowen, . .	330 15 11	85 16 11	61 3 0	477 17 10	301	26,081	85	137	2 0	0 4	2 4
Letterkenny, . .	285 14 7	76 0 11	95 4 1	456 19 7	277	18,314	66	97	2 9	0 8½	3 5½

171	17	9	48	3	8	56	13	6	875	16	9	166	15,868	93	43
116	16	11	39	7	2	25	17	10	175	1	11	216	16,425	55	64
559	16	3	68	1	0	160	17	4	768	16	7	905	36,208	40	183
761	16	8	74	11	5	170	9	6	1,006	10	8	761	47,036	63	243
208	2	10	21	15	11	40	12	9	278	11	6	339	17,067	31	91
1,039	19	8	149	12	11	389	11	0	1,648	16	2	2,005	78,047	39	436
680	6	11	103	9	1	156	11	6	1,189	7	6	1,044	66,765	63	350
553	2	9	116	13	7	91	10	9	701	12	1	338	43,078	78	274
107	12	7	31	17	5	40	1	9	250	11	9	269	11,876	44	76
201	15	8	77	19	9	64	7	4	843	15	9	388	15,480	40	89
640	19	4	116	16	10	200	1	1	937	17	3	774	48,016	61	256
818	4	9	104	12	9	306	19	1	1,224	16	0	1,227	65,575	54	649
315	10	5	71	3	6	135	6	2	555	0	1	628	63,194	55	177
291	1	9	78	17	6	25	10	0	389	6	10	540	88,904	49	140
284	10	6	35	7	9	64	12	6	384	10	8	440	16,104	41	95
430	10	11	76	15	10	65	3	1	572	9	10	785	31,871	40	160
256	19	10	30	9	1	29	13	1	336	16	0	474	10,344	41	102
306	9	5	67	13	10	62	16	2	436	9	5	301	29,128	97	156
104	1	6	25	19	6	19	4	2	149	5	1	158	19,715	80	66
256	16	4	48	13	3	68	2	11	363	9	6	374	16,134	18	95
282	18	5	66	11	5	63	16	9	422	18	6	397	25,771	76	137
449	11	1	65	15	6	83	0	6	658	12	10	794	37,320	47	199
318	19	6	24	17	8	18	10	8	169	7	10	925	9,790	43	57
448	11	3	61	4	8	79	18	5	583	14	4	801	38,258	60	193
304	16	11	60	4	6	115	13	1	720	14	5	1,051	40,789	39	217
5,835	1	0	4,091	5	2	6,719	3	6	33,746	10	2	33,144	1,763,767	53	9,393

No. 8.—Table showing the Expenditure for Provisions, Necessaries, and Clothing of Workhouse Inmates, during the Half-year ended 29th September, 1871 (included in Table No. 3); also, the Number relieved in the Half-year, and the Average Weekly Cost per Head:—163 Unions—*continued*.

Name of Union.	Cost of Provisions consumed.	Cost of Necessaries consumed.	Cost of Clothing.	Total Cost of Provisions, Necessaries, and Clothing.	Total Number of Paupers relieved.	Collective No. of Days for all Paupers relieved in the Half-year.	Average No. of Days of Relief to each Pauper.	Average Daily No. of Paupers in Workhouse.	Average Weekly Cost per head: Provisions and Necessaries.	Average Weekly Cost per head: Clothing.	Average Weekly Cost per head: Total.
Province of Munster:	£ s. d.	£ s. d.	£ s. d.	£ s. d.					s. d.	s. d.	s. d.
Co. of Clare.											
Ballyvaghan, . . .	444 1 3	40 16 7	92 8 10	577 6 8	250	28,069	127	142	2 5	0 5½	2 10½
Corrofin, . . .	322 8 9	37 11 5	80 0 0	439 17 7	281	20,349	72	108	2 5½	0 6½	3 0
Ennis, . . .	1,450 3 1	114 10 9	168 8 4	1,733 2 7	1,025	74,342	73	890	2 11½	0 4½	3 3½
Ennistymon, . . .	904 1 8	110 8 10	203 16 7	1,218 1 1	508	49,919	98	280	2 10½	0 7	3 5½
Killadysert, . . .	422 16 6	41 12 4	103 15 6	568 4 4	255	21,763	85	116	3 0	0 8	3 8
Kilrush, . . .	968 13 5	63 17 9	110 7 7	1,160 18 9	583	52,948	91	282	2 9½	0 3½	3 0½
Scariff, . . .	521 16 6	53 16 6	80 17 4	656 7 5	333	30,378	91	163	2 7½	0 4½	3 0
Tulla, . . .	892 3 4	70 16 4	113 16 1	1,077 0 0	592	64,202	75	835	3 0½	0 4½	3 5
Co. of Cork.											
Bandon, . . .	628 1 7	53 11 9	73 0 5	754 18 9	641	35,051	55	156	2 8½	0 3½	3 0½
Bantry, . . .	231 19 11	18 19 3	29 14 5	280 13 6	341	16,844	49	89	2 1½	0 5	2 6½
Castletown, . . .	276 3 1	28 16 4	60 4 8	405 8 7	360	24,101	67	128	2 0½	0 3½	2 4
Clonakilty, . . .	612 11 9	50 16 8	108 9 0	771 19 5	479	39,042	82	208	2 4½	0 4½	2 9½
Cork, . . .	7,280 6 3	114 16 7	1,501 17 8	8,347 8 1	8,333	872,447	59	1,961	2 11½	0 7	3 6½
Dunmanway, . . .	282 3 0	41 6 10	141 3 2	464 16 0	303	22,585	74	120	2 0	0 10½	2 10½
Fermoy, . . .	644 0 4	102 6 0	150 6 8	896 17 0	856	42,191	49	231	2 5½	0 6	2 11½
Kanturk, . . .	1,134 4 1	176 6 10	141 19 8	1,452 8 7	1,000	67,864	68	369	2 6½	0 3½	3 0
Kinsale, . . .	411 13 10	80 4 9	78 6 4	534 4 11	376	23,141	62	123	2 9½	0 5½	3 3½
Macroom, . . .	702 16 2	49 6 8	100 8 4	852 4 9	570	42,012	74	221	2 6	0 4	2 10
Mallow, . . .	1,190 19 10	226 18 7	280 7 0	1,600 3 5	1,280	67,281	56	338	2 9	0 7	3 4
Midleton, . . .	784 17 11	112 6 1	162 8 4	1,050 9 4	1,157	54,572	47	290	2 3½	0 6	2 9½
Millstreet, . . .	796 6 2	98 10 6	129 17 9	1,024 13 11	735	41,536	57	221	3 0½	0 5½	3 5½
Mitchelstown, . . .	535 10 8	66 19 1	138 16 6	701 4 6	843	36,868	46	207	2 3	0 6	2 9

Skibbereen,	765 17 8	118 13 8	195 15 11	1,090 6 6	599	46,962	79	230	2 7½	0 7	3 3½
Skull,	236 3 11	28 11 8	53 10 6	315 6 3	169	17,130	101	91	2 1½	0 5½	3 7
Youghal,	752 15 2	96 19 0	228 12 10	1,078 0 0	912	50,015	55	206	2 4½	0 7½	3 0
Co. of Kerry.											
Cahersiveen,	336 5 6	49 15 9	47 18 5	433 19 8	381	23,022	60	179	2 5½	0 8½	2 9
Dingle,	478 10 9	64 4 4	57 2 11	599 17 5	366	37,430	75	146	2 9½	0 8½	3 0½
Kenmare,	346 10 8	23 18 1	49 11 5	422 14 0	450	21,594	47	114	2 0½	0 8½	2 9½
Killarney,	1,179 11 10	115 18 9	276 16 1	1,313 6 8	744	58,548	79	311	3 1½	0 8	3 9½
Listowel,	510 17 6	97 14 0	88 5 9	606 17 3	430	27,225	61	146	2 8½	0 4½	3 1½
Tralee,	918 17 0	203 5 0	534 18 7	1,659 0 7	1,090	73,162	69	400	2 1	1 0	3 1
Co. of Limerick.											
Croom,	798 14 0	142 10 10	129 15 6	1,001 0 8	587	42,486	72	228	2 10½	0 5½	3 3½
Glin,	361 7 7	44 16 1	55 5 11	461 9 7	324	20,076	70	110	2 10½	0 4½	3 3
Kilmallock,	1,778 16 11	170 1 9	408 19 10	2,367 18 6	1,486	98,398	67	523	2 9½	0 7	3 4½
Limerick,	4,909 6 8	355 0 6	810 18 8	6,074 5 4	4,848	259,499	56	1,360	2 10	0 6½	3 8½
Newcastle,	835 11 4	123 15 8	122 16 6	1,082 2 2	676	41,231	61	219	3 3	0 5	3 6
Rathkeale,	864 12 1	108 0 3	118 2 10	1,085 15 2	767	37,903	49	201	3 7	0 5½	4 0½
Co. of Tipperary.											
Borrisokane,	375 2 4	41 17 11	78 5 0	493 5 3	285	21,256	73	114	2 6½	0 6	3 3½
Carrick-on-Suir,	1,093 11 2	102 12 5	280 9 0	1,405 12 7	1,076	59,659	55	317	2 7½	0 8	3 3½
Cashel,	1,647 16 7	217 1 4	184 11 11	2,019 9 10	1,366	88,808	70	471	2 11½	0 3½	3 2½
Clogheen,	732 4 10	86 3 0	162 9 9	1,000 17 7	681	45,407	67	212	2 7	0 6	3 1
Clonmel,	1,330 14 2	206 7 4	262 10 8	1,799 15 2	1,416	81,053	57	431	2 7½	0 5½	3 1½
Nenagh,	1,249 14 3	142 17 0	175 13 7	1,569 4 10	920	69,082	75	368	2 10	0 4½	3 2½
Roscrea,	526 13 10	83 16 4	161 2 2	771 14 4	394	29,503	75	157	2 10½	0 9½	3 8
Thurles,	759 4 10	70 7 8	152 2 6	982 15 0	593	42,591	72	237	2 8½	0 6	3 2½
Tipperary,	1,361 6 7	149 19 6	232 1 9	1,743 7 2	1,297	74,259	57	395	2 10½	0 5½	3 3½
Co. of Waterford.											
Dungarvan,	937 16 6	99 13 7	170 0 0	1,207 10 1	1,017	53,808	35	297	2 7½	0 5	3 0½
Kilmacthomas,	567 9 10	54 17 9	137 12 5	760 0 0	545	28,841	53	159	3 0½	0 8	3 6½
Lismore,	519 0 8	67 18 8	129 5 8	716 4 7	598	31,023	60	165	2 7½	0 7	3 2½
Waterford,	2,891 16 9	195 3 2	519 16 8	3,406 17 2	2,241	139,772	63	613	2 7½	0 5½	3 1½
Total Munster (30 Unions),	50,806 1 2	5,248 14 0	9,108 7 4	65,481 9 5	44,742	2,533,043	63	15,093	2 9	0 5½	3 2½

[continued.

No. 8.—Table showing the Expenditure for Provisions, Necessaries, and Clothing of Workhouse Inmates, during the Half-year ended 29th September, 1871 (included in Table No. 3); also, the Number relieved in the Half-year, and the Average Weekly Cost per Head:—163 Unions—*continued.*

Names of Unions.	Cost of Provisions consumed. £ s. d.	Cost of Necessaries consumed. £ s. d.	Cost of Clothing. £ s. d.	Total Cost of Provisions, Necessaries, and Clothing. £ s. d.	Total Number of Paupers relieved.	Collective No. of Days for all Paupers relieved in the Half-year.	Average No. of Days of Relief to each Pauper.	Average Daily No. of Paupers in Workhouse.	Average Weekly Cost per head: Provisions and Necessaries. s. d.	Clothing. s. d.	Total. s. d.
Province of Leinster:											
Co. of Carlow.											
Carlow,	1,330 3 6	167 4 0	352 14 5	1,850 1 11	1,078	61,088	57	337	3 4½	0 8½	4 1
Co. of Dublin.											
Balrothery,	645 18 11	80 11 3	165 2 8	891 12 10	2,386	39,639	17	211	2 7	0 7	3 2
Dublin, North,	7,599 1 2	445 0 7	963 16 1	9,007 17 10	4,410	355,089	81	1,959	3 2	0 4½	3 6½
Dublin, South,	11,846 0 8	1,360 4 10	3,164 14 6	16,371 0 0	6,328	535,210	85	2,963	3 5½	0 10	4 3½
Rathdown,	2,021 3 5	201 2 2	464 5 10	2,686 11 5	1,763	88,144	50	474	3 8	0 6½	4 2½
Co. of Kildare.											
Athy,	858 5 1	130 11 8	224 3 10	1,213 0 9	1,055	53,808	52	296	2 10½	0 7	3 5½
Celbridge,	698 18 8	117 13 2	136 10 4	953 2 2	600	30,006	50	160	3 9½	0 7½	4 5
Naas,	952 13 5	140 17 9	125 16 2	1,219 7 0	1,009	50,386	31	282	3 0½	0 4½	3 4¾
Co. of Kilkenny.											
Callan,	881 4 1	106 3 1	191 11 5	1,178 18 7	989	45,377	49	245	3 0	0 7	3 7
Castlecomer,	528 19 5	89 1 7	114 3 3	731 4 3	648	27,387	50	150	3 2	0 7	3 9
Kilkenny,	1,734 8 6	183 15 10	312 3 6	2,230 8 5	1,842	87,390	47	485	3 0½	0 6	3 6½
Thomastown,	667 8 5	83 9 11	94 3 11	845 2 3	780	41,005	53	218	3 2	0 8¼	3 10½
Urlingford,	615 6 0	51 3 4	125 6 1	791 15 5	414	29,559	71	137	3 2	0 7	3 9
King's County.											
Edenderry,	627 15 0	48 7 8	93 7 0	769 9 8	812	32,761	40	174	2 10½	0 4¾	3 3¼
Parsonstown,	817 10 9	126 18 4	102 11 9	1,047 0 10	582	49,342	84	269	2 8½	0 3¼	2 11¾
Tullamore,	1,049 3 0	102 10 11	173 0 6	1,324 14 5	1,274	61,160	48	325	2 7¾	0 5	3 0¾

Co. of Longford											
Ballymahon, . .	405 4 6	51 4 3	96 4 7	559 13 4	519	23,095	44	123	9 8½	0 7	8 4½
Granard, . . .	603 17 6	136 1 2	181 3 0	940 1 6	619	57,934	73	209	2 9½	0 6	3 5½
Longford, . .	744 3 3	124 17 7	199 10 0	1,067 10 10	922	48,168	69	246	2 6½	0 7	3 1½
Co. of Louth.											
Ardee, . . .	1,014 11 0	87 6 1	126 9 11	1,228 9 0	1,786	44,479	25	287	3 5½	0 4½	3 10½
Drogheda, . .	1,281 17 6	84 12 11	231 7 4	1,597 17 11	8,046	62,216	23	366	2 8½	0 5½	3 2½
Dundalk, . . .	786 4 5	120 3 4	171 16 6	1,078 4 9	1,467	40,386	34	263	2 6½	0 6½	3 0½
Co. of Meath.											
Dunshaughlin, . .	543 15 1	113 15 0	112 9 11	770 0 0	1,338	28,025	20	143	5 5	0 7	4 0
Kells, . . .	743 0 5	122 9 3	134 6 1	1,020 4 9	565	36,390	64	193	3 4	0 7	3 11
Navan, . . .	808 1 6	90 8 4	224 10 6	1,116 0 0	2,311	58,114	17	209	3 3½	0 10	4 1½
Oldcastle, . .	543 10 8	129 6 1	122 11 6	795 6 3	453	34,892	78	163	2 9	0 6	3 3
Trim, . . .	974 17 2	118 4 5	115 14 10	1,203 16 5	1,163	39,093	34	206	5 10½	0 6	4 8½
Queen's County.											
Abbeyleix, . .	404 8 10	86 5 1	107 15 9	698 9 6	659	23,859	48	138	3 1½	0 7	3 8½
Donaghmore, . .	489 4 1	43 18 9	46 18 11	580 1 9	282	16,814	66	84	4 6½	0 5	4 11½
Mountmellick, . .	1,225 19 10	140 15 7	268 5 4	1,634 13 9	1,169	64,384	55	348	2 11½	0 7	3 6½
Co. of Westmeath.											
Athlone, . . .	796 14 2	116 6 1	189 2 6	1,104 1 9	928	62,734	57	290	2 5	0 6	2 11
Delvin, . . .	391 9 7	76 12 11	100 0 0	568 2 6	559	20,853	37	111	3 1½	0 8	3 9½
Mullingar, . .	968 9 2	136 12 2	330 9 9	1,434 11 1	856	66,909	66	303	2 8½	0 10	3 6½
Co. of Wexford.											
Enniscorthy, . .	720 5 11	180 1 6	214 15 5	1,115 2 10	907	61,540	52	274	2 5½	0 7	3 0½
Gorey, . . .	692 10 8	91 1 10	229 1 4	1,012 2 5	734	43,769	60	213	3 1½	0 8½	3 10½
New Ross, . .	1,434 4 10	137 18 0	220 0 0	1,811 17 10	985	77,886	79	414	2 10½	0 4½	3 3
Wexford, . . .	1,416 4 11	108 14 5	400 0 0	1,954 19 4	1,208	81,865	63	435	2 8½	0 8½	3 4½
Co. of Wicklow.											
Baltinglass, . .	712 8 2	177 13 6	228 4 6	1,118 6 2	1,004	38,349	88	204	3 3	0 10	4 1
Rathdrum, . .	1,073 2 11	113 14 4	214 10 7	1,401 7 10	1,245	51,487	41	274	3 2½	0 7	3 9½
Shillelagh, . .	641 9 7	78 8 1	145 3 8	865 14 11	485	34,347	71	163	2 11½	0 7	3 6½
Total Leinster (40 Unions),	32,686 0 6	6,139 16 4	11,249 11 4	70,076 8 2	52,118	2,036,297	51	14,124	3 1½	0 7	3 8½

[continued.

No. 6.—Table showing the Expenditure for Provisions, Necessaries, and Clothing of Workhouse Inmates, during the Half-Year ended 29th September, 1871 (included in Table No. 8); also, the Number relieved in the Half-year, and the Average Weekly Cost per Head:—163 Unions—*continued.*

Name of Union.	Cost of Provisions consumed.	Cost of Necessaries consumed.	Cost of Clothing.	Total Cost of Provisions, Necessaries, and Clothing.	Total Number of Paupers relieved.	Collective No. of Days for all Paupers relieved in the Half-year.	Average No. of Days of Relief to each Pauper.	Average Daily No. of Paupers in Workhouse.	Average Weekly cost per head: Provisions and Necessaries.	Average Weekly cost per head: Clothing.	Average Weekly cost per head: Total.
Province of Connaught:	£ s. d.	£ s. d.	£ s. d.	£ s. d.					s. d.	s. d.	s. d.
Co. of Galway.											
Ballinasloe,	609 11 6	56 10 4	184 13 4	993 16 1	636	48,309	78	257	2 0	0 4	2 10
Clifden,*	309 9 7	63 0 0	46 12 5	400 8 0	249	23,139	67	184	2 5	0 3	2 8
Galway,*	1,140 4 3	161 19 2	101 11 9	1,383 16 2	859	66,266	79	363	2 7	0 2	2 9
Glennamaddy,	461 11 9	66 0 1	64 6 10	601 18 8	441	30,934	70	165	2 5	0 3	2 8
Gort,	473 1 9	86 11 10	01 10 7	570 3 7	394	29,534	76	157	2 5	0 3	2 8
Loughrea,	337 7 4	89 16 8	65 16 10	448 16 4	865	21,313	69	113	2 6	0 5	2 11
Mount Bellew,	448 7 9	84 7 7	84 16 7	551 11 4	400	27,143	68	144	2 [illegible]	0 5½	2 10
Oughterard,*	467 3 6	93 1 10	34 8 0	474 7 4	216	25,048	116	133	2 5	0 2	2 7
Portumna,	427 8 7	48 17 7	60 8 8	534 14 10	294	25,331	89	135	2 7	0 4	2 11
Tuam,	865 14 9	110 9 6	157 8 0	1,133 16 8	724	50,116	69	267	2 8	0 5½	3 2
Co. of Leitrim.											
Carrick-on-Shannon,	526 7 7	36 6 6	139 14 1	702 10 2	457	33,569	73	178	2 4	0 7	2 11
Manorhamilton,	263 19 5	60 15 8	89 5 4	353 0 0	347	21,675	62	110	1 11½	0 7	2 6½
Mohill,	474 11 10	53 4 0	135 18 2	665 9 6	494	32,556	66	173	2 3½	0 7	2 10½
Co. of Mayo.											
Ballina,	375 10 0	54 16 4	74 1 6	504 8 10	470	27,421	50	147	2 2½	0 4½	2 6½
Ballinrobe,	789 14 9	36 16 11	143 3 8	969 10 4	371	45,810	90	244	2 6½	0 6	2 11½
Belmullet,	216 0 8	27 13 4	80 1 6	850 15 6	300	16,417	63	87	2 0½	0 4	2 4½
Castlebar,	364 10 11	34 14 6	73 14 11	478 0 0	390	34,782	75	189	2 3	0 5	2 8
Claremorris,	364 16 4	40 8 3	67 7 9	452 8 9	294	24,083	63	180	2 5½	0 4	2 9½
Killala,	603 3 4	81 11 6	81 5 0	526 0 0	139	16,941	116	61	2 6½	0 3½	3 0
Newport,	105 13 5	39 5 9	32 5 0	257 8 2	171	14,608	63	78	2 8	0 0	3 0
Swineford,	370 10 0	63 9 10	115 18 4	549 6 2	403	24,297	60	130	2 6	0 6	3 2
Westport,	348 15 7	80 15 7	124 15 4	561 6 0	421	29,944	71	159	2 0½	0 7	2 7½

Co. of Roscommon.											
Boyle, . . .	639 7 10	109 6 5	103 14 9	913 0 0	536	49,107	68	809	2 3	0 5½	2 8½
Castlerea, . . .	636 1 2	78 13 0	89 14 11	636 9 1	582	38,071	73	200	2 8¼	0 4	3 0½
Roscommon, . . .	1,104 6 10	166 12 0	105 17 10	1,468 16 8	891	39,681	80	318	2 11½	0 3¼	3 3½
Strokestown, . .	616 1 2	71 9 10	66 2 1	773 13 1	460	35,989	78	169	2 6½	0 4	3 0½
Co. of Sligo.											
Dromore, West, .	167 19 6	22 17 11	24 16 0	259 9 7	140	11,839	85	63	2 6	0 8½	2 9½
Sligo, . . .	971 5 9	123 14 0	235 0 8	1,333 0 5	748	61,824	62	396	2 6	0 7	3 1
Tobercurry, . .	241 5 4	18 7 3	20 12 0	289 4 8	228	16,377	73	58	2 2½	0 8	2 5½
Total Connaught (29 Unions).	14,696 17 11	1,751 16 6	2,723 14 0	19,178 7 6	12,284	932,093	78	4,058	2 8½	0 5	2 10½
SUMMARY OF PROVINCES.											
Ulster, . . .	23,935 1 6	4,091 5 2	5,710 3 6	33,745 10 2	33,144	1,763,787	53	9,208	2 2½	0 5½	2 8½
Munster, . . .	50,309 1 2	5,248 14 0	9,903 7 4	65,461 2 6	44,742	2,535,643	68	15,083	2 9	0 5½	3 3½
Leinster, . . .	52,058 0 0	6,139 16 4	11,848 11 4	70,076 8 2	52,116	2,655,297	51	14,124	3 1½	0 7	3 8½
Connaught, . .	14,696 17 11	1,751 16 6	2,723 14 0	19,178 7 6	12,284	932,093	76	4,058	2 5½	0 5	2 10½
Total Ireland (163 Unions).	141,629 1 1	17,229 11 0	29,186 16 2	188,455 8 8	142,288	8,186,820	56	42,858	2 6½	0 6	3 2½

* The accounts of the Clifden, Galway, and Oughterard Unions have not yet been audited, but the above particulars have been obtained from the Clerks of the Unions.

No. 9.—Statement (in pursuance of Sec. 20 of 12 & 13 Vic., c. 104) relative to the Audit of Union Accounts:—(in continuation of Statement in Twenty-fourth Annual Report, 1871, Appendix B., No. 9).

i. Date up to which the Accounts of Unions have been audited.

The Accounts of all the Unions have been audited to 29th September, 1871, except those of Clifden, Galway, and Oughterard, which have been audited up to 25th March, 1871.

ii. Sums disallowed or found due on Audit of the Accounts of Unions in Ireland, up to 29th September, 1871, and whether recovered or in course of Recovery from the Parties debited.

Unions.	Half-year ended	Date of Audit.	Amount disallowed or found due.	Whether paid or in course of Recovery.	Observations:—Nature of Sums disallowed, &c.
			£ s. d.		
Ballymena,	25 March, 1871,	26 Sept., 1871,	2 5 6	Remitted,	Out-door relief given without due authority. Remitted on explanation from Guardians.
"	29 Sept., 1871,	11 Nov., 1871,	5 10 0	Paid,	Gratuities to Workhouse inmates for their services.
Ballyshannon,	25 March, 1871,	19 July, 1871,	20 12 6	Not enforced,	Value of 31 tons of meal which appeared from the Master's account to be deficient; and of meal and other articles of provisions, for which the Master took credit as "waste" in distribution.
Ballyvaghan,	"	13 June, 1871,	8 19 7	In course of recovery,	Value of clothing illegally given to persons not on relief. Guardians authorizing it surcharged.
Bawnboy,	"	5 Sept., 1871,	1 0 0	Paid,	Out-door relief illegally given. Guardian who authorized it debited with the amount.
"	"	"	1 5 0	Remitted,	Out-door relief given without due authority. Remitted on explanation from Guardians.
"	"	"	2 0 6	Paid,	Overpayment to Clerk as Returning Officer.
Boyle,	"	31 July, 1871,	1 0 8	Not enforced,	An apparent overcharge in Messrs. Leslie's account for drugs. Satisfactorily explained by Messrs. Leslie.
Castlebar,	"	19 "	3 16 10	In course of recovery,	Cash unaccounted for by Relieving Officer; his sureties debited.
"	29 Sept., 1871,	12 January, 1872,	1 6 0	In course of recovery,	Ditto, ditto, ditto.
Cavan,	"	16 Dec., 1871,	0 6 0	Paid,	Out-door relief given without authority. Relieving Officer debited.
Celbridge,	"	3 Nov., 1871,	12 5 4	Paid,	Deficiency in stock of provisions. Debited to Master.
Coleraine,	"	29 Jan., 1872,	2 8 7	Paid,	Overpayment in salaries and superannuation allowances.
Croom,	"	5 "	1 3 6	In course of recovery,	Out-door relief illegally given. Debited to Guardian who authorized it.
Dublin, North,	25 March, 1871,	8 July, 1871,	2 1 6	Paid,	Expenditure for a political purpose. Charged to Guardians who made the payment.
Dublin, South,	"	1 "	11 0 0	Paid,	Wages illegally authorized by late Workhouse Master, Horridge; debited to him.
"	29 Sept., 1871,	30 Jan., 1872,	4 10 0	Paid,	Ditto, ditto, ditto, ditto.
"	"	"	19 6 3	Not enforced,	Leather unaccounted for. Surcharged to Workhouse Shoemaker. Subsequently accounted for.
Dungannon,	25 March, 1871,	30 Sept., 1871,	7 6 2	Paid,	Balance, ascertained to be in hands of a Guardian, of moneys belonging to the Union.
"	29 Sept., 1871,	29 Jan., 1872,	1 0 1	Paid,	Overpayment to late Clerk on postage account.
Dunmanway,	25 March, 1871,	7 June, 1871,	5 14 0	Paid,	[illegible]

			£	s.	d.		
Enniskillen,	23 March, 1871,	11 Sept., 1871,	7	16	3	Not enforced,	The amount disallowed was the difference between the price of buttermilk authorised by the Dietary to be given to a sub-division of Class 3 and that of the new milk alleged to have been given.
Gorey,	„	20 June, 1871,	12	15	9	In course of recovery,	Goods not accounted for. Debited to the Master.
„	„	„	2	15	1	Paid,	Money advanced to late Clerk and not accounted for by him.
Gortin,	„	17 „	0	8	11	Paid,	Illegally paid to a former Nurse as pension, she having received her full salary for the period.
Irvinestown,	„	12 Sept., 1871,	0	19	10	Paid,	Overpayments to certain Medical Officers of Dispensary Districts.
Kenmare,	„	18 June, 1871,	0	7	0	Paid,	Overcharge by Master in his Provision Check Account.
Killarney,	„	17 „	0	7	0	Not enforced,	Unauthorised out-door relief. Relieving Officer subsequently produced Guardian's authority.
Lisnaskea,	29 Sept., 1871,	6 Feb., 1872,	1	7	6	Not enforced,	Value of thirty yards of linen apparently not forthcoming at the end of the half year.
Magherafelt,	„	18 Dec., 1871,	0	15	0	Remitted,	Apparently overpaid to the late Medical Officer of the Bellaghy Dispensary District as vaccination fees.
Mallow,	„	6 Feb., 1872,	11	15	7	In course of recovery,	Deficiency in stock of provisions, &c.
Manorhamilton,	„	1 March, 1872,	2	10	0	Paid,	Excessive payment for election expenses.
Mountmellick,	„	15 Nov., 1871,	18	9	0	In course of recovery.	Deficiency in stock of clothing.
Newcastle,	„	10 Jan., 1872,	0	10	0	Paid,	Overcharge by Master in his Provision Check Account.
Oldcastle,	25 March, 1871,	23 June, 1871,	1	8	0	Not enforced,	Over-issue of stimulants, and deficiency in meal, surcharged to late Workhouse Master, Maguire, who left from ill-health. The Guardians do not enforce payment.
Parsonstown,	„	11 August, 1871,	0	10	6	Not enforced,	Debited against Relieving Officer for coffins illegally supplied.
„	„	„	0	2	8	Paid,	Ditto Clerk for an unvouched payment.
„	29 Sept., 1871,	1 March, 1872,	2	12	11	In course of recovery,	Ditto ditto ditto ditto in his petty cash account.
Rathdown,	„	4 Nov., 1871,	4	10	0	Paid,	Car-hire charged by Relieving Officer, but not expended by him. Debited to his account.
Rathdrum,	„	15 Feb., 1872,	2	2	0	In course of recovery,	Illegal subscription to the Wicklow Fever Hospital. Debited to Guardians who authorised the payment.
Roscrea,	„	8 Nov., 1871,	0	10	0	Remitted,	Unauthorised out-door relief given by Relieving Officer. Subsequently remitted on production of authority from Guardians.
Sligo,	25 March, 1871,	26 July, 1871,	0	5	0	Paid,	Expended by Guardians in releasing from pawn the clothing of an inmate about to leave the Workhouse.
Strabane,	29 Sept., 1871,	26 Jan., 1872,	4	10	0	Remitted,	Out-door relief given without due authority. Remitted on explanation from Guardians.
„	„	„	0	5	1	Paid,	Overpayment in superannuation allowance to the late Relieving Officer, T. G. Gregory.
Tobercurry,	25 March, 1871,	26 July, 1871,	0	11	0	Remitted,	Out-door relief given without due authority. Remitted on explanation from Guardians.
„	29 Sept., 1871,	20 Feb., 1872,	1	0	0	Remitted,	Ditto, ditto, ditto, ditto.
Tralee,	25 March, 1871,	23 May, 1871,	7	8	1	In course of recovery,	Rates unaccounted for by Collectors.
„	29 Sept., 1871,	23 Feb., 1872,	1	18	11	In course of recovery,	Ditto, ditto.
Youghal,	„	18 Jan., 1872,	0	6	0	Paid,	Out-door relief illegally given. Debited to Guardian who authorised it.

No. 10.—Classification of Persons relieved in the Union Workhouses in Ireland, during the Year ended 29th September, 1871.

	Classes of Persons Relieved in the Workhouses.			No. in the Half-year ended 25th March, 1871.	No. in the Half-year ended 29th September, 1871.
	Able-bodied and their Children.				
1	Adults,	Married Couples,	Males,	1,633	2,067
2			Females,	1,623	2,067
3		Other Males,		23,534	29,301
4		Other Females,		24,958	26,091
5	Children under 15, of Able-bodied Inmates,		Illegitimate,	9,098	9,940
6			Other Children,	12,976	14,343
	Not Able-bodied.				
7	Adults,	Married Couples,	Males,	515	575
8			Females,	515	575
9		Other Males,		20,448	22,046
10		Other Females,		16,912	16,778
11	Children under 15.	Of Parents not able-bodied being Inmates	Illegitimate,	556	633
12			Other Children,	1,636	1,719
13		Orphans, or other Children, relieved without Parents,		9,677	10,426
	Lunatics, Insane Persons, and Idiots.				
14	Adult Males,			1,807	1,534
15	Adult Females,			1,614	1,651
16	Children under 15,			113	180
17	Total number of Males,			53,527	55,323
18	Do.	Females,		45,619	49,784
19	Do.	Children under 15,		34,156	37,161
20		Grand Total,		133,305	142,268

No. 11.—Classification of Persons relieved out of the Workhouses in Unions in Ireland, during the Year ended 29th September, 1871, including Persons relieved in Blind and Deaf and Dumb Asylums.

	Class of Persons Relieved.		Number in the Half-year ended 25th March, 1871.	Number in the Half-year ended 29th Sept., 1871.
1	Blind Persons maintained in Asylums,	Males,	83	76
2		Females,	138	143
3	Deaf and Dumb Persons maintained in Asylums,	Males,	161	177
4		Females,	129	140
	Total,		511	536
	RELIEVED UNDER 10 VIC., C. 31, SEC. 1.			
5	Adult Males permanently disabled by old age or infirmity,		8,980	8,140
6	Families of Adult Males under heading 5,	Wives,	1,471	1,493
7		Children under 15,	812	716
8	Adult Males relieved in cases of their own sickness or accident,		3,865	3,830
9	Families of Adult Males under heading 8,	Wives,	2,814	2,717
10		Children under 15,	6,883	6,807
11	Adult Women permanently disabled by old age or infirmity,		7,435	7,630
12	Children under 15, of Women under heading 11,	Legitimate,	188	200
13		Illegitimate,	17	13
14	Adult Women relieved in cases of sickness or accident,		3,637	3,613
15	Children under 15, of Women under heading 14,	Legitimate,	1,810	1,690
16		Illegitimate,	109	182
17	Able-bodied Widows, having two or more legitimate children dependent on them,		1,640	1,642
18	Children under 15, dependent on Widows under heading 17,		5,453	5,445
19	Lunatics, Insane Persons, and Idiots,	Males,	29	25
20		Females,	37	38
21		Children under 15,	8	10
	Total,		37,912	38,390
	PERSONS RELIEVED UNDER 10 VIC., C. 31, NOT RELIEVABLE UNDER SEC. 1.			
22	Adult Males, married or single, relieved on account of want of work,		–	–
23	Families of Adult Males under heading 22,	Wives,	–	–
24		Children under 15,	–	–
25	Able-bodied Women,	Unmarried,	–	–
26		Widows not relievable under sec. 1,	–	–
27	Children of Women under headings 25 and 26,	Legitimate,	–	–
28		Illegitimate,	–	–
	Families relieved without Husband or Father.			
29	Husband or Father in Gaol,	Wives,	–	–
30		Children under 15,	–	–
31	Husband or Father on service in Army or Navy,	Wives,	–	–
32		Children under 15,	–	–
33	Deserted by Husband or Father,	Wives,	–	–
34		Children under 15,	–	–
35	Orphans and children relieved without either parent,		–	–
36	Number of persons relieved provisionally, and not included in the foregoing columns,		690	769
	Total,		690	769
37	Orphans or Deserted Children out at Nurse under sec. 9 of 25 and 26 Vic., c. 83,		1,866	1,723
	Grand Total,		40,979	41,448

No. 12.—Summary of Weekly Returns of Inmates in the Union Workhouses in Ireland, arranged in Provinces, from the 25th February, 1871, to the 17th February, 1872, both inclusive; distinguishing the several Classes, the number of Sick and Deaths in each Week, and the Weekly Rate of Mortality per 1,000; also the Average Weekly Cost of Maintenance per head.

Week ended Saturday.	Provinces.	Number of Paupers in Workhouses.											Average Weekly Cost of Maintenance per head (exclusive of Clothing).	Deaths.	
		Able-bodied.			Healthy Children under 15 years of age.	Sick in Workhouse Hospitals.			All other Classes.			Total Number in Workhouses.			
		Males.	Females.	Total.		Fever Patients.	Other Cases.	Total.	Males aged 15 and upwards.	Females aged 15 and upwards.	Total.		s. d.	No. in the week.	Weekly Rate of Mortality per 1,000.
1871.															
25th February,	Ulster,	634	1,604	2,238	3,380	391	8,558	8,949	1,355	1,391	2,746	17,313	2 2¾	53	4·9
	Munster,	661	1,839	2,500	4,647	327	6,080	6,407	2,019	2,755	4,774	18,328	3 1½	78	4·3
	Leinster,	676	1,523	2,199	3,818	299	6,474	6,773	1,609	2,035	3,644	16,434	3 0	69	4·1
	Connaught,	189	530	719	1,675	117	1,687	1,804	662	753	1,415	5,613	2 5½	11	2·0
	Total,	2,350	5,336	7,685	13,520	1,134	16,799	17,933	5,645	6,931	12,579	51,027	2 7	213	4·1
4th March,	Ulster,	592	1,651	2,243	3,354	364	2,475	2,839	1,323	1,372	2,695	11,131	2 2½	50	4·5
	Munster,	652	1,838	2,490	4,628	308	5,994	6,302	2,094	2,709	4,803	18,223	3 6½	88	4·8
	Leinster,	862	1,446	2,308	3,763	312	6,512	6,824	1,566	2,048	3,614	16,509	3 0	54	3·3
	Connaught,	191	533	724	1,720	67	1,670	1,737	665	739	1,404	5,585	2 5½	27	2·9
	Total,	2,297	5,471	7,765	13,465	1,051	16,651	17,702	5,537	6,959	12,516	51,421	2 7½	219	4·2
11th March,	Ulster,	640	1,644	2,284	3,297	343	2,328	2,680	1,335	1,380	2,715	11,186	2 2¾	50	4·5
	Munster,	673	1,799	2,472	4,531	323	6,043	6,366	1,966	2,801	4,767	18,136	2 8½	76	4·3
	Leinster,	813	1,519	2,332	3,634	306	6,458	6,764	1,763	2,078	3,841	16,571	3 0	73	4·4
	Connaught,	178	520	698	1,696	67	1,668	1,735	651	748	1,399	5,528	2 5½	28	5·1
	Total,	2,304	5,482	7,786	13,158	1,048	16,497	17,545	5,640	7,007	12,542	51,510	2 7½	227	4·4

18th March,	Ulster,	588	1,619	2,207	3,967	343	2,692	3,936	1,349	1,428	2,785	11,174	2 8½	67	4·3
	Munster,	630	1,724	2,354	4,846	313	6,006	6,319	1,950	2,785	4,748	17,967	2 8	88	4·9
	Leinster,	655	1,643	2,298	3,781	308	6,438	6,788	1,553	2,041	3,880	18,110	2 11½	79	4·3
	Connaught,	176	515	691	1,632	71	1,694	1,766	681	741	1,402	5,813	2 5½	18	3·8
	Total,	2,049	5,301	7,350	13,916	1,030	16,730	17,760	5,506	7,003	12,508	51,064	2 7½	222	4·4
25th March,	Ulster,	572	1,566	2,138	3,810	318	2,354	2,672	1,286	1,382	2,668	10,857	2 2½	63	5·8
	Munster,	580	1,697	2,277	4,492	381	5,928	6,249	1,923	2,731	4,680	17,678	2 6½	78	4·1
	Leinster,	806	1,401	2,207	3,890	321	6,338	6,662	1,510	1,898	3,818	16,077	3 0½	57	6·4
	Connaught,	157	500	657	1,638	70	1,654	1,724	656	734	1,392	5,411	2 5½	20	3·7
	Total,	2,115	5,164	7,279	13,039	1,033	16,474	17,507	5,387	6,861	12,258	50,063	2 7½	219	4·8
1st April,	Ulster,	520	1,504	2,024	3,118	306	2,441	2,769	1,263	1,374	2,637	10,348	2 2½	66	6·2
	Munster,	564	1,647	2,211	4,354	304	5,843	6,119	1,889	2,676	4,564	17,278	2 5½	74	4·3
	Leinster,	781	1,362	2,163	3,603	341	6,271	6,610	1,477	1,977	3,454	15,825	3 0	67	5·5
	Connaught,	150	475	625	1,606	88	1,638	1,725	638	726	1,361	5,318	2 2½	16	3·1
	Total.	2,025	4,988	7,013	12,711	1,041	16,215	17,256	5,256	6,753	12,009	48,969	2 7½	245	5·0
8th April,	Ulster,	505	1,412	1,910	3,046	315	2,380	2,695	1,240	1,864	2,604	10,263	2 2½	61	6·2
	Munster,	538	1,630	2,166	4,306	302	5,678	5,980	1,858	2,602	4,456	16,924	2 6½	75	4·4
	Leinster,	790	1,353	2,143	3,630	318	6,176	6,191	1,469	1,950	3,419	15,684	3 0	77	4·9
	Connaught,	140	465	613	1,582	80	1,620	1,700	626	705	1,333	5,237	2 6	18	3·1
	Total,	1,976	4,861	6,839	12,560	1,015	15,854	16,869	5,193	6,621	11,814	48,108	2 7½	223	4·8
15th April,	Ulster,	511	1,453	1,961	3,080	314	2,419	2,733	1,239	1,333	2,673	10,259	2 3½	61	5·9
	Munster,	518	1,594	2,112	4,281	307	5,709	6,016	1,847	2,604	4,451	16,869	2 11½	90	5·3
	Leinster,	755	1,346	2,101	3,604	345	6,183	6,478	1,470	1,904	3,374	15,557	3 3½	74	4·8
	Connaught,	146	469	615	1,601	75	1,640	1,715	680	711	1,331	5,263	2 8½	20	3·6
	Total,	1,930	4,862	6,792	12,346	1,041	15,901	16,941	5,176	6,552	11,728	48,008	2 9½	245	5·1

[continued.

No. 12.—Summary of Weekly Returns of Inmates in Union Workhouses in Ireland—*continued.*

Week ended Saturday.	Province.	Number of Paupers in Workhouses.											Average Weekly Cost of Maintenance per head (exclusive of Clothing).	Deaths.	
		Able-bodied.			Healthy Children under 15 years of age.	Sick in Workhouse Hospitals.			All other Classes.			Total Number in Workhouses.		No. in the week.	Weekly Rate of Mortality per 1,000.
		Males.	Females.	Total.		Fever Patients.	Other Cases.	Total.	Males aged 15 and upwards.	Females aged 15 and upwards.	Total.		s. d.		
1871.															
22nd April,	Ulster,	483	1,445	1,928	3,074	318	2,419	2,737	1,265	1,298	2,563	10,302	2 3½	59	5·7
	Munster,	523	1,594	2,117	4,209	303	5,813	6,116	1,810	2,567	4,377	16,819	2 9¼	67	4·0
	Leinster,	784	1,309	2,093	3,600	370	6,184	6,554	1,450	1,866	3,316	15,563	3 0½	67	5·6
	Connaught,	137	466	603	1,621	66	1,634	1,700	644	709	1,353	5,277	2 6½	24	4·5
	Total,	1,927	4,814	6,741	12,504	1,057	16,050	17,107	5,169	6,440	11,609	47,970	2 6	217	4·9
29th April,	Ulster,	468	1,416	1,884	3,048	330	2,380	2,710	1,845	1,335	3,180	10,822	2 3½	48	4·7
	Munster,	690	1,380	2,070	4,192	299	5,664	5,963	1,807	2,531	4,338	16,563	2 6½	73	4·3
	Leinster,	689	1,304	1,993	3,354	320	6,172	6,492	1,434	1,879	3,313	15,152	3 0½	71	4·6
	Connaught,	142	476	620	1,601	64	1,613	1,677	629	706	1,336	5,234	2 5½	22	4·4
	Total,	1,789	4,778	6,567	12,395	1,013	15,829	16,842	5,715	6,451	11,889	47,380	2 7½	214	4·5
6th May,	Ulster,	446	1,341	1,787	2,893	319	2,401	2,720	1,243	1,322	2,565	10,067	2 3½	40	4·0
	Munster,	634	1,339	1,973	4,130	310	5,327	5,637	1,769	2,526	4,295	16,233	2 9	68	4·2
	Leinster,	661	1,230	1,891	3,494	312	6,021	6,333	1,418	1,920	3,338	15,048	3 0½	60	4·0
	Connaught,	129	457	586	1,571	51	1,614	1,665	634	714	1,348	5,170	2 6½	14	2·7
	Total,	1,870	4,367	6,237	12,088	992	15,363	16,355	5,064	6,480	11,544	46,516	2 7½	182	3·9

13th May,	Ulster,	423	1,244	1,687	2,868	300	2,347	2,867	1,200	1,255	2,495	9,717	2 2½	53	5·5
	Munster,	407	1,600	1,507	4,064	819	5,449	5,728	1,746	2,434	4,210	15,687	2 6	81	3·8
	Leinster,	650	1,279	1,679	3,459	216	5,891	6,210	1,430	1,850	8,290	14,625	3 0	70	4·7
	Connaught,	132	451	563	1,541	81	1,566	1,647	641	700	1,344	5,155	2 5½	13	2·5
	Total,	1,612	4,644	6,036	11,912	1,016	15,256	16,273	5,020	6,289	11,339	45,560	2 7	167	4·3
20th May,	Ulster,	411	1,252	1,663	2,849	313	2,532	2,665	1,193	1,010	2,500	9,480	2 2½	57	5·9
	Munster,	290	1,508	1,698	4,011	317	5,306	5,625	1,714	2,867	4,101	15,653	2 6	73	4·6
	Leinster,	639	1,201	1,640	3,430	319	5,841	6,160	1,406	1,831	3,237	14,607	3 0	67	4·6
	Connaught,	125	436	561	1,519	77	1,583	1,659	645	718	1,257	5,016	2 5½	15	3·5
	Total,	1,565	4,397	5,962	11,808	1,026	15,081	16,107	4,958	6,240	11,198	45,016	2 7	214	4·7
27th May,	Ulster,	418	1,224	1,642	2,636	696	2,309	2,605	1,205	1,795	2,500	9,565	2 2½	43	4·7
	Munster,	355	1,482	1,637	3,979	294	5,340	5,634	1,716	2,306	4,076	16,536	2 6	56	3·6
	Leinster,	616	1,192	1,807	3,400	309	5,630	6,129	1,426	1,821	3,247	14,595	3 11½	72	4·9
	Connaught,	130	436	566	1,537	77	1,597	1,674	636	679	1,325	5,104	3 5	16	3·1
	Total,	1,519	4,334	5,654	11,745	976	15,086	16,049	4,985	6,173	11,158	44,720	2 6½	180	4·3
3rd June,	Ulster,	326	1,203	1,566	2,617	283	2,201	2,584	1,104	1,255	2,459	9,446	2 2½	49	5·3
	Munster,	355	1,466	1,821	3,836	300	5,243	5,543	1,664	2,319	4,023	15,503	2 6½	65	4·4
	Leinster,	604	1,161	1,765	3,356	300	5,779	6,079	1,412	1,626	3,234	14,467	3 11½	57	3·9
	Connaught,	121	421	545	1,518	69	1,577	1,646	623	707	1,330	5,029	2 5	19	2·8
	Total,	1,466	4,270	5,739	11,636	932	14,900	15,659	4,913	6,117	11,030	44,167	2 7	183	4·4
10th June,	Ulster,	357	1,190	1,567	2,914	271	2,283	2,531	1,197	1,367	2,464	9,299	2 2½	43	4·8
	Munster,	338	1,431	1,769	3,867	290	5,231	5,521	1,673	2,307	3,980	15,167	2 6½	64	4·2
	Leinster,	599	1,142	1,741	3,353	279	5,766	6,035	1,375	1,606	3,183	14,519	3 11½	63	4·3
	Connaught,	135	416	550	1,307	53	1,563	1,611	619	703	1,332	4,998	2 5	16	5·9
	Total,	1,469	4,179	5,647	11,571	822	14,812	15,704	4,864	6,085	10,949	43,671	2 7	167	4·3

[continued.

No. 12.—Summary of Weekly Returns of Inmates in Union Workhouses in Ireland—*continued.*

Week ended Saturday.	Provinces.	Number of Paupers in Workhouses. — Able-bodied. — Males.	Able-bodied. — Females.	Able-bodied. — Total.	Healthy Children under 15 years of age.	Sick in Workhouse Hospitals. — Fever Patients.	Sick in Workhouse Hospitals. — Other Cases.	Sick in Workhouse Hospitals. — Total.	All other Classes. — Males aged 15 and upwards.	All other Classes. — Females aged 15 and upwards.	All other Classes. — Total.	Total Number in Workhouses.	Average Weekly Cost of Maintenance per head (exclusive of Clothing).	Deaths. — No. in the week.	Deaths. — Weekly Rate of Mortality per 1,000.
1871.													s. d.		
17th June.	Ulster,	416	1,167	1,501	2,763	283	2,676	2,559	1,187	1,265	2,468	9,839	2 2½	31	3·3
	Munster,	350	1,385	1,735	3,671	287	5,219	5,506	1,630	2,371	3,001	15,013	2 6	50	3·3
	Leinster,	555	1,099	1,654	3,346	234	5,680	5,934	1,376	1,840	3,216	14,154	3 0	61	4·3
	Connaught,	140	412	552	1,302	84	1,363	1,617	605	705	1,308	4,979	2 3	12	2·4
	Total,	1,461	4,063	5,524	11,486	676	14,738	15,616	4,798	6,081	10,879	43,605	2 7	154	3·5
24th June.	Ulster,	430	1,153	1,583	2,737	279	2,233	2,512	1,176	1,265	2,441	9,271	2 2½	43	4·5
	Munster,	334	1,370	1,704	3,635	293	5,148	5,441	1,615	2,263	3,898	14,565	2 8½	51	3·6
	Leinster,	538	1,106	1,694	3,551	240	5,573	5,813	1,370	1,837	3,197	14,053	2 11	53	3·8
	Connaught,	137	412	549	1,524	51	1,326	1,377	626	703	1,329	4,973	2 5	15	3·0
	Total,	1,439	4,041	5,530	11,457	863	14,460	15,343	4,787	6,078	10,865	43,175	2 7	161	3·8
1st July.	Ulster,	405	1,147	1,552	2,740	278	2,206	2,484	1,169	1,271	2,440	9,221	2 8½	46	5·0
	Munster,	332	1,375	1,707	3,736	288	5,111	5,399	1,656	2,284	3,900	11,743	2 8	39	4·0
	Leinster,	567	1,094	1,661	3,393	209	5,470	5,679	1,378	1,851	3,229	13,969	3 0	64	4·6
	Connaught,	141	406	547	1,494	63	1,544	1,607	602	702	1,304	4,995	2 5	11	2·8
	Total,	1,445	4,012	5,467	11,371	838	14,331	15,169	4,805	6,085	10,893	42,629	2 7	160	4·3

.	404	1,147	1,551	2,713	356	2,180	2,455	1,164	1,282	2,446
.	333	1,281	1,614	3,693	179	5,113	5,365	1,602	2,777	3,900
.	573	1,074	1,647	3,234	227	5,480	5,702	1,359	1,336	3,176
.	144	414	555	1,473	51	1,559	1,610	607	720	1,327
.	1,461	3,916	5,367	11,113	800	14,332	15,132	4,732	6,115	10,846
.	410	1,133	1,343	2,690	250	2,153	2,403	1,178	1,289	2,465
.	311	1,260	1,571	3,660	175	5,096	5,271	1,576	2,258	3,836
.	553	1,043	1,695	3,159	347	5,419	5,866	1,340	1,840	3,180
.	144	399	643	1,449	42	1,566	1,508	619	706	1,383
.	1,417	3,835	5,252	10,981	814	14,234	15,048	4,713	6,093	10,806
.	404	1,077	1,461	2,640	236	2,118	2,374	1,170	1,380	2,450
.	320	1,259	1,579	3,639	256	5,134	5,392	1,556	2,308	3,764
.	548	1,036	1,384	3,086	240	5,422	5,670	1,319	1,617	3,136
.	137	407	541	1,436	65	1,531	1,576	608	713	1,321
.	1,409	3,779	5,168	10,801	807	14,205	15,012	4,653	6,018	10,671

No. 12.—Summary of Weekly Returns of Inmates in Union Workhouses in Ireland—*continued.*

Week ended Saturday.	Province.	Number of Paupers in Workhouse. Able-bodied. Males.	Able-bodied. Females.	Able-bodied. Total.	Healthy Children under 15 years of age.	Sick in Workhouse Hospitals. Fever Patients.	Sick in Workhouse Hospitals. Other Cases.	Sick in Workhouse Hospitals. Total.	All other Classes. Males aged 15 and upwards.	All other Classes. Females aged 15 and upwards.	All other Classes. Total.	Total Number in Workhouses.	Average Weekly Cost of Maintenance per head (exclusive of Clothing.)	Deaths. No. in the week.	Deaths. Weekly Rate of Mortality per 1,000.
1871.													s. d.		
13th August,	Ulster,	379	1,066	1,445	2,675	249	2,093	2,342	1,126	1,259	2,385	8,747	2 2½	43	5·1
	Munster,	394	1,227	1,621	3,528	271	4,901	5,172	1,604	2,184	3,788	13,879	2 8½	39	2·8
	Leinster,	337	823	1,460	2,969	185	5,388	5,573	1,275	1,782	3,057	13,061	3 0¼	54	4·1
	Connaught,	186	382	568	1,189	58	1,515	1,573	603	663	1,266	4,775	2 5¼	19	4·0
	Total,	1,296	3,498	4,994	10,361	801	13,862	14,663	4,607	5,888	10,495	40,465	2 7½	157	3·9
19th August,	Ulster,	351	1,038	1,429	2,353	226	2,064	2,292	1,111	1,249	2,360	8,634	2 2¼	36	4·2
	Munster,	293	1,131	1,424	3,493	263	4,833	5,096	1,492	2,180	3,672	13,685	2 8¼	39	2·9
	Leinster,	526	865	1,391	2,647	231	5,399	5,630	1,254	1,723	2,977	12,749	3 0	44	3·5
	Connaught,	134	380	504	1,406	45	1,472	1,517	583	668	1,251	4,680	2 5¼	8	1·7
	Total,	1,326	3,424	4,750	10,241	769	13,668	14,437	4,446	5,835	10,280	39,686	2 7½	137	3·2
26th August,	Ulster,	352	1,060	1,412	2,363	219	2,042	2,261	1,094	1,282	2,376	8,612	2 2½	37	4·3
	Munster,	294	1,145	1,439	3,409	255	4,804	5,059	1,512	2,169	3,681	13,589	2 8½	50	3·7
	Leinster,	533	839	1,374	2,835	222	5,325	5,547	1,227	1,738	2,965	12,719	3 0¼	50	3·9
	Connaught,	126	377	503	1,406	44	1,168	1,212	584	680	1,264	4,687	2 5½	19	2·6
	Total,	1,307	3,421	4,728	10,213	740	13,639	14,379	4,417	5,869	10,286	39,606	2 7½	149	3·6

2nd September,	Ulster,	351	1,039	1,390	2,300	224	2,017	2,215	1,110	1,260	2,370	8,366	2	2½	37	3·2
	Munster,	293	1,171	1,464	3,486	262	4,802	5,081	1,519	2,176	3,695	13,849	2	8½	47	3·4
	Leinster,	513	872	1,387	2,672	219	5,381	5,541	1,439	1,760	2,989	12,799	3	0½	40	3·1
	Connaught,	194	339	463	1,389	43	1,458	1,465	573	676	1,249	4,617	2	5½	13	2·8
	Total,	1,353	3,461	4,784	10,847	752	13,694	14,346	5,441	5,878	10,313	39,630	2	7½	132	3·4
9th September,	Ulster,	341	1,055	1,409	2,448	230	2,018	2,236	1,105	1,240	2,348	8,571	2	2½	35	4·1
	Munster,	313	1,169	1,503	3,475	264	4,630	5,094	1,526	2,205	3,731	13,603	2	8½	44	3·2
	Leinster,	558	962	1,510	2,939	220	5,275	5,485	1,854	1,765	3,039	12,991	3	0½	60	4·6
	Connaught,	124	370	494	1,468	38	1,452	1,490	669	670	1,239	4,500	2	5½	9	3·0
	Total,	1,337	3,556	4,923	10,344	752	13,363	14,835	4,455	5,800	10,355	39,667	2	7½	148	3·7
16th September,	Ulster,	347	1,057	1,404	2,519	226	2,027	2,253	1,109	1,263	2,340	8,548	2	2½	36	4·2
	Munster,	312	1,179	1,491	3,466	259	4,815	5,074	1,544	2,211	3,765	13,816	2	8	59	4·3
	Leinster,	561	969	1,520	2,789	207	5,253	5,460	1,260	1,643	3,123	13,093	3	0½	56	4·3
	Connaught,	129	362	491	1,353	48	1,460	1,508	584	865	1,229	4,541	2	5½	16	3·5
	Total,	1,339	3,567	4,906	10,337	750	13,565	14,305	4,497	6,002	10,499	40,067	2	7½	167	4·2
23rd September,	Ulster,	343	1,084	1,429	2,539	239	2,034	2,273	1,099	1,356	2,254	8,385	2	3	21	2·4
	Munster,	312	1,201	1,513	3,506	253	4,839	5,092	1,543	2,248	3,791	13,992	2	8½	46	3·3
	Leinster,	620	1,130	1,750	2,983	208	5,049	5,257	1,291	1,641	3,138	13,112	3	0	46	3·5
	Connaught,	130	350	480	1,371	41	1,476	1,517	556	665	1,231	4,699	2	5	11	2·4
	Total,	1,407	3,775	5,182	10,399	741	13,396	14,139	4,498	6,010	10,508	40,278	2	7½	124	3·1
30th September,	Ulster,	357	1,119	1,476	2,535	257	2,060	2,317	1,113	1,236	2,369	8,697	2	3	37	4·3
	Munster,	334	1,259	1,593	3,559	257	4,873	5,112	1,048	2,871	3,819	14,053	2	8½	66	4·7
	Leinster,	670	1,174	1,844	3,037	200	5,038	5,238	1,314	1,868	3,182	13,321	3	0½	56	4·2
	Connaught,	130	373	503	1,373	64	1,491	1,337	638	659	1,317	4,630	2	5	10	3·3
	Total,	1,491	3,925	5,416	10,484	740	13,464	14,204	4,533	6,034	10,587	40,491	2	7½	169	4·2

[continued.

No. 12.—Summary of Weekly Returns of Inmates in Union Workhouses in Ireland—*continued.*

Week ended Saturday.	Province.	Number of Paupers in Workhouses. Able-bodied. Males.	Females.	Total.	Healthy Children under 15 years of age.	Sick in Workhouse Hospitals. Fever Patients.	Other Cases.	Total.	All other Classes. Males aged 15 and upwards.	Females aged 15 and upwards.	Total.	Total Number in Workhouses.	Average Weekly Cost of Maintenance per head (exclusive of Clothing). s. d.	Deaths. No. in the Week.	Weekly Rate of Mortality per 1,000.
1871.															
7th October,	Ulster,	350	1,134	1,525	2,616	264	2,066	2,330	1,095	1,247	2,342	8,801	3 2½	35	4·0
	Munster,	366	1,449	1,815	3,555	248	4,960	5,726	1,361	2,298	3,659	14,757	2 9½	66	4·6
	Leinster,	649	1,138	1,817	3,060	165	5,075	5,280	1,330	1,862	3,192	13,329	3 1	59	4·4
	Connaught,	137	370	507	1,389	43	1,461	1,504	562	676	1,238	4,631	2 6	11	3·0
	Total,	1,541	3,951	5,492	10,613	730	13,601	14,332	4,348	6,083	10,631	41,068	2 7¾	174	4·2
14th October,	Ulster,	347	1,159	1,506	2,667	276	2,135	2,411	1,103	1,243	2,346	8,929	2 3½	41	4·6
	Munster,	373	1,264	1,637	3,596	240	5,029	5,269	1,567	2,317	3,884	14,158	2 9½	48	3·4
	Leinster,	667	1,208	1,875	3,033	195	5,076	5,271	1,317	1,695	3,012	13,441	3 1	49	3·7
	Connaught,	134	378	512	1,344	50	1,496	1,546	656	692	1,348	4,690	2 6½	21	4·5
	Total,	1,541	4,009	5,530	10,682	761	13,736	14,497	4,563	6,176	10,739	41,498	2 8	160	3·9
21st October,	Ulster,	386	1,149	1,535	2,656	309	2,099	2,408	1,135	1,232	2,367	8,961	2 3½	36	4·0
	Munster,	374	1,326	1,700	3,639	343	5,441	5,784	1,635	2,366	4,001	14,624	2 9½	41	2·8
	Leinster,	700	1,226	1,926	3,101	214	5,085	5,299	1,341	1,922	3,263	13,691	3 1	55	4·0
	Connaught,	147	386	533	1,366	47	1,486	1,533	551	685	1,236	4,688	2 6½	11	2·3
	Total,	1,607	4,082	5,689	10,762	913	13,711	14,624	4,662	6,225	10,887	41,964	2 8¼	143	3·4

28th October,	Ulster,	460	1,159	1,338	2,435	291	2,077	2,371	1,150	1,380	2,435	8,995	2 3½	36	4·0
	Munster,	341	1,304	1,883	3,670	271	5,026	5,297	1,869	2,429	4,096	14,736	2 9	33	3·6
	Leinster,	712	1,223	1,835	3,037	317	5,130	5,347	1,355	1,853	3,288	15,607	3 1	38	4·5
	Connaught,	110	400	540	1,391	45	1,488	1,531	367	694	1,261	4,715	2 6	13	2·8
	Total,	1,633	4,085	5,718	10,734	925	13,721	14,546	4,741	6,339	11,080	43,073	2 8½	160	3·8
4th November,	Ulster,	437	1,167	1,624	2,626	310	2,126	2,436	1,164	1,296	2,430	9,131	2 4½	40	4·4
	Munster,	396	1,375	1,771	3,760	255	5,063	5,338	1,743	2,450	4,193	16,081	2 9	64	4·2
	Leinster,	751	1,268	2,029	3,072	213	5,183	5,398	1,365	1,932	3,297	13,767	3 1	41	3·0
	Connaught,	147	418	565	1,392	43	1,506	1,549	386	708	1,078	4,762	2 7½	11	2·3
	Total,	1,734	4,218	5,983	10,850	821	13,898	14,719	4,658	6,386	11,218	43,767	2 8½	156	3·6
11th November,	Ulster,	447	1,224	1,671	2,683	302	2,153	2,455	1,101	1,322	2,513	8,322	2 4½	44	4·7
	Munster,	410	1,379	1,789	5,611	344	5,189	5,433	1,779	2,477	4,256	15,899	2 10	40	3·3
	Leinster,	775	1,300	2,075	5,137	305	5,204	5,499	1,405	1,916	3,361	16,092	3 2	55	3·9
	Connaught,	146	418	564	1,376	45	1,552	1,597	385	719	1,304	4,641	2 7½	9	1·9
	Total,	1,778	4,321	6,099	11,807	796	14,188	14,984	4,980	6,494	11,464	45,644	2 9	157	3·6
18th November,	Ulster,	455	1,271	1,726	2,777	329	2,188	2,517	1,238	1,336	2,584	9,604	2 4½	50	5·2
	Munster,	439	1,415	1,854	3,679	212	3,288	3,505	1,797	2,531	4,321	15,650	2 10	73	4·7
	Leinster,	781	1,340	2,122	3,165	250	5,397	5,647	1,406	1,969	3,395	14,349	3 2	56	6·9
	Connaught,	156	428	583	1,410	52	1,553	1,605	605	719	1,384	4,923	2 7	18	3·7
	Total,	1,831	4,454	6,285	11,251	860	14,394	15,274	5,036	6,368	11,634	44,434	2 9	197	4·4
25th November,	Ulster,	494	1,289	1,783	2,842	323	2,257	2,580	1,254	1,387	2,641	9,657	2 4½	52	5·3
	Munster,	465	1,451	1,916	3,932	255	3,274	3,527	1,656	2,575	4,431	15,896	2 10	73	4·6
	Leinster,	826	1,419	2,245	3,291	249	5,438	5,687	1,485	1,992	3,447	11,640	3 2	74	6·1
	Connaught,	156	449	607	1,450	70	1,580	1,650	605	710	1,315	5,015	2 7½	31	4·2
	Total,	1,943	4,608	6,551	11,485	901	14,589	15,439	5,170	6,664	11,834	43,360	2 9	219	4·6

[continued.

No. 12.—Summary of Weekly Returns of Inmates in Union Workhouses in Ireland—*continued.*

Week ended Saturday.	Province.	Number of Paupers in Workhouses. Able-bodied. Males.	Females.	Total.	Healthy Children under 15 years of age.	Sick in Workhouse Hospitals. Fever Patients.	Other Cases.	Total.	All other Classes. Males aged 15 and upwards.	Females aged 15 and upwards.	Total.	Total Number in Workhouses.	Average Weekly Cost of Maintenance per head (exclusive of Clothing). s. d.	Deaths. No. in the week.	Weekly Rate of Mortality per 1,000.
1871.															
2nd December,	Ulster,	486	1,322	1,808	2,835	344	2,545	2,889	1,279	1,418	2,697	10,629	2 4	63	6·3
	Munster,	490	1,506	1,996	4,032	269	5,363	5,632	1,874	2,567	4,441	16,111	2 10	88	4·2
	Leinster,	843	1,437	2,280	3,319	317	6,342	6,659	1,477	2,021	3,498	14,656	3 2½	64	4·6
	Connaught,	169	461	630	1,481	72	1,581	1,653	609	701	1,310	5,084	2 7	31	4·1
	Total,	1,968	4,726	6,694	11,767	1,003	14,761	16,758	5,239	6,707	11,946	46,180	2 9	235	5·1
9th December,	Ulster,	510	1,384	1,894	2,991	340	2,296	2,636	1,292	1,433	2,725	10,245	2 4½	64	6·2
	Munster,	416	1,547	2,089	4,077	300	5,174	5,734	1,919	2,529	4,451	16,334	2 10½	96	6·0
	Leinster,	847	1,470	2,317	3,349	362	6,617	6,979	1,329	2,050	3,379	15,324	3 2	89	5·8
	Connaught,	183	453	636	1,469	75	1,699	1,674	631	703	1,334	5,103	2 7½	83	4·5
	Total.	2,056	4,854	6,909	11,886	1,037	14,986	16,092	5,371	6,706	12,079	46,890	2 9	273	5·8
16th December,	Ulster,	428	1,391	1,869	3,062	336	2,317	2,463	1,813	1,437	2,750	10,394	2 4½	66	5·4
	Munster,	501	1,560	2,061	4,099	252	5,471	5,723	1,891	2,561	4,452	16,335	2 10½	118	6·9
	Leinster,	881	1,496	2,307	3,348	406	5,616	6,021	1,341	2,063	3,404	15,320	3 1½	103	6·9
	Connaught,	135	455	640	1,450	82	1,601	1,683	630	704	1,334	5,167	2 8	26	5·4
	Total.	1,985	4,902	6,897	12,039	1,076	15,038	16,110	5,375	6,765	13,140	47,136	2 9	303	6·4
23rd December,	Ulster,	575	1,430	1,952	3,111	352	2,284	2,636	1,329	1,460	2,789	10,488	2 4½	78	6·9
	Munster,	555	1,555	2,090	4,093	232	5,352	5,581	1,560	2,549	4,402	16,159	2 10½	88	5·5
	Leinster,	680	1,478	2,354	3,370	427	5,508	5,932	1,288	2,071	3,663	15,313	3 2	90	5·9
	Connaught,	138	479	683	1,476	75	1,553	1,628	618	696	1,314	5,083	2 8	25	4·9
	Total.	2,150	4,933	7,035	12,040	1,086	14,695	15,781	5,275	6,717	12,167	47,083	2 9½	276	5·9

30th December,	Ulster,	525	1,436	1,963	3,107	331	2,399	2,749	1,333	1,430	2,769
	Munster,	581	1,566	2,147	4,126	237	3,471	3,708	1,865	2,564	4,430
	Leinster,	899	1,504	2,403	3,424	459	5,632	6,091	1,336	2,081	3,617
	Connaught,	189	490	679	1,495	71	1,581	1,652	604	709	1,313
	Total,	2,194	4,998	7,192	12,152	1,178	15,083	16,200	5,376	6,780	12,165
1872.											
[illegible]th January,	Ulster,	652	1,481	2,033	3,178	355	2,435	2,790	1,354	1,487	2,841
	Munster,	608	1,649	2,257	4,241	318	5,582	5,900	1,931	2,583	4,514
	Leinster,	908	1,557	2,465	3,473	440	5,743	6,183	1,601	2,083	3,621
	Connaught,	197	510	707	1,531	65	1,604	1,669	617	707	1,324
	Total,	2,365	5,197	7,462	12,421	1,098	15,434	16,532	5,493	6,840	12,303
13th January,	Ulster,	562	1,506	2,068	3,234	376	2,518	2,894	1,337	1,498	2,835
	Munster,	687	1,672	2,359	4,380	276	5,824	6,100	1,975	2,646	4,621
	Leinster,	974	1,469	2,443	3,519	479	5,922	6,401	1,599	2,049	3,648
	Connaught,	203	534	736	1,600	64	1,625	1,689	623	730	1,353
	Total,	2,366	5,281	7,647	12,703	1,195	15,890	17,085	5,534	6,923	12,457
20th January,	Ulster,	558	1,518	2,076	3,205	396	2,561	2,959	1,337	1,470	2,807
	Munster,	617	1,683	2,299	4,410	338	5,964	6,302	1,896	2,885	4,681
	Leinster,	981	1,596	2,580	3,625	503	5,968	6,471	1,629	2,110	3,739
	Connaught,	206	533	739	1,693	64	1,663	1,725	630	733	1,363
	Total,	2,366	5,329	7,694	12,731	1,301	16,156	17,457	5,593	6,998	12,390

No. 12.—Summary of Weekly Returns of Inmates in Union Workhouses in Ireland—*continued.*

Week ended Saturday.	Province.	Number of Paupers in Workhouses. Able-bodied. Males.	Able-bodied. Females.	Able-bodied. Total.	Healthy Children under 15 years of age.	Sick in Workhouse Hospitals. Fever Patients.	Sick in Workhouse Hospitals. Other Cases.	Sick in Workhouse Hospitals. Total.	All other Classes. Males aged 15 and upwards.	All other Classes. Females aged 15 and upwards.	All other Classes. Total.	Total Number in Workhouses.	Average Weekly Cost of Maintenance per head (exclusive of Clothing).	Deaths. No. in the Week.	Deaths. Weekly Rate of Mortality per 1,000.
1872.													s. d.		
3rd February,	Ulster,	551	1,539	2,090	3,228	371	2,594	2,965	1,328	1,481	2,809	11,092	3 4½	59	8·3
	Munster,	670	1,750	2,420	4,539	414	6,101	6,515	2,008	2,718	4,726	18,250	2 10½	55	5·3
	Leinster,	583	1,571	2,154	3,321	490	6,173	6,663	1,636	2,111	3,747	16,465	3 2½	122	7·4
	Connaught,	314	521	736	1,613	81	1,678	1,759	633	730	1,363	5,446	3 8	35	6·9
	Total,	2,118	5,361	7,729	12,920	1,336	16,546	17,902	5,604	7,040	12,644	51,263	3 9½	315	6·1
10th February,	Ulster,	553	1,512	2,065	3,160	391	2,615	3,006	1,318	1,466	2,784	11,045	3 4½	66	6·0
	Munster,	654	1,748	2,402	4,646	405	6,122	6,527	2,019	2,698	4,717	18,154	2 10½	123	6·8
	Leinster,	1,209	1,543	2,552	3,491	498	6,107	6,605	1,413	2,293	3,706	16,447	3 2½	110	6·7
	Connaught,	212	510	722	1,603	91	1,686	1,777	652	725	1,377	5,461	3 6	22	4·0
	Total,	2,128	5,313	7,741	12,837	1,385	16,630	18,005	5,602	6,982	12,584	51,167	3 9½	321	6·3
17th February,	Ulster,	558	1,506	2,054	3,169	347	2,615	2,962	1,320	1,461	2,781	10,968	3 4½	69	6·3
	Munster,	563	1,732	2,295	4,841	410	6,128	6,538	2,016	2,749	4,765	18,420	2 10½	64	4·6
	Leinster,	986	1,632	2,617	3,631	483	6,188	6,671	1,595	2,063	3,658	16,477	3 2½	81	4·9
	Connaught,	235	516	751	1,593	108	1,661	1,769	653	741	1,394	5,508	3 7½	18	8·3
	Total,	2,431	5,368	7,807	12,636	1,348	16,610	17,958	5,594	7,007	12,601	51,002	3 9½	232	4·9

No. 13.—Summary of Returns of the Number of Cases of Ophthalmia or other Inflammatory Diseases of the Eye, which were treated in Workhouses in Ireland during the Years 1870 and 1871.

I. Table showing the Number of Cases which occurred during each Month of the Years 1870 and 1871.

Year.	January.*	February.	March.	April.	May.	June.	July.	August.	Sept.	October.	Nov.	Dec.	Total.
1870, .	576	326	339	313	342	381	368	316	306	319	277	238	4,421
1871, .	660	334	370	316	330	331	373	314	339	285	270	239	4,365

II. Table showing the Number of Adults and Children affected by Disease of the Eye, the Number of Cases arising in the Workhouse, the Number labouring under the Disease when admitted, the average Duration of the Disease, and the Result of the Treatment adopted by the Medical Officers.

Year.	Persons above 15 years of age. Males.	Persons above 15 years of age. Females.	Children under 15 years of age. Males.	Children under 15 years of age. Females.	Total.	Number of cases arising in Workhouse during the Year.†	Number of cases labouring under the disease when admitted.†	Duration of Disease. Average duration of disease.	Duration of Disease. Average period in Hospital.	Result. Cured.	Result. Sight partially injured.	Result. One eye lost.	Result. Both eyes lost.	Result. Died from disease of eye.	Result. Died from other diseases while under treatment of eye.	Result. Discharged or left Workhouse before recovery of the eye.	Result. Under treatment on 31st December, 1870.	Result. Removed of result.	Total.
-								Days.	Days.										
1870, .	670	1,586	1,018	1,147	4,421	2,283*	2,184‡	37	31	3,397	161	69	34	1	16	394	513	15	4,421
1871, .	1,043	1,670	1,034	1,017	4,365	2,174†	2,191‡	38	34	3,155	256	71	43	-	24	345	510	42	4,365

* The month of January includes cases which occurred in the previous year, and were still under treatment in January.

† The registry of cases in a few of the Unions does not distinguish whether the disease first arose in or out of the Workhouse; the numbers in these columns do not therefore agree with the number in the previous column, showing the total number of cases.

Note on Columns headed "Result."—From the nature of the headings under the general term "Result," some cases are necessarily twice entered; and consequently the numbers in the several Columns exceed the total entered in the final Column; and even that total must be regarded as indicating a greater prevalence of the disease than has actually existed, inasmuch as the number of cases is usually given by the Medical Officers in their Returns without reference to the fact that the same person may have been under treatment on more than one occasion during the year, thus showing a number of cases greater than the number of persons treated. The extent of this tendency is of course much greater where, as in the case of the last Census Report, the Returns for a series of years are added together.

Also as regards Columns headed "One eye lost," "Both eyes lost."—These columns include many cases in which the sight was lost before admission into the Workhouse.

No. 14.—Abstract of Returns from Clerks of Unions, showing the Number of Persons admitted to the Workhouse during the year ended 29th September, 1871; distinguishing the Number admitted in Sickness; also the Number of Births and Deaths in the Workhouse during the Year.

Unions.	Number of Persons admitted during the Year.						No. of Births in the Workhouse during the year.	No. of Deaths in the Workhouse during the year.
	Number admitted in Sickness.				Number admitted who were well and healthy.	Total number admitted during the year.		
	Suffering under Fever or other dangerous contagious diseases.	Suffering under other diseases.	Suffering from bodily injury.	Total number admitted in sickness.				
Province of Ulster:								
Co. of Antrim.								
Antrim,	10	47	9	66	1,208	1,274	12	43
Ballycastle,	18	143	12	173	218	391	7	13
Ballymena,	21	47	11	79	737	816	13	49
Ballymoney,	20	62	4	86	677	763	9	37
Belfast,	853	2,087	105	3,145	7,697	10,842	155	671
Larne,	31	205	2	238	807	540	7	43
Lisburn,	75	174	16	268	1,382	1,650	16	63
Co. of Armagh.								
Armagh,	71	420	15	506	441	917	22	63
Lurgan,	130	664	24	818	1,651	2,459	60	178
Co. of Cavan.								
Bailieborough,	15	70	5	90	425	515	7	25
Bawnboy,	5	107	18	130	300	430	6	22
Cavan,	47	254	8	309	797	1,106	11	61
Cootehill,	9	56	6	71	412	483	4	25
Co. of Donegal.								
Ballyshannon,	45	31	11	87	282	369	10	32
Donegal,	1	38	5	44	159	203	3	21
Dunfanaghy,	–	20	1	21	21	42	1	5
Glenties,	6	51	5	61	119	176	1	25
Inishowen,	4	61	1	66	161	250	6	19
Letterkenny,	12	20	3	35	272	307	8	25
Milford,	5	42	4	51	98	149	3	15
Stranorlar,	37	65	4	106	173	279	–	16
Co. of Down.								
Banbridge,	29	346	24	399	1,048	1,447	9	60
Downpatrick,	24	236	2	260	766	1,026	13	64
Kilkeel,	9	27	4	40	377	417	6	8
Newry,	60	177	25	255	2,616	2,871	27	89
Newtownards,	117	314	16	450	876	1,326	22	65
Co. of Fermanagh.								
Enniskillen,	32	151	9	192	367	559	9	65
Irvinestown,	9	83	7	99	278	377	7	18
Lisnaskea,	11	107	12	130	425	555	4	21
Co. of Londonderry.								
Coleraine,	32	152	17	201	851	1,052	12	51
Londonderry,	39	157	9	205	1,454	1,659	20	61
Magherafelt,	100	98	12	210	601	811	11	49
Newtownlimavady,	24	57	6	87	658	745	11	31

[continued.

No. 14.—Abstract of Returns from Clerks of Unions—*continued.*

Unions.	Number of Persons admitted during the Year. — Number admitted in Sickness. — Suffering under Fever or other dangerous and infectious diseases.	Suffering under other diseases.	Suffering from accidental injury.	Total number admitted in sickness.	Number admitted who were not sick.	Total number admitted during the year.	No. of Births in the Workhouse during the year.	No. of Deaths in the Workhouse during the year.
Province of Ulster—con.								
Co. of Monaghan.								
Carrickmacross,	–	49	3	54	548	602	8	23
Castleblayney,	29	179	18	226	895	1,121	6	32
Clones,	1	42	2	45	669	714	7	34
Monaghan,	2	36	3	41	220	261	5	27
Co. of Tyrone.								
Castlederg,	–	56	3	62	81	140	1	16
Clogher,	10	102	11	123	450	573	4	16
Cookstown,	10	65	6	81	274	355	5	34
Dungannon,	14	109	12	135	917	1,052	20	81
Gortin,	1	30	6	37	285	322	–	17
Omagh,	67	88	2	147	583	730	24	52
Strabane,	37	93	17	147	1,394	1,511	21	67
Total, Ulster (44 Unions),	[illegible]	7,635	[illegible]	[illegible]	[illegible]	[illegible]	[illegible]	[illegible]
Province of Munster.								
Co. of Clare.								
Ballyvaghan,	6	63	7	76	41	119	4	24
Corrofin,	22	100	13	140	196	336	3	16
Ennis,	133	332	1	466	640	1,106	11	106
Ennistymon,	33	205	21	259	215	474	5	43
Killadysert,	17	67	8	92	170	262	7	15
Kilrush,	44	277	22	343	248	591	6	56
Scariff,	16	57	8	81	231	315	7	28
Tulla,	24	128	11	163	505	668	6	30
Co. of Cork.								
Bandon,	74	240	11	331	235	566	16	42
Bantry,	3	110	1	118	145	264	5	18
Castletown,	6	78	5	88	318	406	4	26
Clonakilty,	2	196	17	215	260	475	3	58
Cork,	304	2,675	154	3,133	4,469	7,602	78	505
Dunmanway,	1	67	5	73	247	320	4	16
Fermoy,	28	291	29	352	761	1,116	17	72
Kanturk,	93	315	65	475	720	1,185	16	60
Kinsale,	12	164	8	212	381	603	15	40
Macroom,	63	151	17	230	365	565	14	47
Mallow,	85	440	26	560	960	1,550	20	63
Midleton,	74	290	35	403	1,156	1,562	10	83
Millstreet,	59	136	6	202	636	836	9	26
Mitchelstown,	25	213	10	246	872	1,120	14	50
Skibbereen,	7	198	5	210	430	640	5	47
Skull,	–	24	–	24	122	146	–	17
Youghal,	95	208	27	330	892	1,222	10	60
Co. of Kerry.								
Cahirciveen,	121	160	10	291	166	457	6	31
Dingle,	7	148	20	175	228	403	4	35

[*continued.*

L 2

No. 14.—Abstract of Returns from Clerks of Unions—*continued.*

Unions.	Number of Persons admitted during the Year. — Number admitted to Workhouse. — Suffering under Fever or other dangerous contagious disease.	Suffering under other diseases.	Suffering from accidental injury.	Total number admitted to workhouse.	Number admitted who were not sick.	Total number admitted during the year.	No. of Births in the Workhouse during the year.	No. of Deaths in the Workhouse during the year.
Province of Munster—*con.*								
Co. of Kerry—con.								
Kenmare, . .	21	83	11	114	428	542	8	20
Killarney, . .	–	164	20	174	544	718	11	60
Listowel, . .	50	161	9	210	340	650	8	33
Tralee, . .	51	330	0	390	884	1,274	14	97
Co. of Limerick.								
Croom, . .	37	259	0	305	803	604	6	39
Glin, . . .	12	92	3	107	252	350	6	20
Kilmallock, .	100	308	29	497	1,390	1,600	36	68
Limerick, . .	380	2,208	93	2,645	3,706	6,351	60	40[illegible]
Newcastle, . .	66	209	5	270	509	639	11	40
Rathkeale, . .	75	240	18	333	661	1,000	17	49
Co. of Tipperary.								
Borrisokane, .	7	43	9	59	280	339	5	10
Carrick-on-Suir, .	103	675	7	784	640	1,421	39	135
Cashel, . .	42	271	8	321	1,039	1,360	21	72
Clogheen, . .	107	111	6	224	503	727	10	60
Clonmel, . .	99	188	23	310	1,497	1,807	26	94
Nenagh, . .	47	214	10	260	700	989	10	56
Roscrea, . .	20	64	7	191	271	458	5	36
Thurles, . .	66	145	12	216	448	672	8	81
Tipperary, . .	122	276	28	429	1,232	1,661	36	170
Co. of Waterford.								
Dungarvan, . .	56	270	4	330	1,121	1,151	16	67
Kilmacthomas, .	57	122	4	183	613	738	5	23
Lismore, . .	55	80	15	150	619	769	6	43
Waterford, . .	217	804	19	1,040	1,597	2,637	43	165
Total, Munster (50 Unions),	2,180	14,729	880	18,[illegible]	[illegible]	[illegible]	707	2,451
Province of Leinster:								
Co. of Carlow.								
Carlow, . .	156	187	10	353	2,015	2,308	17	81
Co. of Dublin.								
Balrothery, .	44	211	16	271	3,626	3,897	0	38
Dublin, North, .	66	2,420	80	2,577	1,984	4,561	61	507
Dublin, South, .	65	2,926	151	3,142	2,900	6,042	94	677
Rathdown, . .	418	725	46	1,216	1,137	2,355	30	104
Co. of Kildare.								
Athy, . . .	21	183	14	241	968	1,208	10	56
Celbridge, . .	135	140	23	307	466	702	11	43
Naas, . . .	46	187	17	253	1,997	2,250	18	56

[*continued.*

No. 14.—Abstract of Returns from Clerks of Unions—*continued.*

Unions.	Number of Persons admitted during the Year.							
	Number admitted in Sickness.							
	Suffering under Fever or other dangerous contagious diseases.	Suffering under other diseases.	Suffering from accidental injury.	Total number admitted in Sickness.	Number admitted who were not sick.	Total number admitted during the year.	No. of Births in the Workhouse during the year.	No. of Deaths in the Workhouse during the year.
Province of Leinster—con.								
Co. of Kilkenny.								
Callan,	47	160	11	218	944	1,170	16	40
Castlecomer,	76	144	18	340	400	640	7	25
Kilkenny,	138	546	14	708	1,641	2,349	33	120
Thomastown,	42	107	6	155	832	987	7	44
Urlingford,	14	87	2	103	410	513	6	21
King's County.								
Edenderry,	24	63	4	91	1,061	1,152	11	32
Parsonstown,	24	59	9	92	484	576	6	61
Tullamore,	66	419	28	513	1,107	1,620	18	76
Co. of Longford.								
Ballymahon,	13	56	6	75	570	645	1	20
Granard,	12	61	6	79	484	563	7	35
Longford,	11	145	20	165	1,080	1,273	13	40
Co. of Louth.								
Ardee,	34	442	45	521	2,491	3,012	18	84
Drogheda,	87	238	20	345	4,526	4,871	14	84
Dundalk,	173	96	14	283	2,114	2,397	13	65
Co. of Meath.								
Dunshaughlin,	3	118	4	125	2,120	2,245	11	31
Kells,	38	191	18	247	448	695	10	26
Navan,	131	271	2	404	3,331	3,735	5	60
Oldcastle,	40	30	15	85	323	408	6	30
Trim,	23	118	20	161	1,004	1,165	17	34
Queen's County.								
Abbeyleix,	30	89	14	133	580	713	8	40
Donaghmore,	27	65	9	101	287	388	3	15
Mountmellick,	111	399	47	557	959	1,516	20	75
Co. of Westmeath.								
Athlone,	12	150	19	181	1,085	1,266	9	80
Delvin,	25	70	6	101	707	808	3	28
Mullingar,	19	139	4	162	954	1,116	15	69
Co. of Wexford.								
Enniscorthy,	129	216	18	363	1,005	1,368	31	80
Gorey,	78	191	10	279	621	900	13	53
New Ross,	117	263	20	400	703	1,103	31	100
Wexford,	234	408	5	647	824	1,471	24	90
Co. of Wicklow.								
Baltinglass,	12	100	14	126	1,288	1,414	12	45
Rathdrum,	36	79	18	133	1,076	1,209	20	70
Shillelagh,	60	99	2	161	425	586	18	81
Total Leinster (40 Unions),	[illegible]	12,[illegible]	[illegible]	16,[illegible]	49,1[illegible]	65,943	446	3,231

No. 14.—Abstracts of Returns from Clerks of Unions—*continued*.

Unions.	Number of Persons admitted during the Year. Number admitted in Sickness. Suffering under Fever or other contagious or epidemic diseases.	Suffering under other diseases.	Suffering from accidental injury.	Total number admitted in sickness.	Number admitted who were not sick.	Total number admitted during the year.	No. of Births in the Workhouse during the year.	No. of Deaths in the Workhouse during the year.
PROVINCE OF CONNAUGHT:								
Co. of Galway.								
Ballinasloe, .	10	132	12	154	591	745	6	31
Clifden, . .	64	40	14	118	104	289	–	23
Galway, . .	62	367	31	460	419	928	14	106
Glennamaddy, .	1	65	4	70	412	482	4	16
Gort, . . .	5	88	14	115	293	404	11	28
Loughrea, . .	–	98	3	101	434	535	10	36
Mount Bellew, .	25	40	3	68	418	487	6	22
Oughterard, .	1	57	3	61	73	134	1	24
Portumna, . .	2	70	7	79	177	250	2	27
Tuam, . .	30	106	15	914	654	868	4	44
Co. of Leitrim.								
Carrick-on-Shan.,	24	77	6	110	405	515	6	20
Manorhamilton, .	7	94	9	110	284	394	1	17
Mohill, . .	15	86	10	111	498	609	5	21
Co. of Mayo.								
Ballina, . .	39	200	21	260	109	353	13	44
Ballinrobe, . .	67	182	19	268	395	663	5	26
Belmullet, . .	6	49	5	63	180	248	7	10
Castlebar, . .	8	136	5	140	164	343	5	20
Claremorris, .	31	69	10	110	216	326	1	23
Killala, . .	1	6	4	11	60	110	2	17
Newport, . .	1	47	4	52	128	180	–	12
Swineford, . .	7	48	3	58	462	520	–	16
Westport, . .	13	151	7	171	275	416	2	32
Co. of Roscommon.								
Boyle, . .	5	154	23	182	334	616	3	26
Castlerea, . .	68	164	34	266	395	641	5	40
Roscommon, .	51	175	16	242	451	666	10	60
Strokestown, .	17	145	30	199	366	564	3	21
Co. of Sligo.								
Dromore West, .	7	51	5	56	67	125	1	9
Sligo, . . .	2	152	–	154	583	737	9	53
Tobercurry, .	1	48	4	54	224	278	3	16
Total, Connaught, (29 Unions),	567	3,343	310	4,176	9,412	13,589	145	820

SUMMARY.

ULSTER, . .	7,880	7,636	356	10,883	34,799	11,277	586	2,419
MUNSTER, .	5,150	14,720	566	18,784	55,469	64,707	767	3,441
LEINSTER, .	2,480	12,830	794	16,421	57,061	68,913	640	3,351
CONNAUGHT, .	567	3,143	340	4,176	9,412	13,588	145	820
TOTAL, IRELAND, (163 Unions)	6,716	38,312	2,040	45,880	131,697	161,033	2,165	10,040

No. 15.—Abstract of Returns showing the Number of Sick Persons who received Medical treatment in the Workhouse Hospitals and Fever Hospitals of Unions in Ireland, during the year ended 29th September, 1871.

Unions.	Under treatment at the commencement of the year.				New Cases.				Total Cases treated in Hospitals during the year.			
	Fever or other contagious diseases.	Other diseases.	Accidentally injured.	Total.	Fever or other contagious diseases.	Other diseases.	Accidentally injured.	Total.	Fever or other contagious diseases.	Other diseases.	Accidentally injured.	Total.
Province of Ulster:												
Co. of Antrim.												
Antrim, . .	14	68	2	84	46	800	17	863	60	868	19	947
Ballycastle, .	5	26	1	32	20	172	12	204	25	198	13	236
Ballymena, . .	2	42	–	44	28	174	11	213	30	216	11	257
Ballymoney, .	–	33	2	35	20	151	4	175	20	184	6	210
Belfast, . .	129	515	12	656	1,272	3,466	156	4,894	1,401	3,981	168	5,550
Larne, . .	2	40	1	43	31	267	2	300	33	307	3	343
Lisburn, . .	3	53	–	56	86	275	16	377	89	328	16	433
Co. of Armagh.												
Armagh, . .	4	62	2	68	94	420	15	529	98	482	17	597
Lurgan, . .	1	79	1	81	175	1,109	23	1,307	176	1,188	24	1,388
Co. of Cavan.												
Bailieborough, .	2	25	1	28	28	102	6	136	30	127	7	164
Bawnboy, . .	1	27	–	28	5	117	18	140	6	144	18	168
Cavan, . .	11	35	–	46	75	405	5	485	86	440	5	531
Cootehill, . .	1	20	–	21	18	92	6	116	19	112	6	137
Co. of Donegal.												
Ballyshannon, .	5	18	5	28	40	144	12	196	45	162	17	224
Donegal, . .	1	26	–	27	3	56	5	64	4	82	5	91
Dunfanaghy, .	–	11	–	11	1	20	1	22	1	31	1	33
Glenties, . .	5	38	2	45	10	98	5	113	15	136	7	158
Inishowen, . .	–	15	–	15	7	65	3	75	7	80	3	90
Letterkenny, .	–	30	–	30	12	120	3	135	12	150	3	165
Milford, . .	–	11	–	11	6	102	4	112	6	113	4	123
Stranorlar, . .	5	25	2	32	38	75	4	117	43	100	6	149
Co. of Down.												
Banbridge, . .	5	38	4	46	29	382	24	435	57	415	28	480
Downpatrick, .	3	122	–	125	40	524	4	568	43	646	4	693
Kilkeel, . .	6	9	–	15	10	99	4	113	16	108	4	128
Newry, . .	4	27	1	32	146	421	36	603	150	448	37	635
Newtownards, .	4	108	2	114	155	456	19	630	159	564	21	744
Co. of Fermanagh.												
Enniskillen, .	4	64	1	69	43	335	13	391	47	399	14	460
Irvinestown, .	3	6	–	9	13	149	7	169	16	155	7	178
Lisnaskea, . .	–	33	3	36	16	151	12	183	16	188	15	228
Co. of Londonderry.												
Coleraine, . .	6	42	4	52	45	282	21	348	51	324	25	400
Londonderry, .	3	32	2	37	48	301	9	358	51	333	11	395
Magherafelt, .	11	6	–	17	107	153	18	278	118	159	18	295
Newtownlimavady,	2	8	–	10	25	148	6	179	27	156	6	189
Co. of Monaghan.												
Carrickmacross, .	–	26	–	26	–	78	6	84	–	104	6	110
Castleblayney, .	–	36	2	38	48	276	19	343	48	312	21	381
Clones, . .	–	32	–	32	11	109	2	122	11	141	2	154
Monaghan, . .	–	44	2	46	8	89	7	104	8	133	9	150

[continued.

No. 13.—Abstract of Returns showing the Number of Sick Persons—*continued.*

Unions.	Under treatment at the commencement of the year.				New Cases.				Total Cases treated in Hospitals during the year.			
	Fever or other dangerous contagious disease.	Other diseases.	Accidentally injured.	Total.	Fever or other dangerous contagious disease.	Other diseases.	Accidentally injured.	Total.	Fever or other dangerous contagious disease.	Other diseases.	Accidentally injured.	Total.
Province of Ulster—con.												
Co. of Tyrone.												
Castlederg, . .	–	13	1	14	–	75	3	78	–	88	4	92
Clogher, . .	3	1	28	31	14	169	12	186	17	163	41	221
Cookstown, . .	6	16	2	24	10	126	6	141	16	141	8	165
Dungannon, . .	–	29	3	32	29	258	15	302	29	287	18	334
Gortin, . .	–	25	–	25	1	37	6	44	1	62	6	69
Omagh, . .	2	31	–	33	57	198	9	264	59	229	9	297
Strabane, . .	2	42	3	47	37	167	17	221	39	209	20	268
Total, Ulster (44 Unions),	596	1,682	67	2,345	2,591	13,918	809	16,716	3,167	15,120	865	19,047
Province of Munster:												
Co. of Clare.												
Ballyvaghan, . .	6	50	1	57	20	157	11	187	32	170	12	214
Corrofin, . .	1	40	1	42	24	128	13	165	25	168	14	208
Ennis, . .	10	56	–	66	164	602	6	772	204	661	6	871
Ennistymon, . .	9	80	1	90	65	232	60	357	74	312	61	447
Killadysert, . .	4	56	–	60	16	75	7	97	19	131	7	157
Kilrush, . .	5	177	4	186	44	401	24	457	49	584	28	673
Scariff, . .	3	54	–	57	22	103	7	167	25	212	7	244
Tulla, . .	4	65	1	70	28	191	1	220	32	256	2	290
Co. of Cork.												
Bandon, . .	–	66	–	66	74	325	11	408	74	389	11	474
Bantry, . .	–	44	–	44	4	127	1	132	4	171	1	176
Castletown, . .	–	23	–	23	17	145	10	172	17	168	10	195
Clonakilty, . .	–	68	5	73	6	303	22	331	6	371	27	404
Cork, . .	16	734	24	774	420	4,203	194	5,217	436	5,041	218	5,791
Dunmanway, . .	–	68	–	56	1	128	7	136	1	186	7	161
Fermoy, . .	3	44	5	52	30	326	26	383	33	368	34	435
Kanturk, . .	6	142	16	164	98	414	65	574	104	549	81	734
Kinsale, . .	6	43	3	52	24	284	20	331	30	327	29	386
Macroom, . .	21	37	2	60	72	242	17	331	93	279	19	391
Mallow, . .	5	68	4	77	116	619	46	784	121	688	52	861
Midleton, . .	6	42	3	51	118	452	33	585	124	473	36	636
Millstreet, . .	8	110	8	121	91	321	8	420	99	431	10	511
Mitchelstown, . .	8	61	–	62	38	351	18	408	46	412	15	473
Skibbereen, . .	3	254	7	264	10	151	5	166	13	405	12	430
Skull, . .	–	42	1	43	15	74	8	100	15	116	9	143
Youghal, . .	16	81	7	104	178	358	35	571	161	439	42	674
Co. of Kerry.												
Cahersiveen, . .	2	66	1	69	148	195	14	358	144	281	15	427
Dingle, . .	1	46	1	48	8	169	20	197	9	215	21	245
Kenmare, . .	9	33	4	46	24	114	11	148	33	147	15	195
Killarney, . .	–	110	4	114	–	445	20	465	–	535	24	579
Listowel, . .	6	62	3	70	66	204	9	279	71	266	12	349
Tralee, . .	4	63	4	71	185	718	14	917	189	781	18	988

[*continued.*

No. 15.—Abstract of Returns showing the Number of Sick Persons—*continued.*

Unions.	Under treatment at the commencement of the year.				New Cases.				Total Cases treated in Hospitals during the year.			
	Fever or other diseases	Other diseases	Accidentally injured	Total	Fever or other diseases	Other diseases	Accidentally injured	Total	Fever or other diseases	Other diseases	Accidentally injured	Total
Province of Munster—con.												
Co. of Limerick.												
Croom, . .	7	69	2	78	49	373	12	434	56	442	14	512
Glin, . . .	–	29	–	29	12	152	6	170	12	181	6	199
Kilmallock, . .	20	64	6	90	245	500	31	776	265	564	37	866
Limerick, . .	22	548	12	579	430	2,488	63	2,981	447	3,030	65	3,567
Newcastle, . .	3	81	–	84	72	410	5	487	75	491	5	571
Rathkeale, . .	15	58	3	76	87	354	18	459	102	412	21	535
Co. of Tipperary.												
Borrisokane, .	1	39	1	41	7	111	5	123	8	153	3	164
Carrick-on-Suir, .	3	63	1	67	107	821	7	930	104	906	8	1,018
Cashel, . .	4	84	3	91	49	619	17	689	53	707	20	780
Clogheen, . .	3	34	2	39	156	303	18	477	159	337	20	516
Clonmel, . .	14	76	3	93	112	429	20	561	126	505	23	654
Nenagh, . .	6	189	2	197	41	326	17	384	47	515	19	581
Roscrea, . .	–	54	3	56	21	217	7	213	21	264	10	278
Thurles, . .	16	40	1	57	97	314	12	423	113	354	13	480
Tipperary, . .	23	51	4	78	205	378	22	605	228	429	26	683
Co. of Waterford.												
Dungarvan, . .	5	44	–	49	64	490	4	558	69	534	4	607
Kilmacthomas, .	18	67	–	85	110	265	4	379	128	332	4	464
Lismore, . .	–	29	2	31	58	215	10	283	58	244	12	314
Waterford, . .	1	279	12	292	263	1,471	115	1,849	264	1,750	127	2,141
Total, Munster (50 Unions),	316	4,798	168	[illegible]	4,318	[illegible]	1,164	[illegible]	[illegible]	[illegible]	[illegible]	[illegible]
Province of Leinster.												
Co. of Carlow.												
Carlow, . .	13	72	2	87	210	478	25	713	223	550	27	800
Co. of Dublin.												
Balrothery, . .	2	56	1	59	46	361	16	423	48	417	17	482
Dublin, North, .	–	1,011	28	1,039	119	3,459	96	3,674	119	4,470	124	4,713
Dublin, South, .	32	1,318	60	1,410	642	6,078	180	6,900	674	7,400	211	8,105
Rathdown, . .	25	254	–	279	486	1,022	56	1,564	511	1,276	56	1,843
Co. of Kildare.												
Athy, . . .	–	38	1	39	44	488	4	536	44	526	5	575
Celbridge, . .	9	49	6	64	179	216	26	421	188	265	32	485
Naas, . . .	–	51	6	57	58	273	17	348	58	324	19	401
Co. of Kilkenny.												
Callan, . .	10	83	4	97	56	357	18	431	66	440	22	528
Castlecomer, .	17	23	2	42	90	265	22	377	107	288	24	419
Kilkenny, . .	9	104	3	116	180	893	11	1,081	189	1,087	16	1,291
Thomastown, .	2	43	2	47	47	150	6	203	49	193	8	250
Urlingford, . .	–	63	–	63	14	250	2	266	14	313	2	329

[continued.

No. 15.—Abstract of Returns showing the Number of Sick Persons—*continued.*

Unions.	Under treatment at the commencement of the year.				New Cases.				Total Cases treated in Hospitals during the year.			
	Fever or other contagious diseases.	Other diseases.	Accidentally injured.	Total.	Fever or other contagious diseases.	Other diseases.	Accidentally injured.	Total.	Fever or other contagious diseases.	Other diseases.	Accidentally injured.	Total.
Province of Leinster—*con.*												
King's Co.												
Edenderry,	1	69	–	70	37	104	5	146	38	173	5	216
Parsonstown,	2	61	1	64	34	264	11	309	36	325	12	373
Tullamore,	12	91	1	104	92	446	29	567	104	537	30	671
Co. of Longford.												
Ballymahon,	1	37	–	38	15	124	6	145	16	161	6	183
Granard,	–	39	1	40	16	190	6	169	16	199	7	226
Longford,	–	52	–	52	30	391	22	450	30	443	29	502
Co. of Louth.												
Ardee,	6	85	5	90	51	517	46	619	63	603	50	718
Drogheda,	12	90	4	106	116	519	21	656	128	609	25	762
Dundalk,	2	38	–	40	172	155	14	341	174	173	14	361
Co. of Meath.												
Dunshaughlin,	–	33	3	36	40	193	8	241	40	226	11	277
Kells,	6	58	–	64	96	273	18	387	102	329	18	451
Navan,	16	63	–	79	130	290	3	423	140	353	3	495
Oldcastle,	2	74	–	76	100	231	15	346	102	303	15	422
Trim,	–	26	–	26	42	353	26	421	42	379	26	447
Queen's Co.												
Abbeyleix,	–	21	1	22	44	203	17	264	44	224	18	286
Donaghmore,	2	32	1	35	27	109	9	145	29	141	10	181
Mountmellick,	15	56	–	71	107	511	50	668	120	569	50	739
Co. of Westmeath.												
Athlone,	2	25	1	28	22	335	13	370	24	358	14	396
Delvin,	2	46	1	49	27	174	6	207	29	220	7	256
Mullingar,	1	66	–	67	28	163	4	195	29	231	4	264
Co. of Wexford.												
Enniscorthy,	3	78	5	86	160	393	18	571	163	471	23	657
Gorey,	3	77	1	81	82	275	10	367	85	352	11	448
New Ross,	1	103	–	104	149	535	21	705	150	641	21	812
Wexford,	10	82	–	92	234	680	8	922	244	771	8	1,020
Co. of Wicklow.												
Baltinglass,	3	61	4	68	73	216	14	303	76	277	18	371
Rathdrum,	7	41	1	49	63	337	16	410	70	378	18	480
Shillelagh,	3	41	–	44	20	220	2	242	23	261	2	286
Total, Leinster (40 Unions),	[illegible]	[illegible]	183	[illegible]	[illegible]	[illegible]	[illegible]	[illegible]	4,117	[illegible]	1,046	[illegible]
Province of Connaught.												
Co. of Galway.												
Ballinasloe,	2	64	–	66	94	311	27	432	96	375	27	498
Clifden,	–	20	–	20	33	60	14	165	53	115	14	212
Galway,	6	65	5	76	110	506	31	647	116	571	36	723

[*continued.*

No. 15.—Abstract of Returns showing the Number of Sick Persons—*continued*.

Unions.	Under treatment at the commencement of the year.				New Cases.				Total Cases treated in Hospitals during the year.			
	Fever or other contagious diseases.	Other diseases.	Accidentally injured.	Total.	Fever or other contagious diseases.	Other diseases.	Accidentally injured.	Total.	Fever or other contagious diseases.	Other diseases.	Accidentally injured.	Total.
Province of Connaught—*con.*												
Co. Galway—con.												
Glennamaddy,	–	39	2	41	1	140	6	152	1	185	7	193
Gort,	1	20	–	20	6	178	14	210	6	217	11	240
Loughrea,	–	51	2	53	–	173	3	176	–	226	5	231
Mount Bellew,	2	41	1	44	26	84	2	112	27	125	4	156
Oughterard,	1	37	2	40	6	127	7	130	6	164	9	179
Portumna,	2	43	–	45	6	193	7	207	4	241	7	252
Tuam,	3	51	1	55	88	340	13	303	41	691	16	448
Co. of Leitrim.												
Carrick-on-Shan.,	2	62	–	64	31	178	2	212	33	234	9	276
Manorhamilton,	1	22	2	25	7	122	2	130	8	144	16	167
Mohill,	4	33	4	41	16	214	16	279	23	275	22	320
Co. of Mayo.												
Ballina,	3	42	7	52	30	639	39	126	53	681	46	780
Ballinrobe,	2	47	2	51	79	280	23	382	81	327	25	433
Belmullet,	1	30	–	31	18	96	2	116	13	120	5	147
Castlebar,	–	39	–	39	8	237	5	250	8	270	5	280
Claremorris,	1	28	–	28	31	102	10	141	32	128	10	170
Killala,	–	55	–	55	4	33	4	41	4	86	4	94
Newport,	–	24	–	24	13	106	5	124	13	130	5	148
Swinford,	2	40	–	42	19	201	4	224	21	241	4	266
Westport,	1	35	–	36	15	189	7	211	16	234	7	257
Co. of Roscommon.												
Boyle,	12	67	4	74	70	290	30	320	82	316	54	413
Castlerea,	7	65	3	75	105	301	36	408	103	429	41	573
Roscommon,	6	121	–	127	67	283	16	366	93	384	18	495
Strokestown,	–	46	3	50	31	269	30	330	31	311	41	380
Co. of Sligo.												
Dromore West,	–	30	1	31	6	64	6	71	3	94	6	102
Sligo,	–	111	–	111	2	309	–	304	2	417	–	419
Tobercurry,	–	35	–	35	1	80	6	87	1	115	6	122
Total, Connaught (29 Unions),	60	1,362	44	1,472	[illegible]	6,237	337	7,817	935	7,486	441	[illegible]

SUMMARY.

ULSTER,	250	1,8[illegible]	67	[illegible]	2,694	13,318	634	16,714	3,187	16,169	[illegible]	19,648
MUNSTER,	310	4,782	160	[illegible]	4,110	[illegible]	1,1[illegible]	[illegible]	[illegible]	[illegible]	[illegible]	[illegible]
LEINSTER,	[illegible]	4,623	130	[illegible]	[illegible]	[illegible]	911	77,167	4,113	[illegible]	[illegible]	[illegible]
CONNAUGHT,	60	1,362	44	1,472	673	6,237	337	7,817	935	7,486	441	[illegible]
TOTAL, IRELAND, (163 Unions),	[illegible]	14,1[illegible]	[illegible]	14,11[illegible]	11,[illegible]	[illegible]	3,017	80,277	12,[illegible]	78,1[illegible]	3,[illegible]	91,110

No. 16.—UNION OFFICERS' SUPERANNUATION.—Statement of Allowances under the 1st section of the Act 28 Vic., c. 26, in force during any portion of the year ended 29th September, 1871; showing also the cases in which the Allowances had terminated during the year. (In continuation of Statement in Twenty-fourth Annual Report, 1871, Appendix B, No. 16.)

Date of Commissioners' Consent.	Union.	Name of Officer.	Office.	Age.	Period of Service as a Union Officer.	Cause of Retirement.	Annual Salary. £ s. d.	Annual Superannuation Allowance. £ s. d.	If terminated, date of termination.
11 June, 1868	Antrim	William Shaw	Master	59	23	Infirmity of body	40 0 0	15 0 0	
10 Nov., 1870	Do.	Anne Stavely	Matron of Workhouse	60	27½	Do.	35 0 0	20 0 0	
7 Sept., 1868	Armagh	Sarah Call	Matron	59	20	Infirmity of mind and body	35 0 0	20 0 0	
14 June, 1869	Do.	Elizabeth M'Arthur	Infirmary Nurse	64	19	Infirmity of body	15 0 0	10 0 0	
13 July, 1868	Do.	Eleanor Wilkin	Schoolmistress	53	14½	Infirmity of mind	25 0 0	10 0 0	
30 Dec. 1868	Athlone	John O'Connell	Medical Officer of Dispensary District.	60	17 7/12	Infirmity of body	100 0 0	66 13 4	
20 June, 1868	Ballinrobe	John Muller	Schoolmaster	43	18	Do.	35 0 0	15 0 0	
1 Nov., 1869	Ballymahon	Jas. Henry M'Manus	Medical Officer of Dispensary District.	72	10 4/12	Do.	60 0 0	40 0 0	
18 July, 1871	Ballymena	James Jeffares	Do.	44	10 11/12	Do.	80 0 0	30 0 0	
18 Jan. 1868	Ballymoney	Hamilton Gault	Porter	61	11	Old age and infirmity	15 0 0	5 0 0	
6 Jan. 1868	Banbridge	Joseph Dickson	Clerk	40	20	Infirmity of mind and body	100 0 0	56 13 4	
16 Oct., 1866	Bandon	Samuel Holland	Porter	44½	15	Infirmity of body	15 0 0	6 0 0	
21 June, 1870	Do.	William Nicolls	Master	66	20	Old age	40 0 0	13 6 8	
24 Jan. 1868	Belfast	David M'Elheran	Do.	65½	27½	Infirmity of body	100 0 0	30 0 0	
11 Dec., 1868	Do.	Echlin Gordon	Relieving Officer	46	19½	Do.	60 0 0	35 0 0	
4 Nov., 1867	Do.	Edward Ring	Apothecary	70	14½	Do.	120 0 0	75 0 0	
6 Nov., 1870	Boyle	Alexander S. Fraser	Relieving Officer.	66	20	Do.	50 0 0	20 0 0	
5 Oct. 1870.	Caherciveen	Thomas H. Bentley	Medical Officer of Dispensary District.	63	16½	Do.	86 0 0	67 4 0	
23 Aug., 1868	Callan	Robert Toomey	Master	69	24½	Old age	60 0 0	30 0 0	
25 May, 1867	Do.	Richard Ryan	Porter	65	27	Do.	12 0 0	8 0 0	
26 April, 1870	Do.	Ellen Harvey	Fever Hospital Nurse	74	21½	Do.	15 0 0	10 0 0	
8 Dec. 1869	Carlow	E. M. Bolton	Medical Officer of Dispensary District.	66	23	Infirmity of body	100 0 0	43 0 0	
20 Jan. 1869	Carrick-on-Suir	Charles Dealy	Clerk	81	28½	Old age	110 0 0	73 6 8	
31 Oct. 1868	Do.	Ellen Collins	Fever Hospital Nurse	63	23	Old age and infirmity	9 2 3	6 1 6	
6 May, 1870	Cashel	M. A. Burke	Matron	61	22	Infirmity of body	30 0 0	20 0 0	
31 Oct., 1870	Do.	William Kennedy	Master Tailor	78	20	Old age and infirmity	26 0 0	17 6 8	
5 June, 1871	Castlebar	Mary Mackle	Matron	66	18½	Infirmity of mind and body	30 0 0	20 0 0	
16 June, 1870	Castlerea	Prudence Galbraith	Do.	54	20	Infirmity of body	30 0 0	18 5 0	

Do.	Andrew Dillon	Medical Officer of Dispensary District	65	19	Do.	110	0	0	17	4	0	
Do.	Charles O'Hara	Porter of Workhouse	70	10	Do.	10	0	0	6	10	4	
Cavan	Hugh Fitzpatrick	Tailor	66	20½	Old age and infirmity	26	0	0	11	4	0	
Do.	Blayney Grier	Clerk	67	21 1/12	Do.	110	0	0	12	0	8	
Claremorris	Bridget Fleming	Nurse in Infirmary and Fever Hospital	66	15	Infirmity of body	8	0	0	5	6	8	
Clonakilty	Jane Hegarthy	Nurse	60	16½	Infirmity of mind and body	15	0	0	7	10	0	
Do.	Timothy Hunt	Relieving Officer	70	19	Infirmity of body	15	0	0	7	10	0	26 Aug. 1872
Clonmel	Michael King	Relieving Officer	64	29½	Old age	60	0	0	40	0	0	
Do.	John H. Prosser	Medical Officer of Dispensary District	56	18 1/12	Infirmity of body	90	0	0	40	0	0	
Coleraine	Isabella Hemphill	Matron	64	25	Old age and infirmity	25	0	0	15	0	0	
Do.	Elizabeth King	Schoolmistress	65	20	Do.	30	0	0	12	6	8	
Cookstown	Mary Murphy	Matron	60	25½	Do.	30	0	0	13	6	8	
Cootehill	William Stuart	Medical Officer of Dispensary District	61	15	Infirmity of mind and body	85	0	0	47	10	0	
Cork	R. J. O'Shaughnessy	Clerk	47	16 1/12	Infirmity of body	350	0	0	200	0	0	
Do.	William Cogan	Porter	70	18	Do.	25	0	0	12	0	0	
Do.	Timothy Lane	Relieving Officer	65	19½	Do.	43	0	0	40	0	0	
Corrofin	Francis M'Mahon	Do.	73	15	Do.	15	0	0	6	0	0	
Croom	William C. Murphy	Medical Officer of Workhouse and Dispensary District	60	21 / 20	Do.	70 / 100	0 / 0	0 / 0	113	6	4	
Dingle	Mary Grey	Matron	68	20½	Do.	35	0	0	22	6	8	
Do.	George Williams	Medical Officer of Workhouse	60	21	Do.	40	0	0	33	6	8	
		Medical Officer of Dispensary District	..	11	Do.	100	0	0	46	10	4	
Do.	Timothy M'Laughlin	Schoolmaster	68	20½	Old age	20	0	0	13	6	8	
Donaghmore	Alicia Delany	Matron	74	16½	Infirmity of body	20	0	0	17	0	0	10 Mar. 1871
Downpatrick	George Patterson	Relieving Officer	75	10	Do.	45	4	0	24	0	0	
Do.	Michael Savage	Relieving Officer and Sanitary Inspector	72	22	Old age	54	10	0	30	0	0	
Drogheda	Maria Dallaghan	Matron	57	22½	Do.	30	0	0	20	0	0	
Dublin, North	Peter Byrne	Shoemaker	65	20	Old age and infirmity	46	16	7	21	5	9	
Do.	James H. Crean	Clerk	60	27	Infirmity of mind and body	250	0	0	160	0	0	
Do.	Jane Blake	Superintendent of Sheds	50	21	Infirmity of body	31	0	0	11	0	0	
Do.	Thomas Hammond	Relieving Officer	71	18½	Do.	60	0	0	30	0	0	
Do.	Daniel Gilligan	Do.	71	22½	Old age and infirmity	60	0	0	40	0	0	
Do.	Frederick Hurford	Assistant Master	48	10	Infirmity of mind	120	0	0	30	13	4	
Dublin, South	Ward Gibson Jones	Relieving Officer	67	16½	Infirmity of mind and body	70	0	0	15	0	0	
Do.	Henry Evans	Do.	62	13	Infirmity of body	70	0	0	18	6	8	
Do.	Andrew M'Loughlin	Assistant Clerk	60	17	Do.	80	0	0	45	0	0	1 April, 1871
Do.	James Brien	Master Tailor	64	20	Old age and infirmity	51	12	0	26 / 10	0 / 0	0 / 0	

No. 16.—Union Officers' Superannuation.—Statement of Allowances under the 1st section of the Act 28 Vic., c. 26, in force during any portion of the year ended 29th September, 1871; showing also the cases in which the Allowances had terminated during the year. (In continuation of Statement in Twenty-fourth Annual Report, 1871, Appendix B, No. 16)—*continued.*

Date of Commissioners' Consent.	Union.	Name of Officer.	Office.	Age.	Period of Service as a Union Officer.	Cause of Retirement.	Annual Salary.	Annual Superannuation Allowance.	If terminated, date of termination.
							£ s. d.	£ s. d.	
30 Mar. 1870	Dublin, South	Peter Kirwan	Scourer	[illegible]	17	Infirmity of body	[illegible] 0 0	27 [illegible] [illegible]	
24 Mar. 1870	Do.	Jane Dollard	Matron	76	30	Old age and infirmity	[illegible] 0 0	[illegible] 0 0	
26 Mar. 1870	Do.	John Duggan	Gate Porter	[illegible]	19	Infirmity of body	[illegible] [illegible] [illegible]	[illegible] [illegible] [illegible]	23 June, 1871
10 Oct. 1870	Do.	Charles M'Crea	Medical Officer of Dispensary District.	71	[illegible]	Do.	100 0 0	66 13 4	
27 April, 1871	Do.	John Johnston	Wardmaster	44	[illegible]	Do.	[illegible] 0 0	[illegible] [illegible] 4	
7 Sept. 1871	Do.	Jas. Thos. Maguire	Medical Officer of Dispensary.	[illegible]	21	Do.	[illegible] 0 0	[illegible] 0 0	
17 Jan. 1870	Dundalk	Bridget Keenan	Fever Hospital Nurse	[illegible]	[illegible]	Do.	[illegible] 0 0	10 0 0	
19 Jan. 1871	Dunfanaghy	Michael [illegible]	Porter of Dispensary	[illegible]	[illegible]	Do.	[illegible] 0 0	[illegible] 0 0	
1 Feb. 1870	Dunshaughlin	Wm. Chas. Byrne	Medical Officer of Workhouse Infirmary, and Medical Officer of Dispensary District.	[illegible]	17 [illegible]; 17 [illegible]	Do.	42 10 0; [illegible] [illegible] 0	70 0 0	
21 June, 1870	Do.	John Cahill	Clerk and Returning Officer	67	[illegible]	Old age	[illegible] [illegible] 0	46 13 4	
25 April, 1871	Do.	Wm. Stuart Johnston	Medical Officer of Dispensary District.	[illegible]	[illegible]	Do.	[illegible] [illegible] 0	[illegible] 0 0	
17 Dec. 1869	Edenderry	Patrick Murphy	Master	[illegible]	[illegible]	Infirmity of body	70 [illegible] 0	[illegible] 0 0	
16 Dec. 1869	Do.	James Fitzsimon	Medical Officer of Dispensary District.	[illegible]	[illegible]	Do.	100 [illegible] 0	66 13 4	
26 July, 1867	Ennis	James Smith	Relieving Officer	[illegible]	10	Do.	[illegible] [illegible] 0	[illegible] 13 4	
19 Oct. 1869	Do.	R. J. M'Namara	Schoolmistress	[illegible]	[illegible]	Do.	[illegible] [illegible] 0	[illegible] 0 0	
10 Aug. 1871	Do.	Honora Fay	Matron	[illegible]	[illegible]	Do.	[illegible] [illegible] 0	[illegible] 0 0	
15 Oct. 1867	Enniscorthy	Margaret Harris	Schoolmistress	[illegible]	[illegible]	Do.	[illegible] [illegible] 0	[illegible] 0 0	
6 April, 1870	Do.	George W. Long	Medical Officer of Dispensary District.	[illegible]	[illegible]	Do.	[illegible] [illegible] 0	[illegible] 0 0	
11 Feb. 1870	Enniskillen	Rebecca Carson	Matron	[illegible]	[illegible]	Old age	[illegible] [illegible] 0	[illegible] 0 0	
16 Oct. 1866	Ennistymon	Timothy Collins	Relieving Officer	[illegible]	[illegible]	Old age and infirmity	[illegible] [illegible] 0	[illegible] [illegible] [illegible]	
8 Dec. 1869	Fermoy	John P. Elgee	Medical Officer of Dispensary District.	[illegible]	[illegible]	Infirmity of body	100 0 0	[illegible] 0 0	
13 Sept. 1871	Galway	Michael Considine	Do.	[illegible]	[illegible]	Do.	[illegible] 0 0	[illegible] 0 0	
19 Mar. 1869	Glenties	Patrick Breslin	Porter	[illegible]	[illegible]	Old age and infirmity	[illegible] 0 0	[illegible] 13 4	22 April, 1871
26 April, 1866	Gort	Catherine M. Behan	Matron	[illegible]	[illegible]	Infirmity of body and mind	[illegible] 0 0	30 0 0	

William Meredith	Porter	60	6	Infirmity of body	4	[illegible]	0
John Riordan	Assistant Medical Officer of Workhouse.	61	20½	Infirmity and old age	40	[illegible]	0
Charles Somerton	Shoemaker	80	23	Old age	25	11	0
Martin Donohue	Porter	70	20[illegible]	Do.	8	9	6
Daniel M'Farland	Clerk	70	29	Infirmity of mind and body	60	0	0
Margaret M'Shane	Fever Hospital Nurse	60	17[illegible]	Infirmity of body	10	0	0
Patrick Shiel	Porter	78	10	Infirmity of body	18	10	0
Kate Clifford	Matron	46	23½	Do.	40	0	0
Henry Pentland	Medical Officer of Dispensary District.	62	18	Do.	100	0	0
Thomas Tuaffe	Do.	68	16	Do.	100	0	0
John Boyd	Clerk	40½	27	Infirmity of body	75	0	0
Charles Nelson	Medical Officer of Workhouse and Dispensary District.	71	20[illegible]	Do.	160	0	0
Thomas Brazill	Relieving Officer	60	12½	Infirmity of mind and body	26	0	0
Edmund Walsh	Do.	78	17	Infirmity of body	30	0	0
Samuel J. Smiley	Do.	68	18	Do.	40	0	0
Patrick J. M'Inerney	Master	63	24	Infirmity of mind and body	150	0	0
James Heffernan	Medical Officer of Dispensary District.	64	18	Infirmity of body	100	0	0
Patrick Hartigan	Relieving Officer	60	21	Old age and infirmity of body.	40	0	0
Robert Moore	Porter	60	20	Infirmity of body	12	18	0
Matilda Walker	Nurse in Fever Hospital	72	10[illegible]	Do.	15	0	0
James Montgomery	Porter	63	20	Infirmity of mind and body	10	0	0
James Hairs	Clerk	61	23[illegible]	Do.	50	0	0
Berrett Fitzmaurice	Relieving Officer	48	17	Do.	31	0	0
William Rogers	Master	56	27½	Infirmity of body	70	0	0
James Stanton	Porter	63	10	Do.	15	0	0
Michael Twohig	Tailor	72	27	Old age and infirmity	18	10	0
William Young	Porter	56	11½	Infirmity of body	4	0	0
Mary Leary	Infirmary Nurse	60½	20[illegible]	Do.	10	0	0
James Phelan	Medical Officer of Workhouse.	60	21	Old age	100	0	0
Timothy Kelly	Porter	70	25	Infirmity of body	15	0	0
Patrick Mulholland	Relieving Officer	62	25	Old age	33	0	0
Margaret Dimond	Matron	64	23[illegible]	Infirmity of mind and body	25	0	0
Geo. Wm. Heron	Relieving Officer and Inspector of Nuisances.	60	21[illegible]	Infirmity of body	46	0	0
Kate Kiernan	Schoolmistress	60	41	Do.	26	0	0
John Gordon	Relieving Officer	60	22	Old age and infirmity of	25	0	0

No. 16.—Union Officers' Superannuation.—Statement of Allowances under the 1st section of the Act 28 Vic., c. 26, in force during any portion of the year ended 29th September, 1871; showing also the cases in which the Allowances had terminated during the year. (In continuation of Statement in Twenty-fourth Annual Report, 1871, Appendix B, No. 16)—*continued.*

Date of the Commissioners' Consent.	Union.	Name of Officer.	Office.	Age.	Period of Service as a Union Officer.	Cause of Retirement.	Annual Salary.	Annual Superannuation Allowance.	If terminated, date of termination.
							£ s. d.	£ s. d.	
1 July, 1868	Nenagh	Ignatius O'Leary	Relieving Officer	73	20½	Old age	25 0 0	18 13 4	
24 Feb. 1871	Do.	John Coughlan	Do.	63	17	Infirmity of body	75 0 0	18 13 4	
14 Mar. 1870	Newcastle	Francis Healy	Medical Officer of Dispensary District.	66	18	Do.	100 0 0	66 13 4	8 Oct. 1870.
18 June, 1867	New Ross	Nicholas Frizelle	Relieving Officer	66	19	Do.	65 0 0	35 0 0	
30 Aug. 1870	Newry	Henry G. Gray	Medical Officer of Dispensary District.	63	19	Do.	90 0 0	60 0 0	
24 Oct. 1867	Newtownlimavady	John Linton	Relieving Officer	79	8½	Do.	30 0 0	10 0 0	
11 Jan. 1870	Do.	Mathew Robinson	Medical Officer of Dispensary District.	61	10	Do.	80 0 0	30 0 0	4 Sept. 1871.
4 Dec. 1867	Omagh	Dorothea Wilkins	Midwife	80	8½	Do.	20 0 0	8 0 0	
26 June, 1868	Do.	Rebecca M'Guinness	Fever Nurse	60	17 1/12	Do.	12 0 0	8 0 0	
20 Sept. 1870	Rathdown	Michael C. Bernard	Medical Officer of Dispensary District.	60	19	Do.	90 0 0	60 0 0	
15 Aug. 1871	Do.	Joseph Lowreth	Do.	66	19	Do.	110 0 0	73 6 8	
7 Sept. 1871	Do.	Bernard M'Cabe	Master Shoemaker	69	22	Old age and infirmity	30 0 0	13 0 0	
10 June, 1870	Ballinrobe	John Hatch	Medical Officer of Dispensary District.	77	10	Infirmity of body	100 0 0	33 6 8	
15 Feb. 1866	Rathkeale	Martha Rourke	Nurse	61	23	Old age	15 0 0	10 0 0	
22 July, 1867	Do.	William Bourke	Porter	60	26	Do.	20 0 0	13 6 8	31 Jan. 1871.
1 Mar. 1869	Do.	John O'Donovan	Schoolmaster	64	4 1/12	Infirmity of body	20 0 0	13 6 8	
11 Jan. 1870	Do.	Thomas Holmes	Medical Officer of Workhouse.	61	20½	Old age	100 0 0	60 0 0	
19 Feb. 1868	Roscommon	Henry Roche, senr.	Relieving Officer	75	20½	Do.	20 0 0	12 0 0	22 Sept. 1871.
13 May, 1868	Shillelagh	Ellen Byrne	Matron	61	21	Infirmity	24 0 0	8 8 8	
4 Aug. 1871	Do.	Robert Smith	Clerk	62½	22 1/12	Infirmity of mind and body	80 0 0	53 6 8	
20 Jan. 1871	Skibbereen	Daniel Donovan	Medical Officer of Workhouse.	62	27½	Old age	80 0 0	53 6 8	
27 Mar. 1871	Do.	Daniel Donovan	Medical Officer of Dispensary	62	18 7/12	Infirmity of body	100 0 0	66 13 4	
4 Dec. 1865	Strabane	John Jones	Ward Master and Fever ward Steward	54	16½	Do.	24 0 0	12 0 0	

26 / 16	Old age	50 / 100	0 / 0	0 / 0	33 / 66	6 / 13	8 / 4
24	Old age and infirmity .	40	0	0	26	0	0
16 [illegible]	Infirmity of body . .	40	0	0	26	13	4
16 [illegible]	Do. . .	[illegible]	[illegible]	0	13	[illegible]	[illegible]
19	Do. . .	100	0	0	66	13	4
22	Do. . .	70	0	0	46	13	4
21	Old age and infirmity .	14	[illegible]	0	7	0	0
18	Infirmity of body . .	110	[illegible]	0	40	0	0
18	Do. . .	[illegible]	[illegible]	0	13	[illegible]	[illegible]
19	Do. . .	[illegible]	[illegible]	0	[illegible]	[illegible]	[illegible]
17 [illegible]	Do. . .	[illegible]	[illegible]	0	14	13	4
25	Old age	[illegible]	[illegible]	0	10	[illegible]	0
21	Old age and infirmity of body.	[illegible]	[illegible]	0	[illegible]	0	0
19	Infirmity of body . .	[illegible]	[illegible]	0	10	[illegible]	0
14	Old age	[illegible]	[illegible]	0	[illegible]	[illegible]	0
14	Infirmity of body . .	31	[illegible]	0	21	0	0

APPENDIX C.

CIRCULARS OF INSTRUCTION AND CORRESPONDENCE UNDER THE MEDICAL CHARITIES ACT, THE VACCINATION ACTS, AND THE SANITARY ACTS.

I.—CIRCULARS.

No. 1.—Annual Appointment of Dispensary Committees and Wardens.

Poor Law Commission Office, Dublin,
30th March, 1872.

Sir,

The Commissioners for administering the Laws for Relief of the Poor in Ireland desire to call your attention to their circular of the 21st of March, 1862, relating to the annual appointment of Dispensary Committees and Wardens, and to the extracts from previous circulars appended thereto; and they request that you will take the necessary steps, as pointed out in the circular referred to, to place before the Board of Guardians, after the annual election, a correct list of the members of the Board entitled to be members of the respective Dispensary Committees in the Union.

This ought to be done by distinct resolution and recorded on the minutes.

As soon as the committee shall have been completed for any Dispensary District, the Guardians should fix a day for the first meeting of such committee, for the special purpose of appointing their honorary officers for the current year, in accordance with articles 5 and 6 of the Dispensary Regulations, and you should give notice thereof to each member of the Dispensary Committee, in accordance with articles 10 and 12 of the Dispensary Regulations.

A form for the return of officers of the several Dispensary Committees in the Union will be forwarded to you in due course.

By order of the Commissioners,

B. Banks, Chief Clerk.

To the Clerk of the Board of Guardians
of each Union.

No. 2.—Return of Officers of Dispensary Committees.

Poor Law Commission Office, Dublin,
5th April, 1872.

Sir,

With reference to their circular of the 30th ultimo, relating to the annual appointment of Dispensary Committees and Wardens, the Commissioners for administering the Laws for Relief of the Poor in Ireland enclose herewith a form for the return of officers of the several Dispensary Committees in the Union.

In the circular above referred to the Commissioners recommended that as soon as the committee should have been completed for any Dispensary District, the Guardians should fix a day for the first meeting of such committee, for the special purpose of appointing their honorary officers for the current year, in accordance with the Dispensary Regulations, and that you should give notice thereof to each member of the Dispensary Committee, in accordance with those regulations; and if this recommendation has not been acted upon in the case of any Dispensary District in the Union, the Commissioners request that you will bring the matter again under the notice of the Board of Guardians.

Articles 6 and 7 of the Dispensary Regulations of 29th November, 1869, relate to the appointment of the honorary officers, and articles 11 and 13 relate to the notice of meeting.

The Commissioners enclose three copies of the form so as to enable you to make the return in duplicate to this office, and to retain a copy for the use of the Board; and they request that you will procure the necessary information with the least practicable delay, and then forward your return to this office.

By order of the Commissioners,

B. Banks, Chief Clerk.

To the Clerk of the Board of Guardians
of each Union.

No. 3.—Appointment of Committees under Sanitary Acts.

Poor Law Commission Office, Dublin,
22nd April, 1871.

Sir,

The Commissioners for administering the Laws for Relief of the Poor in Ireland, having reason to believe that in some instances Boards of Guardians have not, since the recent annual election of Guardians, re-appointed committees under the Sewage Utilization Act, and the Nuisances Removal Act, and as some of the members of the committees which were formerly appointed may not continue to be qualified, not being any longer Guardians of the Union, the Commissioners desire to draw the attention of the Board of Guardians to the subject, as it appears desirable that those committees should be appointed in the same manner as the Dispensary Committees after each annual election of Guardians.

The Commissioners annex, for the information of the Board of Guardians, a copy of their circular letter of the 30th March, 1867, in which they pointed out the constitution and the functions of each of the three different committees that may be appointed under the Sanitary Acts, and of the two circulars dated respectively the 17th October and the 5th December, 1866, which are therein referred to.

By order of the Commissioners,

B. Banks, Chief Clerk.

To the Clerk of each Union.

Circulars referred to in the above Circular Letter of 22nd April, 1871.

(1) *Committees under Sanitary Act.*

Poor Law Commission Office, Dublin,
30th March, 1867.

Sir,

The election of Guardians for the current year in the several Unions being now completed, the Commissioners for administering the Laws for Relief of the Poor in Ireland think it right to draw the attention of the Board of Guardians to the propriety of re-appointing committees, under the provisions of the Sanitary Act, 1866, for the purpose of carrying into effect the provisions of the Sewage Utilization Act and the Nuisances Removal Acts.

On this subject the Commissioners desire to refer the Board of Guardians to their circular letter of the 17th October last, by which it will be seen that the Act contemplates three distinct committees, viz.:—

1. The Sanitary Committee, which is in fact the Dispensary Committee of the district, and whose functions as sanitary committee under the Diseases Prevention Act are only called into action when an order in council under that Act is in force (29 & 30 Vic., c. 90, sec. 53).
2. The Committee of the Nuisance Authority, the action of which is continuous, and which must consist exclusively of members of the body by which it is appointed, that is, members of the Board of Guardians where the Board is the nuisance authority (18 & 19 Vic., c. 121, sec. 5; and 23 & 24 Vic., c. 77, sec. 5).
3. The Committee of the Sewer Authority, the action of which is also continuous, and which must be appointed at a meeting specially convened for the purpose, and may consist partly of ratepayers (29 & 29 Vic., c. 90, sec. 4).

The Guardians may appoint one or more committees for each of the purposes above mentioned (Nos. 2 and 3), and the Commissioners recommend the Guardians to take the subject into consideration, with a view to appointing nuisance and sewer committees for such parts of the Union as are not within the jurisdiction of another sewer and nuisance authority; and the Commissioners think it might be advisable to consider the propriety of dividing the Union into districts consisting of electoral divisions, for those purposes, and appointing committees for each district.

The Commissioners enclose another copy of the circular of the 17th October last, above referred to, and also a copy of another circular, dated the 5th December, on the subject of appointing Sanitary Inspectors, to which the attention of the Guardians is requested.

By order of the Commissioners,

B. Banks, Chief Clerk.

To the Clerk of each Union.

---

(2) *Mode of charging Expenses under Sanitary Act.*

Poor Law Commission Office, Dublin,
17th October, 1866.

Sir,

The Commissioners for administering the Laws for Relief of the Poor in Ireland forward herewith a general order issued by them under the provisions of the Sanitary Act, 1866, prescribing the mode in which certain items of expenditure, incurred under the authority of that Act, are to be charged in the accounts of the Board of Guardians. Such expenditure may be incurred either directly by the Board of Guardians, or through the agency of some committee appointed either for the purposes of the Sewage Utilization Act, the Nuisances Removal Acts, or the Diseases Prevention Act.

It is of much importance that the functions of these several committees should be exercised by the body to which they legally belong, and by no other; for not only might the legality of expenditure, conducted by a wrong agency, be brought in question, but the area of chargeability, as will be seen by the terms of the sealed order, will depend on the question, under what provision of the law, and through what particular agency, it has taken place.

In order to avoid confusion, as far as practicable, the Commissioners have defined the agency of the Dispensary Committee of Management to be that of "The Sanitary Committee," whose function is to assist the Guardians in carrying out the purposes of the "Diseases Prevention Act," when cholera is in the Union. Any committee appointed by the Guardians, acting as sewer authority, should, therefore, for distinction's sake, as well as in conformity with the language of the Act of Parliament, be called, not the "Sanitary Committee," but the "Sewer Committee" of the Union, or other district within the Union for which it may be appointed. Similarly, and for the same reasons, any committee appointed by the Guardians, acting as nuisance authority under the Nuisances Removal Acts, should be called the "Nuisance Committee" for the Union, or other district within the Union for which it may be appointed.

None of these committees are accounting bodies, but agents merely, acting for the Board of Guardians, who must account with the electoral divisions of the Union for expenditure conducted through such agencies, in the same way as for expenditure directly incurred by the Board itself; such expenditure being subject to the inspection and authority of the auditor of the Union, in the same manner as the Poor Law Relief expenditure.

It is desirable, therefore, that as far as possible, the sums expended under the Sanitary Act should be paid by order of the Board of Guardians, by cheque on their treasurer, to the parties entitled to receive them.

If under any sudden emergency or necessity of an urgent kind, cash should be placed at the disposal of a committee, or any member or members thereof, it will at once be apparent that proper vouchers for the disbursement of all sums should be obtained and preserved, and finally deposited with the Clerk of the Union, for the purpose of being submitted to the auditor when auditing the accounts.

By order of the Commissioners,

B. Banks, Chief Clerk.

To the Clerk of each Union.

---

(3) *Sanitary Inspectors.*

Poor Law Commission Office, Dublin,
5th December, 1866.

Sir,

The Commissioners for administering the Laws for Relief of the Poor in Ireland have observed that the Guardians of many Unions which have not yet been attacked by cholera, or in which cholera, having broken out, appears no longer likely to prevail, have shown a disposition to lessen their expenditure under the Sanitary Act of 1866, by discontinuing the services of Inspectors of Nuisances, or Sanitary Inspectors as they are sometimes called.

The fact that the present invasion of cholera commenced almost at the same time with the introduction of the new sanitary law, may, perhaps, have given rise to a supposition, that when the one is disappearing the other ceases to be necessary.

No doubt, on the disappearance of the epidemic from Ireland, and the withdrawal or termination of the order in council, and of the sealed order of the Commissioners relating to treatment and prevention of the spread of the disease, all expenses of an extraordinary nature incurred under the provisions of the latter order will also cease, inasmuch as, in fact, they could not continue to be legally incurred.

But the provisions of the Sanitary Act are not directed against cholera alone, but against every description of dangerous contagious disease, especially the more fatal kinds of fever, which, although not now epidemic, are always prevailing more or less in the country with fatal effects, and may at any time become epidemic.

These diseases are promoted in the same way as cholera, by the impurity of the air, more especially of that within the dwelling-house, and by the use of impure water, unwholesome food, and other like causes.

The removal of nuisances, the maintenance of proper drainage, the supply of pure water to the population of towns and villages, and the prevention of over-crowding in dwelling-houses, are objects which the Legislature has determined shall henceforward be continuously carried out for the security of the public health, and has therefore created permanent powers and imposed permanent responsibilities for that purpose; and there is no Union in Ireland in which, henceforth, it will not be necessary for the Guardians to employ, at all times, one or more Inspectors of Nuisances, in order to enable them to carry out continuously and permanently these objects of the Legislature.

The office of Inspector of Nuisances will necessarily vary much as to the extent of its duties, and the amount of remuneration for their performance according to the circumstances of the district. In some cases it may be proper to employ a person devoting himself wholly to the office; in other cases, especially in rural districts, Relieving Officers or other officers under the control of the Guardians can be invested with the duties; but in the opinion of the Commissioners all territory which is within the district of the Guardians, as a sewer or nuisance authority, should be under some person having authority to act as an Inspector of Nuisances, and responsible for reporting to the Guardians every case requiring any exercise of their powers either as sewer or nuisance authority.

In the discharge of their sanitary duties the Guardians must be prepared to encounter some additional annual expenditure from the poor-rates; but whenever epidemic disease is not present, the ordinary sanitary expenses will be found to be only a light additional burthen; and it must be borne in mind that the continuous and permanent powers, if properly exercised, will obviate the more expensive arrangements which it would become necessary to adopt in the presence of epidemic disease.

By order of the Commissioners,

B. Banks, Chief Clerk.

To the Clerk of each Union.

No. 4.—Dispensary Notices.

Poor Law Commission Office, Dublin,
25th April, 1871.

Sir,

The Commissioners for administering the Laws for Relief of the Poor in Ireland desire to draw your attention to the provisions of Article 4 of the dispensary regulations, under which you are required, after the completion of the dispensary committee in each year, to prepare a notice specifying the persons and their residences to whom application may be made for tickets for medical relief, with various other particulars which are set forth in that article and in the form of notice given in the order (Form N).

This notice is to be posted at each Dispensary in the district to which it relates, and at such other places therein as may be necessary for the due notification of the dispensary arrangements.

As it is desirable that any changes which may have been made, by the formation of the new committee, in the persons authorised to give tickets, should be promptly made known, your immediate attention is requested to this subject if you have not already issued the revised notices.

It would be well to take the opportunity of ascertaining whether the notice board (Form O) remains affixed on the exterior of the Dispensary, and whether it is in good condition and legible.

By order of the Commissioners,

B. Banks, Chief Clerk.

To the Clerk of each Union.

No. 5.—Small-Pox.

Poor Law Commission Office, Dublin,
13th July, 1871.

Sir,

The Commissioners for administering the Laws for Relief of the Poor in Ireland desire to state, for the information of the Guardians, that since their last circular upon small-pox in Ireland, dated 7th February, 1871, they have had reports from Medical Officers of 480 cases, which were distributed through the country as follows :—

Unions.	No. of Cases.	Unions.	No. of Cases.
Antrim,	10	Kinsale,	4
Ardee,	9	Larne,	7
Armagh,	2	Limerick,	1
Ballina,	1	Lisburn,	4
Ballinrobe,	1	Lisnaskea,	1
Ballymena,	15	Londonderry,	3
Ballymoney,	2	Longford,	3
Balrothery,	19	Lurgan,	2
Baltinglass,	1	Magherafelt,	3
Banbridge,	1	Mallow,	1
Ballymahon,	1	Midleton,	1
Belfast,	68	Mountmellick,	1
Carlow,	1	Mullingar,	1
Carrick-on-Suir,	1	Navan,	2
Clonakilty,	2	Newry,	2
Coleraine,	1	Newtownards,	9
Cork,	16	Omagh,	2
Downpatrick,	4	Rathdown,	6
Drogheda,	127	Rathdrum,	10
North Dublin,	23	Rathkeale,	3
South Dublin,	91	Scariff,	1
Dundalk,	7	Strabane,	1
Enniscorthy,	2	Tuam,	15
Enniskillen,	1	Waterford,	3
Fermoy,	1	Wexford,	57
Gorey,	1		
Inishowen,	3	53 Unions.	480
Kilkenny,	1		

Many cases from centres of contagion, like Belfast, have doubtless escaped being reported. It is not often that the source of contagion, when it is within the country, can be ascertained, on account of the ordinary frequent intercourse between any centre of contagion and the places in its vicinity; but the centres to which the contagion, arising internally, has in a few cases been traced, have been Belfast, Drogheda, Dublin, and Wexford, in the two former of which, it will be seen from the preceding figures, the disease had assumed the nearest approach to an epidemic.

The cases, however, in which contagion has been imported from abroad are more easily ascertainable, and during the five months which have elapsed since last circular the following cases of that class have been reported, viz. —

From *Liverpool* to Belfast two cases, to Ardee one, to Dublin four, to Cork twelve, to Downpatrick two, to Coleraine one, to Magherafelt one, to Lisnaskea one, to Londonderry two, to Dundalk two, to Newry one, to Newtownards one, to Rathdown one, to Waterford one, to Carlow one, and to Drogheda two cases; in all thirty-five cases imported into Ireland from Liverpool.

From *Glasgow* to Antrim one case, to Ballymena one, to Ballymoney one, to Dublin one, to Enniskillen one, to Newry one, to Newtownards two, to Omagh one, to Strabane one ; in all ten cases imported from Glasgow.

From Wales to Balrothery one, to Drogheda one, to Dublin one, to Midleton one, to Waterford one ; five cases in all imported from Wales.

From other parts of Great Britain to various parts of Ireland eight cases.

Thus the number of cases known to have been imported from Great Britain into Ireland during the five months was fifty-eight ; which added to thirty-four like cases specified in previous circulars make a total of ninety-two cases imported during the year 1870, and that part which is passed of 1871.

The promptitude with which the Guardians and their officers have met these imported cases, by efficient treatment, isolation, and disinfecting processes of every description, reflects much credit on the several Unions which have been invaded by small-pox, and accounts, at the same time, for the very few instances in which the disease has spread after its introduction.

Of cases which have terminated fatally during the five months very few have been reported in the correspondence, and it is not possible to say what the small-pox mortality during the period in question may have been until the Registrar-General's returns have been published. The last quarterly return published was that for the quarter ended 31st December, 1870, and at that time the present invasion of small-pox had scarcely commenced. The weekly tables, however, for the Dublin Registration District (population 314,000) exhibit eleven deaths, as registered in that district, from the 7th February last, to the present date.

It will probably be found ultimately, from the Registrar-General's returns, that the number of deaths compared even with the imperfect number of cases reported to the Commissioners exhibits a very small rate of mortality, inasmuch as a large proportion of the cases so reported have been described as of a very mild type in consequence of previous vaccination.

The principal inferences to be drawn from the figures above presented are the following :—

1. That the ordinary intercourse prevailing between Great Britain and Ireland has been the cause of introducing small-pox once more into the latter, the earlier cases having been almost all traceable to importation.
2. That considering the number of different localities in Ireland into which small-pox has been so imported, it is surprising that there are so few in which it has taken such hold as to establish a new centre of infection, such having apparently been the case only in Belfast, Dublin, Drogheda, and Wexford.
3. These incidents are due in all probability to the comparatively good state of vaccination in the country, combined with other favourable sanitary conditions, the latter being partly due to the absence of any decided epidemic influences, and partly to the progressive operation of the sanitary laws.

The Guardians will no doubt concur with the Commissioners in believing that the greatest public benefit has been derived from the law of compulsory vaccination, as administered in this country, and from such exertions as have hitherto been made in carrying into effect the Sanitary Act, and will be disposed, under existing circumstances, to continue to use their utmost exertions for the preservation of the public health.

By order of the Commissioners,

B. Banks, Chief Clerk.

To the Clerk of each Union.

No. 6.—Small-Pox.

Poor Law Commission Office, Dublin,
14th July, 1871.

Sir,

The Commissioners for administering the Laws for Relief of the Poor in Ireland transmit herewith, for your information, a copy of a further circular letter which they have addressed to the several Boards of Guardians, in continuation of previous circulars, on the subject of small-pox in Ireland; and the Commissioners do not doubt that the matter will continue to receive your attention.

The Commissioners have been recently in correspondence with the medical branch of the Privy Council in England on the subject of the supply of vaccine lymph from the National Vaccine Establishment of London; and they request that you will inform them by return of post of the sources from which you have derived your supplies since the 1st January, 1871.

By order of the Commissioners,

B. Banks, Chief Clerk.

To each Workhouse and
Dispensary Medical Officer.

No. 7.—Small-Pox.

Poor Law Commission Office, Dublin,
14th July, 1871.

Sir,

The Commissioners for administering the Laws for Relief of the Poor in Ireland transmit to you herewith, for the information of the Committee of Management of the Dispensary district, a copy of a further circular letter which the Commissioners have addressed to the several Boards of Guardians in continuation of previous circulars on the subject of small-pox in Ireland.

The Commissioners have forwarded a copy of the enclosed circular to each Medical Officer, and the Commissioners do not doubt that the matter will continue to receive their attention.

By order of the Commissioners,

B. Banks, Chief Clerk.

To the Honorary Secretary of the Committee
of Management of each Dispensary District.

No. 8.—Supply of Vaccine Lymph.

Poor Law Commission Office, Dublin,
24th January, 1872.

Sir,

The Commissioners for administering the Laws for Relief of the Poor in Ireland desire to draw the attention of the Board of Guardians to their circular letters of the 7th March, 1848, and the 8th July, 1852, in which they recommended the Guardians to make arrangements for procuring supplies of vaccine lymph from time to time, as required by the Medical Officer of the Workhouse, and the Medical Officers of the several Dispensary districts, from the Cow Pock Institution in Dublin, which the Guardians can do by subscribing annually the sum of one guinea for the Workhouse, and half-a-guinea for each Dispensary district.

Generally the Medical Officers should be able to keep up a supply of lymph for themselves, by taking it from the arms of children whom they have vaccinated, preserving it with the aid of Husband's capillary tubes (as recommended in the circular letter of 28th October, 1863); but it occasionally happens, from various circumstances, that this source of supply fails, and it is most important that in such cases the Medical Officers should be in a position to renew the source of supply with promptitude and certainty. This, the Commissioners think, may be effected most satisfactorily by the Guardians subscribing to the Dublin Cow Pock Institution as above suggested, thereby enabling their Medical Officers to demand a fresh supply from that institution whenever their own supply fails; this course also will, in the opinion of the Commissioners, be found more economical than the alternative one of purchasing a supply from time to time as required.

A considerable number of Boards of Guardians are at the present time subscribers to the Dublin Cow Pock Institution both for the Workhouse and the *Dispensaries*, and the Commissioners have received an intimation of the desire of His Excellency the Lord Lieutenant that the practice should be generally adopted. They, therefore, beg to recommend the subject to the consideration of the Board of Guardians.

By order of the Commissioners,

D. Banks, Chief Clerk.

To the Clerk of each Union.

No. 6.—Cholera—Quarantine.

Poor Law Commission Office, Dublin,
3rd August, 1871.

Sir,

The Commissioners for administering the Laws for Relief of the Poor in Ireland desire to call the attention of the Guardians of —— Union to an order issued on the 20th July last, by the Lords of Her Majesty's Most Honorable Privy Council, relating to the apprehended approach of cholera to the shores of the United Kingdom, and containing regulations on the subject of quarantine, which entail specific duties on every nuisance authority within whose jurisdiction any ship shall be found arriving, and having on board any person affected by cholera.

The following are the provisions relating to quarantine in such cases contained in the Privy Council order referred to:—

"1. In this order—

"The term 'Ship' includes vessel or boat.

"The term 'Master' includes the officer or person for the time being in charge or command of a ship.

"The term 'Cholera' includes choleraic diarrhœa.

"The term 'Nuisance authority' has the same meaning as in 'The Sanitary Act, 1866.'

"2. It shall be lawful for any nuisance authority having reason to believe that any ship arriving in its district comes from a place infected with cholera, to visit and examine such ship before it enters any port, or lands any person or thing in the district, for the purpose of ascertaining whether such ship comes within the operation of this order.

"3. The master of every ship within the district of a nuisance authority, having on board any person affected with cholera, or the body of any person dead of cholera, or anything infected with or that has been exposed to the infection of cholera, shall, as long as the ship is within such district, moor, anchor or place her in such position as from time to time the nuisance authority directs

"4. No person shall land from any such ship until the examination hereinafter mentioned has been made.

"5. The nuisance authority shall immediately on the arrival of such a ship, cause all persons on board of the same to be examined by a legally qualified medical practitioner, and shall permit all persons who shall not be certified by him to be suffering from cholera to land immediately.

"6. All persons certified by the examiner to be suffering from cholera shall be dealt with under any rules that may have been made by the nuisance authority under the twenty-ninth section of the Sanitary Act, 1866; or, where no such rules shall have been made, shall be removed, if their condition admits of it, to some hospital or place to be designated for such purpose by the nuisance authority; and no person so removed shall quit such hospital or place until some physician or surgeon shall have certified that such person is free from the said disease.

"7. In the event of any death from cholera taking place on board of such vessel, the body shall be taken out to sea and committed to the deep, properly loaded, to prevent its rising.

"8. The clothing and bedding of all persons who shall have died or had an attack of cholera on board such vessel shall be disinfected or (if necessary) destroyed under the direction of the nuisance authority.

"9. The ship, and any articles therein which may be infected with cholera, shall be disinfected by the nuisance authority.

"10. Every person obstructing the nuisance authority in carrying this order into effect, or otherwise offending against this order, shall be liable, on summary conviction, to a penalty not exceeding twenty pounds."

When a vessel lies in any place which is not within the district of any nuisance authority, section 30 of the Sanitary Act defines it to be for the purposes of that Act in the district of that nuisance authority whose district nearest adjoins the place where such vessel is lying, the distance being measured in a straight line. It is easy, therefore, to distinguish to what nuisance authority, on a ship arriving in adjoining waters, the duty of attending to her belongs.

As the Board of Guardians of —— Union is the nuisance authority of a district on the coast of Ireland, the Commissioners request their especial attention to the terms of the Privy Council order. The Commissioners have, at the same time, to observe that it is the duty of the Board of Guardians to provide proper and convenient hospital accommodation for the treatment of persons affected by cholera, to which they can be removed from any ship lying in quarantine under the terms of the Privy Council order.

The Guardians will also bear in mind that in the event of any vessel arriving with cholera in the waters adjoining any part of the Union, although such part is within the district of another nuisance authority, it is their duty under the Poor Law Acts to provide accommodation and treatment in hospital for all such patients as may be brought ashore by the nuisance authority for that purpose, as well as for cases falling within their own jurisdiction as nuisance authority.

By order of the Commissioners,

B. Banks, Chief Clerk.

To the Clerk of the —— Union.

II.—REPORTS FROM DR. KING, MEDICAL AND POOR LAW INSPECTOR, AS TO THE OUTBREAK AND PROGRESS OF THE EPIDEMIC OF SMALL-POX IN CORK.

No. 1.—Report from Dr. King, Medical and Poor Law Inspector.

1, Belgrave-place, Cork,
17th November, 1871.

Gentlemen,

I have the honour to inform you that there is a case of small-pox at present under treatment at Evergreen, Cork, which is in the Cork Dispensary District, in the person of a sailor named Timothy Driscoll; he is under the care of Dr. O'Flynn (8 district).

This man is twenty-eight years of age; he never was vaccinated; he contracted the disease in Newport, where small-pox was in the house in which he resided; he sailed from Newport in the ship *Minnie* on the 3rd inst., but did not complain until the 11th; the disease at present is simple, and it is expected that the case may progress favourably.

Neither the man himself nor his friends will consent to his removal to hospital, which is much to be regretted, as Evergreen is a densely populated district, and a number of persons reside in the house in which Driscoll lies sick.

Your obedient servant,

Charles Croker King.

To the Poor Law Commissioners.

No. 2.—Report from Dr. King.

Kilmallock, 7th December, 1871.

Gentlemen,

I have the honour to inform you that on Monday last a case of small-pox occurred at 93, Evergreen-street, in Dr. O'Flynn's sub-district (Cork Dispensary); this case was sent to hospital; three additional cases have since appeared in persons aged fifteen, nine, and one and a half years; the two former have been sent to hospital. All these cases showed themselves in the immediate neighbourhood of the sailor who refused to go to hospital, and who had imported the disease from Wales, as stated in my report, and with whom all the patients at present attacked had either direct or indirect intercourse.

I cannot say at present whether these four persons have or have not been vaccinated.

Your obedient servant,

Charles Croker King.

To the Poor Law Commissioners.

No. 3.—Report from Dr. King.

1, Belgrave-place, Cork,
13th December, 1871.

Gentlemen,

I have the honour to inform you that a man named Charles Murphy, from the Ballinlough Road, was admitted into the Cork Union Fever Hospital on this day, labouring under small-pox.

I had an interview with the Mayor of Cork on Monday last, and he seems determined to use every means to prevent as far as possible the further spread of the disease, and has put active sanitary measures in operation. The above case has been promptly communicated to him.

Your obedient servant,

CHARLES CROKER KING.

To the Poor Law Commissioners.

No. 4.—REPORT from Dr. KING.

GENTLEMEN, Cork, 18th December, 1871.

I have the honour to inform you that Richard Ellis, whose case was reported to you as having been admitted to the Cork Fever Hospital on the 6th inst., labouring under small-pox, died of that disease last night. He had not been vaccinated; he was nine years of age; he died on the fifteenth day of the disease.

Your obedient servant,

CHARLES CROKER KING.

To the Poor Law Commissioners.

No. 5.—REPORT from Dr. KING.

GENTLEMEN, Cork, 21st December, 1871.

I have the honour to inform you that Honoria Walsh, aged fourteen years, and Hannah Keeffe, aged seventeen, labouring under small-pox, were admitted into the Cork Union Fever Hospital on yesterday. Honoria Walsh has been one week ill, and Hannah Keeffe five days. I have visited them and on examination find that both of them were vaccinated during infancy, and have well-marked cicatrices on their arm.

So far they are going on favourably. Mary Barry and Charles Murphy, whose cases I have already reported as admitted on the 4th and 13th inst., are now convalescent; and Margaret Eager is progressing favourably.

Hannah Keeffe and Honoria Walsh resided in the neighbourhood of Evergreen, the locality in which small-pox showed itself in the case of the seaman from Wales, who refused to go to hospital.

Your obedient servant,

CHARLES CROKER KING.

To the Poor Law Commissioners.

No. 6.—REPORT from Dr. KING.

1, Belgrave-place, Cork,

GENTLEMEN, 25th December, 1871.

I have the honour to inform you that a boy named Andrew Gleeson, residing at 56, Douglas-street, Cork, was admitted into the Cork Union Fever Hospital on the 23rd inst., labouring under modified small-pox. He had been vaccinated.

Notification has been given to the corporate authorities, in order that precautionary measures may be adopted.

Your obedient servant,

CHARLES CROKER KING.

To the Poor Law Commissioners.

No. 7.—REPORT from DR. KING.

GENTLEMEN, Cork, 24th December, 1871.

I have the honour to inform you that three additional cases of small-pox have occurred in the Cork Union since my last report, namely, Bartholomew Flynn, aged thirty years, admitted into the Union Fever Hospital on last Friday evening; seems to have been vaccinated; he took ill four days ago at 39, Evergreen-street. Notice has been served on the municipal authorities with the view of the necessary steps being taken to prevent (as far as may be) the further spread of the disease.

Three days ago a man named Robert Moore, aged eighteen years, and who had never been vaccinated, took ill of small-pox at Frankfield, in the Douglas Dispensary District. He refuses to be removed to hospital. I requested Dr. White, under whose care he is, to immediately inform Relieving Officer Rooney of the nature of the case, who would carry out such sanitary measures as he (the Medical Officer) should direct.

The third case is a young lady residing near the South Terrace, who is in the first stage of what appears to be small-pox. The eruption is not as yet fully developed, but she suffers from the usual symptoms which usher in a severe case. I believe she has been vaccinated.

Your obedient servant,

CHARLES CROKER KING.

To the Poor Law Commissioners.

No. 8.—REPORT from DR. KING.

GENTLEMEN, Cork, 26th December, 1871.

I have to report the admission of five fresh cases of small-pox into the Union Fever Hospital. Two of the cases occurred in the Workhouse, but the disease was evidently contracted in the Union Fever Hospital, as in both instances the persons had been recently patients in the Fever Hospital, one having had scarlatina the other fever; but having become convalescent they were removed to the main house a few days ago. In addition to these, a boy aged sixteen, suffering from fever, from which he was nearly convalescent, showed symptoms of small-pox this day.

It is quite evident that patients labouring under febrile affections are liable to contract small-pox from the patients labouring under this disease in the same building; in fact, such has happened in the above three instances. I fear we are about to have a sharp outbreak of small pox in this locality; and I think the Guardians ought to make further provision, under the 37th section of the Public Health Act, for such cases of that disease as may arise.

Your obedient servant,

CHARLES CROKER KING.

To the Poor Law Commissioners.

There are at present fourteen cases in all under treatment in the Union Fever Hospital—nine males, five females; some of them very heavy cases, especially when the patients had not been previously vaccinated. I visited them this day.

No. 9.—LETTER from the COMMISSIONERS to Dr. KING.

Poor Law Commission Office, Dublin,
SIR, 29th December, 1871.

The Commissioners for administering the Laws for Relief of the Poor in Ireland acknowledge the receipt of your reports of the 24th, 25th, 26th, and 27th inst., from which it appears that additional cases of small-pox continue to occur in the Cork Union; and that there are at present fifteen cases suffering from that disease in the Union Fever Hospital.

With reference to the suggestion contained in your report of the 26th inst., as to the necessity of providing increased accommodation in the Workhouse for the treatment of such other small-pox cases as may occur, the Commissioners request that you will attend the next meeting of the Board of Guardians, and confer with them specially as to the steps which ought to be taken to meet the outbreak of the disease, apparently now becoming epidemic.

In the two Dublin Unions temporary Workhouse accommodation, specially appropriated for small-pox cases, has been provided on a large scale.

If, as the Commissioners infer from your report of 26th inst., small-pox cases, when admitted to the Workhouse, are placed in the ordinary fever wards, immediate steps should be taken to provide separate wards for such cases, isolated as much as possible from other wards, experience having shown that small-pox is frequently propagated from hospitals in which small-pox patients have been treated in the same wards as ordinary fever patients.

The Commissioners request that you will be good enough to report specially and fully to them on the subject after your conference with the Board of Guardians.

By order of the Commissioners,

D. DANES, Chief Clerk.

To Dr. King, Poor Law Inspector,
1, Belgrave-place, Cork.

No. 10.—REPORT from Dr. KING.

GENTLEMEN, Cork, 27th December, 1871.

I have the honour to inform you that a girl named Bridget Dooly, labouring under small-pox, was admitted yesterday evening from 95, Evergreen-street, into the Cork Union Fever Hospital, in which there are now fifteen patients suffering from that disease.

Your obedient servant,

CHARLES CROKER KING.

To the Poor Law Commissioners.

No. 11.—REPORT from Dr. KING.

GENTLEMEN, Cork, 30th December, 1871.

I have the honour to inform you that a case of small-pox has occurred in the Blarney District, in the person of a young man, aged seventeen, who had been vaccinated in his youth.

He evidently contracted the disease in Cork, where he has been engaged at work. His parents object to his being removed to hospital.

I have written to the Medical Officer of the district, with the view of the patient being isolated so far as the circumstances of his case will permit.

Since my last report nine fresh cases of small-pox have been admitted into the Cork Union Fever Hospital labouring under small-pox, principally from the vicinity of Evergreen-street.

Your obedient servant,

Charles Croker King.

To the Poor Law Commissioners.

No. 12.—Report from Dr. King.

Gentlemen, Cork Workhouse, January 2, 1872.

In compliance with your letter of instructions of the 29th ultimo, I have the honour to submit for your consideration the following report of the progress of small-pox in the Cork Union, and the proposed hospital accommodation for the reception of such cases as may arise.

The present outbreak of small-pox can be traced to the case of a sailor, who, having contracted the disease at Newport, Wales, fell sick in Cork in a street densely inhabited, and called Evergreen, from which locality and neighbourhood the vast majority of the cases admitted into the Cork Union Fever Hospital have been received. The first case was admitted into hospital on the 14th of December, from 73, Evergreen-street, the patient being a girl aged fourteen years; since which thirty-one other cases have been admitted. Of the thirty-two cases admitted, twenty-two had been previously vaccinated; sixteen had the disease modified—of these, fourteen had been vaccinated and two had not; sixteen had the disease in a severe form, mostly confluent—of these, eight had and eight had not been vaccinated; four of the sixteen severe cases died—and of these, three had not been vaccinated but one had.

Up to the present time the hospital accommodation has been of this nature:—The Fever Hospital consists of two large wards and two small wards in each wing. The large wards are capable of accommodating nineteen patients each, the small wards five each, making a total accommodation for ninety-six patients.

The upper wards were appropriated for the reception of female patients, the lower for male patients.

The first cases of small-pox were placed in the small wards, but as the cases increased in number they had to be transferred to the larger wards. One large female ward and one large male ward are at present occupied by small-pox cases.

At the meeting of the Board of Guardians on last Thursday, I brought under the consideration of the Board the necessity of making increased provision for the treatment in hospital of cases of small-pox, and also of more effectually isolating cases of this disease from those of fever, as three patients in the hospital (convalescent from fever) had contracted the disease. I informed the Board that at the Cork Fever Hospital accommodation for small-pox patients could be obtained in an isolated building; but the Guardians would not consent to send future patients there, and they came to the conclusion of transferring their fever cases to the female probationary ward, and instructed Drs. Wall and Wherland to carry out their views. These gentlemen recommended that one wing of the Fever Hospital should be allocated for the accommodation of small-pox patients, the other for fever cases; and made certain suggestions as to the conversion of the new female probationary building into a fever hospital, if necessary. To this latter proposal the most serious objections exist; but as the notion has been abandoned, it is unnecessary to enter into details at present.

On the 29th December, the day after the meeting of the Board, I found that on the previous day so many as nine fresh cases had been admitted. It was thus evident that if something were not done speedily, there would not be sufficient accommodation for small-pox and fever cases in the Union Fever Hospital. I consequently waited on the mayor (who is a person of much energy and determination) and I arranged a meeting of the Cork house committee for the following morning at the dispensary house, and the mayor promised to attend and confer. I also invited Mr. Ballard, one of the principal governors of the Cork Fever Hospital, to be present. At the meeting it appeared that half of the Union Fever Hospital would not afford accommodation for the cases of small-pox (which were rapidly increasing), and it was stated by Mr. Ballard that the Cork Fever Hospital could, at the very most, accommodate thirty-two patients labouring under small-pox. The committee then determined to appropriate the entire of the Union Fever Hospital for the reception of small-pox cases, and to send future fever patients to the Cork Fever Hospital. There is not much fever in the district at present, and even if there were, there is accommodation for a large number of fever patients in the Cork Fever Hospital, and the support of our fever patients there will cost very little more than they cost at present. I believe the governors will take each patient for 7*s.* 0*d.* a head, and the cost in our own fever hospital is 6*s.* 8*d.* a head per week.

It was necessary that the recommendation of the committee should receive the sanction of the Board of Guardians, and I consequently had a special meeting of the Board called for this day, and after a long and warm discussion the recommendation of the committee was adopted.

I have the honour to remain, gentlemen,

Your obedient servant,

CHARLES CROKER KING.

To the Poor Law Commissioners.

No. 13.—REPORT from DR. KING.

1, Belgrave-place, Cork,
GENTLEMEN, 6th February, 1872.

I have the honour to submit for your consideration the following report as to the progress of small-pox in this district, which I compiled this day at the Workhouse. I have been most particular in requesting the Medical Officers of the Workhouse to keep an accurate registry of all cases, as to whether the patients have or have not been vaccinated, and the result of my inquiry has been so far in favour of the influence of vaccination in averting death or modifying the disease, that I consider you should be made acquainted with the results.

	Patients.
Since the present invasion of the disease, there have been admitted into the Cork Union Fever Hospital, . .	232
Of these there were previously vaccinated . .	132
" " not vaccinated	100
Of the vaccinated there died	3
Of those who had not been vaccinated died . . .	39
The disease was mild and modified in	67

	Patients.
Of those in which the disease was mild . . . . . had been previously vaccinated.	80
It thus appears that the number of deaths out of 139 cases in the vaccinated was	3
And out of 100 cases of the unvaccinated	32

There are at present under treatment 124 cases. Of these, thirty-four are not sufficiently advanced in the disease to enable the Medical Officers to say positively whether the disease will be severe or mild; at the same time that the impression is that the disease will generally be mild in cases where the patient has been previously vaccinated.

Your obedient servant,

CHARLES CROKER KING.

To the Poor Law Commissioners.

No. 14.—EXTRACT from Dr. KING'S half-yearly REPORT on the CORK UNION; dated 10th March, 1872.

The sanitary state of the house is favourable, there is no prevailing epidemic, but Cork has suffered from a severe invasion of small-pox, but the general house has so far been kept wonderfully free from that disease. I attribute this in a great measure to the circumstance that the new probationary building enables us to establish a sort of quarantine for women and children, who when admitted (many of them from the neighbourhood in which small-pox is raging) are kept in this building for fourteen days after admission. Several attempts have been made to convert this building either into a small-pox hospital or into a convalescent home, which up to the present I have successfully resisted and by doing so have incurred some odium from a small section of the Board, who wished to save the small expense of erecting a couple of sheds which have answered admirably, and have in my opinion cost less than the alteration of the probationary building, and have averted the serious loss which would be sustained by the diversion of it to other than its legitimate use.

The fever hospital soon became occupied by small-pox patients and this disease having attacked some of the patients during convalescence from fever or scarlatina, an arrangement was entered into with the Cork Fever Hospital for the accommodation of union paupers affected by these diseases, and the fever hospital was appropriated for the treatment of small-pox exclusively, but even this extended accommodation was found insufficient, and consequently a large timber shed, 100 feet long, eighteen wide, and fourteen high, was erected, and subsequently a second shed of the same dimensions which is now ready, but has not as yet been occupied, as there has been a lull in the disease during the last few days, only nine cases having been admitted during the last three days, whereas the admissions have reached 15 a day, and on one day, the 2nd February, amounted to 23.

From the commencement of the epidemic of small-pox to the 8th of March, 463 patients had been admitted, labouring under this disease; amongst these 88 deaths have taken place, 26 of which occurred in children under 5 years of age; 39 died between the ages of 5 and 15, and 23, in persons above 15 years of age; of the 88 deaths, 73 took place in persons who had never been vaccinated.

The clothes of all the small-pox patients are regularly disinfected in the disinfecting room, which is heated for the purpose three times each week.

III.—REPORTS FROM MR. ROBINSON, POOR LAW INSPECTOR, AS TO THE MEANS TAKEN BY THE TWO DUBLIN BOARDS, TO PROVIDE HOSPITAL ACCOMMODATION FOR SMALL-POX CASES.

No. 1.—Letter from the Commissioners to Mr. Robinson, Poor Law Inspector.

Poor Law Commission Office, Dublin,
21st October, 1871.

Sir,

Referring to the recent increase of small-pox in Dublin on both sides of the river, as shown by the reports on the subject received from the Medical Officers of both the north and south city dispensary districts, the Commissioners for administering the Laws for Relief of the Poor in Ireland desire to state that it appears to them that an urgent necessity now exists for the Guardians of each Union (North and South Dublin) to provide themselves with accommodation for small-pox cases independently of the hospitals, maintained by parliamentary grant, or other hospitals, none of which are at present under the control of either of the two Boards.

Some of those hospitals, the Hardwicke in particular, do not profess to treat small-pox patients in perfect isolation from other patients, and several cases are known to have occurred of convalescent fever patients carrying the contagion of small-pox with them from hospital, and spreading it in the city.

The Commissioners request you, therefore, to attend the North and South Dublin Boards next week and bring the subject specially under their consideration.

In the meantime you may perhaps have the opportunity of considering the best locality in each Union for a small-pox hospital, and ascertaining where a proper building could be obtained.

By order of the Commissioners,

B. Banks, Chief Clerk.

To Henry Robinson, esq., Poor Law Inspector,
21, Cambridge-terrace, Kingstown.

No. 2.—Report from Mr. Robinson to the Commissioners.

Gentlemen,

Dublin, October 26th, 1871.

I have the honour to acknowledge the receipt of your letter of the 21st inst., relating to the prevalence of small-pox in Dublin; and I beg to inform you of the steps that I have taken to carry out the instructions contained in your communication.

I attended a meeting of the Guardians of the North Dublin Union yesterday, and brought the subject of the increase of small-pox under their notice, when they at once resolved, on my suggestion, to convert a portion of the auxiliary Workhouse at Glasnevin into a Small-pox Hospital. This auxiliary consists of a number of comfortable, well-ventilated sheds; and the sheds to be occupied by the sick can be separated from the remaining portion of the establishment, and will have a different entrance; and the Medical Officer in charge of it concurs with me in thinking that the arrangement can be adopted without any danger of infection to the inmates of the other part of the auxiliary. The Committee deputed to carry out this measure met to-day, and appointed, provisionally, a Medical Officer, a nurse, and a porter; and it is anticipated that the hospital, which will contain nearly one hundred beds, will be ready for the reception of patients on Saturday next.

I also attended, on this day, a meeting of the South Dublin Board of Guardians, and I made known to them your opinion that it would be advisable that they should establish an hospital independently of the hospitals at present existing in the city of Dublin; but the Board resolved, in the first instance, to inquire how far they could still obtain accommodation for small-pox cases in those hospitals, and they appointed a committee for that purpose; but they also empowered the committee, if it should appear to them to be necessary, to erect forthwith some wooden sheds for hospital purposes.

I understand that the governors of the Meath Hospital will allow the Guardians to erect sheds on their hospital grounds, which was done before during an epidemic of cholera, and this is a course which I believe the committee will at once adopt, should they, at their meeting to-morrow, deem it to be expedient.

Having made inquiry during the last few days as to the extent to which small-pox prevails in the city of Dublin, I think it right to report to you the information I obtained. I ascertained that, during the present month, there were about fifty cases of small-pox brought under the notice of the Medical Officers of the North City Dispensary District, and that there were about twenty-five cases reported in the South City District. I also found that there were yesterday forty-three cases of small-pox in the Hardwicke Hospital, and, on Monday, thirty cases in the Cork-street Hospital, and about seven or eight cases in other hospitals; there are, therefore, at present, about eighty cases of small-pox under treatment in the Dublin hospitals.

I have the honour to be, gentlemen,

Your obedient servant,

HENRY ROBINSON.

The Poor Law Commissioners.

No. 3.—REPORT from Mr. ROBINSON to the COMMISSIONERS.

GENTLEMEN, Dublin, October 28th, 1871.

With reference to my report to you of the 26th inst., I now beg to forward to you the following extract from a letter addressed to me by Mr. Byrne, a member of the committee appointed on Thursday last to provide accommodation for small-pox cases in the South Dublin Union, by which you will observe that wooden sheds, to contain from forty-five to fifty patients, will be erected at once in the grounds of the Meath Hospital:—

"The South Dublin Union Committee to-day met at 16, Peter-street, and adopted a series of resolutions, of which the clerk was directed to forward to you a copy.

"They afterwards saw the authorities of the Meath Hospital, the result of which is that from fifteen to twenty beds for small-pox patients will be at once available there; and in ten days, from forty-five to fifty more, in a wooden building which we propose to erect on the hospital grounds as before."

I have the honour to be, gentlemen,

Your obedient servant,

HENRY ROBINSON.

The Poor Law Commissioners.

No. 4.—Report from Mr. Robinson to the Commissioners.

Gentlemen, Dublin, November 2nd, 1871.

Adverting to my recent reports to you on the subject of hospital accommodation for small-pox cases in the South Dublin Union, I now have the honour to inform you that the Board of Guardians have abandoned the intention of building sheds in the grounds attached to the Meath Hospital, and have converted a portion of the auxiliary Workhouse at Kilmainham into a Small-pox Hospital.

The part of the auxiliary set apart for hospital purposes has been entirely separated from the rest of the establishment, and has a different entrance. A Medical Officer, a nurse, and a porter have been appointed to take charge of it, and it is now ready for the reception of patients.

These arrangements appear to me to be satisfactory, and the hospital will contain about twenty-seven sick persons.

I have the honour to be, gentlemen,

Your obedient servant,

Henry Robinson.

The Poor Law Commissioners.

No. 5.—Extract from Report from Mr. Robinson to the Commissioners, dated 5th December, 1871.

With reference to my former reports to you respecting the hospital provided by the South Dublin Board of Guardians for small-pox patients, I now beg to inform you that the hospital referred to has been enlarged, and that arrangements have this day been made to extend the accommodation still further.

IV.—CORRESPONDENCE ON THE NECESSITY OF PROVIDING SEPARATE WARDS AND CONVALESCENT ACCOMMODATION FOR SMALL-POX PATIENTS.

No. 1.—Letter from the Commissioners to the Under Secretary of the Lord Lieutenant.

Poor Law Commission Office, Dublin,

Sir, 11th January, 1871.

The Commissioners for administering the Laws for Relief of the Poor in Ireland have the honour to transmit to you herewith for the information of His Excellency the Lord Lieutenant, a copy of a circular letter which they issued on the 15th ult., on the subject of an outbreak of small-pox at Belfast.* The Commissioners submit this circular as showing the present danger which exists of small-pox reaching every part of this country from England and Wales and Scotland, as well as from the Continent.

The present state of the epidemic in Belfast is very alarming. Since the Commissioners last addressed His Excellency on the subject (on the

* See Annual Report for 1871, page 258.

14th ultimo), the number of patients suffering from small-pox in the Workhouse Hospital has risen from 37 to 65.

Finding that the neighbouring towns were exposed to contagion from Belfast, the Commissioners on the 9th ultimo wrote to the Boards of Guardians of the Unions of Antrim, Armagh, Ballymena, Banbridge, Cookstown, Downpatrick, Dungannon, Larne, Lisburn, Lurgan, Magherafelt, Newry, and Newtownards, informing them of their danger, and advising the immediate provision of separate small-pox wards in the Workhouse—a measure which has been generally adopted in those Unions. A copy of that letter is also sent herewith for His Excellency's information.*

The Commissioners understand that there are cases of small-pox now under treatment in one of the Dublin Hospitals assisted by Parliamentary grant.

The Commissioners submit to His Excellency's consideration the propriety of calling the attention of the Board of Superintendence of Dublin Hospitals to the subject, with the view of precautions being taken against the epidemic, by establishing in time small-pox wards separate from the other fever hospital wards, experience having shown beyond doubt that the treatment of small-pox in the general fever wards renders the hospital liable to become a means of spreading contagion to the surrounding population.

By order of the Commissioners,

B. Banks, Chief Clerk.

To T. H. Burke, esq., &c., &c.,
Dublin Castle.

No. 2.—Letter from the Under Secretary of the Lord Lieutenant to the Commissioners.

Gentlemen, Dublin Castle, 9th February, 1871.

Referring to your letter of the 11th ultimo, relative to an alleged case of small-pox under treatment in the Meath Hospital, I am directed by the Lord Lieutenant to transmit herewith, for your information, copy of a letter, with its enclosure, received from the Board of Superintendence of the City of Dublin Hospitals on the subject.

I am, gentlemen, your obedient servant,

T. H. Burke.

The Poor Law Commissioners, Custom House.

Enclosures in foregoing Letter.

33, Dawson-street, Dublin,
8th February, 1871.

Sir,

I am directed by the Board of Superintendence of Dublin Hospitals to forward to you the annexed documents, in reference to your letter of the 25th January last (No. 1,463), which, with the previous letters, and those of the Poor Law Commissioners, were laid before the Board yesterday.

I have, &c.,

(Signed) Denis Phelan, Secretary.

T. H. Burke, esq., Under Secretary,
Dublin Castle.

* See Appendix A, No. 1, page 13.

Tuesday.

I am not of opinion that the suggestion of the Poor Law Commissioners that separate wards should be provided in fever hospitals for cases of small-pox is a good one. In the Meath Hospital fever wards I do not remember a communicated case of small-pox in any fever patient for a quarter of a century.

Faithfully yours,

W. Stokes.

C. Fleming, esq., M.D.

Sir, Meath Hospital, 30th January, 1871.

I am directed by the Board of Governors of this Hospital, in answer to your letter of 21st inst. relative to the small-pox in Belfast, to state for the information of the Board of Superintendence of Hospitals, that it is more than doubtful if the case alleged to be under treatment in this hospital was a case of small-pox. The patient left hospital well last Wednesday.

I am, &c.,

(Signed) Edward Stapley.

D. Phelan, esq., M.D.

No. 3.—Letter from the Commissioners to the Under Secretary of the Lord Lieutenant.

Poor Law Commission Office, Dublin,
14th February, 1871.

Sir,

The Commissioners for administering the Laws for Relief of the Poor in Ireland acknowledge the receipt of your letter of the 9th instant, forwarding by direction of His Excellency the Lord Lieutenant, for their information, copy of a letter with its enclosure received from the Board of Superintendence of the City of Dublin Hospitals on the subject of an alleged case of small-pox under treatment in the Meath Hospital, and with regard to the Commissioners' suggestion, referred to by Dr. Stokes, that wards should be provided for the treatment of cases of small-pox, the Commissioners desire to state that the suggestion was founded upon cases of contagion communicated from the Workhouse Fever Hospital at Belfast by patients who left the Fever Hospital convalescent, carrying with them the seeds of disease contracted from patients treated in the same ward.

The Commissioners have the honour to forward for His Excellency's information a copy of a letter which has been addressed to Dr. Curran, Dispensary medical officer, on the subject of the admission of small pox patients to the Mater Misericordiæ Hospital, which shows that a separate ward for small-pox is there the rule.

By order of the Commissioners,

B. Banks, Chief Clerk.

To Thos. H. Burke, esq., &c., &c., Dublin Castle.

Enclosure in foregoing Letter.

Clerk's Office, North Brunswick-street, Dublin,
10th February, 1871.

Sir,

I beg herewith to forward you copy of a letter received from Dr. Curran as regards the admission of small-pox patients into the Mater Misericordiæ Hospital.

I am, sir, your obedient servant,

Thos. H. Atkinson.

H. Robinson, esq.

Convent of our Lady of Mercy,
St. Catherine's, Baggot-street,
MY DEAR DR. CURRAN, February 9th, 1871.

Will you kindly make known to the Committee of the North Union that we shall set apart two wards at the extremity of the new wing of the Mater Misericordiæ Hospital for the reception of cases of small pox, but we cannot bind ourselves to admit more than we have vacancies for in these wards, as this would spread the contagion and endanger the lives of patients under treatment for other diseases. You may be sure the Sisters will not fall short of any assistance they can give the Dispensaries should this terrible disease become prevalent. At the same time we are obliged to have regard to the other patients, and cautiously avoid exposing them to new dangers, or giving them any reason for complaint.

Believe me, dear Dr. Curran,
Faithfully yours in J. C.,
Sister M. E. FORBE.

No. 4.—LETTER from the COMMISSIONERS to the UNDER SECRETARY of the LORD LIEUTENANT.

Poor Law Commission Office, Dublin,
SIR, 7th August, 1871.

With reference to the correspondence which took place in the early part of the present year on the subject of the arrangements for the reception and treatment of small-pox cases in the Dublin Hospitals, the Commissioners for administering the Laws for Relief of the Poor in Ireland forward for the information of His Excellency the Lord Lieutenant the accompanying copy of a letter which they have received from Dr. Gerald Osbrey, one of the medical officers of the North City Dispensary District, reporting the occurrence of a case of small-pox in the person of a girl aged fourteen years, named Eliza Conlan, lately a patient in the Hardwicke Hospital, who states that there were some cases of small-pox in the ward of that hospital in which she had been under treatment for fever.

It would appear from Dr. Osbrey's statement that the disease of small-pox was contracted in the Hardwicke Hospital in this case.

By order of the Commissioners,
B. BANKS, Chief Clerk.

To Thomas H. Burke, esq., &c.,
Dublin Castle.

ENCLOSURE in foregoing LETTER.

North Dublin Union, No. 2 District,
20, Coleraine-street,
GENTLEMEN, July 29th, 1871.

I beg to report that a patient of the name of Eliza Conlan, æt. 14, affected with modified variola, and resident at 12 Greek-street, was sent by me to the Hardwicke Hospital on the 27th instant. The patient stated that she had left the Hardwicke Hospital some day previously to having been visited by me, and that there were some cases of small-pox in the ward in which she had been under treatment for fever. She had been vaccinated in childhood.

Yours, obedient,
GERALD OSBREY.

The Poor Law Commissioners.

No. 5.—LETTER from the COMMISSIONERS to the UNDER SECRETARY of the LORD LIEUTENANT.

Poor Law Commission Office, Dublin,
SIR, 2nd October, 1871.

With reference to their letter of the 28th August last, transmitting a letter from Dr. Fitzgibbon on the subject of the arrangements for the reception and treatment of cases of small-pox in the Dublin Hospitals, the Commissioners for administering the Laws for Relief of the Poor in Ireland have the honour to forward, for the information of their Excellencies the Lords Justices, the accompanying copy of a letter which they have received from Dr. Nowlan, one of the Medical Officers of the North City Dispensary District, reporting the occurrence of a case of small-pox in his district, the patient having, in his opinion, contracted the disease whilst in the Hardwicke Hospital; and several similar cases of persons admitted for fever and other diseases contracting small-pox in hospital, having come under his observation.

By order of the Commissioners,

B. BANKS, Chief Clerk.

To Thomas H. Burke, esq., &c.,
Dublin Castle.

ENCLOSURE in foregoing LETTER.

GENTLEMEN, 46, Talbot-street, 26th September, 1871.

I have to report that Laurence Lawless, of 2, Lower Oriel-street, was this day removed to the Hardwicke Hospital, suffering from small-pox. He was discharged from that hospital some three weeks ago. I have no doubt he contracted the disease whilst in hospital. I take this opportunity of stating that several similar cases of persons admitted for fever and other diseases contracting small-pox in hospital have come under my observation. I believe that isolated special hospital accommodation is essential for successfully limiting the disease.

I remain, gentlemen, your obedient servant,

JOHN P. NOWLAN, Medical Officer,
No. 1, North City Dispensary.

To the Poor Law Commissioners.

No. 6.—LETTER from the CHIEF SECRETARY of the LORD LIEUTENANT to the COMMISSIONERS.

GENTLEMEN, Dublin Castle, 19th October, 1871.

Referring to your letter of the 2nd instant, I am directed by the Lord Lieutenant to transmit to you the accompanying copy of a report which has been received from the Secretary of the Board of Superintendence of the Dublin Hospitals, relative to the case of Laurence Lawless.

I am, gentlemen, your obedient servant,

HARTINGTON.

The Poor Law Commissioners.

ENCLOSURE in foregoing LETTER.

SIR, 35, Dawson-street, 17th October, 1871.

I am directed by the Board of Superintendence of the Dublin Hospitals to acknowledge receipt of yours of the 4th October, No. 17,522, enclosing letter from Poor Law Commissioners, with communication from Dr. Nowlan stating that a patient, Laurence Lawless, had been discharged from the Hardwicke Hospital "some three weeks ago," and that he was readmitted on the 26th of September suffering from small-pox. Dr. Nowlan had no doubt the disease was contracted in that hospital.

In reply I am directed to observe that the period stated to have elapsed—viz., "some three weeks"—between Lawless's leaving the hospital and his re-admission labouring under small-pox, renders it most improbable that it was in the Hardwicke Hospital he contracted the disease.

The Governors and the Medical Officers of the House of Industry Hospitals use their best efforts to prevent the spreading of small-pox.

Were it even desirable to erect "isolated special hospitals," on which there is diversity of opinions, there are no available funds.

I have, &c.,

(Signed) Wm. J. Martin, Secretary.

T. H. Burke, esq., Under Secretary.

No. 7.—Letter from the Commissioners to Dr. Nowlan.

Poor Law Commission Office, Dublin,
24th October, 1871.

Sir,

Adverting to your letter of the 26th ultimo, reporting the occurrence of a case of small pox in your district of the North City Dispensary District, in the person of Laurence Lawless, of 3, Lower Oriel-street, who you were of opinion contracted the disease in the Hardwicke Hospital where he had been previously under treatment, the Commissioners for administering the Laws for Relief of the Poor in Ireland transmit to you herewith a copy of a report on the subject from the Secretary of the Board of Superintendence of the Dublin Hospitals, which has been forwarded to the Commissioners by the Chief Secretary of His Excellency the Lord Lieutenant, and the Commissioners request that you will have the goodness to favour them with your observations thereon.

The Commissioners would feel obliged by your stating, if you can, the date on which Lawless was discharged from the Hardwicke Hospital, and the date on which the disease of small-pox first manifested itself in him.

By order of the Commissioners,

B. Banks, Chief Clerk.

To Dr. Nowlan, Medical Officer, North City
Dispensary District, 40, Talbot-street.

No. 8.—Letter from the Commissioners to the Chief Secretary of the Lord Lieutenant.

Poor Law Commission Office, Dublin,
24th October, 1871.

Sir,

With reference to their letter of the 2nd instant, transmitting a letter from Dr. Nowlan, one of the Medical Officers of the North City Dispensary District of North Dublin Union, on the subject of the arrangements for the reception and treatment of cases of small-pox in the Dublin Hospitals, the Commissioners for administering the Laws for Relief of the Poor in Ireland have the honour to forward, for the information of His Excellency the Lord Lieutenant, as another instance of the dissemination of small-pox from hospital, a copy of a letter which they have received from Dr. Usher, one of the Medical Officers of the Dundrum and Glencullen Dispensary

District of Rathdown Union, reporting the occurrence of a case of small-pox, at Neilstown, in that District, on the 18th instant, in the person of a police-constable named Robert Cody, aged about twenty years, who was lately a patient in the Hardwicke Fever Hospital, and had only returned home from thence a few days before.

By order of the Commissioners,

B. Banks, Chief Clerk.

To the Right Hon. the Marquess of Hartington, M.P.,
Chief Secretary, &c., &c., Dublin Castle.

Enclosure in foregoing Letter.

Dundrum, co. Dublin, 20th October, 1871.

Gentlemen,—In accordance with my instructions, I beg to inform you of a case of "small-pox" that occurred in my district on Wednesday last. I was sent for to see, at his mother's residence, in Neilstown, Police Constable Robert Cody, aged about twenty years, who had been but a few days home from the Hardwicke Fever Hospital, where he had been laid up for some weeks, and where he no doubt contracted the disease which developed itself a few hours before I saw him. Having explained the danger to his family, I *immediately* sent for the police van, and had him conveyed back to the Hardwicke Hospital, where he now lies, going on favourably, as I have been informed.

He had a *good mark* of primary vaccination. I revaccinated all the young members of his family, and had his room cleansed, chloride of lime, &c., being used, hoping thus to prevent the disease spreading.

I remain, gentlemen, your obedient servant,

Isaac W. Usher.

To the Poor Law Commissioners.

No. 9.—Letter from the Commissioners to the Under Secretary of the Lord Lieutenant.

Poor Law Commission Office, Dublin,
1st November, 1871.

Sir,

With reference to the report from the Secretary of the Board of Superintendence of the Dublin Hospitals, relative to the case of Laurence Lawless, a convalescent fever patient, who was recently discharged from the Hardwicke Hospital, and was shortly afterwards found to be suffering from small-pox, a copy of which was forwarded to the Commissioners by direction of His Excellency the Lord Lieutenant, on the 19th ultimo, the Commissioners for administering the Laws for Relief of the Poor in Ireland have now the honour to forward, for the information of His Excellency, a copy of a further report which they have received from Dr. Nowlan, relating to the case, dated the 27th ultimo, in which he adverts also to other cases of a similar nature, and to the danger convalescent patients incur when small-pox cases are treated in or near to the fever wards.

A separate hospital for small-pox cases has now been established by the Board of Guardians of North Dublin Union, and was opened for the reception of patients on Saturday last.

The South Dublin Board have determined, for a similar purpose of treatment and isolation, to erect sheds within the grounds of the Meath Hospital, with the approval of the Governors.

By order of the Commissioners,

B. Banks, Chief Clerk.

To the Under Secretary of His Excellency the
Lord Lieutenant, Dublin Castle.

Enclosure in foregoing Letter.

Gentlemen, 46, Talbot-street, 27th October, 1871.

I received yours of the 24th instant, No. 26,356, enclosing a letter from the Secretary of the Board of Superintendence of the Dublin Hospitals for my observations. I may remark that the date of readmission into hospital is no evidence of the duration of the disease. I visited Lawless the 22nd of September: he was then in the febrile stage of the disease; the period of incubation of small-pox is fixed at from ten to sixteen days. His friends state he sickened a week after leaving hospital, they cannot fix the exact date nearer than it was between the 17th and 22nd of September. Since my report of the father's case, *four cases of small-pox have occurred in this family*, resulting in two deaths. My colleague, Dr. Ferguson, now in charge of this portion of the district, has reported these cases. I entertain no doubt that the admission of small-pox into general hospitals tends to spread the disease. I have procured a list of some cases in my district which I append in proof of my statement. It is but fair to state that the same observations apply to the Mater Misericordiæ Hospital. Sanitary Sergeant Berry has drawn my attention to them and other cases *out of* my district. I have confined myself to those cases of which I have knowledge when they suffered from fever previous to admission into hospital. Within these few days I visited each house, in order to verify the correctness of the fact. Some years ago I remember patients going into the Hardwicke Hospital and contracting *small-pox there*. I spoke to Dr. M'Dowell on the subject; I visited a hospital ward with him, every possible sanitary precaution was taken, but yet without effect. While I believe vaccination can resist the ordinary miasm of small-pox, yet to expose a patient convalescing from fever to an atmosphere highly impregnated with small-pox poison, is to run the risk of producing the disease in its worst form. Each patient discharged from hospital on his or her return home serves as a fresh centre for spreading the disease. I believe isolated special hospitals for treating the disease, with a convalescent hospital some distance from town, where the patient could remain until fully recovered, and all further risk of contagion avoided. I make these observations in the interest of the sick poor, and knowing your anxiety to prevent the further spread of the disease.

I remain, gentlemen, your obedient servant,

John P. Nowlan.

To the Poor Law Commissioners.

List referred to.

No. 1. Henry Loftus, of 4, Gregg's-lane, admitted to the Hardwicke Hospital with fever, readmitted with small-pox.

No. 2. Joseph Loftus, of 4, Gregg's-lane, admitted to the Hardwicke Hospital with fever, readmitted with small-pox.

No. 3. Robert Charleson, of Johnson's-court, admitted to the Hardwicke Hospital with fever, readmitted with small-pox.

No. 4. Edward Molloy, of Strong's-court, admitted to the Hardwicke Hospital with pleurisy, readmitted with small-pox.

No. 5. Jane Meehan, of 4, Courtney place, admitted with fever, got small-pox in hospital.

No. 6. Anne Power, of 9, Kelly's-row, admitted to the Mater Misericordiæ Hospital with fever, returned on the fifth day to the Hardwicke Hospital with small-pox.

No. 7. Bridget Doyle, of 9, Lower Temple-street, admitted to the Mater Misericordiæ Hospital with scarlatina, readmitted on fourth day with small-pox.

No. 8. Her sister, Catharine Doyle, of 9, Lower Temple-street, went to the Mater Misericordiæ Hospital with small-pox and died there.

John P. Nowlan.

28th October, 1871.

No. 10.—EXTRACT from LETTER from the BOARD of SUPERINTENDENCE to the UNDER SECRETARY—referred to the COMMISSIONERS.

Board of Superintendence of the Dublin Hospitals,
SIR, Office, 35, Dawson-street, 2nd November, 1871.

I am directed by the Board of Superintendence of the Dublin Hospitals to acknowledge receipt of your letter of the 27th ultimo.

In reference to case of Police Constable Cody, alleged to have taken small-pox in the Hardwicke Fever Hospital, it does not appear that he was in a ward with small-pox cases, nor is the interval stated that elapsed between his discharge from hospital and the breaking out of the disease; this is a matter on which there should be precision, as the length of interval is of use, in arriving at a probable knowledge of the place in which the infection was caught; hence it does not appear where Cody contracted the disease.

Small-pox patients are admitted to the wards in the Hardwicke Hospital, and always have been since its foundation; it is much better that such practice should continue with its risks, than that small-pox patients should be denied admission, as the disease is more likely to spread its contagion among the poor in their own ill-ventilated and crowded apartments, than in the large and airy wards of the Hardwicke Hospital.

I have, &c.,
WILLIAM J. MARTIN, Secretary.

R. N. Matheson, esq.,
Chief Secretary's Office, Dublin Castle.

No. 11.—LETTER from the CHIEF SECRETARY'S OFFICE to the COMMISSIONERS.

GENTLEMEN, Dublin Castle, 13th November, 1871.

With reference to previous correspondence relative to the arrangements for the reception and treatment of small-pox cases in Dublin Hospitals, I am directed by the Lord Lieutenant to transmit to you copy of a further letter from the Board of Superintendence of the Dublin Hospitals on the subject.

I am, gentlemen, your obedient servant,
R. N. MATHESON.

The Poor Law Commissioners.

ENCLOSURE in foregoing LETTER.

Board of Superintendence of the Dublin Hospitals,
SIR, Office, 35, Dawson-street, 7th November, 1871.

I am directed by the Board of Superintendence of the Dublin Hospitals to acknowledge receipt of your letter, No. 19,300, of the 4th instant, transmitting for their information a communication from the Poor Law Commissioners, together with a letter from Dr. J. Nowlan, of the 27th ult., respecting the dissemination of small-pox, with appended list of cases.

I am directed to inform you, for the information of His Excellency, that the Board do not think it necessary to make any further observations beyond those contained in their letters of the 17th October and the 2nd inst.

I have, &c.,
(Signed) W. J. MARTIN, Secretary.

R. N. Matheson, esq.

No. 12.—LETTER from the COMMISSIONERS to the UNDER SECRETARY.

Poor Law Commission Office, Dublin,
SIR, 27th November, 1871.

The Commissioners for administering the Laws for Relief of the Poor in Ireland return to you herewith the letter from the Board of Superintendence of the Dublin Hospitals, dated the 2nd inst., which was referred to them on the 4th inst., in reference to the case of Police Constable Cody, who was alleged to have taken small-pox while under treatment as a patient in the Hardwicke Hospital; and in reference thereto the Commissioners have the honour to forward for the information of His Excellency the Lord Lieutenant, a copy of a letter dated 17th inst., which they have received from Dr. Usher, by whom the case was originally brought under their notice, from which it appears that Cody left the hospital on the 13th October, and that on the 18th of that month Dr. Usher saw him covered with the eruption.

It would appear from the letter of the Board of Superintendence now returned, as well as from that of the 17th October last (both of which are referred to in their letter of the 7th inst., a copy of which was forwarded to the Commissioners with your letter of the 13th instant), that the practice complained of by Dispensary Medical Officers, and represented by the Commissioners to His Excellency, still continued and was intended to be continued; but the Commissioners have learned, from inquiry recently made by their Inspector, Mr. Robinson, that this is not the case—that wards quite separate from the rest of the hospital have been provided, and are now in use for small-pox cases; and the Commissioners trust, therefore, that there will be no further occasion for the Commissioners to address His Excellency on the subject.

Your obedient servant,

D. BANKS, Chief Clerk.

To R. N. Matheson, esq.,
Chief Secretary's Office, Dublin Castle.

ENCLOSURE in foregoing LETTER.

GENTLEMEN, Dundrum, Co. Dublin, November 17th, 1871.

In answer to your letter dated November 13th, 1871, asking me to report to you what length of time elapsed between Constable Cody's discharge from the Hardwicke Hospital and the breaking out of the small-pox on his person, I beg to inform you that he left said hospital on the 13th of October to go to Nellstown in my district, and on the 18th of same month I was sent for to see him, when I found him covered with the eruption, which clearly shows he brought home the disease, of which he was much afraid when in hospital.

On inquiry this day, I find he is home again from hospital at his own request, and just at a time when he will be most likely to spread the disease.

I remain, gentlemen, your obedient servant,

I. W. USHER.

No. 13.—LETTER from the CLERK of the SOUTH DUBLIN UNION to the UNDER SECRETARY of the LORD LIEUTENANT, referred to the COMMISSIONERS.

South Dublin Union, Clerk's Office, Board Room,
SIR, James's-street, 11th day of January, 1872.

I have the honour to enclose copy of a report laid before the Board of Guardians of this Union by their Relieving Officer, Entwisle, at their meeting this day, on the subject of providing accommodation for persons recovering from small-pox, and to convey their respectful request that you will have the goodness to submit same to His Excellency the Lord Lieutenant.

I have the honour, &c.,

Geo. Hepburn, Clerk of the Union.

To the Under Secretary,
Secretary's Office, Dublin Castle.

Relieving Officer's Report, enclosed in foregoing Letter.

9th January, 1872.

I beg to report for the information of the Board of Guardians of the South Dublin Union, that persons recovering from small-pox have applied to me for admission to the Workhouse. As I believe it would not be safe to admit such persons, fearing it would be the means of communicating the infection to the inmates, I therefore bring this matter under the notice of the Board, and would respectfully urge upon them the necessity of providing some place for their reception; and if the part of Grangegorman Prison cannot be obtained, that, as in the time of the cholera a house in Nicholas-street was provided for persons recovering from that disease, a similar house should at once be provided and fitted up for persons recovering from small-pox.

E. Entwisle, Relieving Officer.

No. 14.—Letter from the Commissioners to the Board of Guardians of South Dublin Union.

Poor Law Commission Office, Dublin,
13th January, 1872.

Sir,

The Commissioners for administering the Laws for Relief of the Poor in Ireland have received from the office of the Chief Secretary of His Excellency the Lord Lieutenant a letter addressed by you to the Under Secretary on the 11th inst., forwarding copy of a report made to the Board of Guardians of South Dublin Union by Mr. Entwisle, relieving officer, suggesting the necessity of providing some separate place for the reception of persons recovering from small-pox, who make application for admission into the Workhouse, and in reference thereto, the Commissioners desire to inform the Board of Guardians that the inquiry made by the medical inspector as referred to in their letter to the Board of Guardians of the 11th inst., has resulted in a report altogether adverse to the proposal of using part of Grangegorman Prison for a convalescent home for small-pox patients.

The Commissioners think no time should be lost by the Guardians of South Dublin Union in providing a convalescent home to be separately occupied under their own control and that of their officers, and that an immediate meeting of the Board should take place for the purpose of making the necessary arrangements.

The Guardians of North Dublin Union have, as the Commissioners are apprized, already taken steps to provide themselves with accommodation for the purpose under their own separate control.

By order, &c.,

B. Banks, Chief Clerk.

To the Clerk of South Dublin Union.

No. 15.—Letter from the Commissioners to the Board of North Dublin Union.

Poor Law Commission Office, Dublin,
Sir, 13th January, 1872.

The Commissioners for administering the Laws for Relief of the Poor in Ireland desire to inform the Board of Guardians of North Dublin Union, that a letter addressed by the Board of Guardians of South Dublin Union on the 11th inst. to the Under Secretary of His Excellency the Lord Lieutenant on the subject of providing a convalescent home for small-pox patients has been forwarded to them, and that the Commissioners have informed the Board of Guardians in reply that the inquiry made by their Medical Inspector, Dr. King, has resulted in a report altogether adverse to the proposal of using part of Grangegorman Prison for a convalescent home for small-pox patients.

The Commissioners think no time should be lost by the Guardians in providing a convalescent home to be separately occupied under their own control and that of their officers, and that an immediate meeting of the Board should take place for the purpose of making the necessary arrangements.

The Commissioners believe that some steps have been already taken by the Board of Guardians of North Dublin Union with this object.

By order, &c.,
B. Banks, Chief Clerk.

To the Clerk of North Dublin Union.

No. 16.—Report from Mr. Robinson, Poor Law Inspector, to the Commissioners.

Gentlemen, Kingstown, January 20, 1872.

With reference to the correspondence that has taken place on the subject of a convalescent home for small-pox patients discharged from hospitals in Dublin, I have now the honour to inform you that the North and South Dublin Boards of Guardians have made arrangements to establish convalescent hospitals in their respective Unions.

In the North Dublin Union a portion of the Auxiliary Workhouse at Glasnevin has been set apart for the purpose, and the convalescent hospital there will be ready for occupation on Monday next; in the South Dublin Union a somewhat similar arrangement has been made at the Auxiliary Workhouse at Kilmainham, and this hospital will be open this evening.

In both Unions all communication has been cut off between the wards and yards allocated to the convalescent small-pox patients and the other parts of the auxiliaries; there is a separate entrance to each department, and the duties of the resident officers will be confined exclusively to the convalescent hospitals in which they are employed.

I have the honour to be, gentlemen,
Your obedient servant,
Henry Robinson.

The Poor Law Commissioners.

No. 17.—LETTER from the COMMISSIONERS to the UNDER SECRETARY of the LORD LIEUTENANT.

Poor Law Commission Office, Dublin,
SIR, 20th January, 1872.

With reference to previous correspondence on the subject the Commissioners for administering the Laws for Relief of the Poor in Ireland have the honour to forward for the inspection of His Excellency the Lord Lieutenant the accompanying copy of a report from their inspector Mr. Robinson, showing the arrangements made by the Boards of Guardians of the North and South Dublin Unions, to establish convalescent hospitals in their respective Unions for the reception of small-pox patients discharged from the Union hospitals.

The letter of relieving officer Entwisle, forwarded to the Chief Secretary's office by the Guardians of South Dublin Union on the 11th inst., and referred to the Commissioners, appears to relate to convalescents from the small-pox hospitals generally, and not to those of the Poor Law Unions only; and the Commissioners fear that the provision made by the Unions, as described in Mr. Robinson's report, being available only for the Poor Law convalescents, will leave it necessary for some similar provision to be made for convalescents from other hospitals.

The Commissioners understand from the public press that the health committee of the Corporation are still looking out for a proper building for a convalescent home; but it occurs to the Commissioners to be worthy of consideration whether this duty does not properly belong to the Board of Superintendence of Dublin Hospitals in relation to the Hardwicke Fever Hospital, which is wholly supported by parliamentary grant, and also to the Cork-street Hospital, which receives an annual subsidy from the same fund, and which, as well as the Hardwicke, is under the superintendence of that Board. It is probable that the funds assigned for the service of the present year are not more than sufficient for the ordinary requirements of the several hospitals subsidised from the annual grant; but it might be practicable to obtain from the Lords of the Treasury permission to exceed the limits of the annual grant on an occasion so pressing as the present, and to remedy the deficiency hereafter by a supplementary estimate.

The letter from the Guardians of South Dublin Union (with its enclosure) is herewith returned.

By order, &c.,
B. BANKS, Chief Clerk.

To Thomas H. Burke, &c., &c.,
Dublin Castle.

No. 18.—LETTER from the UNDER SECRETARY of the LORD LIEUTENANT to the COMMISSIONERS.

GENTLEMEN, Dublin Castle, 15th February, 1872.

With reference to your letter of the 24th ultimo, relative to providing convalescent wards for small-pox patients, I am directed by the Lord Lieutenant to transmit to you herewith copies of communications from the Board of Superintendence of the Dublin Hospitals on the subject, together with copies of the enclosures therein.

I am, gentlemen, your obedient servant,
T. H. BURKE.

The Poor Law Commissioners, Custom House.

ENCLOSURES in foregoing LETTER.

Board of Superintendence of the Dublin Hospitals' Office,
23, Dawson-street, 13th February, 1872.

SIR,

In reference to my letter of the 7th inst. addressed to you, I beg to enclose for the information of His Excellency copies of replies received from the Board of Governors of the House of Industry Hospitals, and from the Managing Committee of the Cork-street Fever Hospital; and to draw His Excellency's attention to the communication from the Board of Governors of the House of Industry Hospitals, from which it appears that by Act 14 & 15 Vic., cap. 68, sec. 19, the Poor Law Commissioners are the "Commissioners for executing the powers and purposes of the Nuisances Removal and Diseases Prevention Act, 1848," and that under that Act on the Poor Law Commissioners devolves the responsibility of taking whatever measures may be necessary for preventing or mitigating epidemic, endemic, or contagious disease.

I have the honour to be, sir,
Your obedient servant,
W. J. MARTIN, Secretary.

Thomas H. Burke, esq.,
Under Secretary, Dublin Castle.

(COPY.)

Fever Hospital, Cork-street, Dublin,
8th February, 1872.

SIR,

I have the honour to acknowledge receipt of your letter of yesterday's date, and am directed to state in reply, that the Governors of this institution have had open for some time a convalescent ward for the exclusive use of small-pox patients. This ward contains beds in proportion to the full number of acute cases of that disease which the Hospital can accommodate.

The Governors also wish to call attention to the fact that the establishment and maintenance of the *special wards* for acute and convalescent patients under *small-pox*, have totally exhausted the ordinary funds at their disposal, and they have been obliged to appeal to the public for means to enable them to continue to keep these wards open; they regret to state that up to the present much success has not attended this effort.

I have the honour to be, sir,
Your obedient servant,
(Signed) T. F. EUSTACE, Registrar.

W. J. Martin, esq., Secretary, Board of
Superintendence of the Dublin Hospitals.

(COPY.)

House of Industry Hospitals, Dublin,
8th February, 1872.

SIR,

I am directed by the Board of Governors of the House of Industry Hospitals (which includes the Hardwicke Fever Hospital) to acknowledge the receipt of your letter of the 7th inst., with enclosures, and to acquaint you in reply, for the information of the Board of Superintendence of the Dublin Hospitals, that the Governors have not the power, nor have they any funds with which to erect or maintain any buildings to serve as Convalescent Hospitals.

The Governors have done all in their power to meet the present epidemic visitation, not only to the full extent to which their funds have enabled them, but they have incurred a considerable debt in continuing their efforts; and they regret they must now contract the admissions, as they cannot feel justified in increasing their debt.

This Board addressed communications to the Poor Law Commissioners and Public Health Committee of the Corporation some months since, informing them that the accommodation of the Hardwicke Fever Hospital was exhausted.

I am further to observe that by the Act 14 & 15 Vic., cap. 68, sec. 19, 1851, the Poor Law Commissioners are appointed the Commissioners for executing in Ireland the powers and purposes of "The Nuisances Removal and Diseases Prevention Act, 1848;" and that under that Act the Poor Law Commissioners are empowered to take measures generally for "preventing or mitigating such epidemic, endemic, or contagious diseases, in such manner as may seem expedient," and may authorize and require Boards of Guardians to carry out such measures.

This Board therefore quite concur in the observations of the Board of Superintendence that the responsibility of providing convalescent hospitals, or whatever extended hospital accommodation is required, devolves wholly on the Poor Law authorities.

I am, sir, your obedient servant,

(Signed) Jas. W. Hughes, Secretary, &c.

W. J. Martin, esq., M.D., Secretary to Board of Superintendence of the Dublin Hospitals.

Board of Superintendence of the Dublin Hospitals' Office,
Sir, 35, Dawson-street, 7th February, 1872.

I am directed by the Board of Superintendence of the Dublin Hospitals to forward to the Governors of the House of Industry Hospitals, and to the Managing Committee of the Cork-street Fever Hospital, copies of your letter of the 2nd inst., No. 1,287, requesting to be informed whether such convalescent hospitals can be provided by the Governors of the above institutions.

I have further to observe as to the advisability of establishing convalescent hospitals, that the Board of Superintendence is of opinion that such a measure would be most desirable, but the Board has no power in the matter, its functions being confined altogether to the supervision of certain hospitals in the city of Dublin, and the economic management of their funds.

The Board of Superintendence understands that the law imposes on the Poor Law Commissioners and the respective Boards of Guardians the duty of providing all such extended hospital accommodation as may be required to meet epidemic visitations.

I have the honour to be, sir,

Your obedient servant,

W. J. Martin, Secretary.

Thomas H. Burke, esq.,
Under Secretary, Dublin Castle.

APPENDIX D.

TABULAR RETURNS IN CONNEXION WITH RELIEF UNDER THE MEDICAL CHARITIES ACT.

[NOTE.—In this series of Tables, the Unions are classed in the Counties and Provinces in which the chief or central place of the respective Unions is situate; but many of the Unions comprise parts of more than one County or Province. The total of Population and Area of the Unions in the respective Counties and Provinces, as arranged in these Tables, will not, therefore, agree with the summaries of those Counties and Provinces in the Census Returns. An Alphabetical Index List of the Dispensary Districts is annexed (No. 6), showing the name of the Union in which each District is situate, and referring to the table and page in which the particulars relating to each District are to be found.]

No. 1.—Statement of the Dispensary Districts formed in the Poor Law Unions in Ireland up to 25th March, 1872, (arranged in Provinces and Counties), according to Orders issued from time to time, by the Commissioners, in pursuance of § 6 of 14 and 15 Vic., c. 68.

Names of Unions and Dispensary Districts.	No. of Electoral Divisions in each.	Population: 1871.	Area in Statute Acres.			Poor Law Valuation: 1871.			No. of Members of Committee of Management.	No. of Medical Officers.	Number of Apothecaries.	Number of Midwives.
Column 1.	2.	3.	4.			5.			6.	7.	8.	9.
PROVINCE OF ULSTER.												
County of Antrim.			A.	R.	P.	£	s.	d.				
Antrim Union.												
1. Antrim, . . .	2	6,283	14,378	1	16	21,828	14	0	19	1	–	–
2. Crumlin, . .	4	8,743	23,418	1	33	23,686	10	0	15	1	–	–
3. Templepatrick, .	3	8,692	21,172	3	19	23,177	6	0	17	1	–	–
4. Dough, . . .	3	6,940	15,292	0	13	19,136	6	0	15	1	–	–
5. Connor, . . .	3	5,975	21,669	2	2	13,651	4	0	15	1	–	–
6. Randalstown, . .	4	9,049	20,617	3	25	20,617	7	0	13	1	–	–
	19	39,682	117,110	0	28	122,116	5	0	91	6	–	–
Ballycastle Union.												
1. Ballycastle, . .	7	8,421	46,205	2	38	19,308	9	0	23	1	–	–
2. Creagh, . . .	4	6,557	22,653	0	9	14,307	12	0	17	1	–	–
3. Cushendall, . .	4	4,675	34,336	2	1	9,861	14	0	15	1	–	–
	15	19,653	103,197	1	8	43,608	15	0	55	3	–	–
Ballymena Union.												
1. Ballymena, . .	2	11,620	8,282	0	22	25,118	13	0	19	1	–	1
2. Galgorm, . .	2	11,166	16,696	0	25	17,437	18	0	22	1	–	–
3. Ahoghill, . .	3	8,269	14,356	3	18	13,441	13	0	17	1	–	–
4. Portglenone, . .	5	10,036	17,205	0	28	17,929	9	0	17	1	–	–
5. Clogh, . . .	4	7,963	38,924	2	24	12,221	11	0	20	1	–	–
6. Broughshane, . .	3	7,976	30,065	2	34	14,373	9	0	13	1	–	–
7. Glenwhirry, . .	3	7,155	32,710	2	18	13,991	12	0	13	1	–	–
8. Toome, . . .	3	8,630	15,714	3	14	12,855	18	0	15	1	–	–
	23	74,397	161,161	1	19	123,490	15	0	136	8	–	1
Ballymoney Union.												
1. Ballymoney, . .	4	10,048	21,633	3	23	24,410	2	0	24	1	–	–
2. Dervock, . .	4	6,901	20,719	0	15	14,705	9	0	20	1	–	–
3. Castle Quarter, .	6	6,510	35,851	0	21	14,692	4	0	20	1	–	–
4. Dirraw, . . .	5	9,140	26,971	3	10	14,945	16	0	23	1	–	–
5. Kilrea, . . .	4	9,660	24,382	1	15	12,864	5	0	16	1	–	–
	22	41,383	127,510	1	27	81,617	16	0	103	5	–	–
Belfast Union.												
1. Belfast, . . .	7	125,875	31,334	2	16	454,220	11	0	89	10	2	3
2. Castlereagh, . .	5	17,634	16,477	0	8	83,639	5	0	40	3	–	1
	12	144,629	47,811	2	24	537,830	16	0	129	13	2	4
Larne Union.												
1. Glenarm, . .	3	5,932	36,210	3	20	13,336	4	0	16	1	–	1
2. Larne, . . .	4	9,119	30,255	1	18	25,518	11	0	21	1	–	–
3. Ballynure, . .	3	5,634	20,306	3	37	13,027	0	0	15	1	–	–
4. Ballycarry, . .	2	4,969	14,157	1	24	16,641	9	0	15	1	–	–
5. Carrickfergus, . .	1	9,423	16,702	0	34	23,366	7	0	21	1	–	1
	13	35,077	117,763	3	8	92,886	11	0	87	5	–	2

[continued.

No. 1.—Statement of Dispensary Districts—*continued.*

Names of Unions and Dispensary Districts.	No. of Electoral Divisions in each.	Population 1861.	Area in Statute Acres.			Poor Law Valuation 1861.			No. of Members of Committee of Management.	No. of Medical Officers.	Number of Apothecaries.	Number of Midwives.
Column 1.	2.	3.	4.			5.			6.	7.	8.	9.
PROVINCE OF ULSTER—*continued.*												
County of Antrim—*con.*			A.	R.	P.	£	s.	d.				
Lisburn Union.												
1. Lisburn,	4	11,671	11,830	1	35	30,336	0	0	25	1	–	–
2. Hillsborough,	4	11,347	18,716	2	32	21,263	0	0	17	1	–	–
3. Knocknadona,	4	6,763	16,325	0	27	20,852	0	0	15	1	–	–
4. Glenavy,	4	6,812	19,173	0	4	19,422	0	0	17	1	–	–
5. Dunmurry,	3	7,848	12,030	2	15	23,468	0	0	21	1	–	–
6. Ballylesson,	2	6,107	12,083	1	31	15,117	0	0	13	1	–	–
7. Saintfield,	6	8,411	12,568	0	13	13,905	0	0	19	1	–	–
8. Annahilt,	3	7,923	17,029	0	19	15,906	0	0	18	1	–	–
	27	66,880	119,842	2	16	167,767	0	0	126	8	–	–
County of Armagh.												
Armagh Union.												
1. Armagh,	3	14,624	13,764	1	21	40,746	7	0	29	1	–	1
2. Blackwatertown,	3	8,276	16,819	1	11	21,049	0	0	15	1	–	1
3. Caledon,	1	2,482	7,640	1	3	9,129	0	0	9	1	–	–
4. Tynan,	3	7,398	19,761	1	24	24,606	7	0	20	1	–	–
5. Keady,	8	16,017	35,920	3	2	82,044	17	0	17	1	–	–
6. Markethill,	4	11,652	25,261	2	37	28,676	12	0	15	1	–	1
7. Rich Hill,	3	9,866	16,869	0	5	25,110	5	0	15	1	–	–
8. Loughgall,	4	10,685	18,057	0	38	21,004	16	0	15	1	–	1
	29	80,910	154,233	0	21	203,067	1	0	135	8	–	4
Lurgan Union.												
1. Lurgan,	4	20,340	15,449	0	22	38,024	0	0	29	2	–	–
2. Aghalee,	3	6,283	12,317	1	27	13,692	0	0	15	1	–	–
3. Moira,	3	8,599	13,903	2	15	20,579	0	0	19	1	–	–
4. Waringstown,	3	11,074	11,856	2	22	17,380	0	0	17	1	–	–
5. Portadown,	3	16,876	11,989	3	21	33,350	0	0	17	1	–	1
6. Tartaraghan,	3	11,538	13,096	3	39	15,437	0	0	18	1	–	–
	19	73,920	78,484	1	37	138,692	0	0	115	7	–	1
County of Cavan.												
Bailieborough Union.												
1. Bailieborough,	5	10,256	21,314	0	2	18,863	2	0	19	1	–	–
2. Shercock,	2	4,125	11,275	1	5	6,610	17	0	11	1	–	–
3. Kingscourt,	3	4,550	13,106	3	6	9,110	7	0	13	1	–	–
4. Crossbane,	1	1,768	5,219	2	23	2,523	5	0	9	1	–	–
5. Termon,	1	1,660	4,800	1	16	2,605	8	0	9	1	–	–
	12	23,079	65,908	0	30	39,569	17	0	61	5	–	–
Bawnboy Union.												
1. Ballyconnell,	7	7,718	32,709	0	26	14,962	19	0	35	1	–	–
2. Ballinamore,	6	7,394	26,498	1	35	10,477	11	0	25	1	–	1
3. Swanlinbar,	6	5,922	28,900	1	19	6,306	3	0	19	1	–	–
4. Newtowngore,	6	5,274	18,404	2	30	7,775	6	0	19	1	–	–
	25	26,308	104,563	2	20	39,529	19	0	100	4	–	1
Cavan Union.												
1. Arvagh,	4	6,294	17,071	3	13	10,091	18	0	19	1	–	–
2. Ballinagh,	4	6,139	16,023	2	25	10,690	7	0	19	1	–	–
3. Ballyhaise,	5	7,619	19,791	3	9	13,733	17	0	27	1	–	–
4. Belturbet,	5	7,676	21,350	1	30	16,138	15	0	26	1	–	–
5. Cavan,	4	10,625	28,254	2	14	23,462	19	0	27	1	–	–
6. Killeshandra,	3	5,569	16,948	2	9	11,595	0	0	18	1	–	–
7. Kilnaleck,	4	7,776	21,111	2	4	13,639	10	0	17	1	–	–
8. Stradone,	4	6,948	21,243	2	32	11,851	2	0	17	1	–	–
	33	58,652	160,663	0	16	111,246	5	0	170	8	–	–

[*continued.*

No. 1.—Statement of Dispensary Districts—*continued.*

Names of Unions and Dispensary Districts.	No. of Electoral Divisions in each.	Population 1871.	Area in Statute Acres.			Poor Law Valuation 1871.			No. of Members of Committee of Management.	No. of Medical Officers.	Number of Apothecaries.	Number of Midwives.
Column 1.	2.	3.	4.			5.			6.	7.	8.	9.
PROVINCE OF ULSTER—*continued.*												
County of Cavan—*con.*			a.	r.	p.	£	s.	d.				
Cootehill Union.												
1. Cootehill,	4	11,888	27,031	2	16	19,629	7	0	19	1	-	-
2. Dawson Grove,	4	7,813	22,124	2	35	17,395	10	0	19	1	-	-
3. Drum,	6	10,488	29,737	3	6	21,069	3	0	19	1	-	-
4. Tullyvin,	5	8,942	26,653	3	27	14,170	19	0	19	1	-	-
	19	38,961	105,848	0	2	72,189	19	0	76	4	-	-
County of Donegal.												
Ballyshannon Union.												
1. Ballyshannon,	6	10,949	25,452	3	10	17,828	18	0	21	1	-	-
2. Belleek,	5	4,779	31,480	0	1	10,837	14	0	23	1	-	-
3. Church Hill,	3	2,804	26,727	0	23	6,675	6	0	11	1	-	-
4. Kinlough,	7	6,153	32,416	1	35	9,735	12	0	17	1	-	-
5. Ballintra,	2	3,497	16,966	1	24	5,861	1	0	11	1	-	-
	21	28,181	182,352	2	11	50,268	10	0	83	5	-	-
Donegal Union.												
1. Pettigo,	3	3,568	36,006	2	10	4,296	15	0	11	1	-	-
2. Laghy,	3	5,736	29,475	0	14	7,912	13	0	11	1	-	1
3. Donegal,	5	7,767	43,439	2	19	9,724	1	0	16	1	-	-
4. Mountcharles,	4	6,214	33,928	3	28	6,674	14	0	15	1	-	1
5. Dunkineely,	3	5,862	17,660	3	12	5,381	17	0	15	1	-	-
	18	31,238	160,411	0	3	34,130	0	0	68	5	-	2
Dunfanaghy Union.												
1. Dunfanaghy,	5	5,767	32,212	0	25	5,773	12	0	17	1	-	-
2. Creeslough,	5	11,559	93,437	3	28	5,690	4	0	17	1	-	-
	10	17,326	125,650	0	13	11,432	16	0	34	2	-	-
Glenties Union.												
1. Dungloe,	8	12,928	72,221	0	37	4,261	2	0	16	1	-	-
2. Glenties,	5	7,084	72,245	3	27	4,259	14	0	15	1	-	-
3. Carrick,	8	8,161	51,128	2	12	3,690	13	0	13	1	-	-
4. Ardara,	5	7,321	44,784	0	8	4,281	13	0	14	1	-	-
5. Killybegs,	3	4,313	16,869	3	25	3,328	16	0	13	1	-	1
	27	39,809	257,129	1	37	19,824	18	0	71	5	-	1
Inishowen Union.												
1. Carndonagh,	6	6,431	35,225	3	31	7,379	12	0	18	1	-	1
2. Clonmany,	5	5,668	23,875	3	30	4,376	1	0	11	1	-	1
3. Moville,	6	10,920	38,696	2	10	12,331	12	0	17	1	-	1
4. Malin,	4	8,190	26,259	0	25	7,574	9	0	15	1	-	-
5. Buncrana,	4	6,094	35,618	1	30	7,023	16	0	14	1	-	1
	21	37,303	159,407	3	36	38,675	1	0	75	5	-	4
Letterkenny Union.												
1. Letterkenny,	5	7,151	23,450	0	4	13,106	11	0	23	1	-	-
2. Manorcunningham,	3	4,650	18,611	2	0	10,861	2	0	15	1	-	-
3. Church Hill,	6	6,831	60,136	1	37	6,976	9	0	21	1	-	-
	14	18,632	101,207	0	1	30,944	2	0	59	3	-	-

[*continued.*

No. 1.—Statement of Dispensary Districts—*continued.*

Names of Unions and Dispensary Districts.	No. of Electoral Divisions in each.	Population 1871.	Area in Statute Acres.			Poor Law Valuation 1874.			No. of Members of Committee of Management.	No. of Medical Officers.	Number of Apothecaries.	Number of Midwives.
Column 1.	2.	3.	4.			5.			6.	7.	8.	9.
PROVINCE OF ULSTER—*continued.*												
County of Donegal—*con.*			A.	R.	P.	£	s.	d.				
Milford Union.												
1. Rathmelton,	3	6,268	19,467	1	18	11,061	5	0	17	1	–	1
2. Rathmullan,	8	3,383	11,834	3	13	3,540	5	0	15	1	–	–
3. Kilmacrenan and Milford,	4	5,977	28,655	1	15	5,621	9	0	15	1	–	–
4. Fanad,	5	7,015	26,819	3	27	6,024	6	0	19	1	–	–
5. Rosguill,	4	5,583	24,484	1	11	3,375	1	0	11	1	–	–
	19	28,236	111,334	3	4	29,623	5	0	77	5	–	1
Stranorlar Union.												
1. Killygordon,	4	6,180	36,757	2	31	11,113	17	0	19	1	–	1
2. Stranorlar,	3	7,467	80,423	3	1	13,081	0	0	18	1	–	1
3. Cloghan,	4	6,231	53,967	0	23	5,448	1	0	13	1	–	1
	11	19,878	121,130	2	14	29,640	18	0	50	3	–	3
County of Down.												
Banbridge Union.												
1. Banbridge,	4	21,547	24,630	1	18	48,257	12	0	29	1	–	–
2. Dromore,	3	10,749	15,003	0	29	21,767	18	0	23	1	–	–
3. [illegible],	3	6,087	16,269	0	30	13,265	19	0	14	1	–	–
4. Ballyward,	4	11,431	24,730	2	19	18,350	0	0	17	1	–	–
5. Loughbrickland,	5	11,594	28,418	3	14	29,778	2	0	29	1	–	–
6. Tanderagee,	4	10,530	17,769	1	0	26,251	14	0	19	1	–	–
	23	71,918	126,823	1	28	156,663	3	0	130	6	–	–
Downpatrick Union.												
1. Downpatrick,	3	8,925	18,703	6	2	20,093	15	0	21	1	–	–
2. Clough,	4	8,830	23,857	2	15	23,576	2	0	17	1	–	–
3. Ballynahinch,	4	10,492	28,234	1	33	27,199	0	0	17	1	–	–
4. Killyleagh,	4	11,483	25,665	2	19	31,686	10	0	19	1	–	–
5. Killough,	6	6,117	17,309	0	38	22,625	12	0	17	1	–	–
6. Strangford,	5	4,861	17,555	2	2	20,185	15	0	17	1	–	–
7. Portaferry,	5	7,281	16,032	2	0	20,248	2	0	17	1	–	1
	34	57,989	147,360	2	28	174,592	16	0	125	7	–	1
Kilkeel Union,												
1. Kilkeel,	5	13,078	47,022	3	19	20,021	2	0	23	2	–	1
2. Bryansford,	3	6,162	21,420	0	6	12,430	16	0	17	1	–	..
3. Rostrevor,	2	3,392	12,626	1	8	8,391	5	0	21	1	–	1
	10	22,814	81,069	0	33	41,042	5	0	61	4	–	2
Newry Union.												
1. Newry,	2	18,758	16,479	2	18	48,166	3	0	23	2	–	–
2. Warrenpoint,	3	6,917	13,168	3	14	15,215	11	0	17	1	–	1
3. Rathfriland,	4	11,868	27,850	0	29	20,086	6	0	15	1	–	–
4. Mullaghglass,	3	9,163	16,129	3	9	19,269	6	0	17	1	–	1
5. Mountnorris,	5	6,369	17,868	2	12	15,360	19	0	17	1	–	–
6. Meigh,	2	6,985	13,648	2	20	18,337	5	0	11	1	–	.
7. Forkhill,	3	5,196	11,190	0	2	7,191	13	0	9	1	–	.
8. Donaghmore,	3	4,843	13,332	1	22	16,510	15	0	11	1	–	–
9. Poyntzpass,	1	3,281	7,305	2	30	10,371	14	0	9	1	–	–
	22	74,311	137,074	3	32	160,502	11	0	129	10	–	2

[*continued.*

No. 1.—STATEMENT of DISPENSARY DISTRICTS—*continued.*

Names of Unions and Dispensary Districts.	No. of Electoral Divisions in each.	Population: 1861.	Area in Statute Acres.			Poor Law Valuation: 1871.			No. of Members of Committee of Management.	No. of Medical Officers.	Number of Apothecaries.	Number of Midwives.
Column 1.	2.	3.	4.			5.			6.	7.	8.	9.
PROVINCE OF ULSTER—*continued.*												
COUNTY OF DOWN—*con.*			A.	R.	P.	£	s.	d.				
NEWTOWNARDS UNION,												
1. Newtownards,	3	18,906	17,336	1	1	27,723	2	0	18	1	–	–
2. Comber,	3	6,916	16,641	0	33	23,865	15	0	13	1	–	–
3. Kilmood,	2	5,758	14,594	1	34	16,807	10	0	13	1	–	–
4. Grey Abbey,	4	9,345	18,676	2	21	23,007	7	0	17	1	–	–
5. Donaghadee,	2	7,449	9,593	0	7	15,238	7	0	18	1	–	–
6. Bangor,	1	8,023	17,026	3	31	27,057	13	0	17	1	–	–
	16	53,128	93,850	2	7	133,694	14	0	90	6	–	–
COUNTY OF FERMANAGH.												
ENNISKILLEN UNION,												
1. Enniskillen,	7	13,621	30,640	2	39	33,130	8	0	49	1	–	1
2. Tempo,	6	8,593	40,912	2	17	14,634	3	0	28	1	–	–
3. Lisbellaw,	3	2,791	10,634	0	9	7,383	16	0	18	1	–	–
4. Boho,	8	6,895	40,261	1	26	19,611	2	0	37	1	–	–
5. Holywell,	10	9,215	49,589	3	20	11,809	14	0	26	1	–	–
6. Florencecourt,	8	8,600	41,576	0	23	17,052	12	0	36	1	–	1
	42	49,718	203,627	3	7	103,114	15	0	189	6	–	2
IRVINESTOWN UNION,												
1. Irvinestown,	7	11,711	36,134	3	16	28,014	16	0	35	2	–	–
2. Ederney,	8	8,730	31,824	3	17	16,426	0	0	38	1	–	–
3. Clonelly,	2	2,287	7,967	2	18	4,099	19	0	13	1	–	–
	17	22,728	75,927	1	11	48,540	15	0	81	4	–	–
LISNASKEA UNION.												
1. Brookeborough,	6	7,676	35,196	2	11	17,631	9	0	21	1	–	1
2. Lisnaskea,	5	6,704	25,132	3	25	17,351	13	0	15	1	–	1
3. Derrylin,	6	7,870	26,884	0	8	13,871	4	0	15	1	–	1
4. Maguiresbridge,	3	3,382	11,131	0	5	8,379	8	0	13	1	–	–
	20	25,632	98,744	2	9	57,596	14	0	64	4	–	3
COUNTY OF LONDONDERRY.												
COLERAINE UNION,												
1. Coleraine,	3	10,783	13,851	3	4	29,051	15	0	29	1	–	–
2. Bushmills,	4	8,317	21,341	0	6	15,692	10	0	27	2	–	–
3. Articlave,	4	5,280	24,072	3	34	11,408	18	0	15	1	–	–
4. Aghadowey,	5	8,858	28,010	2	37	18,932	2	0	23	1	–	–
5. Garvagh,	4	7,427	25,079	3	19	11,842	18	0	20	1	–	–
	20	40,562	112,396	1	18	87,099	3	0	114	6	–	–
LONDONDERRY UNION,												
1. City of Londonderry,	2	20,356	5,059	2	34	57,653	0	0	29	1	1	1
2. Glendermot,	3	8,673	16,804	3	5	19,536	0	0	19	1	–	1
3. Eglinton,	2	6,630	25,290	1	31	16,981	0	0	15	1	–	1
4. Claudy,	4	7,182	30,302	3	31	9,783	0	0	19	1	–	–
5. Kilderry,	4	7,157	28,237	0	33	17,061	0	0	17	1	–	1
6. Burt,	3	4,361	19,931	1	8	11,762	0	0	13	1	–	1
7. Killea,	3	5,043	18,370	0	6	14,912	0	0	15	1	–	1
	21	59,372	143,996	1	31	147,714	0	0	127	7	1	6

[*continued.*

No. 1.—Statement of Dispensary Districts—*continued.*

Names of Unions and Dispensary Districts.	No. of Electoral Divisions included.	Population: 1861.	Area in Statute Acres.			Poor Law Valuation: 1871.			No. of Members of Committee of Management.	No. of Medical Officers.	Number of Apothecaries.	Number of Midwives.
Column 1.	2.	3.	4.			5.			6.	7.	8.	9
PROVINCE OF ULSTER—*continued.*												
Co. of Londonderry—con.			A.	R.	P.	£	s.	d.				
Magherafelt Union.												
1. Magherafelt, . .	5	12,943	21,497	0	20	19,776	0	0	25	1	–	–
2. Bellaghy, . .	4	13,771	26,853	1	37	19,194	15	0	25	1	–	–
3. Maghera, . .	5	13,965	34,796	2	4	18,758	16	0	27	1	–	–
4. Draperstown, . .	5	9,890	41,065	1	29	12,815	15	0	13	1	–	–
5. Moneymore, . .	6	11,680	32,005	3	24	20,757	10	0	17	1	–	–
	25	63,859	156,721	1	27	91,313	16	0	107	5	–	–
New Tn. Limavady Union.												
1. Newtownlimavady, .	4	7,618	24,871	0	34	18,803	6	0	21	1	–	–
2. Ballykelly, . .	4	7,384	30,329	3	0	15,157	13	0	17	1	–	–
3. Bellarena, . .	4	6,803	26,040	0	31	15,812	18	0	19	1	–	–
4. Dungiven, . .	4	8,831	42,317	2	18	12,039	2	0	15	1	–	1
5. Feeny, . . .	3	3,874	22,653	2	4	6,454	17	0	13	1	–	–
	19	38,987	146,712	1	9	68,267	16	0	85	5	–	1
County of Monaghan.												
Carrickmacross Union.												
1. Carrickmacross, .	5	9,258	22,720	1	32	21,278	4	0	21	1	–	1
2. Donaghmoyne, .	5	6,847	20,357	0	16	17,178	8	0	19	1	–	1
3. Rafaragh, . .	4	6,239	17,586	3	20	11,510	12	0	15	1	–	1
	14	22,344	60,664	1	28	49,971	4	0	55	3	–	3
Castleblayney Union.												
1. Castleblayney, . .	5	12,865	27,381	2	11	24,207	10	0	21	1	–	1
2. Ballybay, . .	6	10,980	25,064	0	12	21,245	0	0	23	1	–	1
3. Crossmaglen, . .	5	8,950	19,535	3	36	14,280	10	0	23	1	–	1
4. Newtownhamilton, .	5	9,017	22,221	3	0	14,926	0	0	21	1	–	–
	21	41,812	94,203	1	19	74,626	0	0	88	4	–	3
Clones Union.												
1. Clones, . . .	4	11,298	22,039	0	35	23,532	9	0	31	1	–	–
2. Newtownbutler, .	7	7,832	24,158	2	31	16,928	6	0	23	1	–	–
3. Rosslea, . . .	5	7,569	27,213	1	17	14,812	6	0	19	1	–	–
	16	26,699	73,409	1	3	56,878	1	0	73	3	–	–
Monaghan Union.												
1. Monaghan, . .	8	10,798	17,683	3	26	24,789	7	0	27	1	–	–
2. Glasslough, . .	5	8,515	23,723	3	20	20,891	2	0	23	1	–	–
3. Castleshane, . .	4	9,667	22,618	0	13	18,707	12	0	19	1	–	–
4. Scotstown, . .	5	9,049	28,558	2	11	13,583	0	0	23	1	–	–
5. Kilmore, . .	4	7,435	18,324	1	21	13,533	2	0	21	1	–	–
	21	45,674	112,738	3	11	93,606	2	0	113	5	–	–
County of Tyrone.												
Castlederg Union.												
1. Castlederg & Killeter,	10	13,869	62,051	2	31	21,048	3	0	29	2	–	–
2. Drumquin.	4	3,609	29,733	2	26	5,031	19	0	9	1	–	–
	14	17,478	91,785	1	17	26,081	2	0	38	3	–	–

[*continued.*

No. 1.—Statement of Dispensary Districts—*continued*.

Names of Unions and Dispensary Districts.	No. of Electoral Divisions in each.	Population, 1861.	Area in Statute Acres.			Poor Law Valuation, 1861.			No. of Members of Committees of Management.	No. of Medical Officers.	Number of Apothecaries.	Number of Midwives.
Column 1.	2.	3.	4.			5.			6.	7.	8.	9.
PROVINCE OF ULSTER—*continued*.												
County of Tyrone—*con.*			A.	R.	P.	£	s.	d.				
Clogher Union.												
1. Fivemiletown, . .	4	5,129	28,896	1	23	11,331	2	0	17	1	–	1
2. Clogher, . . .	5	8,297	31,018	0	2	17,931	0	0	23	1	–	1
3. Ballygawley, . .	4	6,843	23,484	2	5	11,638	12	0	21	1	–	–
4. Aughnacloy, . .	5	7,187	23,869	3	7	15,247	5	0	23	1	–	1
	18	27,753	107,678	2	37	56,147	19	0	84	4	–	2
Cookstown Union.												
1. Cookstown, . .	6	14,129	33,979	1	10	27,739	9	0	23	1	–	–
2. Pomeroy, . .	5	8,897	35,323	3	39	11,372	4	0	24	1	–	–
3. Coagh, . . .	2	6,110	11,178	3	10	8,126	11	0	11	1	–	–
4. Stewartstown, . .	3	7,817	16,038	3	33	15,410	7	0	13	1	–	–
	16	37,033	96,720	0	11	63,008	11	0	68	4	–	–
Dungannon Union.												
1. Dungannon, . .	5	15,535	23,168	1	39	30,393	9	0	25	1	–	1
2. Benburb, . .	3	7,754	17,339	1	16	17,430	4	0	18	1	–	1
3. Coal Island, . .	4	18,648	20,293	0	18	18,361	13	0	22	1	–	1
4. Clonavaddy, . .	5	11,654	31,174	2	29	18,530	0	0	19	1	–	1
5. Ballymagran, . .	2	9,283	11,123	3	34	8,496	18	0	9	1	–	–
	18	61,892	104,347	3	16	93,919	4	0	93	5	–	4
Gortin Union.												
1. Gortin, . .	6	9,138	55,586	1	29	11,783	12	0	19	1	–	1
2. Plumb Bridge, .	7	7,488	55,674	3	21	7,631	15	0	19	1	–	–
	13	16,626	111,261	1	6	19,427	7	0	38	2	–	1
Omagh Union.												
1. Omagh, . .	18	22,303	73,080	3	8	36,939	0	0	44	2	–	1
2. Fintona, . .	7	9,385	27,162	0	32	17,911	12	0	21	1	–	1
3. Dromore, . .	4	6,128	24,145	1	13	12,978	7	0	17	1	–	–
4. Drumquin, . .	4	5,224	20,696	1	14	8,875	0	0	16	1	–	–
5. Sixmilecross, .	5	9,796	29,129	3	33	15,694	12	0	24	1	–	1
	38	52,836	174,216	2	14	92,401	11	0	122	6	–	3
Strabane Union.												
1. Donemana, . .	5	7,692	32,091	1	10	14,023	3	0	18	1	–	2
2. Strabane, . .	5	11,380	19,971	1	17	23,170	17	0	15	1	–	2
3. Newtown Stewart, .	5	8,045	29,253	0	31	16,377	16	0	16	1	–	2
4. Castlederg, . .	5	8,675	28,549	0	24	22,386	7	0	20	1	–	2
5. Raphoe, . .	5	7,730	24,484	2	6	18,369	3	0	17	1	–	2
	24	43,604	134,371	2	3	94,329	6	0	83	5	–	10
PROVINCE OF MUNSTER.												
County of Clare.												
Ballyvaghan Union.												
1. Ballyvaghan, . .	11	6,819	71,063	2	26	10,362	11	0	30	1	–	–
	11	6,819	71,063	2	26	10,362	11	0	30	1	–	–
Corrofin Union.												
1. Corrofin, . .	9	7,866	61,286	0	19	20,410	8	0	29	1	–	–
	9	7,866	61,286	0	19	20,410	8	0	29	1	–	–

[*continued*.

No. 1.—STATEMENT of DISPENSARY DISTRICTS—*continued.*

NAMES OF UNIONS AND DISPENSARY DISTRICTS.	No. of Electoral Divisions in each.	Population, 1871.	Area in Statute Acres.			Poor Law Valuation, 1871.			No. of Members of Committees of Management.	No. of Medical Officers.	Number of Apothecaries.	Number of Midwives.
Column 1.	2.	3.	4.			5.			6.	7.	8.	9.
PROVINCE OF MUNSTER—*continued.* COUNTY OF CLARE—*con.*			a.	r.	p.	£	s.	d.				
ENNIS UNION.												
1. Ennis, . . .	4	13,463	23,262	0	4	24,536	14	0	35	2	-	1
2. Crusheen, . .	6	4,572	24,845	1	24	11,378	3	0	19	1	-	-
3. Kilmaley, . .	5	4,845	33,750	1	1	10,076	9	0	11	1	-	-
4. Newmarket, . .	5	7,317	29,191	1	1	26,694	14	0	11	1	-	-
	20	30,097	112,404	3	30	72,685	13	0	76	5	-	1
ENNISTYMON UNION.												
1. Roadford, . .	6	7,187	30,197	0	37	12,423	9	6	17	1	-	-
2. Ennistymon, . .	8	8,729	33,043	1	7	12,978	15	0	25	1	-	-
3. Miltown Malbay, .	6	9,193	35,220	1	37	11,423	5	0	15	1	-	-
	20	25,028	99,291	0	1	36,825	0	0	57	3	-	-
KILLADYSERT UNION.												
1. Labasheeda, . .	5	5,849	26,029	3	38	10,548	8	0	20	1	-	-
2. Ballynacally, . .	6	7,416	36,286	1	8	11,700	14	0	23	1	-	-
	11	13,265	62,319	0	4	25,841	9	0	43	2	-	-
KILRUSH UNION.												
1. Kilrush, . .	8	9,904	28,640	1	31	13,166	18	8	23	1	-	1
2. Kilmihil, . .	6	8,478	31,923	0	19	8,759	0	0	15	1	-	-
3. Cragnock, . .	7	9,688	67,310	0	4	11,931	3	0	21	1	-	-
4. Kilkee, . .	6	8,530	24,815	1	24	10,776	17	0	27	1	-	-
5. Carrigaholt, . .	5	6,620	22,368	3	24	7,603	12	0	14	1	-	-
	27	41,130	156,787	3	12	52,087	16	0	103	5	-	1
SCARIFF UNION.												
1. Mountshannon, .	5	5,857	32,773	3	23	8,563	18	0	15	1	-	-
2. Feakle, . .	8	5,155	34,820	0	6	9,281	2	0	15	1	-	-
3. Annacarriga, .	4	4,601	19,228	0	25	7,878	12	0	15	1	-	-
	17	15,611	86,820	0	14	25,723	12	0	45	3	-	-
TULLA UNION.												
1. Tulla, . . .	7	6,589	38,063	1	29	10,856	12	0	17	1	-	-
2. Quin, . . .	6	4,755	25,463	2	33	12,018	11	0	17	1	-	-
3. Kilkishen, . .	5	4,465	21,196	0	15	9,780	6	0	17	1	-	1
	18	15,759	84,723	0	37	32,650	9	0	51	3	-	1
COUNTY OF CORK. BANDON UNION.												
1. Bandon, . .	9	10,791	21,142	1	39	28,298	15	0	23	1	1	-
2. Innishannon, . .	4	3,730	17,107	3	26	12,104	15	0	15	1	-	-
3. Templemartin, .	6	4,763	24,897	2	13	13,193	0	0	23	1	-	-
4. Murragh, . .	5	4,775	19,801	1	30	11,779	18	0	13	1	-	-
5. Kilbrittain, . .	4	3,297	18,093	2	4	6,749	15	0	13	1	-	-
	28	27,256	101,346	3	15	72,396	0	0	87	5	1	-
BANTRY UNION.												
1. Bantry, . . .	4	6,831	24,400	0	0	10,489	5	0	25	1	-	-
2. Glengariff, . .	5	4,762	58,315	0	25	6,177	17	0	17	1	-	-
3. Durrus & Kilcrohane,	5	4,365	24,130	3	27	4,607	10	0	13	1	-	-
	14	15,958	106,854	3	12	21,273	12	0	55	3	-	-

(continued.

No. 1.—Statement of Dispensary Districts—*continued.*

Names of Unions and Dispensary Districts.	No. of Electoral Divisions included.	Population, 1861.	Area in Statute Acres.			Poor Law Valuation, 1871.			No. of Members of Committee of Management.	No. of Medical Officers.	Number of Apothecaries.	Number of Midwives.
Column 1.	2.	3.	4.			5.			6.	7.	8.	9.
PROVINCE OF MUNSTER—*continued.*												
County of Cork—*con.*			A.	R.	P.	£	s.	d.				
Castletown Union.												
1. Castletown, . .	4	6,822	30,623	1	24	6,155	17	0	15	1	–	–
2. Kilcatherine, . .	3	8,254	33,821	3	29	8,733	3	0	11	1	–	–
	7	15,076	73,445	1	13	15,889	0	0	26	2	–	–
Clonakilty Union.												
1. Rosscarbery, . .	6	9,085	27,353	1	33	16,629	0	0	25	1	–	–
2. Clonakilty, . .	7	10,002	28,602	0	7	18,995	5	0	25	1	–	–
3. Timoleague, . .	7	9,169	24,499	1	4	15,855	15	0	21	1	–	–
	20	28,256	80,454	3	9	50,481	0	0	71	3	–	–
Cork Union.												
1. Dripsey, . . .	8	4,722	16,230	1	30	10,321	14	0	12	1	–	–
2. Blarney, . . .	4	3,836	22,448	0	28	17,254	1	0	10	1	–	–
3. Carrignavar, . .	7	5,134	42,832	3	27	25,767	2	0	31	2	–	–
4. Whitechurch, . .	2	4,470	16,511	1	16	16,277	12	0	21	1	–	–
5. Cork, . . .	1	93,389	13,818	1	24	169,400	10	6	71	9	2	–
6. Carrigaline, . .	2	6,706	8,832	3	1	20,913	10	0	26	1	–	1
7. Douglas, . . .	2	2,620	10,091	0	38	12,769	18	0	15	1	–	–
8. Ballygarvan, . .	3	2,868	13,928	0	14	11,686	5	0	11	1	–	–
9. Ballincollig, . .	8	6,718	17,716	1	18	16,501	18	9	11	1	–	–
10. Queenstown, . .	1	14,607	7,013	0	30	27,514	16	0	23	1	1	–
	29	147,372	169,731	3	14	327,486	7	3	231	10	3	1
Dunmanway Union.												
1. Dunmanway, . .	4	5,838	38,882	2	18	8,712	0	0	15	1	–	–
2. Coolmountain, . .	6	5,653	46,819	0	16	10,129	10	0	18	1	–	–
3. Ballineen, . .	5	5,935	28,192	1	29	13,088	0	0	15	1	–	–
	15	17,426	103,917	0	24	32,929	10	0	48	3	–	–
Fermoy Union.												
1. Fermoy, . . .	3	12,930	19,028	3	9	27,174	10	0	23	1	–	–
2. Rathcormac, . .	4	5,114	37,131	0	35	13,548	15	0	13	1	–	–
3. Ballyhooly, . .	6	6,843	22,025	2	16	20,879	0	0	15	1	–	–
4. Kilworth, . .	6	7,048	31,652	0	9	18,297	10	0	22	1	–	–
5. Ballynoe, . .	5	6,765	33,409	1	35	21,167	15	0	17	1	–	–
	24	37,960	148,258	0	26	103,067	10	0	92	5	–	–
Kanturk Union.												
1. Newmarket, . .	8	7,897	63,477	3	16	14,098	0	0	18	1	–	1
2. Kanturk, . .	11	11,380	47,820	2	7	28,897	5	0	27	1	1	1
3. Milford, . .	7	9,210	40,052	3	35	21,843	15	0	19	1	–	1
4. Boherboy, . .	7	6,893	35,153	0	37	11,424	5	0	10	1	–	–
	33	34,450	186,523	2	18	76,262	5	0	63	4	1	3
Kinsale Union.												
1. Courceys, . .	4	5,575	18,494	3	36	8,560	10	0	9	1	–	–
2. Kinsale, . . .	1	6,335	12,811	1	37	16,612	15	0	21	1	–	–
3. Ballymartle, . .	4	3,347	19,112	1	27	12,156	0	0	13	1	–	–
4. Carrigaline, . .	4	4,431	15,077	3	9	10,824	5	0	11	1	–	–
5. Ballyfeard, . .	6	4,849	10,454	2	37	10,995	0	0	14	1	–	–
	19	23,537	78,851	1	19	58,149	10	0	68	5	–	–

[continued.

No. 1.—Statement of Dispensary Districts—*continued.*

Names of Unions and Dispensary Districts.	No. of Electoral Divisions included.	Population: 1861.	Area: in Statute Acres.			Poor Law Valuation: 1871.			No. of Members of Committee of Management.	No. of Medical Officers.	Number of Apothecaries.	Number of Midwives.
Column 1.	2.	3.	4.			5.			6.	7.	8.	9.
PROVINCE OF MUNSTER—*continued.*												
County of Cork—*con.*			A.	R.	P.	£	s.	d.				
Macroom Union.												
1. Macroom, . .	5	9,728	39,418	1	23	16,833	12	0	29	1	–	–
2. Clondrohid, . .	5	6,579	31,354	1	21	14,109	15	0	21	1	–	–
3. Slievereagh, . .	5	5,444	45,439	0	21	9,219	5	0	19	1	–	–
4. Inchigeelagh, . .	5	4,186	32,457	0	38	7,433	0	0	19	1	–	–
5. Cannaway, . .	5	5,133	26,643	0	13	16,293	0	0	21	1	–	–
	25	31,090	179,108	0	33	63,917	12	0	109	5	–	–
Mallow Union.												
1. Kilshannig, . .	2	6,108	37,650	0	24	16,814	0	0	13	1	–	–
2. Mallow, . . .	2	7,456	12,779	2	25	22,012	15	0	19	1	–	–
3. Rahan, . . .	3	3,970	23,168	2	17	11,169	0	0	15	1	–	–
4. Buttevant (a), . .	5	8,331	53,773	2	8	27,717	10	0	25	2	–	1
5. Ballyclogh, . .	3	3,122	16,504	1	33	11,950	0	0	15	1	–	–
6. Doneraile, . .	6	5,844	29,758	1	25	18,642	0	0	21	1	1	–
	21	34,781	154,357	3	10	109,485	5	0	107	7	1	1
Midleton Union.												
1. Midleton, . .	3	10,873	27,148	3	11	29,477	10	0	25	2	–	–
2. Walshtownmore, East, . .	5	3,838	28,161	1	27	13,173	5	0	16	1	–	–
3. Castlemartyr, . .	4	4,838	20,362	3	33	15,844	5	0	20	1	–	–
4. Aghada, . .	4	7,193	19,015	2	11	17,871	15	0	17	1	–	–
5. Cloyne, . .	3	7,346	16,926	3	24	17,483	15	0	21	1	–	–
	19	34,086	109,354	2	26	93,849	10	0	99	6	–	–
Millstreet Union.												
1. Cullen, . .	6	6,193	29,293	3	35	11,560	5	0	22	1	–	–
2. Millstreet, . .	6	8,604	46,512	3	11	15,773	0	0	18	1	–	–
	12	14,797	71,808	2	10	27,333	5	0	40	2	–	–
Mitchelstown Union.												
1. Mitchelstown, . .	6	8,622	30,831	3	17	19,160	5	0	16	1	–	1
2. Kildorrery, . .	6	6,658	24,631	2	34	15,000	5	0	16	1	–	–
3. Galbally, . .	6	6,967	25,492	3	25	14,935	5	0	16	1	–	–
	18	21,747	80,956	3	6	49,095	15	0	48	3	–	1
Skibbereen Union.												
1. Skibbereen, . .	6	9,628	23,638	3	16	13,921	16	0	35	1	1	–
2. Union Hall, . .	6	8,391	27,283	0	19	13,033	5	0	21	1	–	–
3. Drimoleague, . .	6	7,050	43,125	0	33	10,483	0	0	21	1	–	–
4. Tullagh, . .	5	7,382	20,978	2	5	8,175	6	0	21	1	–	–
	23	32,412	115,025	2	33	45,619	8	0	98	4	1	–
Skull Union.												
1. Skull, . .	6	7,856	34,281	1	12	9,101	13	0	17	1	–	–
2. Goleen, . .	5	5,944	22,887	3	18	5,627	13	0	17	1	–	–
	11	13,800	57,169	0	30	14,729	6	0	34	2	–	–

(a) This district has since been altered by the transfer of the Ardskeagh Electoral Division to the Kilmallock Union.

[continued.

No. 1.—Statement of Dispensary Districts—*continued.*

Names of Unions and Dispensary Districts.	No. of Electoral Divisions.	Population, 1871.	Area in Statute Acres.			Poor Law Valuation, 1871.			No. of Members of Committees of Management.	No. of Medical Officers.	Number of Apothecaries.	Number of Midwives.
Column 1.	2.	3.	4.			5.			6.	7.	8.	9.
PROVINCE OF MUNSTER—*continued.*												
County of Cork—*con.*			A.	R.	P.	£	s.	d.				
Youghal Union.												
1. Youghal, . .	1	8,378	4,830	2	22	16,938	10	0	25	1	–	–
2. Killeagh, . .	3	5,859	18,798	1	8	16,907	0	0	19	1	–	–
3. Templemichael, .	3	2,923	21,228	2	4	8,850	0	0	17	1	–	–
4. Ardagh, . .	4	3,197	13,278	1	11	8,139	15	0	17	1	–	–
5. Clashmore, . .	3	4,014	12,494	1	1	9,505	0	0	15	1	–	–
	14	24,701	70,624	0	6	60,641	5	0	93	5	–	–
County of Kerry.												
Cahirciveen Union.												
1. Cahir, . . .	4	7,232	46,740	2	21	6,150	5	0	18	1	–	–
2. Glanbehy, . .	5	3,598	40,459	3	14	3,627	5	0	15	1	–	–
3. Valencia, . .	2	3,203	10,451	0	19	2,791	0	0	15	1	–	–
4. Kenlagh, . .	7	7,236	65,160	2	3	6,290	15	0	19	1	–	–
5. Derrynane, . .	4	3,946	24,723	3	31	3,168	0	0	15	1	–	–
	22	25,204	187,546	0	8	22,027	5	0	83	5	–	–
Dingle Union.												
1. Dingle, . . .	9	6,066	23,037	3	31	6,866	15	0	13	1	1	1
2. Castlegregory, .	5	5,374	41,049	3	0	5,832	0	0	15	1	–	–
3. Annascaul, . .	5	3,714	29,251	0	39	4,622	15	0	15	1	–	–
4. Ventry, . .	5	5,386	31,943	2	20	5,674	15	0	15	1	–	1
	19	20,539	125,278	2	13	22,983	5	0	58	4	1	2
Kenmare Union.												
1. Kenmare, . .	4	6,700	31,687	2	25	5,690	10	0	19	1	–	–
2. Kilgarvan, . .	4	3,677	57,381	3	0	4,484	0	0	11	1	–	–
3. Tuosist, . .	4	4,310	55,727	0	6	3,947	5	0	9	1	–	–
4. Bonane, . .	4	3,570	58,355	2	32	4,676	10	0	11	1	–	–
	16	18,257	193,152	0	18	18,767	5	0	50	4	–	–
Killarney Union.												
1. Killarney, . .	6	12,321	56,420	2	28	22,360	10	0	55	2	–	–
2. Molahiffe, . .	8	7,770	38,743	1	39	15,939	15	0	27	1	–	–
3. Milltown, . .	4	6,601	25,070	3	16	12,293	15	0	27	1	–	–
4. Killorglin, . .	6	9,119	53,835	3	3	10,176	10	0	27	1	–	1
5. Coom, . . .	7	8,173	77,278	3	11	13,760	0	0	27	1	–	–
	31	43,987	251,296	2	18	74,530	10	0	163	6	–	1
Listowel Union.												
1. Ballylongford, .	9	8,259	36,474	1	28	12,262	15	0	30	1	–	–
2. Listowel, . .	7	12,030	43,241	3	10	16,473	5	0	30	1	1	–
3. Ballyduff, . .	8	8,383	28,238	2	9	11,398	15	0	30	1	–	–
4. Ballybunion, . .	8	6,957	42,946	2	18	12,164	0	0	30	1	–	–
	32	36,531	151,208	1	17	52,048	15	0	120	4	1	–
Tralee Union.												
1. Tralee, . .	8	21,818	46,236	3	13	35,069	15	0	53	2	–	–
2. Castleisland, .	6	6,790	36,324	2	11	14,380	10	0	31	1	–	–
3. Kilgobbin, . .	7	5,789	40,110	2	4	9,915	5	0	25	1	–	–
4. Brosna, . .	6	7,626	60,429	1	29	9,374	15	0	23	1	–	–
5. Ardfert, . .	8	10,042	38,753	1	16	15,235	5	0	19	1	–	–
	35	52,065	221,846	2	26	84,577	16	0	146	6	–	–

[*continued.*

No. 1.—Statement of Dispensary Districts—*continued.*

Names of Unions and Dispensary Districts.	No. of Electoral Divisions, &c.	Population: 1871.	Area in Statute Acres.			Poor Law Valuation: 1871.			No. of Members of Committee of Management.	No. of Medical Officers.	Number of Apothecaries.	Number of Midwives.
Column 1.	2.	3.	4.			5.			6.	7.	8.	9.
PROVINCE OF MUNSTER—*continued.*												
County of Limerick.			A.	R.	P.	£	s.	d.				
Croom Union.												
1. Croom,	6	8,336	29,910	3	5	23,246	10	0	25	1	1	–
2. Castletown,	6	5,801	29,161	3	7	16,013	5	0	19	1	–	–
3. Adare,	6	5,935	23,251	0	5	21,241	10	0	21	1	–	–
	20	21,172	82,323	2	17	60,501	5	0	65	3	1	–
Glin Union.												
1. Shanagolden,	6	8,920	21,235	3	30	13,655	15	0	15	1	–	–
2. Tarbert,	7	9,830	38,710	1	14	14,587	0	0	21	2	–	–
	13	18,750	60,946	1	4	28,242	15	0	36	3	–	–
Kilmallock Union.												
1. Kilmallock,	4	8,193	10,575	0	21	23,450	0	0	23	1	–	1
2. Bruff,	4	8,805	20,720	2	21	23,506	0	0	17	1	1	1
3. Hospital,	4	6,145	15,928	0	17	21,650	0	0	17	1	–	–
4. Kilfinane,	7	9,051	37,489	3	18	23,068	0	0	31	1	1	1
5. Charleville (a),	4	6,473	20,615	2	16	20,374	5	0	17	1	1	–
6. Dromin,	4	4,752	23,029	1	14	21,633	0	0	17	1	–	–
	27	39,539	140,356	2	25	132,727	5	0	124	6	3	3
Limerick Union.												
1. Clarina,	5	6,632	23,079	3	10	21,051	5	0	25	1	–	–
2. Caherconlish,	5	6,965	27,513	1	24	24,738	5	0	19	1	–	–
3. Annacotty,	3	7,376	22,773	2	19	20,605	15	0	24	1	–	–
4. Murroe,	5	6,512	28,046	2	13	13,653	5	0	16	1	–	–
5. City of Limerick,	1	50,060	6,508	3	23	78,135	0	0	32	4	1	–
6. Bridgetown,	9	7,823	41,155	0	1	16,961	10	0	21	1	–	–
7. Castleconnell,	7	5,150	27,314	2	32	16,057	5	0	24	1	–	–
	34	90,758	177,251	0	21	191,083	5	0	179	10	1	–
Newcastle Union.												
1. Ardagh,	5	5,296	30,173	0	31	9,039	0	0	15	1	–	–
2. Abbeyfeale,	7	8,151	38,885	1	1	9,251	15	0	25	1	–	–
3. Newcastle,	4	6,478	17,896	0	23	14,238	15	0	20	1	1	–
4. Feenagh,	5	4,831	20,912	2	21	11,058	0	0	29	1	–	–
5. Broadford,	7	6,748	31,156	1	33	16,756	15	0	25	1	–	–
	28	31,634	113,023	2	34	61,243	5	0	114	5	1	–
Rathkeale Union.												
1. Askeaton,	6	5,703	23,183	1	31	15,013	5	0	17	1	–	–
2. Pallaskenry,	3	5,703	19,944	2	2	13,085	5	0	19	1	–	–
3. Rathkeale,	7	10,649	37,804	0	8	27,961	0	0	25	2	1	–
	16	22,055	79,931	3	31	55,759	10	0	61	4	1	–
County of Tipperary.												
Borrisokane Union.												
1. Terryglass,	4	4,314	29,713	0	3	14,987	2	0	17	1	–	–
2. Borrisokane,	5	4,059	23,142	3	17	12,611	10	0	15	1	–	–
3. Cloughjordan,	4	4,357	28,961	2	29	13,850	10	0	15	1	–	–
	13	12,740	81,819	2	10	41,451	2	0	47	3	–	–

(a) This district has since been altered by the addition of the Ardskeagh Electoral Division from the Mallow Union.

[*continued.*

No. 1.—Statement of Dispensary Districts—*continued*.

Names of Unions and Dispensary Districts.	No. of Electoral Divisions in District.	Population: 1871.	Area: in Statute Acres.			Poor Law Valuation: 1871.			No. of Members of Committee of Management.	No. of Medical Officers.	Number of Apothecaries.	Number of Midwives.
Column 1.	2.	3.	4.			5.			6.	7.	8.	9.
PROVINCE OF MUNSTER—*continued*.												
Co. of Tipperary—*con*.			A.	R.	P.	£	s.	d.				
Carrick-on-Suir Union.												
1. Carrick-on-Suir,	8	12,116	23,248	0	31	24,360	17	0	22	1	1	-
2. Garrangibbon,	1	1,532	9,861	0	35	4,355	5	0	13	1	-	-
3. Piltown,	8	7,818	27,119	3	34	22,108	15	0	21	1	-	-
4. Rathgormuck,	6	4,812	37,807	1	25	17,869	10	0	21	1	-	-
5. Portlaw,	2	4,971	11,167	3	24	9,992	5	0	9	1	-	-
	23	30,254	112,925	2	30	78,879	19	0	87	5	1	-
Cashel Union.												
1. Kilpatrick,	5	5,305	31,819	3	31	22,162	11	0	20	1	-	1
2. Cashel,	5	9,646	32,326	0	10	25,408	16	0	37	1	-	1
3. Tullamain,	5	5,083	33,234	0	31	21,980	18	0	23	1	-	-
4. Fethard,	5	6,908	29,670	1	31	20,884	9	0	25	1	-	1
5. Killenaule,	4	5,925	28,511	1	35	17,236	10	0	25	1	-	-
	24	33,467	156,021	8	18	107,678	18	0	130	5	-	3
Clogheen Union.												
1. Cahir,	4	8,812	33,659	1	7	23,028	5	0	23	1	-	-
2. Ardfinnan,	6	7,985	42,560	0	34	25,078	15	0	23	1	-	-
3. Clogheen,	4	8,451	42,161	1	13	15,464	0	0	21	1	-	1
	14	25,249	118,495	3	14	63,571	0	0	67	3	-	1
Clonmel Union.												
1. Clonmel and St. Mary's,	3	13,789	16,843	1	29	23,327	9	0	40	2	1	-
2. Marlfield,	3	3,183	12,240	1	31	12,576	0	0	21	1	-	-
3. Killaloan,	2	1,831	11,129	1	8	7,931	10	0	18	1	-	-
4. Kilnalevlan,	4	4,589	31,010	0	3	14,804	5	0	21	1	-	-
5. Ballymacarbry,	3	2,582	16,076	3	20	6,464	6	0	11	1	-	-
	14	26,039	86,810	0	6	63,703	5	0	109	6	1	-
Nenagh Union.												
1. Nenagh,	6	12,900	33,509	3	29	31,117	19	0	55	2	-	-
2. Newport,	5	7,709	44,800	1	39	16,518	0	0	21	1	-	-
3. Portroe,	5	6,240	30,434	2	34	16,244	18	0	19	1	-	-
4. Silvermines,	5	4,661	30,759	3	15	8,593	13	0	17	1	-	-
5. Toomavara,	6	6,765	41,504	1	29	20,816	15	0	19	1	-	-
	28	38,277	183,058	1	17	93,290	16	0	131	6	-	-
Roscrea Union.												
1. Roscrea,	7	11,378	45,872	3	14	30,203	18	0	25	2	-	1
2. Shinrone,	8	7,218	37,156	1	14	25,158	12	0	25	2	-	-
3. Bourney,	6	5,977	34,416	2	21	15,823	6	0	15	1	-	-
	21	24,608	116,487	3	9	71,088	16	0	68	5	-	1
Thurles Union.												
1. Thurles,	3	8,812	20,459	2	17	27,089	0	0	25	1	1	-
2. Holycross,	3	4,176	18,894	3	31	12,858	19	0	15	1	-	-
3. Littleton,	6	4,370	33,150	2	30	12,803	17	0	20	1	-	-
4. Moyne,	8	5,071	25,729	1	18	13,978	19	0	15	1	-	1
5. Templemore,	2	6,239	12,721	1	17	14,842	2	0	19	1	-	1
6. Borrisoleigh,	5	7,264	32,063	5	16	18,279	18	0	21	1	-	-
	21	36,159	143,350	2	9	99,887	16	0	115	6	1	2

[*continued*.

No. 1.—Statement of Dispensary Districts—*continued.*

Names of Unions and Dispensary Districts.	No. of Electoral Divisions in each.	Population: 1871.	Area: in Statute Acres.			Poor Law Valuation: 1871.			No. of Members of Committee of Management.	No. of Medical Officers.	Number of Apothecaries.	Number of Midwives.
Column 1.	2.	3.	4.			5.			6.	7.	8.	9.
PROVINCE OF MUNSTER—*continued.*												
Co. of Tipperary—*con.*			A.	R.	P.	£	s.	d.				
Tipperary Union.												
1. Bansha, . . .	3	6,890	41,771	3	33	10,077	6	0	25	1	–	–
2. Golden, . . .	5	4,529	22,678	3	6	17,961	5	0	22	1	–	–
3. Tipperary, . . .	4	12,077	22,628	3	37	22,647	5	0	25	1	–	–
4. Cappagh, . . .	6	8,287	41,947	3	27	14,729	16	0	25	1	–	1
5. Oola, . . .	4	7,704	26,523	3	10	23,273	5	0	20	1	–	–
6. Emly, . . .	6	6,811	24,682	3	18	50,394	15	0	25	1	–	–
	30	47,298	179,967	3	6	189,902	6	0	142	6	–	1
County of Waterford.												
Dungarvan Union.												
1. Ringville, . . .	4	1,295	23,477	1	34	7,113	15	0	13	1	–	–
2. Seskinane, . . .	5	3,681	30,492	2	39	9,581	5	0	15	1	–	–
3. Whitechurch, . . .	5	4,390	17,692	3	35	11,768	5	0	17	1	–	–
4. Dungarvan, . . .	4	11,890	23,440	3	3	23,117	5	0	28	1	–	1
	18	21,316	94,044	0	31	53,870	10	0	73	4	–	1
Kilmacthomas Union.												
1. Kilmacthomas, . .	8	7,380	40,839	0	24	18,558	5	0	23	1	–	–
2. Bonmahon, . .	8	8,114	23,638	3	15	16,180	0	0	23	1	–	–
	16	15,494	64,477	3	39	34,738	5	0	46	2	–	–
Lismore Union.												
1. Ballyduff, . . .	5	3,920	28,764	2	12	10,835	16	0	20	1	–	–
2. Cappoquin, . . .	4	6,186	26,209	3	8	13,316	5	0	21	1	–	–
3. Lismore, . . .	3	6,240	26,021	3	29	13,976	0	0	11	1	–	1
4. Tallow, . . .	4	1,499	16,143	2	22	11,601	7	0	15	1	–	–
	16	29,845	97,160	0	1	49,729	7	0	74	4	–	1
Waterford Union.												
1. Waterford, . . .	4	30,570	17,289	0	28	89,845	5	0	45	2	–	–
2. Ullid, . . .	6	7,613	24,898	3	15	25,303	0	0	27	1	–	–
3. Kilmakevoge, . .	6	6,542	30,769	3	16	16,661	17	0	27	1	–	1
4. Woodstown, . . .	5	6,356	20,936	2	37	17,183	5	0	31	1	–	1
5. Tramore, . . .	3	4,796	18,133	0	30	13,924	15	0	17	1	–	–
6. Kilmeadan, . . .	4	3,291	19,209	3	31	18,556	5	0	20	1	–	–
	30	60,068	125,719	3	3	169,236	7	0	167	7	–	2
PROVINCE OF LEINSTER.												
County of Carlow.												
Carlow Union.												
1. Carlow, . . .	7	13,855	30,074	2	18	36,305	7	0	49	1	–	–
2. Tullow, . . .	8	8,069	33,134	1	35	28,090	15	0	51	1	–	1
3. Borris, . . .	8	6,571	26,334	3	28	16,415	15	0	27	1	–	1
4. Fenagh & Myshall,	7	6,146	31,981	2	0	21,452	13	0	37	1	–	–
5. Leighlinbridge, .	4	5,101	20,104	3	31	12,820	13	0	19	1	–	–
6. Bagenalstown, .	4	5,011	16,834	0	29	16,346	1	0	21	1	–	1
7. Ballickmoyler and Newtown, . .	9	6,936	29,672	0	4	18,404	10	0	28	1	–	1
	43	51,809	185,836	2	15	150,035	16	0	230	7	–	4

[*continued.*

No. 1.—Statement of Dispensary Districts—continued.

Names of Unions and Dispensary Districts.	No. of Electoral Divisions in each.	Population, 1871.	Area in Statute Acres.			Poor Law Valuation, 1871.			No. of Members of Committees of Management.	No. of Medical Officers.	Number of Apothecaries.	Number of Midwives.
Column 1.	2.	3.	4.			5.			6.	7.	8.	9.
PROVINCE OF LEINSTER—continued.												
County of Dublin.			A.	R.	P.	£	s.	d.				
Balrothery Union.												
1. Balbriggan, . .	8	4,779	18,330	0	27	21,453	15	0	25	1	–	1
2. Holmpatrick, . .	1	8,737	7,125	0	37	10,625	15	0	14	1	–	1
3. Lusk, . .	1	3,917	12,049	1	33	13,280	5	0	16	1	–	1
4. Swords, . .	2	3,721	13,978	1	26	18,830	5	0	22	1	–	1
5. Kilsallaghan, . .	3	2,037	16,243	0	12	15,743	5	0	17	1	–	–
6. Malahide, . .	2	2,812	7,459	1	11	14,681	0	0	14	1	–	1
	19	22,016	75,135	2	26	94,819	5	0	107	6	–	5
Dublin, North, Union.												
1. North City, . .	1	109,143	1,697	1	10	230,169	0	0	50	6	3	–
2. Blanchardstown and Castleknock, .	2	7,094	13,246	0	38	25,391	15	0	18	1	–	–
3. Finglas & Glasnevin,	2	6,015	12,867	1	24	29,116	5	0	12	1	–	2
4. Clontarf and Howth,	2	5,297	5,769	0	12	22,672	0	0	18	2	–	–
5. Coolock & Drumcondra,	2	6,376	7,158	2	29	23,620	5	0	19	2	–	1
	9	134,255	40,768	2	22	331,255	5	0	117	12	3	3
Dublin, South, Union.												
1. South City, . .	1	143,665	1,835	2	13	341,214	0	0	51	8	4	–
2. Donnybrook, . .	1	18,756	1,915	1	8	71,891	0	0	19	2	–	–
3. Rathmines, . .	1	15,747	1,399	2	37	67,180	0	0	18	1	–	–
4. Rathfarnham, . .	2	6,358	11,839	3	20	40,190	0	0	23	2	–	1
5. Tallaght, . .	1	3,719	21,176	3	34	15,184	0	0	11	1	–	–
6. Clondalkin, . .	1	2,828	8,302	0	7	12,405	0	0	12	1	–	1
7. Palmerstown, . .	1	6,856	3,606	2	19	15,849	0	0	13	1	–	–
	9	201,963	48,083	0	27	567,235	0	0	153	16	4	2
Rathdown Union.												
1. Dundrum and Glencullen, . .	3	6,336	11,828	1	34	28,016	15	0	15	2	–	2
2. Blackrock & Stillorgan,	2	10,441	4,673	1	20	46,302	5	0	16	2	–	1
3. Killiney, . .	1	4,241	4,598	2	18	25,210	5	0	14	1	–	1
4. Kingstown, . .	1	18,089	1,647	0	31	74,889	10	0	22	2	–	1
5. Bray & Rathmichael,	2	8,832	8,340	2	4	36,227	0	0	23	2	–	1
6. Powerscourt, . .	1	3,018	27,332	0	1	7,984	0	0	12	1	–	1
7. Delgany, . .	1	2,366	8,159	2	8	9,296	10	0	14	1	–	–
	10	53,259	61,519	2	27	228,075	5	0	115	11	–	7
County of Kildare.												
Athy Union.												
1. Athy, . .	6	8,749	20,321	2	16	25,348	0	0	26	1	1	1
2. Monasterevin, .	7	6,654	21,709	3	33	20,718	15	0	20	1	–	1
3. Vicarstown, . .	6	3,751	25,279	2	23	14,629	6	0	18	1	–	1
4. Castledermot, . .	7	4,140	23,711	0	21	16,981	10	0	10	1	–	1
5. Stradbally, . .	6	5,349	26,260	2	28	17,580	6	0	18	1	–	1
6. Ballylinan, . .	6	4,577	21,759	1	0	18,919	12	0	19	1	–	1
	38	33,210	160,281	1	7	109,165	7	0	121	6	1	6
Celbridge Union.												
1. Lucan, . .	3	3,018	11,839	2	34	24,566	13	0	15	1	–	1
2. Celbridge, . .	3	4,769	16,639	0	15	23,335	13	0	15	1	–	1
3. Maynooth, . .	3	3,266	15,659	1	28	19,291	18	0	13	1	–	1
4. Rathcoole, . .	3	3,370	16,937	0	11	20,793	5	0	13	1	–	1
5. Kilcock, . .	4	4,333	25,753	1	18	28,614	7	0	17	1	–	1
	16	19,580	86,837	2	31	114,601	15	0	73	5	–	5

[continued.

No. 1.—Statement of Dispensary Districts—*continued.*

Names of Unions and Dispensary Districts.	No. of Electoral Divisions in each.	Population: 1871.	Area in Statute Acres.			Poor Law Valuation: 1871.			No. of Members of Committee of Management.	No. of Medical Officers.	Number of Apothecaries.	Number of Midwives.
Column 1.	2.	3.	4.			5.			6.	7.	8.	9.
PROVINCE OF LEINSTER—*continued.*												
County of Kildare—*con.*												
Naas Union.			A.	R.	P.	£	s.	d.				
1. Blessington & Ballymore,	6	6,760	60,728	2	30	21,832	7	0	21	1	–	1
2. Robertstown & Kilmeague,	5	4,219	20,470	2	18	8,412	9	0	15	1	–	–
3. Rathmore,	4	2,841	19,094	1	28	17,790	1	0	17	1	–	–
4. Kilcullen,	5	11,967	22,733	3	13	22,631	9	0	17	1	–	–
5. Naas and Carragh,	5	6,600	24,451	3	27	25,043	8	0	17	1	–	1
6. Clane and Timahoe, North,	5	4,649	28,680	0	28	22,194	8	0	16	1	–	1
7. Kildare,	4	4,080	19,307	2	2	17,023	3	0	15	1	–	–
8. Newbridge,	3	6,282	14,073	2	5	15,805	3	0	15	1	–	1
	37	47,398	216,621	2	27	151,891	8	0	135	8	–	4
County of Kilkenny.												
Callan Union.												
1. Ballingarry,	4	5,363	20,276	3	30	14,109	1	0	17	1	–	–
2. Mullinahone,	4	5,163	21,484	1	24	13,001	16	0	14	1	–	–
3. Kilmaganny,	6	6,141	30,309	0	8	21,360	1	0	19	1	–	1
4. Callan,	6	5,080	31,830	2	6	24,234	8	0	25	1	–	–
	20	21,959	104,010	3	20	73,405	6	0	76	4	–	1
Castlecomer Union.												
1. Castlecomer,	4	11,379	39,284	3	30	21,310	10	0	28	2	–	–
2. Ballyragget,	3	4,565	18,535	1	21	10,912	5	0	17	1	–	–
	7	15,937	57,820	1	11	32,223	15	0	45	3	–	–
Kilkenny Union.												
1. Kilkenny,	5	19,463	28,414	3	27	42,378	11	0	38	2	1	1
2. Gowran,	4	5,076	24,307	3	4	18,012	0	0	15	1	–	1
3. Tiscoffin,	4	4,161	22,763	0	28	15,414	0	0	16	1	–	–
4. Freshford,	4	4,063	16,302	1	2	13,469	15	0	13	1	–	–
5. Tullaroan,	4	2,658	10,896	1	11	11,063	0	0	13	1	–	–
	21	35,490	110,948	1	32	100,348	6	0	95	6	1	2
Thomastown Union.												
1. Graigue,	6	5,966	30,183	1	23	13,747	4	0	23	1	–	–
2. Inistioge,	6	4,100	25,106	0	11	10,976	0	0	23	1	–	–
3. Thomastown,	7	5,891	23,880	1	17	20,316	10	0	23	1	–	–
4. Knocktopher,	8	5,148	28,357	1	16	18,868	15	0	23	1	–	–
	27	21,405	107,477	0	27	63,843	9	0	93	4	–	–
Urlingford Union.												
1. Balleen,	4	3,017	17,891	1	1	12,080	15	0	17	1	–	–
2. Johnstown,	4	3,568	20,852	0	5	12,315	15	0	17	1	–	–
3. Urlingford,	4	4,372	19,050	1	21	11,195	3	0	17	1	–	–
4. Kilcooly,	4	4,308	10,255	3	10	9,936	7	0	17	1	–	–
	16	15,265	78,149	1	38	45,469	0	0	60	4	–	–

[*continued.*

No. 1.—Statement of Dispensary Districts—*continued.*

Names of Unions and Dispensary Districts.	No. of Electoral Divisions in each.	Population, 1861.	Area in Statute Acres.			Poor Law Valuation, 1861.			No. of Members of Committee of Management.	No. of Medical Officers.	Number of Apothecaries.	Number of Midwives.
Column 1.	2.	3.	4.			5.			6.	7.	8.	9.
PROVINCE OF LEINSTER—*continued.*												
King's County.			A.	R.	P.	£	s.	d.				
Edenderry Union.												
1. Johnstown,	4	2,734	18,270	1	6	13,339	10	0	13	1	–	–
2. Carbury,	6	3,263	34,050	3	9	17,013	1	0	21	1	–	–
3. Rathangan,	5	3,953	28,168	1	21	11,127	13	0	17	1	–	–
4. Edenderry,	5	5,723	33,311	2	36	17,971	9	0	19	1	–	–
5. Rhode,	5	3,627	29,691	2	18	16,527	16	0	15	1	–	–
6. Ballyboggan,	4	3,650	21,093	3	33	15,394	15	0	13	1	–	–
	29	23,334	172,108	2	35	85,129	4	0	96	6	–	–
Parsonstown Union.												
1. Parsonstown,	9	8,777	11,327	1	33	16,112	12	0	28	1	–	–
2. Killyon,	3	2,325	17,111	0	17	8,908	7	0	22	1	–	–
3. Kinnitty,	6	3,168	33,360	3	20	13,678	17	0	24	1	–	–
4. Frankford,	5	3,930	28,664	0	15	12,920	4	0	23	1	–	–
5. Banagher,	7	7,984	40,023	2	30	19,862	11	0	30	1	–	–
6. Ferbane,	10	8,723	62,515	0	35	20,160	4	0	27	1	–	–
7. Riverstown,	8	3,923	27,427	3	4	12,761	3	0	18	1	–	–
	39	39,350	220,437	1	19	102,313	3	0	172	7	–	–
Tullamore Union.												
1. Killoughy,	7	8,725	42,912	3	14	15,963	19	0	23	1	–	–
2. Philipstown,	6	3,377	33,630	3	25	15,883	17	0	19	1	–	–
3. Kilbeggan,	5	4,359	21,690	2	29	14,251	16	0	21	1	–	–
4. Clara,	5	8,110	23,963	1	27	15,084	13	0	19	1	–	–
5. Tullamore,	5	10,286	33,196	3	32	21,653	7	0	27	1	–	–
	28	33,087	155,394	3	1	82,825	4	0	109	5	–	–
County of Longford.												
Ballymahon Union.												
1. Abbeyshrule,	5	7,163	30,734	0	18	20,749	12	0	21	1	–	–
2. Ballymahon,	5	9,064	30,935	0	10	20,354	7	0	21	1	–	–
3. Ballymore,	8	5,862	38,459	0	22	20,073	14	0	23	1	–	–
	18	22,089	100,128	1	10	61,177	13	0	65	3	–	–
Granard Union.												
1. Granard,	8	8,191	28,824	0	37	20,458	17	0	23	1	–	–
2. Streete,	7	6,314	29,537	0	11	19,931	0	0	21	1	–	–
3. Ballinalee,	8	6,014	22,089	2	4	13,005	18	0	19	1	–	–
4. Scrabby,	5	7,301	21,368	0	1	10,305	10	0	17	1	–	–
5. Finnea,	5	6,084	21,493	1	13	12,035	1	0	17	1	–	–
6. Coole,	3	1,989	11,521	0	38	8,200	7	0	11	1	–	–
	36	36,043	134,005	1	26	84,221	12	0	108	6	–	–
Longford Union.												
1. Longford,	6	13,560	34,306	1	34	28,728	12	0	25	1	–	–
2. Drumlish,	7	11,828	35,838	3	13	13,600	16	0	21	1	–	–
3. Killashee,	6	7,360	39,816	0	10	17,448	10	0	23	1	–	–
	19	32,737	109,961	1	17	59,777	18	0	69	3	–	–

[*continued.*

No. 1.—STATEMENT of DISPENSARY DISTRICTS—*continued.*

NAMES OF UNIONS AND DISPENSARY DISTRICTS.	No. of Electoral Divisions in each.	Population, 1871.	Area: in Statute Acres.			Poor Law Valuation, 1871.			No. of Members of Committee of Management.	No. of Medical Officers.	Number of Apothecaries.	Number of Midwives.
Column 1.	2.	3.	4.			5.			6.	7.	8.	9.
PROVINCE OF LEINSTER—*continued.*												
COUNTY OF LOUTH.			A.	R.	P.	£	s.	d.				
ARDEE UNION.												
1. Ardee,	3	9,174	27,947	1	38	31,673	5	0	24	1	–	1
2. Drumconrath,	2	4,214	23,800	1	34	21,087	15	0	15	1	–	1
3. Collon,	2	2,850	13,431	2	0	8,541	0	0	11	1	–	–
4. Dunleer,	3	4,715	16,790	3	21	15,836	10	0	15	1	–	–
5. Castlebellingham,	3	4,301	11,282	0	38	17,115	2	0	17	1	–	–
	13	25,284	96,210	2	4	94,085	12	0	83	5	–	2
DROGHEDA UNION.												
1. Stamullen,	2	3,060	21,338	2	34	25,482	0	0	21	1	–	1
2. Duleek,	2	3,832	20,703	3	37	19,934	5	0	15	1	–	–
3. St. Mary's,	1	7,346	9,733	1	0	17,511	5	0	15	1	–	–
4. Drogheda,	1	16,158	10,086	0	37	28,834	2	0	25	2	–	–
5. Termonfeckin,	3	6,205	19,231	3	25	18,912	6	0	19	1	–	1
6. Monasterboice,	3	3,373	17,911	0	10	13,874	18	0	17	1	–	–
	12	39,821	99,045	0	18	124,769	7	0	112	7	–	2
DUNDALK UNION.												
1. Dundalk,	3	16,433	17,123	0	16	39,896	10	0	55	1	1	1
2. Louth,	4	6,888	20,085	1	20	17,098	15	0	18	1	–	–
3. Barronstown,	4	7,108	18,082	3	11	15,006	3	0	15	1	–	–
4. Dromiskin,	2	4,102	10,579	1	27	12,483	12	0	11	1	–	–
5. Ravensdale,	3	5,282	17,818	3	30	9,682	7	0	11	1	–	–
6. Carlingford,	3	8,635	19,984	1	31	11,906	19	0	15	1	–	–
	19	46,850	104,434	0	21	106,069	6	0	125	6	1	1
COUNTY OF MEATH.												
DUNSHAUGHLIN UNION.												
1. Dunboyne,	3	3,611	32,522	1	20	33,329	0	0	27	1	–	–
2. Ratoath,	3	3,092	20,801	0	16	27,143	0	0	30	1	–	–
3. Killeen,	3	3,412	21,960	2	0	25,176	0	0	19	1	–	–
4. Garristown,	3	3,391	24,046	1	4	21,978	10	0	17	1	–	–
	12	14,109	108,339	1	0	105,620	10	0	93	4	–	–
KELLS UNION.												
1. Kells,	6	7,230	27,063	3	7	32,817	19	0	27	1	–	–
2. Moynalty,	6	6,053	26,188	3	29	19,520	5	0	31	1	–	–
3. Kilskeer,	7	6,891	25,400	1	10	20,974	18	0	23	1	–	1
4. Nobber,	6	4,036	30,277	2	16	22,420	0	0	17	1	–	1
	25	24,183	108,902	1	21	95,431	17	0	98	4	–	2
NAVAN UNION.												
1. Navan,	4	12,118	37,086	3	7	42,354	18	0	25	1	–	1
2. Painestown,	4	4,718	27,648	2	38	26,124	15	0	17	1	–	–
3. Castletown,	4	5,157	29,730	1	34	29,442	13	0	17	1	–	1
	12	21,993	94,465	3	37	97,921	5	0	57	3	–	2
OLDCASTLE UNION.												
1. Crossakeel,	4	3,010	19,369	0	12	18,734	13	0	17	1	–	–
2. Oldcastle,	4	5,667	24,365	0	8	19,885	4	0	19	1	–	–
3. Virginia,	3	7,773	22,138	2	0	18,245	3	0	15	1	–	–
4. Ballyjamesduff,	3	7,207	18,040	0	10	13,341	0	0	17	1	–	–
	14	23,657	83,911	3	30	82,204	2	0	68	4	–	–

[*continued.*

No. 1.—Statement of Dispensary Districts—*continued.*

Names of Unions and Dispensary Districts.	No. of Electoral Divisions in each.	Population, 1861.	Area in Statute Acres.			Poor Law Valuation, 1871.			No. of Members of Committee of Management.	No. of Medical Officers.	Number of Apothecaries.	Number of Midwives.
Column 1.	2.	3.	4.			5.			6.	7.	8.	9.
PROVINCE OF LEINSTER—*continued.*												
County of Meath—*con.*			A.	R.	P.	£	s.	d.				
Trim Union.												
1. Athboy, . . .	6	7,382	37,046	0	9	31,096	10	0	21	1	–	–
2. Trim, . . .	5	6,469	28,393	1	11	25,605	5	0	17	1	–	–
3. Summerhill, . . .	5	5,095	30,762	0	0	27,851	5	0	17	1	–	1
4. Jamesfield, . . .	4	3,969	23,117	0	23	24,283	0	0	15	1	–	–
	20	23,918	119,318	2	3	108,848	0	0	70	4	–	1
Queen's County.												
Abbeyleix Union.												
1. Abbeyleix, . . .	6	5,365	16,877	2	24	12,323	13	0	19	1	–	–
2. Ballyroan, . . .	4	3,947	20,012	1	35	11,199	16	0	13	1	–	–
3. Durrow, . . .	5	6,169	24,043	2	22	15,894	3	0	20	1	–	1
4. Castletown, . . .	4	3,327	16,630	2	18	12,706	17	0	15	1	–	1
5. Ballinakill, . . .	5	4,592	23,502	1	13	15,813	12	0	20	1	–	–
	22	22,400	107,169	2	32	68,947	3	0	87	5	–	2
Donaghmore Union.												
1. Borris-in-Ossory, .	7	3,791	23,709	1	27	20,575	7	0	27	1	–	–
2. Rathdowney, . .	8	5,713	27,330	1	18	19,625	1	0	23	1	–	1
	15	9,504	51,039	3	5	40,200	8	0	50	2	–	1
Mountmellick Union.												
1. Mountmellick, . .	7	8,331	27,460	0	39	16,087	2	0	29	1	–	–
2. Clonaslee, . . .	6	4,727	32,338	1	29	10,325	13	0	17	1	–	–
3. Coolrain, . . .	6	2,712	28,968	1	12	8,185	18	0	22	1	–	–
4. Mountrath, . . .	5	6,820	23,385	1	37	11,868	11	0	17	1	–	–
5. Maryborough, . .	6	7,301	23,730	1	18	17,875	4	0	25	1	–	–
6. Emo, . . .	6	5,773	32,155	3	32	21,629	18	0	30	1	–	–
7. Clonygowan, . .	6	6,319	25,564	0	31	13,939	1	0	23	1	–	–
	43	42,184	201,622	3	27	101,894	7	0	163	7	–	–
County of Westmeath.												
Athlone Union.												
1. Athlone, . . .	5	13,924	27,619	1	10	22,312	0	0	36	2	–	–
2. Bridgetown, . . .	7	6,834	28,339	1	6	14,698	5	0	25	1	–	–
3. Kiltoom, . . .	6	5,367	27,483	1	15	12,671	5	0	21	1	–	–
4. Glasson, . . .	6	5,438	24,601	0	27	15,000	8	0	19	1	–	–
5. Moate, . . .	7	7,630	32,633	1	7	24,160	0	0	30	1	–	–
	31	38,323	140,769	1	33	88,842	1	0	131	6	–	–
Delvin Union.												
1. Castlepollard, . .	6	5,280	23,490	1	27	17,425	16	0	21	1	–	–
2. Delvin, . . .	7	4,125	27,687	3	37	18,446	3	0	21	1	–	–
3. Clonmellon, . .	6	4,156	23,602	0	12	17,139	4	0	21	1	–	–
	19	13,561	74,778	1	1	53,011	3	0	63	3	–	–
Mullingar Union.												
1. Mullingar, . . .	8	11,816	31,786	3	32	32,449	19	0	31	1	–	1
2. Multyfarnham, . .	6	4,124	22,303	1	12	17,037	0	0	19	1	–	–
3. Ballynacargy, . .	7	6,237	34,441	0	37	26,016	15	0	23	1	–	–
4. Castletown Geoghegan,	7	6,757	35,223	0	19	28,711	10	0	29	1	–	–
5. Tyrrellspass, . .	7	5,875	31,180	2	20	17,128	10	0	21	1	–	1
6. Miltown, . . .	6	8,820	27,491	2	8	16,195	7	0	19	1	–	–
7. Killucan, . . .	7	5,034	25,973	0	1	21,335	13	0	21	1	–	–
	48	48,703	208,400	3	13	157,227	19	0	163	7	–	2

[*continued.*

No. 1.—Statement of Dispensary Districts—*continued.*

Names of Unions and Dispensary Districts.	No. of Electoral Divisions included.	Population: 1851.	Area: in Statute Acres.			Poor Law Valuation: 1851.			No. of Members of Committees of Management.	No. of Medical Officers.	Number of Apothecaries.	Number of Midwives.
Column 1.	2.	3.	4.			5.			6.	7.	8.	9.
PROVINCE OF LEINSTER—*continued.*												
County of Wexford			A.	R.	P.	£	s.	d.				
Enniscorthy Union.												
1. Newtownbarry, . .	5	6,033	31,181	3	23	13,347	0	0	32	1	-	1
2. Killann, . .	5	5,629	34,378	0	14	11,691	0	0	18	1	-	-
3. Ferns, . .	6	4,134	23,082	3	33	13,044	0	0	17	1	-	-
4. Enniscorthy, . .	5	12,404	33,782	2	16	30,130	0	0	33	2	-	-
5. Oulart, . .	6	9,341	30,481	1	33	23,131	0	0	19	1	-	1
6. Clonroche, . .	5	6,345	33,281	1	35	18,105	0	0	19	1	-	1
	32	43,886	186,629	1	35	109,748	0	0	137	7	-	3
Gorey Union.												
1. Gorey, . . .	8	8,324	31,578	0	39	22,590	5	0	23	1	-	-
2. Coolgreany, . .	5	4,660	30,008	3	11	15,671	10	0	15	1	-	-
3. Camolin, . .	7	3,933	33,045	0	6	16,624	10	0	19	1	-	-
4. Killenagh and Wells,	5	6,720	35,073	3	9	23,921	5	0	25	1	-	1
	25	24,037	129,704	3	25	79,216	10	0	82	4	-	1
New Ross Union.												
1. New Ross, . .	1	7,845	4,400	1	30	11,079	5	0	10	1	-	1
2. Old Ross, . .	8	3,743	31,843	3	3	19,619	15	0	35	1	-	1
3. Duncannon, . .	7	5,780	28,478	2	30	18,041	12	0	22	1	-	-
4. St. Mullins, . .	5	5,330	23,134	3	13	9,950	2	0	21	1	-	1
5. Templeudigan, .	4	2,134	17,218	0	19	7,253	10	0	21	1	-	-
6. Carrigbyrne, . .	8	6,474	36,691	3	25	17,180	12	0	29	1	-	1
7. Fethard, . .	6	8,801	34,360	3	19	21,471	7	0	25	2	-	2
	39	44,141	177,230	2	19	104,325	6	0	168	8	-	6
Wexford Union.												
1. Wexford, . .	3	15,250	10,723	1	24	25,164	10	0	35	1	1	-
2. Broadway, . .	6	5,710	21,611	1	11	18,179	5	0	31	1	-	1
3. Bridgetown, . .	7	7,767	28,281	3	16	10,769	15	0	35	1	-	1
4. Bannow, . .	6	8,563	24,214	2	4	16,425	10	0	23	1	-	3
5. Taghmon and Glynn,	7	4,918	23,687	2	24	14,508	17	0	33	1	-	1
6. Crossabeg, . .	4	4,529	16,172	1	27	12,696	15	0	21	1	-	1
	33	43,727	124,801	0	29	107,164	13	0	180	6	1	6
County of Wicklow.												
Baltinglass Union.												
1. Baltinglass, . .	7	6,573	28,659	3	17	22,419	15	0	30	1	-	..
2. Kiltegan, . .	8	5,765	44,642	3	7	15,491	11	0	25	1	-	-
3. Dunlavin, . .	8	6,131	43,634	2	38	18,769	3	0	25	1	-	-
4. Rathvilly, . .	5	3,563	22,080	0	25	17,118	5	0	16	1	-	-
	28	22,032	139,107	2	8	73,797	16	0	96	4		-
Rathdrum Union.												
1. Newcastle, . .	4	6,081	23,585	1	10	20,909	0	0	21	1	-	-
2. Ashford, . .	3	6,490	24,725	0	20	23,751	10	0	21	1	-	-
3. Annamoe, . .	7	4,794	60,562	0	18	11,621	15	0	21	1	-	-
4. Dunganstown, .	4	8,544	25,164	3	37	19,678	15	0	17	1	-	-
5. Arklow, . .	1	7,750	16,793	1	14	12,236	17	0	13	1	-	-
6. Newbridge, . .	4	5,484	16,827	0	22	12,799	7	0	16	1	-	-
7. Rathdrum, . .	4	5,518	36,954	2	6	10,377	0	0	17	1	-	-
8. Aughrim, . .	3	2,724	24,287	0	13	7,078	0	0	15	1	-	-
	30	43,402	227,540	2	21	127,634	4	0	143	8	-	-

[*continued.*

No. 1.—Statement of Dispensary Districts—*continued.*

Names of Unions and Dispensary Districts.	No. of Electoral Divisions in each.	Population: 1861.	Area: in Statute Acres.			Poor Law Valuation: 1861.			No. of Members of Committee of Management.	No. of Medical Officers.	Number of Apothecaries.	Number of Midwives.
Column 1.	2.	3.	4.			5.			6.	7.	8.	9.
PROVINCE OF LEINSTER—*continued.*												
County of Wicklow—*con.*			A.	R.	P.	£	s.	d.				
Shillelagh Union.												
1. Coolattin & Clonegall,	8	6,780	38,356	0	15	20,112	13	0	29	1	–	–
2. Coolkenno and Hacketstown,	7	6,626	31,137	2	37	17,048	11	0	21	1	–	–
3. Tinahely,	6	5,777	40,627	2	33	12,623	12	0	21	1	–	–
	21	19,183	110,121	2	4	50,081	15	0	71	3	–	–
PROVINCE OF CONNAUGHT.												
County of Galway.												
Ballinasloe Union.												
1. Ahascragh,	2	2,479	17,321	1	20	7,804	0	0	20	1	–	–
2. Ballinasloe,	3	7,234	19,173	1	6	16,063	0	0	29	1	1	–
3. Killian,	4	5,841	27,617	3	7	15,041	0	0	20	1	–	–
4. Creagh,	6	6,305	36,425	3	27	17,539	0	0	16	1	–	–
5. Lawrencetown,	5	4,131	31,549	1	35	13,120	0	0	18	1	–	–
6. Kiltormer,	5	4,232	27,919	1	23	14,541	0	0	18	1	–	–
	25	28,272	160,507	1	7	78,719	0	0	118	6	1	–
Clifden Union.												
1. Clifden,	7	12,087	43,893	2	37	7,163	5	0	19	2	–	–
2. Kleyle,	4	4,791	16,754	0	8	4,148	15	0	15	1	–	–
3. Roundstone,	8	8,122	104,318	1	39	5,785	4	0	15	2	–	–
	19	25,000	192,968	1	4	17,397	2	0	49	5	–	–
Galway Union.												
1. Galway,	3	24,880	21,338	0	23	31,750	17	0	51	2	1	–
2. Oranmore,	6	6,816	30,311	1	19	13,325	5	0	21	1	–	–
3. Turloughmore,	8	7,608	46,235	1	33	11,485	13	0	37	1	–	–
4. Aran,	1	3,299	11,287	3	17	1,684	4	0	2	1	–	–
5. Spiddle,	3	5,620	62,364	1	39	3,668	15	0	20	1	–	–
6. Moycullen,	3	3,003	21,949	2	34	3,244	16	0	15	1	–	–
	25	50,821	197,467	0	0	65,227	10	0	150	7	1	–
Glennamaddy Union.												
1. Dunmore,	3	3,037	17,357	1	4	5,880	9	0	16	1	–	–
2. Glennamaddy,	7	8,914	40,161	2	28	11,898	5	0	21	1	–	–
3. Williamstown,	8	10,324	42,799	2	36	14,678	1	0	23	1	–	–
	18	22,469	100,318	2	28	31,801	15	0	60	3	–	–
Gort Union.												
1. Gort,	8	7,168	34,790	0	2	17,194	0	0	20	1	1	–
2. Kinvarra,	6	7,771	36,308	0	23	13,488	9	0	20	1	–	–
3. Ardrahan,	6	5,012	36,821	0	6	12,538	15	0	20	1	–	–
	20	20,[illegible]	107,919	0	31	43,238	16	0	60	3	1	–
Loughrea Union.												
1. Loughrea,	5	7,299	29,611	0	10	17,649	15	0	28	1	–	–
2. Bullaun,	10	6,108	53,914	3	30	22,933	9	0	31	1	–	–
3. Athenry,	11	8,799	56,131	0	27	21,411	10	0	28	1	–	–
4. Woodford,	8	6,933	56,914	2	38	13,434	10	0	23	1	–	–
	34	29,139	196,631	3	35	75,463	4	0	108	4	–	–
Mount Bellew Union.												
1. Killererin,	4	6,694	31,924	0	27	10,219	5	0	15	1	–	1
2. Clonbrock,	5	5,816	29,857	1	17	13,522	18	0	21	1	–	1
3. Mount Bellew,	5	7,476	40,801	3	7	16,719	1	0	21	1	–	–
	14	19,986	102,583	1	21	40,459	4	0	57	3	–	2

[continued.

No. 1.—Statement of Dispensary Districts—*continued.*

Names of Unions and Dispensary Districts.	No. of Electoral Divisions included.	Population: 1871.	Area: in Statute Acres.			Poor Law Valuation: 1871.			No. of Members of Committee of Management.	No. of Medical Officers.	Number of Apothecaries.	Number of Midwives.
Column 1.	2.	3.	4.			5.			6.	7.	8.	9.
PROVINCE OF CONNAUGHT—*continued.*												
County of Galway—*con.*			A.	R.	P.	£	s.	d.				
Oughterard Union.												
1. Clonbur,	5	5,749	88,806	2	9	6,009	10	0	13	2	–	1
2. Oughterard,	4	6,070	69,658	3	23	5,490	14	0	15	1	–	–
3. Lettermore,	5	6,653	44,290	3	37	3,487	16	0	13	1	–	–
	14	18,472	172,745	1	22	14,893	0	0	41	4	–	1
Portumna Union.												
1. Portumna,	8	8,761	45,628	0	34	18,841	9	0	35	2	–	1
2. Eyrecourt,	7	6,178	31,417	1	31	16,681	3	0	27	1	–	–
	15	14,939	77,045	2	25	35,333	12	0	62	3	–	1
Tuam Union.												
1. Tuam,	13	19,379	72,235	2	28	30,537	8	0	37	2	–	–
2. Dunmore,	5	9,708	36,443	0	30	14,628	1	0	23	1	–	–
3. Headford,	9	9,393	46,460	0	28	18,687	0	0	23	1	–	–
4. Abbey,	7	5,959	35,481	0	12	11,865	8	0	21	1	–	–
	34	44,440	190,648	0	30	75,717	17	0	104	5	–	–
County of Leitrim.												
Carrick-on-Shannon Union.												
1. Drumshanbo,	8	8,970	33,787	1	22	8,856	18	0	21	1	–	1
2. Leitrim,	6	7,937	23,110	1	21	10,492	15	0	19	1	–	–
3. Jamestown,	5	8,727	21,973	2	5	14,583	12	0	27	1	–	1
4. Aughrim,	6	6,023	21,855	3	35	14,064	18	0	19	1	–	–
	25	31,677	100,736	1	3	48,100	3	0	86	4	–	2
Manorhamilton Union.												
1. Manorhamilton,	8	10,163	39,701	0	28	11,838	2	0	10	1	–	–
2. Largaboy,	6	6,893	45,850	0	6	10,783	18	0	11	1	–	–
3. Dromahaire,	5	8,490	31,385	3	28	12,606	6	0	11	1	–	–
4. Drumkeerin,	5	7,885	38,920	0	12	8,095	2	0	11	1	–	–
	22	33,443	144,847	0	34	43,319	8	0	43	4	–	–
Mohill Union.												
1. Mohill,	6	9,687	25,757	2	16	13,014	10	0	19	1	–	–
2. Ryan,	7	8,718	28,103	0	6	11,980	3	0	15	1	–	–
3. Rowan,	5	5,590	19,032	2	14	7,129	10	0	11	1	–	–
4. Carrigallen,	5	6,246	18,540	1	1	7,892	8	0	11	1	–	–
	23	30,191	92,433	1	37	39,516	17	0	54	4	–	–
County of Mayo.												
Ballina Union.												
1. Ballina,	11	23,389	78,846	1	10	30,704	15	0	37	1	1	–
2. Crossmolina,	9	9,294	76,566	1	17	15,719	9	0	27	1	–	–
	20	32,683	155,412	2	27	46,424	4	0	64	2	1	–
Ballinrobe Union.												
1. Ballinrobe,	8	14,673	72,217	1	7	23,065	3	0	35	2	–	–
2. Cong,	4	7,555	31,180	2	34	14,917	1	0	23	1	–	–
3. Hollymount,	6	9,310	41,008	1	23	21,925	12	0	21	1	–	–
	18	31,538	144,404	1	21	59,907	16	0	79	4	–	–

[*continued.*

No. 1.—Statement of Dispensary Districts—*continued.*

Names of Unions and Dispensary Districts.	No. of Electoral Divisions (wholly or partly).	Population, 1871.	Area in Statute Acres.			Poor Law Valuation, 1871.			No. of Members of Committee of Management.	No. of Medical Officers.	Number of Apothecaries.	Number of Midwives.
Column 1.	2.	3.	4.			5.			6.	7.	8.	9.
PROVINCE OF CONNAUGHT—*continued.*												
County of Mayo—*con.*			A.	R.	P.	£	s.	d.				
Belmullet Union.												
1. Binghamstown, . .	8	8,075	31,091	2	7	5,735	11	0	19	1	–	–
2. Bangor, . . .	12	9,021	146,841	0	14	5,097	13	0	24	1	–	–
	15	17,096	177,932	2	21	10,933	4	0	43	2	–	–
Castlebar Union.												
1. Castlebar, . .	12	20,029	97,809	1	16	26,003	0	0	36	2	–	–
2. Balla, . . .	6	11,681	48,165	0	27	19,667	0	0	31	1	–	–
	18	31,780	110,997	2	3	45,870	0	0	67	3	–	–
Claremorris Union.												
1. Claremorris, . .	7	9,621	31,841	0	28	14,529	9	0	29	1	–	–
2. Ballindine, . .	6	8,442	34,550	3	16	15,761	9	0	28	1	–	–
3. Ballyhaunis, . .	6	12,007	41,295	3	33	11,635	16	0	25	1	–	–
	19	30,070	110,787	3	37	41,926	15	0	80	3	–	–
Killala Union.												
1. Killala, . . .	3	5,818	25,106	1	25	12,066	7	0	25	1	–	–
2. Ballycastle, . .	5	5,511	79,653	2	29	8,437	10	0	19	1	–	–
	8	11,029	104,083	0	14	20,503	17	0	44	2	–	–
Newport Union.												
1. Newport, . . .	5	8,162	63,968	0	39	8,506	7	0	21	1	–	1
2. Achill, . . .	6	8,188	106,173	3	21	4,313	8	0	23	2	–	1
	11	16,060	170,112	2	20	12,819	15	0	44	3	–	2
Swineford Union.												
1. Swineford, . .	4	11,924	30,695	1	6	10,357	0	0	21	1	–	–
2. Foxford, . . .	3	7,452	21,914	0	19	6,779	10	0	15	1	–	–
3. Kiltamagh, . .	5	8,909	22,499	3	18	8,402	1	0	10	1	–	–
4. Lowpark, . . .	4	11,302	35,985	2	12	6,758	17	0	11	1	–	–
5. Kilkelly, . . .	5	12,377	41,330	3	18	8,161	14	0	17	1	–	–
	21	52,001	152,095	2	23	40,459	2	0	83	5	–	–
Westport Union.												
1. Westport, . . .	8	12,550	62,478	2	14	15,634	4	0	30	2	–	–
2. Louisburgh, . .	9	7,985	80,450	3	12	6,991	14	0	15	2	–	–
3. Islandeady, . .	5	6,328	32,579	2	8	8,190	1	0	19	1	–	–
	22	26,863	175,507	3	34	30,815	19	0	64	5	–	–
County of Roscommon.												
Boyle Union.												
1. Boyle, . . .	9	16,275	52,042	2	18	22,467	12	0	58	2	1	1
2. Ballinameen, . .	7	8,168	18,768	2	31	18,612	16	0	39	1	–	–
3. Gurteen, . . .	8	10,610	22,749	0	12	18,853	13	0	34	1	–	–
4. Keadue, . . .	6	7,107	21,869	0	13	7,289	9	0	17	1	–	–
5. Ballyfarnan, . .	5	5,550	24,768	1	36	9,826	18	0	22	1	–	–
	35	47,750	139,625	3	30	72,651	5	0	127	6	1	1

[*continued.*

No. 1.—STATEMENT of DISPENSARY DISTRICTS—*continued.*

Names of Unions and Dispensary Districts.	No. of Electoral Divisions in each.	Population 1871.	Area in Statute Acres.			Poor Law Valuation 1871.			No. of Members of Committee of Management.	No. of Medical Officers.	Number of Apothecaries.	Number of Midwives.
Column 1.	2.	3.	4.			5.			6.	7.	8.	9.
PROVINCE OF CONNAUGHT—*continued.*												
Co. of Roscommon—*con.*			A.	R.	P.	£	s.	d.				
Castlerea Union.												
1. Ballaghaderreen, .	5	16,032	46,257	3	38	14,501	2	0	20	1	-	-
2. Frenchpark, . .	5	10,283	36,639	3	13	17,180	9	0	21	1	-	-
3. Castlerea, . .	5	13,943	31,011	3	34	18,735	0	0	21	1	-	-
4. Castleplunket, .	4	1,573	28,423	2	30	21,293	12	0	21	1	-	-
	19	48,785	102,363	1	35	71,759	12	0	83	4	-	-
Roscommon Union.												
1. Athleague, . .	6	7,250	36,350	2	29	28,551	0	0	15	1	-	-
2. Roscommon, . .	5	9,492	36,194	1	15	25,008	16	0	19	1	-	-
3. Ballyleague, . .	7	9,760	41,183	1	34	20,252	7	0	19	1	-	-
	18	26,501	114,036	1	38	64,393	12	0	53	3	-	-
Strokestown Union.												
1. Strokestown, . .	7	10,488	31,614	1	15	19,371	3	0	21	1	-	-
2. Roosky, . .	7	8,346	33,270	2	3	12,338	19	0	23	1	-	1
3. Elphin, . .	6	6,561	25,151	2	0	18,928	18	0	31	1	-	-
	20	25,395	90,036	1	18	50,738	12	0	75	3	-	1
County of Sligo.												
Dromore, West, Union.												
1. Easky, . .	6	8,473	43,231	0	3	12,578	4	0	19	1	-	1
2. Skreen, . .	8	6,231	32,734	1	6	13,963	18	0	21	1	-	1
3. Castleconnor, .	3	8,815	21,969	0	30	10,175	6	0	11	1	-	-
	17	16,006	96,985	1	39	36,727	8	0	51	3	-	2
Sligo Union.												
1. Carney, . .	9	12,995	44,551	1	30	18,851	11	0	21	2	-	1
2. Sligo, . .	6	20,198	20,815	0	27	28,464	2	0	41	2	1	2
3. Collooney, . .	5	7,050	25,143	0	19	13,323	17	0	23	1	-	-
4. Ballymote, . .	4	6,774	19,138	3	22	12,817	10	0	15	1	-	-
5. Riverstown, . .	5	6,630	23,551	2	25	13,333	0	0	19	1	-	-
	29	53,901	143,423	1	12	97,475	0	0	119	7	1	3
Tobercurry Union.												
1. Tobercurry, . .	7	10,691	45,316	0	16	16,712	3	0	23	1	-	-
2. Coolaney, . .	8	5,424	34,300	0	19	12,578	13	0	23	1	-	-
3. Aclare, . .	6	11,542	46,157	1	5	11,230	13	0	23	1	-	-
	21	27,657	125,773	2	0	40,523	10	0	69	3	-	-

SUMMARY OF FOREGOING TABLE, No. 1.

Provinces.	No. of Unions.	No. of Dispensary Districts.	No. of Electoral Divisions.	Population in 1871.	Area in Statute Acres.			Poor Law Valuation 1871.			No. of Members of Committees of Management.	No. of Medical Officers.	Number of Apothecaries.	Number of Midwives.
					A.	R.	P.	£	s.	d.				
Ulster, .	41	213	873	1,807,284	5,316,588	2	7	4,021,853	5	0	4,073	251	3	68
Munster, .	50	234	1,073	1,328,877	6,005,103	1	1	3,360,392	15	5	4,229	228	19	27
Leinster, .	40	203	944	1,473,009	4,840,319	1	27	4,503,527	17	0	4,247	229	11	70
Connaught,	32	69	548	869,414	4,050,259	0	21	1,353,609	19	0	2,141	113	6	15
Total, .	163	719	3,438	5,798,564	20,322,613	1	16	13,239,383	16	3	14,700	801	39	180

No. 2.—FINANCIAL and RELIEF RETURNS.—LIST, in pursuance of § 20 of the Medical Charities Act (14 & 15 Vic., c. 68), of all DISPENSARY DISTRICTS in the several Unions in Ireland (arranged in Provinces and Counties):—showing the NUMBER of DISPENSARIES in each, and the EXPENSES of each Dispensary District for the Year ended 29th September, 1871; with a RETURN,—for the Year ended 30th September, 1871,—of the NUMBER of CASES of MEDICAL RELIEF afforded to Patients at the Dispensary and at their own Homes, respectively; the Number of TICKETS for Medical Relief CANCELLED by the Committee of Management, under § 9 of the Act; Number of Cases of VACCINATION; Number of DANGEROUS LUNATICS certified; of Patients attended in BRIDEWELLS, &c.

NOTE ON TABLE, No. 2.

Columns 1 to 3, 5 and 6 inclusive, are abstracted from the sealed Orders of the Commissioners.
Columns 4 and 7 to 15, inclusive, are abstracted from Returns received from the Clerks of Unions.
Columns 16 to 23, inclusive, are abstracted from Returns received from the Medical Officers of Dispensary Districts.
Column 8:—In various instances in which Rent does not appear in this Table as part of the Annual Expense, the Dispensary of the District is held in a house which was used for a Dispensary under the late system, or in a court-house, or other public building; the use of which is obtained by the Guardians for the purpose, or in a house granted by the proprietor, rent free, or at a nominal rent.
Columns 5 and 10:—In some instances two Dispensary Districts, in different but adjoining Unions, are attended by the same Medical Officer.

Name of Union.	Name of Dispensary District.	No. of Dispensaries [illegible]	No. of Officers authorised by Sealed Orders: Med. Officers	Apothecaries	[illegible]	Expenses of Year ended 29th September, 1871: Medicines and Medical Appliances	Rent of Dispensary Buildings	Books, Forms, Stationery, and Printing	Salaries: Medical Officers	Salaries: Apothecaries	Vaccination Expenses: [illegible]	Vaccination Expenses: Other Expenses [illegible]	[illegible]	Total Expenditure for each Dispensary District for Year ended 29th Sept., 1871	Medical Relief afforded in Year ended 30th September, 1871: Number of New Cases attended and registered during the year: Dispensary Tickets	Visiting Tickets	Total	[illegible]	[illegible]	[illegible]	[illegible]	[illegible]
Column 1.	2.	3.	4.	5.	6.	7.	8.	9.	10.	11.	12.	13.	14.	15.	16.	17.	18.	19.	20.	21.	22.	23.
PROVINCE OF ULSTER.						£ s. d.	£ s. d.	£ s. d.	£ s. d.	£ s.	£ s. d.	£ s. d.	£ s. d.	£ s. d.								
COUNTY OF ANTRIM.																						
ANTRIM,	1. Antrim,	1	1	-	-	48 3 10	10 10 0	0 18	1 100 0 0	-	7 11 0	0 18 0	6 6 8	182 19 6	409	392	801	-	134	-	1	1
	2. Crumlin,	1	1	-	-	56 16 3	4 0 0	0 10	6 120 0 0	-	5 6 0	0 18 0	1 8 11	171 1 10	416	230	646	-	157	-	-	-
	3. Templepatrick,	1	1	-	-	83 7 11	5 0 0	0 7	8 65 0 0	-	7 0 0	-	3 8 6	120 14 10	307	104	401	-	163	-	-	-
	4. Doagh,	1	1	-	-	10 3 0	5 0 0	0 7	3 85 0 0	-	7 17 0	-	9 9 8	118 16 11	306	175	481	-	178	1	-	-
	5. Connor,	1	1	-	-	5 8 9	5 0 0	0 7	3 85 0 0	-	8 0 0	-	4 11 9	109 7 8	273	167	440	-	131	-	-	-
	6. Randalstown,	1	1	-	-	77 2 9	-	0 14	8 100 0 0	-	9 16 0	0 10 0	8 13 1	136 16 7	1,016	311	1,327	1	330	-	-	-
		6	6	-	-	289 2 6	30 10 0	3 11	6 555 0 0	-	47 10 0	1 16 0	35 16 7	849 4 3	3,167	1,307	4,[illegible]	1	1,[illegible]	1	1	1

BALLYCASTLE,	1. Ballycastle,	1	1	–	–	[illegible]
	2. Cr[illegible],	1	1	–	–	[illegible]
	3. Cushendall,	1	1	–	–	[illegible]
		3	3	–	–	[illegible]
BALLYMENA,	1. Ballymena,	1	1	–	1	[illegible]
	2. Galgorm,	1	1	–	–	[illegible]
	3. Ahoghill,	1	1	–	–	[illegible]
	4. Portglenone,	1	1	–	–	[illegible]
	5. Clough,	1	1	–	–	[illegible]
	6. Broughshane,	1	1	–	–	[illegible]
	7. Glenwhirry,	1	1	–	–	[illegible]
	8. Toome,	1	1	–	–	[illegible]
		11	8	–	1	[illegible]
BALLYMONEY,	1. Ballymoney,	1	1	–	–	[illegible]
	2. Dervock,	1	1	–	–	[illegible]
	3. Co[illegible],	1	1	–	–	[illegible]
	4. D[illegible],	1	1	–	–	[illegible]
	5. Kilrea,	1	1	–	–	[illegible]
		6	5	–	–	[illegible]
BELFAST,	1. Belfast,	6	10	2	3	[illegible]
	2. Castlereagh,	3	3	–	1	[illegible]
		9	13	2	4	[illegible]
LARNE,	1. Glenarm,	1	1	–	1	[illegible]
	2. Larne,	1	1	–	–	[illegible]
	3. Ballynure,	1	1	–	–	[illegible]
	4. Ballycarry,	1	1	–	–	[illegible]
	5. Carrickfergus,	1	1	–	1	[illegible]
		5	5	–	2	[illegible]

[continued.

No. 2.—Dispensary Districts, with the Expenses, and Amount of Medical Relief afforded, in the several Unions—*continued*.

Name of Union.	Name of Dispensary Districts.	3	No. of Officers: Med. Officers	Apothecaries	Midwives	Expenses of Year ended 29th September, 1871: Medicines and Medical Appliances	Rent of Dispensary Buildings	Books, Forms, Stationery, Printing	Salaries: Medical Officers	Apothecaries	Vaccination Expenses: Amount of Fees paid to Medical Officers	Other Expenses in carrying out the Vaccination Act	Fuel and Attendance, and other Expenses	Total Expenditure for each Dispensary District for Year ended 29th Sept., 1871	Medical Relief afforded in Year ended 29th September, 1871: Number of New Cases attended and registered during the year: Dispensary Tickets	Visiting Tickets	Total	19	20	21	22	23
Column 1.	2.	3	4.	5.	6.	7.	8.	9.	10.	11.	12.	13.	14.	15.	16.	17.	18.	19.	20.	21	22.	23.
PROVINCE OF ULSTER—*continued*.						£ s. d.	£ s. d.	£ s. d.	£ s. d.	£ s. d.	£ s. d.	£ s. d.	£ s. d.	£ s. d.								
County of Antrim—*con.*																						
Lisburn,	1. Lisburn,	1	1	–	–	60 10 3	15 0 0	1 0 0	120 0 0	–	11 0 0	1 0 0	–	194 18 9	1,014	894	1,908	–	290	1	–	–
	2. Hillsborough,	1	1	–	–	80 10 0	10 0 0	0 15 0	120 0 0	–	11 16 0	–	–	151 7 11	301	346	647	–	190	1	–	–
	3. [illegible],	1	1	–	–	30 10 7	7 0 0	0 15 1	75 0 0	–	11 16 0	3 0 0	0 9 4	180 14 3	173	116	289	–	215	–	–	–
	4. Glenavy,	1	1	–	–	34 14 7	10 0 0	0 15 4	77 10 0	–	9 15 0	5 0 0	–	150 16 11	476	187	663	1	174	1	–	–
	5. Dunmurry,	1	1	–	–	16 9 8	10 0 0	1 4 8	75 0 0	–	9 10 0	–	4 0 0	118 6 10	699	217	916	–	191	1	–	–
	6. [illegible],	1	1	–	–	23 17 3	10 10 0	0 15 4	90 0 0	–	[illegible]	1 0 0	1 0 0	195 11 8	370	254	627	–	119	2	–	–
	7. [illegible],	1	1	–	–	9 0 3	4 0 0	0 15 3	36 0 0	–	3 17 0	0 0 0	4 17 0	103 17 7	463	150	613	1	193	3	–	–
	8. Annahilt,	1	1	–	–	11 10 5	4 0 0	1 0 6	77 10 0	–	7 19 0	–	–	104 7 11	316	160	476	–	144	1	–	–
		[illegible]	8	–	–	276 16 4	75 10 0	7 7 3	640 0 0	–	73 0 0	7 0 0	13 6 6	1001 18 10	3,542	2,323	[illegible]	2	1,[illegible]	10	–	–
County of Armagh.																						
Armagh,	1. Armagh,	1	1	–	1	38 12 11	15 0 0	1 12 11	120 0 0	–	11 12 0	2 0 0	43 0 0	270 0 10	3,180	500	1,[illegible]	–	300	[illegible]	–	–
	2. Blackwatertown,	1	1	–	1	13 9 5	11 10 0	1 15 11	130 0 0	–	8 13 0	–	5 3 5	185 10 10	276	107	[illegible]	–	[illegible]	1	–	–
	3. Caledon,	1	1	–	–	0 10 0	7 0 0	0 10 11	45 0 0	–	8 10 0	–	–	70 17 5	230	64	[illegible]	–	50	–	–	–
	4. Tynan,	1	1	–	–	0 10 0	0 10 0	1 0 5	130 0 0	–	7 3 0	1 0 0	3 0 0	145 6 11	[illegible]	141	403	–	164	3	–	–
	5. Keady,	1	1	–	–	13 16 11	7 0 0	0 11 11	120 0 0	–	18 13 0	1 0 0	3 0 0	165 3 10	465	237	[illegible]	–	[illegible]	3	–	–
	6. Markethill,	1	1	–	1	16 11 5	0 0 0	1 19 3	130 0 0	–	10 1 0	6 10 0	11 0 0	175 0 10	360	231	[illegible]	–	[illegible]	–	–	–
	7. Richhill,	1	1	–	–	40 2 5	6 0 0	0 16 11	125 0 0	–	6 11 0	–	6 18 6	191 7 8	[illegible]	237	[illegible]	–	[illegible]	3	–	–
	8. Loughgall,	1	1	–	1	11 7 5	6 0 0	0 14 11	100 0 0	–	11 7 0	3 0 0	15 0 0	213 16 7	[illegible]	[illegible]	[illegible]	–	[illegible]	1	–	–
		8	8	–	4	161 1 3	73 0 0	8 7 1	830 0 0	–	82 11 0	11 10 0	100 18 11	1,397 8 6	[illegible]	[illegible]	[illegible]	–	1,[illegible]	10	–	–
Lurgan,	1. Lurgan,	2	2	–	–	33 15 10	19 0 0	1 5 0	200 0 0	–	31 14 0	–	6 0 0	335 15 10	1,708	774	1,[illegible]	–	[illegible]	2	–	–
	2. Aghalee,	1	1	–	–	7 18 4	8 0 0	1 0 6	73 11 8	–	7 0 0	–	1 10 6	108 17 1	463	[illegible]	[illegible]	–	117	3	–	–
	3. Moira,	1	1	–	–	17 17 3	7 10 0	1 0 0	100 0 0	–	10 17 0	6 17 0	6 10 1	158 10 3	[illegible]	[illegible]	[illegible]	1	[illegible]	–	–	–
	4. Waringstown,	1	1	–	–	7 10 0	4 0 0	3 1 11	79 17 6	–	16 16 0	[illegible]	5 10 0	116 4 0	[illegible]	[illegible]	[illegible]	–	[illegible]	–	–	–
	5. Portadown,	1	1	–	1	34 16 0	21 0 0	1 0 0	120 0 0	–	[illegible]	[illegible]	[illegible]	[illegible]	[illegible]	[illegible]	[illegible]	–	[illegible]	4	–	–
	6. Tartaraghan,	1	1	–	–	17 3 8	10 0 0	1 0 0	100 0 0	–	11 10 0	[illegible]	[illegible]	142 17 3	[illegible]	[illegible]	[illegible]	–	[illegible]	–	–	–
		7	7	–	1	103 7 0	61 10 0	8 11 11	673 17 5	–	97 1 0	[illegible]	61 10 3	[illegible]	[illegible]	[illegible]	[illegible]	1	[illegible]	10	–	–

COUNTY OF CAVAN.																						
BAILIEBOROUGH,	1. Bailieborough,	1	1	–	–	31 18 9	8 0 0	0 10 1	140 0 0	–	16 7 0	6 12 0	1 0 0	145 3 10	932	770	672	4	208	–	–	–
	2. Shercock,	1	1	–	–	27 2 9	10 0 0	1 17 11	77 10 [illegible]	–	1 0 0	1 1 0	1 10 0	146 17 10	198	138	348	–	94	1	–	–
	3. Kingscourt,	1	1	–	–	27 10 11	5 0 0	0 11 11	80 0 0	–	4 7 0	2 1 7	0 0 0	186 17 10	970	174	544	–	98	–	–	–
	4. Cro-[illegible],	1	1	–	–	7 0 0	7 9 0	0 6 3	30 0 0	–	3 10 0	1 1 0	–	40 11 3	164	50	150	–	15	–	–	–
	5. Tergan,	1	1	–	–	9 8 9	5 0 0	1 13 [illegible]	23 0 0	–	–	3 1 0	0 0 0	74 7 9	104	52	100	–	50	–	–	–
		5	5	–	–	122 0 5	50 0 0	5 0 5	330 15 0	–	27 10 0	12 16 0	11 0 6	665 0 0	1,112	435	2,000	4	435	1	–	–
BAWNBOY,	1. Ballyconnell,	1	1	–	–	22 15 11	9 0 0	1 0 9	90 0 0	–	7 6 0	–	1 5 0	134 6 6	590	334	113	–	217	1	–	–
	2. Ballinamore,	1	1	–	*1	10 1 0	9 0 0	0 16 7	91 2 10	–	7 10 0	–	1 0 0	131 11 6	164	109	305	–	310	2	2	3
	3. Swanlinbar,	1	1	–	–	18 6 10	7 10 0	0 17 10	90 0 0	–	6 5 0	–	1 0 0	123 10 5	160	29	316	1	117	1	–	–
	4. Newtowngore,	1	1	–	–	21 14 11	4 0 0	2 2 10	94 10 0	–	11 3 0	–	6 10 4	111 9 7	177	103	276	–	140	–	–	–
		4	4	–	1	80 17 0	30 10 0	5 19 0	370 1 0	–	35 11 0	–	17 15 1	525 10 1	796	580	1,020	1	900	4	2	3
CAVAN,	1. Arvagh,	1	1	–	–	9 10 0	6 0 0	0 11 [illegible]	85 7 7	–	1 10 0	1 10 0	3 6 3	113 17 6	257	192	654	–	195	4	–	–
	2. Ballinagh,	1	1	–	–	18 14 6	4 0 0	0 11 9	85 0 0	–	6 10 0	–	1 5 0	185 13 2	319	87	794	–	172	–	–	–
	3. Ballyhaise,	1	1	–	–	30 15 9	9 0 0	0 14 10	97 3 1	–	11 1 0	1 0 0	3 16 1	111 11 6	116	187	325	–	181	–	–	–
	4. Belturbet,	1	1	–	–	27 11 0	–	0 11 10	65 0 0	–	16 9 0	3 0 0	5 15 8	130 6 1	641	214	580	–	274	2	–	–
	5. Cavan,	1	1	–	–	21 7 3	30 0 0	0 17 [illegible]	102 18 5	–	35 15 0	1 10 0	4 0 1	137 8 9	460	690	720	–	310	9	–	–
	6. Killeshandra,	1	1	–	–	15 15 1	5 0 0	0 11 10	91 16 1	–	8 11 0	2 0 0	3 0 0	105 15 0	320	121	660	–	141	1	–	–
	7. Kilnaleck,	1	1	–	–	11 7 6	4 0 0	0 11 [illegible]	96 0 0	–	11 0 0	–	0 10 0	117 18 1	630	120	660	9	230	2	–	–
	8. Stradone,	1	1	–	–	14 1 2	6 10 0	0 11 10	75 0 0	–	9 8 0	1 0 0	2 2 8	119 10 10	340	60	451	–	197	–	–	–
		8	8	–	–	170 1 0	65 10 0	6 6 6	726 1 3	–	79 0 0	10 0 0	32 10 5	1,030 10 11	4,911	1,369	4,733	9	1,120	19	–	–
COOTEHILL,	1. Cootehill,	1	1	–	–	35 11 10	18 10 0	1 0 0	93 0 0	–	19 7 0	–	–	175 9 10	107	730	811	–	300	6	–	–
	2. D[illegible]grove,	1	1	–	–	13 2 10	10 0 0	0 0 0	40 0 0	–	8 6 0	–	–	116 9 3	841	90	783	–	333	–	–	–
	3. Drum,	1	1	–	–	33 1 9	13 0 0	0 11 10	75 0 0	–	27 0 0	–	1 10 0	155 16 7	307	340	301	1	947	–	–	–
	4. Tullyvin,	1	1	–	–	34 10 0	13 10 0	0 11 0	103 0 0	–	12 18 0	–	17 9 1	137 11 0	737	100	991	10	117	–	–	–
		4	4	–	–	130 12 1	44 0 0	2 9 0	312 0 0	–	68 13 0	–	45 19 1	585 6 8	1,920	300	2,890	10	1,010	6	–	–
COUNTY OF DONEGAL.																						
BALLYSHANNON,	1. Ballyshannon,	1	1	–	–	–	–	–	91 0 0	–	–	0 10 0	3 0 0	170 10 0	1,114	107	500	–	336	2	–	–
	2. Belleek,	1	1	–	–	–	8 10 0	–	103 0 0	–	10 6 0	1 10 0	4 12 0	104 17 5	500	60	149	1	131	–	–	–
	3. Church Hill,	1	1	–	–	–	8 0 0	–	50 0 0	–	3 8 0	0 10 0	2 0 0	45 17 0	70	13	91	–	90	–	–	–
	4. Kinlough,	1	1	–	–	–	15 0 0	–	100 0 0	–	15 17 0	0 10 0	7 0 0	130 7 4	267	119	170	–	200	–	–	–
	5. Ballintra,	1	1	–	–	–	–	4 17 6	73 3 0	–	3 4 0	–	2 10 0	45 11 0	171	20	160	–	109	1	–	–
		5	5	–	–	–	37 10 0	4 17 6	420 3 0	–	31 8 0	2 2 6	23 7 0	317 1 6	1,9[illegible]	31[illegible]	2,[illegible]	1	1,07[illegible]	3	–	–

* Bawnboy Union: Ballinamore District.—The appointment of Midwife appears not yet to have been made.

[continued.

No. 2.—Dispensary Districts, with the Expenses, and Amount of Medical Relief afforded, in the several Unions—continued.

Name of Union.	Name of Dispensary District.	No. of Dispensaries, &c.	No. of Officers authorized by Regulations: Medical Officers	Apothecaries	Wardens	Expenses of Year ended 29th September, 1871: Medicines and Medical Appliances	Rent of Dispensary Buildings	Books, Forms, Stationery, and Printing	Salaries: Medical Officers	Salaries: Apothecaries	Vaccination Expenses: Amount of Fees paid to Medical Officers	Vaccination Expenses: Other Expenses	Fuel and Attendance, Incidental Expenses, &c.	Total Expenditure for each Dispensary District for Year ended 29th Sept., 1871	Medical Relief afforded in Year ended 29th September, 1871: Number of New Cases: Dispensary Tickets	Visiting Tickets	Total	No. of Tickets, &c.	Total Number of Tickets, &c.	No. of Dangerous Lunatics, &c.	No. of Days, &c.	Total, &c.
Column 1.	2.	3.	4.	5.	6.	7.	8.	9.	10.	11.	12.	13.	14.	15.	16.	17.	18.	19.	20.	21.	22.	23.
PROVINCE OF ULSTER—continued.						£ s. d.	£ s. d.	£ s. d.	£ s. d.	£ s. d.	£ s.	£ s. d.	£ s. d.	£ s. d.								
County of Donegal—con.																						
Donegal,	1. Pettigo,	1	1	–	–	–	5 0 0	–	80 0 0	–	6 5	–	9 0 0	[illegible]	[illegible]	[illegible]	[illegible]	–	[illegible]	–	–	–
	2. Laghy,	1	1	–	1	44 12 7	8 10 0	–	80 0 0	–	11 19	1 11 6	20 10 10	170 4 11	[illegible]	[illegible]	[illegible]	–	[illegible]	–	–	–
	3. Donegal,	1	1	–	–	76 3 11	10 0 0	–	100 0 0	–	11 0	–	27 6 11	236 17 10	[illegible]	[illegible]	[illegible]	–	251	5	–	–
	4. Mountcharles,	1	1	–	1	60 6 4	4 0 0	–	100 0 0	–	10 13	–	24 10 9	200 3 5	[illegible]	[illegible]	[illegible]	–	[illegible]	–	–	–
	5. Dunkineely,	1	1	–	–	30 17 6	5 0 0	–	100 0 0	–	15 17	–	4 0 0	161 11 5	[illegible]	97	[illegible]	9	117	–	–	–
		5	5	–	2	212 14 10	32 10 0	–	460 0 0	–	60 8	1 11 6	86 6 9	826 6 1	1,5[illegible]	[illegible]	1,[illegible]	9	791	5	–	–
Dunfanaghy,	1. Dunfanaghy,	1	1	–	–	38 10 7	9 5 0	2 8 6	86 17 [illegible]	–	8 13	1 4 7	7 17 6	156 0 7	[illegible]	[illegible]	406	–	[illegible]	–	–	–
	2. Creeslough,	1	1	–	–	42 6 8	10 0 0	0 12 10	100 0 0	–	24 1	6 1 2	1 2 3	196 1 10	[illegible]	[illegible]	170	13	[illegible]	–	–	–
		2	2	–	–	80 16 8	19 5 0	3 1 4	186 17 [illegible]	–	33 14	7 6 0	11 19 9	340 9 5	[illegible]	[illegible]	576	13	[illegible]	–	–	–
Glenties,	1. Dungloe,	1	1	–	–	30 3 6	10 12 6	0 8 11	100 0 0	–	25 14	1 8 6	9 16 0	177 9 1	[illegible]	160	[illegible]	1	[illegible]	5	–	–
	2. Glenties,	1	1	–	–	16 8 2	10 0 0	0 1 8	100 0 0	–	–	–	–	126 9 7	[illegible]	[illegible]	[illegible]	8	[illegible]	–	–	–
	3. Carrick,	1	1	–	–	13 14 9	11 15 0	0 1 8	100 0 0	–	17 8	–	17 0 0	167 16 2	[illegible]	110	[illegible]	–	177	–	–	–
	4. Ardara,	1	1	–	–	17 8 10	6 0 0	0 1 8	80 0 0	–	4 10	1 0 0	–	109 1 3	[illegible]	[illegible]	[illegible]	–	239	2	–	–
	5. Killybegs,	1	1	–	1	4 5 6	6 0 0	0 1 8	90 0 0	–	7 16	–	9 0 0	106 4 10	200	97	[illegible]	1	165	1	–	–
		5	5	–	1	81 1 9	57 11 6	0 14 7	470 0 0	–	56 1	2 8 6	30 16 0	702 10 11	1,467	[illegible]	2,[illegible]	13	1,167	13	–	–
Inishowen,	1. Carndonagh,	1	1	–	1	–	12 0 0	0 6 10	80 0 0	–	8 8	–	19 0 0	120 15 10	[illegible]	100	[illegible]	–	[illegible]	3	–	–
	2. Clonmany,	1	1	–	1	16 1 1	3 0 0	1 0 1	[illegible]	–	10 15	–	2 0 0	127 18 5	[illegible]	[illegible]	[illegible]	–	66	[illegible]	–	–
	3. Moville,	1	1	–	1	29 7 0	9 11 0	0 6 11	[illegible]	–	27 11	–	12 0 0	207 19 11	[illegible]	[illegible]	[illegible]	–	410	–	–	–
	4. Malin,	1	1	–	–	15 14 3	16 0 0	0 6 10	120 0 0	–	8 16	–	3 0 0	164 16 1	[illegible]	[illegible]	[illegible]	3	[illegible]	1	–	–
	5. Buncrana,	1	1	–	1	30 0 11	10 0 0	0 5 10	[illegible]	–	9 9	1 10 0	3 2 6	128 17 5	[illegible]	167	516	–	134	8	–	–
		5	5	–	4	91 7 3	50 11 0	2 7 9	[illegible]	–	66 17	1 10 0	39 2 6	750 4 6	1,[illegible]	[illegible]	2,[illegible]	3	8[illegible]	5	–	–

LETTERKENNY,	1. Letterkenny,	1	1	–	–	11	16	7	11	0	0	0	12	6	100	0	0	–	13	11	1	1	6	1	0	0	170	10	9	619	772	891	–	101	–	1	4
	2. [illegible]	1	1	–	–	10	5	5	0	0	0	0	9	0	100	0	0	–	6	6	1	1	6	4	0	0	140	6	5	610	190	941	8	128	2	–	–
	3. Church Hill,	1	1	–	–	15	0	7	6	0	0	0	9	0	100	0	0	–	7	3	4	1	0	0	0	0	130	1	2	188	176	385	–	100	–	–	–
		3	3	–	–	45	11	8	30	0	0	1	11	6	300	0	0	–	35	17	6	3	0	11	15	0	440	19	3	1,387	644	1,227	8	330	2	1	4
MILFORD,	1. Rathmelton,	1	1	–	1	17	19	6	6	0	0	1	3	6	100	0	0	–	7	16	0	0	6	20	0	1	163	3	0	619	264	717	–	162	–	–	–
	2. Rathmullen,	1	1	–	–	16	8	8	6	0	0	0	4	3	100	0	0	–	4	3	0	0	7	0	13	5	187	3	1	450	145	814	–	114	–	–	–
	3. Kilmacrenan and Milford,	1	1	–	–	4	7	6	10	0	0	0	1	11	90	0	0	–	7	1	0	0	7	7	19	6	119	10	4	570	130	663	–	130	1	–	–
	4. Fannet,	1	1	–	–	25	12	0	5	0	0	0	4	11	100	0	0	–	7	18	6	10	7	4	10	11	167	10	4	301	107	663	17	101	8	–	–
	5. Rosguill,	1	1	–	–	34	10	6	5	0	0	0	5	11	100	0	0	–	10	5	0	0	7	5	1	0	142	0	9	120	101	230	–	105	1	–	–
		5	5	–	1	106	17	0	30	0	0	2	3	2	490	0	0	–	38	6	0	13	6	39	14	0	782	0	1	2,080	734	2,305	17	630	5	–	–
STRANORLAR,	1. Killygordon,	2	1	–	1	32	15	5	17	0	0	0	8	9	100	0	0	–	4	1	–			10	0	0	176	6	5	300	189	470	–	164	–	–	–
	2. Stranorlar,	2	1	–	1	57	10	1	10	0	0	1	6	9	100	0	0	–	7	11	–			5	16	0	106	5	1	577	300	720	1	168	–	–	–
	3. Clogher,†	2	1	–	11	–			10	0	0	0	1	9	100	0	0	–	16	0	–			9	9	6	120	0	3	170	90	360	6	370	3	–	–
		6	3	–	3	90	5	6	41	0	0	1	16	9	300	0	0	–	20	0	–			26	4	6	407	11	9	949	589	1,550	7	633	3	–	–
COUNTY OF DOWN. BANBRIDGE,*	1. Banbridge,	1	1	–	–	11	15	2	11	0	0	1	10	2	130	0	0	–	6	0	3	6	7	10	0	9	140	17	8	1,134	804	1,369	–	411	1	–	–
	2. Dromore,	1	1	–	–	41	1	6	10	0	0	1	6	1	100	0	0	–	10	0	1	12	10	6	16	5	195	0	10	630	643	1,073	17	873	–	–	–
	3. Gransha,	1	1	–	–	0	1	1	0	16	0	1	0	1	170	0	0	–	4	0	1	5	0	6	7	9	123	10	11	346	152	470	–	198	9	–	–
	4. Hollywood,	1	1	–	–	82	13	9	8	0	0	0	10	7	100	0	0	–	41	3	8	3	7	3	1	0	147	10	11	677	819	861	–	981	4	–	–
	5. Loughbrickland,	1	1	–	–	7	15	4	10	10	0	0	15	2	80	0	0	–	4	2	2	11	10	4	0	0	114	15	0	110	167	257	–	119	–	–	–
	6. Tanderagee,	1	1	–	–	22	1	0	9	0	0	0	11	1	100	0	0	–	0	0	1	11	0	5	0	6	100	0	3	600	877	1,010	–	310	2	–	–
		6	6	–	–	132	5	10	43	0	0	0	16	1	610	0	0	–	55	18	12	13	6	30	17	11	901	16	10	2,300	2,119	5,000	17	1,000	9	–	–
DOWN-PATRICK,‡	1. Downpatrick,	1	1	–	–	27	1	0	15	0	0	1	4	2	90	0	0	–	70	15	8	10	0	20	4	1	104	15	7	777	887	1,193	–	957	4	–	–
	2. Clough,	1	1	–	–	21	0	3	11	7	0	0	10	2	90	0	0	–	11	0	–			1	10	0	115	7	4	441	825	486	–	738	1	–	–
	3. Ballynahinch,	1	1	–	–	82	18	1	15	0	0	1	14	6	140	0	0	–	54	15	4	0	9	5	13	0	179	10	7	395	710	616	–	374	–	–	–
	4. Killyleagh,	1	1	–	–	34	9	11	14	0	0	0	14	8	90	0	0	–	12	15	1	2	0	2	15	0	168	0	7	631	221	254	–	852	1	–	–
	5. Kilkeel,	1	1	–	–	85	10	8	5	10	0	0	13	6	90	0	0	–	27	0	0	5	0	0	12	8	135	0	4	429	165	733	–	497	2	–	–
	6. Strangford,	1	1	–	–	83	14	2	6	0	0	1	3	2	90	0	0	–	0	6	–			5	10	0	133	0	4	350	231	483	–	93	–	–	–
	7. Portaferry,	3	1	–	11	34	7	7	9	10	0	1	15	6	80	0	0	–	15	10	3	0	0	4	0	1	141	0	3	804	200	600	–	107	1	–	–
		11	7	–	1	188	19	5	74	7	0	7	16	9	600	0	0	–	138	11	10	17	0	35	4	4	1,051	17	0	3,800	1,000	5,200	–	3,690	0	–	–
KILKEEL,	1. Kilkeel,	2	2	–	1	38	1	0	6	10	0	1	0	7	170	0	0	–	16	1	6	0	0	27	0	11	181	7	1	481	400	841	–	390	5	–	–
	2. Bryansford,	1	1	–	–	23	0	3	4	0	0	1	3	3	111	10	0	–	7	3	0	10	4	10	19	0	361	12	7	466	174	785	–	100	1	–	–
	3. Rostrevor,	1	1	–	1	16	18	6	10	0	0	0	13	7	60	0	0	–	2	1	0	13	0	13	10	3	129	17	1	350	179	424	8	71	2	–	–
		4	4	–	3	78	1	1	20	10	0	3	18	11	351	10	9	–	24	5	0	0	0	38	4	1	661	17	0	1,361	730	2,118	8	560	5	–	–

* Banbridge Union: Clonduff and Banagher Districts.—No appointment of Midwife appears to have been made in these Districts.
† Stranorlar Union: Clogher District.—No appointment of Midwife appears to have been made.
‡ Downpatrick Union: Portaferry District.—No appointment of Midwife appears to have been made.

(continued)

No. 2 g.—Dispensary Districts, with the Expenses, and Amount of Medical Relief afforded, in the several Unions—*continued.*

Name of Union.	Names of Dispensary Districts	[illegible]	No. of Officers appointed by Sealed Order: Med. Officers	Apothecaries	Midwives	Expenses of Year ended 29th September, 1871: Medicines and Medical Appliances	Rent of Dispensary Buildings	Books, Forms, Stationery, and Printing	Salaries: Medical Officers	Apothecaries	Vaccination Expenses: [illegible]	[illegible]	[illegible]	Total Expenditure [illegible] for Year ended 29th Sept., 1871	Medical Relief afforded in Year ended 29th September, 1871: Number of New Cases attended and Prescribed during the year: Dispensary Tickets	Visiting Tickets	Totals	[illegible]	[illegible]	[illegible]	[illegible]	[illegible]
Column 1.	2.	3.	4.	5.	6.	7.	8.	9.	10.	11.	12.	13.	14.	15.	16.	17.	18.	19.	20.	21.	22.	23.
PROVINCE OF ULSTER—*continued.*						£ s. d.	£ s. d.	£ s. d.	£ s. d.	£ s. d.	£ s. d.	£ s. d.	£ s. d.	£ s. d.								
County of Down—*con.*																						
Newry,	1. Newry,	1	2	–	–	17 0 8	25 0 0	2 6 2	119 6 0	–	[illegible]	1 0 0	31 10 0	224 19 11	1,657	770	[illegible]	6	377	6	10	9
	2. Warrenpoint,	1	1	–	1	10 4 1	10 0 0	0 15 [illegible]	106 5 0	–	1 9 0	0 5 0	18 10 0	160 8 1	272	[illegible]	[illegible]	1	156	–	–	–
	3. Rathfriland,	1	1	–	–	16 15 0	16 10 0	1 4 0	105 3 0	–	16 19 0	1 3 0	6 13 6	166 6 3	[illegible]	[illegible]	[illegible]	–	[illegible]	8	–	–
	4. Mullaghglass,	1	1	–	1	16 0 4	10 0 0	0 15 0	100 3 0	–	12 12 0	0 5 0	25 0 0	180 16 4	[illegible]	[illegible]	[illegible]	–	[illegible]	3	–	–
	5. [illegible],	1	1	–	–	6 16 11	16 0 0	0 15 0	105 3 0	–	5 15 0	0 5 0	6 17 0	130 4 11	[illegible]	[illegible]	[illegible]	–	[illegible]	–	–	–
	6. Meigh,	1	1	–	–	10 13 1	6 0 0	0 15 0	105 0 1	–	12 19 0	0 5 0	6 0 0	138 1 6	[illegible]	[illegible]	[illegible]	–	[illegible]	–	–	–
	7. Forkhill,	1	1	–	–	18 7 0	4 10 0	0 15 0	109 9 1	–	6 10 0	0 5 0	4 0 6	146 17 1	[illegible]	[illegible]	[illegible]	–	[illegible]	1	–	–
	8. Donaghmore,	1	1	–	–	6 16 11	10 0 0	0 15 0	101 10 0	–	4 6 0	1 0 0	–	128 6 6	[illegible]	[illegible]	[illegible]	–	67	–	–	–
	9. Poyntzpass,	1	1	–	–	18 10 3	8 0 0	0 16 0	101 10 0	–	3 10 0	0 5 0	–	126 17 0	[illegible]	[illegible]	[illegible]	–	[illegible]	1	–	–
		10	10	–	[illegible]	164 1 1	94 0 0	6 15 [illegible]	1056 17 [illegible]	–	91 11 0	1 16 [illegible]	123 10 3	1446 11 0	1,[illegible]	2,[illegible]	6,[illegible]	7	1,[illegible]	[illegible]	10	9
Newtownards,	1. Newtownards,	1	1	–	–	40 14 0	10 0 0	1 4 [illegible]	150 0 0	–	10 10 0	–	10 8 10	185 8 11	2,[illegible]	672	3,[illegible]	–	[illegible]	–	–	–
	2. Comber,	1	1	–	–	26 0 6	8 0 0	1 15 [illegible]	[illegible] 0 0	–	9 10 0	1 0 0	5 1 1	139 10 1	[illegible]	[illegible]	[illegible]	–	[illegible]	1	–	–
	3. Kilmood,	1	1	–	–	20 4 5	9 10 0	1 4 [illegible]	[illegible] 0 0	–	7 10 0	0 15 [illegible]	2 8 0	183 8 1	[illegible]	[illegible]	[illegible]	–	[illegible]	–	–	–
	4. Grey Abbey,	[illegible]	1	–	–	40 0 8	8 0 0	1 3 [illegible]	[illegible] 0 0	–	11 10 0	0 10 0	6 15 4	1[illegible] 5 5	1,1[illegible]	[illegible]	1,[illegible]	–	[illegible]	–	–	–
	5. Donaghadee,	1	1	–	–	22 10 6	7 0 0	0 15 [illegible]	[illegible] 0 0	–	9 0 0	0 14 0	7 3 6	182 15 3	[illegible]	[illegible]	[illegible]	–	[illegible]	–	–	–
	6. Bangor,	1	1	–	–	67 14 3	16 0 0	0 16 [illegible]	100 0 0	–	9 10 0	1 0 0	4 11 6	197 10 6	1,[illegible]	[illegible]	1,[illegible]	–	[illegible]	8	–	–
		7	6	–	–	277 8 11	37 10 0	10 6 [illegible]	[illegible] 0 0	–	57 0 0	6 5 0	36 8 0	1042 18 3	[illegible]	2,[illegible]	[illegible]	–	1,[illegible]	2	–	–
County of Fermanagh.																						
Enniskillen,	1. Enniskillen,	1	1	–	1	65 10 1	12 0 0	3 0 5	100 0 0		17 0 0	–	27 2 10	224 13 7	[illegible]	[illegible]	1,[illegible]	–	[illegible]	2	–	–
	2. Tempo,	1	1	–	–	7 8 6	12 0 0	1 12 5	1[illegible] 0 0	–	1 7 0	1 0 0	–	130 10 7	[illegible]	[illegible]	[illegible]	–	[illegible]	–	–	–
	3. Lisbellaw,	1	1	–	–	6 3 9	7 10 0	2 1 1	70 0 0	–	1 10 0	–	6 11 0	95 6 6	[illegible]	[illegible]	[illegible]	6	[illegible]	–	–	–
	4. Ely,	1	1	–	–	–	9 10 0	1 12 6	100 0 0	–	13 10 0	–	10 16 [illegible]	136 1 1	[illegible]	[illegible]	[illegible]	–	[illegible]	–	–	–
	5. Holywell,	1	1	–	–	15 1 0	10 10 0	1 3 7	1[illegible] 0 0	–	11 10 0	–	6 0 0	137 10 7	[illegible]	[illegible]	[illegible]	–	[illegible]	3	–	–
	6. Florencecourt,	1	1	–	1	13 0 6	10 0 0	1 12 5	100 0 0	–	9 0 0	–	11 0 0	137 13 11	[illegible]	[illegible]	[illegible]	3	[illegible]	1	–	–
		6	6	–	2	100 16 4	61 15 0	12 0 10	540 0 0	–	61 10 0	1 0 0	82 10 0	679 13 6	2,[illegible]	[illegible]	3,[illegible]	9	1,[illegible]	7	–	–

Union	Dispensary District	Returns
Irvinestown,	1. Irvinestown,	[illegible]
	2. Ederney,	[illegible]
	3. Clonelly,	[illegible]
	(Total)	[illegible]
Lisnaskea,	1. Brookeborough,	[illegible]
	2. Lisnaskea,	[illegible]
	3. Derrylin,*	[illegible]
	4. Maguiresbridge,	[illegible]
	(Total)	[illegible]
County of Londonderry. Coleraine,	1. Coleraine,	[illegible]
	2. Bushmills,	[illegible]
	3. Articlave,	[illegible]
	4. Aghadowey,	[illegible]
	5. Garvagh,	[illegible]
	(Total)	[illegible]
Londonderry,	1. City of Londonderry,	[illegible]
	2. Glendermott,	[illegible]
	3. Eglinton,	[illegible]
	4. Claudy,	[illegible]
	5. [illegible],	[illegible]
	6. Burt,	[illegible]
	7. Ballou,	[illegible]
	(Total)	[illegible]
Magherafelt,	1. Magherafelt,	[illegible]
	2. Bellaghy,	[illegible]
	3. Maghera,	[illegible]
	4. Draperstown,	[illegible]
	5. Moneymore,	[illegible]
	(Total)	[illegible]

* Lisnaskea Union: Derrylin District.—No appointment of Midwife appears to have been made.

[continued.

No. 2.—Dispensary Districts, with the Expenses, and Amount of Medical Relief afforded, in the several Unions—*continued*.

Name of Union.	Names of Dispensary Districts.	No. of Dispensary Stations	No. of Officers: Med. Officers	Apothecaries	Midwives	Expenses of Year ended 29th September, 1871: Medicines and Medical Appliances	Rent of Dispensary Buildings	Books, Forms, Stationery, and Printing	Salaries: Medical Officers	Salaries: Apothecaries	Vaccination Expenses: Amount of Fees paid to Medical Officers	Vaccination Expenses: Other Expenses	Fuel and Attendance, and other incidental expenses	Total Expenditure for each Dispensary District for Year ended 29th Sept., 1871	Medical Relief: Dispensary Tickets	Visiting Tickets	Total	[illegible]	[illegible]	[illegible]	[illegible]	[illegible]
Column 1.	2.	3.	4.	5.	6.	7.	8.	9.	10.	11.	12.	13.	14.	15.	16.	17.	18.	19.	20.	21.	22.	23.
						£ s. d.	£ s. d.	£ s. d.	£ s. d.	£ s. d.	£ s. d.	£ s. d.	£ s. d.	£ s. d.								
PROVINCE OF ULSTER—continued.																						
Co. of Londonderry—con.																						
Newtown-Limavady.	1. N.T.Limavady,	1	1	–	–	–	7 0 0	1 18 9	95 0 0	–	14 18 0	–	1 0 0	121 8 1	[illegible]	124	511	–	105	–	6	4
	2. Ballykelly,	1	1	–	–	27 8 6	10 0 0	1 16 0	80 0 0	–	13 19	–	2 0 0	116 4 5	[illegible]	144	697	–	271	1	–	–
	3. Bellarena,	1	1	–	–	16 6 3	–	1 6 6	90 0 0	–	5 7 0	–	2 13 1	119 12 10	[illegible]	137	[illegible]	–	111	–	–	–
	4. Dungiven,	1	1	–	1	20 11 7	8 0 0	1 11 0	70 4 0	–	3 10 0	–	10 0 0	116 3 7	[illegible]	[illegible]	[illegible]	–	142	–	–	–
	5. Feeny,	1	1	–	–	24 13 7	4 0 0	1 11 6	140 10 6	–	8 4 0	–	14 0 3	180 11 6	[illegible]	[illegible]	[illegible]	2	[illegible]	1	–	–
		5	5	–	1	90 1 10	31 0 0	8 17 9	505 10 6	–	41 13 0	–	30 1 4	704 2 3	2,[illegible]	[illegible]	3,[illegible]	2	[illegible]	2	6	4
County of Monaghan,																						
Carrickmacross.	1. Carrickmacross,	1	1	–	1	16 16 10	10 10 0	0 11 6	160 0 0	–	26 11 0	4 10 0	19 3 6	244 3 9	[illegible]	187	[illegible]	–	190	–	–	–
	2. Donaghmoyne,	1	1	–	1	29 8 1	10 0 0	0 16 7	80 0 0	–	11 9 0	1 1 6	16 10 6	150 12 11	[illegible]	1[illegible]	[illegible]	14	174	–	–	–
	3. Raferagh,	1	1	–	1	25 15 0	6 0 0	1 9 6	80 0 0	–	13 0 3	1 0 0	13 13 4	145 18 9	[illegible]	145	[illegible]	3	191	–	–	–
		3	3	–	3	81 9 2	26 10 0	2 17 7	320 0 0	–	50 16 3	6 11 6	49 6 4	540 15 5	1,131	176	1,[illegible]	17	555	–	–	–
Castleblayney.	1. Castleblayney,	1	1	–	1	68 14 1	10 0 0	0 16 6	100 0 0	–	26 15 0	6 5 6	21 1 1	244 17 9	1,[illegible]	605	2,[illegible]	[illegible]	316	–	2	1
	2. Ballybay,	1	1	–	1	45 5 10	8 0 0	1 14 0	100 0 0	–	16 1 0	–	7 3 1	182 3 9	[illegible]	[illegible]	773	1	313	1	–	–
	3. Crossmaglen,	1	1	–	1	27 8 9	8 0 0	0 18 6	100 0 0	–	21 18 0	2 12 6	14 8 0	178 6 5	[illegible]	[illegible]	[illegible]	1	735	2	–	–
	4. Newtownhamilton,	1	1	–	–	12 11 4	8 0 0	1 8 10	100 0 0	–	13 10 0	2 10 0	6 7 1	152 17 9	[illegible]	[illegible]	614	1	252	4	–	–
		4	4	–	3	154 0 6	34 0 0	7 12 10	450 0 0	–	79 19 0	11 16 6	52 1 6	790 1 6	2,[illegible]	1,267	4,107	37	1,[illegible]	7	2	1
Clones.	1. Clones,	1	1	–	–	27 4 11	15 0 0	0 10 0	130 0 0	–	12 0 0	0 10 6	28 14 7	213 6 0	[illegible]	[illegible]	785	1	[illegible]	6	–	–
	2. Newtownbutler,	1	1	–	–	16 4 1	0 0 0	0 2 6	110 0 0	–	6 2 0	1 17 9	5 6 0	122 16 1	[illegible]	162	[illegible]	–	187	–	–	–
	3. Rosslea,	1	1	–	–	11 [illegible] 6	4 0 0	0 2 6	110 0 0	–	7 4 0	1 18 3	4 13 8	111 17 3	[illegible]	103	[illegible]	–	[illegible]	–	–	–
		3	3	–	–	54 17 6	25 0 0	0 15 0	340 0 0	–	25 9 0	5 6 6	38 17 1	450 19 7	1,[illegible]	[illegible]	1,[illegible]	1	[illegible]	6	–	–

MONAGHAN,	1. Monaghan,	1	1	–	–	27 4 6	15 0 0	0 14 11	100 0 0	–	11 10 [illegible]	2 0 0	5 1 8	109 5 0	394	204	1,291	–	270	5	–	–
	2. Glaslough,	0	1	–	–	41 16 7	16 0 0	0 20 5	100 0 0	–	4 0 [illegible]	–	5 7 5	171 5 0	810	161	904	–	179	–	–	–
	3. Castleblayney,	2	1	–	–	10 12 3	8 0 0	0 11 11	100 0 0	–	11 11 0	–	11 12 3	116 11 5	681	114	343	1	217	–	–	–
	4. Scotstown,	1	1	–	–	25 7 8	15 10 0	0 10 11	100 9 0	–	13 17 0	2 0 0	12 12 5	102 19 2	641	[illegible]	346	5	204	1	–	–
	5. Kilmore,	2	1	–	–	37 16 10	10 0 0	0 13 10	100 0 0	–	6 10 0	–	5 0 8	157 11 6	367	93	462	1	139	–	–	–
		6	5	–	–	148 19 4	84 10 0	3 13 0	500 2 0	–	56 0 0	4 0 0	44 14 0	610 19 6	2,488	[illegible]	3,303	6	1,012	6	–	–
COUNTY OF TYRONE. CASTLEDERG	1. Castlederg and Killeter,	2	2	–	–	27 15 8	12 0 0	–	100 0 0	–	20 5 0	–	15 13 10	110 11 1	370	115	457	–	115	–	–	–
	2. Drumquin,	1	1	–	–	–	4 0 0	–	10 0 0	–	4 13 0	–	1 16 0	85 6 6	48	34	165	–	91	–	–	–
		3	3	–	–	27 15 3	16 0 0	–	200 0 0	–	24 18 0	–	18 8 10	197 8 1	408	157	567	–	494	–	–	–
CLOGHER,	1. Fivemiletown,	1	1	–	1	16 1 0	6 0 0	0 17 7	100 0 0	–	6 7 0	–	21 19 7	162 5 2	121	114	547	–	311	–	–	–
	2. Clogher,	2	1	–	1	17 2 9	5 0 0	1 19 0	110 0 0	–	11 1 0	–	19 0 8	167 3 6	450	228	671	2	221	1	11	7
	3. Ballygawley,	1	1	–	–	18 19 11	4 0 0	0 17 0	100 0 0	–	7 16 0	–	6 6 0	155 13 5	199	92	208	–	154	1	–	–
	4. Augher,	1	1	–	1	20 4 5	10 0 0	1 6 1	100 0 0	–	11 19 0	–	21 13 0	178 1 8	487	195	428	–	196	–	–	–
		5	4	–	3	81 8 1	28 0 0	5 0 11	410 0 0	–	39 20 0	–	68 12 7	624 3 7	1,250	630	1,950	2	405	4	14	7
COOKSTOWN	1. Cookstown,	1	1	–	–	36 12 1	9 15 0	0 11 0	165 0 0	–	13 17 0	1 16 0	5 6 8	164 16 1	470	254	880	1	328	4	–	–
	2. Pomeroy,	1	1	–	–	31 19 2	6 0 0	0 0 4	100 0 0	–	11 17 0	0 0 0	4 15 0	130 15 7	424	128	616	4	311	1	–	–
	3. Coagh,	1	1	–	–	12 8 11	2 0 0	0 5 1	75 0 0	–	7 8 0	0 16 0	1 0 0	180 7 3	491	242	480	2	162	–	–	–
	4. Stewartstown,	1	1	–	–	20 7 5	10 0 0	0 10 0	60 0 0	–	5 0 0	0 5 0	6 15 0	194 1 6	360	131	463	0	107	3	–	–
		4	4	–	–	100 2 7	32 3 0	1 15 6	390 0 0	–	39 14 0	3 4 0	16 1 8	776 3 1	1,739	[illegible]	2,613	9	912	8	–	–
DUNGANNON,	1. Dungannon,	1	1	–	1	30 14 3	4 0 0	0 11 11	136 10 0	–	21 13 0	–	16 5 0	240 3 8	450	439	977	–	450	2	5	5
	2. Benburb,	1	1	–	1	30 9 1	7 0 0	3 6 11	110 0 0	–	7 10 0	–	18 8 4	217 11 4	360	270	791	1	197	3	–	–
	3. Coal Island,	1	1	–	1	41 15 3	5 5 0	1 10 11	150 0 0	–	13 11 0	–	22 13 2	204 15 6	359	430	963	–	278	1	–	–
	4. Clonoe(?),	1	1	–	1	13 10 3	9 0 0	0 2 6	110 0 0	–	12 10 0	–	18 15 0	205 2 8	361	170	690	–	300	–	–	–
	5. Ballymagran(?),	1	1	–	–	16 6 2	2 0 0	0 2 4	50 0 0	–	1 4 0	–	2 1 3	75 16 1	90	35	130	–	70	–	–	–
		5	5	–	4	160 10 6	35 5 0	8 18 5	545 19 6	–	56 14 0	–	64 17 9	850 9 5	2,000	1,280	3,500	1	1,315	12	5	5
OMAGH(?),	1. Gortin,	1	1	–	31	19 13 4	10 0 0	1 19 1	100 0 0	–	18 10 0	2 0 0	1 10 11	124 10 9	277	112	520	1	167	4	–	–
	2. Plumb Bridge,	1	1	–	–	20 14 6	11 0 0	1 5 6	100 0 0	–	13 10 0	–	2 10 0	131 7 6	280	102	416	16	194	–	–	–
		2	2	–	1	40 7 10	21 0 0	3 4 6	200 0 0	–	32 0 0	2 0 0	3 0 11	255 18 3	557	214	936	17	361	4	–	–

* Carrickmacross Union.—Midwives.—One person acts for the three Districts.
† Castle-Blayney Union.—No appointment of Midwife appears to have been made in the Crossmaglen District.
‡ Gortin Union: Gortin District.—No appointment of Midwife appears yet to have been made.

[continued.

No. 2.—Dispensary Districts, with the Expenses, and Amount of Medical Relief afforded, in the several Unions—*continued.*

Name of Union	Name of Dispensary District	[illegible]	No. of Tickets cancelled by Guardians' Order: [illegible]	[illegible]	[illegible]	Medicines and Medical Appliances	Rent of Dispensary Buildings	Books, Forms, Stationery, and Printing	Salaries: Medical Officers	Salaries: Apothecaries	Vaccination Expenses: [illegible]	Vaccination Expenses: [illegible]	[illegible]	Total Expenditure for each Dispensary District for Year ended 29th Sept. 1871	Number of New Cases attended during the year: Dispensary Tickets	Visiting Tickets	Total	[illegible]	[illegible]	[illegible]	[illegible]	[illegible]
Column 1.	2.	3.	4.	5.	6.	7.	8.	9.	10.	11.	12.	13.	14.	15.	16.	17.	18.	19.	20.	21.	22.	23.
						£ s. d.	£ s. d.	£ s. d.	£ s. d.	£ s. d.	£ s. d.	£ s. d.	£ s. d.	£ s. d.								
PROVINCE OF ULSTER—continued.																						
County of Tyrone—con.																						
Omagh,	1. Omagh,	[illegible]	2	–	1	84 3 0	[illegible]	[illegible]	[illegible]	–	[illegible]	[illegible]	[illegible]	[illegible]	[illegible]	[illegible]	[illegible]	–	[illegible]	4	–	–
	2. Tattoid,	[illegible]	1	–	1	[illegible]	[illegible]	[illegible]	[illegible]	–	[illegible]	[illegible]	[illegible]	[illegible]	[illegible]	[illegible]	[illegible]	–	[illegible]	1	–	–
	3. Dromore,	[illegible]	[illegible]	–	–	[illegible]	[illegible]	[illegible]	[illegible]	–	[illegible]	[illegible]	[illegible]	[illegible]	[illegible]	[illegible]	[illegible]	–	[illegible]	[illegible]	–	–
	4. Drumquin,	[illegible]	1	–	–	[illegible]	[illegible]	[illegible]	[illegible]	–	[illegible]	[illegible]	[illegible]	[illegible]	[illegible]	[illegible]	[illegible]	–	[illegible]	–	–	–
	5. [illegible],	1	[illegible]	–	1	7 1 0	[illegible]	[illegible]	[illegible]	–	[illegible]	[illegible]	[illegible]	[illegible]	[illegible]	[illegible]	[illegible]	–	[illegible]	1	–	–
		[illegible]	[illegible]	–	3	[illegible]	[illegible]	[illegible]	[illegible]	–	[illegible]	[illegible]	[illegible]	[illegible]	[illegible]	[illegible]	[illegible]	–	[illegible]	[illegible]	–	–
Strabane,	1. [illegible],	[illegible]	[illegible]	–	[illegible]	[illegible]	[illegible]	[illegible]	[illegible]	–	[illegible]	[illegible]	[illegible]	[illegible]	[illegible]	[illegible]	[illegible]	–	[illegible]	1	–	–
	2. [illegible],	[illegible]	[illegible]	–	[illegible]	[illegible]	–	[illegible]	[illegible]	–	[illegible]	[illegible]	[illegible]	[illegible]	[illegible]	[illegible]	[illegible]	–	[illegible]	1	–	–
	3. Newtown Stewart,	[illegible]	[illegible]	–	[illegible]	[illegible]	[illegible]	[illegible]	[illegible]	–	[illegible]	[illegible]	[illegible]	[illegible]	[illegible]	[illegible]	[illegible]	–	[illegible]	–	–	–
	4. Castle Finn,	[illegible]	[illegible]	–	[illegible]	[illegible]	[illegible]	[illegible]	[illegible]	–	[illegible]	[illegible]	[illegible]	[illegible]	[illegible]	[illegible]	[illegible]	1	[illegible]	[illegible]	–	–
	5. Raphoe,	[illegible]	[illegible]	–	[illegible]	[illegible]	[illegible]	[illegible]	[illegible]	–	[illegible]	[illegible]	[illegible]	[illegible]	[illegible]	[illegible]	[illegible]	1	[illegible]	–	–	–
		[illegible]	[illegible]	–	[illegible]	[illegible]	[illegible]	[illegible]	[illegible]	–	[illegible]	[illegible]	[illegible]	[illegible]	[illegible]	[illegible]	[illegible]	[illegible]	[illegible]	[illegible]	–	–
PROVINCE OF MUNSTER																						
County of Clare.																						
Ballyvaghan,	1. Ballyvaghan,	[illegible]	1	–	–	[illegible]	[illegible]	[illegible]	[illegible]	–	[illegible]	–	[illegible]	[illegible]	[illegible]	[illegible]	[illegible]	–	[illegible]	–	–	–
		[illegible]	1	–	–	[illegible]	[illegible]	[illegible]	[illegible]	–	[illegible]	–	[illegible]	[illegible]	[illegible]	[illegible]	[illegible]	–	[illegible]	–	–	–
Corrofin,	1. Corrofin,	[illegible]	1	–	–	[illegible]	[illegible]	[illegible]	[illegible]	–	[illegible]	–	[illegible]	[illegible]	[illegible]	[illegible]	[illegible]	–	[illegible]	[illegible]	–	–
		[illegible]	1	–	–	[illegible]	[illegible]	[illegible]	[illegible]	–	[illegible]	–	[illegible]	[illegible]	[illegible]	[illegible]	[illegible]	–	[illegible]	[illegible]	–	–

Ennis,	1. Ennis,	2	2	-	1	34 6 7	6 0 0	0 16 4	120 0 0	-	13 0 0	0 10 6	80 16 6	235 14 11	1,970	611	2,5[illegible]	-	102	7	-	-
	2. Crusheen,	3	1	-	-	29 9 6	12 0 0	1 0 0	90 0 0	-	17 30 0	0 10 6	13 17 5	130 1 6	351	80	431	-	107	4	-	-
	3. Kilmaley,	1	1	-	-	9 1 0	5 0 0	0 9 6	101 0 0	-	0 180 0	0 10 6	3 0 0	179 2 0	277	74	349	-	1[illegible]	3	-	-
	4. Newmarket,	2	1	-	-	21 10 10	6 10 0	1 1 4	120 0 0	-	0 180 0	0 10 6	3 11 5	130 0 0	1,3[illegible]	107	1,4[illegible]	-	[illegible]	-	-	-
		8	5	-	1	111 10 7	32 10 0	5 15 0	404 0 0	-	20 170 0	2 2 0	110 7 0	653 5 10	3,0[illegible]	[illegible]	4,[illegible]	-	3[illegible]	15	-	-
Enniskillen,	1. Enniskillen(?),	2	1	-	-	84 12 6	15 0 0	1 7 0	120 0 0	-	0 180 0	1 0 0	9 4 6	160 16 0	[illegible]	113	[illegible]	-	20[illegible]	1	-	-
	2. Enniskillen(?),	2	1	-	-	41 1 6	11 10 0	1 17	6 180 0 0	-	9 70 0	0 10 6	10 1 7	100 8 4	[illegible]	3[illegible]	1,0[illegible]	1	1[illegible]	-	-	-
	3. [illegible],	2	1	-	-	10 9 1	13 0 0	1 10	4 105 14 0	-	16 80 0	0 10 6	26 5 6	214 7 10	[illegible]	[illegible]	[illegible]	1	1[illegible]	3	-	-
		6	3	-	-	150 2 2	40 10 0	5 10	0 209 14 0	-	31 80 0	3 1 6	55 11 1	464 18 0	1,7[illegible]	7[illegible]	2,67[illegible]	2	[illegible]	6	-	-
Killadysert,	1. Labasheeda,	1	1	-	-	17 9 4	6 0 0	0 16	3 100 0 0	-	-	1 0 0	8 0 0	137 7 7	3[illegible]	164	40[illegible]	-	66	-	-	-
	2. Ballynacally,	2	1	-	-	-	4 10 0	0 15	8 100 0 0	-	-	-	6 10 0	113 13 0	[illegible]	1[illegible]	791	-	21[illegible]	-	-	-
		3	2	-	-	17 9 1	10 10 0	1 11	11 200 0 0	-	-	1 0 0	20 19 0	2[illegible] 1 3	1,0[illegible]	[illegible]	1,3[illegible]	-	[illegible]	-	-	-
Kilrush,	1. Kilrush,	1	1	-	[1]‡	38 8 1	-	3 0	9 97 1 9	-	15 80 0	1 1 0	16 10 7	180 14 0	1,9[illegible]	[illegible]	2,[illegible]	-	10[illegible]	8	8	8
	2. Kilmihil,	2	1	-	-	14 6 2	5 0 0	1 5	0 100 0 0	-	10 60 0	1 1 0	12 2 0	140 1 5	3[illegible]	[illegible]	4[illegible]	-	16[illegible]	-	-	-
	3. Cooraclare(?),	2	1	-	-	24 15 3	11 0 0	1 5	0 100 0 0	-	23 60 0	1 1 0	9 17 5	191 4 [illegible]	[illegible]	[illegible]	[illegible]	1	231	1	-	-
	4. Kilkee,	1	1	-	-	4 18 0	10 0 0	1 5	6 100 0 0	-	7 140 0	1 1 0	11 0 0	135 19 11	[illegible]	1[illegible]	[illegible]	-	1[illegible]	1	-	-
	5. Carrigaholt,	1	1	-	-	15 2 4	10 0 0	1 4	6 100 0 0	-	5 40 0	1 1 0	10 1 1	144 0 11	5[illegible]	3[illegible]	[illegible]	-	11[illegible]	-	-	-
		7	5	-	1	123 10 3	37 0 0	6 0	3 497 1 9	-	61 380 0	6 5 0	40 6 7	792 8 10	4,331	1,5[illegible]	5,5[illegible]	1	[illegible]	4	3	3
Scariff,	1. Mountshannon,	2	1	-	-	30 4 3	8 10 0	0 8	10 90 10 5	-	11 119 0	1 10 0	3 10 0	135 2 0	[illegible]	11[illegible]	[illegible]	-	15[illegible]	-	-	-
	2. Feakle,	3	1	-	-	40 12 8	10 17 6	0 8	10 90 0 0	-	9 80 0	1 0 0	6 12 0	143 0 11	[illegible]	[illegible]	[illegible]	-	[illegible]	2	-	-
	3. Annamerriga,	2	1	-	-	17 14 6	12 0 0	0 8	10 90 17 6	-	5 70 0	1 0 0	1 5 6	104 14 9	[illegible]	1[illegible]	[illegible]	-	2[illegible]	1	2	2
		7	3	-	-	88 11 5	34 6 4	1 0	6 270 7 6	-	2[illegible] 49 0	3 10 0	11 8 6	402 2 4	[illegible]	3[illegible]	1,2[illegible]	-	611	3	2	2
Tulla,	1. Tulla,	2	1	-	-	26 13 0	9 0 0	-	105 0 0	-	19 113 0	0 12 6	5 17 10	156 16 0	3[illegible]	10[illegible]	61[illegible]	-	19[illegible]	-	6	3
	2. Quin,	2	1	-	-	28 3 10	9 0 0	-	100 12 10	-	10 100 0	2 5 6	9 11 6	170 10 4	[illegible]	[illegible]	[illegible]	-	1[illegible]	-	-	-
	3. Killaloe,	2	1	-	[1]§	30 3 6	5 10 0	-	100 0 0	-	6 100 0	0 15 6	10 10 4	154 10 4	[illegible]	[illegible]	[illegible]	-	[illegible]	-	-	-
		6	3	-	1	85 9 9	23 10 0	-	305 12 10	-	35 0 0	3 11 6	26 1 10	479 19 8	[illegible]	[illegible]	1,[illegible]	-	43[illegible]	-	6	3
COUNTY OF CORK. Bandon,	1. Bandon,	1	1	1	-	24 10 10	1 1 0	1 0	9 100 0 0	10 11 6	12 30 0	0 10 6	23 15 4	194 12 1	1,2[illegible]	[illegible]	1,5[illegible]	-	[illegible]	1	-	-
	2. Inishannon,	1	1	-	-	28 9 4	4 0 0	0 10	0 65 0 0	-	3 60 0	0 10 6	5 10 0	143 11 0	3[illegible]	1[illegible]	[illegible]	-	7[illegible]	2	-	-
	3. Templemartin,	1	1	-	-	31 3 3	5 0 0	-	95 0 0	-	7 170 0	0 10 6	1 6 0	130 11 3	3[illegible]	16[illegible]	[illegible]	-	1[illegible]	6	-	-
	4. Murragh,	1	1	-	-	13 18 8	4 0 0	-	92 0 0	-	5 140 0	4 10 6	0 10 0	198 3 11	[illegible]	[illegible]	[illegible]	-	1[illegible]	-	-	-
	5. Kilbrittain,	2	1	-	-	23 10 10	10 10 0	-	90 0 0	-	[illegible] 130 0	0 10 6	3 7 4	188 11 0	[illegible]	[illegible]	1[illegible]	-	77	-	-	-
		6	5	1	-	121 13 1	25 11 0	1 10	9 440 0 0	10 11 6	32 170 0	6 10 6	34 17 11	715 0 7	7,5[illegible]	1,1[illegible]	3,[illegible]	-	5[illegible]	6	-	-

* Omagh Union: [illegible] District.—No appointment of Midwife appears yet to have been made.

† Strabane Union: Strabane District.—Only one Midwife appears to have been appointed for the Strabane District.

‡ Kilrush Union: Kilrush District.—No appointment of a Midwife appears to have been made.

§ Tulla Union: Killaloe District.—No appointment of a Midwife appears to have been made.

[continued.

No. 2.—Dispensary Districts, with the Expenses, and Amount of Medical Relief afforded, in the several Unions—*continued.*

Name of Union.	Name of Dispensary District.	No. of Dispensary Stations	No. of Officers: Med. Officers	Apothecaries	Midwives	Medicines and Medical Appliances	Rent of Dispensary Buildings	Books, Forms, Stationery, and Printing	Salaries: Medical Officers	Salaries: Apothecaries	Vaccination Expenses: Amount of Fees paid to Medical Officers	Vaccination Expenses: Other Payments	Fuel and Attendance, and other Expenses	Total Expenditure for each Dispensary District for Year ended 29th Sept., 1872	New Cases: Dispensary Tickets	New Cases: Visiting Tickets	New Cases: Total	19.	20.	21.	22.	23.
Column 1.	2.	3.	4.	5.	6.	7.	8.	9.	10.	11.	12.	13.	14.	15.	16.	17.	18.	19.	20.	21.	22.	23.
						£ s. d.	£ s. d.	£ s. d.	£ s. d.	£ s. d.	£ s. d.	£ s. d.	£ s. d.	£ s. d.								
PROVINCE OF MUNSTER—*continued.*																						
County of Cork—*con.*																						
Bantry,	1. Bantry,	1	1	–	–	36 17 4	–	0 11 7	100 0 0	–	10 10 0	–	65 5 9	182 10 6	486	275	761	2	221	3	11	6
	2. Glengarriff,	1	1	–	–	16 8 [illegible]	5 0 0	0 3 8	100 0 0	–	9 6 0	–	0 15 2	139 11 6	115	104	220	–	175	–	–	–
	3. Durrus and Kilcrohane,	1	1	–	–	16 3 8	4 0 0	0 2 7	100 0 0	–	7 19 0	0 12 0	6 10 0	135 6 10	240	171	411	–	300	1	–	–
		3	3	–	–	69 5 8	9 0 0	0 16 2	300 0 0	–	27 15 0	0 12 0	30 10 11	462 9 0	1,043	550	1,715	2	702	4	11	6
Castletown,	1. Castletown,	2	1	–	–	39 13 5	18 0 0	1 3 9	100 0 0	–	20 0 0	–	6 11 2	173 [illegible] 4	1,099	256	1,355	–	404	–	–	–
	2. Kilcatherine,	2	1	–	–	15 13 0	4 11 6	1 3 9	110 0 0	–	16 16 0	–	4 19 6	180 3 0	1,162	201	1,363	–	300	–	–	–
		4	2	–	–	55 6 5	18 11 6	2 7 6	200 0 0	–	36 16 0	–	11 10 8	357 12 1	2,261	457	2,718	–	704	–	–	–
Clonakilty,	1. Rosscarbery,	1	1	–	–	35 6 10	5 0 0	–	85 0 0	–	16 11 0	0 10 1	4 1 7	157 0 0	649	280	929	–	311	–	–	–
	2. Clonakilty,	1	1	–	–	30 10 2	2 14 0	–	85 0 0	–	14 15 0	0 10 9	12 16 0	136 4 0	1,037	270	1,307	9	289	1	–	–
	3. Timoleague,	1	1	–	–	21 11 5	3 0 0	–	100 15 0	–	11 11 0	0 16 2	8 18 0	160 10 7	349	321	670	–	170	–	–	–
		3	3	–	–	87 8 5	10 14 0	–	270 15 0	–	42 17 0	2 16 0	30 11 1	453 15 0	1,835	971	2,806	9	651	1	–	–
Cork,	1. Dripsey,	1	1	–	–	37 11 2	4 0 0	0 18 10	120 0 0	–	11 3 0	–	5 16 0	176 0 0	1,361	379	1,720	1	115	1	–	–
	2. Blarney,	2	1	–	–	35 17 4	20 0 0	0 18 10	110 0 0	–	5 17 0	–	16 7 1	209 0 2	630	107	737	–	102	1	–	–
	3. Carrignavar,	1	1	–	–	40 9 2	20 0 0	1 15 8	148 0 0	–	18 18 0	–	14 19 0	250 0 10	672	244	916	–	180	–	–	–
	4. Whitechurch,	2	1	–	–	41 16 4	15 0 0	0 15 10	110 0 0	–	4 9 0	–	25 16 0	173 3 11	231	184	415	–	95	1	–	–
	5. Cork,	1	2	2	–	515 0 9	91 0 0	35 0 1	987 19 1	180 0 0	67 10 0	0 0 0	113 0 0	2047 19 11	24,782	3,077	28,[illegible]	–	1,6[illegible]	15	8	8
	6. Carrigaline,	2	1	–	1	60 0 1	13 18 0	1 13 10	150 0 0	–	6 11 0	–	25 2 6	250 19 0	854	298	1,152	–	167	2	–	–
	7. Douglas,	1	1	–	–	30 15 1	3 0 0	0 15 10	140 0 0	–	1 17 0	–	10 7 4	186 15 0	337	241	578	1	88	–	–	–
	8. Ballygarvan,	1	1	–	–	3 13 2	7 0 0	0 14 10	100 0 0	–	8 3 0	–	14 17 0	157 19 6	102	104	206	–	61	–	–	–
	9. Ballincollig,	1	1	–	–	86 16 11	5 0 0	1 18 10	120 0 0	–	8 0 0	–	7 7 1	165 10 10	266	197	463	–	180	–	–	–
	10. Queenstown,	1	1	1	–	46 10 11	10 0 0	7 11 8	149 10 0	75 0 0	13 6 0	–	83 5 1	341 11 9	2,110	803	2,913	8	201	7	8	4
		19	19	3	1	[illegible] 5 8	210 18 0	60 11 7	2073 11 7	255 0 0	164 10 0	0 0 0	361 10 2	3565 17 1	31,0[illegible]	4,3[illegible]	35,[illegible]	4	3,041	25	10	7

Expenses of Year ended 29th September, 1872. Medical Relief afforded in Year ended 29th September, 1871.

Union	Dispensary District					£ s. d.	£ s. d.	£ s. d.	£ s. d.	£ s. d.	£ s. d.	£ s. d.	£ s. d.	£ s. d.								
Dunmanway,	1. Dunmanway,	1	1	–	–	8 3 11	7 0 0	–	97 18 0	–	6 10 0	–	14 11 5	131 2 1	421	[illegible]	404	2	17[illegible]	–	[illegible]	3
	2. Coolmountain,	2	1	–	–	3[illegible] 8 0	3 0 0	–	100 0 0	–	10 0 0	–	8 15 9	103 17 9	363	13[illegible]	400	4	7[illegible]	–	–	–
	3. Ballineen,	1	1	–	–	62 16 11	5 0 0	–	97 3 4	–	10 6 0	2 0 0	8 2 8	153 2 2	343	1[illegible]	3[illegible]	–	[illegible]	2	–	–
		4	3	–	–	88 17 10	14 0 0	–	295 16 1	–	29 18 0	2 0 0	32 0 9	4[illegible] 2 1	1,[illegible]	[illegible]	1,[illegible]	6	[illegible]	2	8	3
Fermoy,	1. Fermoy,	2	1	–	–	64 7 6	11 0 0	0 10 4	100 0 0	–	18 7[illegible]	0 6 0	8 5 8	211 17 6	1,077	631	1,3[illegible]	8	[illegible]	6	8	4
	2. Rathcormack,	2	1	–	–	[illegible] 15 3	8 10 0	0 7 6	114 15 0	–	5 14 0	–	0 12 0	1[illegible] 4 1	6[illegible]	[illegible]	[illegible]	–	[illegible]	–	–	–
	3. Ballyhooly,	2	1	–	–	19 16 7	10 18 0	1 5 4	1[illegible] 0 0	–	19 11 0	–	2 3 8	[illegible] 9 3	[illegible]	14[illegible]	[illegible]	–	[illegible]	–	–	–
	4. Kilworth,	3	1	–	–	36 2 6	10 4 0	0 7 3[illegible]	100 0 0	–	11 3[illegible]	–	7 7 6	139 5 1	[illegible]	10[illegible]	[illegible]	2	[illegible]	2	–	–
	5. Ballynoe,	2	1	–	–	35 11 8	7 15 0	0 7 4	100 0 0	–	7 16 0	–	10 2 2	161 14 6	[illegible]	156	[illegible]	1	[illegible]	–	–	–
		10	5	–	–	221 11 10	56 9 0	1 12 7	[illegible] 19 0	–	60 16 0	0 6 6	38 1 1	887 13 9	3,3[illegible]	1,[illegible]	4,[illegible]	5	[illegible]	8	8	4
Kanturk,	1. Newmarket,*	2	1	–	0 1	35 6 8	16 0 0	0 11 10	100 0 0	–	19 11 0	–	6 5 8	179 11 11	736	[illegible]	[illegible]	–	[illegible]	1	–	–
	2. Kanturk,	2	1	1	1	66 1 1	6 10 0	3 0 6	100 0 0	85 0 0	6 13 0	1 16 0	21 10 9	[illegible] 18 5	1,[illegible]	[illegible]	1,[illegible]	–	[illegible]	1	–	–
	3. Millford,	2	1	–	1	90 11 3	12 0 0	2 11 10	100 0 0	–	19 11 0	–	27 17 4	[illegible] 11 1	7[illegible]	10[illegible]	[illegible]	–	[illegible]	–	–	–
	4. Boherboy,	3	1	–	–	25 13 11	14 0 0	2 11 10	100 0 0	–	20 10 0	–	3 18 9	1[illegible] 11 5	3[illegible]	1[illegible]	478	–	[illegible]	–	–	–
		9	4	1	3	217 11 3	50 10 0	11 3 10	400 0 0	85 0 0	76 17 0	1 16 0	59 1 8	841 18 11	3,4[illegible]	[illegible]	4,[illegible]	–	1,7[illegible]	2	–	–
Kinsale,	1. Courceys,	1	1	–	–	10 13 9	5 0 0	1 10 10	[illegible] 10 0	–	1 14 0	–	6 10 6	1[illegible] 16 3	7[illegible]	[illegible]	16[illegible]	–	[illegible]	1	–	–
	2. Kinsale,	1	1	–	–	11 8 0	–	3 6 8	[illegible] 10 0	–	14 1 0	–	7 11 9	1[illegible] 15 3	[illegible]	[illegible]	[illegible]	–	[illegible]	3	4	1
	3. Ballymartle,	1	1	–	–	15 4 1	4 0 0	1 10 0	[illegible] 10 0	–	3 0 0	–	4 16 1	117 0 0	671	[illegible]	[illegible]	–	71	–	–	–
	4. Carrigaline,	1	1	–	–	0 17 1	4 0 0	0 15 0	[illegible] 10 0	–	–	–	4 5 3	1[illegible] 0 1	1[illegible]	11[illegible]	[illegible]	–	11[illegible]	–	–	–
	5. Ballyfeard,	1	1	–	–	6 15 9	6 0 0	0 10 11	[illegible] 10 0	–	6 16 0	–	0 10 11	1[illegible] 1 6	[illegible]	[illegible]	[illegible]	–	[illegible]	–	–	–
		5	5	–	–	57 13 11	22 0 0	0 0 0	412 10 0	–	30 13 0	–	34 3 6	5[illegible] 9 9	1,5[illegible]	[illegible]	2,[illegible]	–	[illegible]	1	4	1
Macroom,	1. Macroom,	1	1	–	–	21 6 1	10 0 0	1 3 4	100 0 0	–	17 6 0	–	10 6 2	1[illegible] 18 7	[illegible]	3[illegible]	1,[illegible]	–	[illegible]	–	–	–
	2. Clondrohid,	1	1	–	–	19 8 4	4 0 0	1 3 4	100 0 0	–	9 16 0	–	6 1 4	1[illegible] 12 10	[illegible]	16[illegible]	1,[illegible]	–	[illegible]	–	–	–
	3. Kilnamartery,	2	1	–	–	30 6 7	4 0 0	2 3 1	100 0 0	–	28 3[illegible]	–	6 16 0	1[illegible] 1 11	[illegible]	[illegible]	[illegible]	–	[illegible]	–	–	–
	4. Inchigeelagh,	1	1	–	–	11 19 10	4 10 0	2 3 4	100 0 0	–	4 15 0	–	1 0 0	1[illegible] 18 2	[illegible]	[illegible]	[illegible]	1	[illegible]	–	–	–
	5. Coachford,	1	1	–	–	22 6 1	5 0 0	2 3 4	100 0 0	–	8 15 0	–	1 0 0	1[illegible] 4 5	[illegible]	[illegible]	[illegible]	–	1[illegible]	–	–	–
		6	5	–	–	1[illegible] 19 1	[illegible] 15 0	10 14 [illegible]	[illegible] 0 0	–	55 18 0	–	30 0 8	[illegible] 13 11	3,[illegible]	[illegible]	4,[illegible]	1	1,[illegible]	–	–	–
Mallow,	1. Kilshannig,	2	1	–	–	78 10 11	8 5 0	0 15 10	100 0 0	–	[illegible] 15 0	–	0 13 0	191 0 3	8[illegible]	[illegible]	2,0[illegible]	–	[illegible]	1	–	–
	2. Mallow,	1	1	–	–	61 6 6	12 0 0	0 11 4	100 0 0	–	12 3[illegible]	–	11 6 1	1[illegible] 10 6	1,[illegible]	[illegible]	2,0[illegible]	–	[illegible]	1	43	[illegible]
	3. Kilbolane,	1	1	–	–	27 7 2	5 0 0	0 11 4	100 0 0	–	5 14 0	2 0 0	1 19 4	1[illegible] 19 6	[illegible]	[illegible]	[illegible]	–	11[illegible]	–	–	–
	4. Buttevant,	1	2	–	1†	36 18 3	12 16 10	5 4 3	100 0 0	–	3 5 3	–	21 12 0	[illegible] 17 6	1,3[illegible]	[illegible]	1,01[illegible]	2	17[illegible]	–	–	–
	5. Ballyclough,	2	1	–	–	65 1 1	8 10 0	1 3 6	100 0 0	–	1 17 0	–	10 11 9	1[illegible] 18 3	7[illegible]	[illegible]	[illegible]	1	13[illegible]	1	–	–
	6. Doneraile,	1	1	1	–	21 4 7	8 10 0	0 11 4	100 0 0	70 2 4	2 11 0	–	3 16 8	1[illegible] 4 11	[illegible]	[illegible]	1,2[illegible]	–	1[illegible]	–	–	–
		13	7	1	1	2[illegible] 1 6	57 1 10	2 6 5	600 0 0	70 2 4	71 16 3	2 0 0	52 1 5	1,1[illegible] 0 11	6,[illegible]	1,[illegible]	7,6[illegible]	10	1,[illegible]	3	43	[illegible]

* Kanturk Union; Newmarket District.—No appointment of Midwife appears to have been made for this District.
† Mallow Union; Buttevant District.—Office of Midwife vacant.

[continued.

No. 3.—Dispensary Districts, with the Expenses, and Amount of Medical Relief afforded, in the several Unions—continued.

Name of Union.	Name of Dispensary District.	[illegible]	No. of Officers: Med. Officers.	Apothecaries.	Midwives.	Medicines and Medical Appliances.	Rent of Dispensary Buildings.	Books, Forms, Stationery, and Printing.	Salaries: Medical Officers.	Salaries: Apothecaries.	Vaccination Expenses	Vaccination Expenses	[illegible]	Total Expenditure for Year ended 29th Sept., 1871.	Number of New Cases attended and registered during the year: Dispensary Tickets.	Visiting Tickets.	Total.	[illegible]	[illegible]	[illegible]	[illegible]	[illegible]
Column 1.	2.	3.	4.	5.	6.	7.	8.	9.	10.	11.	12.	13.	14.	15.	16.	17.	18.	19.	20.	21.	22.	23.
						£ s. d.	£ s. d.	£ s. d.	£ s. d.	£ s. d.	£ s. d.	£ s. d.	£ s. d.	£ s. d.								
PROVINCE OF MUNSTER—continued.																						
County of Cork—con.																						
Midleton,	1. Midleton,	2	1		-	70 0 0	8 0 0	0 8 5	180 0 0	-	30 0 0	1 4 0	10 16 3	300 6 10	1,306	650	1,956	-	570	1	17	1
	2. Walshtown-more, East,	1	1	-	-	19 9 7	1 10 0	0 8 6	100 0 0	-	3 10 0	1 0 0	16 12 6	144 10 1	[illegible]	164	[illegible]	-	[illegible]	-	-	-
	3. Castlemartyr,	1	1	-	-	25 0 4	7 0 0	0 3 6	100 0 0	-	5 16 0	0 10 0	9 8 0	188 11 10	[illegible]	[illegible]	[illegible]	-	144	-	-	-
	4. Aghada,	1	1	-	-	27 16 5	7 0 0	0 5 0	125 0 0	-	12 2 0	0 10 0	6 10 0	195 5 5	401	243	[illegible]	1	270	1	-	-
	5. Cloyne,	1	1	-	-	43 0 9	8 0 0	1 15 0	150 0 0	-	11 10 0	0 15 0	13 8 4	243 15 3	[illegible]	227	[illegible]	-	[illegible]	-	-	-
		6	6	-	-	190 8 1	34 10 0	2 7 7	620 0 0	-	[illegible]	3 16 0	[illegible]	[illegible] 6 4	[illegible]	[illegible]	[illegible]	1	[illegible]	3	17	4
Mallow,	1. Cullen,	1	1	-	-	10 3 9	5 16 0	1 18 6	80 0 0	-	[illegible]	1 13 6	8 10 0	116 16 9	[illegible]	[illegible]	[illegible]	-	[illegible]	-	-	-
	2. Millstreet,	1	1	-	-	29 1 7	10 0 0	1 13 4	100 0 0	-	[illegible]	[illegible]	7 16 0	204 16 5	1,410	[illegible]	[illegible]	-	[illegible]	-	-	-
		2	2	-	-	[illegible]	15 16 0	3 6 10	180 0 0	-	[illegible]	[illegible]	16 6 0	[illegible]	[illegible]	[illegible]	[illegible]	-	[illegible]	-	-	-
Mitchelstown,	1. Mitchelstown,	2	1	-	1	[illegible]	10 0 0	[illegible]	[illegible]	-	9 18 0	-	16 5 5	290 3 7	[illegible]	[illegible]	[illegible]	-	[illegible]	1	3	1
	2. Kildorrery,	2	1	-	-	5 5 3	10 0 0	[illegible]	[illegible]	-	-	-	17 18 9	[illegible]	[illegible]	177	[illegible]	-	[illegible]	-	-	-
	3. Galbally,	2	1	-	-	[illegible]	15 0 0	1 7 6	100 0 0	-		[illegible]	11 3 6	152 19 9	[illegible]	211	[illegible]	-	141	-	-	-
		6	3	-	1	[illegible]	35 0 0	[illegible]	[illegible]	-	9 18 0	[illegible]	45 7 8	[illegible]	[illegible]	[illegible]	[illegible]	-	[illegible]	1	3	1
Skibbereen,	1. Skibbereen,	1	1	1	-	39 10 1	8 0 0	[illegible]	150 0 0	30 0 0	[illegible]	0 10 6	[illegible]	[illegible]	[illegible]	[illegible]	[illegible]	-	[illegible]	5	4	3
	2. Union Hall,	1	1	-	-	23 17 10	8 0 0	1 16 1	100 0 0	-	13 10 0	0 10 6	32 7 6	[illegible]	[illegible]	[illegible]	[illegible]	-	271	1	-	-
	3. Drimoleague,	1	1	-	-	[illegible]	5 0 0	[illegible]	100 0 0	-	19 10 0	0 1 6	5 11 0	173 11 0	[illegible]	[illegible]	[illegible]	-	[illegible]	-	-	-
	4. Tullagh,	[illegible]	1	-	-	28 7 10	9 0 0	1 1 1	[illegible]	-	24 0 0	0 19 6	5 5 10	182 16 3	[illegible]	[illegible]	[illegible]	2	[illegible]	-	-	-
		[illegible]	4	1	-	[illegible]	31 0 0	[illegible]	[illegible]	30 0 0	[illegible]	[illegible]	[illegible]	[illegible]	[illegible]	[illegible]	[illegible]	2	[illegible]	6	[illegible]	3

SKULL,	1. Schull,	1	1	-	-	14 17 3	6 0 0	0 12 6	120 0 0	-	16 10 0	-	4 5 8	121 12 0	1,010	150	1,171	-	956	7	-	-
	2. Goleen,	1	1	-	-	5 11 5	6 0 0	0 19 [illegible]	100 0 0	-	4 10 0	-	3 14 4	105 14 1	[illegible]	[illegible]	[illegible]	-	[illegible]	-	-	-
		2	2	-	-	20 8 8	12 0 0	1 11 8	220 0 0	-	21 0 0	-	8 19 9	227 6 1	[illegible]	[illegible]	[illegible]	-	[illegible]	1	-	-
YOUGHAL,	1. Youghal,	1	1	-	-	31 4 11	30 0 0	1 0 5	120 0 0	-	7 10 0	6 15 0	15 10 3	185 15 6	1,060	[illegible]	[illegible]	-	16[illegible]	1	-	-
	2. Killeagh,	1	1	-	-	[illegible] 0 6	7 0 0	0 12 7	100 0 0	-	6 0 0	-	0 9 3	165 17 1	[illegible]	[illegible]	[illegible]	-	[illegible]	-	-	-
	3. Templemichael,	1	1	-	-	0 9 6	5 0 0	0 12 7	100 0 0	-	5 10 0	-	0 12 5	100 10 4	[illegible]	[illegible]	[illegible]	-	[illegible]	-	-	-
	4. Ardmore,	1	1	-	-	30 1 1	6 0 0	0 13 2	116 16 0	-	9 12 0	-	5 16 4	160 19 7	[illegible]	[illegible]	[illegible]	1	[illegible]	-	-	-
	5. Clashmore,	1	1	-	-	20 6 5	5 0 0	1 6 6	120 0 0	-	4 10 0	0 16 0	5 15 0	130 11 7	276	101	367	-	11[illegible]	-	-	-
		5	5	-	-	125 11 5	53 0 0	4 14 11	546 16 0	-	47 10 0	1 11 0	44 12 11	773 6 10	2,677	[illegible]	3,[illegible]	1	[illegible]	1	-	-
COUNTY OF KERRY. CAHERSIVEEN,	1. Cahir,	1	1	-	-	80 19 6	6 0 0	1 8 3	80 0 0	-	-	1 1 0	-	188 16 10	276	[illegible]	[illegible]	-	[illegible]	[illegible]	-	-
	2. Glenbehy,	2	1	-	-	-	6 17 6	2 1 10	80 0 0	-	-	1 1 0	4 0 0	150 0 0	452	[illegible]	[illegible]	-	[illegible]	-	-	-
	3. Valentia,	2	1	-	-	11 3 3	11 10 0	5 10 6	120 13 11	-	7 15 0	1 1 0	11 5 10	227 11 6	[illegible]	[illegible]	[illegible]	-	[illegible]	[illegible]	-	-
	4. Emlagh,	2	1	-	-	59 14 8	7 0 0	6 7 10	80 0 0	-	7 10 0	1 1 0	5 19 5	171 4 8	[illegible]	[illegible]	[illegible]	9	[illegible]	-	-	-
	5. Derrynane,	2	1	-	-	16 17 11	10 0 0	1 11 7	105 16 0	-	5 0 0	1 1 0	4 0 0	143 0 6	[illegible]	[illegible]	[illegible]	-	[illegible]	-	-	-
		9	5	-	-	160 7 9	40 7 11	17 18 0	466 5 11	-	19 5 0	5 5 0	[illegible] 5 6	797 8 4	1,5[illegible]	[illegible]	1,[illegible]	9	1,[illegible]	4	-	-
DINGLE,	1. Dingle,	1	1	1	†1	31 11 8	-	1 16 3	100 0 0	10 15 3	11 10 0	0 10 6	53 10 9	[illegible] 7 11	1,813	[illegible]	1,[illegible]	1	[illegible]	1	-	-
	2. Castlegregory,	2	1	-	-	40 17 11	11 0 0	0 5 3	120 0 0	-	9 11 0	-	-	173 17 8	[illegible]	[illegible]	1,1[illegible]	4	[illegible]	-	-	-
	3. Annascaul,	1	1	-	-	17 0 5	7 0 0	0 5 3	100 0 0	-	7 10 0	1 6 0	6 10 6	140 10 1	[illegible]	151	[illegible]	-	[illegible]	-	-	-
	4. Ventry,	2	1	-	†1	0 16 10	15 0 0	2 15 0	120 0 0	-	11 0 0	1 10 0	11 2 6	165 5 6	[illegible]	[illegible]	[illegible]	-	[illegible]	-	-	-
		6	4	1	2	110 6 4	33 0 0	5 6 11	440 0 0	10 15 3	42 10 0	3 6 6	101 17 6	780 8 6	3,43[illegible]	[illegible]	4,1[illegible]	5	[illegible]	1	-	-
KENMARE,	1. Kenmare,	1	1	-	-	36 13 6	10 0 0	0 7 8	100 0 0	-	7 10 0	-	10 10 6	175 0 7	1,271	[illegible]	1,[illegible]	-	[illegible]	2	11	2
	2. Kilgarvan,	1	1	-	-	22 7 6	4 0 0	0 10 0	100 0 0	-	7 10 0	-	6 2 11	146 19 7	[illegible]	[illegible]	1,[illegible]	-	[illegible]	-	-	-
	3. Tuosist,	2	1	-	-	0 5 3	7 10 0	0 5 6	100 0 0	-	0 30 0	-	7 11 0	104 14 3	[illegible]	[illegible]	[illegible]	1	[illegible]	2	-	-
	4. Sneem,	1	1	-	-	10 10 11	6 0 0	0 5 0	100 0 0	-	7 10 0	-	0 10 10	126 17 8	[illegible]	[illegible]	[illegible]	-	[illegible]	2	-	-
		5	4	-	-	70 6 7	27 10 0	1 17 7	400 0 0	-	29 0 0	-	30 3 5	573 13 8	2,09[illegible]	[illegible]	3,1[illegible]	1	1,[illegible]	6	11	2
KILLARNEY,	1. Killarney,	1	2	-	-	75 0 9	-	0 15 0	220 0 0	-	35 10 0	0 10 6	61 4 0	398 5 3	1,405	501	[illegible]	-	[illegible]	3	1	2
	2. Molahiffe,	2	1	-	-	7 7 10	7 0 0	0 7 6	100 0 0	-	13 10 0	0 10 6	117 11 6	248 0 7	[illegible]	[illegible]	[illegible]	-	[illegible]	-	-	-
	3. Milltown,	1	1	-	-	30 3 5	8 0 0	0 7 0	110 0 0	-	20 10 0	0 10 6	0 3 6	197 17 11	1,704	[illegible]	2,1[illegible]	-	[illegible]	-	-	-
	4. Killorglin,	1	1	-	‡1	34 16 5	11 0 0	0 15 0	170 0 0	-	16 0 0	0 10 6	9 8 4	259 10 5	2,1[illegible]	[illegible]	[illegible]	2	[illegible]	1	-	-
	5. Coom,	2	1	-	-	11 10 6	3 0 0	0 7 0	100 0 0	-	20 10 0	0 10 6	10 7 8	167 0 2	[illegible]	[illegible]	[illegible]	-	[illegible]	-	-	-
		7	6	-	1	160 18 11	29 0 0	2 12 6	640 0 0	-	100 10 0	2 12 6	1[illegible] 8 2	1,112 0 6	6,3[illegible]	1,[illegible]	[illegible]	2	1,[illegible]	7	1	2
LISTOWEL,	1. Ballylongford,	1	1	-	-	19 1 11	7 0 0	1 1 0	100 0 0	-	17 10 0	-	3 5 0	140 0 5	[illegible]	211	[illegible]	-	[illegible]	-	-	-
	2. Listowel,	2	1	1	-	40 12 0	3 10 0	1 11 4	100 0 0	10 0 0	31 10 0	-	3 3 10	201 16 8	[illegible]	561	1,[illegible]	-	[illegible]	3	2	6
	3. Ballyduff,	1	1	-	-	50 0 0	0 0 0	1 0 0	100 0 0	-	30 17 0	0 10 0	-	180 5 0	[illegible]	386	1,1[illegible]	3	[illegible]	-	-	-
	4. Ballybunion,	2	1	-	-	15 12 11	10 0 0	1 11 2	100 0 0	-	-	-	0 7 0	159 7 1	[illegible]	355	[illegible]	-	[illegible]	1	-	-
		6	4	1	-	125 19 0	24 10 0	7 13 4	400 0 0	10 0 0	79 17 0	0 10 0	6 10 10	729 15 2	2,0[illegible]	1,461	[illegible]	3	1,1[illegible]	4	2	6

* Mitchelstown Union: Mitchelstown District.—Office of Midwife vacant.
† Dingle Union: Dingle and Ventry Districts.—A Midwife authorised for each district; but one person acts for both Districts.
‡ Killarney Union: Killorglin District.—No appointment of Midwife appears to have been made.

(continued.

No. 2.—Dispensary Districts, with the Expenses, and Amount of Medical Relief afforded, in the several Unions—*continued*.

Name of Union.	Name of Dispensary District.	No. of Dispensary Stations in each District	No. of Officers authorised by Sealed Order: Med. Officers	Apothecaries	Midwives	Expenses of Year ended 29th September, 1871: Medicines and Medical Appliances	Rent of Dispensary Buildings	Books, Forms, Stationery, and Printing	Salaries: Medical Officers	Apothecaries	Vaccination Expenses: Amount of Fees paid to Medical Officers	Other Expenses	Fuel and all other Expenses	Total Expenditure for each Dispensary District for Year ended 29th Sept., 1871	Medical Relief afforded in Year ended 29th September, 1871: Number of New Cases attended and registered during the year: Dispensary Tickets	Visiting Tickets	Total	Col. 19	Col. 20	Col. 21	Col. 22	Col. 23
Column 1.	2.	3.	4.	5.	6.	7.	8.	9.	10.	11.	12.	13.	14.	15.	16.	17.	18.	19.	20.	21.	22.	23.
						£ s. d.	£ s. d.	£ s. d.	£ s. d.	£ s. d.	£ s. d.	£ s. d.	£ s. d.	£ s. d.								
PROVINCE OF MUNSTER—*continued*.																						
County of Kerry—*con.*																						
Tralee,	1. Tralee,	1	1	–	–	317 14 9	31 0 0	1 16 9	100 0 0	–	21 0 0	–	46 0 6	417 0 1	2,191	1,277	3,468	–	560	6	5	8
	2. Castle Island,	1	1	–	–	61 4 7	4 0 0	4 8 3	100 0 0	–	20 12 7	–	10 10 10	160 16 6	2,274	264	2,488	–	300	3	1	1
	3. Kilgobban,	3	1	–	–	16 4 0	21 10 0	4 8 0	100 0 0	–	20 0 0	–	20 3 4	182 19 6	[illegible]	116	[illegible]	–	345	–	–	–
	4. Brosna,	2	1	–	–	25 11 8	20 3 0	3 9 9	100 0 0	–	17 3 0	–	9 6 9	191 13 9	[illegible]	171	1,211	–	200	1	–	–
	5. Ardfert,	2	1	–	–	4 5 7	16 0 0	4 5 9	100 0 0	–	8 10 0	–	10 9 6	164 17 1	[illegible]	[illegible]	[illegible]	–	124	–	–	–
		10	6	–	–	255 3 7	75 15 0	22 14 6	500 0 0	–	92 5 6	–	115 15 0	1,100 11 6	4,294	2,161	8,085	–	1,316	7	6	6
County of Limerick.																						
Croom,	1. Croom,	2	1	1	–	22 16 1	11 0 0	–	166 16 8	30 0 0	8 9 0	–	10 10 10	[illegible]	2,374	190	[illegible]	–	67	–	–	–
	2. Castletown,	2	1	–	–	35 4 3	11 0 0	–	100 0 0	–	9 10 0	–	6 13 6	180 0 11	[illegible]	[illegible]	516	–	162	1	–	–
	3. Adare,	2	1	–	–	34 13 8	18 0 0	–	100 0 0	–	6 4 0	–	6 18 7	183 10 1	361	171	664	–	122	1	–	–
		6	3	1	–	103 16 0	40 0 0	–	366 16 8	30 0 0	24 3 0	–	23 10 11	601 13 3	[illegible]	609	[illegible]	–	380	2	–	–
Glin,	1. Shanagolden,	2	1	–	–	29 0 8	35 0 0	0 3 3	100 11 5	–	10 16 0	–	6 10 0	178 14 9	671	326	[illegible]	–	371	1	–	–
	2. Tarbert,	2	2	–	–	11 19 3	11 0 0	2 1 3	100 0 0	–	13 13 0	–	3 2 10	157 16 6	767	679	[illegible]	–	373	2	–	–
		4	3	–	–	66 19 11	50 0 0	2 4 6	200 11 5	–	24 9 0	–	7 12 10	310 16 3	[illegible]	[illegible]	[illegible]	–	644	3	–	–
Kilmallock	1. Kilmallock,	1	1	–	–	25 10 8	8 0 0	0 11 6	100 0 0	–	8 16 0	8 15 3	10 10 4	137 11 0	[illegible]	[illegible]	[illegible]	–	198	–	–	–
	2. Bruff,	1	1	2	1	42 4 6	8 0 0	0 1 6	100 0 0	65 0 0	7 10 0	1 1 0	21 17 1	[illegible]	[illegible]	310	[illegible]	–	131	–	–	–
	3. Hospital,	1	1	–	–	20 15 0	5 0 0	1 6 7	100 0 0	–	8 16 0	0 3 0	18 15 1	139 11 0	[illegible]	176	[illegible]	–	199	2	–	–
	4. Kilfinane,	1	1	1	1	32 11 11	8 0 0	0 17 3	110 0 0	65 0 0	15 16 0	1 11 0	34 0 1	[illegible]	[illegible]	[illegible]	[illegible]	1	200	–	–	–
	5. Charleville,	1	1	1	–	13 12 7	–	0 18 6	100 0 0	65 0 0	8 10 0	1 1 0	13 6 0	155 16 1	[illegible]	[illegible]	[illegible]	–	149	–	–	–
	6. Bruree,	1	1	–	–	17 10 6	6 0 0	[illegible]	100 0 0	–	6 15 0	3 1 0	11 2 3	105 11 3	1,207	250	[illegible]	–	104	–	–	–
		6	6	3	2	177 8 6	31 0 0	3 11 6	636 0 0	195 0 0	50 10 0	11 10 3	110 11 11	1,073 3 0	7,457	1,320	8,777	1	1,027	2	–	–

Limerick,	1. Clarina,	[illegible]
	2. Caherconlish,	[illegible]
	3. Annacotty,	[illegible]
	4. Murroe,	[illegible]
	5. City of Limerick,	[illegible]
	6. Bridgetown,	[illegible]
	7. [illegible],	[illegible]
		[illegible]
Newcastle,	1. Ardagh,	[illegible]
	2. Abbeyfeale,	[illegible]
	3. Newcastle,	[illegible]
	4. Toomagh,	[illegible]
	5. Broadford,	[illegible]
		[illegible]
Rathkeale,	1. Askeaton,	[illegible]
	2. Pallaskenry,	[illegible]
	3. Rathkeale,	[illegible]
		[illegible]
County of Tipperary. Borrisokane,	1. Terryglass,	[illegible]
	2. Borrisokane,	[illegible]
	3. Cloghjordan,	[illegible]
		[illegible]
Carrick-on-Suir,	1. Carrick-on-Suir,	[illegible]
	2. Garrangibbon,	[illegible]
	3. Piltown,	[illegible]
	4. [illegible],	[illegible]
	5. Portlaw,	[illegible]
		[illegible]
Cashel,	1. Kilpatrick,	[illegible]
	2. Cashel,	[illegible]
	3. Tullamain,	[illegible]
	4. Fethard,	[illegible]
	5. Killenaule,	[illegible]
		[illegible]

* Cashel Union: Fethard District.—No appointment of Midwife appears to have been made.

[continued.

No. 2.—Dispensary Districts, with the Expenses, and Amount of Medical Relief afforded, in the several Unions—*continued.*

Name of Union.	Names of Dispensary Districts.	[illegible]	No. of Officers authorised by Sealed Orders: Med. Officers	Apothecaries	Midwives	Medicines and Medical Appliances	Rent of Dispensary Buildings	Books, Forms, and Stationery, and Printing	Salaries: Medical Officers	Apothecaries	Vaccination Expenses: Amount of Fees paid to Medical Officers	Other Expenses	[illegible]	Total Expenditure for each Dispensary District for Year ended 29th Sept., 1871	Number of New Cases attended and registered during the year: Dispensary Tickets	Visiting Tickets	Total	[illegible]	[illegible]	[illegible]	[illegible]	[illegible]
Column 1.	2.	3.	4.	5.	6.	7.	8.	9.	10.	11.	12.	13.	14.	15.	16.	17.	18.	19.	20.	21.	22.	23.
PROVINCE OF MUNSTER—*continued.*						£ s. d.	£ s. d.	£ s. d.	£ s. d.	£ s. d.	£ s. d.	£ s. d.	£ s. d.	£ s. d.								
COUNTY OF TIPPERARY—*con.*																						
Clogheen,	1. Cahir,	3	1	–	–	14 11 8	10 0 0	6 3 9	120 0 0	–	10 6 9	1 8 6	8 6 10	138 7 9	734	282	1,016	–	160	1	6	9
	2. Ardfinnan,	2	1	–	–	19 9 1	17 10 0	6 6 0	100 0 0	–	13 7 6	1 0 0	11 14 8	184 1 8	[illegible]	129	[illegible]	–	[illegible]	–	–	–
	3. Clogheen,	1	1	–	1	27 12 11	18 0 0	6 8 10	100 0 0	–	9 3 0	–	4 6 7	169 11 1	1,079	[illegible]	1,324	–	[illegible]	–	–	–
		[illegible]	3	–	1	54 13 8	46 10 0	[illegible]	300 0 0	–	32 16 9	[illegible]	[illegible]	[illegible]	2,139	[illegible]	2,995	–	[illegible]	1	6	9
Clonmel,	1. Clonmel and St. Mary's,	1	[illegible]	1	–	61 16 1	–	6 13 9	236 16 8	65 0 0	[illegible]	[illegible]	77 1 7	445 11 8	3,919	1,191	5,110	–	[illegible]	5	–	–
	2. Moyfield,	2	1	–	–	16 9 3	15 0 0	[illegible]	100 0 0	–	12 [illegible]	–	19 5 8	177 14 9	[illegible]	[illegible]	[illegible]	–	[illegible]	1	–	–
	3. Kilsheelan,	1	1	–	–	3 11 7	[illegible]	[illegible]	34 1 0	–	1 [illegible]	–	1 12 5	79 3 3	[illegible]	[illegible]	[illegible]	1	[illegible]	[illegible]	–	–
	4. Killenaule,	1	1	–	–	18 3 2	5 0 0	[illegible]	100 0 0	–	5 [illegible]	2 0 0	6 17 0	151 8 6	[illegible]	[illegible]	[illegible]	–	[illegible]	1	–	–
	5. Ballymacarbry,	1	1	–	–	7 6 6	6 10 0	[illegible]	75 1 6	–	10 [illegible]	–	5 7 1	104 7 6	147	61	[illegible]	–	[illegible]	–	–	–
		6	6	1	–	[illegible]	36 10 0	6 7 3	601 1 9	65 0 0	[illegible]	[illegible]	[illegible] 5 0	956 8 7	3,116	1,784	7,150	1	[illegible]	9	–	–
Nenagh,	1. Nenagh,	2	2	–	–	20 1 6	16 10 0	0 17 6	200 0 0	–	18 [illegible]	3 1 0	[illegible] 9 2	280 0 0	1,221	613	1,834	–	[illegible]	–	–	–
	2. Newport,	1	1	–	–	14 6 9	8 0 0	4 16 0	120 0 0	–	9 [illegible]	1 5 0	4 0 0	161 14 0	[illegible]	[illegible]	[illegible]	–	[illegible]	–	7	2
	3. Portroe,	2	1	–	–	18 13 0	16 0 0	0 16 0	100 0 0	–	7 [illegible]	6 1 1	0 6 0	148 18 1	[illegible]	[illegible]	[illegible]	–	[illegible]	–	–	–
	4. Silvermines,	1	1	–	–	0 10 0	[illegible]	[illegible]	100 0 0	–	6 [illegible]	1 0 0	4 0 0	118 15 3	[illegible]	[illegible]	[illegible]	–	[illegible]	–	–	–
	5. Toomevara,	1	1	–	–	0 10 6	10 0 0	[illegible]	100 5 0	–	6 [illegible]	3 16 0	5 3 3	135 2 11	[illegible]	[illegible]	[illegible]	1	[illegible]	–	–	–
		7	6	–	–	[illegible] 6 2	34 16 0	3 16 0	[illegible] 0 0	–	[illegible]	[illegible]	[illegible] 17 5	[illegible] 6 6	[illegible]	[illegible]	4,574	1	[illegible]	–	7	2
Roscrea,	1. Roscrea,	2	[illegible]	–	1	73 6 8	6 0 0	3 6 0	180 0 0	–	32 7 0	1 13 0	[illegible] 7 6	277 1 6	[illegible]	[illegible]	1,010	–	[illegible]	6	1	1
	2. Shinrone,	2	2	–	–	45 6 9	16 10 0	2 3 11	150 0 0	–	11 [illegible]	2 1 0	15 6 1	215 1 3	[illegible]	[illegible]	[illegible]	–	[illegible]	1	–	–
	3. Bourney,	3	1	–	–	[illegible] 9 0	16 0 0	1 0 10	100 0 0	–	–	1 1 0	3 7 9	132 17 10	[illegible]	[illegible]	[illegible]	6	[illegible]	8	–	–
		7	[illegible]	–	1	[illegible] 3 4	[illegible] 10 0	6 10 9	350 0 0	–	[illegible]	1 16 0	48 0 8	[illegible] 0 8	1,679	[illegible]	[illegible]	6	[illegible]	7	1	1

and Relief Returns of Dispensary Districts.

6 10	–	16 17 4	930 0 7	884	154	1,[illegible]	–	213	1	–	–
3 60	–	8 5 4	166 8 3	804	335	1,[illegible]	–	92	–	–	–
11 0	–	10 3 8	610 18 1	2,[illegible]	165	2,[illegible]	–	194	–	1	1
13 6	–	11 9 0	197 18 1	680	237	450	–	173	1	–	–
6 60	–	6 15 7	116 11 0	670	167	766	–	166	1	–	–
8 10	1 10 0	17 1 6	180 4 5	694	154	683	–	155	–	–	–
50 50	1 10 0	47 9 5	2,183 10 5	5,[illegible]	1,442	7,[illegible]	–	1,161	3	1	2
6 20	0 15 0	9 16 4	185 8 3	885	201	608	–	80	–	–	–
14 170	1 10 0	31 8 8	183 12 4	366	[illegible]	800	–	66	–	–	–
6 160	2 0 0	7 13 10	150 17 4	617	195	319	–	101	–	–	–
15 60	2 0 0	11 16 8	326 1 4	2,782	634	3,217	–	254	–	–	–
42 110	6 5 0	61 5 0	743 1 5	4,800	918	5,[illegible]	–	540	–	–	–
18 156	–	2 8 6	191 15 3	1,101	124	2,035	–	245	1	–	–
13 80	1 5 0	12 11 4	178 12 4	1,[illegible]	528	1,300	8	170	–	–	–
25 36	1 5 0	16 19 0	370 8 5	3,011	650	3,364	8	420	1	–	–
14 60	–	63 16 9	918 11 1	707	102	859	3	145	1	–	–
7 08	1 0 0	1 1 3	141 4 0	488	230	1,144	–	164	3	–	–
6 98	–	7 15 0	117 16 7	1,556	890	1,967	11	190	–	1	1
5 160	0 5 0	5 1 9	131 10 5	478	108	304	–	114	–	–	–
33 90	1 6 0	81 0 9	660 7 1	3,[illegible]	704	4,[illegible]	14	613	4	1	1
63 10	–	64 9 6	710 18 1	3,[illegible]	1,761	5,130	–	1,243	29	25	32
11 100	–	8 18 0	175 19 0	827	215	1,212	–	150	2	–	–
6 90	–	14 19 10	160 7 11	640	604	3,[illegible]	–	111	1	1	1
9 90	–	13 9 6	203 13 6	567	321	920	–	356	–	–	–
13 150	–	3 1 6	240 5 7	460	390	776	–	164	3	–	–
–	–	17 0 11	164 17 11	297	104	681	–	64	–	–	–
103 80	–	130 0 3	1,600 1 0	6,972	3,059	10,830	–	2,210	80	34	34

No. 2.—Dispensary Districts, with the Expenses, and Amount of Medical Relief afforded, in the several Unions—*continued*.

Name of Union.	Names of Dispensary Districts.	[illegible]	No. of Officers appointed by Sealed Order: Med. Officers.	Apothecaries.	Midwives.	Expenses of Year ended 29th September, 1877: Medicines and Medical Appliances.	Rent of Dispensary Buildings.	Books, Forms, Stationery, Printing.	Salaries: Medical Officers.	Apothecaries.	Vaccination Expenses: [illegible]	[illegible]	Fuel and Attendance, [illegible]	Total Expenditure for each Dispensary District for Year ended 29th Sept., 1877.	Medical Relief afforded in Year ended 29th September, 1877: Number of New Cases attended and registered during the year: Dispensary Tickets.	Visiting Tickets.	Total.	[illegible]	[illegible]	[illegible]	[illegible]	[illegible]
Column 1.	2.	3.	4.	5.	6.	7.	8.	9.	10.	11.	12.	13.	14.	15.	16.	17.	18.	19.	20.	21.	22.	23.
PROVINCE OF LEINSTER.						£ s. d.	£ s. d.	£ s. d.	£ s. d.	£ s. d.	£ s. d.	£ s. d.	£ s. d.	£ s. d.								
County of Carlow.																						
Carlow,	1. Carlow,	1	1	–	–	73 11 9	15 0 0	8 15 7	103 15 4	–	6 7 0	–	30 6 10	251 10 6	2,096	394	2,474	–	119	1	–	–
	2. Tullow,	1	1	–	1	95 9 6	–	1 18 4	100 0 0	–	7 0 0	–	7 19 6	166 9 9	[illegible]	[illegible]	1,140	–	116	[illegible]	–	–
	3. Borris,	1	1	–	1	13 10 11	9 0 0	1 18 4	100 0 0	–	21 7 0	–	38 15 10	113 1 6	694	[illegible]	[illegible]	1	413	–	–	–
	4. Fenagh and Myshall,	2	1	–	–	36 16 0	16 0 0	1 18 2	100 0 0	–	6 10 0	–	14 10 0	157 0 5	[illegible]	[illegible]	472	–	119	–	–	–
	5. Leighlinbridge,	1	1	–	–	22 0 0	16 0 0	5 6 10	100 0 0	–	28 13 0	–	11 6 0	176 17 2	[illegible]	[illegible]	422	–	371	–	–	–
	6. Bagenalstown,	1	1	–	1	20 0 1	9 0 0	13 11 7	100 0 0	–	20 5 0	–	64 5 1	[illegible] 10 6	[illegible]	[illegible]	[illegible]	1	[illegible]	–	–	–
	7. Ballickmoyler and Newtown,	2	1	–	1	17 8 6	16 0 0	4 12 4	135 0 0	–	5 11 0	–	19 16 0	249 0 0	836	[illegible]	1,116	–	160	1	–	–
		9	7	–	4	[illegible] 6 8	77 0 0	[illegible]	738 15 4	–	104 10 0	–	[illegible] 15 0	1,365 2 11	5,767	1,[illegible]	7,[illegible]	2	2,[illegible]	6	–	–
County of Dublin.																						
Balrothery,	1. Balbriggan,	2	1	–	1	25 10 1	9 0 0	0 7 8	100 0 0	–	40 13 6	8 10 6	20 19 0	[illegible] 11 1	471	611	1,[illegible]	1	691	–	–	–
	2. Holmpatrick,	1	1	–	1	11 9 9	–	–	100 0 0	–	4 0 0	1 10 6	25 11 0	[illegible] 0 3	576	710	[illegible]	–	177	[illegible]	–	–
	3. Lusk,	2	1	–	1	29 16 9	13 0 0	–	100 0 0	–	5 5 0	0 10 6	33 5 5	161 17 9	[illegible]	134	[illegible]	–	416	1	–	–
	4. Swords,	2	1	–	1	21 13 1	11 0 0	–	100 0 0	–	5 1 0	0 10 6	37 16 5	[illegible] 1 1	406	257	[illegible]	–	[illegible]	2	–	–
	5. Kilsallaghan,	2	1	–	–	20 16 4	11 0 0	–	100 0 0	–	–	–	2 0 0	153 16 4	[illegible]	64	117	–	[illegible]	–	–	–
	6. Malahide,	2	1	–	1	25 17 1	15 0 0	–	100 0 0	–	27 0 2	0 10 6	20 18 3	195 5 1	[illegible]	190	[illegible]	–	347	–	–	–
		11	6	–	5	136 3 7	60 0 0	0 7 8	600 0 0	–	95 10 3	[illegible]	150 1 2	1,067 15 0	3,[illegible]	1,[illegible]	4,[illegible]	1	2,611	9	–	–
Dublin, North,	1. North City,	3	6	3	–	700 18 11	101 15 5	41 1 5	[illegible] 7 8	[illegible]	83 0 0	–	327 11 8	[illegible] 8 1	13,[illegible]	10,[illegible]	23,[illegible]	–	2,[illegible]	130	–	–
	2. Blanchardstown & Castleknock	2	1	–	–	3[illegible] 7 1	22 0 0	1 15 11	185 15 1	–	29 0 0	–	0 10 4	313 10 2	730	[illegible]	1,[illegible]	–	131	–	–	–
	3. Finglas and Glasnevin,	2	1	–	2	60 3 10	14 10 0	2 4 10	125 15 1	–	6 15 0	1 10 0	15 0 2	230 1 11	[illegible]	473	1,[illegible]	–	150	–	–	–
	4. Clontarf and Howth,	3	2	–	–	61 18 5	30 0 0	0 5 0	[illegible] 0 1	–	7 1 0	–	0 0 0	[illegible] 1 6	1,[illegible]	[illegible]	1,[illegible]	–	190	1	–	–
	5. Coolock and Drumcondra,	3	2	–	1	15 5 0	30 0 0	3 11 4	172 13 9	–	6 12 0	–	0 0 0	2[illegible] 7 6	[illegible]	[illegible]	1,[illegible]	–	367	1	–	–
		13	12	3	3	[illegible] 9 6	201 5 5	[illegible]	1,413 6 [illegible]	[illegible]	164 11 6	1 10 0	[illegible]	[illegible] 6 9	17,[illegible]	14,[illegible]	[illegible]	–	3,[illegible]	[illegible]	–	–

...ntrim and ...nstown,	8	2 –	8	34 13 9	12 10 0	6 19 3	697 13 4	–	6 11 0	–	48 16 6	418 1 8	[illegible]	[illegible]	[illegible]	–	394	–	–	–
...chrach and ...thorpe,	8	2 –	1	112 19 8	17 0 0	7 10 8	116 13 1	–	17 6 0	–	36 8 7	420 18 11	1,231	[illegible]	1,980	–	801	–	–	–
...ltney,	8	1 –	1	62 10 1	20 0 0	3 13 0	117 18 4	–	16 9 0	–	38 4 0	380 18 9	[illegible]	138	540	–	349	–	–	–
...ngstown,	8	2 –	1	50 0 7	20 0 0	6 16 8	[illegible] 9 8	–	6 6 0	–	13 17 10	418 16 8	2,601	917	3,001	1	133	6	–	–
...y and Rath-...tobart,	6	1 –	1	71 6 9	21 9 11	4 18 6	218 13 4	–	11 5 0	–	31 15 9	300 17 6	1,261	462	1,764	–	304	–	–	–
...werscourt,	5	1 –	1	50 6 3	8 0 0	9 19 8	100 7 6	–	3 13 0	0 0	34 7 0	104 10 8	417	168	406	5	97	–	–	–
...agany,	8	1 –	–	15 8 9	9 0 0	8 19 5	118 6 6	–	6 11 0	–	9 0 4	101 9 3	344	136	1,034	–	136	–	–	–
	44	11 –	7	118 8 4	119 10 11	36 8 2	3350 15 2	–	71 19 0	0 0	243 0 3	1947 10 11	7,0[illegible]	3,5[illegible]	11,053	5	1,734	6	–	–
...LDARE. ...by,	1	1 1	1	66 8 4	10 0 0	3 8 6	130 8 8	20 0 0	9 1 0	0 0	37 6 0	258 3 8	1,114	318	1,387	–	390	–	–	–
...monstown,	8	1 –	1	40 13 8	16 0 0	1 3 4	100 0 0	–	5 19 0	–	38 5 7	311 1 8	1,016	346	1,309	–	168	–	–	–
...stown,	3	1 –	1	29 18 3	16 0 0	1 14 4	100 0 0	–	3 6 0	–	17 7 0	170 10 6	981	109	341	–	91	–	–	–
...lindermot,	1	1 –	1	60 8 7	14 0 0	1 5 4	100 0 0	–	–	–	87 18 6	193 4 5	725	337	1,362	–	111	–	–	–
...mitally,	1	1 –	1	81 4 0	15 0 0	1 18 1	100 0 0	–	1 17 0	–	8 12 0	187 14 10	1,050	366	1,777	–	120	–	–	–
...Kilteel,	1	1 –	1	30 7 1	8 0 0	1 3 4	100 0 0	–	1 17 0	0 0	35 18 9	173 6 9	540	404	642	–	101	1	–	–
	9	6 1	6	276 0 11	74 0 0	10 12 6	640 0 0	20 0 0	20 11 0	0 0	181 8 10	1,299 10 3	5,[illegible]	1,873	6,6[illegible]	–	976	1	–	–
...ran,	8	1 –	1	69 12 8	18 6 0	3 13 7	114 0 4	–	–	1 0	17 18 10	914 17 5	516	177	403	2	84	–	–	–
...bridge,	2	1 –	1	39 0 4	16 0 0	0 0 3	100 0 0	–	11 1 6	1 0	16 9 3	191 16 10	1,073	324	1,734	–	118	2	–	–
...nstown,	9	1 –	1	3 10 9	10 0 0	1 15 4	100 0 0	–	3 6 0	1 0	12 1 8	181 12 11	1,067	366	1,720	–	30	–	–	–
...lbeggie,	3	1 –	1	34 0 8	16 0 0	0 7 9	100 0 0	–	7 1 0	1 0	33 8 1	186 6 6	616	254	607	–	118	–	5	–
...leath,	5	1 –	1	30 2 11	30 0 0	0 7 9	100 0 0	–	8 3 0	1 0	10 0 0	177 17 8	548	164	406	–	97	2	–	–
	11	5 –	5	194 10 6	100 6 0	6 1 10	520 6 1	–	38 13 0	5 0	88 17 10	946 3 4	3,811	1,136	4,619	2	826	4	–	–

* Carlow Union: Tullow and Ballinkillin and Newtown Districts.—No appointment of Midwife appears to have been made in these Districts.
† North Dublin Union: Coolock and Drumcondra District.—No appointment of Midwife appears to have been made.
‡ Athy Union: Fontstown District.—No appointment of Midwife appears to have been made.

[continued.

No. 2.—Dispensary Districts, with the Expenses, and Amount of Medical Relief afforded, in the several Unions—continued.

Name of Union.	Name of Dispensary District.	No. of Dispensary Stations	No. of Officers employed by Committee: Med. Off.	Apothecaries	Midwives	Medicines and Medical Appliances	Rent of Dispensary Buildings	Books, Forms, Stationery, and Printing	Salaries: Medical Officers	Salaries: Apothecaries	Vaccination Expenses: Amount of Fees paid to Medical Officers	Vaccination Expenses: Other Expenses	Fuel and Attendance, Repairs, and all other Expenses	Total Expenditure for each Dispensary District for Year ended 29th Sept., 1871	Number of New Cases: Dispensary Tickets	Number of New Cases: Visiting Tickets	Number of New Cases: Total	19.	20.	21.	22.	23.
Column 1.	2.	3.	4.	5.	6.	7.	8.	9.	10.	11.	12.	13.	14.	15.	16.	17.	18.	19.	20.	21.	22.	23.
						£ s. d.	£ s. d.	£ s. d.	£ s. d.	£ s. d.	£ s. d.	£ s. d.	£ s. d.	£ s. d.								
PROVINCE OF LEINSTER —continued.																						
County of Kildare—con.																						
Naas,	1. Blessington & Ballymore,	2	1	–	1	9 10 6	16 0 0	10 12 [illegible]	100 0 0	–	2 [illegible]	–	33 0 0	147 10 10	736	192	[illegible]	–	130	1	–	–
	2. Robertstown and Kilmeague,	1	1	–	–	[illegible] 1 0	4 0 0	1 13 [illegible]	114 0 0	–	0 10	–	0 0 0	163 16 10	[illegible]	119	[illegible]	–	135	1	–	–
	3. [illegible],	1	1	–	–	[illegible] 9 11	10 0 0	0 12	75 0 0	–	3 10 0	–	–	109 16 1	224	[illegible]	[illegible]	–	[illegible]	1	–	–
	4. Kilcullen,	1	1	–	–	7 16 1	10 0 0	0 12	100 0 0	–	6 3 0	0 1 6	5 0 0	120 17 11	17[illegible]	131	[illegible]	–	190	–	–	–
	5. Naas & Curragh,	1	1	–	1	21 5 [illegible]	10 0 0	1 2	100 0 0	–	6 10 0	0 11 0	20 0 0	1[illegible] 1 5	[illegible]	[illegible]	[illegible]	–	316	3	–	–
	6. Clane and Timahoe, North,	2	1	–	1	[illegible] 7 0	10 0 0	3 15	120 2 1	–	4 17 0	2 1 [illegible]	–	172 0 2	417	161	[illegible]	7	81	–	–	–
	7. Newbridge,	1	1	–	1	11 6 4	15 0 0	2 16 10	100 0 0	–	17 16 0	–	4 0 0	140 10 2	[illegible]	3[illegible]	1[illegible]	–	17[illegible]	1	–	–
	8. Kildare,	1	1	–	–	46 10 5	12 0 0	3 3 1	100 0 0	–	1 0 0	–	0 5 8	170 13 2	[illegible]	[illegible]	[illegible]	1	16[illegible]	1	–	–
		11	8	–	4	136 10 7	109 0 0	13 5 [illegible]	[illegible] 11 2 1	–	64 10 0	2 16 6	60 12 8	1206 17 7	3,0[illegible]	1,[illegible]	[illegible]	11	1,[illegible]	5	–	–
County of Kilkenny.																						
Callan,	1. Ballingarry,	1	1	–	–	16 14 5	6 0 0	1 0 6	100 0 0	–	5 10 0	1 [illegible] 6	4 10 3	137 3 11	[illegible]	12[illegible]	2[illegible]	–	101	1	–	–
	2. Mullinahone,	1	1	–	–	[illegible] 1 7	4 10 0	0 11 9	90 0 0	–	4 6 0	1 1 0	4 16 6	111 4 10	[illegible]	[illegible]	[illegible]	–	[illegible]	–	–	–
	3. Kilmaganny,	3	1	–	1	[illegible] 19 4	11 0 0	3 0 11	110 10 0	–	3 0 0	2 10 0	19 10 1	1[illegible] 1 4	114	160	[illegible]	–	91	–	–	–
	4. Callan,	1	1	–	–	21 1 6	6 0 0	0 10 10	123 1 0	–	17 0 6	3 17 0	4 10 2	176 1 0	1,[illegible]	2[illegible]	1,[illegible]	–	171	3	–	–
		6	4	–	1	79 2 3	31 10 0	6 7 3	[illegible] 12 0	–	[illegible]	0 0 6	43 12 9	619 11 3	2,1[illegible]	[illegible]	3,[illegible]	–	[illegible]	4	–	–
Castle-comer,	1. Castlecomer,	3	2	–	–	33 4 5	82 16 0	–	[illegible] 10 6	–	17 0 0	0 10 3	11 1 4	320 10 4	1,317	[illegible]	1,[illegible]	1	2[illegible]	2	–	–
	2. Ballyragget,	1	1	–	–	10 12 10	6 10 0	–	112 1 0	–	6 7 0	2 0 0	7 10 1	145 13 8	816	1[illegible]	[illegible]	–	[illegible]	1	–	–
		4	3	–	–	43 [illegible] 3	89 0 0	–	[illegible] 4 0	–	[illegible]	2 10 3	18 19 5	[illegible] 6 0	2,133	410	2,7[illegible]	1	11[illegible]	3	–	–
Kilkenny,	1. Kilkenny,	1	7	1	11	77 3 6	35 0 0	5 7 9	200 0 0	[illegible]	7 0 0	5 6 0	41 17 0	453 5 10	[illegible]	2[illegible]	3,[illegible]	–	[illegible]	2	–	–
	2. Gowran,	1	1	–	11	29 5 6	7 0 0	5 15	100 0 0	–	10 0 0	1 10 0	7 11 2	161 11 10	310	2[illegible]	[illegible]	–	166	–	–	–

Union	Dispensary District	Returns
	3. Tiscoffin,	[illegible]
	4. Freshford,	[illegible]
	5. Tullaroan,	[illegible]
		[illegible]
Thomastown,	1. Graigue,	[illegible]
	2. Inistioge,	[illegible]
	3. Thomastown,	[illegible]
	4. Knocktopher,	[illegible]
		[illegible]
Urlingford,	1. Ballina,	[illegible]
	2. Johnstown,	[illegible]
	3. Urlingford,	[illegible]
	4. Kilcooley,	[illegible]
		[illegible]
King's County. Edenderry,	1. Johnstown,	[illegible]
	2. Carbury,	[illegible]
	3. Rathangan,	[illegible]
	4. Edenderry,	[illegible]
	5. Rhode,	[illegible]
	6. Ballyboggan,	[illegible]
		[illegible]
Parsonstown,	1. Parsonstown,	[illegible]
	2. Killyon,	[illegible]
	3. Kinnitty,	[illegible]
	4. Frankford,	[illegible]
	5. Banagher,	[illegible]
	6. Ferbane,	[illegible]
	7. Riverstown,	[illegible]
		[illegible]
Tullamore,	1. Kilmanaghan,	[illegible]
	2. Philipstown,	[illegible]
	3. Kilbeggan,	[illegible]
	4. Clara,	[illegible]
	5. Tullamore,	[illegible]
		[illegible]

* Naas Union: Clane and Timahoe, North, Districts.—No appointment of Midwife appears to have been made.
† Kilkenny Union: Kilkenny and Gowran Districts.—No appointment of Midwife appears to have been made.

[continued.

No. 2.—Dispensary Districts, with the Expenses, and Amount of Medical Relief afforded, in the several Unions—*continued.*

Name of Union.	Name of Dispensary District.	3.	4. Med. Officers	5. Apothecaries	6. Midwives	7. Medicines and Medical Appliances	8. Rent of Dispensary Buildings	9. Books, Forms, Stationery, and Printing	10. Salaries: Medical Officers	11. Salaries: Apothecaries	12. Vaccination Expenses	13. Vaccination Expenses	14.	15. Total Expenditure for each Dispensary District	16. Number of New Cases: Dispensary Tickets	17. Visiting Tickets	18. Total	19.	20.	21.	22.	23.
Column 1.	2.	3.	4.	5.	6.	7.	8.	9.	10.	11.	12.	13.	14.	15.	16.	17.	18.	19.	20.	21.	22.	23.
						£ s. d.	£ s. d.	£ s. d.	£ s. d.	£ s. d.	£ s. d.	£ s. d.	£ s. d.	£ s. d.								
PROVINCE OF LEINSTER—*continued.* COUNTY OF LONGFORD.																						
Ballymahon,	1. Abbeyshrule,	1	1	–	–	17 15 10	10 0 0	–	100 0 0	–	18 18 6	1 0 6	12 0 0	193 19 10	581	262	833	20	161	1	–	–
	2. Ballymahon,	3	1	–	–	40 6 8	23 10 0	–	100 0 0	–	13 10 0	0 10 6	10 15 0	208 7 6	1,055	117	1,172	–	161	1	–	–
	3. Ballymore,	1	1	–	–	17 2 11	10 0 0	–	100 0 0	–	9 13 0	1 16 6	1 10 0	130 11 8	498	127	625	1	157	1	–	–
		6	3	–	–	75 3 11	43 10 0	–	300 0 0	–	35 9 0	3 12 6	24 5 0	533 1 8	2,134	636	2,770	21	477	3	–	–
Granard,	1. Granard,	1	1	–	–	67 6 5	6 0 0	0 9 4	100 0 0	–	9 14 0	11 10 6	8 8 6	194 18 9	417	355	772	6	173	–	–	–
	2. Street,	2	1	–	–	38 1 8	17 4 0	0 9 4	106 0 0	–	5 4 0	1 15 0	3 0 0	193 15 0	354	217	571	–	177	–	–	–
	3. Ballinalee,	1	1	–	–	30 15 1	9 0 0	0 9 4	100 0 0	–	7 11 0	6 14 6	1 10 0	146 19 11	409	231	640	–	117	–	–	–
	4. Scrabby,	1	1	–	–	28 17 8	8 0 0	0 9 4	100 0 0	–	11 15 0	5 18 6	8 1 1	163 1 7	290	181	471	–	153	–	–	–
	5. Finnea,	1	1	–	–	21 15 8	8 0 0	0 9 4	100 0 0	–	6 10 0	3 5 6	12 10 0	160 4 0	516	224	740	–	186	–	–	–
	6. Coole,	1	1	–	–	80 13 11	7 0 0	0 9 4	50 0 0	–	–	1 4 6	1 17 0	152 4 8	216	97	313	–	37	–	–	–
		7	6	–	–	262 13 11	56 0 0	2 16 0	556 0 0	–	42 3 0	34 7 6	41 0 7	981 0 0	2,248	1,306	3,553	6	943	–	–	–
Longford,	1. Longford,	2	1	–	–	37 19 4	12 10 1	1 5 6	180 0 0	–	26 11 0	1 10 6	0 6 0	188 7 11	1,271	215	1,386	–	867	3	–	–
	2. Drumlish,	1	1	–	–	17 14 7	12 0 0	1 5 7	87 0 0	–	27 11 0	9 0 0	9 17 8	177 17 8	432	163	595	–	630	2	–	–
	3. Killashee,	1	1	–	–	6 7 11	10 0 0	1 5 6	90 0 0	–	16 15 0	1 10 0	5 11 6	168 0 11	196	153	349	6	193	–	–	–
		4	3	–	–	60 1 10	44 16 1	3 16 7	277 0 0	–	70 17 0	3 0 0	17 15 0	473 15 6	1,701	531	2,232	6	1,790	5	–	–
COUNTY OF LOUTH. Ardee,	1. Ardee,	4	1	–	1	35 3 5	6 0 0	1 17 10	187 18 6	–	19 6 0	1 1 0	48 16 9	301 14 6	1,100	208	1,308	–	1,015	2	–	–
	2. Drumconrath,	2	1	–	1	9 18 1	11 10 0	0 13 6	111 8 6	–	20 10 0	1 1 0	25 9 8	180 1 1	377	102	479	–	200	–	–	–
	3. Collon,	2	1	–	–	15 0 11	16 0 0	0 15 7	100 0 0	–	8 0 0	1 1 0	6 15 6	155 9 7	222	136	358	–	226	1	–	–
	4. Dunleer,	2	1	–	–	16 6 11	11 0 0	0 10 0	140 0 0	–	17 0 0	1 1 0	–	186 19 11	328	171	499	–	660	–	–	–
	5. Castlebellingham,	5	1	–	–	17 1 0	12 10 0	0 17 0	101 6 7	–	13 13 0	1 1 0	0 2 0	153 6 7	279	101	380	–	376	1	–	–
		10	3	–	2	100 4 4	55 0 0	4 16 0	643 6 7	–	116 10 0	5 5 0	76 1 9	917 17 8	2,300	1,112	3,412	–	2,476	4	–	–

DROGHEDA,	1. [illegible],	3	1	–	1	–	12 0 0	1 12 9	118 0 0	–	21 2 9	1 1 0	31 3 0	190 0 0	1,170	188	[illegible]	–		[illegible]	–	–	–
	2. Duleek,	[illegible]	1	–	–	11 5 10	10 0 0	[illegible]	118 0 0	–	13 18 0	5 1 0	[illegible] 3 0	161 13 10	[illegible]	132	[illegible]	–		[illegible]	–	–	–
	3. St. Mary's,	1	1	–	–	10 12 6	10 10 0	1 3 11	50 0 0	–	38 5 0	0 0 0	1 10 0	151 10 11	[illegible]	[illegible]	[illegible]	–		[illegible]	1	–	–
	4. Drogheda,	1	1	–	–	[illegible] 1 6	11 0 0	2 13 [illegible]	150 0 0	–	73 0 0	0 0 0	17 5 0	303 16 6	1,817	1,178	2,1[illegible]	–		1,3[illegible]	2	–	–
	5. Termonfeckin,*	3	1	–	*1	[illegible] 14 0	12 0 0	1 16 [illegible]	110 0 0	–	22 17 0	1 1 0	8 15 0	177 2 6	[illegible]	113	318	1		[illegible]	–	–	–
	6. Monasterboice,	8	1	–	–	34 10 3	13 0 0	1 13 [illegible]	111 19 9	–	13 1 0	0 10 0	3 5 0	173 0 0	771	175	413	–		[illegible]	2	–	–
		18	[illegible]	–	2	[illegible] 5 7	64 10 0	9 8 4	711 19 9	–	[illegible]	[illegible]	26 14 6	[illegible] 10 6	3,376	1,602	4,7[illegible]	–	1	3,[illegible]	3	–	–
DUNDALK,	1. Dundalk,	1	1	1	1	50 6 3	20 0 0	1 11 6	190 0 0	10 0 0	16 11 0	0 10 0	40 11 8	333 17 11	1,704	[illegible]	2,[illegible]	–		1,[illegible]	3	–	–
	2. Louth,	1	1	–	–	25 15 1	8 0 0	3 16 10	100 0 0	–	27 5 0	0 15 0	3 18 0	171 11 11	641	337	871	–		[illegible]	1	–	–
	3. Ravensdown,	2	1	–	–	39 10 7	9 0 0	3 7 6	100 0 0	–	16 0 0	–	16 3 6	341 19 3	1,401	[illegible]	1,6[illegible]	–		[illegible]	–	–	–
	4. Dromiskin,	1	1	–	–	13 10 9	3 0 0	3 7 1	60 0 0	–	3 0 0	–	5 18 10	61 9 1	[illegible]	150	171	–		[illegible]	–	–	–
	5. Ravensdale,	1	1	–	–	13 4 11	20 0 0	8 17 3	152 13 0	–	7 0 0	1 10 0	7 7 3	137 6 5	[illegible]	105	819	–		[illegible]	1	–	–
	6. Carlingford,	3	1	–	–	15 6 5	14 0 0	3 11 10	100 0 0	–	16 16 0	2 0 0	1 7 0	152 15 3	447	[illegible]	787	1		[illegible]	2	–	–
		8	6	1	1	151 9 5	66 0 0	22 10 1	653 13 0	10 0 0	[illegible]	5 15 6	75 8 6	1180 11 1	6,577	3,153	7,[illegible]	1		3,373	7	–	–
COUNTY OF MEATH.																							
DUNSHAUGHLIN,	1. Dunboyne,	2	1	–	–	21 19 6	11 10 0	3 7 1	90 0 0	–	6 16 0	1 10 0	94 4 6	221 0 11	487	1[illegible]	626	–		1[illegible]	–	–	–
	2. Ratoath,	1	1	–	–	11 1 8	10 0 0	1 15 [illegible]	80 0 0	–	3 14 0	–	[illegible]	1[illegible] 4 9	[illegible]	[illegible]	2[illegible]	–		[illegible]	–	–	–
	3. Killeen,	1	1	–	–	[illegible] 1 4	10 0 0	0 10 1	85 0 0	–	–	–	21 4 7	161 7 2	[illegible]	[illegible]	[illegible]	–		[illegible]	–	–	–
	4. Garristown,	1	1	–	–	10 1 6	10 0 0	1 11 1	95 0 0	–	3 7 0	0 10 0	12 16 10	163 16 5	[illegible]	97	2[illegible]	–		[illegible]	–	–	–
		6	4	–	–	73 4 6	53 10 0	9 11 1	350 0 0	–	13 7 0	2 15 0	159 7 4	636 9 8	1,579	611	2,1[illegible]	–		373	–	–	–
KELLS,	1. Kells,	1	1	–	–	37 18 9	12 3 0	2 1 0	115 0 0	–	87 17 0	1 2 6	98 16 10	333 17 1	1,[illegible]	[illegible]	1,[illegible]	–		[illegible]	3	–	–
	2. Moynalty,	1	1	–	–	43 5 1	12 0 0	0 9 10	115 0 0	–	11 0 0	3 7 6	16 7 11	159 16 5	[illegible]	[illegible]	[illegible]	–		[illegible]	1	–	–
	3. Kilskeer,	1	1	–	–	18 3 0	6 0 0	0 10 3	115 0 0	–	11 10 0	0 11 4	[illegible]	162 5 3	[illegible]	[illegible]	[illegible]	–		[illegible]	–	–	–
	4. Nobber,	8	1	–	1	30 6 5	11 0 0	6 7 2	115 0 0	–	29 16 0	2 7 4	94 11 8	309 8 6	[illegible]	[illegible]	6[illegible]	2		[illegible]	2	–	–
		4	4	–	1	178 2 5	13 3 0	8 6 3	460 0 0	–	[illegible]	15 11 0	[illegible]	911 1 5	[illegible]	1,[illegible]	1,[illegible]	2		1,71[illegible]	6	–	–
NAVAN,	1. Navan,	1	1	1	1	35 6 4	–	2 15 6	130 0 0	7 10 0	11 15 0	1 0 0	17 0 0	217 7 10	1,44[illegible]	412	1,[illegible]	–		330	2	1	1
	2. Painestown,	8	1	–	–	7 0 3	11 0 0	1 1 0	110 0 0	–	9 13 0	1 1 0	18 0 0	138 7 3	[illegible]	13[illegible]	331	–		11[illegible]	–	–	–
	3. Castletown,	1	1	–	1	[illegible] 14 5	11 0 0	2 2 0	115 0 0	–	9 16 0	5 1 0	16 1 11	185 18 7	[illegible]	[illegible]	[illegible]	–		21[illegible]	1	–	–
		3	3	1	2	77 3 2	22 0 0	7 1 6	355 0 0	7 10 0	31 9 0	7 2 0	53 1 11	545 6 6	[illegible]	77[illegible]	2,[illegible]	–		[illegible]	10	1	1
OLDCASTLE,	1. Crossakeel,	1	1	–	–	16 4 0	6 0 0	0 1 10	90 0 0	–	3 20 0	2 6 0	7 15 6	119 13 10	[illegible]	131	[illegible]	–		77	1	–	–
	2. Oldcastle,	1	1	–	–	17 5 1	5 0 0	0 1 10	90 0 0	–	6 16 0	2 15 0	9 8 1	151 1 1	[illegible]	113	5[illegible]	–		112	1	–	–
	3. Virginia,	1	1	–	–	17 13 0	8 0 0	0 15 2	90 0 0	–	11 6 0	1 0 0	1 4 1	128 10 11	[illegible]	181	[illegible]	–		1[illegible]	–	–	–
	4. Ballyjamesduff,	3	1	–	–	73 4 9	10 10 0	1 4 1	90 0 0	–	7 11 0	3 0 0	18 3 5	193 15 5	4[illegible]	[illegible]	[illegible]	–		10[illegible]	2	–	–
		5	4	–	–	[illegible] 10 11	33 10 0	2 3 1	330 0 0	–	30 15 0	8 0 0	33 16 10	577 10 1	1,49[illegible]	43[illegible]	2,1[illegible]	–		41[illegible]	4	–	–

* Drogheda Union: Termonfeckin District.—No appointment of Midwife appears to have been made.

[continued.

No. 3.—Dispensary Districts, with the Expenses, and Amount of Medical Relief afforded, in the several Unions—*continued.*

Name of Union.	Name of Dispensary District.	No. of Dispensary Stations	No. of Officers appointed by Sealed Order: Med. Officers	Apothecaries	Midwives	Expenses of Year ended 29th September, 1871: Medicines and Medical Appliances	Rent of Dispensary Buildings	Books, Forms, Stationery, and Printing	Salaries: Medical Officers	Salaries: Apothecaries	Vaccination Expenses: Amount of Fees paid to Medical Officers	Vaccination Expenses: Other Expenses	Fuel and Light, and all other Expenses	Total Expenditure for each Dispensary District for Year ended 29th Sept., 1871	Medical Relief: Dispensary Tickets	Visiting Tickets	Total	Col. 19	Col. 20	Col. 21	Col. 22	Col. 23
Column 1.	2.	3.	4.	5.	6.	7.	8.	9.	10.	11.	12.	13.	14.	15.	16.	17.	18.	19.	20.	21.	22.	23.
PROVINCE OF LEINSTER—*continued.*						£ s. d.	£ s. d.	£ s. d.	£ s. d.	£ s. d.	£ s. d.	£ s. d.	£ s. d.	£ s. d.								
County of Meath—*con.*																						
Trim,	1. Athboy,	2	1	–	–	14 8 5	4 0 0	1 4 5	100 0 0	–	–	1 6 0	–	125 1 1	[illegible]	[illegible]	1,339	–	322	2	–	–
	2. Trim,	1	1	–	–	16 0 0	20 0 0	1 4 4	105 0 0	–	8 18	3 6 0	32 8 11	220 14 0	[illegible]	[illegible]	1,074	–	119	–	–	–
	3. Summerhill,	2	1	–	1	13 7 1	15 0 0	1 0 5	110 15 1	–	3 10 0	1 6 0	9 11 0	167 0 9	[illegible]	[illegible]	[illegible]	–	209	4	–	–
	4. Innfield,	2	1	–	–	16 16 1	25 0 0	0 19 1	93 6 8	–	3 10 0	1 0 0	–	126 7 7	[illegible]	[illegible]	[illegible]	–	101	1	–	–
		7	4	–	1	60 12 1	43 0 0	5 0 0	420 0 0	–	15 16 6	7 4 0	42 11 7	640 8 9	[illegible]	[illegible]	3,941	–	679	5	–	–
Queen's County.																						
Abbeyleix,	1. Abbeyleix,	1	1	–	–	8 10 0	20 10 0	0 1 6	115 0 0	–	6 10 0	0 10 6	5 1 4	143 19 4	[illegible]	[illegible]	[illegible]	–	137	–	–	–
	2. Ballyroan,	2	1	–	–	–	8 15 0	0 1 6	105 0 0	–	15 10 0	0 10 6	10 9 1	130 7 1	[illegible]	[illegible]	[illegible]	–	152	3	–	–
	3. Durrow,	1	1	–	1	62 14 2	7 10 0	0 19 6	92 10 10	–	15 0 0	0 10 6	20 5 0	195 13 8	[illegible]	[illegible]	[illegible]	–	75	–	–	–
	4. Castletown,	1	1	–	1	27 16 11	4 0 0	0 1 6	98 0 0	–	4 4 0	–	31 15 1	160 5 6	[illegible]	[illegible]	[illegible]	1	[illegible]	–	–	–
	5. Ballinakill,	2	1	–	–	11 11 8	16 0 0	0 1 6	108 0 0	–	3 3 0	0 10 0	13 6 9	169 16 3	[illegible]	[illegible]	[illegible]	–	131	2	–	–
		7	5	–	2	109 10 7	58 15 0	1 5 6	518 11 10	–	43 10 0	2 2 9	80 10 0	816 1 10	2,934	[illegible]	3,116	1	540	5	–	–
Donagh-more,	1. Borris-in-Ossory,	1	1	–	–	90 7 1	9 0 0	4 2 11	92 10 0	–	6 10 0	0 10 6	1 10 0	121 16 7	[illegible]	[illegible]	[illegible]	–	[illegible]	2	2	1
	2. Rathdowney,	1	1	–	1	34 13 1	12 0 0	3 7 3	103 10 0	–	7 0 0	0 10 6	21 5 6	202 10 4	[illegible]	[illegible]	[illegible]	3	116	–	–	–
		2	2	–	1	75 0 3	21 0 0	7 10 2	195 0 0	–	13 10 0	1 1 0	25 5 6	324 6 11	[illegible]	[illegible]	1,135	3	184	2	2	1
Mountmel-lick,	1. Mountmellick,	2	1	–	–	18 19 2	20 10 0	0 12 0	112 0 0	–	3 10 0	1 0 0	3 6 6	161 18 7	[illegible]	[illegible]	[illegible]	–	[illegible]	–	–	–
	2. Clonaslee,	1	1	–	–	7 14 0	7 0 0	0 11 0	100 0 0	–	1 10 0	–	0 1 8	108 4 4	[illegible]	[illegible]	[illegible]	–	[illegible]	–	–	–
	3. Coolrain,	1	1	–	–	11 7 3	8 10 0	0 13 0	91 1 0	–	3 10 0	–	1 1 10	121 3 3	[illegible]	[illegible]	[illegible]	–	[illegible]	–	–	–
	4. Mountrath,	1	1	–	–	19 1 0	10 10 0	0 15 0	100 0 0	–	7 10 0	1 0 0	0 1 5	136 10 5	[illegible]	[illegible]	[illegible]	–	132	–	–	–
	5. Maryborough,	2	1	–	–	14 7 5	16 0 0	1 0 1	100 0 0	–	–	–	7 7 3	139 14 9	[illegible]	[illegible]	[illegible]	–	156	–	–	–

	6. Emo,	2	1	-	-	37 11 6	10 0 0	0 13 6	160 0 0	-	6 7 0	-	1 7 4	170 1 10	[illegible]	217	1,0[illegible]	-	11[illegible]	-	-	-
	7. Clonygowan,	3	1	-	-	26 0 9	11 0 0	0 13 0	109 0 0	-	6 14 0	-	0 16 1	119 8 10	7[illegible]	31[illegible]	1,0[illegible]	-	1[illegible]	-	-	-
		10	7	-	-	183 10 1	76 10 0	4 15 1	1,[illegible] 6 8	-	31 4 0	8 8 0	12 3 10	964 15 0	1,[illegible]	1,37[illegible]	[illegible]	-	9[illegible]	-	-	-
COUNTY OF WESTMEATH. ATHLONE,	1. Athlone,	1	1	-	-	108 18 4	-	8 16 6	228 0 0	-	17 10	4 1 0	10 10 1	344 18 3	2,[illegible]	7[illegible]	3,1[illegible]	2	[illegible]	2	-	-
	2. Bridgewell,	1	1	-	-	31 17 8	4 0 0	-	120 0 0	-	0 17 0	7 1 0	9 16 0	182 18 8	[illegible]	[illegible]	[illegible]	-	[illegible]	-	-	-
	3. Kilkenny,	1	1	-	-	[illegible] 2 6	7 0 0	-	166 13 0	-	7 10 0	5 1 0	7 9 6	[illegible] 9 0	[illegible]	[illegible]	[illegible]	1	13[illegible]	-	-	-
	4. Glasson,	1	1	-	-	15 6 11	-	0 8 0	140 0 0	-	10 0 0	1 12 0	7 10 0	1[illegible] 10 11	[illegible]	1[illegible]	[illegible]	-	[illegible]	3	-	-
	5. Moate,	1	1	-	-	[illegible] 5 7	9 0 0	0 15 0	111 1 1	-	11 10 0	2 11 0	11 10 0	173 10 4	[illegible]	[illegible]	[illegible]	-	13[illegible]	1	-	-
		5	6	-	-	[illegible] 1 [illegible]	[illegible] 0 0	3 7 6	[illegible] 11 1	-	[illegible]	5 [illegible]	46 5 7	1,0[illegible] 10 2	[illegible]	1,[illegible]	5,7[illegible]	2	9[illegible]	6	-	-
DELVIN,	1. Castlepollard,	2	1	-	-	38 15 0	10 0 0	-	97 11 0	-	4 11 0	-	-	1[illegible] 16 8	[illegible]	1[illegible]	[illegible]	-	1[illegible]	-	-	-
	2. Delvin,	3	1	-	-	21 [illegible] 5	16 0 0	-	97 3 6	-	7 11 0	-	6 10 0	135 12 5	[illegible]	1[illegible]	[illegible]	-	1[illegible]	-	-	-
	3. Clonmellon,	3	1	-	-	40 11 1	17 0 0	-	97 2 8	-	0 10	-	-	[illegible] 10 1	1[illegible]	11[illegible]	[illegible]	-	1[illegible]	3	-	-
		8	3	-	-	144 15 2	41 0 0	-	281 15 0	-	21 0 0	-	6 10 0	[illegible] 0 2	[illegible]	[illegible]	1,2[illegible]	-	[illegible]	1	-	-
MULLINGAR,	1. Mullingar,	1	1	-	1	37 18 10	4 0 0	20 4 6	1[illegible] 11 [illegible]	-	15 10 0	-	[illegible] 12 0	[illegible] 7 0	[illegible]	[illegible]	9[illegible]	-	[illegible]	-	-	-
	2. Multyfarnham,	8	1	-	-	16 8 1	9 0 0	0 15 0	99 11 [illegible]	-	6 11 0	-	3 7 10	137 6 2	[illegible]	17[illegible]	[illegible]	-	1[illegible]	3	-	-
	3. Ballymacarigy,	1	1	-	-	18 16 2	8 0 0	0 15 0	99 11 5	-	9 17 0	0 0 0	9 10 0	141 11 4	[illegible]	[illegible]	[illegible]	-	171	-	-	-
	4. Castletown Geoghegan,	1	1	-	-	19 0 6	10 0 0	0 15 0	99 11 [illegible]	-	5 10	2 0 3	4 7 0	151 10 1	3[illegible]	1[illegible]	4[illegible]	-	[illegible]	4	-	-
	5. Tyrrellspass,	1	1	-	1	[illegible] 16 10	-	0 15 0	1[illegible] 11 [illegible]	-	4 13 0	0 3 0	30 19 3	[illegible] 14 9	[illegible]	11[illegible]	[illegible]	-	[illegible]	-	-	-
	6. Milltown,	1	1	-	-	15 2 4	7 0 0	0 15 0	1[illegible] 11 [illegible]	-	3 0 0	1 0 0	2 4 6	1[illegible] 13 6	[illegible]	1[illegible]	[illegible]	-	[illegible]	1	-	-
	7. Kilbeggan,	2	1	-	-	16 2 19	6 4 0	1 4 0	109 14 0	-	7 16 0	-	7 2 2	1[illegible] 2 6	1,1[illegible]	[illegible]	1,2[illegible]	-	1[illegible]	-	-	-
		6	7	-	2	1[illegible] 5 9	[illegible] 4 0	[illegible] 1 [illegible]	[illegible] 3 8	-	49 12 0	5 3 0	[illegible] 6 7	1,162 15 11	3,771	1,[illegible]	4,[illegible]	-	[illegible]	[illegible]	-	-
COUNTY OF WATERFORD. ENNISCORTHY,	1. Newtownbarry,	1	1	-	*1	40 7 0	10 0 0	7 0 11	60 0 0	-	14 10 0	3 15 0	1 0 10	1[illegible] 14 9	[illegible]	[illegible]	[illegible]	1	[illegible]	7	-	-
	2. Killann,	1	1	-	-	10 6 1	4 0 0	1 16 6	140 0 0	-	3 15 0	1 10 0	19 0 0	1[illegible] 9 9	[illegible]	1[illegible]	[illegible]	-	61	-	-	-
	3. Ferns,	1	1	-	-	12 13 7	4 10 0	1 14 5	90 0 0	-	10 10 0	1 10 0	3 5 0	1[illegible] 11 0	[illegible]	1[illegible]	[illegible]	-	[illegible]	-	-	-
	4. Enniscorthy,	3	1	-	-	[illegible] 2 2	10 10 0	2 7 0	1[illegible] 0 0	-	31 10 0	0 10 0	45 7 1	2[illegible] 5 7	1,115	[illegible]	1,[illegible]	-	510	4	-	-
	5. Oulart,	1	1	-	1	1 6 6	9 0 0	7 19 [illegible]	90 0 0	-	20 0 0	0 10 0	30 3 4	1[illegible] 17 6	41[illegible]	17[illegible]	[illegible]	-	3[illegible]	3	-	-
	6. Clonegal,	1	1	-	1	22 19 4	16 0 0	3 1 11	90 0 0	-	11 0 0	2 10 0	20 4 7	1[illegible] 1 0	[illegible]	[illegible]	[illegible]	-	[illegible]	3	-	-
		9	7	-	3	[illegible] 19 11	[illegible] 0 0	16 11 [illegible]	[illegible] 0 0	-	[illegible]	10 4 0	1[illegible] 15 1	1,[illegible] 1 7	3,1[illegible]	[illegible]	1,[illegible]	1	1,[illegible]	12	-	-
GOREY,	1. Gorey,	1	1	-	-	67 18 1	7 0 0	-	126 16 8	-	15 0 0	0 0 0	6 7 1	[illegible] 1 0	[illegible]	34[illegible]	1,[illegible]	2	[illegible]	8	1	1
	2. Coolgreany,	2	1	-	-	[illegible] 14 10	17 0 0	-	100 0 0	-	4 11 0	1 10 0	8 10 0	13[illegible] 10 4	47[illegible]	[illegible]	[illegible]	-	[illegible]	-	-	-
	3. Camolin,	3	1	-	-	31 16 10	10 0 0	-	100 0 0	-	18 30	1 15 0	0 14 10	136 8 0	[illegible]	1[illegible]	[illegible]	-	1[illegible]	2	-	-
	4. Killenagh and Wells,	3	1	-	-	41 17 8	13 0 0	-	1[illegible] 0 0	-	16 0 0	1 10 0	1 4 0	1[illegible] 3 0	[illegible]	[illegible]	7[illegible]	-	17[illegible]	2	-	-
		7	6	-	-	[illegible] 17 5	57 0 0	-	1[illegible] 16 8	-	66 0 1	7 10 0	[illegible] 10 9	7[illegible] 6 0	2,0[illegible]	[illegible]	2,9[illegible]	2	7[illegible]	6	1	1

* Enniscorthy Union: Newtownbarry District.—No appointment of Midwife appears yet to have been made

(continued.

No. 2.—Dispensary Districts, with the Expenses, and Amount of Medical Relief afforded, in the several Unions—continued.

Name of Union.	Names of Dispensary Districts.	3.	4. Med. Officers	5. Apothecaries	6. Midwives	7. Medicines and Medical Appliances	8. Rent of Dispensary Buildings	9. Books, Forms, Stationery, and Printing	10. Salaries: Medical Officers	11. Salaries: Apothecaries	12. Vaccination Expenses	13.	14.	15. Total Expenditure for each Dispensary District for Year ended 29th Sept., 1871	16. Dispensary Tickets	17. Visiting Tickets	18. Total	19.	20.	21.	22.	23.
Column 1.	2.	3.	4.	5.	6.	7.	8.	9.	10.	11.	12.	13.	14.	15.	16.	17.	18.	19.	20.	21.	22.	23.
PROVINCE OF LEINSTER—continued.						£ s. d.	£ s. d.	£ s. d.	£ s. d.	£ s. d.	£ s. d.	£ s. d.	£ s. d.	£ s. d.								
County of Wexford—con.																						
New Ross, .	1. New Ross, .	1	1	–	1	14 8 5	4 0 0	0 17 10	100 0 0	–	11 10 0	–	20 1 0	171 0 0	[illegible]	[illegible]	1,618	–	[illegible]	–	–	–
	2. Old Ross, .	1	1	–	1	25 16 3	3 10 0	1 10 0	100 0 0	–	20 3 9	–	24 6 6	209 6 6	661	159	820	–	171	1	–	–
	3. Dunganstown, .	3	1	–	–	22 17 9	10 7 6	2 1 0	101 0 0	–	12 1 0	0 14 0	12 1 0	170 1 9	281	134	415	–	150	2	–	–
	4. St. Mullins, .	1	1	–	1	9 9 1	1 16 0	0 10 [illegible]	70 0 0	–	9 1 0	–	20 0 0	113 16 7	151	97	248	–	100	–	–	–
	5. Templeudigan, .	1	1	–	–	5 9 7	9 10 0	0 13 6	50 0 0	–	3 16 3	–	1 1 0	70 1 1	[illegible]	[illegible]	[illegible]	–	54	–	–	–
	6. Carrickbyrne, .	1	1	–	1	38 0 11	6 0 0	0 19 6	100 0 0	–	11 6 0	2 0 0	27 6 6	186 1 11	911	139	1,050	–	174	1	–	–
	7. Fethard, .	1	3	–	2	5 10 3	25 10 0	0 10 0	100 0 0	–	26 16 6	–	10 0 0	177 9 9	279	[illegible]	[illegible]	–	200	5	–	–
		10	7	–	6	155 10 3	62 0 0	7 11 4	605 0 0	–	120 15 0	2 15 0	140 9 4	1117 16 1	3,366	1,000	4,465	–	1,425	9	–	–
Wexford, .	1. Wexford, .	1	1	1	–	34 19 1	15 0 0	0 11 0	180 0 0	50 0 0	31 6 0	4 0 0	2 11 3	348 11 2	744	478	1,222	–	861	4	–	–
	2. Broadway, .	2	1	–	1	24 3 9	12 17 6	0 16 7	100 0 0	–	70 16 0	1 0 0	30 10 0	196 1 5	185	134	319	–	[illegible]	–	–	–
	3. Bridgetown, .	2	1	–	1	16 16 10	9 0 0	1 0 0	100 0 0	–	79 13 2	2 0 0	33 16 0	195 1 1	667	155	822	–	355	2	–	–
	4. Bannow, .	1	1	–	1	27 9 4	4 0 0	–	105 0 0	–	4 19 3	–	30 10 4	183 5 0	614	234	848	1	274	1	–	–
	5. Taghmon and Ulyss, .	2	1	–	1	9 18 0	11 10 0	–	100 0 0	–	50 15 0	7 0 0	19 18 3	198 16 5	817	197	1,014	–	824	–	–	–
	6. Crossabeg, .	1	1	–	1	20 15 0	10 0 0	–	80 0 0	–	15 0 0	2 0 0	11 18 0	170 1 4	211	128	339	–	390	–	–	–
		9	6	1	5	165 16 10	65 7 6	2 10 [illegible]	665 0 0	50 0 0	257 15 0	12 0 0	165 11 5	1117 1 10	3,348	1,266	4,604	1	2,704	8	–	–
County of Wicklow.																						
Baltinglass, .	1. Baltinglass, .	3	1	–	–	89 18 11	25 0 0	0 14 0	100 0 0	–	8 16 0	0 16 0	–	286 19 11	475	216	691	–	330	1	80	10
	2. Kiltegan, .	2	1	–	–	–	10 0 0	0 10 6	97 3 10	–	5 6 0	0 10 0	8 10 0	121 4 10	231	115	346	–	95	–	–	–
	3. Dunlavin, .	3	1	–	–	14 10 2	24 0 0	0 16 0	100 0 0	–	6 11 0	0 10 6	–	147 16 2	327	176	503	–	154	1	–	–
	4. Rathvilly, .	2	1	–	–	12 14 7	15 0 0	1 11 11	65 11 3	–	6 17 0	0 10 6	17 10 1	111 2 7	140	123	263	–	92	–	–	–
		10	4	–	–	43 12 8	60 0 0	4 1 5	340 19 1	–	28 10 0	4 2 0	20 0 1	634 5 6	1,467	687	2,110	–	798	2	80	10

Rathdrum,	1. Newcastle,	[illegible]
	2. Ashford,	[illegible]
	3. Annamoe,	[illegible]
	4. Dunganstown,	[illegible]
	5. Arklow,	[illegible]
	6. Newbridge,	[illegible]
	7. Rathdrum,	[illegible]
	8. Aughrim,	[illegible]
		[illegible]
Shillelagh	1. [illegible] and [illegible],	[illegible]
	2. [illegible] and Hacketstown,	[illegible]
	3. Tinahely,	[illegible]
		[illegible]
PROVINCE OF CONNAUGHT. County of Galway.		
Ballinasloe.	1. Ahascragh,	[illegible]
	2. [illegible],	[illegible]
	3. Killian,	[illegible]
	4. Creagh,	[illegible]
	5. Lawrencetown,	[illegible]
	6. Kiltormer,	[illegible]
		[illegible]
Clifden,	1. Clifden,	[illegible]
	2. Renvyle,	[illegible]
	3. Roundstone,	[illegible]
		[illegible]
Galway,	1. Galway,	[illegible]
	2. Arran,	[illegible]
	3. Oranmore,	[illegible]
	4. Turloughmore,	[illegible]
	5. Moycullen,	[illegible]
	6. Spiddal,	[illegible]
		[illegible]

* Ballinasloe Union: Ballinasloe District.—Apothecary directions—duty performed by the Medical Officer.

[continued.

No. 2.—Dispensary Districts, with the Expenses, and Amount of Medical Relief afforded, in the several Unions—*continued.*

Name of Union.	Names of Dispensary Districts.	No. of Dispensary Stations	No. of Officers appointed by Relief Order: Med. Officers	Apothecaries	Midwives	Expenses of Year ended 29th September, 1871: Medicines and Medical Appliances	Rent of Dispensary Buildings	Books, Forms, Stationery, and Printing	Salaries: Medical Officers	Salaries: Apothecaries	Vaccination Expenses: Amount of Fees paid to Med. Officers	Vaccination Expenses: Other Expenses	Fuel and all other incidental Expenses	Total Expenditure for each Dispensary District for Year ended 29th Sept., 1871	Medical Relief afforded in Year ended 29th September, 1871: Number of New Cases: Dispensary Tickets	Visiting Tickets	Total	No. of Visits	Total Cases of Vaccination during the year	Total Dispensary Cases	No. of Days	Total
Column 1.	2.	3.	4.	5.	6.	7.	8.	9.	10.	11.	12.	13.	14.	15.	16.	17.	18.	19.	20.	21.	22.	23.
						£ s. d.	£ s. d.	£ s. d.	£ s. d.	£ s. d.	£ s. d.	£ s. d.	£ s. d.	£ s. d.								
PROVINCE OF CONNAUGHT—*continued.* County of Galway—*con.*																						
Glenamaddy,	1. Dunmore,	1	1	–	–	19 3 0	–	0 13 9	33 0 0	–	3 10 0	1 1 0	6 0 0	64 7 9	167	79	246	–	87	–	–	–
	2. Glenamaddy,	1	1	–	–	80 11 6	–	5 0 1	85 0 0	–	15 10 0	1 1 0	6 10 6	183 13 11	774	180	954	–	256	–	–	–
	3. Williamstown,	1	1	–	–	31 5 7	13 0 0	0 11 8	100 0 0	–	13 11 0	0 1 0	7 0 0	171 16 9	631	147	778	–	300	–	–	–
		3	3	–	–	131 0 0	13 0 0	1 15 6	220 0 0	–	32 3 0	5 3 0	18 18 6	427 18 11	1,572	406	[illegible]	–	633	–	–	–
Gort,*	1. Gort,	2	1 1	–	–	30 16 3	7 0 0	–	100 0 0	24 0 0	15 15 0	–	1 19 0	197 4 3	836	303	1,139	–	339	3	4	–
	2. Ballinderreen,	3	1 1	–	–	33 11 0	25 0 0	–	140 0 0	–	21 0 0	1 0 0	–	217 13 6	953	344	1,297	–	301	2	–	–
		5	2 2	–	–	64 1 11	32 0 0	–	240 0 0	24 0 0	36 17 0	1 0 0	1 19 0	395 17 11	1,791	601	2,432	–	640	5	4	–
Loughrea,	1. Loughrea,	2	1	–	–	18 0 0	5 0 0	0 3 8	100 0 0	–	13 0 0	–	–	163 14 0	309	291	600	–	138	3	19	4
	2. Bullaun,	1	1	–	–	0 19 6	5 4 0	0 6 1	100 0 0	–	9 17 0	–	10 1 0	130 12 0	174	117	291	–	106	–	–	–
	3. Athenry,	2	1	–	–	36 6 3	12 0 0	0 4 1	100 0 0	–	21 10 0	–	5 0 0	176 2 4	449	132	581	–	332	4	–	–
	4. Woodford,	3	1	–	–	18 0 0	4 0 0	0 3 6	100 0 0	–	8 4 0	–	3 0 0	139 16 [illegible]	97	77	174	–	100	–	–	–
		8	4	–	–	70 11 3	25 1 [illegible]	0 10 6	400 0 0	–	58 10 0	–	18 1 0	525 11 11	1,111	601	1,6[illegible]	–	727	7	19	8
Mount Bellew,	1. Killererin,	1	1	–	1	13 11 11	5 0 0	1 16 0	100 0 0	–	16 15 0	1 5 0	23 10 10	180 8 9	1,0[illegible]	137	1,1[illegible]	–	166	–	–	–
	2. Clonbrock,	1	1	–	1	17 8 1	5 0 0	1 0 11	100 0 0	–	8 10 0	3 0 0	15 0 0	184 19 6	1,254	132	1,386	1	166	2	–	–
	3. Mount Bellew,	1	1	–	–	16 9 6	5 0 0	0 19 5	100 0 0	–	11 11 6	2 0 6	1 0 0	161 1 6	1,[illegible]	15[illegible]	1,517	–	616	3	–	–
		3	3	–	2	47 3 6	16 0 0	3 16 11	300 0 0	–	36 10 6	6 6 6	39 5 10	473 18 8	3,[illegible]	406	4,1[illegible]	1	[illegible]	5	–	–

and Relief Returns of Dispensary Districts.

[illegible]	[illegible]	[illegible]	[illegible]	[illegible]	[illegible]	[illegible]	[illegible]
[illegible]	[illegible]	[illegible]	[illegible]	[illegible]	[illegible]	[illegible]	[illegible]
[illegible]	[illegible]	[illegible]	[illegible]	[illegible]	[illegible]	[illegible]	[illegible]

No. 2.—Dispensary Districts, with the Expenses, and Amount of Medical Relief afforded, in the several Unions—*continued*.

Name of Union.	Names of Dispensary Districts.	No. of Dispensaries or Stations in each District.	No. of Officers authorised by Sealed Order: Medical Officers.	Apothecaries.	Midwives.	Expenses of Year ended 29th September, 1871: Medicines and Medical Appliances.	Rent of Dispensary Buildings.	Books, Forms, Stationery, and Printing.	Salaries: Medical Officers.	Apothecaries.	Vaccination Expenses: Amount of Fees paid to Medical Officers.	Other Expenses in carrying out the Vaccination Acts.	Fuel and other miscellaneous expenses.	Total Expenditure for each Dispensary District for Year ended 29th Sept., 1871.	Medical Relief afforded in Year ended 29th September, 1871: Number of New Cases attended and registered during the year: Dispensary Tickets.	Visiting Tickets.	Total.	No. of Visits.	No. of Cases of Vaccination during the year.	Total Dispensary Districts.	Col. 22.	Col. 23.
Column 1.	2.	3.	4.	5.	6.	7.	8.	9.	10.	11.	12.	13.	14.	15.	16.	17.	18.	19.	20.	21.	22.	23.
PROVINCE OF CONNAUGHT—*continued*. COUNTY OF MAYO—*con*.						£ s. d.	£ s. d.	£ s. d.	£ s. d.	£ s. d.	£ s. d.	£ s. d.	£ s. d.	£ s. d.								
Ballinrobe,	1. Ballinrobe,	2	2	–	–	13 10 11	8 0 0	0 15 9	170 0 0	–	23 15 0	1 10 6	15 15 0	295 17 4	1,026	467	1,493	–	101	4	–	–
	2. Cong,	2	1	–	–	30 19 1	8 0 0	0 15 0	170 0 0	–	11 10 0	–	16 19 8	171 13 1	726	176	902	1	226	1	–	–
	3. Hollymount,	1	1	–	–	31 6 6	8 0 0	0 15 0	100 0 0	–	13 17 6	1 5 6	6 3 0	161 8 8	466	210	467	–	154	1	–	–
		5	4	–	–	110 17 8	24 0 0	2 5 0	500 0 0	–	47 4 0	2 10 6	48 17 0	630 12 5	2,217	853	3,070	1	481	7	–	–
Belmullet,	1. Binghamstown	1	1	–	–	11 17 5	7 10 0	–	90 0 0	–	21 15 0	3 0 0	5 0 1	143 2 9	420	30	451	–	242	–	–	–
	2. Bangor,	2	1	–	–	0 10 6	15 0 0	1 0 0	125 0 0	–	31 10 0	3 0 0	8 14 7	184 15 1	356	183	541	–	427	–	–	–
		3	2	–	–	12 7 11	22 10 0	1 0 0	215 0 0	–	56 5 0	6 0 0	13 14 11	327 17 10	776	183	959	–	670	–	–	–
Castlebar,	1. Castlebar,	4	2	–	–	74 15 10	16 7 3	10 7 4	210 0 0	–	20 2 6	6 8 0	22 12 1	362 7 11	742	510	1,252	–	541	4	–	–
	2. Balla,	2	1	–	–	30 7 3	13 16 4	5 4 0	105 11 4	–	10 12 0	0 12 9	10 6 8	185 18 9	296	220	516	–	872	2	–	–
		6	3	–	–	105 2 1	29 3 7	15 11 4	315 11 4	–	30 15 0	7 11 4	32 18 9	533 0 8	1,048	727	1,773	–	839	6	–	–
Claremorris,	1. Claremorris,	1	1	–	–	–	–	0 3 3	150 0 0	–	10 10 0	3 15 6	6 11 8	187 9 6	240	134	374	–	308	1	–	–
	2. Ballindine,	1	1	–	–	32 17 3	6 0 0	3 17 7	100 0 0	–	22 9 0	3 15 6	9 8 4	177 7 3	497	231	728	8	439	–	–	–
	3. Ballyhaunis,	1	1	–	–	13 5 0	5 0 0	0 1 10	100 0 0	–	10 10 0	2 10 8	0 3 8	145 19 10	493	161	754	–	609	3	–	–
		3	3	–	–	46 2 3	11 0 0	3 2 8	350 0 0	–	43 7 6	10 1 8	25 3 7	410 16 7	1,237	549	1,856	8	1,356	4	–	–
Killala,	1. Killala,	1	1	–	–	30 12 0	6 0 0	0 12 0	150 11 10	–	5 10 0	5 0 0	22 17 6	179 10 1	293	87	380	8	183	–	–	–
	2. Ballycastle,	2	1	–	–	13 10 3	9 10 0	1 8 0	125 0 0	–	6 15 0	1 0 0	10 6 7	150 9 4	505	123	628	10	168	2	–	–
		3	2	–	–	44 2 3	15 10 0	2 0 0	275 11 10	–	11 6 0	6 0 0	33 4 1	329 19 5	798	210	1,008	18	351	2	–	–

NEWPORT, .	1. Newport, .	1	1	–	*1	30 16 [illegible]	10 0 0	1 15 6	201 19 [illegible]	–	10 15 0	11 3 0	6 8 12	171 11 [illegible]	[illegible]	[illegible]	564	–	[illegible]	–	–	–
	2. Achill, .	4	1	–	*1	95 1 11	34 0 0	1 3 4	100 0 0	–	8 15 0	11 1 0	3 10 6	345 18 1	[illegible]	[illegible]	915	–	307	–	–	–
		6	2	–	2	126 8 7	34 0 0	2 19 5	301 16 0	–	18 10 0	22 4 0	9 8 5	517 10 1	1,491	419	1,9[illegible]	–	891	–	–	–
SWINEFORD,	1. Swineford, .	1	1	–	–	31 6 5	9 0 0	2 19 0	190 0 0	–	15 0 7	5 8 0	5 3 10	171 19 3	604	230	629	–	479	1	10	4
	2. Foxford, .	1	1	–	–	18 9 9	5 0 0	1 14 4	106 13 0	–	10 0 0	3 10 6	3 0 0	103 0 11	503	157	1,0[illegible]	–	592	–	–	–
	3. Kiltamagh, .	1	1	–	–	21 15 7	11 0 0	2 1 6	100 0 0	–	13 15 0	5 10 0	4 18 0	157 6 7	334	130	116	–	3[illegible]	1	–	–
	4. Lowpark, .	1	1	–	–	30 0 4	10 0 0	1 11 9	190 0 0	–	20 0 0	2 10 0	3 0 0	176 8 7	904	60	1,030	–	145	2	–	–
	5. Kilkelly, .	1	1	–	–	45 11 9	10 0 0	2 2 6	100 0 0	–	25 10 8	11 10 0	3 7 6	211 14 3	795	464	1,006	–	422	–	–	–
		5	5	–	–	160 9 10	45 0 0	10 10 1	696 13 0	–	103 14 0	29 10 0	19 9 1	858 6 7	3,5[illegible]	981	6,300	–	2,045	4	10	0
WESTPORT,	1. Westport, .	2	1	–	–	31 0 5	–	5 17 10	173 10 0	–	10 18 0	6 15 0	9 0 6	175 13 11	790	19[illegible]	6[illegible]	–	349	2	–	–
	2. Louisburgh, .	1	1	–	–	15 0 3	15 0 0	2 17 7	110 10 0	–	13 15 0	9 15 0	11 13 5	195 0 0	1,7[illegible]	203	1,300	–	362	–	–	–
	3. Islandeady, .	1	1	–	–	20 3 6	9 0 0	8 10 2	65 14 0	–	9 18 0	6 10 0	18 13 6	137 6 2	[illegible]	119	750	–	177	–	–	–
		5	3	–	–	75 13 1	30 0 0	16 11 8	351 16 0	–	47 5 0	20 7 0	45 6 6	525 0 7	2,9[illegible]	370	3,80[illegible]	–	907	2	–	–
COUNTY OF ROSCOMMON. BOYLE, .	1. Boyle, .	1	1	1	1	10 0 10	–	5 6 0	100 0 0	13 0 0	41 10 0	3 0 0	26 18 6	418 3 1	547	369	759	–	454	–	–	–
	2. Ballinameen, .	1	1	–	–	21 3 2	3 0 0	6 5 0	100 0 0	–	11 10 0	2 0 0	6 3 0	114 3 4	302	131	4[illegible]	–	[illegible]	1	–	–
	3. Gurteen, .	1	1	–	–	27 11 5	10 0 0	1 10 1	170 0 0	–	[illegible] 0 0	2 0 0	18 9 5	160 0 5	316	107	601	2	311	1	–	–
	4. Keadue, .	1	1	–	–	34 2 0	–	0 15 0	110 0 0	–	11 10 0	2 10 0	10 0 0	161 13 2	900	71	314	–	[illegible]	–	–	–
	5. Ballyfarnan, .	1	1	–	–	27 0 3	5 0 0	0 6 0	100 0 0	–	19 10 0	5 10 0	18 10 0	308 11 0	194	70	872	–	183	1	–	–
		5	6	1	1	123 16 1	20 0 0	8 19 10	590 0 0	13 0 0	109 10 0	15 2 0	80 6 6	1274 11 3	2,071	750	2,900	2	1,287	6	–	–
CASTLEREA,	1. Ballaghaderin,	2	1	–	–	37 18 11	16 10 0	4 2 0	110 0 0	–	–	0 10 0	11 12 1	308 19 9	1,46[illegible]	107	1,40[illegible]	–	350	–	–	–
	2. Frenchpark, .	1	1	–	–	26 13 4	10 0 0	3 5 6	170 0 0	–	18 17 0	0 10 0	15 8 4	190 14 0	1,06[illegible]	217	3,0[illegible]	–	300	2	–	–
	3. Castlerea, .	2	1	–	–	29 12 1	10 0 0	3 0 0	111 0 0	–	42 17 0	2 10 0	4 0 0	230 3 1	1,131	150	1,41[illegible]	–	[illegible]	–	1	1
	4. Castleplunket,	3	1	–	–	6 19 3	6 0 0	2 0 0	75 0 0	–	–	8 10 0	11 0 0	160 17 11	[illegible]	61	3[illegible]	–	[illegible]	0	–	–
		8	4	–	–	111 0 0	42 10 0	12 7 6	375 0 0	–	56 16 0	6 2 0	39 0 6	790 1 5	1,5[illegible]	51[illegible]	5,11[illegible]	–	1,24[illegible]	4	1	1
ROSCOMMON,	1. Athleague, .	1	1	–	–	21 0 1	10 0 0	–	100 0 0	–	9 0 0	–	–	178 0 1	650	103	670	–	170	4	–	–
	2. Roscommon,	1	1	–	–	23 9 3	5 0 0	–	100 0 0	–	9 10 3	1 7 0	10 11 8	152 16 0	937	180	1,0[illegible]	–	250	–	–	–
	3. Ballyleague, .	1	1	–	–	60 1 5	9 0 0	–	100 0 0	–	12 15 0	–	5 3 0	176 5 5	1,077	46	1,1[illegible]	–	311	2	–	–
		3	3	–	–	103 11 0	24 0 0	–	300 0 0	–	33 3 3	1 7 0	16 17 8	442 7 5	2,447	313	2,784	–	670	6	–	–

* Newport Union: Newport and Achill Districts.—No appointment of Midwife appears to have been made.

[continued.

No. 2.—Dispensary Districts, with the Expenses, and Amount of Medical Relief afforded, in the several Unions—continued.

Name of Union.	Names of Dispensary Districts.	3.	No. of Officers authorized by Sealed Order: Med. Officers.	Apothecaries.	Midwives.	Expenses of Year ended 29th September, 1871: Medicines and Medical Appliances.	Rent of Dispensary Buildings.	Books, Forms, Stationery, and Printing.	Salaries: Medical Officers.	Apothecaries.	Vaccination Expenses: Amount of Fees paid to Med. Officers.	Other Expenses of Vaccination.	14.	Total Expenditure for each Dispensary District for Year ended 29th Sept. 1871.	Medical Relief afforded in Year ended 29th September, 1871: Number of New Cases attended and registered during the year: Dispensary Tickets.	Visiting Tickets.	Total.	19.	20.	21.	22.	23.
Column 1.	2.	3.	4.	5.	6.	7.	8.	9.	10.	11.	12.	13.	14.	15.	16.	17.	18.	19.	20.	21.	22.	23.
						£ s. d.	£ s. d.	£ s. d.	£ s. d.	£ s.	£ s. d.	£ s. d.	£ s. d.	£ s. d.								
PROVINCE OF CONNAUGHT—continued. County of Roscommon—con.																						
Strokestown,	1. Strokestown,	1	1	–	–	20 13 8	5 0 0	4 0 0	100 0 0	–	12 14 0	–	6 11 1	136 18 6	1,001	673	1,674	1	179	1	–	–
	2. Rooskey,	1	1	–	1	22 11 8	5 10 0	4 3 0	100 0 0	–	15 3 0	1 0 0	22 3 0	170 19 9	1,946	136	1,1[illegible]	–	307	1	–	–
	3. Elphin,	1	1	–	–	47 10 7	12 0 0	4 0 0	100 0 0	–	0 0 0	–	7 0 0	171 10 7	430	118	548	–	119	5	–	–
		3	3	–	1	90 16 7	25 10 0	12 0 0	300 0 0	–	33 10 0	4 0 0	40 14 1	507 9 0	3,710	640	3,350	1	606	7	–	–
County of Sligo.																						
Dromore, West,	1. Easky,	1	1	–	*1	30 10 0	–	–	80 0 0	–	16 7 8	1 1 0	1 16 0	140 1 11	1,357	130	1,497	–	300	1	–	–
	2. Skreen,	1	1	–	*1	25 1 1	8 0 0	–	100 0 0	–	9 16 8	1 1 0	3 0 0	152 16 6	1,057	130	1,187	3	331	–	–	–
	3. Castleconnor,	1	1	–	–	38 1 9	–	–	30 0 0	–	6 10 0	1 1 0	0 0 0	81 15 9	470	15	485	–	300	–	–	–
		3	3	–	2	93 1 10	8 0 0	–	230 0 0	–	32 13 6	3 3 0	10 16 0	380 13 9	2,934	270	3,169	3	642	1	–	–
Sligo,	1. Carney,	2	2	–	1	36 16 11	25 0 0	2 12 9	177 0 5	–	17 13 0	7 10 0	20 0 10	317 8 5	1,626	821	1,447	–	449	7	–	–
	2. Sligo,	1	2	1	1	40 2 7	6 0 0	1 7 7	268 0 0	30 0	31 4 0	6 12 0	72 1 6	633 6 7	1,721	643	2,364	–	1,043	–	–	–
	3. Collooney,	1	1	–	–	15 0 0	10 0 0	2 8 4	100 0 0	–	5 3 0	3 11 0	4 11 0	165 0 6	282	142	424	–	126	–	–	–
	4. Ballysadare,	1	1	–	–	24 11 10	5 3 0	1 7 8	100 0 0	–	9 1 0	5 10 0	16 15 8	163 11 8	922	189	1,111	–	275	1	–	–
	5. Riverstown,	1	1	–	–	4 0 0	19 0 0	1 17 5	100 0 0	–	17 10 0	5 10 0	5 7 6	153 16 5	267	163	430	–	240	–	–	–
		6	7	1	2	140 16 10	61 3 0	10 6 4	688 0 5	30 0	120 14 0	28 2 0	116 3 11	1423 10 11	4,738	1,939	6,677	–	1,218	8	–	–
Tobercurry,	1. Tobercurry,	1	1	–	–	25 9 3	–	1 10 3	100 0 0	–	8 1 0	–	2 0 0	130 0 0	985	300	1,285	2	183	–	–	–
	2. Coolaney,	1	1	–	–	20 0 0	10 0 0	0 18 6	125 0 0	–	12 16 0	–	1 0 0	170 15 3	612	22	634	4	107	–	–	–
	3. Achonry,	2	1	–	–	28 10 0	15 0 0	0 18 6	100 0 0	–	16 16 0	–	2 0 0	150 0 0	774	187	1,051	4	416	–	–	–
		4	3	–	–	75 14 0	25 0 0	4 1 3	325 0 0	–	37 13 0	–	0 0 0	450 0 0	2,380	390	2,770	10	706	–	–	–

* Dromore, West, Union.—Easky and Skreen Districts.—No appointment of Midwife appears to have been made.

SUMMARY OF FOREGOING TABLE, No. 2.

PROVINCES.	Number of Unions.	Number of Dispensary Districts.	Number of Dispensaries or Stations.	Number of Officers appointed by Boards of Guardians: Medical Officers.	Apothecaries.	Midwives.	Expenses of year ended 29th September, 1871: Medicines and Medical Appliances.	Rent of Dispensary Buildings.	Books, Forms, Stationery, and Printing.	Salaries: Medical Officers.	Salaries: Apothecaries.	Vaccination Expenses: [illegible]	Vaccination Expenses: [illegible]	Fuel, Committee Rooms, Salaries, and other Incidental Expenses not included in the preceding Columns.	Total Expenses of Dispensary Districts, for year ended 29th Sept. 1871.	Medical relief afforded in year ended 29th September, 1871: Number of New Cases attended and registered during the year: Dispensary Tickets.	Visiting Tickets.	Total.	[illegible]	[illegible]	[illegible]	[illegible]
Column 1.	2.	3.	4.	5.	6.	7.	8.	9.	10.	11.	12.	13.	14.	15.	16.	17.	18.	19.	20.	21.	22.	[illegible]
							£ s. d.	£ s. d.	£ s. d.	£ s. d.	£ s. d.	£ s. d.	£ s. d.	£ s. d.	£ s. d.							
ULSTER,	[illegible]	[illegible]	[illegible]	[illegible]	[illegible]	[illegible]	[illegible]	[illegible]	[illegible]	[illegible]	[illegible]	[illegible]	[illegible]	[illegible]	[illegible]	[illegible]	[illegible]	[illegible]	[illegible]	[illegible]	[illegible]	[illegible]
MUNSTER,	[illegible]	[illegible]	[illegible]	[illegible]	[illegible]	[illegible]	[illegible]	[illegible]	[illegible]	[illegible]	[illegible]	[illegible]	[illegible]	[illegible]	[illegible]	[illegible]	[illegible]	[illegible]	[illegible]	[illegible]	[illegible]	[illegible]
LEINSTER,	[illegible]	[illegible]	[illegible]	[illegible]	[illegible]	[illegible]	[illegible]	[illegible]	[illegible]	[illegible]	[illegible]	[illegible]	[illegible]	[illegible]	[illegible]	[illegible]	[illegible]	[illegible]	[illegible]	[illegible]	[illegible]	[illegible]
CONNAUGHT,	[illegible]	[illegible]	[illegible]	[illegible]	[illegible]	[illegible]	[illegible]	[illegible]	[illegible]	[illegible]	[illegible]	[illegible]	[illegible]	[illegible]	[illegible]	[illegible]	[illegible]	[illegible]	[illegible]	[illegible]	[illegible]	[illegible]
Totals,	[illegible]	[illegible]	[illegible]	[illegible]	[illegible]	[illegible]	[illegible]	[illegible]	[illegible]	[illegible]	[illegible]	[illegible]	[illegible]	[illegible]	[illegible]	[illegible]	[illegible]	[illegible]	[illegible]	[illegible]	[illegible]	[illegible]

No. 3.—General Summary of previous Tables, in Provinces:—containing, 1. Dispensary Districts formed under § 6 of the Medical Charities Act, 14 & of Dispensaries, Officers, &c.:—2. Financial Statement; showing the 1870, to 29th September, 1871:—and 3. Relief Return; showing the Home, respectively; the Number of Cases in which Tickets for Medical Vaccination performed; Number of Cases of Dangerous Lunatics certified; year ended 30th September, 1871.

Heads of Particulars in foregoing Tables.	Ulster.		Munster.	
Column 1.	2.	3.	4.	5.
Statistics of Unions and Districts:				
Population of Unions, in Provinces,—1861,	. .	1,907,284	. .	[illegible]
Area of Unions and Dispensary Districts, in statute acres,	. .	5,816,860	. .	6,000,[illegible]
Poor Law Valuation of Unions, in Provinces,—1871,	. .	£4,021,663	. .	£3,04[illegible]
Number of Unions,	. .	44	. .	[illegible]
" Electoral Divisions,	. .	875	. .	[illegible]
" Dispensary Districts,	. .	218	. .	[illegible]
" Dispensaries or Dispensary Stations therein,	. .	229	. .	[illegible]
" Medical Officers authorised to be appointed for Dispensary Districts,	. .	230	. .	[illegible]
" Apothecaries,	. .	2	. .	19
" Midwives,	. .	65	. .	26
Expenditure in Year ended 29th September, 1871:—				
	£		£	
Medicines and Medical Appliances,	6,484	. .	7,166	. .
Rent of Dispensary Buildings,	2,030	. .	2,011	. .
Books, Forms, Stationery, Printing, and Advertising,	358	. .	808	. .
Salaries of Medical Officers,	23,068	. .	23,231	. .
" Apothecaries,	374	. .	[illegible]	. .
Vaccination Expenses,	2,576	. .	2,378	. .
Fuel, Attendance, and Incidental Expenses,	2,704	. .	2,403	. .
Total Expenditure in year ended 29th September, 1871,	. .	£38,980	. .	£39,[illegible]

STATISTICAL STATEMENT; showing the number of Unions, Electoral Divisions, and
15 Vic., c. 68; the total and average Population, Area, and Valuation; Number
Expenditure under the Medical Charities Act for the year from 29th September,
Number of Cases of Medical Relief afforded at the Dispensary and at the Patient's
Relief have been Cancelled by the Dispensary Committee; the Number of Cases of
Number of Patients attended at Bridewells or Houses of Correction, &c.; during the

No. 4.—Vaccination:—Return of the Number of Persons Vaccinated in the Workhouses and Auxiliary Establishments of the several Unions in Ireland, by the Medical Officers of those Institutions; and of the Number Vaccinated in the several Dispensary Districts, by the Medical Officers of Dispensaries under the Medical Charities Act, in the Year ended 30th September, 1871:—abstracted from Returns made by the respective Medical Officers.—Also a Return of the Expenses incurred in each Union for Vaccination in the several Dispensary Districts, under the Act 21 & 22 Vic., cap. 64.

Names of Unions.	No. Vaccinated in Workhouses by the Medical Officers thereof			No. of Cases Vaccinated by Medical Officers of Dispensary Districts.	Total No. of Cases vaccinated in Columns 4 and 5.	Vaccination Expenses in the Dispensary Districts of each Union.								
	Successful Cases.	Unsuccessful Cases.	Total.			Amount of Fees paid to Medical Officers.			Other Expenses in carrying out the Vaccination Act.			Total Vaccination Expenses.		
Column 1.	2.	3.	4.	5.	6.	7.			8.			9.		
PROVINCE OF ULSTER.						£	s.	d.	£	s.	d.	£	s.	d.
Co. of Antrim.														
Antrim,	9	–	9	1,028	1,037	47	6	0	1	14	0	49	0	0
Ballycastle,	7	–	7	784	791	35	2	0	3	18	0	39	0	0
Ballymena,	13	14	27	2,344	2,371	105	5	8	9	3	0	114	9	8
Ballymoney,	17	–	17	896	913	46	15	0		—		46	15	0
Belfast,	42	6	48	5,153	5,201	284	11	0	19	10	0	304	1	0
Larne,	9	1	10	904	914	47	6	0	6	15	0	54	1	0
Lisburn,	5	–	5	1,056	1,061	75	0	0	8	0	0	83	0	0
Co. of Armagh.														
Armagh,	29	2	31	1,763	1,794	82	11	0	11	10	0	94	1	0
Lurgan,	35	6	41	2,186	2,227	97	18	0	11	12	6	109	5	6
Co. of Cavan.														
Bailieborough,	24	1	25	651	676	27	12	0	13	10	0	41	2	0
Bawnboy,	5	1	6	953	959	35	11	0		—		35	11	0
Cavan,	9	–	9	1,528	1,537	70	0	0	10	0	0	80	0	0
Cootehill,	8	8	16	1,010	1,026	63	15	0		—		63	15	0
Co. of Donegal.														
Ballyshannon,	7	–	7	1,058	1,065	34	8	0	3	2	0	37	10	0
Donegal,	5	12	17	791	808	60	2	0	1	14	0	61	16	0
Dunfanaghy,	1	–	1	687	688	30	14	0	7	8	0	38	2	0
Glenties,	5	1	6	1,157	1,163	59	4	0	3	8	8	62	12	8
Inishowen,	5	–	5	983	988	65	17	0	1	10	0	67	7	0
Letterkenny,	5	–	5	526	531	26	17	0	6	3	0	33	0	0
Milford,	2	3	5	836	841	38	0	0	0	13	0	38	13	0
Stranorlar,	6	0	6	874	880	23	3	0		—		23	3	0
Co. of Down.														
Banbridge,	20	–	20	1,526	1,546	53	17	0	13	13	6	67	10	6
Downpatrick,	31	5	36	2,420	2,456	136	14	0	10	17	6	147	11	6
Kilkeel,	4	–	4	598	602	25	8	0	6	6	0	31	14	0
Newry,	21	–	21	1,836	1,857	91	11	0	4	16	0	96	7	0
Newtownards,	23	15	38	1,506	1,544	67	0	0	4	5	0	71	5	0
Co. of Fermanagh.														
Enniskillen,	6	–	6	1,410	1,416	61	5	0	1	0	0	62	5	0
Irvinestown,	4	–	4	837	841	51	15	0		—		51	15	0
Lisnaskea,	5	–	5	927	932	33	6	0	2	2	0	35	8	0

[continued.

No. 4.—Return of Number of Persons Vaccinated, &c.—*continued.*

Names of Unions.	No. Vaccinated in Workhouses by the Medical Officers thereof.			No. of Cases Vaccinated by Medical Officers of Dispensary Districts.	Total No. of Cases returned in Columns 4 and 5.	Vaccination Expenses in the Dispensary districts of each Union.								
	Successful Cases.	Unsuccessful Cases.	Total.			Amount of Fees paid to Medical Officers.			Other Expenses in carrying out the Vaccination Act.			Total Vaccination Expenses.		
Column 1.	2.	3.	4.	5.	6.	7.			8.			9.		
PROVINCE OF ULSTER—con.						£	s.	d.	£	s.	d.	£	s.	d.
Co. of Londonderry.														
Coleraine,	7	–	7	950	963	40	13	0	—			40	13	0
Londonderry,	19	–	19	1,553	1,572	97	13	6	0	7	0	98	0	6
Magherafelt,	16	2	18	1,960	1,978	103	11	0	13	12	6	117	3	0
Newtownlimavady,	3	–	3	768	771	44	11	0	—			44	11	0
Co. of Monaghan.														
Carrickmacross,	3	–	3	551	554	30	10	6	0	11	6	43	7	6
Castleblayney,	16	11	27	1,041	1,068	70	19	0	11	16	6	91	5	2
Clones,	14	7	21	685	706	33	9	0	5	6	6	88	15	6
Monaghan,	7	–	7	1,013	1,020	56	8	0	4	0	0	60	8	0
Co. of Tyrone.														
Castlederg,	–	6	6	486	492	24	18	0	—			24	18	0
Clogher,	8	–	8	675	683	39	2	0	—			39	2	0
Cookstown,	7	3	10	917	927	39	10	0	3	4	6	43	0	6
Dungannon,	16	–	16	1,815	1,831	58	16	9	—			58	19	6
Gortin,	4	–	4	378	382	26	5	0	3	0	0	28	5	0
Omagh,	25	2	27	1,260	1,287	60	8	0	9	10	0	76	18	0
Strabane,	18	–	18	1,053	1,071	48	7	0	8	12	6	67	19	6
Total of Ulster,	816	102	918	63,850	64,768	3,648	5	9	227	15	4	3,870	0	6
PROVINCE OF MUNSTER.														
Co. of Clare.														
Ballyvaghan,	6	–	6	141	147	13	11	0	—			13	11	0
Corrofin,	–	–	–	176	176	8	4	3	—			8	4	3
Ennis,	20	5	25	822	847	40	17	0	2	2	0	42	19	0
Ennistymon,	–	–	–	929	929	51	8	0	2	1	0	53	9	0
Killadysert,	8	–	8	883	891	—			1	0	0	1	0	0
Kilrush,	–	–	–	849	849	61	10	0	0	5	0	67	15	0
Scariff,	–	–	–	611	611	20	6	9	3	10	0	29	16	9
Tulla,	6	1	7	427	434	28	0	9	5	11	6	33	19	3
Co. of Cork.														
Bandon,	5	–	5	637	642	37	17	0	0	12	0	44	0	0
Bantry,	3	8	11	703	714	27	4	0	0	12	0	27	16	0
Castletown,	10	–	10	788	798	38	16	0	—			38	16	0
Clonakilty,	4	3	7	851	858	43	17	0	2	16	0	45	13	0
Cork,	78	–	78	3,040	3,118	154	19	0	2	0	0	156	19	0
Dunmanway,	3	–	3	567	570	29	19	0	2	0	0	31	19	0
Fermoy,	6	–	6	969	975	49	10	0	0	4	6	49	14	6
Kanturk,	12	8	20	1,734	1,754	70	17	9	1	15	0	78	12	9
Kinsale,	11	2	13	646	658	26	13	0	—			26	13	0
Macroom,	17	–	17	1,093	1,110	55	8	6	—			55	8	6
Mallow,	19	–	19	1,366	1,385	71	16	3	2	0	0	73	16	3
Midleton,	11	–	11	908	919	44	15	0	3	15	0	48	10	0
Millstreet,	11	–	11	1,059	1,070	49	12	0	4	3	6	53	15	0
Mitchelstown,	15	5	20	596	616	9	18	0	0	5	6	10	3	6
Skibbereen,	7	17	24	1,408	1,432	73	18	0	3	13	0	70	3	0
Skull,	2	–	2	460	462	21	3	0	—			21	3	0
Youghal,	9	2	11	616	627	27	1	9	1	1	0	28	2	9

[*continued.*

No. 4.—RETURN of Number of Persons VACCINATED, &c.—*continued.*

NAMES OF UNIONS.	No. Vaccinated in *Workhouses* by the Medical Officers thereof.			No. of Cases Vaccinated by Medical Officers of *Dispensary Districts.*	Total No. of Cases returned in Columns 4 and 5.	Vaccination Expenses in the Dispensary districts of each Union.								
	Successful Cases.	Unsuccessful Cases.	Total.			Amount of Fees paid to Medical Officers.			Other Expenses in carrying out the Vaccination Act.			Total Vaccination Expenses.		
Column 1.	2.	3.	4.	5.	6.	7.			8.			9.		
PROVINCE OF MUNSTER—*con.*						£	s.	d.	£	s.	d.	£	s.	d.
CO. OF KERRY.														
Cahersiveen, . .	21	23	44	1,588	1,632	19	5	0	5	5	0	24	10	0
Dingle, . . .	5	–	5	862	867	43	10	0	3	0	6	46	2	6
Kenmare, . . .	8	–	8	1,154	1,162	32	6	0		—		32	6	0
Killarney, . . .	15	–	15	1,606	1,621	100	16	3	2	12	0	103	8	3
Listowel, . . .	7	–	7	1,140	1,147	75	13	0	0	10	0	76	3	0
Tralee, . . .	12	1	13	1,016	1,029	81	5	0		—		81	5	0
CO. OF LIMERICK.														
Croom, . . .	3	–	3	304	307	24	3	0		—		24	3	0
Glin, . . .	3	–	3	444	447	24	7	0		—		24	7	0
Kilmallock, . .	17	–	17	1,075	1,092	50	10	0	11	10	3	62	0	3
Limerick, . . .	73	17	90	1,787	1,877	65	14	9	1	0	0	66	14	9
Newcastle, . . .	11	–	11	982	993	43	17	0	6	0	0	49	17	0
Rathkeale, . . .	9	–	9	551	560	26	6	0	7	11	11	33	17	11
CO. OF TIPPERARY.														
Borrisokane, . .	10	–	10	270	280	17	5	0	3	11	6	20	16	6
Carrick-on-Suir, .	21	10	31	1,025	1,056	33	2	0	8	2	0	41	4	0
Cashel, . . .	25	–	25	1,016	1,041	70	15	6	8	15	0	79	10	6
Clogheen, . . .	10	–	10	688	698	32	15	0	2	0	0	34	15	0
Clonmel, . . .	23	5	28	880	908	46	18	0	2	12	0	49	10	0
Nenagh, . . .	13	–	13	880	893	41	17	0	16	4	7	58	1	7
Roscrea, . . .	5	–	5	403	408	34	1	0	4	15	0	38	16	0
Thurles, . . .	35	37	72	767	839	41	11	0		—		41	11	0
Tipperary, . . .	14	–	14	1,161	1,175	65	5	6	1	10	0	66	15	6
CO. OF WATERFORD.														
Dungarvan, . .	12	–	12	540	552	58	17	0	6	5	0	65	2	0
Kilmacthomas, . .	6	–	6	321	327	26	3	6	1	3	0	27	6	6
Lismore, . . .	16	–	16	637	653	33	10	3	1	4	0	34	14	3
Waterford, . . .	66	20	86	2,250	2,336	102	2	0		—		102	2	0
Total of Munster,	690	167	857	45,741	46,598	2,228	2	5	145	6	6	2,373	8	11
PROVINCE OF LEINSTER.														
CO. OF CARLOW.														
Carlow, . . .	17	2	19	2,132	2,151	104	18	0		—		104	18	0
CO. OF DUBLIN.														
Balrothery, . .	6	–	6	2,011	2,017	95	10	3	5	12	6	101	2	9
Dublin, North, .	89	–	89	3,235	3,324	146	11	0	1	10	0	148	1	0
Dublin, South, .	88	28	116	5,277	5,393	214	18	0	4	15	0	219	13	0
Rathdown, . . .	35	–	35	1,750	1,785	71	19	0	5	0	0	76	19	0
CO. OF KILDARE.														
Athy, . . .	28	28	56	978	1,034	30	14	0	4	0	0	34	14	0
Celbridge, . . .	5	–	5	696	701	29	13	0	5	5	0	34	18	0
Naas, . . .	8	17	25	1,037	1,062	64	5	0	2	16	6	67	1	6

[*continued.*

No. 4.—Return of Number of Persons Vaccinated, &c.—*continued.*

Names of Unions.	No. Vaccinated in *Workhouses* by the Medical Officers thereof.			No. of Cases Vaccinated by Medical Officers of *Dispensary Districts.*	Total No. of Cases returned in Columns 4 and 5.	Vaccination Expenses in the Dispensary districts of each Union.								
	Successful Cases.	Unsuccessful Cases.	Total.			Amount of Fees paid to Medical Officers.			Other Expenses in carrying out the Vaccination Act.			Total Vaccination Expenses.		
Column 1.	2.	3.	4.	5.	6.	7.			8.			9.		
PROVINCE OF LEINSTER—*con.*						£	s.	d.	£	s.	d.	£	s.	d.
Co. of Kilkenny.														
Callan,	19	24	43	401	164	25	10	6	9	0	6	34	11	0
Castlecomer,	16	–	16	444	460	21	13	0	2	10	8	24	3	8
Kilkenny,	29	62	91	794	885	40	14	0	7	16	0	48	11	8
Thomastown,	3	1	4	636	640	21	1	0	5	15	0	26	16	0
Urlingford,	3	14	17	303	320	14	11	0	1	1	0	15	12	0
King's County.														
Edenderry,	14	–	14	675	686	22	3	0	6	6	0	28	9	0
Parsonstown,	9	–	9	013	922	43	4	6	0	13	0	62	18	0
Tullamore,	14	4	18	061	679	36	2	0	9	2	6	45	4	6
Co. of Longford.														
Ballymahon,	2	–	2	477	479	35	8	9	3	13	6	39	2	3
Granard,	6	1	0	943	950	42	3	0	34	7	0	76	10	6
Longford,	8	10	18	1,209	1,297	68	17	0	5	0	0	73	17	0
Co. of Louth.														
Ardee,	26	37	63	2,478	2,511	110	1	0	5	5	0	121	6	0
Drogheda,	11	–	11	3,369	3,410	172	18	0	8	8	0	181	0	6
Dundalk,	12	9	21	3,377	3,398	126	8	0	5	15	0	132	8	0
Co. of Meath.														
Dunshaughlin,	6	–	6	873	881	13	2	0	2	15	0	15	17	0
Kells,	6	–	6	1,717	1,723	69	11	0	16	14	0	85	5	0
Navan,	16	–	16	748	765	31	9	0	7	9	0	38	4	0
Oldcastle,	6	4	10	617	527	23	15	0	8	0	0	31	15	0
Trim,	14	–	14	670	683	15	16	6	7	4	0	23	0	6
Queen's County.														
Abbeyleix,	2	5	7	563	570	43	1	0	2	2	0	45	3	0
Donaghmore,	–	–	–	164	164	11	11	0	1	1	0	12	12	0
Mountmellick,	21	10	31	926	957	31	4	0	2	0	0	33	4	0
Co. of Westmeath.														
Athlone,	11	32	43	934	973	64	10	4	22	5	0	86	15	4
Delvin,	6	–	6	400	405	21	9	0		—		21	9	0
Mullingar,	17	16	33	946	970	49	19	0	4	5	0	54	15	0
Co. of Wexford.														
Enniscorthy,	13	2	15	1,736	1,751	98	14	0	26	5	0	124	19	0
Gorey,	8	–	8	782	790	46	0	1	7	18	0	55	10	1
New Ross,	40	64	104	1,823	1,028	130	15	0	2	18	6	133	13	6
Wexford,	31	111	146	2,709	2,854	137	18	0	11	0	0	148	18	0
Co. of Wicklow.														
Baltinglass,	11	–	11	496	507	28	10	0	4	2	0	32	12	0
Rathdrum,	20	1	30	1,026	1,080	92	17	2	23	16	9	116	16	11
Shillelagh,	6	–	6	400	400	23	3	0		—		24	3	0
Total of Leinster,	715	477	1,192	51,679	62,871	2,418	4	11	291	1	2	2,708	0	1

[continued.

No. 4.—Return of Number of Persons Vaccinated, &c.—*continued.*

Names of Unions.	No. Vaccinated in *Workhouses* by the Medical Officers thereof. Successful Cases.	Unsuccessful Cases.	Total.	No. of Cases Vaccinated by Medical Officers of *Dispensary Districts.*	Total No. of Cases contained in Columns 4 and 5.	Vaccination Expenses in the Dispensary districts of each Union. Amount of Fees paid to Medical Officers. £	s.	d.	Other Expenses in carrying out the Vaccination Act. £	s.	d.	Total Vaccination Expenses. £	s.	d.
Column 1.	2.	3.	4.	5.	6.	7.			8.			9.		
PROVINCE OF CONNAUGHT.														
Co. of Galway.														
Ballinasloe,	20	—	20	587	607	25	9	0	21	19	0	47	8	0
Clifden,	12	—	12	1,443	1,455	41	0	0	8	10	6	50	0	0
Galway,	23	3	26	1,334	1,360	35	5	0	5	15	6	41	3	6
Glennamaddy,	24	10	34	605	639	33	3	0	5	3	0	38	6	0
Gort,	10	—	10	659	669	34	17	0	1	0	0	35	17	0
Loughrea,	8	—	8	727	735	50	16	0	—			50	16	0
Mountbellew,	6	—	6	644	650	35	10	0	5	0	0	41	0	0
Oughterard,	4	—	4	686	690	36	17	0	1	10	0	38	7	0
Portumna,	5	—	5	352	357	24	2	0	4	14	9	28	16	9
Tuam,	8	—	8	2,604	2,612	89	9	0	8	15	0	98	4	0
Co. of Leitrim.														
Carrick-on-Shannon	50	11	61	775	836	45	13	0	—			45	13	0
Manorhamilton,	9	3	12	1,145	1,157	45	11	0	6	3	2	51	14	2
Mohill,	1	—	1	838	839	54	16	0	8	14	6	63	10	6
Co. of Mayo.														
Ballina,	18	13	31	1,082	1,113	25	9	3	6	0	6	31	9	9
Ballinrobe,	6	—	6	921	927	54	4	0	9	10	6	63	14	6
Belmullet,	3	—	3	670	673	50	5	0	4	0	0	54	5	0
Castlebar,	2	—	2	819	821	36	14	0	7	14	0	44	8	0
Claremorris,	—	17	17	1,156	1,173	58	7	0	10	1	6	68	8	6
Killala,	2	—	2	362	364	14	8	0	9	6	0	23	14	0
Newport,	3	—	3	574	577	18	10	0	22	4	6	41	3	6
Swineford,	—	—	—	2,036	2,036	103	14	0	20	10	0	124	4	0
Westport,	2	—	2	907	909	42	5	0	20	7	2	62	12	2
Co. of Roscommon.														
Boyle,	32	56	88	1,387	1,475	103	2	0	12	2	0	115	4	0
Castlerea,	12	—	12	1,343	1,355	58	14	0	6	2	0	64	16	0
Roscommon,	9	5	14	670	684	33	3	6	1	7	3	34	10	9
Strokestown,	3	—	3	605	608	23	16	0	4	9	0	28	5	0
Co. of Sligo.														
Dromore, West,	1	—	1	547	548	30	13	6	3	3	0	33	16	6
Sligo,	17	—	17	2,315	2,332	100	14	0	20	2	0	120	16	0
Tobercurry,	2	1	3	702	705	37	13	0	—			37	13	0
Total of Connaught,	289	124	413	28,619	29,032	1,305	11	6	242	14	9	1,548	6	3
Summary of Provinces.														
Ulster,	514	102	616	53,850	54,466	2,648	6	2	227	15	4	2,876	0	6
Munster,	690	167	857	45,741	46,598	2,228	2	6	145	6	5	2,373	8	11
Leinster,	715	477	1,192	51,679	52,871	2,478	4	11	291	1	2	2,769	6	1
Connaught,	289	124	413	28,619	29,032	1,305	11	6	242	14	9	1,548	6	3
Total of Ireland,	2,208	870	3,078	179,889	182,967	8,720	4	1	906	17	8	9,627	1	9

No. 5.—Number of Cases of Scarlatina, Smallpox, and Fever, reported by Medical Officers of Dispensaries in Ireland, as having been attended in the Quarters ended 31st December, 1870, 31st March, 30th June, and 30th September, 1871.

Provinces.	Quarters ended	Scarlatina.	Smallpox.	Fever.
Ulster, . .	December 31st, 1870, . .	465	45	771
	March 31st, 1871, . .	265	99	1,012
	June 30th, 1871, . .	221	71	1,042
	September 30th, 1871, . .	190	122	1,043
Munster, . .	December 31st, 1870, . .	561	2	956
	March 31st, 1871, . .	397	6	1,162
	June 30th, 1871, . .	519	11	1,539
	September 30th, 1871, . .	793	11	1,132
Leinster, . .	December 31st, 1870, . .	670	1	1,184
	March 31st, 1871, . .	661	93	1,265
	June 30th, 1871, . .	769	157	1,235
	September 30th, 1871, . .	588	124	1,083
Connaught, . .	December 31st, 1870, . .	76	11	390
	March 31st, 1871, . .	163	4	614
	June 30th, 1871, . .	147	7	611
	September 30th, 1871, . .	169	9	613
Summary.				
Ireland, . .	December 31st, 1870, . .	1,965	59	3,301
	March 31st, 1871, . .	1,379	202	4,043
	June 30th, 1871, . .	1,656	246	4,460
	September 30th, 1871, . .	1,740	266	3,770
	Total, ...	6,780	773	15,574

No. 6.—Index List of Dispensary Districts; with Names of Unions in which they are situate, and References to Pages in which the Districts are to be found in the Appendix.

Name of Dispensary District.	Union in which situate.	References to [illegible]	References to [illegible]
		Page	Page
Abbey,	Tuam,	[illegible]	[illegible]
Abbeyfeale,	Newcastle,	[illegible]	[illegible]
Abbeyleix,	Abbeyleix,	[illegible]	[illegible]
Abbeyshrule,	Ballymahon,	[illegible]	[illegible]
Achill,	Newport,	[illegible]	[illegible]
Aclare,	Tobercurry,	[illegible]	[illegible]
Adare,	Croom,	[illegible]	[illegible]
Aghada,	Midleton,	[illegible]	[illegible]
Aghadowey,	Coleraine,	[illegible]	[illegible]
Aghalee,	Lurgan,	[illegible]	[illegible]
Ahascragh,	Ballinasloe,	[illegible]	[illegible]
Ahoghill,	Ballymena,	[illegible]	[illegible]
[illegible],	Rathdrum,	[illegible]	[illegible]
Annacarriga,	Scariff,	[illegible]	[illegible]
Annacotty,	Limerick,	[illegible]	[illegible]
Annahilt,	Lisburn,	[illegible]	[illegible]
Antrim,	Antrim,	[illegible]	[illegible]
Ardagh,	Newcastle,	[illegible]	[illegible]
Ardara,	Glenties,	[illegible]	[illegible]
Ardee,	Ardee,	[illegible]	[illegible]
Ardfert,	Tralee,	[illegible]	[illegible]
Ardfinnan,	Clogheen,	[illegible]	[illegible]
Ardmore,	Youghal,	[illegible]	[illegible]
Ardrahan,	Gort,	[illegible]	-
Arklow,	Rathdrum,	[illegible]	[illegible]
Armagh,	Armagh,	[illegible]	[illegible]
Arran	Galway,	[illegible]	[illegible]
Articlave,	Coleraine,	[illegible]	[illegible]
Arvagh,	Cavan,	[illegible]	[illegible]
Ashford,	Rathdrum,	[illegible]	[illegible]
Askeaton,	Rathkeale,	[illegible]	[illegible]
Athboy,	Trim,	[illegible]	[illegible]
Athenry,	Loughrea,	[illegible]	[illegible]
Athleague,	Roscommon,	[illegible]	[illegible]
Athlone,	Athlone,	[illegible]	[illegible]
Athy,	Athy,	[illegible]	[illegible]
Aughnacloy,	Clogher,	[illegible]	[illegible]
Aughavas,	Carrick-on-Shannon,	[illegible]	[illegible]
Aughrim,	Rathdrum,	[illegible]	[illegible]
[illegible],	Dingle,	[illegible]	[illegible]
Bagenalstown,	Carlow,	[illegible]	[illegible]
Bailieborough,	Bailieborough,	[illegible]	[illegible]
Balbriggan,	Balrothery,	[illegible]	[illegible]
Balla,	Castlebar,	[illegible]	[illegible]
Ballaghaderreen,	Castlerea,	[illegible]	[illegible]
Balleen,	Urlingford,	[illegible]	[illegible]
Ballickmoyler and Newtown,	Carlow,	[illegible]	[illegible]
Ballina,	Ballina,	[illegible]	[illegible]
Ballinakill,	Abbeyleix,	[illegible]	[illegible]
Ballinalee,	Granard,	[illegible]	[illegible]
Ballinameen,	Boyle,	[illegible]	[illegible]
Ballingeary,	Bantry,	[illegible]	[illegible]
Ballinamore,	Ballinasloe,	[illegible]	[illegible]
Ballincollig,	Cork,	[illegible]	[illegible]
Ballinderreen,	Gort,	-	[illegible]
Ballindine,	Claremorris,	[illegible]	[illegible]
Ballineen,	Dunmanway,	[illegible]	[illegible]
Ballingarry,	Callan,	[illegible]	[illegible]
Ballinrobe,	Ballinrobe,	[illegible]	[illegible]
Ballintra,	Ballyshannon,	[illegible]	[illegible]
Ballybay,	Castleblayney,	[illegible]	[illegible]
Ballyboggan,	Edenderry,	[illegible]	[illegible]
Ballycarry,	Larne,	[illegible]	[illegible]
Ballycastle,	Ballycastle,	[illegible]	[illegible]
Ballycastle,	Killala,	[illegible]	[illegible]
Ballyclough,	Mallow,	[illegible]	[illegible]
Ballyconnell,	Bawnboy,	[illegible]	[illegible]
Ballyduff,	Lismore,	[illegible]	[illegible]
Ballyduff,	Listowel,	[illegible]	[illegible]
Ballyfarnan,	Boyle,	[illegible]	[illegible]
Ballyfeard,	Kinsale,	[illegible]	[illegible]
Ballygarvan,	Cork,	[illegible]	[illegible]
Ballygawley,	Clogher,	[illegible]	[illegible]
Ballyhaise,	Cavan,	[illegible]	[illegible]
Ballyhaunis,	Claremorris,	[illegible]	[illegible]
Ballyhooly,	Fermoy,	[illegible]	[illegible]
Ballyheigue,	Listowel,	[illegible]	[illegible]
Ballyjamesduff,	Oldcastle,	[illegible]	[illegible]
Ballykelly,	Newtown-Limavady,	[illegible]	[illegible]
Ballyleague,	Roscommon,	[illegible]	[illegible]
Ballylesson,	Lisburn,	[illegible]	[illegible]
Ballylongford,	Listowel,	[illegible]	[illegible]
Ballylynan,	Athy,	[illegible]	[illegible]
Ballymacarbery,	Clonmel,	[illegible]	[illegible]
Ballymagorry,	Strabane,	[illegible]	[illegible]
Ballymahon,	Ballymahon,	[illegible]	[illegible]
Ballymartle,	Kinsale,	[illegible]	[illegible]
Ballymena,	Ballymena,	[illegible]	[illegible]
Ballymoney,	Ballymoney,	[illegible]	[illegible]
Ballymore,	Ballymahon,	[illegible]	[illegible]
Ballymote,	Sligo,	[illegible]	[illegible]
Ballymurphy,	Enniscorthy,	[illegible]	[illegible]
Ballynacargy,	Mullingar,	[illegible]	[illegible]
Ballynahinch,	Downpatrick,	[illegible]	[illegible]
Ballynoe,	Fermoy,	[illegible]	[illegible]
Ballynure,	Larne,	[illegible]	[illegible]
Ballyragget,	Castlecomer,	[illegible]	[illegible]
Ballyroan,	Abbeyleix,	[illegible]	[illegible]
Ballyshannon,	Ballyshannon,	[illegible]	[illegible]
Ballyvaughan,	Ballyvaughan,	[illegible]	[illegible]
Ballyward,	Banbridge,	[illegible]	[illegible]
Baltinglass,	Baltinglass,	[illegible]	[illegible]
Banagher,	Parsonstown,	[illegible]	[illegible]
Banbridge,	Banbridge,	[illegible]	[illegible]
Bandon,	Bandon,	[illegible]	[illegible]
Bangor,	Belmullet,	[illegible]	[illegible]
Bangor,	Newtownards,	[illegible]	[illegible]
Bannow,	Wexford,	[illegible]	[illegible]
Bansha,	Tipperary,	[illegible]	[illegible]
Bantry,	Bantry,	[illegible]	[illegible]
Barronstown,	Dundalk,	[illegible]	[illegible]
Belfast,	Belfast,	[illegible]	[illegible]
Bellaghy,	Magherafelt,	[illegible]	[illegible]
Bellananagh,	Cavan,	[illegible]	[illegible]
Bellarena,	N.-T.-Limavady,	[illegible]	[illegible]
Belleek,	Ballyshannon,	[illegible]	[illegible]
Belturbet,	Cavan,	[illegible]	[illegible]
Benburb,	Dungannon,	[illegible]	[illegible]

[continued.

[continued.

[continued.

(continued.

(continued.

Names of Dispensary Districts.	Towns in which situate.	Reference to — [illegible]	Reference to — [illegible]
		Page	Page
St. Mary's,	Drogheda,	221	[illegible]
St. Mullin's,	New Ross,	721	240
Scotstown,	Monaghan,	219	241
Scrabby,	Granard,	[illegible]	[illegible]
Seskinan,	Dungarvan,	277	257
Shanagolden,	Glin,	[illegible]	254
Shercock,	Bailieborough,	715	241
Shinrone,	Roscrea,	[illegible]	[illegible]
Silverstream,	Newry,	[illegible]	[illegible]
Six Mile Cross,	Omagh,	[illegible]	[illegible]
Skibbereen,	Skibbereen,	[illegible]	254
Skreen,	Dromore West,	[illegible]	[illegible]
Skull,	Skull,	[illegible]	[illegible]
Skreverragh,	Macroom,	[illegible]	[illegible]
Sligo,	Sligo,	[illegible]	[illegible]
Suncroft,	Kilcullen,	[illegible]	[illegible]
South City,	South Dublin,	[illegible]	[illegible]
Spiddle,	Galway,	[illegible]	[illegible]
Stamullen,	Drogheda,	221	[illegible]
Stewartstown,	Cookstown,	[illegible]	[illegible]
Strabane,	Strabane,	[illegible]	[illegible]
Stradbally,	Athy,	[illegible]	[illegible]
Stradone,	Cavan,	216	241
Strangford,	Downpatrick,	217	243
Stranorlar,	Stranorlar,	217	[illegible]
Streete,	Granard,	[illegible]	[illegible]
Strokestown,	Strokestown,	[illegible]	[illegible]
Summerhill,	Trim,	[illegible]	[illegible]
Swanlinbar,	Bawnboy,	715	241
Swineford,	Swineford,	[illegible]	271
Swords,	Balrothery,	[illegible]	[illegible]
Taghmon and Glynn,	Wexford,	[illegible]	[illegible]
Tallaght,	South Dublin,	[illegible]	[illegible]
Tallow,	Lismore,	[illegible]	[illegible]
Tandragee,	Banbridge,	217	243
Tarbert,	Glin,	[illegible]	254
Tartaraghan,	Lurgan,	215	240
Templecarrig,	Rathdown,	221	240
Templemolaga,	Youghal,	[illegible]	[illegible]
Templemore,	Thurles,	[illegible]	257
Templepatrick,	Antrim,	711	[illegible]
Templeludigan,	New Ross,	[illegible]	240
Tempo,	Enniskillen,	219	211
Termon,	Bailieborough,	715	241
Termonfeckin,	Drogheda,	221	[illegible]
Terryglass,	Borrisokane,	[illegible]	[illegible]
Thomastown,	Thomastown,	[illegible]	251
Thurles,	Thurles,	[illegible]	257
Timoleague,	Clonakilty,	[illegible]	[illegible]
Tinahely,	Shillelagh,	[illegible]	[illegible]
Tipperary,	Tipperary,	277	257
Tiscoffin,	Kilkenny,	[illegible]	251
Tobercurry,	Tobercurry,	717	271
Toome,	Ballymena,	[illegible]	[illegible]
Toomevara,	Nenagh,	[illegible]	[illegible]
Tralee,	Tralee,	[illegible]	[illegible]
Tramore,	Waterford,	277	257
Trim,	Trim,	[illegible]	[illegible]
Tuam,	Tuam,	[illegible]	[illegible]
Tulla,	Tulla,	[illegible]	[illegible]
Tullagh,	Skibbereen,	[illegible]	[illegible]
Tullamain,	Cashel,	[illegible]	[illegible]
Tullamore,	Tullamore,	[illegible]	[illegible]
Tullaroan,	Kilkenny,	[illegible]	251
Tullow,	Carlow,	[illegible]	[illegible]
Tullyvin,	Cootehill,	216	241
Tynan,	Keady,	[illegible]	[illegible]
Turloughmore,	Galway,	[illegible]	[illegible]
Tynan,	Armagh,	215	240
Tyrrellspass,	Mullingar,	[illegible]	[illegible]
Ullid,	Waterford,	277	257
Union Hall,	Skibbereen,	[illegible]	[illegible]
Urlingford,	Urlingford,	[illegible]	[illegible]
Valentia,	Cahirciveen,	[illegible]	[illegible]
Ventry,	Dingle,	[illegible]	[illegible]
Virginia,	Oldcastle,	[illegible]	[illegible]
Walshestownmore, East,	Midleton,	[illegible]	[illegible]
Waringstown,	Lurgan,	215	240
Warrenpoint,	Newry,	217	[illegible]
Waterford,	Waterford,	277	257
Westport,	Westport,	[illegible]	[illegible]
Wexford,	Wexford,	[illegible]	[illegible]
Whitechurch,	Cork,	[illegible]	[illegible]
Whitechurch,	Dungarvan,	277	257
Williamstown,	Glennamaddy,	[illegible]	[illegible]
Woodford,	Loughrea,	[illegible]	[illegible]
Woodstown,	Waterford,	277	257
Youghal,	Youghal,	[illegible]	[illegible]

Dublin: Printed by Alexander Thom, 87 & 88, Abbey-street,
For Her Majesty's Stationery Office.

www.ingramcontent.com/pod-product-compliance
Lightning Source LLC
Chambersburg PA
CBHW032058220426
43664CB00008B/1048
* 9 7 8 3 7 4 1 1 0 4 7 1 8 *